WHAT THE KORAN REALLY SAYS

What the Koran Really Says

LANGUAGE, TEXT, AND COMMENTARY

EDITED WITH TRANSLATIONS BY

Ibn Warraq

Prometheus Books
59 John Glenn Drive
Amherst, New York 14228-2197

Published 2002 by Prometheus Books

Inquiries should be addressed to
Prometheus Books
59 John Glenn Drive
Amherst, New York 14228–2197
VOICE: 716–691–0133, ext. 207
FAX: 716–564–2711
WWW.PROMETHEUSBOOKS.COM

06 05 04 03 02 5 4 3 2 1

Library of Congress Cataloging-in-Publication Data

What the Koran really says : language, text, and commentary / edited with translations by Ibn Warraq.
p. cm.
Includes bibliographical references.
ISBN 1–57392–945–X (alk. paper)
1. Islam—Controversial literature. 2. Koran—Language, style. 3. Koran—Criticism, interpretation, etc. I. Ibn Warraq.

BP169 .W48 2002
297.1'226—dc21

2001048789

Printed in Canada on acid-free paper

To

ODILE

Uxori Dilectissimae

Respect for the faith of sincere believers cannot be allowed either to block or deflect the investigation of the historian . . .

Maxime Rodinson

CONTENTS

PART 4. SOURCES OF THE KORAN: ESSENIAN, CHRISTIAN, COPTIC

PART 5. SURAS, SURAS, SURAS

PART 6. EMENDATIONS, INTERPOLATIONS

PART 7. RICHARD BELL: INTRODUCTION AND COMMENTARY

PART 8. POETRY AND THE KORAN

PART 9. MANUSCRIPTS

APPENDICES

Preface and Acknowledgments

My wish, in the first part of the introduction, is to dispel the sacred aura surrounding the Arabic language, the Arabic script, and the Holy Arabic Scripture—to *desacralize*, if I may coin a term[1]—and put them into their historical, linguistic, and Middle Eastern sectarian milieu; to show that each—language, script and text—is inexorably related to the Semitic, Aramaic/Nabataean, and Monotheist background respectively, and that each can and must be explained by the normal mechanisms of human history.

In the second part I have tried to give specific examples of the obscurities and grammatical and logical difficulties of the Koran, and then argued that the ninth-century explosion of Muslim scholarly activity—in the composition of Arabic grammars, the exegesis of the Koran, the elaboration of the theories of abrogation and the occasions of revelations (*asbāb al-nuzūl*), the fabrication of *ḥadīth* and the details of the life of the Prophet—revealed the Muslims' ignorance of the meaning of the Koran, and that, indeed, this activity was designed to make sense of this opaque text.

I then briefly look at the various answers proposed by non-Muslim scholars—such as Casanova, Lüling, and Luxenberg—to explain the source of the Koranic difficulties.

I end with a plea for a long overdue examination of the methodological assumptions of the Islamologists, suggesting that the latter could learn some lessons from the work of a new generation of biblical scholars who are much more open to the methods of other disciplines like anthropology, sociology, social history, linguistics, and literary criticism.

The articles in this collection reflect the above concerns. Nevo gives the archaeological data that seem to contradict the traditional accounts of the rise of Islam. The essays in part 3 discuss matters of language: the growth of Classical Arabic, and the importance of Aramaic for our understanding of the Koran. The scholars in part 4 give the Qumranian and Christian background, proposing possible Essenian, Coptic, and other Christian influence on the text of the Koran; while the authors in part 5 not only point to the difficulties in various suras, but also suggest, rejecting the traditional accounts, possible alternative interpretations. The Islamologists in part 6, in an attempt to elucidate some of the obscurities of the Koran show that only emendations can give us a comprehensible text. In part 7, substantial passages from Richard Bell's *Introduction to the Qu'ran* and his *Commentary to Sura II* underline the nature of the difficulties, and provide valuable exegesis. What Bell says of poetry in the Koran should be particularly helpful for understanding Rudolf Geyer's article in the following section. Finally, A. Grohmann discusses Koranic manuscripts, and Gerd Puin gives us a preliminary discussion of the finds in the Yemen.

The articles by Michael Schub (5.9, 5.10), C. Heger (5.8), and Ibn Rawandi (8.3) are published for the first time, while the articles by M. Philonenko (4.3, 4.4), Raimund Kobert (4.7, 4.8, 4.9), Claude Cahen (5.3), J. Barth (6.1), A. Fischer (6.2, 6.3), Rudolf Geyer (8.1), and J. Wellhausen (8.2) are here translated into English for the first time.

A work such as the present compilation owes it very existence to the research of others. We are all heavily indebted to the great scholars of the past—Barth, Fischer, Bell, et al.—represented here. But I also received help of a more personal kind from contemporary scholars, without which this anthology would not have been possible. As with my previous book, I am truly touched by all the help accorded me: at my first steps in Syriac and Hebrew; at the translation and transliteration of at least four Semitic and two Indo-European languages; at the providing of difficult-to-obtain articles, and so on. I was particularly grateful for the translations from the rather abstruse German. It is not only a duty but a pleasure to acknowledge all this kindness and generosity. I should have liked to have given the names of these scholars—indeed, it would make an impressive list of "who's who" in the world of Islamic studies, from professors at distinguished universities in seven countries to Dominican and Capuchin friars. Unfortunately, as on previous occasions, it was thought prudent to protect them by not mentioning them, since Ibn Warraq is still, "mad, bad, and dangerous to know." While naming names might enhance my credibility, it may tarnish theirs, and endanger them physically. However, there is someone I can thank by name, since he writes under a protective pseudonym, Ibn Rawandi (*il miglior fabbro*). Ibn Rawandi helped me in countless ways, providing me with books, articles, and advice, for which I am truly beholden; but above all for accepting to write an essay especially for this collection.

Finally, it remains for me to stress that the opinions expressed, and any errors that persist especially in the introduction, are entirely my responsibility.

Ibn Warraq
January 2001

NOTE

1. Or more precisely, borrow one from the French.

TRANSLITERATION AND OTHER TECHNICAL MATTERS

There is no universally accepted system of transliteration (transcription) of the Semitic scripts. The authors in this anthology use two different systems for the Arabic alphabet. As some editors in whose journals the articles first appeared insisted that we not change one single letter as a precondition for allowing us to reproduce them, I was unable to standardize all the articles and adopt just one system. However, the two systems are not that difficult to come to grips with. For Arabic they are:

(1) ʾ, b, t, th, j, ḥ, kh, d, dh, r, z, s, sh, ṣ, ḍ, ṭ, ẓ, ʿ, gh, f, q, k, l, m, n, h, w, y. *Short vowels*: a, u, i. *Long vowels*: ā, ū, ī

(2) ʾ, b, t, ṯ, ǧ, ḥ, ḫ, d, ḏ, r, z, s, š, ṣ, ḍ, ṭ, ẓ, ʿ, ġ, f, q, k, l, m, n, h, w, y. *Short vowels*: a, u, i. *Long vowels*: ā, ū, ī

The journal *Studia Islamica* uses and recommends system (1) above; on the whole I have used this system in my own introduction and translations.

The journal *Arabica*, on the other hand uses system (2); thus, the articles from this journal included in this anthology follow suit. (Readers are also likely to encounter, though not often in this anthology, the following variations: *dj* for *j*, and *ḳ* for *q*, for example, in *EI2*.)

For the Hebrew and Syriac, I use the following:

ʾ, b, g, d, h, w, z, ḥ, ṭ, y, k, l, m, n, s, ʿ, p, ṣ, q, r, ś/š, t.

All long vowels are overlined. The small raised ^{e} stands for a hurried or neutral vowel. Underlined letters (as in bē<u>t</u>) are pronounced as fricatives, thus <u>t</u> = English "th" as in "thin"; <u>p</u> = "ph" as in "phial."

Right up to the 1930s, Western scholars used the edition of the Koran by Gustav Flügel (sometimes spelled Fluegel), *Corani Textus Arabicus* (1834), whose numbering of verses differs from what has now become the "official" or Standard Egyptian edition, first published in 1928. Again, not only was it obviously much easier for me to leave the original Flügel numbering in the pre-1928 articles included in this anthology, but in the case of Richard Bell it was even essential not to interfere with the original numbering, since his entire two-volume *Commentary*, his *Introduction to the Qur'an*, and his *Translation of the Qur'an* only referred to Flügel's edition. To have changed this in the extracts from the *Commentary* and *The Introduction to the Qur'an* included here to the Standard Egyptian edition would have impaired the concordance of Bell's *Commentary* and *Introduction to the Qur'an* with his *Translation*. Bell also refers to Fischer and Barth, both of whom are included in this anthology; again, all his references would have been out of synchronization had I changed them to the Standard Egyptian edition. Finally, as one scholar reminded me, attempting to change the numbering would only have increased the possibility of further errors. Thus to help readers I have included a table of differences (appendix B), which should ease their passage from one system of numbering to the other. In my introduction, however, I have used the Official Egyptian system, even where I quote from Bell.

TRANSCRIPTION/TRANSLITERATION

Consonants

ا	alif		ض	ḍād	ḍ
ب	bāʾ	b	ط	ṭāʾ	ṭ
ت	tāʾ	t	ظ	ẓāʾ	ẓ
ث	thāʾ	th/ṯ	ع	ʿayn	ʿ
ج	jīm	j/ǧ/dj	غ	ghayn	gh/ġ
ح	ḥāʾ	ḥ	ف	fāʾ	f
خ	khāʾ	kh/ḫ/x	ق	qāf	q/ḳ
د	dāl	d	ك	kāf	k
ذ	dhāl	dh/ḏ	ل	lām	l
ر	rāʾ	r	م	mīm	m
ز	zay	z	ن	nūn	n
س	sīn	s	ه	hāʾ	h
ش	shīn	sh/š	و	wāw	w
ص	ṣād	ṣ	ى	yāʾ	y

(ء hamza ʾ)

Vowels

ا	ā/â	َ	fatḥa	a
و	ū	ُ	ḍamma	u
ى	ī	ِ	kasra	i

Dipthongs : aw, ay

آ	ʾalif-madda	ʾā	لا	lām-ʾalif lā
ة	tāʾmarbūṭa	-at-	ّ	shadda (doubling consonant)
ى	alif maqṣūra (pronounced like lengthening alif) ā			

Part 1

INTRODUCTION

1.1

Introduction

Ibn Warraq

1. KORAN TRANSLATED INTO ARABIC!

Muslims in general have a tendency to disarm any criticisms of Islam and in particular the Koran by asking if the critic has read the Koran in the original Arabic, as though all the difficulties of their sacred text will somehow disappear once the reader has mastered the holy language and has direct experience, aural and visual, of the very words of God, to which no translation can do justice.

In a letter to Mme. du Deffand, who wished to compare Virgil to Alexander Pope, Voltaire wrote "Vous le connaissez par les traductions: mais les poètes ne se traduisent point. Peut-on traduire de la musique?" ("You know him through translations: but poets are not translatable. Can one translate music?" May 19, 1754) As John Hollander remarks, Voltaire's opinion "seems to prefigure the views of a later century, in associating with music not the beauty, or decoration, but a strange sort of ineffable, incomprehensible, and (hence?) untranslatable core of pure poetry."[1] This, I think, captures the Muslim's almost mystical and rather irrational attitude to the untranslatability of the Koran very well.

Jackson Mathews also singles out another feature that is most difficult to translate: "Rhythm is the one feature of a foreign language that we can probably never learn to hear purely. Rhythm and the meaning of rhythm lie too deep in us. They are absorbed into the habits of the body and the uses of the voice along with all our earliest apprehensions of ourselves and the world. Rhythm forms the sensibility, becomes part of the personality; and one's sense of rhythm is shaped once and for all on one's native tongue."[2] Thus, we can grant that in any translation, whatever the language concerned, there will be inevitable loss of melody and evocative power. However matters are, as we shall see, even more complicated when it comes to Arabic.

First, of course, the majority of Muslims are not Arabs or Arabic-speaking peoples. The non-Arabic speaking nations of Indonesia, with a population of 197 million; Pakistan, with 133 million; Iran, with 62 million; Turkey, with 62 million; and India, with a Muslim population of about 95 million, outnumber by far the total number of native Arabic speakers in about thirty countries in the world, estimated as 150 million. Many educated Muslims whose native tongue is not Arabic do learn it in order to read the Koran; but then again, the vast majority do not understand Arabic, even though many do learn parts of the Koran by heart without understanding a word.

In other words, the majority of Muslims have to read the Koran in translation in order to understand it. Contrary to what one might think, there have been translations of the Koran into, for instance, Persian, since the tenth or eleventh century, and there are translations into Turkish and Urdu. The Koran has now been translated into over a hundred languages, many of them by Muslims themselves, despite some sort of disapproval from the religious authorities.[3]

Even for contemporary Arabic-speaking peoples, reading the Koran is far from being a straightforward matter. The Koran is putatively (as we shall see, it is very difficult to decide exactly what the language of the Koran is) written in what we call Classical Arabic (CA), but modern Arab populations, leaving aside the problem of illiteracy in Arab countries,[4] do not speak, read, or write, let alone think, in CA. We are confronted with the phenomenon of *diglossia*,[5] that is to say, a situation where two varieties of the same language live side by side. The two variations are high and low. High Arabic is sometimes called Modern Literary Arabic or Modern Standard Arabic; is learned through formal education in school, like Latin or Sanskrit; and would be used in sermons, university lectures, news broadcasts, and for mass media purposes. Low Arabic, or Colloquial Arabic, is a dialect native speakers acquire as a mother tongue, and is used at home conversing with family and friends, and also in radio or television soap operas. But, as Kaye points out, "the differences between many colloquials and the classical language are so great that a *fallāḥ* who had never been to school could hardly understand more than a few scattered words and expressions in it without great difficulty. One could assemble dozens of so-called Arabs (*fallāḥīn*) in a room, who have never been exposed to the classical language, so that not one could properly understand the other."[6]

In the introduction to his grammar of Koranic and Classical Arabic, Wheeler M. Thackston writes, ". . . the Koran established an unchanging norm for the Arabic language. There are, of course, certain lexical and syntactic features of Koranic Arabic that became obsolete in time, and the standardization of the language at the hands of the philologians of the eighth and ninth centuries emphasized certain extra-Koranic features of the Arabic poetic *koine* while downplaying other, Koranic usages; yet by and large not only the grammar but even the vocabulary of a modern newspaper article display only slight variation from the established norm of classicized Koranic Arabic."[7]

Though he does allow for some change and decay, Thackston it seems to me, paints a totally misleading picture of the actual linguistic situation in modern Arabic-speaking societies. He implies that anyone able to read a modern Arabic newspaper should have no difficulties with the Koran or any Classical Arabic text. Thackston seems totally insensitive "to the evolution of the language, to changes in the usage and meaning of terms over the very long period and in the very broad area in which Classical Arabic has been used."[8] Anyone who has lived in the Middle East in recent years will know that the language of the press is at best semiliterary,[9] and certainly simplified as far as structure and vocabulary are concerned. We can discern what would be called grammatical errors from a Classical Arabic point of view in daily newspapers or on television news. This semiliterary language is highly artificial, and certainly no one thinks in it. For an average middle-class Arab it would take considerable effort to construct even the simplest sentence, let alone talk, in Classical Arabic. The linguist Pierre Larcher has written of the "considerable gap between Medieval Classical Arabic and Modern Classical Arabic [or what I have been calling Modern Literary Arabic], certain texts written in the former are today the object of explanatory texts in the latter." He then adds in a footnote that he has in his library, based on this model, an edition of the *Risāla* of Shāfiʿī (died 204/820) that appeared in a collection with the significant title *Getting Closer to the Patrimony*.[10]

As Kaye puts it, "In support of the hypothesis that modern standard Arabic is ill-defined is the so-called 'mixed' language or 'Inter-Arabic' being used in the speeches of, say, President Bourguiba of Tunisia, noting that very few native speakers of Arabic from any Arab country can really ever master the intricacies of Classical Arabic grammar in such a way as to extemporaneously give a formal speech in it."[11]

Pierre Larcher[12] has pointed out that wherever you have a linguistic situation where two varieties of the same language coexist, you are also likely to get all sorts of linguistic mixtures, leading some linguists to talk of *triglossia*. Gustav Meiseles[13] even talks of *quadriglossia*: between Literary Arabic and Vernacular Arabic, he distinguishes a Substandard Arabic and an Educated Spoken Arabic. Still others speak of *pluri-* or *multi-* or *polyglossia*, viewed as a continuum.[14]

The style of the Koran is difficult, totally unlike the prose of today, and the Koran would be largely incomprehensible without glossaries, indeed, entire commentaries. In conclusion, even the most educated of Arabs will need some sort of translation if he or she wishes to make sense of that most gnomic, elusive. and allusive of holy scriptures, the Koran.

2. THE CLASSIFICATION AND NATURE OF ARABIC

According to Barbara F. Grimes[15] of the Summer Institute of Linguistics, there are 6,703 living languages in the world.[16] These living languages, and the dozens of extinct languages whose structure are known and have been studied, are classified either typologically, that is, in terms of their structural properties (for example, according to the number and kinds of vowels they use, or according to the order of the subject, verb, and object in a simple sentence)[17]—or genetically—that is, on the basis of common origin.

Genetically related languages have developed or evolved from a common parent language. As scholar I. M. Diakonoff put it, "The only real criterion for classifying certain languages together as a family is the common origin of their most ancient vocabulary as well as of the word elements used to express grammatical relations. A common source language is revealed by a comparison of words from the supposedly related languages expressing notions common to all human cultures (and therefore not as a rule likely to have been borrowed from a group speaking another language) and also by a comparison of the inflectional forms (for tense, voice, case, or whatever)."[18]

3. AFRO-ASIATIC: SEMITIC, ARAMAIC, SYRIAC, AND ARABIC

All the world's languages are classified into large groups or *phyla* (sometimes very loosely called "families"). Merrit Ruhlen[19] classifies all languages into twenty independent groups, each group containing genetically related languages. Arabic belongs to the group (or family) now called Afro-Asiatic, though formerly it was called Hamito-Semitic, Semito-Hamitic, or even Erythraean. This family of genetically related languages can be subdivided into six primary branches, all descendants of the original parent language, namely: (1) Ancient Egyptian (from which Coptic, the liturgical language of the Monophysite Christians of Egypt, is descended); (2) Berber (widespread in Morocco and Algeria); (3) Chadic; (4) Omotic; (5) Cushitic; and (6) Semitic. Arabic, like Hebrew, Syriac, and Aramaic, is a Semitic language. The Semitic languages are further subdivided, sometimes into four groups and sometimes into two. I have chosen Robert Hetzron's and Merrit Ruhlen's classification (see language tree appendix D and E), which divides Semitic languages into two groups. As one can see, Arabic belongs to the Central Semitic group, which is further subdivided into two subgroups, Aramaic and Arabo-Canaanite (sometimes rather confusedly called South-Central Semitic; I have avoided this term to underline that Arabic does not belong to the same subgroup as South Semitic, containing Epigraphic South Arabian, Modern South Arabian, and Ethiopian or Ethiopic).

One of the distinctive features of all Semitic languages is the triliteral or triconsonantal root, composed of three consonants separated by vowels. The basic meaning of a word is expressed by the consonants, as well as different shades of this basic meaning are indicated by vowel changes, as well as prefixes and as suffixes. For example, the root *ktb* refers to writing, and the vowel pattern *-a-i* implies "one who does something"; thus *kātib* means "one who writes"; *kitāb* means "book"; *maktūb*, "letter"; and *kataba*, "he wrote." The two genders, masculine and feminine, are found in Semitic languages, the feminine often indicated by the suffixes *-t* or *-at*. The Semitic verb is distinguished by its ability to form from the same root a number of derived stems that express new meanings based on the fundamental sense, such as passive, reflexive, causative, and intensive.[20] The close relationship of the languages to one another in the Semitic family is attested by the persistence of the same roots from one language to another—*slm*, for example, means "peace" in Assyro-Babylonian, Hebrew, Aramaic, Arabic, and other languages.

Aramaic is the name of a group of related dialects once spoken, by various Aramaean tribes, for centuries in what is Syria today. There is evidence for it since the beginning of the first millennium B.C.E. As the Aramaeans moved into Assyria and Babylonia, their language spread to all of the Near East, replacing Akkadian, Hebrew, and other languages, eventually becoming the official language of the Persian Empire. In this period it is spoken of as Imperial Aramaic. Aramaic was itself replaced by Arabic after the rise of Islam in the seventh century C.E. Large parts of the biblical books of Ezra (Ezra 4:8–6:18; Ezra 7:12–26) and Daniel (Dan. 2:4b–7:28), and smaller parts of Genesis (Gen. 31:47) and Jeremiah (Jer. 10:11) are in Aramaic. Jesus' native tongue was Palestinian Aramaic; some words of Jesus in the New Testament (e.g., "*Talitha cum*" in Matt. 5:41) are Aramaic. On the cross, Jesus is said to have quoted Psalm 22:1 in Aramaic.

The Babylonian Talmud was written in Eastern Aramaic, a language close to Syriac, the language of the Christian city of Edessa (until the thirteenth century C.E.), still the liturgical language of the Nestorian and Jacobite Christian Churches.[21]

Edessa was an important center of early Christianity in Mesopotamia. (These early Christians gave the Greek name "Syriac" to the Aramaic dialect they spoke when the term "Aramaic" acquired the meaning of "pagan" or "heathen.") Edessene Syriac rapidly became the literary language of all non-Greek Eastern Christianity, and was instrumental in the Christianization of large parts of central and south-central Asia. Despite the fifth-century schism between the monophysite Jacobite Church in Syria and the Nestorian Church of the East, Syriac remained the liturgical and theological language of both these national churches. Syriac is still the classical tongue of the Nestorians and Chaldeans of Iran and Iraq, and the liturgical language of the Jacobites of Eastern Anatolia and the Maronites of Greater Syria. Missionary activity spread the Syriac language and script to India and Mongolia, and rather surprisingly, even the Mongolian script, though written vertically, is derived from the Syriac script.[22]

The importance of Syriac literature for our understanding of the rise of Islam was discussed by A. Mingana, J. B. Segal, Sebastian Brock, and Claude Cahen, and, of course, by Patricia Crone and Michael Cook.[23] But Syriac also played an important role as an intermediary through which Greek learning and thought passed into the emerging Islamic civilization, since it was Syriac-speaking scholars who first translated late Hellenistic science and philosophy from Syriac into Arabic at the *Dār al-Ḥikma* in Baghdad.[24] Other scholars such as Mingana, Margoliouth, and now Luxenberg want to argue that Syriac greatly influenced not only the vocabulary of the Koran, but its theological and philosophical ideas. How this happened is not yet clearly understood.

The oldest Syriac script, which dates back to the first century C.E., evolved from the Aramaic alphabet,[25] which is also the ancestor of Arabic writing. Perhaps I should add here that in Hebrew, Arabic, and Syriac writing, vowels were at first omitted; symbols to indicate the vowels probably date from only the eighth century C.E.

4. ARABIC

The Arabic language, like any other language—and we must not forget that Arabic is like any other language, especially those in the Semitic group of the Afro-Asiatic family—has a history. It did not appear fully fledged out of nowhere, but slowly evolved over a period of time. Little is known about Old or Proto-Arabic. Early Arabic is the name given to the period from the third to sixth century C.E. "when over a large part of Arabia dialects quite distinct from Old Arabic, but approaching Classical Arabic were spoken, and during which Classical Arabic itself must have evolved."[26] Hundreds of Aramaic loanwords entered the language during this period, through Jewish and Christian contacts.[27]

The earliest Arabic texts seem to have been Christian inscriptions, suggesting that the Arabic script was invented by Christian missionaries probably at Ḥīra or Anbār.

> It is probable that at least partial Bible translations into Arabic existed before Islam. Stylistic reminiscences of the Old and New Testaments are found in the Koran. A. Baumstark claimed a pre-Islamic date for the text of some Arabic Bible manuscripts. There is also a fragment of the Psalms in Arabic in Greek characters. Examination of this and two of Baumstark's texts shows a language slightly deviating from Classical Arabic towards the colloquials. This is typical for Christian-Arabic literature, for early papyri and for the language of scientific writing; it may be early colloquial influence, but also Classical Arabic not yet standardized by grammarians. . . .
>
> Wellhausen plausibly suggested that Classical Arabic was developed by Christians at al-Ḥīra. Muslim tradition names among the first persons who wrote Arabic Zayd b.Ḥamād (ca. 500 A.D.) and his son, the poet ʿAdī, both Christians of Ḥīra. ʿAdī's language was not considered fully *faṣīḥ*, which may be taken as meaning that Classical Arabic was still in course of evolution.[28]

What we know as Classical Arabic was academically, and some would say artificially (because of its almost too perfect algebraic-looking grammar [root and pattern morphology]),[29] standardized between the third Muslim/ninth Christian and fourth Muslim/tenth Christian centuries. "Its grammar, syntax, vocabulary and literary usages were clearly defined under systematic and laborious research."[30] We shall return to the issue of the evolution of Classical Arabic later.

Arabic words fully exhibit the typical Semitic word structure already mentioned (see above). An Arabic word is composed of the root of usually three consonants, providing the basic lexical meaning of the word, and the pattern, which consists of vowels and gives grammatical meaning to the word. This feature has been a positive boon to Muslim commentators, who have shown real genius in their inventivesness when confronted with an obscure word in the Koran in need of elucidation. They would often simply turn to the dictionary meaning of the root of an obscure word and try to employ an etymological interpretation of the word.[31]

Arabic "also makes use of prefixes and suffixes, which act as subject markers, pronouns, prepositions, and the definite article."

> Verbs in Arabic are regular in conjugation. There are two tenses: the perfect, formed by the addition of suffixes, which is often used to

> express past time; and the imperfect, formed by the addition of prefixes and sometimes containing suffixes indicating number and gender, which is often used for expressing present or future time. In addition to the two tenses there are imperative forms, an active participle, and a verbal noun. Verbs are inflected for three persons, three numbers (singular, dual, plural), and two genders. In Classical Arabic there is no dual form and no gender differentiation in the first person, and the modern dialects have lost all dual forms. The classical language also has forms for the passive voice.
>
> There are three cases (nominative, genitive, and accusative) in the declensional system of Classical Arabic nouns; nouns are no longer declined in the modern dialects. Pronouns occur both as suffixes and independent words.[32]

Arabic, also like any other world language, has its peculiar strengths and weaknesses. For Bernard Lewis, Classical Arabic is a precise and accurate vehicle of thought, a language of remarkable clarity and an almost peerless instrument of philosophical and scientific communication.[33] While according to Rabin, "Classical Arabic had an extremely rich vocabulary, due partly to the bedouin's power of observation and partly to poetic exuberance; some of the wealth may be due to dialect mixture. It was not rich in forms or constructions, but sufficiently flexible to survive the adaptation to the needs of a highly urbanised and articulate culture without a disruption of its structure."[34] Here is how A. Schaade assesses the strengths of Arabic: "Comparing it first of all with the other Semitic tongues we notice that the possibilities of syntactic distinctions are in Arabic developed to a far greater extent and brought out with greater precision than in any of the others. Where other languages have to content themselves with simple co-ordination, Arabic commands a large number of subordinating conjunctions."[35]

Looking at the limitations of Arabic, Shabbir Akhtar, who taught for three years at the Malaysian Islamic University, contradicts Lewis: "In modern analytical philosophy, there is hardly anything in Arabic or any other Islamic tongue. Philosophical discussion is best conducted in English. Owing to the grammatical limitations of Arabic, it is impossible to express most philosophical claims with an acceptable degree of rigour and clarity. Moreover, Arabic is a devotional language lacking the vocabulary requisite for detached discussion of controversial matters."[36] Lewis and Akhtar are, of course, talking of two different historical periods; for Lewis does add the caveat, ". . . [Arabic's] only peer until modern times was Greek."[37] Furthermore, Akhtar qualified his remarks a few months later, ". . . I concede that the attack on . . . on the suitability of Arabic for philosophical discussion was unfair. Arabic, like Hebrew, has the capacity to generate novel words and expressions from existing roots. . . ."[38]

Schaade points to other limitations:

> In one respect however Classical Arabic as well as its sisters compares unfavourably with the Aryan languages: while for the noun it has created a great number of subtle distinctions which enable it to express even the most abstract concepts, the development of the verb has been one-sided. We seek in vain for a distinction between inchoative and permansive forms of expression: *qāma* means "he was standing" and "he rose." Similarly the different grades of the simple meaning of the verb which we render by means of various auxiliary verbs, are frequently left unexpressed: *yaqra'u* "he reads" and "he is able to read." The expression of the tenses also often lacks precision, in spite of the development of a number of verbal exponents with a temporal force (*qad*, *kāna*, *sawfa*, etc.).[39]

5. *DIGLOSSIA*, THE ORIGINS OF CLASSICAL ARABIC, AND THE LANGUAGE OF THE KORAN

What was the nature of Arabic before and after the rise of Islam, particularly between the third and sixth centuries, and then between seventh and ninth centuries? When did the break between the spoken and written language (the phenomenon of *diglossia*) take place? Out of what and when did Classical Arabic develop? In what language was the Koran written?

Let us begin with the last two questions. According to Muslims, the Koran was written in the dialect of the Quraysh of Mecca, and CA was born out of the Meccan dialect, which was considered the linguistic norm. The language of the Koran, which is identical to the poetical *koine,* is one of the two bases of CA; Muhammad, being from Mecca, could only have received the revelation in his original dialect, that of the Quraysh.

Nöldeke seems to accept the traditional Muslim view that the Koran and pre-Islamic poetry (poetical *koine*) were the two sources of CA, and that the Koran was written in the Meccan dialect: "For me it is highly unlikely that Muhammad in the Koran had used a form of language absolutely different from the usual one in Mecca, that he would have used case and mood inflexions if his compatriots had not used them."[40]

However there are a certain number of objections to the Muslim view. First, it is unlikely that there existed a linguistic norm. Mecca, being an important commercial town and center of pilgrimage, must have been open to the linguisitic influence of the Yemen, Syria, and Najd. Second, Muhammad's preaching had at least Pan-Arab pretensions, but these pretensions would seem hardly realizable if he was using only his local dialect. Surely Muhammad's preaching in the urban language of Mecca would have had no meaning for the nomads, whose language was considered more prestigious.

For some Western scholars, like Blachère,[41] CA was derived from pre-Islamic poetry and the language of the Koran. But for Blachère, the language of the Koran has nothing to do with the dialect of Mecca, but is rather the language of pre-Islamic poetry (the so-called poetical *koine*). As Schaade put it, "The earliest specimens of classical Arabic known to us are found in the pre-Islamic poems. The problem arises how the poets (who for the most part must have been ignorant of writing) came to possess a common poetical language,—either (perhaps with the object of securing for their works a wider field of circulation?) they used for their purposes a language composed of elements from all the different dialects, such as may have been created by the necessities of trade, and which it only remained for them to ennoble, or the dialect of any particular tribe (perhaps owing to political circumstances?) achieved in pre-historic times special pre-eminence as a language of poetry."[42]

Blachère certainly accepts the idea that *diglossia* is an old phenomenon going back to pre-Islamic times. That is to say, scholars like Blachère, Vollers,[43] Wehr,[44] and Diem,[45] believe that the poetical *koine*, the language of pre-Islamic poetry, was a purely literary dialect, distinct from all spoken idioms and supertribal. This situation, in which two varieties, literary and spoken, of the same language live side by side, is called *diglossia*. Other scholars, like Nöldeke,[46] Fück,[47] and Blau,[48] agree with the traditional Arab view that *diglossia* developed as late as the first

Islamic century as a result of the Arab conquests, when non-Arabs began to speak Arabic.

Karl Vollers upset many people when he argued at the beginning of the twentieth century that the Koran was written, without *iʿrāb*, inflection, or case endings, in a dialect of Najd, and was a result of editing and emendation carried out long after Muhammad with a view to harmonizing the sacred text with the language of so-called pre-Islamic poetry, which is that of Najd. Vollers is certain that the Koran as we have it today is not linguistically the revelation as it was received by Muhammad. One must take into account the numerous phonetic variants preserved in the commentaries and special treatises. These variants of a dialectal origin attest to the contrast between the speech of the Ḥijāz and that of Najd. The Koran preserves everywhere certain linguistic features maintained in Najd and on the way to disappearance in the Ḥijāz, according to Muslim grammarians; thus, the Koran represents the speech of Najd. The Koran is the result of adaptation, and issues from the emendations of the text by readers of Najdian atavism or influenced by the nomadic dialects of this region. As to the linguistic identity of the Koran and pre-Islamic poetry, it is explained by the fact that Muslim scholars unified them one by the other during the course of the establishment of the grammar. Vollers concludes that the Koran and pre-Islamic poetry are truly the two sources of CA, but with this reservation that the Koran is an adaptation of the Ḥijāzi dialect to the norms of the poetical language.

Blachère contended that Vollers made too much of the putative contrast between the western dialect and eastern dialect. The contrast between the Ḥijāz and Najd is not as clear-cut as Vollers makes out. Vollers also seems to accept certain linguistic features as true of the time of Muhammad, but which, in reality, were the creations of much later Muslim philologists. If there had been harmonization of the Koranic text with the dialects of Najd, one would expect to find the essential character of these dialects, the *taltala*. One would find traces of this adaptation in the vocabulary and syntax.

Wansbrough has his own reasons for rejecting Vollers's theory: "The basic error lay in Vollers' adherence to an arbitrary and fictive chronology, though that may have been less important than his contention that the refashioned language of scripture could be identified as the CA of the Arabic grammarians. Neither from the point of view of lexicon nor from that of syntax could the claim be justified."[49] In other words, the language of the Koran is not Classical Arabic.

However, Vollers's theory was revived in 1948 by Paul Kahle (chap. 3.3), who sees in a saying of al-Farrāʾ promising reward to those reciting the Koran with *iʿrāb* support for Vollers's view that the original Koran had no *iʿrāb*.[50]

Corriente also makes the point in his classic paper[51] that the language of the Koran is not CA. For Corriente, CA was standardized by the grammarians in eighth and ninth centuries C.E., on the whole depending on a central core of Old Arabic dialects as koineized in pre-Islamic poetry and rhetoric, and the speech of contemporary Bedouins. Grammarians did not invent the *iʿrāb* system, which must have existed in the texts they edited. (*Iʿrāb* is usually translated as "inflexion," indicating case and mood, but the Arab grammarians define it as "the difference that occurs, in fact or virtually, at the end of a word, because of the various antecedents that govern it.")[52] They did come with their preconceptions about what constituted good Arabic, but they nonetheless respected what they learned from their Bedouin informants in order to standardize the language, and thus fix what came to be CA. However, some did reject certain utterances of the Bedouins as being incorrect.

Koranic Arabic is structurally intermediate between OA *koine* and Eastern Bedouin Arabic and Middle Arabic, and, of course, the Koran cannot have been written in CA since this was only finally standardized over a period of time during the eighth and ninth centuries.

Native tradition identifies two groups of dialects, Ancient West and East Arabian, neither of them identical to the OA *koine*. Corriente adds a third kind of Arabic, Nabataean, the immediate forerunner of the Middle Arabic of Islamic cities. It was very widespread indeed.

Finally, Corriente calls attention to the fact that Bedouin vernaculars themselves must also have been undergoing change under various sociolingusitic pressures, a point perhaps overlooked by the romanticization of Bedouin speech by overeager Muslim grammarians.

All the above accounts rest on a number of assumptions that are not always either spelled out or subjected to rigorous questioning. For example, all our knowledge about the early dialects of Najd, the Ḥijāz, and the highland area of the southwest seems to have been gathered during the second and third Islamic centuries, when these dialects were already declining. Much of our data are preserved only in late works whose sources we cannot check.[53] Second, these accounts also accept without hesitation the traditional Muslim chronology and the accounts of the compilation of the Koran. The first scholar in modern times to radically question these accounts is, of course, John Wansbrough, who wrote:

> To draw from the same data conclusions about the origins and evolution of CA involves implicit acceptance of considerable non-linguisitic material often and erroneously supposed to be "historical fact." I refer to such assumptions as that of the isolation of speakers/writers of Arabic within the Arabian peninsula up to the seventh century, or that of the existence of *ne varietur* text of the Islamic revelation not later than the middle of the same century.[54]

Wansbrough points out that the Muslim accounts of the origins of CA have as their aim the establishment of the Ḥijāz as the cradle of Islam, in particular Mecca, and in the polemical milieu of eighth century C.E. Near East, to establish an independent Arab religious identity, with a specifically Arabic Holy Scripture.

> Suppression of claims made on behalf of other tribal groups to the title *afṣaḥ al-ʿarab* [the most eloquent of the Arabs] is symbolized in the account ascribed to Farrāʾ of how the inhabitants of cosmopolitan (!) Mecca (i.e. Quraysh) were in a position to recognize and adopt the best ingredients from each of the bedouin dialects in Arabia.[55] Besides drawing attention to the role of Mecca as cultic and commercial center, this tradition, like the ones it eventually replaced, served to identify the northern regions of the Arabian peninsula as the cradle of CA at a date prior to the proclamation of Islam.[56]

Nor can we uncritically accept Muslim claims that the language spoken by the bedouins must be identical with that of the poetry called pre-Islamic. The bedouins were hardly disinterested referees. But more important, "for our purposes it is well to remember that the written record of transactions between bedouin and philologist dates only from the third/ninth century, and is thus coincident with the literary stabilization of both Quranic exegesis and Muslim historiography."[57]

The polemical importance of "pre-Islamic poetry" for Muslims is also well explained by Wansbrough:

> Whatever may have been the original motives for collecting and recording the ancient poetry of the Arabs, the earliest evidence of such activity belongs, not unexpectedly, to the third/ninth century and the work of the classical philologists. The manner in which this material was manipulated by its collectors to support almost any argument appears never to have been very successfully concealed. The procedure, moreover, was common to all fields of scholarly activity: e.g. the early dating of a verse ascribed to the mukhaḍrami poet Nābigha Jaʿdī in order to provide a pre-Islamic proof text for a common Quranic construction (finite verb form preceded by direct object), Mubarrad's admitted invention of a *ʿJāhilī*ʾ [pre-Islamic] verse as a gloss to a lexical item in the hadith, and Abū ʿAmr b. ʿAlā's candid admission that save for a single verse of ʿAmr b.Kulthūm, knowledge of Yawm Khazāz would have been lost to posterity. The three examples share at least one common motive: recognition of pre-Islamic poetry as authority in linguistic matters, even where such contained non-linguistic implications. Also common to all three is another, perhaps equally significant feature: Ibn Qutayba, who adduced the verse of Nābigha to explain/justify Quranic syntax, lived at the end of the third/ninth century, as did Mubarrad; Abū ʿAmr, of whom no written works were preserved, lived in the second half of the second/eighth century, but this particular dictum was alluded to only in Jāḥiẓ (third/ninth century) and explicitly in Ibn ʿAbd Rabbih (fourth/tenth century). Now, that pre-Islamic poetry should have achieved a kind of status as linguistic canon some time in the third/ninth century may provoke no quarrel. That it had achieved any such status earlier must, I think, be demonstrated. The fact that it had not, in one field at least, can be shown: the absence of poetic *shawāhid* in the earliest form of scriptural exegesis might be thought to indicate that appeal to the authority of *Jāhilī* (and other) poetry was not standard practice before the third/ninth century. Assertions to the contrary may be understood as witness to the extraordinary influence exercised by the concept of *faṣāḥat al-jāhiliyya*.[58]

In other words, the putative eloquence of pre-Islamic poetry became commonplace only in the third/ninth century; there are no references to pre-Islamic poetry in the early, pre-third-century works of Koranic exegesis.

There are even a number of scholars, such as Alphonse Mingana[59] and D. S. Margoliouth,[60] who think that all pre-Islamic poetry is forged, inspired by Koranic preoccupations. The Egyptian Ṭaha Ḥusayn, in *Of Pre-Islamic Literature*,[61] the second of his two famous books, concludes that most of what we call pre-Islamic literature was forged, though he seems to accept the authenticity of some poems, albeit a tiny number. This cautious acceptance of some pre-Islamic poetry as authentic seems to have been shared by several Western scholars, such as Goldziher, Tor Andrae, W. Marçais, and Tritton, who reject the total skepticism of Margoliouth, but shy away from the too generous credulity of Nöldeke and Ahlwardt.[62] Of course, if all pre-Islamic poetry is forged, then there was no such thing as a poetical *koine*, and the language of the Koran obviously could not owe anything to this fictive poetical language. We would have to look elsewhere for the origins of the language of the Koran.

If the Koran did not originally have *iʿrāb*, then the present rhyme scheme[63] to be found in the Koran must be a later addition, since rhyme depends on *iʿrāb*, and the changes required in the Koranic text must have been considerable. The lack of original *iʿrāb* in the Koran, if true, also suggests that there is less of a relationship between poetry and the Koran than previously thought, and that the text of the Koran is primary.

6. THE DIFFICULTIES OF THE KORAN

> *Reading the Koran on its own terms, trying to interpret it without resorting to commentaries, is a difficult and questionable exercise because of the nature of the text—its allusive and referential style and its grammatical and logical discontinuities, as well as our lack of sure information about its origins and the circumstances of its composition. Often such a reading seems arbitrary and necessarily inconclusive.*[64]
>
> G. R. Hawting

Ironically, far from increasing our understanding of the contents, as devout Muslims would have us believe, a look at the Koran in the original Arabic only increases the confusion. As Gerd-R. Puin said, "The Koran claims for itself that it is 'mubeen' or 'clear.'[65] But if you look at it, you will notice that every fifth sentence or so simply doesn't make sense. . . . The fact is that a fifth of the Koranic text is just incomprehensible. . . ."[66]

As Hirschfeld once remarked, Why would the Koran need to superfluously repeat that it is written in clear or plain Arabic three times, if it had really been written in plain Arabic?[67] Of course, there is much in it that is not Arabic at all, both in terms of the vocabulary, subject matter, and inspiration; further sources of obscurities are not only the large number of foreign words but the "new meanings pressed into service."[68]

Muslim scholars themselves are aware of the difficulties and obscurities of their sacred text. Fuat Sezgin lists no less than eighteen treatises by Muslim philologists, such as Abān b.Taghlib (died 758) and Niftawayh (died 859), for the period between the mid-eighth century and the mid-ninth century entitled *Gharīb al-Qur'ān*, *The Rare* [i.e., strange] *Expressions of the Quran*.[69]

Muslim Exegetes divide the words of the Koran into four classes:[70] *Khāṣṣ*, words used in a special sense; *'Āmm*, collective or common; *Mushtarak*, complex words that have several meanings, and *Mu'awwal*, words that have several meanings, all of which are possible, and thus require a special explanation.

As an example of the latter class of words, *Mu'awwal*, we could look at two differing translations of Sura CVIII.2:

Sale: Wherefore pray unto thy Lord; and slay (the victims).
M. Ali: So pray to thy Lord and sacrifice.

The word translated "slay" is in Arabic *inḥar,* from the root *naḥr*, which has several meanings. The Ḥanafites, followers of Abū Ḥanifa (700–767) a leading fiqh scholar and theologian, translate it as "sacrifice adding the words "the victims" in parenthesis. However, the followers of Ibn Ash-Shāfi'ī (767–820) founder of the school of law named after him, say it means "placing the hands on the breast in prayers."[71]

The sentences (*'Ibārah*) of the Koran are divided into two classes, *Ẓāhir*, obvious, and *Khafī* (or *bāṭin*), hidden. Let us look at just the latter class. *Khafī* sentences are either *Khajī*, *Mushkil*, *Mujmal*, or *Mutashābih.*

Khajī sentences contain words that are understood to have hidden beneath their literal meaning a reference to other things or persons. The word "thief," *sāriq*, for instance, has as its hidden references both pickpockets and highway robbers. *Mushkil* sentences are ambiguous, and hence, their meanings are very difficult to ascertain. *Mujmal* sentences may have a variety of interpretations, owing to the words in them being capable of several meanings. In this case, it is the tradition (*ḥadīth*) that settles the meaning and must be accepted. *Mujmal* sentences may also contain rare words whose meaning is not at all clear. Hughes gives the following example of the first kind of *mujmal* sentence: "Stand for prayer (*ṣalāt*) and give alms (*zakāt*)." Both *ṣalāt* and *zakāt* are *Mushtarak* words. Muslims had recourse to tradition (*ḥadīth*) for an explanation. According to the appropriate *ḥadīth*, Muhammad explained that *ṣalāt* might mean the ritual of public prayer, standing to say the words "God is Great," or standing to repeat a few verses of the Koran; or it might mean private prayer. Whereas, *zakāt* comes from the root word meaning to grow, *zakā*. Muhammad, "however, fixed the meaning here to that of 'alsmgiving,' and said, 'Give of your substance one-fortieth part.' "[72]

Mutashābih sentences are "intricate" sentences, or expressions whose meaning is impossible for man to ascertain, though it was known to Muhammad. As Patricia Crone puts it,

> The Qur'ān is generally supposed to have originated in a social, cultural and linguistic environment familiar to the early commentators, whose activities began shortly after Muhammad's death and many of whom were natives of the two cities in which he had been active; yet they not infrequently seem to have forgotten the original meaning of the text. It is clear, for example, that they did not remember what Muhammad had meant by the expressions *jizya 'an yad*, *al-ṣamad*, *kalāla* or *īlāf*; indeed, the whole of Sura 106 (Quraysh) in which the *īlāf* occurs, was as opaque to them as it is to us; and the same is true of the so-called "mysterious letters." *Kalāla* is a rather unusual case in that several traditions (attributed to 'Umar) openly admit that the meaning of this word was unknown; more commonly the exegetes hide their ignorance behind a profusion of interpretations so contradictory that they can only be guesswork.
>
> "It might," as Rosenthal observes, "seem an all too obvious and unconvincing argument to point to the constant differences of the interpreters and conclude from their disgreement that none of them is right. However, there is something to such an argument." There is indeed. Given that the entire exegetical tradition is characterized by a proliferation of diverse interpretations, it is legitimate to wonder whether guesswork did not play as great a role in its creation as did recollection; but the tradition is not necessarily right even when it is unanimous.[73]

The Koran itself admits to its own ambiguous passages whose meaning is known only to God: Sura II.7: "It is He who has revealed to you the Book. Some of its verses are precise in meaning—they are the foundation of the book—and others ambiguous. Those with an evil inclination in their heart seek after what is unclear in it, wishing to trouble people's minds and wishing to interpret it. But no one but God knows its interpretation. Those who are firmly rooted in knowledge say: 'We believe in it; it is all from our Lord.' "

We also have the curious phenomenon of a word that can have two contradictory meanings. For instance, at Koran XX.15: *ʾinna -s- sāʿata ʾātiyatun ʾakādu ʾukhfīha lituj zā kullu nafsim bimā tasʿā.*

Khafā is said to have the two opposite meanings, "to be hid" and "to reveal." M. Ali translates verse 15 above as: "Surely the Hour is coming—I am about to make it manifest—so that every soul may be rewarded as it strives."[74]

Pickthall has: "Lo! the Hour is surely coming. But I will to keep it hidden, that every soul may be rewarded for that which it striveth."[75]

I have gone through Bell's splendid two-volume commentary on the Koran, and have noted some of his comments and judgments on the various difficulties and obscurities of sense and reference. However, I have confined my search mainly to Sura II. I have also referred to Jeffery,[76] Penrice's *Dictionary*,[77] Lane's *Arabic-English Lexicon*,[77] Blachère's French translation of the Koran,[79] and the two articles in the present anthology by Margoliouth and Mingana.[80] I have classified the difficulties into five fairly loose and sometimes overlapping categories in this way, and, of course, the lists make no pretensions of being complete:

[6.1] Individual words whose meaning is not certain.

[6.2] Phrases or sentences whose meaning is not clear, and passages whose reference is not clear (who or what putative historical event they refer to).

[6.3] Passages and words that are thought to be interpolations, insertions, or evidence for revisions.

[6.4] Sentences containing grammatical errors from the Classical Arabic point of view.

[6. 5] Phrases, sentences, and verses that do not seem to fit the context, and thus must have been transposed. These transposed or displaced verses are responsible for the disorder and incoherence that abounds in the Koran.

[6.1] Individual words whose meaning is not certain.

[6.1.1] LXXX.28. *Qaḍb*: meaning not certain, probably "green herbs" of some kind.

[6.1.2] LXXX.31. *ʾAbb*: meaning not certain, probably "pasture." Cf. Hebrew: *ēbh*; Syriac: *ʾebbāʾ*; as Jeffery notes, "The early authorities in Islam were puzzled by the word as is evident from the discussion by Ṭabarī on the verse, and the uncertainty evidenced by Zamakhsharī and Bayḍāwī in their comments, an uncertainty which is shared by the Lexicons (cf. Ibn Manẓur, *Lisān al-ʿArab*, 20 vols. Cairo: A. H., 1300–1308 i, p. 199; Ibn al-Athīr, *Al- Nihāya fī gharīb al-ḥadīth*, 4 vols. Cairo: A. Ḥ, 1322, i,10)."[81]

[6.1.3] IV.51. *Jibt*: no explanation has been found. As Jeffery observes, "the exegetes knew not what to make of it, and from their works we can gather a score of theories as to its meaning, whether idol, or priest, or sorcerer, or sorcery, or satan, or what not."[82]

[6.1.4] LXIX.36. *Ghislīn*: according to Blachère,[83] the Muslim exegetes do not know the meaning of this term. However, most translators, including Bell, seem to follow Ibn al-Kalbī in interpreting it as "what exudes from the bodies of the inmates of the Fire (i.e. Hell)." Blachère finds this unacceptable because of the use of the word *ṭaʿāmun* at the beginning of the verse, which reads, "Not any other food (= *ṭaʿāmun*) but *ghislīn*." *Ṭaʿāmun* usually indicates solid food. Blachère thinks the word is of foreign origin.

[6.1.5] LXXXIX.7. *Iram:* as Jeffery says, the number of variant readings of this word "suggests of itself that [it] was a foreign one of which the exegetes could make nothing."[84] It is perhaps the name of a city or country with which ʿĀd was associated; usually taken to be of South Arabian origin. But as Blachère notes, "It is naturally impossible to know what this verse could have meant for Muhammad's generation."[85]

[6.1.6] XLVI.28. *Qurbān/Qurabān*: verse 28: "Did those help them, whom they had taken for qurban [as] gods [*ʾālihatan*] to the exclusion of Allah."

The word *Qurbān* as it appears in III.182 and V.27 evidently means "sacrifice," but, according to Jeffery, here, at XLVI.28, it means "favorites of a prince."[86] For Penrice, this word must be translated " 'as a means of access to God,' the false deities there mentioned being supposed to be on familiar terms with God, and therefore likely to act as intercessors with Him."[87]

Barth takes the word following *qurbān*, that is, *ʾālihatan*, meaning "Gods" as a gloss on *qurbān*. This seems to be accepted by Wensinck[88] and Bell, but is totally rejected by Blachère, though he does not say why. Blachère admits to being completely baffled by this term in this verse.[89]

Bell adds that another reading, *qurubān* could be taken as a plural of *qārib*, "neighbour," and accordingly his own translation reads: "Why helped them not those whom they had chosen apart from Allah as neighbours gods?" Bell adds as a footnote to neighbors, "i.e. patrons or intercessors."[90]

[6.1.7] II.62. *Ṣābiʿīn*: as Bell says, this word has "baffled all investigators." Literally, it may mean "the baptizers." According to Bell, the whole verse is out of place, while Blachère believes that the words "the Christians, the *Ṣābiʿīn*" seem not to belong with the natural flow of the sentence; perhaps they were added later to fill out the expression "those who believe in God . . . and do good." Some even hold that "the *Ṣābiʿīn*" must be a post-Muhammadan interpolation.[91] It is unlikely to refer to the Sabaeans of Harran who were pagans and certainly did not practice "baptism," and cannot be considered the people of the Book. Perhaps the Mandaeans, a Judeo-Christian sect practising the rite of baptism, are meant.[92]

[6.1.8] II.78. (a) *ʾummiyyūn*

(b) *ʾamāniyya*

- (i) Bell: "Some of them are common people [*ʾummiyyūn*] who do not know the Book except as things taken on trust [*ʾamāniyya*] and who only cherish opinions."
- (ii) Blachère: "While among them are the Gentiles who do not know the Scripture only chimaeras, and only make conjectures."
- (iii) Dawood: "There are illiterate men among them who, ignorant of the Scriptures, know of nothing but lies and vague fancies."
- (iv) Pickthall: "Among them are unlettered folk who know the Scripture not except from hearsay. They but guess."
- (v) Muhammad Ali: "And some of them are illiterate; they know not the Book but only (from) hearsay, and they do but conjecture."

(a) *ʾummiyyūn*

Dawood, Pickthall, and Muhammad Ali follow the Muslim tradition in translating *ʾummiyyūn* (plural of *ʾummi*) as "illiterate," one who neither writes nor reads a writing.[93]

Bell thinks *ʾummiyyūn* means belonging to the *ʾummah* or community, while Blachère translates it as "Gentiles," in the sense of "pagan." For the French scholar it is clear that the word *ummi* designates pagan Arabs, who, unlike the Jews and Christians, had not received any revelation and were thus living in ignorance of the divine law. Ṭabarī does indeed quote some traditions that give this sense to the word *ummi*: according to Ibn ʿAbbās, "*ʾummiyyūn* (refers to) some people who did not believe in a prophet sent by God, nor in a scripture revealed by God; and they wrote a scripture with their own hands. Then they said to ignorant, common people: 'This is from God.' "[94] However, Ṭabarī himself does not accept this interpretation, instead gives a totally unconvincing and improbable account of the derivation of this word: "I am of the opinion that an illiterate person is called *ummī*, relating him in his lack of ability to write to his mother (*umm*), because writing was something which men, and not women, did, so that a man who could not write and form letters was linked to his mother, and not to his father, in his ignorance of writing. . . ."[95]

There is even a series of traditions in Ibn Saʿd[96] that show Muhammad himself writing his political testament. However, Muslim orthodoxy translates *ummi* as "illiterate" for apologetic reasons, to show that the Koran must have been of divine origin since it was revealed to an illiterate, who thus could not have plagiarized, as often accused, the Jewish or Christian scriptures.

(b) *ʾamāniyya*

The meaning of *ʾamāniyya* is not at all clear. For Bayḍāwī it is the plural of *ʾumniyyah,* from the root *mny.* But Bell prefers to derive it from the root *ʾmn*, giving it the meaning "tradition, dogma, a thing taken on trust."[97]

[6.1.9] II.89. *yastaftahūna*: the sense is not clear.[98]

[6.1.10] II.243. *ʾulūf*: probably plural of *ʾalf*, thousand, but possibly an unusual form plural of *ʾilf*, "intimate friend."[99]

[6.1.11] II.260. *ṣur* in *ṣur-hunna*: variously pointed, but is usually taken as the imperative of *ṣwr*, taken here to mean "cause to come," a very unusual meaning of the verb. Blachère translates it, intuitively, as "press" or "squeeze,"[100] Muhammad Ali as "tame," Arberry as "twist," while Mahmoud Ayoub, relying on Muslim exegetes, translates it as "cut into pieces." Scholars remain puzzled.

[6.1.12] II.53, 185; III.3; VIII.29, 41; XXI.48; XXV.1: *Furqān*

First Jeffery:

> In all passages save VIII.42, it is used as though it means some sort of a Scripture sent from God. Thus "we gave to Moses and Aaron the *Furqān*, and an illumination." (xxi.49), and "We gave to Moses the Book and the *Furqān*" (II.50), where it would seem to be the equivalent of the Taurah [Torah]. In III.2, it is associated with the Taurah and the *Injīl* [Gospel], and XXV.1, and II.181, make it practically the equivalent of the Qurʾan, while in VIII.29, we read, "if ye believe God, he will grant you a *Furqān* and forgive your evil deeds." In VIII.42, however, where the reference is to the Battle of Badr, "the day of the *Furqān*, the day when the two hosts met," the meaning seems something quite different. . . .
>
> The [Muslim] philologers, however, are not unanimous as to its meaning.[101]

Rāzī in his discussion of II.53 goes through several possible meanings of the word *Furqān*:

> The *Furqān* [separator, or that by which things may be distinguished] could be either the Torah as a whole or in part. It may also refer to something other than the Torah, perhaps one of the miracles of Moses, such as his staff, and so forth. It may mean relief and victory, as God said concerning the Apostle, "and what we sent down to our servant on the day of the criterion [*Furqān*], the day when the two parties met" (Koran VIII.41). The word *Furqān* may refer to the splitting [*infiraq*] of the sea, or as some have said, to the Quʾran, which was also sent down to Moses.

Rāzī rejects the latter view as a false interpretation. He concludes, "The *Furqān* is that by which truth may be distinguished from falsehood. Thus it may either be the Torah or something external to it."[102]

[6.1.13] CV. 3.

ʾAbābīl. Bell accepts without a great deal of enthusiasm *ʾAbābīl* as the plural of *ʾibbālah*, meaning "a bundle," "flock." This verse is sometimes translated as "Did He not send against them flocks of birds . . . ?" But the sense of this term is not clear, and the word is rare. Kasimirski and Montet see in it a proper name; hence Montet's translation reads, "Did He not send against them the birds *ʾAbābīl.*" Lane, referring to al-Akhfash and as-Sijjani as his authorities, explains that verse 3 means "Birds in distinct, or separate, flocks or bevies: [or] birds in companies from this and that quarter: or following one another, flock after flock."[103]

As Jeffery points out, the long account in Ibn Manẓur, *Lisān al-ʿArab* (xiii, 5), makes it clear that the philologers did not know what to make of the word.

Some have suggested that the word has nothing to do with birds but is another calamity in addition, connecting the word with smallpox. Whereas Carra de Vaux would take *ṭayran ʾAbābīl* (flock of birds) as a mistaken reading for *tīr bābīl,* meaning "Babylonian arrows," which caused the destruction of the army. The word is very probably of foreign origin, though this origin is so far unknown.[104]

[6.1.14] *Sijjīl*: XI.82; XV.74; CV.4.

Ṭabarī and others seem to have derived it from the Middle Persian words *sang*, meaning "stone," and *gīl*, meaning "mud."

It seems to designate stones resembling lumps of clay, fired or sun-dried,[105] and this is corroborated by sura LI.33–4 ". . . that we may loose on them stones of clay, marked by your lord for the prodigal."

As Ṭabarī tells us, some took it to mean the lowest heaven, others connected it with the word *kitāb*. Bayḍā wī points to those who took it to be a variant of *sijin*, meaning hell. More recently, F. Leemhuis[106] has argued that *sijjīl* is in origin a non-Semitic, apparently Sumerian word appearing in Akkadian as *sikillu* or *shigillu*, denoting a smooth kind of stone found in the Aramaic of Hatra, as *sgyl* or *sgl*, with a specialised meaning of "altar stone." From Mesopotamia, it must have entered the various Arabic dialects in Syria and elsewhere, but acquiring the meaning of "hard, flintlike stone."[107]

[6.1.15] *Sijjīn*: LXXXIII.7,8.

Here is Vacca's account from the first edition of the *Encyclopaedia of Islam*:

> *Sijjīn*, one of the mysterious words of the Koran, "Verily the register of the wicked is surely in *Sijjīn*. And what shall make thee understand what is *Sijjīn*? A book written." Explained by commentators as a place where

a record of the deeds of the wicked is kept, and also as that record itself. It is said to be a valley in Hell; the seventh and lowest earth, where *Iblīs* is chained; a rock beneath the earth or the seventh earth; a place beneath *Iblīs*, where spirits of the wicked are; a register comprising the deeds of the wicked, of the *djinn* and of mankind, or of the devils and unbelievers. Without the article it is a proper name of hell-fire. Also said to mean anything hard, vehement, severe, lasting, everlasting (interpretation influenced by the word's likeness to *sijjīl*, [see above], erroneously connected with the root *s-j-l*).

Though [al- Suyūṭī's] *Itqān* classes it among non-Arabic words, no acceptable etymology is supplied . . . ; . . . lexicographers give it as a synonym of *sijn*, prison, and this last word has evidently influenced the prevailing interpretation of *Sijjīn* by Muslim commentators as a place where the record of the wicked is kept, rather than as that record itself. The text of the Koran admits of both interpretations, and most European translators, following Maracci, have preferred the latter.[108]

[6.1.16] *Sijill*: XXI.104.

As Jeffery tells us, the meaning of *sijill* in this passage from XXI.104 was unknown to the early interpreters of the Koran. Some took it to be the name of an angel, or of the Prophet's amanuensis, but the majority seem to be in favor of its meaning some kind of writing or writing material. Baghawī takes it to be an Arabic word, while others admit that it was a foreign word of Abyssinian or Persian origin. It is, however, derived from the Greek, σιγιλλον, in Latin, *sigillum,* used in Byzantine Greek for an imperial edict.[109]

[6.1.17] *kalāla*: IV. 12b.

The last five or so lines of Sura IV.12 have been the source of much controversy among Muslim commentators. Ṭabarī devotes seven pages to these few lines. As David Powers tells us: "Almost every word in the opening line of the verse is subject to dispute, and there may be as many as four or five different opinions, espoused by an even greater number of authorities, for every point in question." Powers shows that precise meaning of *kalāla* also remains a subject of controversy, with Ṭabarī citing twenty-seven separate definitions by various authorities. It is not clear if this word *kalāla* refers to the deceased himself (*al-mawrūth*) or to the heirs of the deceased (*al-waratha*).[110]

It is of the greatest consequence as to how one reads this particular verse, and the above example shows that the uncertainties of meaning and the obscurities in the Koran are not a trivial matter. Powers himself gives his own novel interpretation, arguing that *kalāla* was originally a kinship term referring to a female in-law.

[6.2] Phrases or sentences whose meaning is not clear, and passages whose reference is not clear (which historical person or what putative historical event they refer to).

[6.2.1] II.27. "Who violate the covenant of Allah after making a compact with Him, and separate what Allah hath commanded to be conjoined, and cause corruption in the land; these are the losers."

Bell comments, "what is meant by 'separating what Allah hath commanded to be conjoined' is not clear, but it may refer to their rejection of part of the Book (verse 85) or to their rejection of Muhammad while claiming to believe in Allah."

Ibn Kathīr, however, explains this verse differently:

> The covenant [*ʿahd*] is either the primordial covenant between God and humanity [*mīthāq*] [Koran VII,172], the measure of the knowledge of God which He has implanted in the minds of human beings as proof against them or the reference may be to the Jews and Christians with whom the Prophet came into contact. That "which God commanded to be joined" means honoring the obligations of blood relationship or any relationship in general.[111]

[6.2.2] II.29. "He it is who created for you what is in the earth, as a whole, then straightened Himself up to the heaven, and formed them seven heavens; He doth know everything." As Blachère points out, the plural pronoun "them" in this verse has resisted all explanation.[112] It is significant that certain translators find it hard to resist translating this passage as ". . . and He fashioned IT into seven heavens,"[113] while others such as Arberry keep closely to the text and translate literally. Ṭabarī gets out of the difficulty by insisting that *samāʾ* (heaven) is a collective noun which is to be treated as a plural.[114]

[6.2.3] II.101–103.

Verse 101: When a messenger has come to them from Allah confirming what is with them, a part of those to whom the Book has been given cast the Book of Allah behind their backs as if they did not know.

Verse 102: "And follow what the satans used to recite in the reign of Solomon. Solomon did not disbelieve, but the satans disbelieved, teaching the people magic and what had been sent down to the two angels in *Bābil—Hārūt and Mārūt*; they do not teach anyone without first saying: 'We are only a temptation, so do not disbelieve.' So they learn from them means by which they separate man and wife, but they do not injure anyone thereby, except by the permission of Allah; and they learn what injures them and does not profit, though they know that he who buys it has no share in the Hereafter; a bad bargain did they make for themselves, if they had known."

Verse 103: "If they had believed and acted piously, assuredly, a reward from Allah would have been better, if they had known."

Bell thinks that "what the satans used to recite in the reign of Solomon" may be a reference to the Rabbinic Law. Bell continues, "The mention of *Bābil* may further suggest the Babylonian Talmud. But the whole verse is obscure. It has been extended to undue length by the insertion of clauses designed to obviate misconceptions:

> *Wa-mā kafara . . . as-siḥr* [and Solomon did not disbelieve . . . magic]
> *Wa-mā yuʿallimāni . . . takfur* [and they do not teach . . . disbelieve]
> *Wa -mā hum . . . Allāh* [but they do not . . . Allah]

"Finally the verse [102] having perhaps given rise to misconceptions was discarded, and the short verse 103 substituted for it; this is shown by the repetition of the rhyme-phrase."[115]

As Ayoub confesses, verse 102 "has been the subject of much controversy. Commentators have disagreed concerning every phrase and even word in it."[116] I shall give just Ṭabarī's discussion of the meaning of "and what had been sent down to the two angels *in Bābil—Hārūt and Mārūt*" (*wa-mā ʾunzila ʿalā ʾl-malakayni bi-bābila hārūta wa-mārūta*), though I suspect the reader will be confused rather than enlightened by the end of it.

Ṭabarī[117] gives several opinions about the meaning of *mā* at the beginning of this passage. According to one, it is a particle of negation, and the corresponding interpretation of this verse is: They follow the sorcery which the satans recited during the reign of Solomon; but neither was Solomon an unbeliever, nor did God send sorcery down to the two angels, rather satans disbelieved and taught sorcery to the people in *Bābil—Hārūt* and *Mārūt*. In this case, Ṭabarī tells us, the two angels are Gabriel and Michael, because Jewish sorcerers falsely claimed that God sent down sorcery to Solomon through Gabriel and Michael, and the Koran denies this; and *Hārūt* and *Mārūt* are the names of the two men to whom they taught sorcery in *Bābil*. Ṭabarī recounts a second opinion: *mā* means "that which" (or "what"), and thus *Hārūt* and *Mārūt* are the names of two angels to whom sorcery—different from that which the satans received—was sent down at *Bābil*.

According to a third opinion *mā* means "that which," but it refers specifically to the knowledge of how to sunder a man from his wife. A fourth opinion allows *mā* as both a negative particle and as a relative pronoun. Ṭabarī himself prefers the interpretation of *mā* as a relative pronoun, and of *Hārūt* and *Mārūt* as the names of the two previously mentioned angels. Ṭabarī goes through further opinions, though he rejects them since they seem to create further difficulties in interpreting the rest of the verse.[118]

Many of the commentators took this opportunity to develop the story of *Hārūt* and *Mārūt* for a theological purpose, to prove or emphasize a point of Islamic law. Ibn Kathīr and Ṭabarsī, for instance, give various traditions about *Hārūt* and *Mārūt*, the chief purpose of which seems to have been to show the evils of drinking wine.[119]

Western commentators have not been idle, either: Geiger, Sidersky, Horovitz, and Wensinck have tried to show that the Muslims Commentators were inspired variously by the Babylonian Talmud, by an Ethiopian version of the Book of Enoch, and so on. Dumezil traces the origins of these myths to the Indian epic *Mahabharata*, while de Lagarde identifies *Hārūt* and *Mārūt* as the two secondary divinities associated with the cult of Mazda in the Avesta, the Zoroastrian scriptures: *Haurvatat* (Integrity) and *Ameretat* (the Undying).[120]

[6.2.4] II.114. "But who does greater wrong than those who bar the places of Allah's worship from having the name of Allah remembered in them, and who strive to destroy them? It was not for them to enter them but in fear. For them is (in store) humiliation in this life, and in the Hereafter a mighty punishment."

As Bell says, verse 114 is difficult to understand. Bayḍāwī suggests that it refers to the Romans and their destruction of the temple at Jerusalem, or the Meccans who prevented the Muslims from visiting the Kaʿbah at the time of the Treaty of Ḥudaybiyya. It is typical of Muslim commentators to try to find links in such Koranic passages to putative events in the life of Muhammad. Conservative Western Orientalist scholars have followed suit. These attempts rest on vast assumptions about the reliability of the sources on which our knowledge of the rise of Islam is based. But as Lammens and other revisionists have tried to argue, many so-called events in the life of Muhammad were invented to explain obscure and difficult passages in the Koran. Similarly, once the largely fabricated story of the collection of the Koran was accepted by the Muslim scholars, the Muslim commentators set about trying to interpret in greater detail each and every general Koranic passage, amenable to every possible interpretation, within the framework of the traditional story of the rise of Islam, the life of the Prophet, and the compilation of the Koran. Bayḍāwī's suggestions are a prime example of this activity.

But once again we have vastly divergent Muslim interpretations, each supposedly backed up by impeccable *isnāds* (the chain of authority upon which a report is based); thus showing, once again, they did not have a clue as to what the verse really referred to, or what it really meant. Wāḥidī, relying on al-Suddī and Qatāda, claims that Bukhtnassar (Nebuchadnezzar?) destroyed Jerusalem with the aid of some Byzantine Christians. Then, this time depending on the authority of Ibn ʿAbbās, Wāḥidī reports that this verse was sent down concerning the associators of Mecca when they prevented the Muslims from visiting and worshipping at the Kaʿbah, perhaps at the time of Ḥudaybiyya. Nīsābūrī, also relying on the authority Ibn ʿAbbās, tells us that "the King of the Christians attacked the holy house [the temple at Jerusalem], which he destroyed and desecrated with dead carcasses. He besieged the inhabitants of Jerusalem, killed them, and took their women and children captive. He also burned the books of the Torah. Jerusalem, moreover, remained in ruins until the Muslims rebuilt it during the time of ʿUmar ibn al-Khaṭṭāb. Thus the verse was sent down concerning the sanctuary of Jerusalem."[121]

Ṭabarsī, on the other hand, claims that the people of Quraysh are being referred to. Finally, Bell, a rather conservative Western scholar, who, on the whole, accepted the traditional Muslim account of the rise of Islam, finds the use of the plural *masājid*, "places of worship," difficult to explain. Bells adds, "The *Kaʿbah* is usually distinguished as *al-masjid al-ḥarām*, and it is doubtful if there was more than one definitely Muslim 'mosque' in existence at this time. *Masjid*, however, is not limited to this, cf. XXII.40, and particularly XVII.1. The reference might therefore quite well be to Christian churches in Jerusalem. Jerusalem was still the *qiblah,* but was in Persian hands, the Jews having aided them in its capture. Even this, however, seems far-fetched. . . ."[122]

[6.2.5] Here are some more verses where the references are not clear: II.2: *dhālika*; II.6-7; *alladhīna kafarū*; II.45; II.80; II.153-167; *those who have done wrong*; II.175; II.205; II.210; II.259.

[6.3] Passages and words that are thought to be interpolations, insertions, or evidence for revisions.

[6.3.1] II.105. According to Bell, the word "idolators" in verse 105 may be a later insertion; the grammar is uneven.

[6.3.2] II.219. The latter part of this verse, according to Bell, is a formal rhyme-phrase, which was probably added at a much later revision.

[6.3.3] II.221 ff. Bell observes, "verse 221 f. is not like the surrounding verses, an answer to a question, but it may belong to the same period. If, however, "idolators" includes Jews and Christians the verse must be large, but this is hardly correct. The rhyme clause is again formal and has no doubt been added later."[123]

[6.3.4] II.217. The phrase in the middle of the verse *wa-l-masjid . . . minhu* is an insertion from later date, argues Bell, when the duty of pilgrimage had been recognized, and the Meccan opposition was preventing the duty being fulfilled.[124]

[6.3.5] II.229. The clause *ʾillā . . . bihi* is a later insertion, it shows a mixture of pronouns.[125]

[6.4] Sentences containing grammatical errors[126] from the Classical Arabic point of view.

John Burton[127] in a celebrated article, "Linguistic Errors in the Qurʾān," points out that Muslim scholars have been aware of the grammatical lapses in the Holy Book. But "the errors have never been removed. Either they have been complacently explained away on this grammatical ground or that, or, at best, serious efforts have been made to justify them as actually conforming with the usage of the Arabs."[128] Burton then quotes some hadith where the errors are recognized:

> When the copies of the revelations which he had ordered to be made were submitted to him, ʿUthmān noted several irregularities, "Do not change them," he ordered, "the Arabs will change (or will correct them) as they recite."[129]

Burton next quotes a version from al-Farrāʾ, where ʿUrwah questions ʿĀʾishah about a number of verses, IV.162, V.69, [discussed below] XX.63, "ʿĀʾishah replied: 'That was the doing of the scribes. They wrote it out wrongly.' "[130]

[6.4.1] V.69. Bell agrees with Torrey that *aṣ-ṣābiʿūna* must be an interpolation here since it is grammatically out of order; after *ʾinna* it should have been *aṣ-ṣābiʿina*, i.e., in the accusative.[131]

[6.4.2] VII.160. "We divided them into twelve tribes" (*wa qaṭṭa ʿnāhum- th natay ʿashrata ʾasbāṭan*).

Strict grammar requires the singular, since the numerals from 11 to 99 are followed by the noun in the accusative singular, hence *ʾasbāṭan* should read *sibṭan.*[132]

[6.4.3] IV.162. *al-muqīmīna* is wrong grammatically; it should read *al-muqīmūna*, i.e., in the nominative case, like the other preceding substantives in the nominative, *al-rāsikhūna,* and *al-muʾminūna*, and those coming after it, *al-muʾtūna* and *al-muʾminūna.*

[6.4.4] VII.56. "Surely the mercy of God is nigh . . ." The Arabic word for "nigh," *qarīb*, should agree in gender with the Arabic word for "mercy," *raḥmah*, which is feminine, and thus should read *qarībatun*, and not *qarībun*, as it is in this verse.

[6.4.5] XXII.19. These are two disputants who have contended about their Lord.

Hādhāni khaṣmāni—khtaṣamū fī rabbihim

There are three numbers in Arabic: singular (*mufrad*), dual (*muthanna*), and plural (*jamʿ*). The verb *ikhtaṣamū* should have the dual ending, and not the plural, since two individuals (or two parties) are involved, and thus should read *ikhtaṣamā.*

[6.4.6] IX.69. "... You plunged about (in talk) as they plunged about ..." (or, more literally, "... as they who plunged").

"*Wa-khuḍttum ka-l-ladhī khāḍū.*"

The word "as" is a translation of the Arabic *ka*, "like" or "as," and the relative pronoun *alladhī*, "who, which, that," together forming *kalladhī*. But in Arabic, the relative pronoun is declined, and in this verse, it should be in the plural since it refers to a plural pronoun. Hence it should read *kalladhīna*. instead of *kalladhī*.[133]

[6.4.7] LXIII.10. "O My Lord, wouldst Thou not defer me a little while, that I may give alms, and become one of the upright?"

Rabbi lawla'ā 'akh-khartanī 'ī 'ilā 'ajalin qarībin fa 'aṣṣaddaqa wa 'akun mina-ṣ-ṣāliḥīna.

As Wright tells us in *Grammar*, the subjunctive mood occurs in subordinate clauses, and is governed by particles such as *fa-*, when this particle introduces a clause that expresses the result or effect of a preceding clause. The preceding clause must express a wish or hope. Hence the verb *'akun* should be in the subjunctive, and should read, *'akūna*.[134]

[6.4.8] XI.10. "If We cause him to experience prosperity after *[ba'da]* the dearth [*ḍarrā'ā*] which has affected him, he will assuredly say: 'The evil (deeds) have departed from me'; lo, he is rejoicing, boastful."

All prepositions (e.g., *ba'da*) are followed by the noun in the genitive, and thus *ḍarrā'ā* should in fact be *ḍarrā'i*.[135]

[6.4.9] XXXVII.123–130. "Elias was surely one of those sent. ... Peace be on Elias."

Many of the verses in this sura end with the rhyme *-īn*. For the sake of this rhyme, the second instance of Elias (verse 130) is rendered *Ilyāsīn*, as though it were a plural; a good example of poetic license.

[6.4.10] XCV.1–3. "By the fig and the olive! And Mount Sinai! [*sīnīn*]
And this city made secure [*al-'amīn*]

(Inflectional vowels at the end of a verse are disregarded for the sake of the rhyme.)

Similarly, in this verse grammar is sacrificed for the rhyme. Sinai (in Arabic, *sīnā'a*) is changed for *sīnīn* for the sake of preserving the *-īn* ending; another example of poetic license.

[6.4.11] II.80. "The Fire shall not touch us but for a few days."

... *illā 'ayyāman ma'dūdatan.*

Arabic has two forms of plural, the plural of abundance and the plural of paucity. The latter is used only of persons and things that do not exceed ten in number, while the former is used for the rest. In this case, clearly a small number of days is meant; the emphasis is on the "fewness." Thus the plural of paucity would seem to be appropriate, *maʿdūdāt* (when declined in the above verse it would then be *maʿdūdātin*) rather than *maʿdūda* (in the above verse, when declined, it is *maʿdūdatan*).[136]

[6.4.12] II.177. "Righteousness does not consist in whether you face the East or the West, but virtuous conduct is (that of) those who have believed in Allah and the Last Day and the angels and the Book and the prophets . . . and practice regular charity, to fulfil [*al-mūfūna*] the contracts you have made, and to be firm and patient [*aṣ-ṣābirīna*] in pain and adversity. . . ."

The whole verse is rather tortuous and inelegant; many of the verbs are in the past tense in the original Arabic (*ʾāmana, ʾātā, ʾaqāma*), when the present would have been more appropriate. Indeed, the translations certainly read more naturally in English when the present tense is used.

Second, in the original Arabic the verse begins rather clumsily: "But the piety [*al-birr*] is he who believes . . ."

Blachère and others prefer to read *al-barru* instead of *al-birr*, giving the more logical reading, "the pious man is he who believes . . ."

There is, however, one undoubted grammatical error: *aṣ-ṣābirīna* is incorrectly in the accusative, it should, like *al-mūfūna*, be in the nominative, and thus should read: *aṣ-ṣābirūna*.[137]

[6.4.13] III.59. Arberry: "The likeness of Jesus, in God's sight is as Adam's likeness. He created him of dust, then said He unto him, 'Be' and he was."

Pickthall: "Lo! the likeness of Jesus with Allah is as the likeness of Adam. He created him of dust, then He said unto him: Be! and he is."

Pickthall translates more literally, and keeps close to the original Arabic tenses. However, it would be more consistent to use, as Arberry does, the verb "to be" in the past, "he was," to agree with the past tense of "he said . . ." The Arabic *yakūn* (is) should thus be *kāna* (was).

It is worth pointing out that another analysis of the above verse is possible.[138]

[6.4.14] XII.15. "So, when they had taken him away, and agreed to place him in the bottom of the cistern and We suggested to him the thought: 'Thou wilt certainly tell them of this affair of theirs, when they are not aware.' "

Fa-lammā dhahabū bihi wa ʾajmaʿū ʾny-yaj ʿ alūhu fighayābati-l-jubbi wa ʾawḥaynā ʾlayhi latunabbiʾannahum bi ʾamrihim hādhā wa hum lā yashʿurūna.

Bell comments: "In verse 15 there is no principal clause, unless we omit one of the connectives, either that before *ʾajmaʿū*, or that before *ʾawḥaynā*; as the clause introduced by the latter breaks the narrative, and verse 16 is short, there has possibly been an insertion. Verse 16 being the original close of verse 15, and *wa* being added."[139]

6.5 Phrases, sentences, and verses that do not seem to fit the context, and thus must have been transposed. These transposed or displaced verses are responsible for the disorder and incoherence that abounds in the Koran.

[6.5.1.] XLVIII.8–9. "Surely We have sent you as a witness [*shāhidan*], as a bringer of glad tidings, and as a warner: In order that you may believe in Allah and His Apostle [*rasūl*], that you may assist [*tuʿazzirūhu*] and honor Him and celebrate his praises [*tusabbiḥūhu*] morning and evening."

Bell remarks, "Verse 9 cannot possibly be in its original form, for the *-hu* [him] in *tusabbiḥūhu* cannot refer to the *rasūl*, while that in the *tuʿazzirūhu* most naturally would; the middle of the verse must therefore have been inserted later, probably to adapt the verses as an introduction to verse 10."[140]

There is hopeless confusion about the pronoun "him" throughout the verse.

[6.5.2] Even scholars who seem to, on the whole, accept the Muslim chronology and the traditional account of the compilation of the Koran admit to difficulties of sense and reference, and point to the frequent breaks in logic and coherence in the Holy Text. Goldziher, for instance, wrote:

> Judgments of the Quran's literary value may vary, but there is one thing even prejudice cannot deny. The people entrusted, during the reigns of Abū Bakr and ʿUthmān, with the redaction of the unordered parts of the book occasionally went about their work in a very clumsy fashion. With the exception of the earliest Meccan suras, which the Prophet had used

before his emigration to Medina as liturgical texts, and which consist of self-contained pieces so brief as to make them less vulnerable to editorial confusion the parts of the holy book, and particularly certain Medinese suras, often display a disorder and lack of coherence that caused considerable difficulty and toil to later commentators who had to regard the established order as basic and sacrosanct. If scholars undertake one day "a real critical edition of the text, reflecting all the results of scholarly research"—a project recently urged in these words by Rudolf Geyer,—they will have to pay attention to the transposition of verses out of their original contexts and to interpolations.[141] The fact of editorial confusion appears clearly from Nöldeke's survey of the arrangement of individual suras.[142]

The assumption of inapposite interpolations can on occasion help us get around difficulties in understanding the text. I would like to illustrate this by an example. Sura 24 (from verse 27 on) deals with the way virtuous people visit one another,how they should announce themselves, greet the people of the house, how women and children are to behave on such occasions. The rules for such situations became confused because in verses 32–34 and 35–36 two digressions, only loosely related to the main theme, were interpolated.

Then in verse 58 the theme of announcing one's visit is reintroduced, and discussed through verse 60. Then verse 61 reads: "There is no restriction on the blind, no restriction on the lame, no restriction on the sick, nor on yourselves, if you eat in one of your houses, or the houses of your fathers, or the houses of your mothers, or the houses of your brothers, or the houses of your sisters, or the houses of your paternal uncles, or the houses of your paternal aunts, or the houses of your maternal uncles, or the houses of your maternal aunts, or in one whose keys you hold or in one belonging to your friend. It will not render you guilty of a sin, whether you eat together or apart. And when you enter houses, greet one another with a greeting from Allah, a blessed and goodly one."

In this passage Muhammad permits his followers to join their relatives at table without any restriction, and even to go as guests to the houses of female blood relations. One cannot fail to notice that the first words of verse 61, which extend this freedom to the blind, lame, and sick, do not fit the natural context very well. A writer on medicine in the Qur'ān took this juxtaposition very seriously, and offered the critique that while the dinner company of the halt and the blind is unobjectionable, a meal in the company of a sick man may be dangerous for one's health; Muhammad would have done better not to combat the aversion to it.[143]

On closer study we see that the passage out of place in this context strayed into it from another group of rules. Its original reference is not to taking part in meals at the houses of others, but to taking part in the military campaigns of early Islam. In Sura 48, verses 11–16, the Prophet inveighs against "the Arabs who were left behind," those who did not participate in the campaign just undertaken. He threatens them with severe divine punishments. He appends to this verse 17: "It is no compulsion for the blind (*laysa . . . ḥarajun*), no compulsion for the lame, and no compulsion for the sick"—the text agrees literally with 24:61—i.e., people handicapped in these or other serious ways may be excused if they abstain. This phrase was inserted into the other context, to which it is foreign. It evidently influenced the redaction of the verse, whose original beginning cannot be reconstructed with certainty. Muslim commentators too have attempted, naturally without assuming an interpolation, to explain the words in keeping with their natural sense as an excuse for the abstention from war of those bodily unfit for service, but they had to accept the rejection of such an explanation for the reason that if the words were so understood, "they would not be in harmony with what precedes and follows them."[144]

[6.5.3] II.238 f.

As Bell argues, "verses 238 and following have no connection with the context. They seem designed for those on some military expedition."[145]

[6.5.4.] II.243

Bell again

"Verse 243 is enigmatical; it is unconnected with the context, and the reference is unknown. Bayḍā wī gives two stories:

(a) that of the people of Dwardān, said to be a village near Wāsiṭ associated in legend with Ezekiel, who were stricken by a pestilence and fled; Allah caused them to die, but afterwards brought them to life;

(b) that of some of the Israelites who refused to fight when summoned to do so by their king; they were caused to die but restored to life after eight days.

The latter is evidently founded on a wrong interpretation of the verse, which has no connection with fighting, but is designed to enforce the doctrine of the resurrection. . . .[146]

7. KORANIC OBSCURITIES AND KORANIC COMMENTARIES

In September 1996 the Ibn Khaldun Society was launched in London as an independent forum for moderate Muslims. At the inaugural conference, the participants reached, among others, the following conclusions:

> Muslims must become independent of tradition. Just as our forebears found their own way, Muslims today must find theirs. In the process, they need to re-evaluate the Islamic tradition.
>
> The only reliable and relevant source of faith is the Qur'ān. Muslims need new scientific research into the Qur'ān, and a re-examination of the Qur'ānic message and its meaning in the 21st century. . . .[147]

All moderate Muslims would no doubt wholeheartedly endorse these laudable goals, but one wonders how many of them realize how much their putative understanding of the Koran rests entirely on Islamic traditions.

The Muslim tradition has woven a fantastic spiderweb around its holy scripture from which even modern scholarship has not managed to disentangle itself. For all Muslims, much of the Koran remains incomprehensible without the commentaries; indeed, that is the very reason there are so many Muslim commentaries. As Leemhuis put it, ". . . The more of the Qur'ān that became obscure in the course of time, the more of it became provided with an explanation."[148] One would hardly need them if the Koran were truly *mubeen*, "clear." But, as all my examples above show, despite all the thousands of pages devoted to clarifying the text, the Koran still remains incomprehensible, even for those Western scholars who accept the traditional, specially chronological Muslim framework for the Koran.

Muslim Koranic exegesis of such influential scholars as Ṭabarī tended to be *tafsīr bi'l-ma'thūr* (interpretation following tradition), rather than *tafsīr bi'l-ra'y* (interpretation by personal opinion). Ṭabarī's great work, *Jāmiʿ al-bayān ʿan taw' īl āy al-Qur'ān*, is full of exegetical *ḥadīths*, where the Prophet gives his explanation of various obscure verses. Similarly, Ibn Kathīr advises that if we are unable to elucidate some passage of the Koran by some other Koranic passage, then one must examine the prophetic *sunna,* and if that fails, then one must have resort to the sayings of the companions of Muhammad.[149]

However, if we accept the negative conclusions of Goldziher, Schacht, Wansbrough, Crone, and Cook about the authenticity of *ḥadīths* in general, then we must be equally skeptical of the *ḥadīths* concerning exegesis of the Koran. In other words, we cannot separate discussions of the compilation and meaning of the Koran from the questions about the authenticity of *ḥadīth* and the *sīrah*, the life of Muhammad.[150]

It is Muslim tradition that has unfortunately saddled us with the fiction that such and such verse in the Koran was revealed at such and such time during Muhammad's ministry. As early as 1861, the Reverend Rodwell wrote in his preface to the translation of the Koran, "It may be considered quite certain that it was not customary to reduce to writing any traditions concerning Muhammad himself, for at least the greater part of a century. They rested entirely on the memory of those who have handed them down, and must necessarily have been coloured by their prejudices and convictions, to say nothing of the tendency to the formation of myths and to actual fabrication, which early shews itself, especially in interpretations of the Koran, to subserve the purposes of the contending factions of the Umayyads and ʿAbbāsids." Even the writings of historians such as Ibn Isḥāq are "necessarily coloured by the theological tendencies of their master and patron. . . . Traditions can never be considered as at all reliable, unless they are traceable to some common origin, have descended to us by independent witnesses, and correspond with the statements of the Koran itself—always of course deducting such texts as (which is not unfrequently the case) have themselves given rise to the tradition. It soon becomes obvious to the reader of Muslim traditions and commentators that both miracles and historical events have been invented for the sake of expounding a dark and perplexing text; and that even the earlier traditions are largely tinged with the mythical element."[151]

The above passage is a remarkable anticipation of the works of not only Goldziher but also Henri Lammens. The former showed by 1890 the entirely spurious and tendentious nature of the *ḥadīth*, and the latter that "on the fabric of the Koranic text, the *ḥadīth* has embroidered its legend, being satisfied with inventing names of additional actors presented or with spinning out the original theme." It is the Koran, in fact, that has generated all the details of the life of the Prophet, and not vice versa: "one begins with the Koran while pretending to conclude with it." Muslim tradition has often been able to do this because of the often vague and very general way events are referred to, such that they leave open the possibility of any interpretation that the Muslim exegetes care to embroider.

Michael Schub shows that the traditional interpretation of sura IX.40 is suspect, and is more probably derived from the Old Testament, 1 Sam. 23:16 ff. "Faithful Muslims will forever believe that Quran IX.40: 'If ye help him not, still Allah helped him when those who disbelieve drove him forth, the second of two; when they two were in the cave, when he said unto his comrade: Grieve not. Lo! Allah is with us. Then Allah caused His peace of reassurance to descend upon him and supported him with hosts ye cannot see, and made the word of those who disbelieved the nethermost, while Allah's word it was that became uppermost. Allah is mighty, wise' refers to the Prophet Muhammad and Abū Bakr, although not one word of the Quranic text supports this."[152]

Rippin has also argued that certain passages in the Koran that are traditionally interpreted as referring to Muhammad are not necessarily historical. Citing Sura XCIII, Rippin states that "there is nothing absolutely compelling about interpreting [Sura XCIII] in light of the life or the lifetime of Muhammad. The 'thee' [in verse 3: 'The Lord has neither forsaken thee nor hates thee'] of this passage does not have to be Muhammad. It certainly could be, but it does not have to be. (I might also point out that Arberry's translation also suggests the necessity of 'he' as God [i.e., 'He'] which is also not necessarily compelling.) All the elements in the verses are motifs of religious literature (and indeed, themes of the Qur᾿ān) and they need not be taken to reflect historical 'reality' as such, but, rather, could well be understood as the foundational material of monotheist religious preaching."[153] One of Rippin's conclusions is that "the close correlation between the sira and the Qur᾿ān can be taken to be more indicative of exegetical and narrative development within the Islamic community rather than evidence for thinking that one source witnesses the veracity of another. To me, it does seem that in no sense can the Qur᾿ān be assumed to be a primary document in constructing the life of Muhammad. The text is far too opaque when it comes to history; its shifting referents leave the text in a conceptual muddle for historical purposes. This is the point of my quick look at the evidence of the 'addressee' of the text; the way in which the shifts occur renders it problematic to make any assumption about the addressee and his (or her) historical situation. If one wishes to read the Qur᾿ān in a historical manner, then it can only be interpreted in light of other material."[154]

8. KORANIC DIFFICULTIES AND ARABIC WRITING

[8.1] Aramaic Alphabet[155]

The North Semitic alphabet, which was used in Syria from the eleventh century B.C.E. onward, is the direct or indirect ancestor of all subsequent alphabetic scripts (including the South Semitic scripts such as Ethiopic, though there is no scholarly consensus on this point).[156] It gave rise to the Phoenician and Aramaic alphabets. The Aramaic alphabet was developed in the tenth and ninth centuries B.C.E.; the oldest inscription in Aramaic script dates from about 850 B.C.E. Both the language and the script were used as a lingua franca throughout the Middle East. The Aramaic alphabet has twenty-two letters, all indicating consonants, and is written, like Arabic and Hebrew, from right to left. "It is ancestral to Square Hebrew and the modern Hebrew alphabet, the Nabataean and modern Arabic scripts, the Palmyrene alphabet, and the Syriac, as well as hundreds of other writing systems used at some time in Asia east of Syria. Aramaic also has been influential in the development of such alphabets as the Georgian, Armenian, and Glagolitic [Slavonic]."[157]

[8.2] Arabic Alphabet

The origins of the Arabic alphabet are still imperfectly understood. It very probably developed in the fourth century C.E. as a direct descendant of the Nabataean alphabet, which in turn comes down from Aramaic. Some scholars, however, think the Nabataean inscriptions found on a tombstone in Umm al-Jimal (see appendix J), and dated approximately to 250 C.E. are examples of at least proto-Arabic writing. Some scholars would claim that earliest example of Arabic script that we know of is a royal funerary inscription, found in Namāra in 1901 (see appendix J), of the Nabataeans dating from 328 C.E. Others argue that this inscription, though it shows some of the characteristics of Arabic, is essentially Aramaic, and insist that the earliest extant example of Arabic writing is a trilingual inscription in Greek, Syriac, and Arabic discovered at Zabad (see appendix J), dating from 512 C.E.

John Healey[158] sums up the two theories as to the origins of the Arabic script:

> Basically the view that has become prevalent, despite some dissent, is that the early cursive Arabic script, evidenced in seventh-century papyri (mostly from Egypt and Nessana in the Negev), derived from the Nabataean script. I have argued[159] that it derived specifically from the cursive [used for less formal everyday purposes] variety of the Nabataean script (a view for which the evidence is now strengthened by the publication on microfiches of more of the cursive Nabataean papyri).[160] . . . The alternative view has sought a Syriac origin for the Arabic script. This view, associated especially with the name of the late Jean Starcky and advocated particularly by the French school, argues from the broader issue of the basic design of the Syriac and Arabic scripts, specifically the fact that both "sit" upon the line of writing, while the Nabataean script "hangs" from an upper line.[161] This point is apposite, though somewhat weakend by the existence of Nabataean inscriptions and papyri in which the lower line seems to be more significant. It remains the fact, however, that a number of the Arabic letters could not have been derived from the Syriac. . . . It would seem, in fact, that there is a fairly even split in the Arabic inventory of letters: eleven of the Arabic letters could be either of Nabataean or Syriac origin, while ten are much more plausibly related to Nabataean are hard to explain from Syriac, formal or cursive. It may be also noted that none of the Arabic letters is impossible to explain from Nabataean.

It is very likely that both Hebrew and Arabic owe to Syriac their own system of vowel notation by supralinear and sublinear markings.[162]

The Arabic alphabet, written from right to left, has twenty-eight letters, twenty-two of them being those of the Semitic alphabet, from which it is descended; the remaining six letters represent sounds not used in the languages written in the earlier alphabet. All the letters represent consonants, and thus, as M. Cohen once put it, "the orthography always comprises an element of interpretation by the reader, an ideographic element."

The shape of each letter differs according to its position at the beginning, middle or end of the word (initial, medial and final respectively); a fourth form of the letter is when it is written alone (see appendix K).

Certain letters of the Arabic alphabet are identical in shape, and are only differentiated by the presence or absence of a dot, for instance, to distingush an *r* from a *z*; *j*, and an *ḥ*, from a *kh*, other pairs are *s* and *sh*; *d* and *dh*; *ṭ* and *ẓ*; and so on. But as Beeston[163] reminds us, in some cases the differentiation is not simply by presence or absence of a dot, but between varieties in the number and placing of dots: initial and medial *b*, *t*, *th*, *n*, and *y* all have dots differing in number and placing, and in word-end position only *n* and *y* are distinctive without the aid of dots. Thus, a great many variant readings are possible according to the way the text is pointed (has dots added; these dots are usually called diacritic dots or even "diacritical points"—in Arabic, *nuqaṭ* [see appendix L]) In the first two centuries of Islam, diacritical dots were hardly used at all. When they were eventually introduced, there were additional problems since many of the dots were often written at some distance above or below the letter itself. Thus it was often difficult to detect which of two adjacent letters the dotting was intended to affect.

Parallel to the problem of diacritics to differentiate the consonants was the problem of indicating the vowels. Following earlier Semitic script traditions, the earliest Arabic used "the letters *w* and *y* ambivalently, both as true consonants and as indicators of the long vowels *ū*-, and *ī*-; but long *ā*- was noted (by an originally consonantal letter) only at the end of the word, hardly ever in the middle of the word. . . . As for the short vowels, these were . . . normally omitted altogether in writing."[164]

> In the very earliest Qurʾān codices, and in inscriptions, coins and papyri, no marking at all is found for short vowels or for *a*- in the middle of a word. By the early second /eighth century, some Qurʾān codices used coloured dots as indications of vowels, though only to a limited extent, where misreading was particularly likely.[165]

Short vowels eventually came to be represented by three orthographical signs—taking the form of a slightly slanting dash placed below or above the line, or a comma placed above the line. Using different vowels, of course, gave different readings. Compounding these problems was the lack of an adequate punctuation system. The Koran was indeed written in a *scripta defectiva*; *scripta plena*, which allowed a fully voweled and pointed text, was not perfected until the late ninth century.

Thus every Arabic text consists of three layers:

(1) the basic (unpointed) form, shape or drawing of the individual word; in Arabic, *rasm*.
(2) the diacritical points, in Arabic, *nuqaṭ*, the function of which is to

differentiate letters of the basic *rasm*; there are seven letters which are the unmarked members of pairs where the other member has over-dotting.

(3) Signs for the short vowels, to be read with the consonants denoted by the basic drawing (*rasm*) and the diacritical points (*nuqaṭ*).

Günter Lüling gives the following example of the ambiguity of the unpointed Arabic script; the word *rasm*, if pointed and vowelled differently, gives at least six possible readings: *zanaytum*, "you have fornicated"; *zayyantum*, "you have adorned"; *rabbaytum*, "you have educated"; *rannaytum*, "you have delected"; *rana'tum*, "you have looked at, or you have walked heavily"; *ra'aytum*, "you have seen."

It should be clear by now that the ground layer of the Arabic script, that is, the *rasm*, or basic drawing, without the diacritical points and signs is very difficult to interpret, and very easy to misinterpret.[166]

The traditional explanation of the existence of variants goes something like this. The problems posed by the *scripta defectiva* inevitably led to the growth of different centers with their own variant traditions of how the texts should be pointed or vowelized. Despite ʿUthmān's order to destroy all texts other than his own, older codices must have survived. As Charles Adams says, "It must be emphasized that far from there being a single text passed down inviolate from the time of ʿUthman's commission, literally thousands of variant readings of particular verses were known in the first three (Muslim) centuries. These variants affected even the ʿUthmanic codex, making it difficult to know what its true form may have been."[167]

Muslim scholars themselves, from the early days of Islam, have acknowledged the existence of variants. This tradition has led to the compilation of all variants in a mammoth work of eight volumes, *Muʿjam al-qira'āt al-qur'āniyyah*,[168] edited in Kuwait recently. This dictionary lists over ten thousand variants, of which about a thousand are variants of or deviations in the *rasm*. Gerd-R. Puin, the German scholar most closely involved with the classification of the approximately sixteen thousand sheets or parchments of Koranic fragments discovered in Ṣanʿā', Yemen, has uncovered even more variants in the *rasm* that are not found in the above-mentioned eight-volume dictionary. By comparing the *rasm* of the

Cairo *Muṣḥaf* with a fragmentary *Ḥijāzī Muṣḥaf* consisting of eighty-three sheets, which can be tentatively dated to the early eighth century C.E. on stylistic grounds, Puin discovered that the deviations in the *Ḥijāzī Muṣḥaf* by far outnumber the deviations that have been recorded by the Muslim authorities on the *qirā'āt* and which have been collected in the above-mentioned encyclopaedia. This observation is not specific to the Koranic manuscripts of Yemeni provenance, but it is true for more or less all of the extant manuscripts preserved in Ḥijāzī style.

The Ḥijāzī Korans show differences in the sytem of counting of verses from the two dozen or so schools of counting; even the sequence of suras is often at variance not only with the Standard Egyptian edition but with the sequence of suras as recorded for the Korans of Ibn Mas'ūd and Ubayy b. Ka'b. These deviations cannot be dismissed as mere scribal errors (*lapsus calami*), since the so-called errors are repeated with the same word several times in several fragments studied by Puin. Thus, as Puin emphasizes, it makes common philological sense to look for a rationale. The recurrent deviations from the Standard Egyptian text must be taken seriously, and cannot be swept under the carpet and attributed to scribal inadequacy.

One of Puin's conclusions is that though there was an oral tradition (otherwise the Koranic text could not have been read at all), there were deliberate changes in the oral tradition of Koran reading/recitation. Thus this oral tradition was not very stable or elaborate—changes must have occurred as can be seen in the variant orthography to be found in the Ḥijāzī manuscripts, in general.

As Guillaume says, the variants are not always trifling in significance.[169] As an example of a variant reading on the level of vocalization though not of the rasm, we might cite the last two verses of Sura LXXXV, *al-Burūj*, which read: (21) *huwa qur'ānum majīdun*; (22) *fī lawḥim maḥfūẓun/in*. The last syllable is in doubt. If it is in the genitive *-in*, it gives the meaning "It is a glorious Koran on a preserved tablet"—a reference to the Muslim doctrine of the Preserved Tablet. If it is the nominative ending *-un*, we get "It is a glorious Koran preserved on a tablet."

In IV.117, the standard text ended in an obscure word: "They do not invoke in lieu of Allah other than . . ."; the last word was usually read *'ināthan* ("females"). The problem is that many of the pre-Islamic deities were male. In XXIX.16, we find, "You only worship in lieu of Allah *ʾauthānan* [idols]." Thus, an emendation gives us idols instead of females; however, the form *ʾauthānan* involved the insertion of a letter, whereas the form *uthunan* was doubtful Arabic.[170]

Other examples include III.11, where, in the account of the miracle of Badr, the nature of the miracle varies seriously according as we read "you saw them" or "they saw them."[171]

It is clear that many hundreds of variants, though not all, were invented by Muslim grammarians, philologists, and exegetes of the third and fourth Muslim centuries to explain all sorts of obscurities of the Koran, whether of sense or reference; Koranic grammatical aberrations;[172] or, even more seriously, for doctrinal reasons to defend some particular theological position.[173] A kind of ethics of variants had developed by the ninth century C.E., according to which only variants that were not too far from Islamic orthodoxy or doctrines, or not too ungrammatical, were to be accepted and preserved. Hence, if there had been startling deviations or variants, they would have been suppressed. Thus, the variants that do remain are not always very significant. But we need to make a distinction between the variants fabricated by the Muslim exegetes, and the variants to be found in the *rasm* in manuscripts such as those examined by Puin. The sheer number of variants in the orthography in the earliest manuscripts certainly cast doubt on the traditional account of the compilation of the Koran. The Ḥijāzī fragments seem to suggest that, even in the eighth century C.E., the text of the Koran was yet to be defined, and the "reading" options that the meagre *rasm* allowed had to be limited by officially recognizing only a part of them as admissible *qirāʾāt*.

9. KORANIC CONTRADICTIONS AND ABROGATION

Spotting contradictions in the Koran is something of a growth industry, particularly in the context of Muslim-Christian polemics, with Muslims desperately trying to keep their finger in the leaking dike.[174]

Contradictions do abound in the Koran, and the early Muslims were perfectly well aware of them; indeed, they devised the science of abrogation to deal with them. It is a very convenient doctrine that, as one Christian unkindly put it, "fell in with that law of expediency which appears to be the salient feature in Muhammad's prophetical career."[175] According to this doctrine, certain passages of the Koran are abrogated by verses revealed afterward, with a different or contrary meaning. This was supposedly taught by Muhammad at Sura II.105: "Whatever verses we [i.e., God] cancel or cause you to forget, we bring a better or its like." According to al-Suyūṭī the number of abrogated verses has been estimated from five to five hundred. As Margoliouth remarked, "To do this, withdraw a revelation and substitute another for it was, [Muhammad] asserted, well within the power of God. Doubtless it was, but so obviously within the power of man that it is to us astonishing how so compromising a procedure can have been permitted to be introduced into the system by friends and foes."[176]

Al-Suyūṭī gives the example of Sura II.240 as a verse abrogated (superseded) by verse 234, which is the abrogating verse. How can an earlier verse abrogate a later verse? The answer lies in the fact that the traditional Muslim order of the suras and verses is not chronological, the compilers simply having placed the longer chapters at the beginning. The Muslim commentators, for whom the Koran and the Sīra are necessarily and inexorably joined, have to decide the chronological order for doctrinal reasons. Western scholars, wedded to the traditional Muslim account, have also worked out a chronological scheme; though there are many differences of detail, there seems to be a broad—but by no means complete—agreement as to which suras belong to the Meccan (i.e., early) period of Muhammad's life and which belong to the Medinan (i.e., later) period. It is worth noting how time-bound the "eternal" word of God is.

Let us take an example: everyone knows that Muslims are not allowed to drink wine in virtue of the prohibition found in the Koran (Sura II.219), and yet many would no doubt be surprised to read in the Koran at Sura XVI.67, "And among fruits you have the palm and the vine, from which you get wine and healthful nutriment: in this, truely, are signs for those who reflect" (Rodwell). Dawood has "intoxicants" and Pickthall, "strong drink," and Sale, with eighteenth-century charm, has "inebriating liquor" in place of "wine." While Yusuf Ali pretends that the Arabic word concerned, *Sakar*, means "wholesome drink," and in a footnote insists that nonalcoholic drinks are being referred to; and then at the last moment concedes that if "*sakar* must be taken in the sense of fermented wine, it refers to the time before intoxicants were prohibited: this is a Meccan Sura and the prohibition came in Medina."[177]

Now we can see how useful and convenient the doctrine of abrogation is in bailing scholars out of difficulties—though, of course, it does pose problems for apologists of Islam, since all the passages preaching tolerance are found in Meccan (i.e., early suras), and all the passages recommending killing, decapitating and maiming, the so-called Sword Verses, are Medinan (i.e., later); "tolerance" has been abrogated by "intolerance." For example, the famous Sword verse, *āyat al-sayf*, at Sura IX.5, "Slay the idolaters wherever you find them," is said to have canceled 124 verses that enjoin toleration and patience.[178]

Here are the supposedly early suras preaching tolerance:

> CIX: "Recite: O Unbelievers, I worship not what you worship, and you do not worship what I worship. I shall never worship what you worship. Neither will you worship what I worship. To you your religion, to me my religion."
>
> L. 45: "We well know what the infidels say: but you are not to compel them."
>
> XLIII. 88,89: "And [Muhammad] says, 'O Lord, these are people who do not believe.' Bear with them and wish them 'Peace.' In the end they shall know their folly."

The exceptions are to be found in Sura II, which is usually considered Medinan (i.e., late):

> II.256: "There is no compulsion in religion."
>
> II.62: "Those who believe [i.e., Muslims] and those who follow the Jewish scriptures, and the Christians and the Sabians, and who believe in God and the Last Day and work righteousness, shall have their reward with their Lord, on them shall be no fear, nor shall they grieve."

Unfortunately, as he gained in confidence and increased his political and military power, so the story goes, Muhammad turned from being a persuader to being a legislator, warrior, and dictator. Hence, the Medinan chapters such as Suras IX, V, IV, XXII, XLVII, VIII, and II reveal

Muhammad at his most belligerent, dogmatic, and intolerant—that is, for those who want to closely link the Koran with the life of the Prophet.

> XXII.19: "As for the unbelievers for them garments of fire shall be cut and there shall be poured over their heads boiling water whereby whatever is in their bowels and skins shall be dissolved and they will be punished with hooked iron rods."

The Koran also enjoins all Muslims to fight and kill nonbelievers:

> XLVII.4: "When you meet the unbelievers, strike off their heads; then when you have made wide slaughter among them, carefully tie up the remaining captives."
>
> IX.29: "Declare war upon those to whom the Scriptures were revealed but believe neither in God nor the Last Day, and who do not forbid that which God and His Apostle have forbidden, and who refuse to acknowledge the true religion [that is, the Jews], until they pay the tribute readily, being brought low."
>
> IX.5–6: "Kill those who join other gods with God wherever you may find them."
>
> IV.76: "Those who believe fight in the cause of God . . ."
>
> VIII.12: "I will instill terror into the hearts of the Infidels, strike off their heads then, and strike off from them every fingertip."
>
> VIII.38–39: "Say to the Infidels: If they desist from their unbelief,what is now past shall be forgiven them; but if they return to it, they have already before them the doom of the ancients! Fight then against them till strife be at an end, and the religion be all of it God's."

It is a grave sin for a Muslim to shirk the battle against the unbelievers, those who do will roast in hell:

> IX.39: "If you do not fight, He will punish you severely, and put others in your place."

Those who die fighting for the only true religion, Islam,will be amply rewarded in the life to come:

IV.74: "Let those fight in the cause of God who barter the life of this world for that which is to come; for whoever fights on God's path, whether he is killed or triumphs, We will give him a handsome reward."

We might give the following further examples of contradictions, though it seems rather doubtful if the doctrine of abrogation can deal with all of them.

The omnipotence of God is everywhere asserted in the Koran; man's will is totally subordinate to God's will to the extent that man cannot be said to have a will of his own. Even those who disbelieve in Him do so because it is God who wills them to disbelieve. This leads to the Muslim doctrine of predestination, which prevails over the doctrine of man's free will, also to be found in the Koran. As Macdonald says, "the contradictory statements of the Kuran on free-will and predestination show that Muhammad was an opportunist preacher and politician and not a systematic theologian."[179]

"*Taqdīr*, or the absolute decree of good and evil, is the sixth article of the Muhammadan creed, and the orthodox believe that whatever has, or shall come to pass in this world, whether it be good or bad, proceeds entirely from the Divine Will, and has been irrevocably fixed and recorded on a preserved tablet by the pen of fate."[180] Here are some quotes from the Koran illustrating this doctrine:

LIV.49: "All things have been created after fixed decree."

III.145: "No one can die except by God's permission according to the book that fixes the term of life."

LXXXVII.2–3: "The Lord has created and balanced all things and has fixed their destinies and guided them."

VIII.17: "God killed them, and those shafts were God's, not yours."

IX.51: "By no means can anything befall us but what God has destined for us."

XIII.31: "All sovereignty is in the hands of God."

XIV.4: "God misleads whom He will and whom He will He guides."

XVIII.101: "The infidels whose eyes were veiled from my warning and had no power to hear."

> XXXII.13: "If We had so willed, We could have given every soul its guidance, but now My Word is realized—'I shall fill Hell with jinn and men together.' "
>
> XLV.26: "Say unto them, O Muhammad: Allah gives life to to you, then causes you to die, then gathers you unto the day of resurrection . . ."
>
> LVII.22: "No disaster occurs on earth or accident in yourselves which was not already recorded in the Book before we created them."

But there are, inevitably, some passages from the Koran that seem to give man some kind of free-will:

> LXXIV.54–55: "Nay, it is surely a Reminder. So whovever pleases may mind it."
>
> LXXVI.3: "We have truly shown him the way; he may be thankful or unthankful."
>
> LXXVI.29: "Surely this is a Reminder; so whoever will, let him take a way to his Lord."
>
> XII.17: "As to Thamud, We vouchsafed them also guidance, but to guidance did they prefer blindness."
>
> XVIII.29: "The truth is from your Lord: let him then who will, believe; and let him who will, be an unbeliever."

Faced with this mass of contradictions, Muslim scholars, leaning on verses from Suras XVI.101, XXII.52, II.106, LXXXVII.6 ff., devised the doctrine of abrogation by which the earlier Koranic passages were abrogated by chronologically later ones. Essentially, "abrogation [*naskh*] involved the suppression of a ruling without the suppression of the wording. That is to say, the earlier ruling is till to be found in the Qur'ān, and is still to this day recited in worship, but it no longer has any legal force."[181]

Some Muslim scholars also postulated two further types of abrogation:

(a) where both the ruling and wording have been suppressed
(b) where the wording has been suppressed but the ruling is still in force (e.g., the famous stoning verse that condemns men and women to death by stoning for sexual immorality—*zinā'*)[182]

It is very doubtful that the verses adduced to back the Muslim scholars' arguments really have anything to do with abrogation at all; on the contrary, the context indicates that the verses can interpreted very differently. Burton tried to show that the word *āya* in Sura II.106 refers to an individual ritual or legal obligation, and the verb *yansakh* means "modification." Thus, II.106 would refer to the modification of an earlier, Jewish ritual or legal regulation by a later, Islamic one.[183]

> A second reason for scepticism about the classical theory of abrogation is that there has never been a consensus among jurists about which Qur'anic passages it affects. Az-Zuhrī (d.742), an early authority on the subject, held that 42 ayahs [verses] had been abrogated. After his time, the number steadily increased until an upper limit was reached in the eleventh century, with Ibn Salāma claiming that there were 238 abrogated ayahs, and al-Fārisī claiming that there were 248. In subsequent generations, a reaction set in: the Egyptian polymath al-Suyūṭī (d. 1505) claimed that there were only 20, and Shah Walī Allāh of Delhi (d.1762) whittled the number down to 5.[184]

We might add two other scholars whose calculation of the number of abrogated verses varies considerably: al-Naḥḥās, 138; Ibn al-ʿAtāʾiqī, 231.[185]

The sura lists of Muslim scholars purporting to indicate which belonged to the Meccan (early) period and which to the Medinan (later) seem at first promising.

> Although no two lists are exactly the same, they all have a family likeness, and some of the lists are supported by *isnāds* [chain of transmitters] ostensibly tracing them back to the period of the Companions. It seems probable, however, that these lists were compiled during the first quarter of the eighth century, at very earliest, and that they reflect the opinion of scholars whe were active at that time. The broad agreement amongst these scholars about which surah are Meccan and which Madinan is understandable, as in the majority of cases this can be deduced from the content. On the other hand, the differences of opinion about the precise order in which the surahs were revealed probably reflect rival views concerning the *asbāb al-nuzūl* [the supposed occasions when such and such sura was revealed to Muhammad, see below] and abrogation. In short, there is insufficient evidence for holding that these lists

are based on independent ancient traditions, although that possibility cannot of course be entirely ruled out.[186]

What of the so-called *asbāb al-nuzūl*, the occasions of revelation, when, according to Muslim tradition, such and such verse was revealed to Muhammad?

Surely, they settle definitively the chronology of the Koran, and decide which verses are Meccan and which Medinan?

In his *Quranic Studies*, John Wansbrough had expressed the view that *asbāb* material had its major reference point in halakic works, that is to say, works concerned with deriving laws from the Koran. Andrew Rippin,[187] however, examined numerous texts, and concluded that the primary purpose of the *sabab* material was in fact not halakic, but rather haggadic: "that is, the *asbāb* functions to provide an interpretation of a verse within a broad narrative framework." This puts the origin of the *asbāb* material in the context of the *quṣṣāṣ*: "the wandering storytellers, and pious preachers and to a basically popular religious worship situation where such stories would prove both enjoyable and edifying." He also notes that the primary purpose of such stories is to historicize the text of the Koran in order to prove that "God really did reveal his book to humanity on earth," and that in arguments over conflicting *asbāb* reports *isnād* (chain of transmission) criticism was a tool that could be "employed when needed and disregarded when not."

As Hawting points out, "The very diversity of these 'occasions of revelation' (*asbāb al-nuzūl*), the variety of the interpretations and historical situations the tradition provides for individual koranic verses, is an argument for the uncertain nature of the explanations that are provided. One often feels that the meaning and context supplied for a particular verse or passage of the Koran is not based on any historical memory or upon a secure knowledge of the circumstances of its revelation, but rather reflect attempts to establish a meaning. That meaning, naturally, was established within a framework of accepted ideas about the setting in which the Prophet lived and the revelation was delivered. In that way, the work of interpretation also defines and describes what had come to be understood as the setting for the revelation."[188]

I shall end this section with what I wrote in an earlier book:

Juynboll once said that Wansbrough's theories were so hard to swallow because of the obvious disparity in style and contents of Meccan and Medinan suras.[189] There is indeed a difference in language, style and even message between the so-called Meccan and Medinan suras. But all that shows is that there are two quite different styles in the Koran, and of course, Muslim exegetes solved this problem by assigning one set to Mecca and the other to Medina, with considerable tinkering (verses from the "Medinese" suras assigned to Mecca and vice versa). But why should we accept the Medinan and Meccan labels? What is the source or sources of this difference? To accept these labels is simply to accept the entire traditional Muslim account of the compilation of the Koran, the biography of the Prophet, and the Rise of Islam. Again, this is precisely what is at stake: the reliability of the sources. The differences, if anything, point to a history far more extensive than the short life of Muhammad as found in the Sīra, and they do not have to be interpreted biographically through the history of the life of Muhammad in Mecca and Medina. There is nothing natural about the Meccan/Medinan separation. It is clear from Lammens, Becker and others that large parts of the sira and hadith were invented to account for the difficulties and obscurities encountered in the Koran, and these labels also proved to be convenient, for the Muslim exegetes for the same reason. The theory of abrogation also gets the exegetes out of similar difficulties, and obviates the need to explain the embarrassing contradictions that abound in the Koran.[190]

10. ARCHAEOLOGICAL EVIDENCE

The full implications of the sixty or so inscriptions found in and around Mecca, Saudi Arabia, have yet to be worked out.[191] Some of these inscriptions, incised on white limestone, which have been dated to 80 A.H. and others to 84 A.H., 98 A.H., and 189 A.H., consist of what seem like quotations from the Koran. There are clearly recognizable phrases from the Koran but there is never a complete verse, and often one sentence is found to contain Koranic quotes from two different suras; others show considerable deviations from the Standard Edition. One could argue that they are not Koranic quotes at all, or that the "writer" has simply badly remembered the Koran. One could also argue that, once again, the Koran had not yet been standardized, or even reduced to a written form.

11. THE SOURCE OF THE DIFFICULTIES AND OBSCURITIES

Given the above examples of some of the difficulties, any critical reading of the Koran should prompt the exasperated but healthy response, "What on earth is going on here?" The fact that so many, but thankfully not all, scholars of the last sixty years have failed to even ask this question, let alone begin to answer it, shows that they have been crushed into silence out of respect for the tender sensibilities of Muslims, by political correctness, postcolonial feelings of guilt, and dogmatic Islamophilia, and have been practicing "Islamic scholarship" rather than scholarship on Islam.

Some scholars did pose pertinent questions, and gave us important insights. I have tried to include their work in this anthology. And yet, so often their keen and just observations were vitiated by a faulty chronology, that is, they all accepted the traditional historical framework fabricated by Muslim tradition. It seems to me that their work makes far more sense within a broad revisionist structure provisionally constructed by Wansbrough and his disciples.

To give a plausible account of the rise of Islam we must put back the last of the three monotheist religions in its Near Eastern geographical, religious, historical, and linguistic (Hebrew, Aramaic, Syriac) context. Scholars have been well aware of the influences of Talmudic Judaism, heretical Christianity, and now even Essenians, on Islam, but relying on the fictive chronology of Muslim tradition has often meant the invention of ingenious but ultimately far-fetched scenarios of how Christian monks, Jewish rabbis, or Essenians fleeing Romans had whispered their arcane knowledge into the ears of an Arabian merchant.

So many scholars have also accepted totally uncritically the traditional account of the compilation of the Koran. But this account is, in the words of Burton, "a mass of confusion, contradictions and inconsistencies,"[192] and it is nothing short of scandalous that Western scholars readily accept "all that they read in Muslim reports on this or that aspect of the discussions on the Qur'ān."[193]

Given that so much of the Koran remains incomprehensible despite hundreds of commentaries, surely it is time to look for some more plausible historical mechanism by which the Koran came to be the Koran, and to restore the original text.

Despite Barth's pioneering work, there is still a reluctance to impugn the putative authenticity of the Koran, and talk of emendations. Bellamy, for instance, makes the following pertinent remarks,

> . . . one seeks in vain for a systematic application of the techniques of textual criticism to the textual problems of the Koran, although classicists and Biblical scholars have for centuries made continuous efforts to improve the quality of the texts that are the bases of their disciplines. . . . Whatever the reasons, Western scholarship, with very few exceptions has chosen to follow the Muslim commentators in not emending the text. When faced with a problem, the Westerners have resorted to etymologizing and hunting for foreign words and foreign influences. They have produced a great deal of valuable scholarship important for our study of the Koran and the origins of Islam, but where they exercised their skill on corrupt texts, they, of course, produced only fantasies.[194]

And yet Bellamy ends his article with almost an apology: "It should not be assumed that in making these emendations, I am in any way trying to diminish the remarkable achievement of Zayd b. Thābit and his colleagues in producing the Uthmanic recension of the Koran." Even Bellamy, it seems, accepts the traditional compilation story.

Bellamy is quite right that among classicists emendations, and even the assumption of interpolations, practically comprise the definition of textual criticism. Here the typically trenchant remarks of the eminent classicist A. E. Housman[195] are of the greatest relevance:

> Textual criticism is a science, and, since it comprises recension and emendation, it is also an art. It is the science of discovering error in texts and the art of removing it. That is its definition, that is what the name denotes.[196]

> . . . [T]extual criticism is not a branch of mathematics, nor indeed an exact science at all. It deals with a matter not rigid and constant, like lines and numbers, but fluid and variable; namely, the frailties and aberrations of the human mind, and of its insubordinate servants, the human fingers.[197]

> . . . the amount of sub-conscious dishonesty which pervades the textual criticism of the Greek and Latin classics is little suspected except by those who have had occasion to analyse it. People come upon this field

> bringing with them prepossessions and preferences; they are not willing to look all facts in the face, nor to draw the most probable conclusion unless it is also the most agreeable conclusion.[198]

> Interpolation is provoked by real or supposed difficulties, and is not frequently volunteered where all is plain sailing; whereas accidental alteration may happen anywhere. Every letter of every word lies exposed to it, and that is the sole reason why accidental alteration is more common. In a given case where either assumption is possible, the assumption of interploation is equally probable, nay more probable; because action with a motive is more probable than action without a motive. The truth therefore is that in such a case we should be loth to assume accident and should rather assume interpolation; and the circumstance that such cases are comparatively uncommon is no reason for behaving irrationally when they occur.[199]

Barth and Fischer's important work (translated here for the first time) on emendations and interpolations, though it did influence Richard Bell in the writing of his commentary on the Koran, was unfortunately not followed up. Even Bell, on the whole, is unwilling to accept emendations too readily, and most scholars seem to agree with Nöldeke that the Koran is free of omissions and additions. But as Hirschfeld says, "Considering the way in which the compilation was made, it would have been a miracle, had the Qoran been kept free of omissions, as well as interpolations."[200] Some scholars did question the authenticity of certain verses: Antoine-Isaac Silvestre de Sacy was doubtful about sura III.138; Weil of Suras III.182, XVII.1, XXI.35–36, XXIX.57, XLVI.14, XXXIX.30; and Sprenger, LIX.7.[201] Hirschfeld questioned the authenticity of verses containing the name Muhammad, regarding it as rather suspicious that such a name, meaning "praised," should be borne by the Prophet:

> . . . that name [Muhammad] could not have come into practical use until a period of the Prophet's life when the material of the Qoran was all but complete. Now it might be objected that the texts of the missionary letters which Muhammad commenced to send in the seventh of the Hijra to unconverted Arab chiefs, as well as to foreign potentates were headed by the phrase: "From Muhammad, the Messenger of Allah, to, etc." The authenticity of the majority of these letters . . . is very doubtful, and besides, even if the genuineness of the texts of the documents be

admitted, the superscription may have been added by the traditionists who took it for granted.[202]

Watt and Bell try to answer Hirschfeld by essentially assuming the reliablity and authenticity of the traditions: "[The name, Muhammad,] occurs, not only in the Qurʾan but in the documents handed down by Tradition, notably the constitution of Medina and the treaty of al-Ḥudaybiyya; in the latter the pagan Quraysh are said to have objected to the title rasūl Allāh, and to ar-Raḥmān as a name of God, but raised no question about the name Muhammad."[203] This is an astonishingly naive and circular argument. First, it is the reliability of tradition that is the crux of the matter, and if tradition is capable of inserting the name Muhammad into the Koran, then it is equally capable of inventing the story where the Quraysh do not object to this name, for it is tradition that is our only source for the story of the reception of the treaty of al-Ḥudaybiyya. We do not have independent means of verifying the story. It is tradition that interpolated the name into the Koran, but it is also tradition that embroidered or spun out the details of the biography of the Prophet. As is so often the case, traditions contradict one another: Some traditions even claim that at birth Muhammad had received the name Qutham.[204] It would seem arbitrary to pick on just one of them; as Burton said, "We must either accept all hadiths impartially with uncritical trust, or one must regard each and every hadith as at least potentially guilty of a greater or lesser degree of inherent bias, whether or not this is immediately visible to Western eyes."[205]

Another scholar who has dared to question the authenticity of the Koran is Paul Casanova, whose ideas are rather perfunctorily dismissed by Watt and Bell. Casanova finished his study *Mohammed et la fin du Monde* in 1921, but in recent years his work has been, I believe unjustly, ignored.[206] I suspect one reason for this neglect has nothing to do with the force of his arguments or the quality of his scholarship, but the simple unavailability of all three volumes of his work; volume three, pages 169–244, being particularly difficult to come by.[207]

Casanova wrote:

It is generally admitted that the text of the Koran, such as it has come down to us, is authentic and that it reproduces exactly the thought of

> Muhammad, faithfully gathered by his secretaries as the revelations gradually appeared. We know that some of his secretaries were highly unreliable, that the immediate successor of the Prophet made a strict recension, that, a few years later, the arrangement of the text was altered. We have obvious examples of verses suppressed, and such a bizarre way in which the text is presented to us (in order of the size of the chapters or surahs) shows well the artificial character of the Koran that we possess. Despite that, the assurance with which Muslims—who do not refrain from accusing Jews and Christians of having altered their Scriptures—present this incoherent collection as rigorously authentic in all its parts has imposed itself upon the orientalists, and the thesis that I wish to uphold will seem very paradoxal and forced.
>
> I maintain, however, that the real doctrine of Muhammad was, if not falsified, at least concealed with the greatest of care. I shall set out soon the extremely simple reasons which led first Abū Bakr, then ʿUthmān, to alter thoroughly the sacred text, and this rearrangement was done with such skill that, thenceforth, it seemed impossible to reconstitute the Ur-Koran or the original Koran. If however my thesis was accepted, it could serve as a point of departure for this reconstitution, at least for everything that concerns the original revelations, the only really interesting ones from my point of view, the only ones, moreover, that there was any advantage in reworking, by means of either very light changes of the text, or by deplacements. There is abundant evidence that the first Muslims, despite the undoubtedly powerful memories of the Arabs, were profoundly ignorant of the Koran, and one could, with Muhammad dead, recite them verses of which they had not, at their own admission, the slightest idea. A rearrangement which did not change the exterior forms of the verses was thus the easiest. Sprenger, who had had a vague intimation of the thesis that I advocate, accuses Muhammad of having thrown the incoherence into his text himself, in order to get rid of the trace of imprudent words.[208] I say in fact that it is for a reason of this kind that the incoherence was introduced, but not by the author—by his successors.[209]

According to Casanova, Muhammad, under the influence of a Christian sect, put great emphasis on the imminent end of the world in his early proclamations. When the approaching end failed to take place, the early followers of the Prophet were forced to refashion or rework the text of the Koran to eliminate that doctrine from it.

Casanova provides some very convincing arguments for the presence of interpolations in the Koranic text, and further points up its general incoherence. Whether they prove what he wanted to prove is another matter. But it is certainly unfair of Watt and Bell to pronounce dismissively that Casanova's thesis is "founded less upon the study of the Qur'an than upon investigation of some of the byways of early Islam."[210] Casanova has anticipated just such a criticism, and we can see the following as an implicit anwser to Watt/Bell-type accusations:

> Already, at this period [Caliph, ʿAbd al-Malik, reigned 685–705 C.E.] the book [Koran] was hardly understood. "If obscurity and lack of coherence with the context in our modern Koran ought to be considered as proof of non-authenticity, I fear that we ought to condemn more than one verse," says Nöldeke.[211]
>
> I confess that as for me I accept these premises and this conclusion. Obscurity and incoherence are the reasons, not to deny absolutely, but to suspect the authenticity [of the Koran], and they permit all effort to restore a more clear and more coherent text.
>
> Permit me some characteristic examples. I have collected them by a careful study of the Koranic text,[212] I could have multiplied them but that would have uselessly padded out this book. Besides, in most cases, all the while feeling the strangeness and obscurity of terms, that the naive exegesis of the commentators only brings out the better, one is very perplexed to propose a rational solution, a credible restoration. I ought to be on my guard the more so because people will not fail to accuse me (that has already been done) of declaring falsified such and such passages because they go counter to my theories. To defend myself from this reproach, I shall add to this list of alterations a short analysis of those which have been noted before me by scholars totally unaware of my aforementioned thesis."[213]

There then follow examples of interpolations, displacement of verses, and so on; in other words, all the evidence of the general incoherence of the Koran.

Watt and Bell's defense depends completely on tightly linking the Koran to the biography of the Prophet, this linkage is,of course, entirely derived from Muslim tradition: "As to [Casanova's] main thesis, it is true that the Qur'an proclaims the coming Judgement and the end of the world. It is true that it sometimes hints that this may be near; for example, in

XXI.1 and XXVII.71–73 f. In other passages, however, men are excluded from knowledge of times, and there are great differences in the urgency with which the doctrine is proclaimed in different parts of the Qur'an. All this, however, is perfectly natural if we regard the Qur'an as reflecting Muhammad's personal problems and the outward difficulties he encountered in carrying out a task to which he had set his mind. Casanova's thesis makes little allowance for the changes that must have occurred in Muhammad's attitudes through twenty years of ever-changing circumstances. Our acceptance of the Qur'an as authentic is based, not on any assumption that it is consistent in all its parts, for this is not the case; but on the fact that, however difficult it may be to understand in detail, it does, on the whole, fit into a real historical experience, beyond which we discern an elusive, but, in outstanding characteristics, intelligible personality."[214]

It requires little reflection to see, once again, the circularity of Watt and Bell's argument. If by "authentic" we mean that the Koran was the word of God, as passed on, either directly from God or through the intermediary of an angel, to a historical figure called Muhammad, supposedly living in Arabia, then clearly we need some independent confirmation of this extraordinary claim. We cannot say the Koran is authentic because "it does fit . . . into a real historical experience."

For this circular reasoning would give us the following tautology: "the Koran is authentic, that is, it fits into a real historical experience, because it fits into a real historical experience."

Some have scholars have, of course, been trying to prise the Koranic text away from the supposed historical fit with the Sīra, the life of Muhammad. Lammens,[215] Tor Andrae,[216] and more modestly Andrew Rippin,[217] and Michael Schub.[218] But perhaps the most radical thesis is that of Gunter Lüling, who, argues very persuasively, that at least a third of the Koran predates Islam, and thus, of course, has nothing whatsoever to do with someone called Muhammad. A third of the Koran was originally a pre-Islamic Christian hymnody that was reinterpreted by Muslims, whose task was made that much easier by the ambiguity of the rasm, that is, the unpointed and unvowelled Arabic letters. Thus both Casanova and Lüling point to the present incoherence of the Koranic text as evidence for its later editing, refashioning, emending, and "re-interpretation" and manipulation. It is interesting to note that though he finds Lüling's evidence "unsound, and his method undisciplined,"[219] Wansbrough nonetheless thinks that the "recent conjectures of Lüling with regard to the essentially hymnic character of Muslim scripture are not unreasonable, though I [Wansbrough] am unable to accept what seems to me [Lüling's] very subjective reconstruction of the text. The liturgical form of the Qur'ān is abundantly clear even in the traditional recension, as well as from the traditional literature describing its communal uses. The detection of strophic formation is certainly not difficult, and the theological (as opposed to rhetorical) nature of orthodox insistence upon the absence from scripture of poetry and even (though less unanimous) of rhymed prose must be acknowledged."[220]

Lüling is reviving a theory first put forward by H. Müller,[221] according to which it was possible to find in the Koran, as in the Bible, an ancient poetical form, the strophe or stanza. This form was present in seventeen suras, particularly Suras LVI and XXVI. For Müller, composition in strophes was characteristic of prophetic literature. Rudolph Geyer[222] took up the theory, and thought he had proved the presence of a strophic structure in such suras as Sura LXXVIII. These ideas were dismissed at the time, but perhaps make more sense now, if we see, as Lüling does, in the Koran pre-Islamic Christians texts.

Lüling's thorough grounding in Semitic languages enables him to show that we cannot hope to understand the Muslim tradition's reworking of the Koranic text without an understanding of Hebrew, Aramaic, and Syriac. Following in the footsteps of Mingana, Jeffery, and Margoliouth, but going way beyond them, is Christoph Luxenberg,[223] who also tries to show that many of the obscurities of the Koran disappear if we read certain words as being Syriac and not Arabic. In order to elucidate passages in the Koran that had baffled generations of scholars, Muslim and non-Muslim, Luxenberg used the following method:

(1) He went carefully through Ṭabarī's great commentary on the Koran, and also consulted Ibn al-Manẓūr's celebrated dictionary of the Arabic language, *Lisān al-ʿArab,* in order to see if Western scholars of the Koran had not omitted any of the plausible explanations proposed by the Muslim commentators and philologists. If this preliminary search did not yield any solutions, then

(2) he tried to replace the obscure Arabic word in a phrase or sentence that had hitherto mystified the Muslim commentators, or that had resulted in unconvincing, strained, or far-fetched explan-

tions with a Syriac homonym, which had a different meaning (though the same sound), but which made more sense in the context. If this step did not yield a comprehensible sentence, then

(3) he proceeded to the first round of changes of the diacritical points, which, according to Luxenberg's theory, must have been badly placed by the Arabic readers or whoever was the original redactor or copier of the Koran, and which had resulted in the actual obscurity of the Koranic passage concerned. In this way, he hoped to obtain another more logical reading of the Arabic. If this also failed to give any results, Luxenberg

(4) then proceeded to the second round of changes of the diacritical points in order to eventually obtain a more coherent *Syriac* reading, and not an Arabic one. If all these attempts still did not yield any positive results,

(5) he tried to decipher the real meaning of the Arabic word, which did not make any sense in its present context, by retranslating it into Syriac to deduce from the semantic contents of the Syriac root the meaning best suited to the Koranic context.

In this way, Luxenberg was able to explain not only the so-called obscure passages, but a certain number of passages that he considers were misunderstood, and whose meaning up to now no one had doubted. He was also able explain certain orthographic and grammatical analomies which abound in the Koran.

This method allows Luxenberg, to the probable horror of all Muslim males dreaming of sexual bliss in the Muslim hereafter, to conjure away the wide-eyed houris promised to the faithful in Suras XLIV.54 and LII.20. According to Luxenberg, the new analysis yields "white raisins" of "crystal clarity" rather than doe-eyed and ever-willing virgins. Luxenberg claims that the context makes it clear that it is food and drink that is being offerred, and not unsullied maidens. Similarly, the immortal, pearl-like ephebes or youths of suras such as LXXVI.19 are really a misreading of a Syriac expression meaning "chilled raisins (or drinks)" that the Just will have the pleasure of tasting in contrast to the "boiling drinks" promised the unfaithful and damned.

Luxenberg's work has only recently been published in Germany, and we must await its scholarly assessment before we can pass any judgments.

12. CRITICAL THOUGHT AND THE SKEPTICAL ATTITUDE: A NOTE ON HISTORICAL METHODOLOGY

Credulity does not become an historian.

P. R. Davies[224]

The sources for that historical event [seventh-century Hijaz] are exclusively literary, predominantly exegetical, and incarcerated in a grammar designed to stress the immediate equivalence of word and world. Or, I might be inclined to add: all we know is what we have been told. With neither artifact nor archive, the student of Islamic origins could quite easily become victim of a literary and linguistic conspiracy. He is, of course, mostly convinced that he is not. Reason for that must be confidence in his ability to extrapolate from the literary version(s) what is likely to have happened. The confidence is certainly manifest; the methodological premises that ought to support, or, at least, accompany it, are less so.

John Wansbrough[225]

Surely it is time for a critical examination of the methodological assumptions that have gone totally unscrutinized for so long. Despite the fact that Wansbrough's literary analysis of the sources has undermined the traditional account of the origin of Islam, the Sīra, and the coming into being of the Koran, scholars, who made their reputations from taking the Muslim account at face value, have carried on as if nothing has happened. Conveniently ignoring the full implications of Wansbrough's theories, these conservative scholars have not even seriously tried to answer him.[226]

But as P. R. Davies says, "it is not acceptable for an historian to trust the text or its unknown author. Credulity does not become a historian. Scepticism, rather, is the proper stance, just as in turn that historian's own text must earn trust too, and not demand credence."

In their Positivist classic of historical methodology, Langlois and Seignobos[227] make a similar point:

> For criticism is antagonistic to the normal bent of the mind. The spontaneous tendency of man is to yield assent to affirmations, and to reproduce them. . . . It takes a special reason to induce us to take the trouble to examine into the origin and value of a document on the history of

> yesterday; otherwise, if there is no outrageous improbability in it, and as long as it is not contradicted, we swallow it whole, we pin our faith to it, we hawk it about, and, if need be, embellish it in the process. Every candid man must admit that it requires a violent effort to shake off *ignavia critica*, that common form of intellectual sloth, that this effort must be continually repeated, and is often accompanied by real pain.
>
> . . . [C]riticism is not a natural habit, it must be inculcated, and only becomes organic by dint of continued practice.
>
> Historical work is, then, pre-eminently critical; whoever enters upon it without having first been put on his guard against his instinct is sure to be drowned in it.

While they warn against hypercriticism, Langlois and Seignobos make it clear that it is credulity that is the main enemy of scientific method. Certain historians "are content to examine whether the author was roughly *contemporary* with the events, whether he was an ocular *witness,* whether he was *sincere* and *well-informed*, whether he knew the truth and desired to tell it, or even—summing up the whole question in a single formula—whether he was *trustworthy.*

> This superficial criticism is certainly better than no criticism at all, and has sufficed to give those who applied it the consciousness of incontestable superiority. But it is only a halfway house between common credulity and scientific method. Here, as in every science, the starting point must be methodical doubt. All that has not been proved must be temporarily regarded as doubtful. . . .[228]

> The historian ought to distrust *a priori* every statement of an author, for he cannot be sure that it is not mendacious or mistaken. . . . We must not postpone doubt till it is forced upon us by conflicting statements in documents, we must *begin* by doubting.[229]

An author may have any number of motives for violating the truth:

(1) He or she may seek to gain a practical advantage; the author knowingly gives false information, he or she has an interest in deceiving. This is the case with most official documents.
(2) The author was placed in a situation that compelled him to violate truth. This happens whenever he has to draw up a document

in conformity with rule or custom, while the actual circumstances are in some point or other in conflict with rule or custom.

(3) "The author viewed with sympathy or antipathy a group of men (nation, party, denomination, province, city, family), or an assemblage of doctrines or institutions (religion, school of philosophy, political theory), and was led to distort facts in such a manner as to represent his friends in a favourable and his opponents in an unfavourable light."

(4) "The author desired to please the public, or at least to avoid shocking it. He has expressed sentiments and ideas in harmony with the morality or the fashion of his public; he has distorted facts in order to adapt them to the passions and prejudices of his time. . . . The purest types of this kind of falsehood are found in ceremonial forms, official formulae, declarations prescribed by etiquette, set speeches, polite phrases."

(5) "The author endeavoured to please the public by literary artifices. He distorted facts in order to embellish them according to his own aesthetic notions."[230]

Outside the more general need for methodological doubt and skepticism, there is an equally urgent, if more specific, necessity to put Islam firmly within the gradual development of Middle Eastern monotheism outside Arabia; that is, within the Judaeo-Christian sectarian milieu. This milieu necessarily includes not only the theological and polemical framework and assumptions of the various contending sects, but also the linguistic background. Arabic itself must be placed squarely back in its Semitic surroundings; its relationship to Hebrew, Aramaic, and Syriac must be reexamined. Placing the Koran in its Hebrew and Syriac milieu has already given us the startlingly new theories of Lüling and Luxenberg.

What a new generation of biblical scholars, such as P. R. Davies,[230] Keith Whitelam,[232] N. P. Lemche,[233] T. L. Thompson,[234] J. van Seters,[235] and G. Garbini,[236] has achieved by its openness to the methods of other disciplines like anthropology, sociology, social history, linguisitics, and literary criticism is very instructive indeed. "In order to deal with the reports of seventh-century Arabia," Wansbrough "divided the field into 'constants' and 'variables': the former representing the 'basic categories' common to most descriptions of monotheism; the latter representing 'local components,' that give each version its special character. . . . The constants were prophet, scripture, and sacred language; the variables were the specifically Arabian features of these. . . . "[237] What the new biblical scholars conclude about the Bible, history, and Ancient Israel is readily applicable to Islam, since these conclusions refer to "constants" common to most descriptions of monotheism. For instance, Lemche writes, "It is certainly not unusual for people to possess their own foundation myth. It is as a matter of fact quite common, almost universal phenomenon, that any group—ethnic, national, political, religious, and occupational—will be in possession of a narrative about its foundation known to and accepted by its membership. . . . The myth of the exile and return has a similar story to tell."[238]

> History is one of the remedies open to the creators of ethnicity, and as has become conspicuous recently, it is of little importance whether this history is a real history or an invented one. History is written in order to create identity among the members of certain society, congregation, or whatever ethnic group we may speak about. The only important thing seen in the perspective of the author, who created this history, would be that it must be acceptable for its readership; its readers must be able to identify with the history as it has been told to them.
>
> The biblical history about Israel . . . is simply a reflection of the self-understanding of the people who created this history and for whom it was created. This community will have to be understood as a religious community, not an ordinary living organism such as a normal people; it is the people of God, now past its punishment and redeemed by its God. It is a community with a firm conviction of belonging to a specific place, which it alone is entitled to possess because it is the gift of its God, and because its membership are all one and the same family, the descendants of the patriarchs, Abraham, Isaac, and Jacob.[239]

Further on, Lemche[240] writes that Israel in the Old Testament is an artificial creation, which has little in common with the Israel that existed once in Palestine. Similarly, Hawting[241] has tried to argue that the pre-Islamic Arabia found in Muslim tradition is essentially a literary and ideological construct with probably little in common with the "real Arabia."

Wansbrough emphasizes two points whose full implications are perhaps too disturbing for most scholars to draw: first, there is no Muslim literature which can be dated, in the form in which it is available to us, earlier than 800 C.E. (end of the second century of the Islamic era); the other is that Islam is a complex phenomenon the development of which must have taken many generations and occupied an extended geographical area before it attained a form resembling that which we know today.

Although it is true that there are a few traditional texts conventionally attributed to figures who died before 800 C.E. (notably Ibn Isḥāq and Mālik b. Anas), we only have those works in recensions made by Muslim scholars of later generations, and none of the works available to us were put into the form in which we know them earlier than the ninth century C.E. (the third century of Islam).We have no biography of Muhammad, no commentary on the Koran, no law book, no collection of Hadiths, no history of early Islam, etc., which can be said to predate, in the form in which have it, the beginning of the third Islamic century. And, given the impulse in traditional Islamic scholarship to attribute to great figures of the past texts which have been formed over a considerable period of time and which stabilized comparatively late, it may be suspected that the conventional attribution to "authors" living in the early ninth century of a number of important works may be too generous.

Wansbrough's work exhibits severe scepticism about these attempts to push our Muslim sources back earlier than the form in which we know them and he shows no interest in reconstructing or analyzing the *isnads*. His position seems to be that even were it possible to accept the accuracy and authenticity of the *isnads* (which seems doubtful for the most important, earliest, alleged links in the transmission), there would nevertheless be little possibility of assessing the transformation of the accompanying traditions as they were subject to the vicissitudes of transmission over many generations. Variant wording, the introduction of glosses, the removal of material from its original context, abbreviation, summary and expansion, incomplete transmission, and other features can all be assumed to have taken place. Above all, even though our earliest Muslim literature undoubtedly recycles and reworks material which originated much earlier, that material exists because it answers to the needs of the generations in whose work we finds it.[242]

Finally, Wansbrough can teach us one further lesson that places him directly within the revisionist tradition of biblical scholars mentioned above:

> The concept of Islam as an evolution from the sectarian monotheism of Mesopotamia in the wake of Arab migration and the establishment of Arab rule; the analysis of that evolution as a gradual elaboration of a series of ideas, practices, and institutions expressive of the independent identity of the community; and the understanding that an elaboration of an account of its own origins is a part of that evolution; these seem to me the especially liberating aspects of Wansbrough's approach.[243]

While modern biblical studies has made great progress building on the works of such pioneers as Wellhausen and Graf, Koranic studies is still lying contentedly, self-satisfied in the procrustean bed prepared by Muslim tradition more than a thousand years ago. As Wansbrough himself said, "As a document susceptible of analysis by the instruments and techniques if Biblical criticism [the Koran] is virtually unknown. The doctrinal obstacles that have traditionally impeded such investigation are, on the other hand, very well known. Not merely dogmas such as those defining scripture as the uncreated Word of God and acknowledging its formal and substantive inimitability, but also the entire corpus of Islamic historiography, by providing a more or less coherent and plausible report of the circumstances of the Quranic revelation, have discouraged examination of the document as representative of a traditional literary type."[244]

Rippin endorses Wansbrough's frustration:

> . . . I have often encountered individuals who come to the study of Islam with a background in the historical study of the Hebrew Bible or early Christianity, and who express surprise at the lack of critical thought that appears in introductory textbooks on Islam. The notion that "Islam was born in the clear light of history" still seems to be assumed by a great many writers of such texts. While the need to reconcile varying historical traditions is generally recognized, usually this seems to pose no greater problem to the authors than having to determine "what makes sense" in given situation. To students acquainted with approaches such as source criticism, oral formulaic composition, literary analysis and structuralism, all quite commonly employed in the study of Judaism and Christianity, such naive historical study seems to suggest that Islam is being approached with less than academic candour.[245]

Conservative scholars such Watt or Welch have never given us an epistemologically or psychologically plausible, or even simply commonsensical account as to how the Koran came into being. If they believe that the Koran is "authentic," how do they think Muhammad received his "revelations"? Do they believe that Muhammad literally went into a trance and somehow saw visions of angels who recited various verses to him, which he then revealed to his companions, who then wrote them down verbatim? Some of the passages and stories in the Koran are very long indeed. Are we to understand that Muhammad remembered several hundred lines of rhymed prose that were "revealed" to him in his trance? Do we assume that all his companions were literate, and able to write down his every word, all the time believing that their Prophet was in direct communion with an angel? What in fact is a revelation or revelation in general? How does it operate psychologically and epistemologically? "We do not yet possess a usable cross-cultural theory or typology of revelations. . . ."[246]

What exactly does "authentic" mean to non-Muslim scholars? Is there a coherent definition of "authentic"? Is there then a valid, i.e., noncircular, argument to show that the Koran is authentic?

These are crucial questions that have never been asked, let alone answered. Then what exactly are the implications of the research of scholars such as Geiger, Sidersky, Hirschfeld, Speyer, Katsch, Torrey, Schapiro, among a host of others,[247] who have shown the various Judaic or Christian elements that have gone into the making of the Koran? Did Muhammad read the Babylonian Talmud in Aramaic? How did he then incorporate what he had read into his "revelatory trances" that were then written down "exactly as revealed" by literate companions, who were already aware that their leader was a prophet from God?

Even scholars skeptical of the sources of our knowledge of Islam are willing to accept the Koran as "authentic." I have already given the example of Watt and Bell arguing in a circle on this point. F. E. Peters is another very distinguished scholar who seems to want it both ways: "The Holy Book of Islam is text without context, and so this prime document, which has a very strong claim to be authentic, is of almost no use for reconstructing the events of the life of Muhammad."[248] How can we know that the Koran is "authentic" if we cannot trust any of our sources for the rise of Islam and the life of Muhammad?[249] It was Lammens who showed how the text of the Koran generated virtually every element that Muslim tradition attributes to the life of its prophet; as Lammens put it, "One begins with the Koran while pretending to conclude with it."[250] Furthermore, Peters himself believes that "Lammens' critical attack has never been refuted."[251] And yet Peters continues to talk in traditional terms of early Meccan suras and later Medinan ones, and seems confident we can "reconstruct to some degree what appears to be an evolution in Muhammad's own thinking about God."[252] A little later Peters tells us that "Goldziher, Lammens, and Schacht were all doubtless correct. A great deal of the transmitted material concerning early Islam was tendentious—not only the material that was used for legal purposes but the very building blocks out of which the earliest history of Muhammad and the Islamic community was constructed." If this is true why take the traditional Muslim account seriously?[253]

One of the strongest arguments against the traditional account, or rather contradictory accounts, of the compilation of the Koran is what we have learned from biblical studies about the canonization process. Why and how are certain texts included in an anthology of texts and then elevated to the status of scripture? It is a long complex process and the Muslim account(s) of the Koran are far too simplistic: neither religions nor sacred texts are born fully-fledged.

It is also an extraordinary situation that in the twenty-first century we still do not have a definitive, scholarly text of the Koran. The situation is truly chaotic, with scholars content to work without specifying which manuscript or edition they are relying on, or more probably tacitly using the so-called Standard Egyptian Edition, sometimes also referred to as the 1342 Cairo text. However even the latter text, as Adrian Brockett pointed out, did not have an official status in northwest Africa or Iran: "In the last decade [Brockett is writing in 1984], for instance, even in central Muslim countries like Saudi Arabia and Qatar, texts differing considerably in orthography from the 1342 Cairo text have been printed under official approval."[254] Brockett goes on to examine a number of printed Ḥafṣ copies available in the 1970s, and finds that they fall into five broad traditions: Iranian, Indian, Turkish, Egyptian, and northwestern. "The differences between these Traditions comprise script, orthography, recitative details and textual division. . . . In some respects the two outlying Traditions, the Indian and the northwest African, are makedly different from the other more centrally situated ones. They have also retained a few fossil elements of orthography lost from the central ones."[255] Neither Western scholars nor ordinary Muslims have, it seems, something called *the* Koran, they all make do with *a* Koran.

GUIDE TO FURTHER READING

The following is a selected list of books for further reading, but it does not include all the books cited or mentioned in my introduction and its footnotes.

Reference works

The Encyclopaedia of Islam. 9 vols. 2d ed. Leiden: E. J. Brill, 1954.
Hughes, T. P. *Dictionary of Islam*. Calcutta: Rupa & Co., 1988.

Grammar

Wright, W. *A Grammar of the Arabic Language*. Cambridge, 1967.

Dictionaries

Dozy, R. P. A. *Supplément aux dictionnaires arabes*. 2 vols. Paris, 1881. Reprint, 1960.
de Biberstein-Kazimirski, A. *Dictionnaire arabe-française*. 4 vols. Paris, 1860.
Lane, E. W. *An Arabic-English Lexicon*. 8 vols. 1863–1893. Reprint, Beirut, 1968.
Penrice, J. *A Dictionary and Glossary of the Koran*. 1873. Reprint, Delhi, 1990.
Wehr, Hans. *A Dictionary of Modern Written Arabic*. 1st Eng. ed. Ithaca, N.Y.: Cornell University Press, 1961.

Muhammad

Cook, Michael. *Muhammad,* Oxford, 1983
Hishām, Ibn. *The Life of Muhammad*. Edited and translated by A. Guillaume. London, 1955.
Warraq, Ibn, ed. *The Quest for the Historical Muhammad*. Amherst, N.Y.: Prometheus Books, 2000.
Watt, W. M. *Muhammad: Prophet and Statesman*. London, 1961.

Koran

Ayoub, M. *The Qur'ān and Its Interpreters*. Vol. 1. Albany, 1984.

Beeston, A. F. L. *Baiḍāwī's Commentary on Sūrah 12 of the Qur'ān: Text Accompanied by an Interpretative Rendering and Notes*. Oxford, 1963.
Bell, Richard. *Introduction to the Qur'ān*. Edinburgh, 1953. Revised by W. M. Watt, 1970.
———. *A Commentary on the Qur'ān*. Manchester, 1991.
Blachère, Régis. *Introduction au Coran*. 1958. Reprint, Paris, 1991.
Burton, John. *The Collection of the Qur'ān*. Cambridge, 1979.
Cook, Michael. *The Koran: A Very Short Introduction*. Oxford, 2000.
Flügel, G. *Corani Textus Arabicus*. Leipzig,1834.
———. *Corcordantiae Corani Arabicae*. Leipzig, 1842.
Goldziher, I. *Muslim Studies*. 2 vols. London, 1967, 1971.
Jeffery, Arthur. *The Foreign Vocabulary of the Qur'ān*. Baroda, 1938.
———. *Materials for the History of the Text of the Qur'ān*. Leiden, 1937.
Lüling, Günter. *Über den Ur-Qoran*. Erlangen, 1993.
Margoliouth, D. S. *Chrestomathia Baidawiana: The Commentary of el- Baiḍāwī on Sura III Translated and Explained for the Use of Students of Arabic*. London, 1894.
Nöldeke, T. *Geschichte des Qorāns*. 3 vols. 2d ed. Leipzig, 1909–1938.
Schacht, Joseph. *The Origins of Muhammadan Jurisprudence*. Oxford, 1950.
Sfar, Mondher. *Le Coran est-il authentique*? Paris, 2000.
Shaikh, A. *Islam, Sex and Violence*. Cardiff, 1999.
Wansbrough, John. *Qur'ānic Studies*. Oxford, 1977.
———. *The Sectarian Milieu*. Oxford, 1978.
Warraq, Ibn, ed. *The Origins of the Koran*. Amherst N.Y.: Prometheus Books, 1998.

Translations of the Koran

Ali, Muhammad. *The Holy Qur-an*. Woking, 1917.
Arberry, Arthur. *The Koran Interpreted*. Oxford, 1964.
Bell, Richard. *The Qur'an, Translated with a Critical Re-arrangement of the Surahs*. 2 vols. Edinburgh, 1937.
Blachère, Régis. *Le Coran*. Paris, 1949–51.
Dawood, N. J. *The Koran*. Harmondsworth, 1990.
Palmer, E. Ḥ *The Qur'an*. Oxford, 1880.
Paret, Rudi. *Der Koran: Übersetzung*. Stuttgart, 1962.
———. *Der Koran: Kommentar und Konkordanz*. Stuttgart, 1971.
Pickthall, Marmaduke. *The Meaning of the Glorious Koran*. New York, 1930.
Rodwell, J. M. *The Koran Translated from the Arabic*. London, 1861.
Sale, George. *The Koran*. London, 1734.
Yusuf Ali, A. *The Holy Qur'an: Translation and Commentary*. Lahore, 1934.

Arabic Commentaries

Bayḍāwī. *Beidhawii commentarius in Coranum.* Edited by H. O. Fleischer, 2 vols. Leipzig, 1846–48.

Jalālain al-Maḥallī, Jalāl ad-Dīn, and as-Suyūṭī, Jalāl ad-Dīn. *Tafsīr al-Jalālain,* in *Al -futūḥāt al-ilāhiyya bi-tau ḍī ḥ tafsīr al- Jalālain li-daqā'iqal-khafiyya ta'līf Sulaymān ibn ʿUmar al-ʿUyaylī ash-Shāfiʿī.* 4 vols. Cairo, 1337 A.H./ 1957–58.

Ibn Kathīr, *Tafsīr al-Qur'ān al-Karīm.* 7 vols. Beirut: 1385 A.H.

Al-Ṭabarī. *The Commentary on the Qur'ān.* Vol. 1. Translated by J. Cooper. Oxford, 1987.

Az-Zamakhsharī. *Tafsīr al-Kashshāf.* 4 vols. Cairo, 1373 A.H./1953–55.

NOTES

1. J. Hollander, "Versions, Interpretations, Performances," in *On Translation*, ed. Reuben A. Brower (Cambridge: Harvard University Press, 1959), p. 208, where Hollander also quotes Voltaire.

2. Jackson Mathews, "On Translating Poetry," in *On Translation*, ed. Reuben A. Brower (Cambridge: Harvard University Press, 1959), p. 70.

3. See appendix, "Bibliography of Translations," in *Arabic Literature to the End of the Umayyad Period*, ed. Beeston, Johnstone, et al. (Cambridge: Cambridge University Press, 1983), pp. 502–20.

4. In Egypt, the rate of illiteracy is placed as high as 49.8 percent. See *Information Please Almanac* (Boston, 1997), p. 180.

5. Charles Ferguson, "Diglossia," *Word* 15, no. 2 (1959): 325–40; William Marçais, "La diglossie arabe," *L'Enseignement public—Revue Pédagogique* 104, no. 12 (1930): 401–409; Alan S. Kaye, "Arabic," in *The Major Languages of South Asia, the Middle East and Africa*, ed. Bernard Comrie (London, Routledge, 1990), p. 181.

6. Kaye, "Arabic," p. 173.

7. Wheeler M. Thackston, *An Introduction to Koranic and Classical Arabic* (Bethesda, Md.: Iranbooks, 1994), p. xii.

8. B. Lewis, *Islam and the West* (Oxford: Oxford University Press, 1993), p. 65.

9. It is in fact becoming more and more westernized, i.e., de-Semitized under the influence of the international news agencies.

10. P. Larcher, "Les Incertitudes de la Poesie Arabe Archaique," *La Revue des Deux Rives*, no. 1 (1999): 129.

11. Kaye, "Arabic," p. 183.

12. P. Larcher, "La Linguistique Arabe d'Hier a Demain: Tendances Nouvelles de la Recherche," *Arabica* 45 (1998): 409–29.

13. Gustav Meiseles, "Educated Spoken Arabic and the Arabic Language Continuum," *Archivum Linguisticum* 11, no. 2 (1980): 118–42; quoted in Larcher, "Les Incertitudes de la Poesie Arabe Archaique."

14. A. S. Kaye, "Formal vs. Informal in Arabic: Diglossia, Triglossia, Tetraglossia, etc., Polyglossia—Multiglossia Viewed as a Continuum," *ZAL* 27 (1994): 47–66.

15. Barbara F. Grimes, *Ethnologue, Languages of the World*, 13th ed. (Dallas, 1996).

16. Everything, of course, depends on our definition of language and dialect; that is why estimates as to the number of languages in the world vary from five thousand to nearly seven thousand.

17. Merrit Ruhlen, *A Guide to the World's Languages*, vol. 1 (Stanford, 1991), p. 1.

18. I. M. Diakonoff, "Afro-Asiatic Languages," in *Encyclopaedia Britannica* [EB] (2000), at www.britannica.com.

19. M. Ruhlen, *A Guide to the World's Languages*, p. 380.

20. "Hamito-Semitic Languages," in *The Columbia Encyclopedia*, 6th ed. (New York, 2000).

21. R. Hetzron, "Semitic Languages," in *The Major Languages of South Asia, the Middle East and Africa*, ed. B. Comrie (London: Routledge, 1990), p. 162.

22. Wheeler M. Thackston, *Introduction to Syriac* (Bethesda, Md.: Iranbooks, 1999), p. vii.

23. S. Brock in G. H. A. Juynboll, ed., *Studies in the First Century of Islamic Society* (Chicago, 1982); Segal in Bernard Lewis and P. M. Holt, eds., *Historians of the Middle East* (London, 1962); Mingana in *The Origins of the Koran*, ed. Ibn Warraq (Amherst, N.Y.: Prometheus Books, 1998). Cahen in *Arabica*, vol. 1 (1954); Cook and Crone, *Hagarism* (Cambridge, 1977).

24. Thackston, *Introduction to Syriac*, p. viii.

25. "Syriac," in *The Columbia Encyclopedia*, 6th ed. (New York, 2000).

26. C. Rabin, "ʿArabiyya," in *EI2*.

27. S. Fraenkel, *Aramaeischen Fremdwörter im Arabischen* (Leiden, 1886).

28. Rabin, "ʿArabiyya"; emphasis added by the author.

29. Kaye, "Arabic," p. 171.

30. Rabin, "ʿArabiyya."

31. A. Rippin, "Epigraphical South Arabian and Qur'anic Exegesis," *JSAI* 13 (1990): 155–74.

32. "Arabic language," in *EB* (1999).

33. B. Lewis, *Islam and the West* (Oxford: Oxford University Press, 1993), p. 68.

34. Rabin, "ʿArabiyya," p. 566b.

35. A. Schaade, "Arabia(e). Arabic Language. Classical Arabic," in *EI1* vol. 1, p. 394.

36. S. Akhtar, "Ex-defender of the Faith," *Times Higher Educational Supplement* [*THES*], August 22, 1997.

37. Lewis, *Islam and the West*, p. 68; emphasis added by the author.

38. S. Akhtar, in *THES*, February 13, 1998.

39. Schaade, "Arabia(e). Arabic Language. Classical Arabic," p. 394.

40. T. Nöldeke, *Beiträge zur Kenntniss der Poesie der alten Araber* (Hanover, 1864), p. 2.

41. R. Blachère, *Histoire de la Littérature Arabe. Des Origines à la fin du XVe siècle de-J.-C.*, vol. 1 (Paris, 1952), p. 79.

42. Schaade, "Arabia(e). Arabic Language. Classical Arabic," p. 393.

43. Karl Vollers, *Volkssprache und Schriftsprache im alten Arabien* (Strassburg, 1906).

44. Hans Wehr, "Review of Fück (1950)," *ZDMG* 102 (1952): 179–84.

45. Werner Diem, "Die nabatäischen Inschriften und die Frage der Kasusflexion im Altarabischen," in *ZDMG* 123 (1973): 227–37.

46. T. Nöldeke, "Zur Sprache des Korans," in *Neue Beiträge zur semitischen* (Strassburg: Sprachwissenschaft, 1910).

47. Johann Fück, *Arabiya: Untersuchungen zur arabischen Sprach—und Stilgeschichte* [Abhandlungen de Sächsischen Akademie der Wissenschaften zu Leipzig, Philologisch—historische Klasse 45/1] (Berlin, 1950).

48. J. Blau, "The Jahiliyya and the Emergence of the Neo-Arabic Lingual Type," *JSAI* 7 (1986): 35–43.

49. J. Wansbrough, *Quranic Studies* (Oxford, 1977), p. 102.

50. Rabin, "ʿArabiyya," p. 566a.

51. F. Corriente, "From Old Arabic to Classical Arabic, the Pre-Islamic Koine: Some Notes on the Native Grammarians' Sorces, Attitudes and Goals," *JSS* 21 (1976): 62–98.

52. "Iʿrāb" in *EI2*, quoting al-Jurjānī.

53. Rabin, "ʿArabiyya," p. 565.

54. Wansbrough, *Quranic Studies*, p. 85.

55. [J.Wansbrough's note: "Suyūṭī, *Muzhir* i, 221; cf. Kahle, *'Readers,'*

pp. 70–71: the story was pressed into the service of a number of distinct but related causes; for the literary effect of similar traditions see also above (*Quranic Studies*, pp. 42–3; pp. 69–70).”]

56. Wansbrough, *Quranic Studies*, p. 94.

57. Ibid., p. 95.

58. Ibid., pp. 97–98.

59. A. Mingana, *Odes and Psalms of Solomon*, ii, 1920, p. 125.

60. D. S. Margoliouth, *JRAS* (1925): 415–49.

61. Ṭ Ḥusayn, *Fī l-adab al-jāhili* (Cairo, 1927).

62. For full bibliography, see Blachère, *Histoire de la Littérature Arabe*, vol. 1, pp. xviii–xxxiii.

63. The rhyme may have been there originally to aid memorization; the recording of rhyme depends on *iʿrāb,* but the use of rhyme does not.

64. G. R. Hawting, *The Idea of Idoltatry and the Emergence of Islam: From Polemic to History* (Cambridge, 1999), p. 48.

65. E.g., Sura XXVI.195; XLIII.1; XII.1.

66. T. Lester, *What is the Koran*? (New York: Atlantic Monthly Press, 1999); chap. 1.2 in this volume.

67. H. Hirschfeld, *New Researches into the Composition and Exegesis of the Qoran* (London, 1902), p. 6.

68. Ibid., p. 7.

69. Fuat Sezgin, *GAS*, band I, p. 24.

70. T. P. Hughes, *Dictionary of Islam* (1885; reprint, Calcutta: Rupa & Co., 1988), pp. 518 ff.

71. Ibid. p. 518.

72. Ibid., p. 519.

73. P. Crone, “Two Legal Problems Bearing on the Early History of the Quran,” *JSAI* 18 (1994): 1–37.

74. M. Ali, *The Holy Qur'ān* (Columbus, Ohio, 1995), p. 611.

75. M. Pickthall, *The Meaning of the Glorious Koran* (London, 1948), p. 318

76. A. Jeffery, *The Foreign Vocabulary of the Qur'an* (Baroda, 1938).

77. J. Penrice, *A Dictionary and Glossary of the Koran* (1873; reprint, Delhi, 1990).

78. E. W. Lane, *An Arabic-English Lexicon* (London, 1863–1893).

79. R. Blachère, *Le Coran* (Paris, 1949–51).

80. See chaps. 3.1 and 3.2, respectively.

81. Jeffery, *The Foreign Vocabulary of the Qu'ran*, p. 43.

82. Ibid., pp. 99–100.

83. Blachère, *Le Coran*, vol. 1, p. 61.

84. Jeffery, *The Foreign Vocabulary of the Qu'ran*, p. 53.

85. Blachère, *Le Coran*, vol. 1, p. 117.

86. Jeffery, *The Foreign Vocabulary of the Qu'ran*, p. 234 n. 4.

87. Penrice, *A Dictionary and Glossary of the Koran*, p. 117.

88. A. J. Wensinck, "Kurbān," in *EI1*.

89. Blachère, *Le Coran*, vol. 2, p. 662.

90. Richard Bell, *Translation of the Qur'ān* (Edinburgh, 1939), p. 511 n. 2.

91. Blachère, *Le Coran*, vol. 2, pp. 743–44 n. 59.

92. See J. D. McAuliffe, "Exegetical Identification of the Sabi'un," *MW* 72 (1982): 95–106; C. Buck, "The Identity of the Sabi'un: An Historical Quest," *MW* 74 (1984): 172–86.

93. Abū'l Qāsim al-Ḥusayn al-Rāghib al-Iṣfahānī, *Al-Mufradāt fī-Gharīb al-Qur'ān* (Cairo, 1324 A.H.).

94. Al-Ṭabarī, *The Commentary on the Qu'ran*, trans. J. Cooper (Oxford: Oxford University Press, 1987), p. 410.

95. Ibid.

96. Ibn Sa'd, *Kitāb al-ṭabaqāt al-kabīr*, ed. Sachau et al. (Leiden, 1925-28), vol. 2, pp. 36–38.

97. Richard Bell, *A Commentary on the Qu'ran* (Manchester, 1991), vol. 1, p. 14.

98. Ibid., p. 17.

99. Ibid., p. 51.

100. Blachère, *Le Coran*, vol. 2, p. 809 n. 262.

101. Jeffery, *The Foreign Vocabulary of the Qu'ran*, pp. 225–26.

102. Fakhr al-Dīn al-Rāzī, *al-Tafsīr al-Kabīr* (Cairo: al-Matba'ah al-Bahiyah, n.d.), vol. 3, p. 77; quoted in M. Ayoub, *The Qur'an and Its Interpreters* (Albany, 1984), vol. 1, p. 102.

103. E. W. Lane, *An Arabic-English Lexicon* (London 1863), vol. 1, p. 9.

104. Jeffery, *The Foreign Vocabulary of the Qur'an*, pp. 43–44.

105. "Sidjdjil," in *EI2*.

106. F. Leemhuis, "Quranic sijjīl and Aramaic sgyl," *JSS* 27 (1982): 47–56.

107. "Sidjdjil," in *EI2*.

108. V. Vacca, "Sidjdjil," in *EI1*.

109. Jeffery, *The Foreign Vocabulary of the Qur'an*, pp. 163–64.

110. David Powers, *Studies in Qur'an and Ḥadīth: The Formation of the Islamic Law of Inheritance* (Berkeley, 1986), pp. 22–23.

111. Quoted in Ayoub, *The Qur'an and Its Interpreters*, vol. 1, p. 70.

112. Blachère, *Le Coran*, vol. 2, p. 736 n. 27.

113. E.g., Dawood, Pickthall.

114. Ṭabarī, *The Commentary on the Quran*, p. 201.

115. Bell, *A Commentary on the Qur'an*, vol. 1, pp. 18–19.

116. Ayoub, *The Qur'an and Its Interpreters*, vol. 1, p. 128.

117. Ṭabarī, *The Commentary on the Quran*, p. 482.

118. Ibid., p. 483.

119. Ayoub, *The Qur'an and Its Interpreters*, vol. 1, p. 132.

120. Blachère, *Le Coran*, vol. 2, pp. 755–56.

121. Ayoub, *The Qur'an and Its Interpreters*, vol. 1, p. 145.

122. Bell, *A Commentary on the Qur'an*, vol. 1 p. 21.

123. Ibid., p. 46.

124. Ibid., p. 45.

125. Ibid., p. 47.

126. Students wishing to test their knowledge of Arabic grammar should perhaps see if they can spot the errors in II.61; II.83; II.84; II.187; II.238; II.253; III.146; IV.1; IV.13/14; IV.69; IV.78–79; IV.80; IV.136; IV.171; V.54; VI.25; VI.95; VII.178; IX.3; IX.107; X.92; XI.46; XI.46; XI.111; XII.30; XII.85; XV.51–52; XVI.13; XVI.69; XVI.101; XXIII.14; XXV.38; XXVI.16; XXX.30; XXXIII.63; XXXVII.6; XXXIX.21; XL.2–3; XLIII.81; LIII.20b; LIV.50; LV.39; LVI.13–14; LVII.18.

127. J. Burton, "Linguistic Errors in the Qur'ān," *JSS* 33, no. 2 (1988): 181–96.

128. Ibid., p. 181.

129. Abū ʿUbayd al-Qāsim b.Sallām, *Faḍ'il al-Qur'ān*, MS., Tübingen, Ma, VI, 96, f.40b.

130. Yaḥyā Ziyād al-Farrā', *Maʿānī al-Qur'ān* (Beirut 1955, 1980), vol. 1, p. 105; cf. Jalāl al-Dīn al-Suyūṭī, *al-Itqān fī ʿulūm al-Qur'ān* (Cairo, 1354), vol. 1, pp. 182 ff.

131. W. Wright, *A Grammar of the Arabic Language*, 3rd. ed. (Cambridge, 1967), vol. 11, pp. 78–79.

132. Bell, *A Commentary on the Qur'an*, vol. 1 p. 255; Wright, *A Grammar of the Arabic Language*, vol. 1, p. 256D.

133. W. Wright, *A Grammar of the Arabic Language*, vol. 1, pp. 270–71.

134. Ibid., vol. 2, pp. 24–34; vol. 1, p. 60: On the subjunctive having a fatha.

135. Ibid., vol. 1, pp. 278 ff.: prepositions.

136. Ibid., p. 234.

137. Blachère, *Le Coran*, vol. 2, pp. 776–77 n. 172.

138. Indeed this verse is considered by many grammarians and linguists as

a good example of aspect in Arabic. "Aspect" is a technical term used in the grammatical description of verbs referring primarily to the way the grammar marks the duration or type of temporal activity denoted by the verb; the contrast is often between perfective and imperfective, between the completion of an action, and duration without specifying completion. Blachère and Gaudefroy-Demombynes write: "He said [to Adam]: 'Be,' and he was . . . , that is to say: he started to exist and continued to live; the use of the perfect would have supposed an accepted fact, established, without the notion of duration." Blachère and Gaudefroy, *Grammaire de l'arabe classique*, 3 ed. (Paris, Maisonneuve et Larose, 1952), p. 254.

While the verb *qāla* indicates that we are in the past, *yakūnu* is presented as posterior (since it follows *fa-*) to the utterance of the imperative *kun*, whereas in French and English "he was" is coordinated to "he said" and presented as past.

139. Bell, *A Commentary on the Qur'an*, vol. 1, p. 378.

140. Ibid., vol. 2, p. 282.

141. Cf. August Fischer, "Eine Qoran-Interpolation," in this volume, chap. 6.2.

142. T. Nöldeke et al., *Geschichte des Qorans,* lst ed. (Göttingen, 1860), pp. 70–174; 2nd ed. (Leipzig, 1909–1938), pp. 87–234.

143. Karl Opitz, *Die Medizin im Koran* (Stuttgart, 1906), p. 63.

144. See Bayḍā wī, *Anwār al-tanzīl wa-asrār al-ta'wil*, ed. H. O. Fleischer (Leipzig, 1846–1848), vol. 2, p. 6. I. Goldziher, *Introduction to Islamic Theology and Law*, trans. A. & R. Hamori (Princeton, N.J.: Princeton University Press, 1981), pp. 28–30.

145. Bell, *A Commentary on the Qur'an*, vol. 1, p. 49.

146. Ibid., pp. 50–51.

147. *TransState Islam*, Special Double Issue (spring 1997): 23.

148. F. Leemhuis, "Origins and Early Development of the tafsīr Tradition," in *Approaches to the History of the Interpretation of the Qu'ran*, ed. A. Rippin (Oxford, 1988), p. 14.

149. J. D. McAuliffe, "Quranic Hermeneutics: The Views of al-Ṭabarī and Ibn Kathīr," in *Approaches to the History of the Interpretation of the Qu'ran,* ed. A. Rippin (Oxford, 1988), pp. 46–62.

150. See H. Berg, *The Development of Exegesis in Early Islam: The Debate over the Authenticity of Muslim Literature from the Formative Period* (London: Curzon Press, 2000).

151. Rev. J. M. Rodwell, *The Koran Translated* (1861; reprint London: E. P. Dutton, 1921), p. 7; emphasis added by the author.

152. M. Schub, "Dave and the Knave in the Cave of the Brave," *ZAL* 38 (2000): 88–90.

153. A. Rippin, "Muhammad in the Qur'an: Reading Scripture in the 21st Century," in *The Biography of Muhammad: The Issue of the Sources*, ed. H. Motzki (Leiden: Brill, 2000), pp. 299–300.

154. Ibid., p. 307.

155. "North Semitic Alphabet," "Aramaic Alphabet," "Arabic Alphabet," in *EB* (1999–2000).

156. I. J. Gelb, *A Study of Writing*, 2d, ed. (Chicago: University of Chicago Press, 1962), reflecting the state of research up to the end of the 1950s, seems to think that even South Semitic must be descended from the Phoenician syllabary, as much as Aramaic. Equally, Beeston thinks that the southern alphabets derive from the same stock as the Phoenician one: "Background Topics," in *Arabic Literature to the End of the Umayyad Period*, ed. Beeston, Johnstone, et al. (Cambridge: Cambridge University Press, 1983), p. 10. However, the article "Arabic Alphabet," in *EB* (1999–2000) seems to be more cautious.

157. "Aramaic Alphabet," in *EB* (1999–2000).

158. J. F. Healey, "The Early History of the Syriac Script, A Reassessment," *JSS* 45, no. 1 (spring 2000): 64–65.

159. J. F. Healey, "The Nabataean Contribution to the Development of the Arabic Script," *Aram* 2 (1990): 93–98; "Nabataean to Arabic: Calligraphy and Scropt Development among the Pre-Islamic Arabs," *Manuscripts of the Middle East* 5 (1990–91): 41–52.

160. E. Tov, ed., *Companion Volume to the Dead Sea Scrolls Microfiche Edition* (Leiden, 1995).

161. F. Briquel-Chatonnet, "De l'araméen à l'arabe: quelques réflexions sur la genèse de l'écriture arabe," in *Scribes et manuscrits du Moyen-Orient*, ed. F. Déroche and F. Richard (Paris, 1997), pp. 135–49.

162. J. F. Healey, *The Early Alphabet* (Los Angeles, 1990), p. 51.

163. "Background Topics," p. 11.

164. Ibid., p. 12.

165. Ibid., p. 13.

166. G. Luling, *On the Pre-Islamic Koran* (Amherst, N.Y.: Prometheus Books, forthcoming), pp. 1–4.

167. C. J. Adams, "Quran: The Text and Its History," in *ER*, ed. M. Eliade (New York: Macmillan, 1987), pp. 157–76.

168. ʿAbd al-ʿĀl Sālim Makram (wa-) Aḥmad Mukhtār ʿUmar (Iʿdād): *Muʿjam al-qiraʾāt al-qurʾāniyyah, maʿa maqadimmah fī l-qiraʾāt wa-ashar al-qurrāʾ*, I–VIII (Al-Kuwayt: Dhāt as-Salāsil 1402–1405/1982–1985).

169. A. Guillaume, *Islam* (Harmondsworth, Penguin Books, 1978), p. 189.

170. D. S. Margoliouth, "Textual Variations of the Koran," in *The Origins of the Koran*, ed. Ibn Warraq (Amherst, N.Y.: Prometheus Books, 1998), p. 159.

171. Ibid.

172. See A. Rippin, "Qur'ān 21:95: A Ban Is Upon Any Town," *JSS* 24 (1979): 43–53: ". . . the variants still show traces of their original intention: to explain away grammtical and lexical difficulties. While obviously this is not true of all variant readings in the Qur'an, many variants being too slight to alleviate any problem, in Sūrah 21:95 and in many others the exegetical nature of *Qur'ānic* variants is apparent" (p. 53).

173. See A. Rippin, "Qur'ān 7:40, Until the Camel Passes through the Eye of the Needle," *Arabica* 27, fasc. 2, pp. 107–13. "Variants such as those for Sūrah 7:40 were created when polemically based pressures on the exegetes were the strongest and the attitudes towards the Qur'anic text less confining" (p. 113).

174. See especially Answering Islam: A Christian-Muslim Dialog, http://www.answering-islam.org.

175. Rev. T. Hughes, *Dictionary of Islam* (1885; reprint, Delhi, 1988), p. 520

176. D. Margoliouth, *Mohammed and the Rise of Islam* (London, 1905), p. 139

177. A. Yusuf Ali, *The Holy Qur'ān* (Lahore, 1934), vol. 1, p. 673.

178. Ibn Salāma, *al-Nāsikh wa'l-mansūkh* (Cairo, 1899), p. 184, referred to by D. Powers, "The Exegetical Genre nāsikh al-Qur'ān," in *Approaches to the History of the Interpretation of the Qur'ān,* ed. A.Rippin (Oxford, 1988), p. 130.

179. D. B. Macdonald, "Kadar," in *EI1*.

180. Hughes, *Dictionary of Islam*, p. 472.

181. Neal Robinson, *Discovering the Qur'an* (London, 1996), p. 65.

182. Ibid., p. 66.

183. John Burton, *The Collection of the Qur'an* (Cambridge, 1977), pp. 235–37.

184. Robinson, *Discovering the Qur'an*, p. 67.

185. D. Powers, "The Exegetical Genre nasikh al-Qur'an," in *Approaches to the History of the Interpretation of the Qu'ran,* ed. A. Rippin (Oxford, 1988), p. 123.

186. Robinson, *Discovering the Qur'an,* p. 75.

187. A. Rippin, "The Function of the *asbāb al-nuzūl* in Qur'ānic Exegesis," *BSOAS* 51 (1988): 1–20, also in Ibn Warraq, ed., *The Quest for the Historical Muhammad* (Amherst, N.Y.: Prometheus Books, 2000), pp. 392–419.

188. G. R. Hawting, *The Idea of Idolatry and the Emergence of Islam. From Polemic to History* (Cambridge, 1999), pp. 31–32.

189. G. H. A. Juynboll, review of *Quranic Studies* by John Wansbrough, in *JSS* 24 (1979): 293–96.

190. Warraq, *The Quest for the Historical Muhammad*, pp. 74–75.

191. Al-Rāshid, Sa'd 'Abd al-'Azīz, in *Kitābāt islām iyyah min Makkah al-mukarramah* (al-Riyāḍ: Makt.al-Malik Fahd al-Waṭaniyyah, 1416/1995).

192. Burton, *The Collection of the Qur'an*, p. 225.

193. Ibid., p. 219.

194. J. Bellamy, "Some Proposed Emendations to the Text of the Koran," in this volume, p. ___.

195. A. E. Housman, *Selected Prose*, ed. John Carter (Cambridge, 1961), pp. 131–44.

196. Ibid., p. 131.

197. Ibid. p. 132.

198. Ibid., p. 135.

199. Ibid., pp. 144–45.

200. H. Hirschfeld, *New Researches into the Composition and Exegesis of the Qoran* (London, 1902), p. 137.

201. S. de Sacy, *Journal des savants* (1832), p. 535 sq.; G. Weil, *Historisch-Kritische Einleitung in den Koran,* 2d ed. (Bielefeld, 1878), p. 52, A. Sprenger, *Das Leben und die Lehre des Mohammad* (Berlin, 1861–65), vol. 3, p. 164.

202. Hirschfeld, *New Researches into the Composition and Exegesis of the Qoran*, p. 139.

203. W. M. Watt and Richard Bell, *Introduction to the Qur'ān* (Edinburgh, 1970), p. 53.

204. Ibn al-Jawzī, *Wafa,* p. 32a; idem *Talqih* (ms. Asir effendi, Istanbul), II, p. 3a; Anonymous, *Sīra* (Berlin, no. 9602), p. 155a; al-Barizi (Berlin, no. 2569), p. 81b; Maqrīzī, *Imta*, III; Sibt ibn al-Jawzī, *Mirat at az-zaman*, II (ms. Kuprulu, Istanbul), p. 149b.

205. Burton, *The Collection of the Qur'an*, pp. 233–34.

206. I hope to publish extracts in English in an anthology in the near future.

207. I was lucky enough to obtain a photocopy of the third volume at New York Public Library. Two of the greatest modern scholars of the Koran did not possess the third volume, and were happy to receive a photocopy from me. What I have called volume three is, in fact, Notes Complementaires II of *Deuxième Fascicule*.

208. A. Sprenger, *Das Leben und die Lehre des Mohammad*, 2d ed., p. 533.

209. P. Casanova, *Mohammed et la Fin du Monde* (Paris, 1911–21), pp. 3–4.

210. Watt and Bell, *Introduction to the Qur'an*, pp. 53–54.

211. Nöldeke, *Gesch. des Q.*, p. 202.

212. My emphasis.

213. Casanova, *Mohammed et la Fin du Monde*, pp. 147 ff.

214. Watt and Bell, *Introduction to the Qur'an*, pp. 53–54.

215. H. Lammens, "Koran and Tradition," in *The Quest for the Historical Muhammad*, ed. Ibn Warraq (Amherst, N.Y.: Prometheus Books, 2000), pp. 169–87.

216. T. Andrae, "Die Legenden von der Berufung Muhammeds," *Le Monde Oriental* 6 (1912): 5–18.

217. A. Rippin, "Muhammad in the Qur'an: Reading Scripture in the 21st Century," in *The Biography of Muhammad: The Issue of the Sources,* ed. H. Motzki (Leiden, Brill, 2000), pp. 299–300.

218. M. Schub, "Quran 9.40, Dave and the Knave in the Cave of the Brave," *ZAL* 38 (2000): 88–90.

219. J. Wansbrough, *The Sectarian Milieu* (Oxford, 1978), p. 52.

220. Ibid., p. 69.

221. H. Müller, *Die Propheten in ihrer ursprünglichen Form* (Vienna, 1896).

222. R. Geyer, "Zur Strophik des Qurans," *WZKM* 22 (1908): 265–86, chap. 8.1 in present volume.

223. C. Luxenberg, *Die Syro-Aramaische Lesart des Koran* (Berlin, Verlag Das Arabische Buch, 2000).

224. P. R. Davies, *In Search of "Ancient Israel"* (1992; reprint, Sheffield, 1999), p. 13.

225. John Wansbrough, *Res Ipsa Loquitur: History and Mimesis* (Jerusalem: Israel Academy of Sciences and Humanities, 1987), p. 10.

226. David Hall, "History, Literature and Religion," in *New Humanist* (September 2000): 13.

227. C. V. Langlois and C. Seignobos, *Introduction to the Study of History*, trans. G. G. Berry (London, 1898), p. 69.

228. Ibid., p. 156; italics in original.

229. Ibid., p. 157; italics in original.

230. Ibid., pp. 166–70.

231. Davies, *In Search of "Ancient Israel."*

232. K. W. Whitelam, *The Invention of Ancient Israel: The Silencing of Palestinian History* (London and New York: Routledge, 1996).

233. N. P. Lemche, *The Israelites in History and Tradition* (London: SPCK, 1998).

234. T. L. Thompson, *Early History of the Israelite People: From the Written and Archaeological Sources* (Leiden: E. J. Brill, 1992).

235. J. van Seters, *Prologue to History: The Yahwist as Historian in Genesis* (Westminster: John Knox Press, 1992).

236. G. Garbini, *History and Ideology in Ancient Israel* (London: SCM Press, 1988).

237. Wansbrough, *Res Ipsa Loquitur*, p. 11.

238. Lemche, *The Isrealites in History and Tradition*, p. 88.

239. Ibid., p. 96.

240. Ibid., p. 165.

241. G. R. Hawting, *The Idea of Idolatry and the Emergence of Islam. From Polemic to History* (Cambridge, 1999).

242. G. R. Hawting, "John Wansbrough, Islam, and Monotheism," in *The Quest for the Historical Muhammad*, pp. 516–17.

243. Ibid., p. 521.

244. J. Wansbrough, *Quranic Studies* (Oxford, 1977), p. ix.

245. A. Rippin, *Muslims. Their Religious Beliefs and Practices,* Vol. 1:The Formative Period (London, 1991), p. ix.

246. W. J. Hanegraaf, *New Age Religion and Western Culture: Esotericism in the Mirror of Secular Thought* (Brill, 1996), pp. 25–26.

247. A. Geiger, "Judaism and Islam," in *The Origins of the Koran*; H. Hirschfeld, *Judische Elemente im Koran* (Berlin, 1878); *Beitrage zur Erklarung des Koran* (Leipzig, 1886); *New Researches into the Composition and Exegesis of the Qoran*; A. Katsch, *Judaism in Islam* (New York, 1954); D. Sidersky, *Les Origines des légendes musulmanes dans le Coran* (Paris, 1933); H. Speyer, *Die Biblischen Erzahlungen im Qoran* (Hildesheim, 1961); B. Heller, "Récits et personnages bibliques dans la légende mahométane," *REJ* 85 (1928): 113–36; "La légende biblique dans I'Islam," *REJ* 98 (1934): 1–18; P. Jensen, "Das Leben Muhammeds und die David-Sage," *Der Islam* 12 (1922): 84–97; I. Schapiro, *Die haggadischen Elemente im erzalenden Teil des Korans*, vol. 1 (Leipzig, 1907); H. Schwarzbaum, "The Jewish and Moslem Versions of Some Theodicy Legends," *Fabula* 3 (1959–60): 119–69; C. Gilliot, "Les 'informateurs' juifs et chrétiens de Muhammad. Reprise d'un problème traité par Aloys Sprenger et Theodor Nöldeke," *JSAI* 22 (1998): 84–126; C. C. Torrey, *The Jewish Foundation of Islam* (New York, 1933), reprinted in *The Origins of the Koran.*

248. F. E. Peters, "The Quest of the Historical Muhammad," in *The Quest for the Historical Muhmmad*, p. 455.

249. Hall, "History, Literature and Religion," pp. 10–14.

250. H. Lammens, "Koran and Tradition—How the Life of Muhammad Was Composed," in *The Quest for the Historical Muhammad*, p. 455.

251. F. E. Peters, "The Quest of the Historical Muhammad," p. 458.

252. Ibid., p.455

253. Hall, "History, Literature and Religion," p. 12.

254. A. Brockett, "Studies in Two Transmissions of the Qur'ān" (Ph.D. diss., University of St. Andrews, 1984), p. 13.

255. Ibid., p. 19.

1.2

WHAT IS THE KORAN?

Toby Lester

In 1972, during the restoration of the Great Mosque of Sana'a, in Yemen, laborers working in a loft between the structure's inner and outer roofs stumbled across a remarkable grave site, although they did not realize it at the time. Their ignorance was excusable: mosques do not normally house graves, and this site contained no tombstones, no human remains, no funereal jewelry. It contained nothing more, in fact, than an unappealing mash of old parchment and paper documents—damaged books and individual pages of Arabic text, fused together by centuries of rain and dampness, gnawed into over the years by rats and insects. Intent on completing the task at hand, the laborers gathered up the manuscripts, pressed them into some twenty potato sacks, and set them aside on the staircase of one of the mosque's minarets, where they were locked away—and where they would probably have been forgotten once again, were it not for Qadhi Isma'il al-Akwa', then the president of the Yemeni Antiquities Authority, who realized the potential importance of the find.

Al-Akwa' sought international assistance in examining and preserving the fragments, and in 1979 managed to interest a visiting German scholar, who in turn persuaded the German government to organize and fund a restoration project. Soon after the project began, it became clear that the hoard was a fabulous example of what is sometimes referred to as a "paper grave"—in this case the resting place for, among other things, tens of thousands of fragments from close to a thousand different parchment codices of the Koran, the Muslim holy scripture. In some pious Muslim circles it is held that worn-out or damaged copies of the Koran must be removed from circulation; hence the idea of a grave, which both preserves the sanctity of the texts being laid to rest and ensures that only complete and unblemished editions of the scripture will be read.

Some of the parchment pages in the Yemeni hoard seemed to date back to the seventh and eighth centuries C.E., or Islam's first two centuries—they were fragments, in other words, of perhaps the oldest Korans in existence. What's more, some of these fragments revealed small but intriguing aberrations from the standard Koranic text. Such aberrations, though not surprising to textual historians, are troublingly at odds with the orthodox Muslim belief that the Koran as it has reached us today is quite simply the perfect, timeless, and unchanging Word of God.

The mainly secular effort to reinterpret the Koran—in part based on textual evidence such as that provided by the Yemeni fragments—is disturbing and offensive to many Muslims, just as attempts to reinterpret the Bible and the life of Jesus are disturbing and offensive to many conservative Christians. Nevertheless, there are scholars, Muslims among them, who feel that such an effort, which amounts essentially to placing the Koran in history, will provide fuel for an Islamic revival of sorts—a reappropriation of tradition, a going forward by looking back. Thus far confined to scholarly argument, this sort of thinking can be nonetheless very powerful and—as the histories of the Renaissance and the Reformation demonstrate—can lead to major social change. The Koran, after all, is currently the world's most ideologically influential text.

LOOKING AT THE FRAGMENTS

The first person to spend a significant amount of time examining the Yemeni fragments, in 1981, was Gerd-R. Puin, a specialist in Arabic calligraphy and Koranic paleography based at Saarland University, in Saarbrücken, Germany. Puin, who had been sent by the German government to organize and oversee the restoration project, recognized the antiquity of some of the parchment fragments, and his preliminary inspection also revealed unconventional verse orderings, minor textual variations, and rare styles of orthography and artistic embellishment. Enticing, too, were the sheets of the scripture written in the rare and early Hijazi Arabic script: pieces of the earliest Korans known to exist, they were also palimpsests—versions very clearly written over even earlier, washed-off versions. What the Yemeni Korans seemed to suggest, Puin began to feel, was an *evolving* text rather than simply the Word of God as revealed in its entirety to the Prophet Muhammad in the seventh century C.E.

Since the early 1980s more than fifteen thousand sheets of the Yemeni Korans have painstakingly been flattened, cleaned, treated, sorted, and assembled; they now sit ("preserved for another thousand years," Puin says) in Yemen's House of Manuscripts, awaiting detailed examination. That is something the Yemeni authorities have seemed reluctant to allow, however. "They want to keep this thing low-profile, as we do too, although for different reasons," Puin explains. "They don't want attention drawn to the fact that there are Germans and others working on the Korans. They don't want it made public that there is work being done *at all*, since the Muslim position is that everything that needs to be said about the Koran's history was said a thousand years ago."

To date just two scholars have been granted extensive access to the Yemeni fragments: Puin and his colleague H.-C. Graf von Bothmer, an Islamic-art historian also based at Saarland University. Puin and Von Bothmer have published only a few tantalizingly brief articles in scholarly publications on what they have discovered in the Yemeni fragments. They have been reluctant to publish partly because until recently they were more concerned with sorting and classifying the fragments than with systematically examining them, and partly because they felt that the Yemeni authorities, if they realized the possible implications of the discovery, might refuse them further access. Von Bothmer, however, in 1997 finished taking more than thirty-five thousand microfilm pictures of the fragments, and has recently brought the pictures back to Germany. This means that soon von Bothmer, Puin, and other scholars will finally have a chance to scrutinize the texts and to publish their findings freely—a prospect that thrills Puin. "So many Muslims have this belief that everything between the two covers of the Koran is just God's unaltered word," he says. "They like to quote the textual work that shows that the Bible has a history and did not fall straight out of the sky, but until now the Koran has been out of this discussion. The only way to break through this wall is to prove that the Koran has a history too. The Sana'a fragments will help us to do this."

Puin is not alone in his enthusiasm. "The impact of the Yemeni manuscripts is still to be felt," says Andrew Rippin, a professor of religious studies at the University of Calgary, who is at the forefront of Koranic studies today. "Their variant readings and verse orders are all very significant. Everybody agrees on that. These manuscripts say that the early history of the Koranic text is much more of an open question than many have suspected: the text was less stable, and therefore had less authority, than has always been claimed."

COPYEDITING GOD

By the standards of contemporary biblical scholarship, most of the questions being posed by scholars like Puin and Rippin are rather modest; outside an Islamic context, proposing that the Koran has a history and suggesting that it can be interpreted metaphorically are not radical steps. But the Islamic context—and Muslim sensibilities—cannot be ignored. "To historicize the Koran would in effect delegitimize the whole historical experience of the Muslim community," says R. Stephen Humphreys, a professor of Islamic studies at the University of California at Santa Barbara. "The Koran is the charter for the community, the document that called it into existence. And ideally—though obviously not always in reality—Islamic history has been the effort to pursue and work out the commandments of the Koran in human life. If the Koran is a historical document, then the whole Islamic struggle of fourteen centuries is effectively meaningless."

The orthodox Muslim view of the Koran as self-evidently the Word of God, perfect and inimitable in message, language, style, and form, is strikingly similar to the fundamentalist Christian notion of the Bible's "inerrancy" and "verbal inspiration" that is still common in many places today. The notion was given classic expression only a little more than a century ago by the biblical scholar John William Burgon.

> The Bible is none other than *the voice of Him that sitteth upon the Throne!* Every Book of it, every Chapter of it, every Verse of it, every

word of it, every syllable of it . . . every letter of it, is the direct utterance of the Most High!

Not all the Christians think this way about the Bible, however, and in fact, as the *Encyclopaedia of Islam* (1981) points out, "the closest analogue in Christian belief to the role of the Koran in Muslim belief is not the Bible, but Christ." If Christ is the Word of God made flesh, the Koran is the Word of God made text, and questioning its sanctity or authority is thus considered an outright attack on Islam—as Salman Rushdie knows all too well.

The prospect of a Muslim backlash has not deterred the critical-historical study of the Koran, as the existence of the essays in *The Origins of the Koran* (1998) demonstrate. Even in the aftermath of the Rushdie affair the work continues: In 1996 the Koranic scholar Günter Lüling wrote in the *Journal of Higher Criticism* about "the wide extent to which both the text of the Koran and the learned Islamic account of Islamic origins have been distorted, a deformation unsuspectingly accepted by Western Islamicists until now." In 1994 the journal *Jerusalem Studies in Arabic and Islam* published a posthumous study by Yehuda D. Nevo, of the Hebrew University in Jerusalem, detailing seventh- and eighth-century religious inscriptions on stones in the Negev Desert which, Nevo suggested, pose "considerable problems for the traditional Muslim account of the history of Islam." That same year, and in the same journal, Patricia Crone, a historian of early Islam currently based at the Institute for Advanced Study, in Princeton, New Jersey, published an article in which she argued that elucidating problematic passages in the Koranic text is likely to be made possible only by "abandoning the conventional account of how the Qur'an was born." And since 1991 James Bellamy, of the University of Michigan, has proposed in the *Journal of the American Oriental Society* a series of "emendations to the text of the Koran"—changes that from the orthodox Muslim perspective amount to copyediting God.

Crone is one of the most iconoclastic of these scholars. During the 1970s and 1980s she wrote and collaborated on several books—most notoriously, with Michael Cook, *Hagarism: The Making of the Islamic World* (1977)—that made radical arguments about the origins of Islam and the writing of Islamic history. Among *Hagarism's* controversial claims were suggestions that the text of the Koran came into being later than is now believed ("There is no hard evidence for the existence of the Koran in any form before the last decade of the seventh century"); that Mecca was not the initial Islamic sanctuary ("[the evidence] points unambiguously to a sanctuary in north-west Arabia . . . Mecca was secondary"); that the Arab conquests preceded the institutionalization of Islam ("the Jewish messianic fantasy was enacted in the form of an Arab conquest of the Holy Land"); that the idea of the *hijra*, or the migration of Muhammad and his followers from Mecca to Medina in 622, may have evolved long after Muhammad died ("No seventh-century source identifies the Arab era as that of the *hijra*"); and that the term "Muslim" was not commonly used in early Islam ("There is no good reason to suppose that the bearers of this primitive identity called themselves 'Muslims' [but] sources do . . . reveal an earlier designation of the community [which] appears in Greek as 'Magaritai' in a papyrus of 642, and in Syriac as 'Mahgre' or 'Mahgraye' from as early as the 640s").

Hagarism came under immediate attack, from Muslim and non-Muslim scholars alike, for its heavy reliance on hostile sources. ("This is a book," the authors wrote, "based on what from any Muslim perspective must appear an inordinate regard for the testimony of infidel sources.") Crone and Cook have since backed away from some of its most radical propositions—such as, for example, that the Prophet Muhammad lived two years longer than the Muslim tradition claims he did, and that the historicity of his migration to Medina is questionable. But Crone has continued to challenge both Muslim and Western orthodox views of Islamic history. In *Meccan Trade and the Rise of Islam* (1987) she made a detailed argument challenging the prevailing view among Western (and some Muslim) scholars that Islam arose in response to the Arabian spice trade.

Gerd-R. Puin's current thinking about the Koran's history partakes of this contemporary revisionism. "My idea is that the Koran is a kind of cocktail of texts that were not all understood even at the time of Muhammad," he says. "Many of them may even be a hundred years older than Islam itself. Even within the Islamic traditions there is a huge body of contradictory information, including a significant Christian substrate; one can derive a whole Islamic *antihistory* from them if one wants."

Patricia Crone defends the goals of this sort of thinking. "The Koran is a scripture with a history like any other—except that we don't know this history and tend to provoke howls of protest when we study it.

Nobody would mind the howls if they came from Westerners, but Westerners feel deferential when the howls come from other people: who are you to tamper with *their* legacy? But we Islamicists are not trying to destroy anyone's faith."

Not everyone agrees with that assessment—especially since Western Koranic scholarship has traditionally taken place in the context of an openly declared hostility between Christianity and Islam. (Indeed, the broad movement in the West over the past two centuries to "explain" the East, often referred to as "Orientalism," has in recent years come under fire for exhibiting similar religious and cultural biases.) The Koran has seemed, for Christian and Jewish scholars particularly, to possess an aura of heresy; the nineteenth-century Orientalist William Muir, for example, contended that the Koran was one of "the most stubborn enemies of Civilisation, Liberty, and the Truth which the world has yet known." Early Soviet scholars, too, undertook an ideologically motivated study of Islam's origins, with almost missionary zeal: in the 1920s and in 1930 a Soviet publication titled *Ateist* ran a series of articles explaining the rise of Islam in Marxist-Leninist terms. In *Islam and Russia* (1956), Ann K. S. Lambton summarized much of this work, and wrote that several Soviet scholars had theorized that "the motive force of the nascent religion was supplied by the mercantile bourgeoisie of Mecca and Medina"; that a certain S. P. Tolstov had held that "Islam was a social-religious movement originating in the slave-owning, not feudal, form of Arab society"; and that N. A. Morozov had argued that "until the Crusades Islam was indistinguishable from Judaism and . . . only then did it receive its independent character, while Muhammad and the first Caliphs are mythical figures." Morozov appears to have been a particularly flamboyant theorist: Lambton wrote that he also argued, in his book *Christ* (1930), that "in the Middle Ages Islam was merely an off-shoot of Arianism evoked by a meteorological event in the Red Sea area near Mecca."

Not surprisingly, then, given the biases of much non-Islamic critical study of the Koran, Muslims are inclined to dismiss it outright. A particularly eloquent protest came in 1987, in the *Muslim World Book Review*, in a paper titled "Method Against Truth: Orientalism and Qur'anic Studies," by the Muslim critic S. Parvez Manzoor. Placing the origins of Western Koranic scholarship in "the polemical marshes of medieval Christianity" and describing its contemporary state as a "cul-de-sac of its own making," Manzoor orchestrated a complex and layered assault on the entire Western approach to Islam. He opened his essay in a rage.

> The Orientalist enterprise of Qur'anic studies, whatever its other merits and services, was a project born of spite, bred in frustration and nourished by vengeance: the spite of the powerful for the powerless, the frustration of the "rational" towards the "superstitious" and the vengeance of the "orthodox" against the "non-conformist." At the greatest hour of his worldly-triumph, the Western man, coordinating the powers of the State, Church and Academia, launched his most determined assault on the citadel of Muslim faith. All the aberrant streaks of his arrogant personality—its reckless rationalism, its world-domineering phantasy and its sectarian fanaticism—joined in an unholy conspiracy to dislodge the Muslim Scripture from its firmly entrenched position as the epitome of historic authenticity and moral unassailability. The ultimate trophy that the Western man sought by his daredevil venture was the Muslim mind itself. In order to rid the West forever of the "problem" of Islam, he reasoned, Muslim consciousness must be made to despair of the cognitive certainty of the Divine message revealed to the Prophet. Only a Muslim confounded of the historical authenticity or doctrinal autonomy of the Qur'anic revelation would abdicate his universal mission and hence pose no challenge to the global domination of the West. Such, at least, seems to have been the tacit, if not the explicit, rationale of the Orientalist assault on the Qur'an.

Despite such resistance, Western researchers with a variety of academic and theological interests press on, applying modern techniques of textual and historical criticism to the study of the Koran. That a substantial body of this scholarship now exists is indicated by the recent decision of the European firm Brill Publishers—a long-established publisher of such major works as *The Encyclopaedia of Islam* and *The Dead Sea Scrolls Study Edition*—to commission the first-ever *Encyclopaedia of the Qur'an*. Jane McAuliffe, a professor of Islamic studies at the University of Toronto and the general editor of the encyclopedia, hopes that it will function as a "rough analogue" to biblical encyclopedias and will be "a turn-of-the-millennium summative work for the state of Koranic scholarship." Articles for the first part of the encyclopedia are currently being edited and prepared for publication later this year.

The *Encyclopaedia of the Qur'an* will be a truly collaborative enterprise, carried out by Muslims and non-Muslims, and its articles will present multiple approaches to the interpretation of the Koran, some of which are likely to challenge traditional Islamic views—thus disturbing many in the Islamic world, where the time is decidedly less ripe for a revisionist study of the Koran. The plight of Nasr Abu Zaid, an unassuming Egyptian professor of Arabic who sits on the encyclopedia's advisory board, illustrates the difficulties facing Muslim scholars trying to reinterpret their tradition.

"A MACABRE FARCE"

"The Koran is a text, a *literary* text, and the only way to understand, explain, and analyze it is through a literary approach," Abu Zaid says. "This is an essential theological issue." For expressing views like this in print—in essence, for challenging the idea that the Koran must be read literally as the absolute and unchanging Word of God—Abu Zaid was in 1995 officially branded an apostate, a ruling that in 1996 was upheld by Egypt's highest court. The court then proceeded, on the grounds of an Islamic law forbidding the marriage of an apostate to a Muslim, to order Abu Zaid to divorce his wife, Ibtihal Yunis (a ruling that the shocked and happily married Yunis described at the time as coming "like a blow to the head with a brick").

Abu Zaid steadfastly maintains that he is a pious Muslim, but contends that the Koran's manifest content—for example, the often archaic laws about the treatment of women for which Islam is infamous—is much less important than its complex, regenerative, and spiritually nourishing latent content. The orthodox Islamic view, Abu Zaid claims, is stultifying; it reduces a divine, eternal, and dynamic text to a fixed human interpretation with no more life and meaning than "a trinket . . . a talisman . . . or an ornament."

For a while Abu Zaid remained in Egypt and sought to refute the charges of apostasy, but in the face of death threats and relentless public harassment he fled with his wife from Cairo to Holland, calling the whole affair "a macabre farce." Sheikh Youssef al-Badri, the cleric whose preachings inspired much of the opposition to Abu Zaid, was exultant. "We are not terrorists; we have not used bullets or machine guns, but we have stopped an enemy of Islam from poking fun at our religion. . . . No one will even dare to think about harming Islam again."

Abu Zaid seems to have been justified in fearing for his life and fleeing: in 1992 the Egyptian journalist Farag Foda was assassinated by Islamists for his critical writings about Egypt's Muslim Brotherhood, and in 1994 the Nobel prize-winning novelist Naguib Mahfouz was stabbed for writing, among other works, the allegorical *Children of Gabalawi* (1959)—a novel, structured like the Koran, that presents "heretical" conceptions of God and the Prophet Muhammad.

Deviating from the orthodox interpretation of the Koran, says the Algerian Mohammed Arkoun, a professor emeritus of Islamic thought at the University of Paris, is "a very sensitive business" with major implications. "Millions and millions of people refer to the Koran daily to explain their actions and to justify their aspirations," Arkoun says. "This scale of reference is much larger than it has ever been before."

MUHAMMAD IN THE CAVE

Mecca sits in a barren hollow between two ranges of steep hills in the west of present-day Saudi Arabia. To its immediate west lies the flat and sweltering Red Sea coast; to the east stretches the great Rabʾ al-Khālī, or Empty Quarter—the largest continuous body of sand on the planet. The town's setting is uninviting: the earth is dry and dusty, and smolders under a relentless sun; the whole region is scoured by hot, throbbing desert winds. Although sometimes rain does not fall for years, when it does come it can be heavy, creating torrents of water that rush out of the hills and flood the basin in which the city lies. As a backdrop for divine revelation, the area is every bit as fitting as the mountains of Sinai or the wilderness of Judea.

The only real source of historical information about pre-Islamic Mecca and the circumstances of the Koran's revelation is the classical Islamic story about the religion's founding, a distillation of which follows.

In the centuries leading up to the arrival of Islam, Mecca was a local pagan sanctuary of considerable antiquity. Religious rituals revolved around the Kaʿba—a shrine, still central in Islam today, that Muslims believe was originally built by Ibrāhīm (known to Christians and Jews as Abraham) and his son Ismāʾīl (Ishmael). As Mecca became increasingly prosperous in the sixth century C.E., pagan idols of varying sizes and shapes proliferated. The traditional story has it that by the early seventh century a pantheon of some 360 statues and icons surrounded the Kaʾba (inside which were found renderings of Jesus and the Virgin Mary, among other idols).

Such was the background against which the first installments of the Koran are said to have been revealed, in 610, to an affluent but disaffected merchant named Muhammad bin ʿAbdallāh. Muhammad had developed the habit of periodically withdrawing from Mecca's pagan squalor to a nearby mountain cave, where he would reflect in solitude. During one of these retreats he was visited by the Angel Gabriel—the very same angel who had announced the coming of Jesus to the Virgin Mary in Nazareth some six hundred years earlier. Opening with the command "Recite!" Gabriel made it known to Muhammad that he was to serve as the Messenger of God. Subsequently, until his death, the supposedly illiterate Muhammad received through Gabriel divine revelations in Arabic that were known as *qurʾan* ("recitation") and that announced, initially in a highly poetic and rhetorical style, a new and uncompromising brand of monotheism known as *Islam*, or "submission" (to God's will). Muhammad reported these revelations verbatim to sympathetic family members and friends, who either memorized them or wrote them down.

Powerful Meccans soon began to persecute Muhammad and his small band of devoted followers, whose new faith rejected the pagan core of Meccan cultural and economic life, and as a result in 622 the group migrated some two hundred miles north, to the town of Yathrib, which subsequently became known as Medina (short for Medinat al-Nabi, or City of the Prophet). (This migration, known in Islam as the *hijra*, is considered to mark the birth of an independent Islamic community, and 622 is thus the first year of the Islamic calendar.) In Medina, Muhammad continued to receive divine revelations, of an increasingly pragmatic and prosaic nature, and by 630 he had developed enough support in the Medinan community to attack and conquer Mecca. He spent the last two years of his life proselytizing, consolidating political power, and continuing to receive revelations.

The Islamic tradition has it that when Muhammad died in 632, the Koranic revelations had not been gathered into a single book; they were recorded only "on palm leaves and flat stones and in the hearts of men." (This is not surprising: the oral tradition was strong and well established, and the Arabic script, which was written without the vowel markings and consonantal dots used today, served mainly as an aid to memorization.) Nor was the establishment of such a text of primary concern: the Medinan Arabs—an unlikely coalition of ex-merchants, desert nomads, and agriculturalists united in a potent new faith and inspired by the life and sayings of Prophet Muhammad—were at the time pursuing a fantastically successful series of international conquests in the name of Islam. By the 640s the Arabs possessed most of Syria, Iraq, Persia, and Egypt, and thirty years later they were busy taking over parts of Europe, North Africa, and Central Asia.

In the early decades of the Arab conquests many members of Muhammad's coterie were killed, and with them died valuable knowledge of the Koranic revelations. Muslims at the edges of the empire began arguing over what was Koranic scripture and what was not. An army general returning from Azerbaijan expressed his fears about sectarian controversy to the Caliph ʿUthmān (644–656)—the third Islamic ruler to succeed Muhammad—and is said to have entreated him to "overtake this people before they differ over the Koran the way the Jews and Christians differ over their Scripture." ʿUthmān convened an editorial committee of sorts that carefully gathered the various pieces of scripture that had been memorized or written down by Muhammad's companions. The result was a standard written version of the Koran. ʿUthmān ordered all incomplete and "imperfect" collections of the Koranic scripture destroyed, and the new version was quickly distributed to the major centers of the rapidly burgeoning empire.

During the next few centuries, while Islam solidified as a religious and political entity, a vast body of exegetical and historical literature evolved to explain the Koran and the rise of Islam, the most important elements of which are *hadith*, or the collected sayings and deeds of the Prophet Muhammad; *sunna*, or the body of Islamic social and legal custom; *sira*, or biographies of the Prophet; and *tafsīr*, or Koranic commentary and explication. It is from these traditional sources—compiled in written form mostly from the mid-eighth to the mid-tenth century—that all accounts of the revelation of the Koran and the early years of Islam are ultimately derived.

"FOR PEOPLE WHO UNDERSTAND"

Roughly equivalent in length to the New Testament, the Koran is divided into 114 sections, known as *suras*, that vary dramatically in length and form. The book's organizing principle is neither chronological nor thematic—for the most part the suras are arranged from beginning to end in descending order of length. Despite the unusual structure, however, what generally surprises newcomers to the Koran is the degree to which it draws on the same beliefs and stories that appear in the Bible. God (*Allah* in Arabic) rules supreme: he is the all-powerful, all-knowing, and all-merciful Being who has created the world and its creatures; he sends messages and laws through prophets to help guide human existence; and, at a time in the future known only to him, he will bring about the end of the world and the Day of Judgment. Adam, the first man, is expelled from Paradise for eating from the forbidden tree. Noah builds an ark to save a select few from a flood brought on by the wrath of God. Abraham prepares himself to sacrifice his son at God's bidding. Moses leads the Israelites out of Egypt and receives a revelation on Mount Sinai. Jesus—born of the Virgin Mary and referred to as the Messiah—works miracles, has disciples, and rises to heaven.

The Koran takes great care to stress this common monotheistic heritage, but it works equally hard to distinguish Islam from Judaism and Christianity. For example, it mentions prophets—Hūd, Ṣaliḥ, Shuʾayb, Luqmān, and others—whose origins seem exclusively Arabian, and it reminds readers that it is "A Koran in Arabic, / For people who understand." Despite its repeated assertions to the contrary, however, the Koran is often extremely difficult for contemporary readers—even highly educated speakers of Arabic—to understand. It sometimes makes dramatic shifts in style, voice, and subject matter from verse to verse, and it assumes a familiarity with language, stories, and events that seem to have been lost even to the earliest of Muslim exegetes (typical of a text that initially evolved in an oral tradition). Its apparent inconsistencies are easy to find: God may be referred to in the first and third person in the same sentence; divergent versions of the same story are repeated at different points in the text; divine rulings occasionally contradict one another. In this last case the Koran anticipates criticism and defends itself by asserting the right to abrogate its own message ("God doth blot out / Or confirm what He pleaseth").

Criticism did come. As Muslims increasingly came into contact with Christians during the eighth century, the wars of conquest were accompanied by theological polemics, in which Christians and others latched on to the confusing literary state of the Koran as proof of its human origins. Muslim scholars themselves were fastidiously cataloging the problematic aspects of the Koran—unfamiliar vocabulary, seeming omissions of text, grammatical incongruities, deviant readings, and so on. A major theological debate in fact arose within Islam in the late eighth century, pitting those who believed in the Koran as the "uncreated" and eternal Word of God against those who believed in it as created in time, like anything that isn't God himself. Under the Caliph al-Maʾmūn (813–833) this latter view briefly became orthodox doctrine. It was supported by several schools of thought, including an influential one known as Muʿtazilism, that developed a complex theology based partly on a metaphorical rather than simply literal understanding of the Koran.

By the end of the tenth century the influence of the Muʿtazili school had waned, for complicated political reasons, and the official doctrine had become that of *iʾjāz*, or the "inimitability" of the Koran. (As a result, the Koran has traditionally not been translated by Muslims for non-Arabic-speaking Muslims. Instead it is read and recited in the original by Muslims worldwide, the majority of whom do not speak Arabic. The translations that do exist are considered to be nothing more than scriptural aids and paraphrases.) The adoption of the doctrine of inimitability was a major turning point in Islamic history, and from the tenth century to this day the mainstream Muslim understanding of the Koran as the literal and uncreated Word of God has remained constant.

PSYCHOPATHIC VANDALISM?

Gerd-R. Puin speaks with disdain about the traditional willingness, on the part of Muslim and Western scholars, to accept the conventional understanding of the Koran. "The Koran claims for itself that it is '*mubeen,*' or 'clear,' " he says. "But if you look at it, you will notice that every fifth sentence or so simply doesn't make sense. Many Muslims—and Orientalists—will tell you otherwise, of course, but the fact is that a fifth of the Koranic text is *just incomprehensible*. This is what has caused the traditional anxiety regarding translation. If the Koran is not comprehensible—if it can't even be understood in Arabic—then it's not translatable. People fear that. And since the Koran claims repeatedly to be clear but obviously is not—as even speakers of Arabic will tell you—there is a contradiction. Something else must be going on."

Trying to figure out that "something else" really began only in this century. "Until quite recently," Patricia Crone, the historian of early Islam, says, "everyone took it for granted that everything the Muslims claim to remember about the origin and meaning of the Koran is correct. If you drop that assumption, you have to start afresh." This is no mean feat, of course; the Koran has come down to us tightly swathed in a historical tradition that is extremely resistant to criticism and analysis. As Crone put it in *Slaves on Horses*,

> The Biblical redactors offer us sections of the Israelite tradition at different stages of crystallization, and their testimonies can accordingly be profitably compared and weighed against each other. But the Muslim tradition was the outcome, not of a slow crystallization, but of an explosion; the first compilers were not redactors, but collectors of debris whose works are strikingly devoid of overall unity; and no particular illuminations ensue from their comparison.

Not surprisingly, given the explosive expansion of early Islam and the passage of time between the religion's birth and the first systematic documenting of its history, Muhammad's world and the worlds of the historians who subsequently wrote about him were dramatically different. During Islam's first century alone a provincial band of pagan desert tribesmen became the guardians of a vast international empire of institutional monotheism that teemed with unprecedented literary and scientific activity. Many contemporary historians argue that one cannot expect Islam's stories about its own origins—particularly given the oral tradition of the early centuries—to have survived this tremendous social transformation intact. Nor can one expect a Muslim historian writing in ninth- or tenth-century Iraq to have discarded his social and intellectual background (and theological convictions) in order accurately to describe a deeply unfamiliar seventh-century Arabian context. R. Stephen Humphreys, writing in *Islamic History: A Framework for Inquiry* (1988), concisely summed up the issue that historians confront in studying early Islam.

> If our goal is to comprehend the way in which Muslims of the late 2nd/8th and 3rd/9th centuries [Islamic calendar/Christian calendar] understood the origins of their society, then we are very well off indeed. But if our aim is to find out "what really happened," in terms of reliably documented answers to modern questions about the earliest decades of Islamic society, then we are in trouble.

The person who more than anyone else has shaken up Koranic studies in the past few decades is John Wansbrough, formerly of the University of London's School of Oriental and African Studies. Puin is "rereading him now" as he prepares to analyze the Yemeni fragments. Patricia Crone says that she and Michael Cook "did not say much about the Koran in *Hagarism* that was not based on Wansbrough." Other scholars are less admiring, referring to Wansbrough's work as "drastically wrongheaded," "ferociously opaque," and a "colossal self-deception." But like it or not, anybody engaged in the critical study of the Koran today must contend with Wansbrough's two main works—*Quranic Studies: Sources and Methods of Scriptural Interpretation* (1977) and *The Sectarian Milieu: Content and Composition of Islamic Salvation History* (1978).

Wansbrough applied an entire arsenal of what he called the "instruments and techniques" of biblical criticism—form criticism, source criticism, redaction criticism, and much more—to the Koranic text. He concluded that the Koran evolved only gradually in the seventh and eighth centuries, during a long period of oral transmission when Jewish and Christian sects were arguing volubly with one another well to the north of Mecca and Medina, in what are now parts of Syria, Jordan, Israel, and Iraq. The reason that no Islamic source material from the first century or so of Islam has survived, Wansbrough concluded, is that it never existed.

To Wansbrough, the Islamic tradition is an example of what is known to biblical scholars as a "salvation history": a theologically and evangelically motivated story of a religion's origins invented late in the day and projected back in time. In other words, as Wansbrough put it in *Quranic Studies*, the canonization of the Koran—and the Islamic traditions that arose to explain it—involved the

> attribution of several, partially overlapping, collections of *logia* (exhibiting a distinctly Mosaic imprint) to the image of a Biblical prophet (modified by the material of the Muhammadan *evangelium* into an Arabian man of God) with a traditional message of salvation (modified by the influence of Rabbinic Judaism into the unmediated and finally immutable word of God).

Wansbrough's arcane theories have been contagious in certain scholarly circles, but many Muslims understandably have found them deeply offensive. S. Parvez Manzoor, for example, has described the Koranic studies of Wansbrough and others as "a naked discourse of power" and "an outburst of psychopathic vandalism." But not even Manzoor argues for a retreat from the critical enterprise of Koranic studies; instead he urges Muslims to defeat the Western revisionists on the "epistemological battlefield," admitting that "sooner or later [we Muslims] will have to approach the Koran from methodological assumptions and parameters that are radically at odds with the ones consecrated by our tradition."

REVISIONISM INSIDE THE ISLAMIC WORLD

Indeed, for more than a century there have been public figures in the Islamic world who have attempted the revisionist study of the Koran and Islamic history—the exiled Egyptian professor Nasr Abu Zaid is not unique. Perhaps Abu Zaid's most famous predecessor was the prominent Egyptian government minister, university professor, and writer Ṭaha Ḥusayn. A determined modernist, Ḥusayn in the early 1920s devoted himself to the study of pre-Islamic Arabian poetry and ended up concluding that much of that body of work had been fabricated well after the establishment of Islam in order to lend outside support to Koranic mythology. A more recent example is the Iranian journalist and diplomat Ali Dashti, who in his *Twenty Three Years: A Study of the Prophetic*

Career of Mohammed (1985) repeatedly took his fellow Muslims to task for not questioning the traditional accounts of Muhammad's life, much of which he called "myth-making and miracle-mongering."

Abu Zaid also cites the enormously influential Muhammad ʿAbduh as a precursor. The nineteenth-century father of Egyptian modernism, ʿAbduh saw the potential for a new Islamic theology in the theories of the ninth-century Muʿtazilis. The ideas of the Muʿtazilis gained popularity in some Muslim circles early in this century (leading the important Egyptian writer and intellectual Ahmad Amin to remark in 1936 that "the demise of Muʿtazilism was the greatest misfortune to have afflicted Muslims; they have committed a crime against themselves"). The late Pakistani scholar Fazlur Rahman carried the Muʿtazilite torch well into the present era; he spent the later years of his life, from the 1960s until his death in 1988, living and teaching in the United States, where he trained many students of Islam—both Muslims and non-Muslims—in the Muʿtazilite tradition.

Such work has not come without cost, however: Ṭaha Ḥusayn, like Nasr Abu Zaid, was declared an apostate in Egypt; Ali Dashti died mysteriously just after the 1979 Iranian revolution; and Fazlur Rahman was forced to leave Pakistan in the 1960s. Muslims interested in challenging orthodox doctrine must tread carefully. "I would like to get the Koran out of this prison," Abu Zaid has said of the prevailing Islamic hostility to reinterpreting the Koran for the modern age, "so that once more it becomes productive for the essence of our culture and the arts, which are being strangled in our society." Despite his many enemies in Egypt, Abu Zaid may well be making progress toward this goal: there are indications that his work is being widely, if quietly, read with interest in the Arab world. Abu Zaid says, for example, that his *The Concept of the Text* (1990)—the book largely responsible for his exile from Egypt—has gone through at least eight underground printings in Cairo and Beirut.

Another scholar with a wide readership who is committed to reexamining the Koran is Mohammed Arkoun, the Algerian professor at the University of Paris. Arkoun argued in *Lectures du Coran* (1982), for example, that "it is time [for Islam] to assume, along with all of the great cultural traditions, the modern risks of scientific knowledge," and suggested that "the problem of the divine authenticity of the Koran can serve to reactivate Islamic thought and engage it in the major debates of our age." Arkoun regrets the fact that most Muslims are unaware that a different conception of the Koran exists within their own historical tradition. What a reexamination of Islamic history offers Muslims, Arkoun and others argue, is an opportunity to challenge the Muslim orthodoxy from within, rather than having to rely on "hostile" outside sources. Arkoun, Abu Zaid, and others hope that this challenge might ultimately lead to nothing less than an Islamic renaissance.

The gulf between such academic theories and the daily practice of Islam around the world is huge, of course—the majority of Muslims today are unlikely to question the orthodox understanding of the Koran and Islamic history. Yet Islam became one of the world's great religions in part because of its openness to social change and new ideas. (Centuries ago, when Europe was mired in its feudal Dark Ages, the sages of a flourishing Islamic civilization opened an era of great scientific and philosophical discovery. The ideas of the ancient Greeks and Romans might never have been introduced to Europe were it not for the Islamic historians and philosophers who rediscovered and revived them.) Islam's own history shows that the prevailing conception of the Koran is not the only one ever to have existed, and the recent history of biblical scholarship shows that not all critical-historical studies of a holy scripture are antagonistic. They can instead be carried out with the aim of spiritual and cultural regeneration. They can, as Mohammed Arkoun puts it, demystify the text while reaffirming "the relevance of its larger intuitions."

Increasingly diverse interpretations of the Koran and Islamic history will inevitably be proposed in the coming decades, as traditional cultural distinctions between east, west, north, and south continue to dissolve, as the population of the Muslim world continues to grow, as early historical sources continue to be scrutinized, and as feminism meets the Koran. With the diversity of interpretations will surely come increased fractiousness, perhaps intensified by the fact that Islam now exists in such a great variety of social and intellectual settings—Bosnia, Iran, Malaysia, Nigeria, Saudi Arabia, South Africa, the United States, and so on. More than ever before, anybody wishing to understand global affairs will need to understand Islamic civilization, in all its permutations. Surely the best way to start is with the study of the Koran—which promises in the years ahead to be at least as contentious, fascinating, and important as the study of the Bible has been in this century.

EDITOR'S SUGGESTIONS FOR FURTHER READING

(Authors mentioned or discussed in this article are marked with an asterisk.)

*Arkoun, M. *Lectures du Coran*. Paris, 1983.

Azmi, M. M. *Studies in Early Hadith Literature*. Indianapolis, 1978.

Bashear, S. *Arabs and Others in Early Islam*. New Jersey, 1997.

*Bellamy, J. "Some Proposed Emendations to the Text of the Koran." *JAOS*, 13 (1993): 562–73 (chap. 6.6 in this volume).

Brock, S. "Syriac Views of Early Islam." In *Studies on the First Century of Islamic Society*, edited by G. H. A. Juynboll (1982), pp. 9–21.

Burton, J. "Those are the High-Flying Cranes." *JSS* 15, no. 2 (1970): 246–65.

———. *Collection of the Qur'an*. Cambridge, 1977.

———. Review of Watt and McDonald, *The History of Al-Ṭabarī*, vol. 6, *Muhammad at Mecca*. *BSOAS* 53 (1990): 328–31.

Calder, N. "From Midrash to Scripture: The Sacrifice of Abraham in Early Islamic Tradition." *Le Museon* 101 (1988): 375–402.

*Cook, M. *Early Muslim Dogma: A Source Critical Study*. Cambridge, 1981.

———. *The Koran. A Very Short Introduction*. Oxford, 2000.

Conrad, L. "Abraha and Muhammad: Some Observations à propos of Chronology and Literary Topoi in the Early Arabic Historical Tradition." In *The Quest for the Historical Muhammad*, edited by Ibn Warraq. Amherst, N.Y.: Prometheus Books, 2000.

*Crone, P., and M. Cook, *Hagarism: The Making of the Muslim World*. Cambridge, 1977.

*Crone, P., and Martin Hinds. *God's Caliph; Religious Authority in the First Centuries of Islam*. Cambridge, 1986.

*Crone, P. *Slaves on Horses: The Evolution of the Islamic Polity*. Cambridge, 1980.

———. *Meccan Trade and the Rise of Islam*. Oxford, 1987.

———. *Roman, Provincial and Islamic Law: The Origins of the Islamic Patronate*, Cambridge, 1987.

———. "Two Legal Problems Bearing on the Early History of the Qur'an." *JSAI* 18 (1994): 1–37.

*Dashti, Ali. *Twenty-Three Years: A Study of the Prophetic Career of Mohammed*. London, 1985.

*Farag, Foda. *Qabl al-Suqut* (*Before the Fall*). Cairo, 1985.

Goldziher, I. *Muslim Studies*. 2 vols. London, 1966, 1971.

*Humphreys, R. S. *Islamic History: A Framework for Inquiry*. New Jersey, 1991.

*Ṭaha Ḥusayn. *Fī al –Shi'r al-jāhili* (*On Pre-Islamic Poetry*), Cairo, 1926

———. *Fī l-adab al-jāhili* (*On Pre-Islamic Literature*). Cairo, 1927.
*Luling, G. *Uber den Urkoran*. Erlangen, 1973.
———. *On the Pre-Islamic Christian Strophe Poetical Texts in the Koran* (translation of above: forthcoming)
———, "Preconditions for the Scholarly Criticism of the Koran and Islam, with Some Autobiographical Remarks." *Journal of Higher Criticism* 3 (spring 1996): 73–109.
*Manzoor, S. P. "Method Against Truth: Orientalism and Qur'anic Studies." *Muslim World Book Review* (1987).
*Muir, W. *The Life of Muhammad*. 1 vol. London, 1894.
*Nevo, Y. D. "Towards a Prehistory of Islam." *JSAI* 17 (1994): 108–41 (chap. 2 in this volume).
*Nevo, Y. D., and Koren, J. "Methodological Approaches to Islamic Studies." In *The Quest for the Historical Muhammad* edited by Ibn Warraq, pp. 420–43. Amherst, N.Y.: Prometheus Books, 2000.
———. "The Origins of the Muslim Descriptions of the Jahili Meccan Sanctuary." *JNES* 49 (1990): 23–44.
———. *Crossroads to Islam*. Forthcoming.
*Puin, Gerd-R. "Observations on Early Qur'ān Manuscripts in Ṣan'ā'." In *The Qur'ān as Text*, edited by Stefan Wild. 1996, (chap. 9.2 in this volume).
———. *Orthographic Peculiarities Observed in the Most Archaic Fragments of Yemeni Korans: The Case of "Alif Maqsurah."* Forthcoming.
———. *Leuke Kome in the Qur'ān: A Way Out of the "Tanglewood."* Forthcoming.
*Rahman, Fazlur. *Islam*. 2d. ed. Chicago, 1979.
———. *Major Themes of the Qur'ān*. Chicago, 1980.
*Rippin, A. *Muslims, Their Religious Beliefs and Practices*, vol. 1: *The Formative Period.* London, New York: Routledge, 1990.
———. *Muslims, Their Religious Beliefs and Practices*, vol. 2: *The Contemporary Period.* London, New York: Routledge, 1993.
———. "Literary analysis of Qur'ān, Sīra and Tafsīr: The Methodologies of John Wansbrough." Reprinted in Ibn Warraq, *The Origins of the Koran*, edited by Ibn Warraq. Amherst, N.Y.: Prometheus Books, 1998, pp. 351–63, 403–408.
———. "Qur'ān 21:95: 'A ban is upon any town.' " *Journal of Semitic Studies* 24 (1979): 43–53.
———. "Qur'ān 7.40: 'Until the Camel Passes Through the Eye of the Needle.' " *Arabica* 27 (1980): 107–13.
———. "Ibn 'Abbās's *Al-lughāt fī'l-Qur'ān*." *Bulletin of the School of Oriental and African Studies* 44 (1981): 15–25.

———. "The Present Status of Tafsīr Studies." *Muslim World* 72 (1982): 224–38. Also published in *Hamdard Islamicus* 6, no. 4 (1983): 17–31.
———. "Qur'ān 78.24: A Study in Arabic Lexicography." *Journal of Semitic Studies* 28 (1983): 311–20.
———. "The Function of *asbāb al-nuzūl* in Qur'ānic Exegesis." *Bulletin of the School of Oriental and African Studies* 51 (1988): 1–20.
———. "Muhammad in the Qur'ān: Reading Scripture in the Twenty-first Century." In *The Biography of Muhammad, The Issue of Sources*, edited by H. Motzki. Leiden, 2000.
———, ed. *The Qur'ān: Formative Interpretation*. Aldershot: Ashgate/Variorum, forthcoming.
———, ed. *The Qur'ān: Style and Contents*. Aldershot: Ashgate/Variorum, forthcoming.
Schacht, J. *The Origins of Muhammadan Jurisprudence*. Oxford, 1950.
Sfar, Mondher. *Le Coran est-il authentique*? Paris, 2000.
*Smirnov, N. A. *Russia and Islam*. Translated by A. Lambton. London, 1954.
*Wansbrough, J. *Quranic Studies: Sources and Methods of Scriptural Interpretation*. Oxford, 1977.
———. *The Sectarian Milieu: Content and Composition of Islamic Salvation History*. Oxford, 1978.
———. Review of Burton's *The Collection of the Qur'ān*. *BSOAS* 41 (1978): 370–71.
———. Review of Crone and Cook's *Hagarism: The Making of the Muslim World*. *BSOAS* 41 (1978): 155–56.
———. *Res Ipsa Loquitur: History and Mimesis*. Seventh Einstein Memorial Lecture, Jerusalem, Israel Academy of Sciences and Humanities, delivered 1986, published 1987.
*Warraq, Ibn, *Why I Am Not A Muslim*. Amherst, N.Y.: Prometheus Books, 1995.
———, ed. *The Origins of the Koran*. Amherst, N.Y.: Prometheus Books, 1998.
———, ed. *The Quest for the Historical Muhammad*. Amherst, N.Y.: Prometheus Books, 2000.
*Zaid (Zayd), Nasr Hamid Abu. *Naqd al-Khitab al-Dini* (*The Criticism of Religious Discourse*). Cairo, 1994.
———. *Al-Itijah al-Aqli fi al-Tafsir* (*The Rational Approach to Interpretation*). Cairo, 1993.
———. *Falsfat al-Ta'wil* (*The Philosophy of Interpretation*). Cairo, 1993.

Part 2

BACKGROUND

2.1

Towards a Prehistory of Islam

*Yehuda D. Nevo**

To Professor Yohanan Friedmann for faith, encouragement and lifegiving funding

There exist today in Islamic studies two paradigms for the rise of Islam. The traditional paradigm sees Islam as arising in the Ḥijāz of the early seventh century A.D. in essentially its final form, to take its place in a world populated by discrete monotheistic religions: Judaism, and several varieties of Christianity. The problem with this view is that it denies Islam a prehistory: a period of development prior to the formulation of orthodoxy and scriptural canonization, such as is attested for other religions. Moreover, as has often been noted, the sources upon which this paradigm are based are all very late, so that

> what they do not, and cannot, provide is an account of the "Islamic" community during the 150 years or so between the first Arab conquests and the appearance, with the *sīra-maghāzī* narratives, of the earliest Islamic literature. (Wansbrough, *SM* 119).

This is no problem for the traditional view, which accepts the accounts in the late sources regarding what happened during the period from which

Yehuda D. Nevo, "Towards a Prehistory of Islam," *JSAI* 17 (1994): 108–41. Reprinted with the permission of the Institute of Asian and African Studies, The Hebrew University, Jerusalem.

*The author died on February 12, 1992. The article was seen through the press by the editors.

sources are absent, maintaining that they are absent only because they have not survived.

The new paradigm, based upon the work of Wansbrough and previous works[1] sees the Muslim sources as representing a late stage in the development of Islam, reflecting the stage (and process) during which orthodoxy was imposed and scriptural canonization achieved. According to this view, we have no orthodox Muslim sources dating from the first 150 years of the Hijra era simply because none ever existed during that period. Rather, we should expect to find, in those first 150 years, at least remnants of evidence for the development of the Arab religion from some point of origin towards Islam. Wansbrough has demonstrated that the point of departure is to be sought in inter-sectarian polemic, in which Judaic and Judaeo-Christian notions are much more prominent than Christian ones. And Pines has attested the importance of Judaeo-Christianity as a factor both in al-Šām and Mesopotamia, and in the Christology of the Qur'ān. From this it would appear that Islam arose in the areas conquered by the Arabs, not in the Ḥijāz, that the starting point of its development was some form of Judaeo-Christianity, and that this process began considerably later than the date of the Arab conquest.

This viewpoint does indeed give us our missing Islamic prehistory, but it has until recently lacked enough evidence on which to amplify and base its conclusions. What it needs, in short, is the missing link between the religion of the Muslim texts from the late second century A.H. on, and the (apparently Judaeo-Christian) religious environment of the first century A.H., attested by non-Muslim sources.[2]

Just such a series of missing links is provided by the Arabic rock inscriptions scattered all over the Syro-Jordanian deserts and the Peninsula, and specifically the Negev, where most of the work of collecting and analyzing them has been carried out to date. Moreover, in view of these inscriptions, the official texts already long familiar—such as those in the papyri, the Dome of the Rock and the Arab-Sassanian coins—should be seen in a new light. It is my intention in the present paper to point out the existence of a considerable corpus of Arab religious texts dating from the first century and a half of Arab rule, exhibiting an Arab monotheistic creed which is demonstrably not Islam, but from which Islam could have developed. It is my opinion that Islam did in fact develop from some variant of this creed, mainly during the first century A.H., but this paper will not be concerned with the process of that development. Here I wish only to indicate that the very existence of this corpus of texts poses considerable problems for the traditional Muslim account of the history of Islam, whereas the alternative paradigm finds in them some, at least, of the evidence it needs to confirm its hypotheses.

I start with a fact to which too little attention has been paid. A distinctive feature of all the Arab religious institutions during the Sufyānī and on into the Marwānid one is the complete absence of any reference to Muḥammad. Neither the Prophet himself nor any Muḥammadan formulae appear in any inscription dated before the year 71/691. This is true whether the religious content of the inscriptions is its main purpose, as in supplications (*ʾadʿiya,* sg. *duʿāʾ*), or whether it is part of a commemorative inscription with a religious emphasis (Muʿāwiya's dam inscription near Ṭāʾif). When an inscription is religious, the absence of any Muḥammadan locution is an *argumentum e silencio* of considerable weight. It is a fact that the name of the Prophet Muḥammad and the use of set phrases or formulae which can be shown to be connected with his name occur in the Arab inscriptions only after ca. 70/690. We can, in fact, be more precise: The first occurrence of "Muḥammad" and the Triple Confession of Faith, viz. 1. *tawḥīd* (with or without *ʿadam al-širk* but always with the word *waḥdahu* ["alone"], and not, for example, the words *illā huwa* ["but He"]); 2. *Muḥammad rasūl Allāh*; 3. the human nature of Jesus (*ʿĪsā*) as merely *rasūl Allāh wa-ʿabduhu* is in ʿAbd al-Malik's inscription in the Dome of the Rock in Jerusalem, dated in the inscription itself A.H. 72/691–92. And the first dated occurrence of the phrase *Muḥammad rasūl Allāh* is from just one year before that, from an Arab-Sassanian coin of Xālid b. ʿAbdallah from the year 71/691 which was struck in Damascus![3] Xālid could perhaps have brought it with him when he returned to Baṣrah from Damascus after the Marwānids succeeded in defeating the Zubayrites in Irāq. And after 72/691–92 and all through the Marwānid dynasty, Muḥammad's name occurs as a rule whenever religious formulae are employed: on coins, milestones and papyrus "protocols."

If no religious text dating from before 72/691–92 had been discovered, we might have concluded that it took time for *any* religious notions to penetrate the Arabic inscriptions. But the first Arabic papyrus, an *entaqion* (receipt for taxes paid) from Egypt dated 22/642, is headed by the *basmala* in both Greek and Arabic (in that order). While the *basmala* is a monotheistic preamble-formula, it betrays no specific creed: it is unquestionably not Christian, but neither is it Muslim per se. The religious content is more pronounced in the rock inscriptions, which start in about the 40s of the first century A.H., and on the Arab-Sassanian coins prior to 71/691–92. These bear religious texts, but with no mention of the Prophet or of Muḥammadan formulae. This means that the official Arab religious confession did not include Muḥammad or Muḥammadan formulae in its repertoire of set phrases at this time. I will refer to this religious stage as "pre-Muḥammadan."

The pre-Muḥammadan texts exhibit what I call "indeterminate monotheism": a monotheistic form of belief, but one which contains no features specific to a known monotheistic religion. The Muḥammadan texts differ greatly from them. The introduction of Muḥammadan variables indicates the imposition of new confessional notions on a preexisting stratum of belief. Muḥammadanism is a previously unattested Marwānid introduction. And the result became—overnight!—the state's *only* form of official religious declaration, to be used in certain kinds of formal documents and inscriptions, as, for example, the papyrus "protocols." In short, the state decided, as a political act, to adopt Muḥammadanism as its official creed.

CLASSIFICATION OF THE TEXTS

The inscriptions found in the Negev may be divided into several classes on the basis of religious content:[4]

1) The common texts. These occur all over the Middle East from the mid-first century A.H. (40–60 A.H.) through the later Islamic periods. Their most prominent feature is the lack of any indication of a specific creed—Islam, Christianity or Judaism—and their lack of any hint of Muḥammadanism. The *tawḥīd* is not mentioned, and they do not engage in the polemics which is the heart of the later, Muslim texts. The term *janna* appears, but the concept it expresses is unclear. There is no mention of a prophet, such as Moses, Jesus, Aaron or Abraham. The only deity mentioned is Allāh, who is also referred to as *Allahumma* (*ʾallhm*) or *rabb/rabbī*, though no other

trait is assigned to Him. I call this class "common texts" both because of their wide distribution, and because their vocabulary continued to be used into the Muḥammadan period.

2) The basic class. These are inscriptions from the mid-first century A.H., currently attested only from the Sde Boqer site. They are distinguishable from the common texts by their style, and in fact this class was discerned by text analysis. All the texts of this group exhibit a characteristic language and content, and many of them were inscribed by, or on behalf of, a small number of individuals whose names recur. They may contain references to Moses and Jesus, but nothing at all that is definable as Muslim. Inclusion of inscriptions in this class was made on the basis of the unmistakable occurrence of certain formulae in them, or because the author of the inscription was also the named author of other inscriptions which were unmistakably of this class. It is quite possible that this class is in fact only a subset of the common texts. There is one recognizable subclass of basic class inscriptions, distinguished by their reference to Allāh as "Lord of Moses and Jesus" (*rabb Mūsā wa-ʿĪsā*).
3) The second class, which immediately followed the basic class (through the end of the first century A.H.).
4) The Muḥammadan inscriptions, which are Marwānid but cannot be more precisely dated.
5) The Marwānid Islamic inscriptions, which seem to be somewhat later than the Muḥammadan texts, and continue through the second century A.H. They are definitely Islamic in language and content, without necessarily reflecting *orthodox* Islam.
6) Muslim (ʿAbbāsid) inscriptions from the second century A.H. on. This class, though Muslim, is still not in perfect harmony with Muslim orthodoxy.

THE PRE-MUḤAMMADAN TEXTS

The basic class texts are recognizable by the use of *rabb Mūsā wa-ʿĪsā* in their opening phrase, and/or by a certain set of phrases and allusions in the text itself, such as *ḥayyan wa-mayyitan*, and *ġayr hālik wa-lā mafqūd*.

(Examples of these and others may be seen in the attached translations and notes to them.) I would be inclined to read Old Testament (and not New Testament) connotations in at least some of them. Though some phrases and formulae are found in the Qurʾān, these texts do not seem to me Qurʾānic; rather, they appear to belong to a certain body of sectarian literature which developed Judaeo-Christian conceptions in a particular literary style. The resulting creed, basically indeterminate monotheism with the addition of Judaeo-Christian variables, is scarcely identifiable as that of a defined sect, but rather is the expression of belief of one group of indeterminate monotheists among many.

PROPHETICAL *LOGIA*

Wansbrough introduced the term "prophetical *logia*" to designate sub-canonical versions of scripture,[5] i.e., the components from which the canonical text was composed. These may have been produced by any Arab group affiliated to one or other of the Christian or Judaeo-Christian sects in the area. Wansbrough's "emphatically provisional conclusion"[6] was that

> the canonical text of scripture exhibited separate [prophetical] *logia* collections which had for some time prior to their final redaction been in liturgical and homiletic use in one or several related communities (*SM* 57 para. 3).

However, an attempt to investigate this thesis was, he found, hindered by a lack of texts for comparison:

> The practical quest for *prototypes of Qurʾānic diction* is hindered both by the transmission history of the document and the absence of trustworthy comparative material (ibid. 69 para. 2, emphasis added).

Nevertheless, with the aid of Wansbrough's terminology, it became easy to see that the hundreds of rock inscriptions scattered over the Near Eastern deserts are in fact sub-canonical texts, providing in some measure those prototypes of Qurʾānic diction which Wansbrough found so sorely lacking. The inscriptions of the first century and the early half of the second century A.H. include *logia* and formulae which are prototypes of Qur'ānic diction, exhibiting what Abbott referred to as "Koranic flavour."[7] They are, of course, pre-Islamic, within the framework of the Schacht-Wansbrough hypothesis concerning the Qur'ān's creation and canonization. Thus now, some ten years after Wansbrough's work, we may regard as overly pessimistic his conclusion that

> we are no closer than we have ever been to the actual forms of pre-Islamic Arabic and . . . a change in these conditions seems unlikely (Wansbrough, loc. cit.).

For not only are the religious texts of the rock inscriptions pre-Islamic, but the language of the chancery papyri can also furnish examples of "actual forms of pre-Islamic Arabic."[8]

Sde Boqer is to date the only site to yield texts with Judaeo-Christian variables in Arabic. But Judaeo-Christian Christology is inscribed in Arabic on the octagon of the Dome of the Rock. All that is written there, with the exception of several repetitious Muḥammadan formulae, is a declaration of the official state opinion (i.e., decision!) concerning Pauline Christology. Muḥammad is introduced merely as *a* messenger of Allāh, with no further clarification. This is also the treatment Muḥammad receives in the Qur'ān. The Judaeo-Christian *content* of the Dome of the Rock inscription is no novelty to theologians of the seventh century A.D., and Pines's work[9] has shown that the Christology of the Qur'ān is also Judaeo-Christian. The Christological text of the Dome of the Rock is composed of verses which occur in the Qur'ān verbatim (the Muḥammad text is not Qur'ānic). I see the Christological text as composed of quotations of prophetical *logia*, i.e., of "sub-canonical versions of scripture"; but the very fact that such logia were inscribed on the royal shrine of the newly emerged state creed may be considered a form of canonization of this text. One would not expect this text to be altered by those who refer to it as being the declaration of the official state faith. This canonical status is demonstrated in the papyrus "protocols" and on the coins, where formulae/*logia* are reproduced in great numbers *invariatur* (though not always in full). This is not, of course, evidence for the existence of "Umayyad scripture," but for a process of ongoing determination of the formulae to be included in an official state confession, expressed in authorized texts whose formulae must not be altered after promulgation. This process is what I call "canonization of state *logia*," which were, to use Wansbrough's phrase, "separated from an extensive corpus of prophetical *logia*."[10]

The Muḥammadan texts were not accepted by the public as promptly as they were officially employed. For years after their appearance in state declarations, and not withstanding the exclusive use of Muḥammadan formulae by the state in official contexts, people continued to include non-Muḥammadan legends in personal inscriptions. In fact, Muḥammadanism was not in common use even for routine chancery writing. Thus Qurra b. Šarīk fails to include set Muḥammadan phrases in his Arabic and Greek correspondence, though he obeys the rule of inscribing Muḥammadan formulae on papyrus "protocols" bearing his name and title. Muḥammadan formulae began to be used in the popular rock inscriptions of the central Negev only in Hišām's days (105–125/724–43). For instance:

> *Allahumma, ṣalli ʿalā Muḥammad al-nabīʾ wa-ʿalā man yuṣallī ʿalayhi* (inscr. HS 3154(6), not reproduced here, dated 117/735).

And there are other (dated) Muḥammadan inscriptions from these years, in the Negev and also in Jabal Usays, east of Damascus.[11]

It thus seems that the period 71–105/690–723 is marked by the use of Muḥammadan formulae for official purposes, but not by the general population. But by Hišām's days, about thirty years—a generation—after the introduction of Muḥammadanism by ʿAbd al-Malik, it had taken root in some circles, apart from its official use by the state, and was perhaps gathering momentum. However, while these texts are Muḥammadan, they cannot yet be called Muslim.[12] Texts which qualify as Muslim started to appear in the Negev only at the end of the second century A.H., approximately coinciding with the appearance of the first written traditional Muslim accounts.

Having given the general background of stages of development, I would like to take the two ends of the process—the pre-Muḥammadan and the Muslim texts—and make a preliminary attempt to compare their language and religious concepts. My intention in so doing is to highlight the differences between them: to demonstrate that by any criteria of literary context analysis, the pre-Muḥammadan texts cannot have been produced by the same religious conceptual system that gave rise to the Muslim ones. In other words, it is very difficult to define as Muslim the religion found in popular expressions of faith dating from the first century of Arab rule.

THE MUSLIM CLASS

The Muslim class of epigraphical texts can be distinguished from the Muḥammadan class by the occurrence of various terms and concepts, and in general by their idiom. I am still hesitant concerning the precision of my typology of texts as Muḥammadan and Muslim, but the two dated groups of Muḥammadan texts from Hišām's days found in the central Negev so far (one dated 112/730, the other 117/735) do not appear to use the same diction as the ʿAbbāsīd texts from the same area.[13] I shall refer to the latest dated inscriptions we possess from the central Negev (second century A.H., facs. 1.25–26) as examples of Muslim texts, and compare their, with the Judaeo-Christian texts from Sde Boqer.[14] The latter are a category of basic class texts with Judaeo-Christian variables, which we tentatively date to the mid-first century A.H. or a little after.

I draw my examples of Muslim texts from three inscriptions. The first two, reproduced in facs. 1.25 and 1.26, belong to Saʿīd b. Yazīd and are dated 164/780 and 170/786 respectively. They were found in two wādīs in close proximity to each other, Wādī-Ḥafīr/Naḥal Laʿanah and Wādī Idṯār/Naḥal Yeter in the central Negev. The third inscription is the lower part (lines 5–12) of facs. 1.12, which was made by one ʿAbdallah, the son of the author of lines 1–4 (as he indicates in the last line). Facs. 1.12 is thus a composite text. The father's part is classifiable as a basic class inscription, while the son's is Muḥammadan or Muslim. All three inscriptions are Muḥammadan; two are also typically Muslim, while the third is less so. A careful reading of them will enable us to distinguish between such Muslim texts and the basic class, with or without Judaeo-Christian variables.

Chart 1 presents a content analysis of concepts in these three inscriptions, and the phraseology in which they are expressed (see p. 152). The verbs of entreaty are significant, and serve as identifying attributes:

Table 1

Word/Class	Basic (Negev)	Muḥammadan (Negev)	Muslim (Negev)
ġ.f.r.	100%	83%	10%
ṡ.l.y.	—	6%	49%

Distribution of two opening words in three classes of texts: basic class (second half of first century A.H.); Muḥammadan class (late first-second century); Muslim class (third century A.H.).

Source: Statistical pilot study made on a sample group, 1982.

As Table 1 shows, in the basic class *ġ.f.r* is the only verb of entreaty found in an opening phrase;[15] it is still frequent in the Muḥammadan texts, but very uncommon in the Muslim ones. In the Muḥammadan texts *ṡly* starts to occur, although infrequently, and it is very frequent in the Muslim texts (those in the table are from ca. A.H. 300/912). The verb *raḍiya* (*r.ḍ.w.*) (not included in the table) is not common in an opening phrase, and has not been found in basic class inscriptions, but it does occur in the Muḥammadan/Muslim ones. The fact that *ġ.f.r.* is so uncommon in the Muslim texts means that they are devoid of the "sinners' load" which is the major—in fact almost the only—notion governing the basic class forms of entreaty and supplication.

SOLICITING GOD'S FAVOUR

In considering whether a text is Muslim or basic class, both content and form of expression must be considered: both what the text says, and the words it uses to say it. As I noted at the Third International Colloquium on "From Jāhiliyya to Islam" in 1985, the Muḥammadan (there called "Islamic") supplication texts exhibit a new attitude,

> that of approaching God to settle personal affairs. This is a new type of supplication, aimed at securing God's benevolence in order to procure a very personal list of *desiderata*, temporal as well as spiritual. The *janna* is only one of the desired items . . . and recorded in the Negev

inscriptions there are still others which together form a rather impressive list of requests.

Gone are the stereotyped expressions of pleading for forgiveness for undisclosed and general transgressions; instead there is optimism, an expectation to receive God's grace: *ʾurzuqhu min faḍlika* ("provide for him from your bounty"); *ʾatimma ʿalayhi niʿmataka/niʿamaka* ("Bestow Your favour/s wholly upon him"); *ijʿalhu min al-mufliḥīn* ("make of him one of the prosperous") and more.

The verb *saʾala*, "requested, asked for" is common as a soliciting verb in the Muḥammadan and Muslim texts, e.g., *ʾannī ʾasʾaluka niʿmataka*: "I request of you your favors upon Bišr b. Tamīm" (inscr. HR 522, ca. 300/912). In addition, in a Muḥammadan (or Muslim) text from Sde Boqer we find: *ʾasʾal Allāh al-janna*: "I request of Allāh *al-janna*" (here facs. 1.12:8). In the basic class, where *janna* is not yet found, a supplicant noted *wa-huwa yasʾal Allāh al-majanna*: "and also he entreats Allāh [to grant him] this sanctuary (*majanna*)" (facs. 1.9:5).

Like *saʾala*, the verb *daxala* ("entered") is also common in Muḥammadan and Muslim texts which solicit God's favour in accepting the supplicant unto Allāh's *raḥma* or, again, letting him enter *al-janna*. This verb is almost absent from the basic class; there is only one instance of it, in connection with an interesting occurrence of a Qurʾānic *topos* (the *jannāt al-naʿīm*): *ʾadxil* [*Xālid b. Ḥumrān*] *jannāt al-naʿīm*: "let [PERSONAL NAME][16] enter *jannāt al-naʿīm*" (facs. 1.19:3–35). The terms *janna* and *jannāt al-naʿīm* in these texts are, I suspect, not yet well understood; the "obvious" translation, "paradise," is very doubtful.

GIVING TESTIMONY

Verbs from the root *š.h.d.* are not known from basic class inscriptions—or common texts in general—or from Muḥammadan texts.[17] I therefore consider their occurrence to be a Muslim trait. The very notion of testimony—giving witness as the mode of announcing one's faith—is Muslim, and is a significant aspect of the polemical features of the Muslim texts. It seems not to occur earlier than the ʿAbbāsid period, or late in the Marwānid period. Thus in the Muslim texts, the claim "I witness" (*ašhadu* or a similar expression) is very common. This is seen in inscriptions 1.25:2–4 and 1.26 passim, which routinely incorporate *š.h.d.* into the text. The basic class and Muḥammadan texts, on the other hand, seem to lack it entirely. With this may be compared the fact that words derived from the root *š.h.d.*, with the meaning of "to give witness," are not rare in the Qur'ān. In fact, the idea of giving witness is Qur'ānic:

> *ʾa-ʾinnakum la-tašhadūna ʾanna maʿa Allāhi ʾālihatan ʾuxrā, qul: lāʾ ašhadu, qul: ʾinnamā huwa ʾilāhun wāḥidun* (Q 6:19)

> Can ye possibly bear witness that there are other gods (*ʾālihat*) associated with Allāh? Say: I shall not/cannot bear witness. Say: but in truth (*innamā*) He is God, one and only (translation following Yusuf Alī and Ben-Shemesh).

niʿma al-mawlā wa niʿma al-naṣīr

This expression is found in the Muslim text 1.25. This exact phrasing is not in the Qur'ān, but the concept of Allāh as overlord (patron) and helper is well attested there, e.g., *ʾiʿtaṣimū bi-llāhi huwa mawlākum fa-niʿma al-mawlā* (Q 22:78): "Strengthen yourselves with Allāh, He is your Overlord (Patron), a Gracious Patron and a Gracious Helper" (translation following Ben-Shemesh). There is also *wa-mā lakum min dūni-llāhi min waliyyin wa-lā naṣīrin* (Q 2:107): "Beside Him ye have neither Overlord (Patron) nor Helper." In Syria, in a text from Hišām's time, we have also *Allāh waliyy* [PN],[18] and *Allahumma kun ʾanta waliyy Yazīd b. ʿAbd al-Waḥīd al-ʾAsadī*.[19] This concept is not found in the basic class.

kafā bi-llāhi šahīdan ["And Allāh is sufficient as a witness"]

This expression occurs in 1.26:8–9. The expression *kafā bi-llāhi, bi-rabbika* is commonly attested in the Qur'ān, e.g., Q 4:6, 4:45, 4:69–70, 4:132, 4:78–79; 48:28. But the phrase *kafā bi-llāhi* does not occur in the pre-Muḥammadan texts: it is Qur'ānic and Muslim only. In its occurrences in the Qur'ānic and Muslim texts, I would distinguish between the different *kinds of patron* referred to: the one who *counts* his deeds or money (Q 4:6); the helper (Q 4:45); the one who knows (Q 4:69–70); the overlord, who is in charge of someone (Q 4:132); and finally, the phrase *kafā bi-llāhi šahīdan*: "and Allāh suffices *as a witness*":

> It is He who has sent His Messenger with Guidance and the true *dīn*, to proclaim/to exalt[20] it over the entire (other) *dīn*—and Allāh suffices as a witness (Q 48:28).

The notion of giving testimony to divine truth is another monotheistic concept well-attested in Rabbinic Judaic and Christian sources, where it is connected with the concept of self-sacrifice for the sake of such divine truth.[21] In the Qur'ān there is no question of bringing witness from scripture, canonical or otherwise. Allāh himself gives witness, through his messenger(s), with no recourse to a book. Those who bear witness from scripture are not the true believers, but the *'ahl al-kitāb*. This, I think, reflects the inter-sectarian polemic, current before the Qur'ān was put together from the existing sectarian *logia*, in which the adherents of a prophet, who lack a scripture of their own, maintain that under the new dispensation of their prophet such a scripture is in fact unnecessary. It is, in these circumstances, ironic that these phrases found their way into the canon.

lā ḥawla wa-lā quwwata . . .

The famous expression *lā ḥawla wa-lā quwwata illa bi-llāhi al-ʿalī al-ʿaẓīm*, "there is no strength or power but through Allāh, the High, the Great," is not Qur'ānic, but a saying in *ḥadīṯ*,[22] and various meanings have been proposed for the word *ḥawl* in this context.[23] A very similar phrasing occurs in facs. 1.12. This inscription is undated, but its Muḥammadan idiom and its genealogical context (the continuation of a basic class text written by the owner's father) lead me to date it to Hišām's days (r. 105–25/724–43). Again, this expression does not occur in the basic class.

jamīʿu-l-xalā'iq

The expressions *jamīʿu-l-xalā'iq*, "all the created beings" (1.26:6–7); *jamīʿ xalqihi*, "all His created beings" (1.25:2); and *al-nās 'ajmaʿīn*, "all humankind" (1.13:4-5) have the same referent as *ʿālamīn* in *rabb al-ʿālamīn*, "Lord of Creation" (1.12:3-4; 1.13:4-5), an expression attested in basic class texts as well a ʿ as later ones. We should consider this concept, Lord of Creation, one of the constants of monotheism. In the basic class it is expressed only via the phrase *rabb al-ʿālamīn*, while in the Muslim texts the religious vocabulary has widened to included the phrases given above.

al-nār

This is a Qurʾānic concept, the opposite of *janna*:

> *balā man kasaba sayyiʾatan . . . fa-ʾulāʾika aṣḥābu al-nāri hum fīhā xālidūna; wa-allaḏīna ʾāmanū wa-ʿamilū al-ṣāliḥāti ʾulāʾika aṣḥābu al-janna hum fīhā xālidūna.*
>
> "They who accumulate evil (deeds on their account) . . . such are inmates of the fire, where they will remain forever; but the faithful who perform good deeds, they are the inmates of *al-janna*, to remain there forever" (Q 2:81-82, translation following Ben-Shemesh).

It would also seem to be one of the constants of the monotheism of late antiquity, yet it is not attested in the common texts, including, of course, the basic class. There are at least two possible reasons for this. One is that not all indeterminate monotheists of the late sixth and seventh centuries A.D. shared this concept, although it of course existed in the other monotheistic religions of the area. The other is that our basic class authors did not mention either *janna* or *nār* when entreating Allāh for forgiveness of transgression, because of their specific beliefs or religious attitudes. For instance, one of the most striking features of these texts is their heavy atmosphere of dread because of undisclosed transgressions; it is clear that the writers regarded themselves as "sinners" in a general sense. It could therefore be that they did not mention *al-janna* because they believed that a sinner should not request such a great favour for himself.[24] And perhaps *nār* was not mentioned in order to avoid naming the unspeakable horror.[25] *Janna* is, however, requested in the second class.

Although *al-nār* is, as stated, a Qurʾānic concept, its context in these texts is somewhat different from that in the Qurʾān. The writer of our inscriptions mentions *al-nār* in the context of seeking protection from it: *ʾaʿūḏu bi-hi/bi-llāhi min al-nār*, "I seek protection through Allāh from the fire" (facs. 1.12:9). In Hišām's days we find, *ʾasʾalu al-janna wa-ʾaʿūḏu bi-hi min al-nār* in Syria,[26] but in the Qurʾān, *ʿ.w.d.* (*aʿūdu*), "I seek protection," refers mostly to protection from Šayṭān, "Satan," and the fire is not mentioned in this connection.

Allāh

The texts consider Allāh in various ways, which I shall first list and then discuss.

1. *Hypostatic definitions*[27] lie at the root of the Trinitarian Christological controversy.
2. *Subordination* is the doctrine that everything is Allāh's creation and subordinated to Him, including angels and prophets, and among the latter, Jesus. This, of course, contradicts any Pauline Trinitarian confession.
3. *Allāh's qualities* are distinguished from His *predicates*, and both are detailed in the text.

1. The nature of Allāh

In the earliest Muḥammadan confession of faith, namely the Dome of the Rock, S:A4–5,[28] we find the maxim that God was not born and does not give birth. However, this is not attested in any other early (i.e., Muḥammadan but non-Muslim) inscriptions, either from the Negev or elsewhere. It occurs in the Qurʾān (Q 112), and in our Muslim texts (e.g., facs. 1.26:9-11). It therefore seems most likely that it signals the Muslim layer of confessional phraseology. Our understanding of how it came to occur in the Dome of the Rock but in no other Muḥammadan text must await further research.

God's singularity, expressed by the *tawḥīd* in full, concluded by the *ʿadam al-širk*, appears in the Dome of the Rock and is attested in the later (ca. 300/913) texts. It is not rare, either, in earlier *Muslim* texts from the central Negev. And in the Qaṣr al-Ḥayr, lines 1–3, we have *basmala*, the *tawḥīd* in full, and *Muḥammad rasūl Allāh* (DKI 211, by the people of Ḥimṣ, dating from 110/728–29). This is an official construction text:

ʾamara bi-ṣināʿat hāḏā al-madīna [= fortress(?)] ʿAbd Allāh Hišām ʾamīr al-muʾminīn:

"This fortress (?) was constructed by order of *ʿAbd Allāh* (title!) *Hišām, ʾamīr al-muʾminīn.*"

But the *tawḥīd* does not appear in dated Muḥammadan popular inscriptions, nor do we find it in the group of Marwānid texts published by Muḥammad al-ʿUšš in *JUI*. I have thus concluded that the official Marwānid convention was to inscribe the *tawḥīd* (with or without the concluding *ʿadam al-širk*) in official texts, but that the writers of the popular texts did not employ this formula.

The idea of God's singularity appears in the Muḥammadan -Muslim *tawḥīd* in a form slightly different from that found in the Qurʾān. In the *tawḥīd*, the reference to God's singularity ends with the word *waḥdahu*, "him alone," e.g., in the Dome of the Rock, S:A1–2 and passim. In the Qurʾān, singularity is expressed by the words *wāḥid* and *illā huwa*. This would appear to be a minute difference, but I consider it to be significant, for the following reason. Most of the text of the Dome of the Rock is familiar verbatim from the Qurʾān, but the locutions that are not Qurʾānic are precisely the conspicuously Muḥammadan ones, which make their first appearance in the Dome of the Rock: *tawḥīd; ʿadam al-širk; wa al-salām ʿalayhi wa-raḥmat Allāh; wa-taqabbal šafāʿatahu yawm al-qiyāma fī ummatihi*; and finally, *ṣallā Allāh ʿalayhi*. We also find *Allahumma ṣalli ʿalā rasūlika wa-ʿabdika ʿĪsā b. Maryama*: "*Allahumma* incline toward Your messenger, Jesus the son of Maryam" (Dome of the Rock, NW–W:B11).[29] This verse is not only non-Qurʾānic, but also foreign to the context of the Qurʾānic verses relating to Jesus. And the expression *ṣallā Allāh ʿalā* does not occur in the Qurʾān. In fact, the idiom *Allahumma ṣalli ʿalā/ṣallā Allāh ʿalā*, so common in the *ṣalʿam*, is not Qurʾānic but Muḥammadan—i.e., Marwānid—in origin, appearing first in relation to Jesus. I would therefore ascribe importance even to small linguistic differences between Qurʾānic and non-Qurʾānic locutions.[30]

To sum up the question of the description of Allāh's nature in our texts: the source for the details of the hypostatic definition found in our Muslim texts is the Qurʾān; the same verbatim description is also found in the Dome of the Rock. But in the latter there occur a few formulae which cannot be found in the Qurʾān. These same formulae also occur as official Marwānid texts, to be used on papyrus "protocols," coins, milestones and construction texts. They continued to be employed under the ʿAbbāsids and have been used ever since, becoming commonplace Muslim locutions. But these official formulae did not, it would seem, take root at a more popular level, for in our Muḥammadan popular rock inscriptions they seldom if ever occur.

2. *Subordination*

This was a question of great ideological significance: Are all creatures subordinated to God, or are there exceptions? The idea that all of creation is subordinate is explicit in *rabb al-ʿālamīn*, "Lord of Creation," and in the phrase *rabb al-nās ajmaʿīn*, "Lord of the people, all of them" (facs. 1.13:4–5). The absolute superiority of Allāh over all seems to be another monotheistic constant, though in the form in which it appears in the Arabic inscriptions it cannot be accepted by Trinitarian (Pauline) Christians. It is therefore interesting that one of our Muslim inscriptions (facs. 1.26:4–7) finds it necessary to declare that Muḥammad, Jesus, Ezra (ʿUzayr) and (or: as well as) all creation —*jamīʿu al-xalāʾiq*—are "subordinated worshippers"—*ʿibād marbūbīn* (for *marbūbūn*). I read this as an addendum to Q 9:30:

> *wa-qālat al-Yahūd: ʿUzayr ʾibnu Allāh, wa-qālat al-Naṣārā: al-Masīḥ ʾibnu Allāh*
>
> The Jews say: ʾUzayr (= Esdras/Ezra) is the son of Allāh, and the Christians say: al-Masīḥ is the son of Allāh.[31]

Our inscription (lines 4–7) pursues an internal Muslim controversy regarding the status of Muḥammad. It denies that anyone, Muḥammad included, can be so close to Allāh as to merit the description "son of God," which implies a share in the Godhead. In the late first–early second centuries A.H., there were those who considered Muḥammad to be qualitatively different from the messengers of the past, and awaited his second coming, another Judaic and Christian monotheistic constant. Nor was Muḥammad the only one whose position was open to doubt. There are

Muslim inscriptions from the Negev in which the supplicant entreats not only Allāh but also His whole retinue to bestow favour upon him:

> *Allahumma ṣalli anta wa-malāʾikatuka al-muqarrabīn waʾanbiyāʾuka al-mursalīn wa-ʿibāduka al-ṣā liḥīn ʿalā PN*
>
> Allāh! You and Your angels who are nigh unto You, and Your prophets who were sent and Your righteous worshippers, be inclined (in favour) unto ʾImru al-Qays b. Tamīm (BR 5117, from the Negev, 300/912; not reproduced here).

This phrasing does not state that Allāh's entourage is subordinate to Him; whether such was understood to be the case has yet to be proved. By contrast, a common text inscription from Iraq (near Karbalah) dated 64/684 (the interregnum; Muxtār in Iraq) has:

> *Allahumma rabb Jibrīl wa-Mīkāʾīl wa-Isrāfīl iġfir li PN*
>
> Allahumma, Lord of Gabriel, Michael and ʾIsrāfil,[32] forgive PN (DKI 163:5–8; source *GAP* fig. 45).

This is a subordinationist declaration regarding the three archangels: Allāh is their *rabb*, i.e., they are subordinate to Him. And from the same period, there are a few basic class (i.e., in my opinion, Judaeo-Christian) inscriptions from Sde Boqer which contain a similar subordinationist formula regarding Moses and Jesus: Allāh is *rabb Mūsā wa-ʿĪsā*. This is not a variation on the theme of Q 9:20, but a reference to a different layer of Judaeo-Christian concepts. Coupling Jesus with Moses, the lawgiver who spoke to God face-to-face, gives to Jesus the highest rank attainable by the most pious of human beings, and has him sharing with Moses the honor of serving as an identifier of God. Nonetheless, it makes Allāh's supreme position, and Jesus' subordination, quite clear.

3. God's Qualities and God's Predicates

Eulogizing God is a common feature of religious discourse, and an essential element of doxology. The wording of the descriptions of God in our texts can indicate, to some degree, the author's confession. This method of classifying texts is, however, at a very rudimentary stage; as more information is gathered and sorted in future research, it will, it is hoped, be possible to improve our discernment of different groups of texts, and to penetrate their laconic language to an understanding of their authors' practical conception of God.

In the basic class God's qualities are expressed succinctly, via predicates composed of single words, as in the Beautiful Names: *ʾal-ʾasmāʾ al-ḥusnā*. There may be minimal elaboration of the predicate phrase, e.g.:

> *ʾarḥam al-rāḥimīn wa-ʾaḥkam al-ḥākimīn*
>
> the most loving among the loving ones and the best ruler among the rulers (facs. 1.3).

These predicates are also found strung together in basic class inscriptions, to form a chain which itself constitutes the main content of the inscription (e.g., facs. 1.9). Such a string of predicates implies that liturgical use was the main avenue of development; elaboration such as "the most loving among those who love" (facs. 1.3) or "the one who knows what is hidden" (facs. 1.20) may be seen as similarly rooted in liturgy. For such phrases must be placed in their proper literary context, the communal, liturgical environment of a particular sect, which cannot be understood by a study of the texts that confines itself to thematic classification or philological and literary comparisons.

In the Qurʾān these and similar predicates also occur, but their usage differs. They occur as pausal phrases, e.g., *fa-ʾ ʿlamū anna Allāh ʿazīz ḥakīm* (Q 2:209); *fa-ʾinna Allāh šadīd al-ʿiqāb* (Q 2:211). We may see here the employment, for literary ends (to demarcate the component *logia* and point out their moral, whether actually implicit in them or attributed to them), of the phrases already familiar from liturgical use. Thus again, the use of these phrases in pausal function in the Qurʾān implies that they were part of the *liturgical*, not just the *conceptual*, environment of the sect that used them. It was the phrases thus familiar from liturgical use that were employed for literary purposes in the formation of Scripture.

CONCLUSION

The real meaning of the many inscriptions from all over the Near East lies in the insight they can give us into the spiritual and social phenomena which eventually matured into Islam. Insofar as we may judge from the evidence so far presented, it would appear that the common texts represent the writings of a (probably Judaeo-Christian) Arab sect, but not the sect whose *logia* were adopted to form the Qur'ān. The subset I call the basic class were certainly left by a Judaeo-Christian group, whose *logia* similarly were not adopted into the Arab Scripture. Apart from linguistic evidence, such as that given here, regarding the absence of various words and phrases in their inscriptions versus their occurrence in the Qur'ān and Muslim texts, there is also the fact that the *logia* of the basic class are not attributed to a prophet specific to that sect, or presented as the words of such a prophet, in sharp contradistinction to the logia which form the Qur'ān. Nonetheless, the texts (prophetical *logia*, in Wansbrough's terminology) out of which the Qur'ān *was* canonized reflect a Judaeo-Christian environment lacking in specifically Muslim concepts. The basic class texts reflect, similarly, a Judaeo-Christian environment and attest its existence, in the Negev at least, in the late first and early second centuries A.H., while the common texts reflect the most widespread form of Arab monotheistic belief during the first century, the stratum upon which, as it were, the more complicated religious edifices were built. From the fact that the Qur'ān exhibits a "prophetical" Judaeo-Christianity and the basic class does not, I conclude that the general Judaeo-Christian sectarian environment was widespread, including at least one group defined by adherence to a prophet, whose corpus of *logia* form the basis of the Qur'ān. From the fact that the Qur'ān contains many phrases present in the Muslim inscriptions of the late second century A.H. and later, but absent from the inscriptions of Hišām's days or earlier, I would conclude that it was canonized quite late, i.e., after these phrases had entered the religious vocabulary. Our texts demonstrate that this scarcely happened before the ʿAbbāsid era.

ACKNOWLEDGMENTS

The survey I have been conducting is part of the ongoing Negev Archaeological Project: Early Arab Period (Research of Rural Settlement), headed by Professor Myriam Rosen-Ayalon of the Institute of Archaeology of the Hebrew University of Jerusalem. This work, which includes excavations and an epigraphical survey as well as a survey of sites of cultic activity and inhabitation, has been possible due to the continuous assistance unselfishly given since 1983 by Kibbutz Sde Boqer, many of its members and its three secretaries during that period: Mr. Zeʾev Zivan, Mr. Razi Yahel and Mrs. Brenda Habshush. Professor Emmanuel Marx, head of the Centre for Social Studies at the Blaustein Institute for Desert Research, appointed me an honourary fellow of the Institute, thereby enabling me to continue my research uninterruptedly in close proximity to the site of excavation and the area surveyed. The funds for the ongoing research were supplied by the Ministry of Science, the Hebrew University and the Israel Academy of Sciences and Humanities. To all of these people and institutions, my warmest thanks.

The survey could not have been carried out, nor its results made known, without the devoted efforts of a selected few who gave unreservedly of their time and energy: Nurit Tsafrir, who helped me to trace the inscriptions over an extended period of time and no less extended area of the Negev; Zmirah Cohen, who helped us decipher the results, which in many cases were apparently unreadable scribbles and might have remained so but for her aid; Amnon Rothenberg, who together with me excavated the site of Sde Boqer, and recorded and computed the findings; Mali Borenstein, whose research assistance was invaluable; Dalia Heftmann, who persuaded the computer to analyze the results and handled all the technical drawing and graphical work of producing the survey; and finally Judith Koren, who translated ideas into English. Our work is not yet finished, and I know how inadequate are the phrases of an acknowledgment to describe their ongoing contributions.

Chart 1: Content analysis of concepts in three Muslim inscriptions

- verbs of entreaty: (note that verbs derived from root *ġ.f.r.* were not employed)

1.26 : 1	رَضِيَ الله عن
1.2 : 5	صَلَّى الله على
1.12 : 8	أَسَل الله

- verbs of confession:

1.25 : 2	شهد
1.26 : 3,4,8	
1.12	

- confession of faith:

1.25 : 1–2	نِعْم المولا و نعم النصير
1.26 : 8–9	كَفَا بِاللهِ شَهِيدًا
1.12 : 10–11	لا حَوْلَ و لا قُوَّةَ إِلَّا بالله العظيم

- Allāh *(tawḥīd) (ʿadam al-širk)* (Christological definitives)

1.25 : 3	انه لا اله الا الله وحده لا شريك له
1.26 : 9–11	انه احدا احدا [الـ] صمـد لا والد و لا ولد
1.12	

- Muḥammad

1.25 : 4	و ان محمد عبده و رسوله
1.26 : 5–7	ان محمد و عيسى و عزير . . . عباد مربوبين
[1.12 : 6–7]	[محمد عليه السلم ورحمة الله]
[1.12 : 5–6]	[صلى الله على محمد]

- humankind/all the created ones

1.25 : 2	جميع خلقه
1.26 : 6–7	جميع الخلائق
1.12	

- requests

1.25	
1.26	
1.12 : 8–9	اسل الله الجنة و اعوذ به من النار

Sources: Inscriptions from central Negev, nos. MA 4205(14), here facs. 1.12:5–12 (the father), no date: EKI 261, here facs. 1.25, A.H. 164/780/81; ST 640(34), here facs. 1.26, A.H. 170/786.

Selected facsimiles

1.1 MA 409

1 غفر الله رب
2 موسى
3 لدحشم بن
4 عمرو

1.2 MA 420A

1 بسم [الـ]له الرحمن الرحيم
2 اللهـ[م] [غـ]فر محجن بن سعيد (ما)
3 تقدم من ذنبه وما تاخر انك
4 انت الـ[ ] العليم العز[يز] الحكم (= الحكيم) امين
5 رب العلمين غفر
6 غفر ا
7 غفر

[in a different hand]

1.3 MA 419

1 اللهم اغفر لاشعث بن عصام حيا وميتا فاغفر له كل ذنب اذنبه قط
2 ارحم الرحمين واحكم الحكمين

1.4 MA 4101

1 غفر ربي
2 لخالد بن حمران
3 ذنبه كله

1.5 MA 4102

1 غفر ربي
2 [لـ]خالد بن حمران
3 حيا وميتا

1.6 MA 4114

1 غـ[فـ]ر الله رب
2 موسى لدحشم
3 بن عمر كل ذنب

1.7 MA 4132

1 غفر ربي

2 لدحشم بن عمر

3 ذنبه كله

4 امين رب العلمين

1.8 MA 4137

1 غفر رب موسى

2 لدحشم بن عمر

3 حيا وميتا

1.9 MA 4138

1 اللهم اغفر لا

2 شعث بن عصام

3 ما تقدم من ذنبه وما تاخر انك انت

4 السميع العليم العلي العظيم العزيز لحكيم الرؤف

5 الرحيم واغفر له حيا وميتا و[هـ]و يسل الله المجنة ان لا يقوم

6 عن مجنة حتا يتسن له الظعون

7 [in a different hand, illegible]

1.10 MA4168

1 غفر رب مـ[و]سى

2 لوضين بن عبد الله

3 حيا غير ها

4 لك ولا مفقود

5 [illegible]

1.11 MA 4204A

1 غفر رب عيسى وموسى لـ[؟]

1.12 MA 4205

1 غفر الله لـ[؟]ى بن و [؟]

2 غير ها<ل> ـــــــــك

3 ولا مفقود امين [ر]ب

4 العـــــــلمين

5 صلى الله عـــــــلى

6. محمد [عـ]ـــليه
7 السلم ورحـــــمة الله
8 اسل الله ا[لجـ]ـــــنة
9 واعوذ به من النار
10 لا حول لنـ[ـا] ولا قوة
11 الا بالله العـــــظيم
12 ولعبد الله بن [ ] ى

MA 4210 1.13

1 غفر الله رب
2 موسى <و>عـ[يـ]سى لقيس
3 بن [؟] حيا وميتـ[ـا]
4 امين رب العلمين رب
5 الناس اجمعين

MA 4254 1.14

1 اللهم يا من تمت كلمته و
2 من في السماء عرشه و
3 الارض موضع قدمه اغـ[فر]
4 لخالد بن حمران كـل
5 ذنب اذنبـه
6 قط

[attempted defacement]

MA 4269 1.15

1 [غـ]ـفر الله رب
2 موسى وعيسى
3 لخالد بن حمران
4 حيا وميتا

MA 4293 1.16

1 غفر رب
2 موسى لعا [

MA 4319 1.17

1 بسم الله [ا]لرحمن الرحيم

2 اللهم اغفر لمحجن بن
3 سعيد ما تقدم من ذ
4 نبه وما تاخر انك
5 [ا]نت [ا]لسميع العليم
6 [ ] العـ[ـ] [ا]مين

MA 4342 1.18

1 غفر الله
2 رب
3 موسى
4 لاشعث

MA 4369 1.19

1 اللهم يا حليم يا كر
2 يم يا رب العرش العظيم
3 ادخل [خالد] بن [حمرا]
4 [ن] جنات
5 النعيم

[obliterated]

MA 4371 1.20

1 غفر ربي لخالد بن حمران
2 ذنبه كله صغيره وكبيره
3 وحديثه وقديمه وسره
4 وعلانيته انك علام
5 الغيوب

MA 4345 1.21

1 اللهم اغفر لخالد [بن] حمـ[ران] ذو الجلال والاكرام
2 انك انت العلي المتعال وانت على كل شىء قدير

MA 4464 1.22

1 غفر الله لمن
2 كتب
3 هذا الكتاب
4 غير هالك

MA 4467 1.23

1 غفر ربي

2 [مـ]وسى

3 وعيسى

4 لر دســ

MA 4900 1.24

1 غفر ربي لعمر بن

2 جابر غير هالك

3 ولا مفقود امين [رب] العلـ[مين]

4 رب مو[ســ]ى وعـ[يـ]سى

AH 164/AD 780–81 EKI 261 1.25

1 الله و[ربـ]ي (؟) سعيد بن يزيد فنعم المولا ونعم

2 النصير سعيد يشهد الله وجميع خلقه

3 انه لا اله الا الله وحده لا شريك له

4 [drawing?] وان محمد عبده ورسوله

5 وكتب سنة اربع وستين

6 ومائة

AH 170/786 ST 640(34) 1.26*

1 رضى الله عنك

2 يا سعيد هذا

3 ما يشهد سعيد

4 يشهد ان محمد

5 وعيسى وعزيز

6 و جميع الخلا

7 ئق عباد مربوبين

8 ويشهد لله وكفا

9 بالله شهيدا ا[نـ]ه احدا

10 احدا صمد لا والد

11 و لا ولد و كتب

12 في سنة سبعين ومائة

*This reading was arrived at with the assistance of Professor Kister.

TRANSLATION

Note: The following are translations of only some of the texts. Repeated locutions are translated once only.

Facsimile 1.2. (related to 1.17).

: 1	basmala
: 2	Allāh, forgive Miḥjan b. Saʿīd
: 2–3	his transgressions, the first ones and those that followed
: 3–4	verily you are (list of predicates, cf. translation of 1.9:3–5).

Facsimile 1.3

: 1	Allāh, forgive Ašʿaṯ b. ʿIṣām as he lives and when he dies; thus forgive him any transgression he may have committed (= at any time).
: 2	(You are) the most Loving/Compassionate among those who love, the most qualified to rule among those who rule.

Facsimile 1.9

: 1–2	Allāh, forgive Ašʿat b. ʿIṣām
: 3	his transgressions, the first ones and those that followed
: 3–5	verily You are the Listener, the Omniscient, the One who is on high, Enormous, Mighty, the Ruler, the Considerate, the Loving one [or: the Compassionate/the Merciful].
: 5	Thus forgive him as he lives and when he dies
: 5–6	and also he asks Allāh (to grant him) the/this sanctuary, so that he shall not desist from being in retreat until he is ready to depart.
: 7	Forgive my Lord [in a different hand].

Facsimile 1.10

: 1–2	Forgive, Lord of Moses, Waḍīn b. ʿAbdallah

: 3–4 as he lives: alive and well (lit.: not perished and not missing).

Facsimile 1.12

: 1 Forgive Allāh [PN] Y̲ b. W[. . .]
: 2–3 alive and well
: 3–4 Amen Lord of Creation
: 5–6 May Allāh bless/incline to Muḥammad
: 6–7 [Let] peace be upon him with Allāh's love
: 8 I request of Allāh *al-janna*
: 9 and I seek protection through Him from the Fire
: 10–11 There is no strength for us or power but through Allāh the Enormous
: 12 and to ʿAbdallah b. [. . .]Y̲

Facsimile 1.14

: 1–3 Allāh, You whose word was accomplished/fulfilled, You whose throne is in the sky and earth is your footstool

: 3–4 forgive Xālid b. Ḥumrān
: 4–6 any transgression he may have committed (= at any time)

Note: This recalls Isaiah 66:1: "Thus saith the Lord: the heavens are my throne and the earth is my footstool." We may ask whether the phrase was not a part of the common stock of monotheistic *logia*, see 1.19 for another *ʿarš*.

Facsimile 1.20

: 1 Forgive my Lord Xālid b. Ḥumrān
: 2–4 his transgression(s)—of every kind—the small one and the great, together with (*wā-*) the latest one and the earliest (previous), the concealed and the disclosed one
: 4–5 verily You are the Knower of the unknown

Facsimile 1.24

: 10–2 Forgive my Lord ʿUmar b. Jābir
: 2–3 alive and well
: 3–4 Amen Lord of Creation, Lord of Moses and Jesus

Facsimile 1.25

: 1 Allāh [and my Lord(?)][33] Saʿīd b. Yazīd
: 1–2 and He is (f̱-) an excellent Patron and excellent Helper
: 2 Saʿīd asks Allāh and the whole of His creation to testify
: 3 that there is no God but Allāh alone, He has no companion with Him (or: nothing is compounded with Him)[34]
: 4 and also that Muḥammad is His slave and messenger
: 5 (this was) written in the year 164.

Facsimile 1.26

: 1–2 Let Allāh be pleased with you, O Saʿīd
: 2 this is the testimony of Sa ʿīd
: 3–7 (and he) testifies that Muḥammad and/as well as Jesus and/as well as ʿUzayr (= Ezra) and all creation are subordinated worshippers
: 8–9 and he testifies unto Allāh, and Allāh suffices as a witness
: 9–10 that He is One, One, Indivisible[35]
: 10–11 He does not give birth nor was He born
: 11–12 (This was) written in the year 170.

1.1 MA409

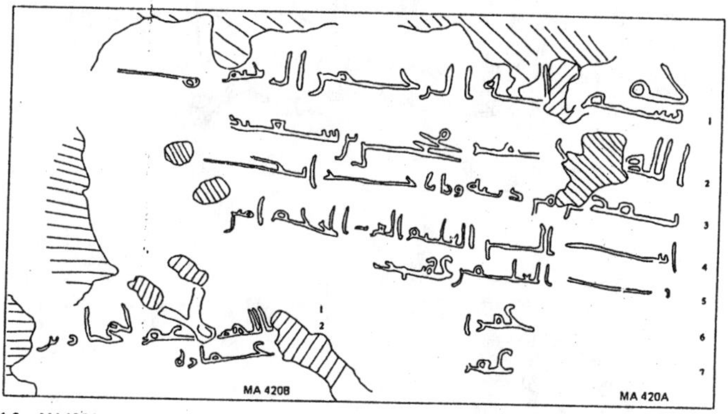

1.2 MA420A

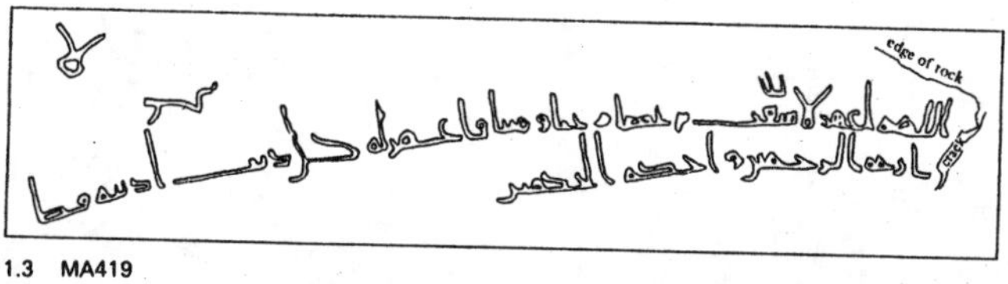

1.3 MA419

1.4 MA4101

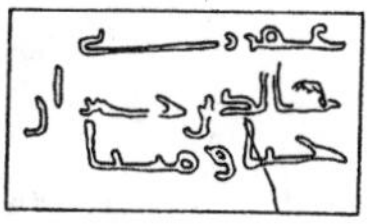

1.5 MA4102

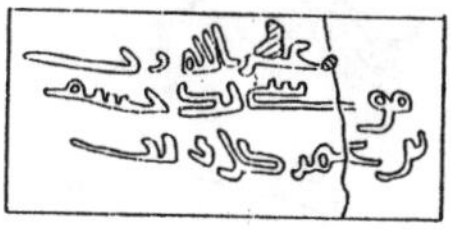

1.6 MA4114

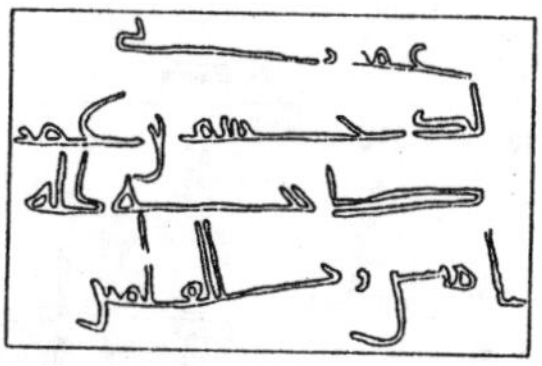

1.7 MA4132

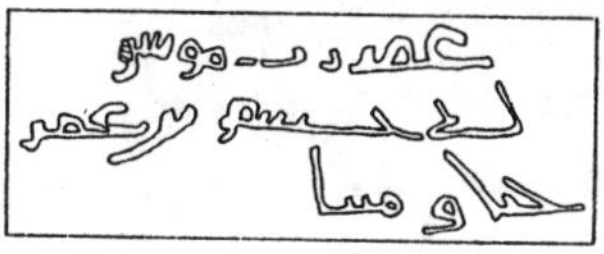

1.8 MA4137

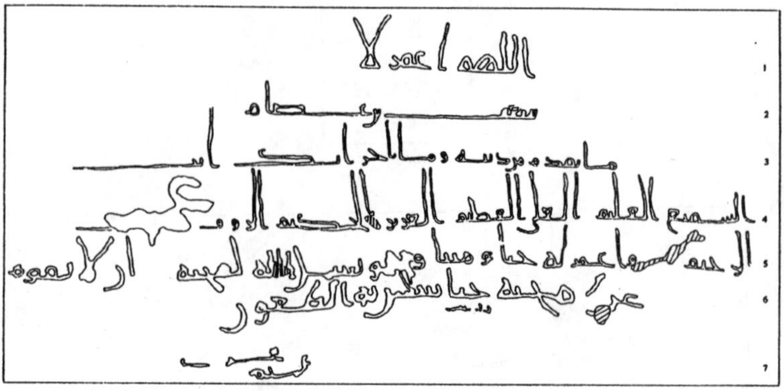

1.9 MA4138

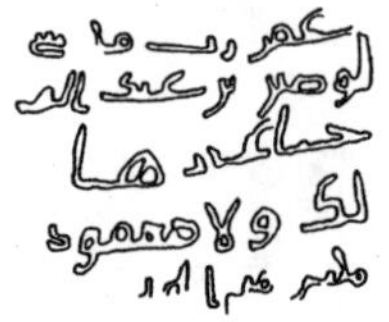

1.10 MA4168

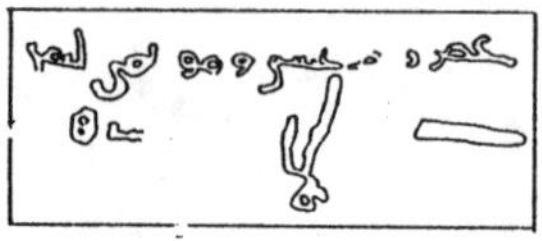

1.11 MA4204A

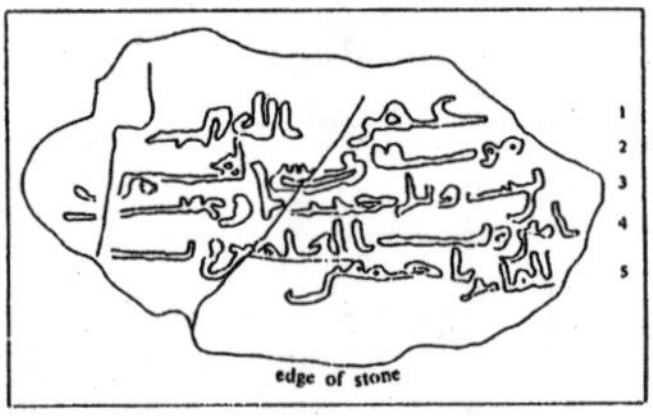

1.13 MA4210

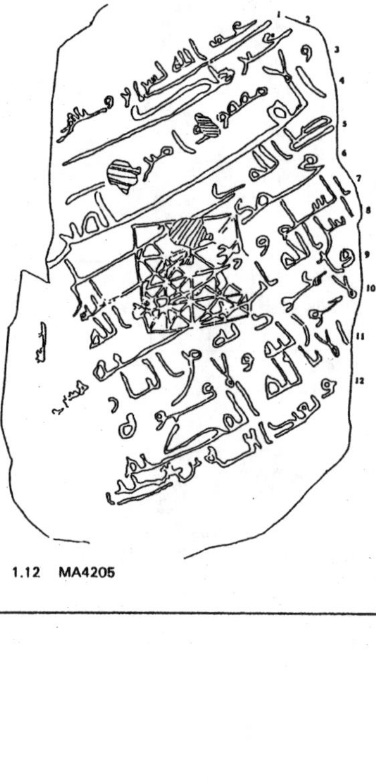

1.12 MA4205

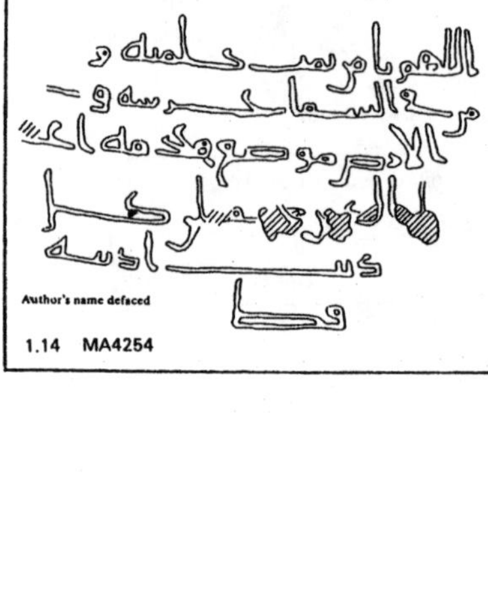

1.14 MA4254

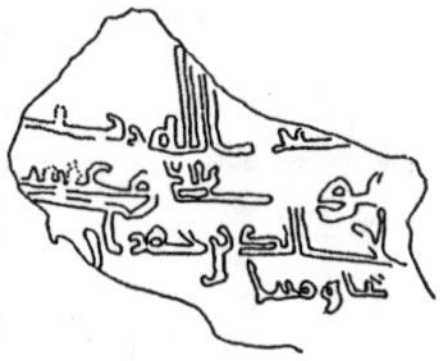

1.15 MA4269

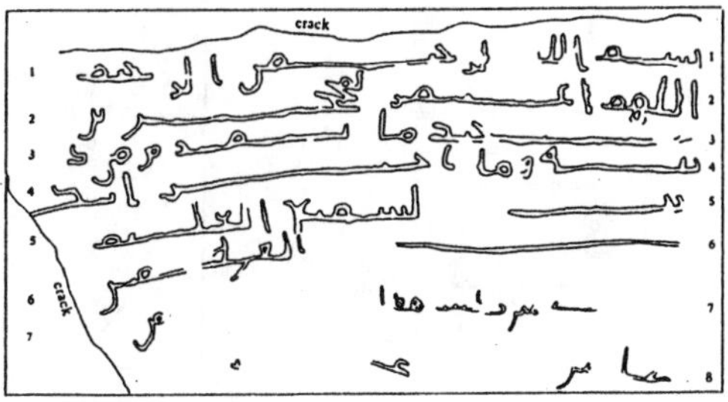

1.17 MA4319

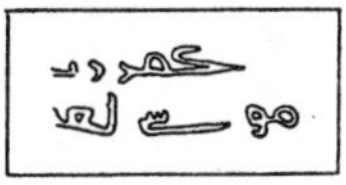

1.16 MA4293

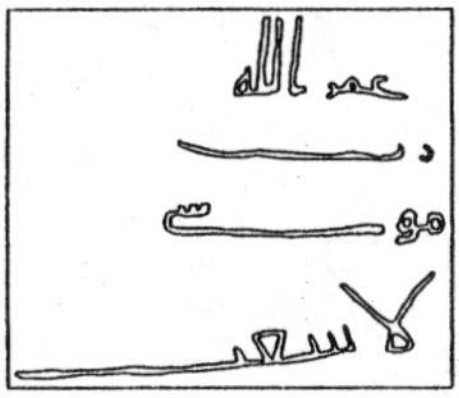

1.18 MA4342

1.19 MA4369

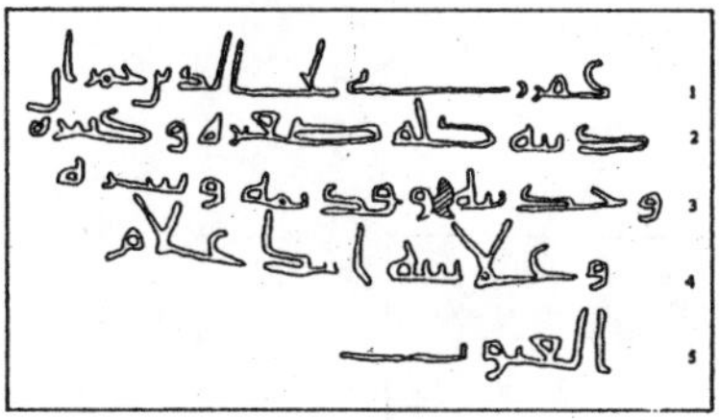

1.20 MA4371

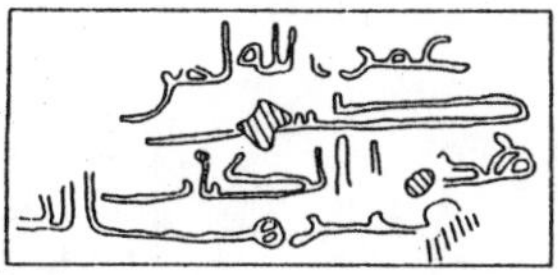

1.22 MA4464

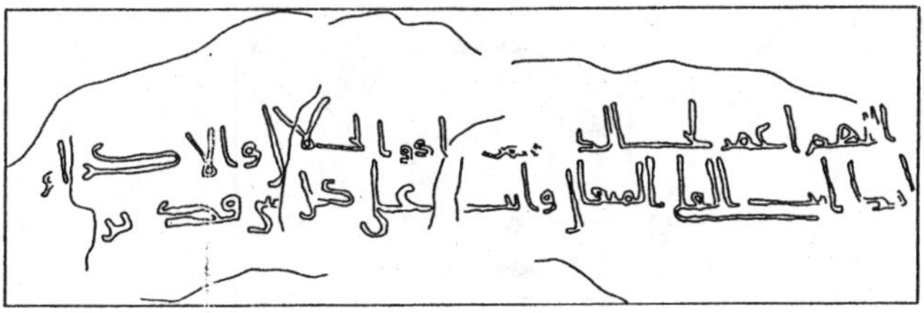

1.21 MA4345

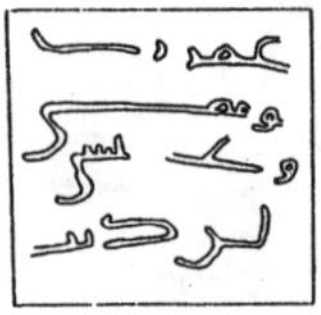

1.23 MA4467

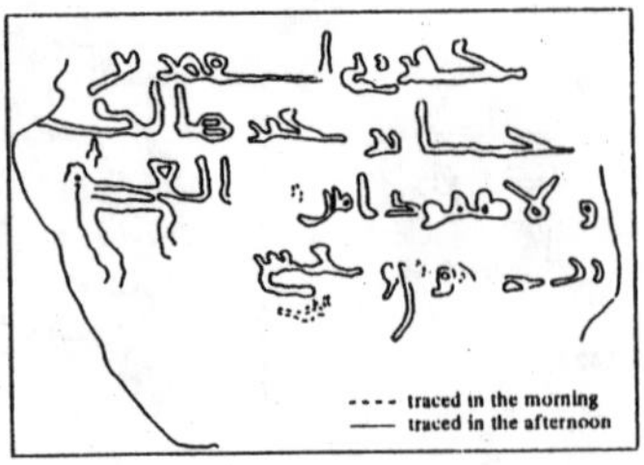

1.24 MA4900

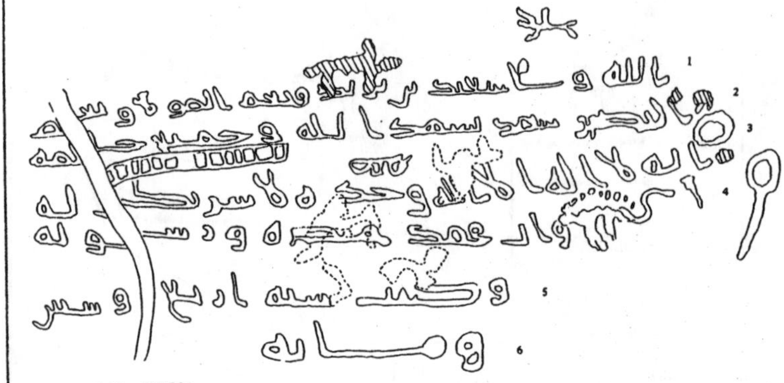

1.25 EKI 261

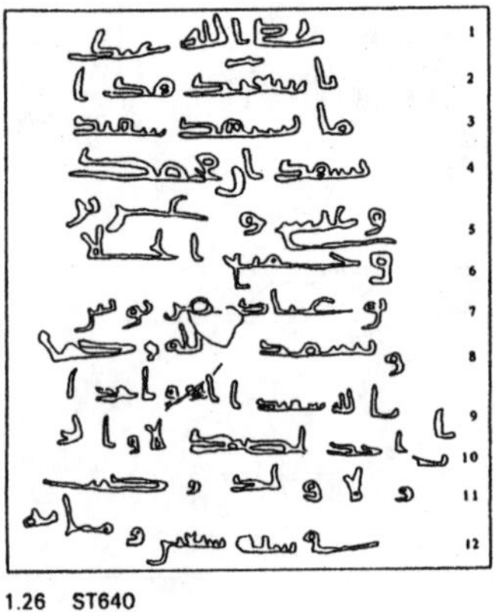

1.26 ST640

BIBLIOGRAPHY

Abbot, Nabia (1946). "The Kaṣr Khrānah Inscription," *Ars Islamica* 11–12 (1946), 190–195 + Fig. 1.

Ben Shemesh, A. (1971). *Ha-Qur'ān: Sefer ha-sefarim shel ha-Islam.* Ramat Gan, 1971.

DKI = Corpus of Dated Kufic Inscriptions, collection of Yehuda D. Nevo.

GAP = Grohmann, Adolf. Arabische Paläographie, Band 2, Teil 2. Graz-Koln, Hermann Bohlaus, 1971.

JUI = al-'Ušš, Muḥammad Abū al-Faraj (1964). "Kitābāt ʿarabiyya ġayr manšūra fī Jabal 'Usays" (Arabic Inscriptions from Jabal 'Usays). *Al-Abḥāt* 17 (1964), 227–316.

Lampe, *Lexicon* = *A Patristic Greek Lexicon*, ed. G. W. H. Lampe. Oxford University Press, 1961.

Lane, Edward William. *An Arabic-English Lexicon.* London, 1863.

ODCC = *The Oxford Dictionary of the Christian Church.* Oxford University Press, various editions.

Pines, Shlomo (1966). "The Jewish Christians of the Early Centuries of Christianity According to a New Source," *Proceedings of the Israel Academy of Sciences and Humanities*, vol. 2, no. 13 (1966).

Pines, Shlomo (1984). "Notes on Islam and on Arabic Christianity and Judaeo-Christianity." *JSAI* 4 (1984), 135–152.

Pines, Shlomo (1990). "Jāhiliyyah and ʿIlm." *JSAI* 13 (1990), 175–194.

Schacht, Joseph. *The Origins of Muḥammadan Jurisprudence.* Oxford, Clarendon, 1950.

Al-ʿUšš, Muḥammad Abū al-Faraj (1964). "Kitābāt ʿarabiyya ġayr manšūra fī Jabal 'Usays" (Arabic Inscriptions from Jabal 'Usays). *Al-Abḥaṯ* 17 (1964), 227–316.

Yūsuf ʿAlī, ʿAbd Allāh (1946). *The Holy Qur'ān. Text, Translation and Commentary.* New York, 1946.

Walker, John (1941). *A Catalogue of the Arab-Sassanian Coins.* London, Trustees of the British Museum, 1941.

Wansbrough, John. *QS* = *Quranic Studies: sources and methods of scriptural interpretation.* Oxford University Press, 1977.

Wansbrough, John. *SM* = *The Sectarian Milieu.* Oxford University Press, 1978.

NOTES

1. Schacht (1950).
2. Pines (1984, 1985).
3. Walker (1941) lviii. The early coins of al-Šām are not dated, and in any case do not bear religious legends.
4. This classification is the fourth so far attempted, and like its predecessors will no doubt prove to be temporary.
5. Wansbrough, *SM* 2.
6. Ibid., 57.
7. Abbott, N. (1946).
8. Wansbrough, referring to epigraphical linguistic evidence, notes that:

> "It is important to remember that from the beginning of [Classical Arabic's linguistic] evolution to its end the evidence is always that of a written language, whatever its pre-history may have been. The material is thus always witness to *formal and/or formalized communication*, for which emergence of a standard of excellence was not only its organizing principle but also its logical conclusion" (Wansbrough, QS 92, emphasis added),

I accept his point, but I would argue that the documents of the first and early second centuries A.H., both chancery and popular inscriptions, provide us with evidence and examples of the (written) idiom of the pre-Islamic period—what we may call the prehistory of Islam.

9. In several articles, listed in the bibliography.
10. Wansbrough, *QS* 1.
11. Al-ʾUšš, *JUI*.
12. I distinguish between Muḥammadan and Muslim texts, at least at present, according to the conceptions expressed and the idiom employed, not merely by whether the Prophet's name and the Triple Confession formulae are mentioned, for these are common to both the Muḥammadan and the Muslim texts.
13. Those from Hišām's days are recorded under the site codes SC and HS, but are not reproduced here. The ʿAbbāsid texts (al-Mahdī and first year of Hārūn's reign) are reproduced here as facs. 1.25-26; they were found at two different sites, YT and ST respectively.
14. Reproduced here as facs. 1.1–1.20.
15. Two verbs of entreaty have been found in the basic class texts at Sde Boqer, construed as a request as part of the supplication, not as its opening phrase (here facs. 1.9:5 and 1.19:3).

16. Henceforth PN.

17. In one Muḥammadan text this root does occur, but in the form *ʾistišhād* "to take part in battle," not with the meaning "to give testimony" (inscription HS 3155:5, not reproduced here).

18. *JUI* no. 103, 108/729.

19. *JUI* no. 105, undated.

20. I am not happy with either translation, though they do not matter much here, since the excerpt given is intended only to demonstrate the context of the *kafā* phrase.

21. Compare the terms *martyreō*, *martyrion*, *martys* in Lampe, *Lexicon*, 828 col. 1–830 col. 2; and the various forms of bearing witness regarding particulars of faith, common in the Rabbinic literature.

22. Lane, *Lexicon* 2, 675 col. 3.

23. Idem, 676 col. 1.

24. Even in this case I would still argue that *janna* did not mean "paradise."

25. In the Muslim texts of ca. 300/913 we have, similarly, cases where the word *šarīk* of the *ʿadam al-širk* was replaced by a dash: *lā—lahu* (HR 507); *lā—k* (BR 5135). Neither is reproduced here. This I also understand as avoidance of pronouncing the unspeakable.

26. *JUI* no. 72, from ca. 113/732.

27. The term *hypostasis* (literally "substance") "also came to mean individual reality and, from the middle of the fourth century onwards, especially in Christological contexts, a 'person' " (*ODCC*, s.v.).

28. S = the south face, first strip (Sʾ indicates the south face, second strip); A = the first subdivision of the text of the first strip, and similarly B = the second subdivision, etc.

29. See note 22 for an explanation of the divisions of the Dome of the Rock text.

30. The phrase "there is no God but Him" is known from Christian intersectarian polemic; cf. Pines (1984).

31. Esdras/Ezra: i.e., he who, according to anti-Jewish tradition, rewrote the Torah from the memory of the Elders after the copy transmitted by Moses had been lost when the First Temple was destroyed. This allegation is the "fact" upon which was based the claim that the book which the Jews call the Torah is not that which Moses transmitted to the Children of Israel.

32. *ʾIsrāfīl*: the angel who is to blow the horn on the day of resurrection (*Tafsīr al-Jalalāyn* on Q 6:73; Lane, *Lexicon* 4, 1351 col. 3).

33. I suspect here a scribal blunder, and that the first line should be reconstructed thus: [This is the testimony of] Saʿīd b. Yazīd: Allāh [is] my Lord, and He is an excellent patron (etc.).

34. I understand *širk* as the Greek *synthetos*, equal to *murakkab* or *mušakkal* in meaning. It belongs to the vocabulary of polemic: *synthetos* was used derogatively to denounce inter-confessional opponents (see Lampe, *Lexicon*).

35. *Ṣmd*: I propose that it means an integer, an indivisible whole, a substance which cannot be split apart or compounded.

Part 3

A Question of Language

3.1

Syriac Influence on the Style of the Koran

Alphonse Mingana

The time has surely come to subject the text of the Qur'ān to the same criticism as that to which we subject the Hebrew and Aramaic of the Jewish Bible, and the Greek of the Christian Scriptures. Apart from some stray comparative remarks by a few eminent scholars, the only comprehensively critical work on the subject is still that of Nöldeke, printed in 1860. It is to be regretted that in the new edition of Nöldeke's classical work undertaken by Schwally and Bergsträsser—which contains most useful references to an astounding number of Arabic printed books and manuscripts—the editors have not seen fit to multiply the critical and comparative remarks on the sacred text itself. Much useful information can also be gathered from another classical study of Nöldeke: the *Neue Beiträge*.[1]

A very recent study on the historical narratives of the Qur'ān has lately been written by J. Horovitz.[2] The section dealing with proper names (pp. 85–155) is a hill of erudition, but I think that in some places he has built too much on the Muslim tradition and on the so-called pre-Islamic or early Arabian poetry. Setting aside as irrelevant the South Arabian and other inscriptions—I believe that we have not a single Arabic page on which we can lay our hands with safety and say that it is pre-Islamic, and I hold with Margoliouth[3] that all the edifice of pre-Islamic poetry is shaky and unstable, and that the Qur'ān is the first genuine

Alphonse Mingana, "Syriac Influence on the Style of the Koran," *Bulletin of the John Rylands Library* 11 (1927): 77–98.

Arabic book that we possess. It is in place here to repeat what I wrote on this subject in 1920:

> Before the seventh century we are not in a position to know how the Arabic poetry was constituted. The numerous poetical compositions known as "early Arabian poetry," and represented chiefly by the well-known *Mufaḍḍaliyāt, Muʿallaqāt*, *Ḥamāsah* and *Jamharah* are enveloped in a thick mist of prehistoricity and spuriousness, and in the present state of our knowledge we may assert that till fuller light dawns they can hardly stand in the domain of a positive study.[4]

As we believe the Qur'ān to be the first Arabic book,[5] its author had to contend with immense difficulties. He had to adapt new words and new expressions to fresh ideas, in a language that was not yet fixed by any grammar or lexicography. The risk of not being understood did probably deter him from coining many new words. The best policy was to use for his new idea of Islam the words that were understood by his hearers and found in a language akin to his that had become an ecclesiastical and religious language centuries before his birth and the adherents of which were surrounding him in all directions in highly organized communities, bishoprics, and monasteries. This is the reason why the style of the Qur'ān is so unlike that of any other classical Arabic book.

In this respect, the author of the Qur'ān has certainly much merit and originality, and his linguistic difficulties were much more formidable than those experienced, for instance, by Paul and by the first Christian evangelists, who had to express their new ideas in the language of Homer. The language of Homer had a fine literature behind it; the language of the Qur'ān had not. As the first Christian writers have left in their lucubrations stylistic peculiarities that clearly point to their country of origin, which was not the old Athens but the Syrian Hellenistic Palestine, so the author of the Qur'ān has exhibited stylistic idiosyncrasies that stamp his work as being somewhat different from the classical Arabic known to us from the eighth century downward; his style suffers from the disabilities that always characterize a first attempt in a new literary language that is under the influence of an older and more fixed literature. This older and more fixed literature is, in our judgment, undoubtedly Syriac more than any other.

Among modern scholars who have treated of the question of the foreign words found in the Qur'ān mention should here be made of

Fraenkel,[6] and Dvorak,[7] in the publications of the Vienna Academy. If I do not refer more often to these two scholars it is simply because I am loath to multiply footnotes without great necessity, but it is hardly necessary to state that I do not always consider all their conclusions as irrefragable; this applies more specially to the second work. Some good information may also be gathered here and there from A. Siddiki's *Studien über die Persischen Fremdwörter im Klass. Arabisch*, 1919.

So far as the Muslim authors are concerned, the number of those who treated of stray the Qur'ānic words of foreign origin is indeed considerable, and there is no need to mention them here by name. Among those who attempted to collect such words in a more or less systematic way, we will refer to the short poetical pieces of Tāj ud-Dīn b. Subki and abul-Faḍl b. Ḥajar. Both of them, however, have been easily eclipsed by Jalāl ad-Dīn Suyūṭī—the best Qur'ānic critic of Islam—who devoted to the subject a special chapter of his well-known *Itqān,*[8] and wrote on it a short and precise treatise entitled *Mutawakkili.*[9] We must remark, however, that the very restricted knowledge that all the Muslim authors had of the other Semitic languages besides Arabic often renders their conclusions very unreliable and misleading, and the critic should use great caution in handling their books, which at best are only good as historical preambles to the subject under consideration.

I am convinced that a thorough study of the text of the Qur'ān independent of Muslim commentators would yield a great harvest of fresh information. The only qualification needed is that the critic should be armed with a good knowledge of Syriac, Hebrew, and Ethiopic. In my opinion, however, Syriac is much more useful than Hebrew and Ethiopic, as the former language seems to have a much more pronounced influence on the style of the Qur'ān. The only Hebrew textual influence I was able to discover bore on the biblical Hebraisms already found in the Syriac Peshitta.[10] We are also apt to exaggerate in our Qur'ānic studies the legendary biblical element that emanates from Jewish folklore beliefs, and to overlook the fact that these legends were already found in scores of apocryphal books circulating among the members of the Syrian churches of South Syria and Arabia. In this connection we may state with some confidence that taking the number 100 as a unit of the foreign influences on the style and terminology of the Qur'ān Ethiopic would represent about 5 percent of the total; Hebrew, about 10 percent; the Greco-Roman languages, about 10 percent; Persian, about 5 percent; and Syriac (including Aramaic and Palestinian Syriac), about 70 percent.

In the following pages we propose to discuss very briefly a *first* list of words bearing on some aspects of this Syriac influence on the linguistic peculiarities of the Qur'ān. The list ought to be carefully examined, because if its points are established they will modify to a large extent our Qur'ānic conclusions, which are mainly derived from Muslim writers, the best of whom flourished some two hundred years after the events.

The Syriac influence on the phraseology of the Qur'ān may be considered under six distinct headings: (a) proper names, (b) religious terms, (c) common words, (d) orthography, (e) construction of sentences, and (f) foreign historical references.

For the sake of conciseness and in order to save our limited space, we shall not add any critical remarks to the words that to us seemed to be self-evident and clear even to the nonexpert eye.[11] We propose to deal with the logical conclusions to be drawn from the present pages at the end of the second list of words, which we will publish in the near future.

So far as the etymology of the common words is concerned, it is, of course, always difficult to decide with tolerable certainty whether a given Arabic word used in the Qur'ān is derived directly from the Syriac, Hebrew, or Ethiopic languages, or not derived from any of them at all. There are thousands of concrete lexicographical words that are identical in all the Semitic languages, and no responsible scholar will ever contend that any of them is derived from this or that Semitic language. This applies especially to *primitive* vocables such as "head," "hand," and the like. Such words belong to the common Semitic stock found in *all* the Semitic languages. For the words that are not primitive and common to all the Semitic languages but found in *some* of them only, to the exclusion of others, I have found the following considerations worthy of attention:

(a) With all words, whether concrete or abstract, we must consider first the grammatical and lexicographical genius of this or that Semitic language and see how the Qur'ānic words fit in with it; and second, the nearest form presented by the Qur'ānic words as compared with the corresponding words found in this or that Semitic language.
(b) With exclusively concrete words we must consider the history,

and the geography and topography of the land, of this or that Semitic people, and examine the extent to which the Qur'ānic words fall in harmony with them.

(c) With exclusively abstract words we must consider which of the Semitic nations first acquired literary civilization, and which of them by force of circumstances or by its proximity to the Ḥijāz was more likely to exercise a direct influence on its language in this or that special branch of literature.

For a general view of the mutual relations that bind all the Semitic languages together, the following works need no special recommendation from me: Wright's *Comprehensive Gram. of the Sem. Lang.*, Brockelmann's *Grundriss*, Zimmern's *Verg. Gram. d. Sem. Sprachen*, and the well-known works of Nöldeke on the subject.

I. PROPER NAMES

The proper names of biblical personages found in the Qur'ān are used in their Syriac form. Such names include those of Solomon, Pharaoh, Isaac, Ishmael, Israel, Jacob, Noah, Zachariah, and Mary. The other biblical names used in the Jewish sacred books have the same spelling in Syriac and in Hebrew. The following names need some explanation.

Solomon and Pharaoh. The Hebrew names are *slōmōh* and *prʿh* with a final *hé*, and for Solomon with two vowels *ō*; so the Arabic *Sulayman* and *Firʿawn* (with a final *nūn*) of the Qur'ān could only have emanated from the Syriac forms of the two names *šlymwn* and *prʿwn*. (The Ethiopic form of the last name has the vowel *i* under the *pé*.) The penultimate *aliph* of the modern pronunciation *Sulaymān* is a later addition of the scribes. We must here remark that the penultimate *wāw* of the Syriac name is also missing in many ancient books, and the name appears as *šlmn* in manuscripts written before the time of Muhammad. See the Brit. Mus. Syr. MS. Add., 14, 602 ff., 82a and 84b.[12] The manuscript itself is of the end of the sixth or at the latest of the beginning of the seventh Christian century.

Isaac. Here also the Arabic *Isḥaq* is without doubt derived from the Syriac *ʾysḥq* and not from the Hebrew *yṣḥq* or *yśḥq* (with a *yōdh*).[13]

Ishmael and Israel. The same remark applies to Ishmael and Israel.

Their Qurʾānic equivalents, Ismaʿīl (or Ismāʿīl) and Isrāʾīl (with or without *hamzah*), are exactly the Syriac *ʾšmʿyl* and *ʾsrʾyl* or *ʾsr yl* and not the Hebrew *yšmʿʾl* [*yišᵉmāʿēʾl*] and *yśrʾl* [*yiśrāʾēl*]. For references to some Arabic inscriptions bearing on the name "Ishmael," see Horovitz, *Koranische*, p. 92, and Hartmann's *Arabische Frage*, pp. 182, 252 *sqq*.

Jacob. To a certain extent the form of the name of Jacob is also more Syriac than Hebrew: *Yaʿqūb* (Arabic) = *yʿqwb* (Syriac), but in Hebrew *yʿqb* [*yaᶜᵃqōḇ*] with a short *pataḥ* for the *ʿé* and without a long vowel. The name occurs five times only in the Hebrew Massoretic text with the long vowel [*yaʿqōḇ*] and a quiescent *ʿé* as in Arabic and Syriac, and it is very probable that they represent a more modern pronunciation of the name.

Noah. The Hebrew *nōḥa* is somewhat remote and the Arabic *Nūḥ* is exactly the Syriac and the Ethiopic: *nwḥ*.

Zachariah. Here also the Arabic *Zakariyyāʾ* is the Syriac *zkryʾ* with an *alaph* and not its Hebrew form with a *hé*, or the Ethiopic *Zakarias* (taken from the Greek).

Mary. Note the difference in the first vowel of the word; Arabic and Syriac *Mar*, but the Massoretic text *Mir*. It should be observed, however, that according to the Massorah to the Targum of Onkelos[14] on Exod. 15:20, *Maryam* was also the Targumic pronunciation. In Ethiopic both syllables are long; *Māryām*.

There is not a single biblical name with an exclusively Hebrew pronunciation in the whole of the Qurʾān. So far as the names Ishmael, Israel, and Isaac are concerned, we may remark that their deviation from the Hebrew pronunciation is all the more remarkable because in them the author (or the editor of the Qurʾān) is running counter to the genius of the Arabic and Hebrew languages to follow that of Syriac. It is well known that the letter of the third person singular of the aorist is both in Hebrew and Arabic a *yōdh*, which in Hebrew precedes the above proper names, and it would have been much more natural that their Arabic form should have been, for instance, *Yasmaʿil*, and *Yasḥaq* with a *yāʾ* than *ʾIsmāʿīl* and *ʾIsḥāq* with an *aliph*—forms which have been used by the Syrians in order to retain as much as possible the original pronunciation of the Hebrews, inasmuch as the letter of the third person singular of the aorist is in their language a *nūn* and not a *yōdh* as in Arabic and Hebrew.

Another very remarkable fact emerging from all the above words is their pronunciation. I am at present engaged in the study of the early history of Christianity in Arabia as a sequel to my *Early Spread of Christianity in Central Asia*, and *Early Spread of Christianity in India*, published in 1925 and 1926, respectively. From that study it will be seen that the majority of the Christians round about Ḥijāz and South Syria belonged to the Jacobite community and not to that of the Nestorians. This was the state of affairs even in the middle of the ninth Christian century, in which a well-informed Muslim apologist, ʿAli b. Rabban al-Ṭabarī, was able to write: "What (Christians) are found among the Arabs except a sprinkling of Jacobites and Melchites."[15]

Now the pronunciation used in the Arabic proper names mentioned above is that of the Nestorians and not that of the Jacobites. The latter say *ishmōʿīl*, *isrōīl* and *Isḥōq*, etc., and not *Ishmāʿīl*, *Isrāʿīl,* and *Isḥāq*, as they appear in the Qurʾān.

The Greco-Roman world is seemingly represented by two names only: that of the prophet Jonas, who figures as *yūnus*, and that of the prophet Elijah, whose name is written *Ilyās*, and once as *Ilyāsīn (sic)* for the sake of the rhyme (XXXVII.130). It is highly probable, however, that these two names were borne by Christian Syrians and that they were taken direct from them; indeed, many men of the Jacobite, Nestorian, Melchite, and Maronite Syrians had from the third Christian century names either completely Greek or with a pronounced Greek termination only. The number of such men literally amounts to thousands. As an illustration of the final *sīn*, we may remark here that many Syrians were called *Yoḥannis* for *Yoḥanna* (John), *Mattaeus* for *Mattai* (Matthew), *Thomas* for *Thoma* (Thomas), and so on.

That the view we have here exposed is the only right one is borne out by the fact that in Palestinian Syriac the form of the two names is *Ilyās*[16] and *Yūnus*,[17] as in the Qurʾān. In Ethiopic both names appear also as *Ilyās* and *Yūnus*, but from the Syriac vocable (dhu-n) *nūn*, "(he of the) fish," by which the Qurʾān names Jonah (XXI.87), it is more probable to suppose that he got his name also from the Syrians.

By applying the Syriac method of proper names, we will be able to throw light on some strange forms of names used in the Qurʾān. To express "John" the Qurʾān of our days has the strange form *Yaḥya*. I believe, with Margoliouth,[18] that the name is almost certainly the Syriac *Yoḥannan*. In the early and undotted Qurʾāns the word stood as ىحى which could be read *Yoḥanna, Yoḥannan,*or *Yaḥya*, and the Muslim qurrāʾ

who knew no other language besides Arabic, adopted the erroneous form *Yaḥya*. I am absolutely unable to agree with Lidzbarski[19] that this curious name is an old Arabic one.

So far as the word *ʿĪsa* (the name given to Jesus in the Qurʾān) is concerned, it was apparently in use before Muhammad, and it does not seem probable that it was coined by him. A monastery in South Syria, near the territory of the Christian Ghassanid Arabs, bore in 571 C.E. the name *ʿIsanīyah*, that is to say, "of the followers of Jesus," i.e., of the Christians. See fol. 84b of the Brit. Mus. Syr. MS. Add., 14, 602, which is of the end of the sixth, or at the latest of the beginning of the seventh century.[20] The Mandean pronunciation *ʿIso*[21] is of no avail as the guttural *ʿé* has in Mandaic the simple pronunciation of a *hamzah*. The Mandean pronunciation is rather reminiscent of *ʿIso*, as the name of Jesus was written in the Marcionite Gospel used by the Syrians.[22]

II. RELIGIOUS TERMS

Almost all the religious terms found in the Qurʾān are derived from Syriac. In this category we will include such terms as:

Arabic		*Syriac*
kāhin	from	*khnʾ*, priest (LII.29; LXIX.42)
masīḥ	from	*mšyḥʾ*, the Christ (III.40 and passim)
qissīs	from	*qšyšʾ*, Christian priest[23] (V.85)
dīn	(in the sense of)	last judgment from *dynʾ* (I.3, etc)
safara	from	*sprʾ*, scribes (LXXX.115)
mathal	from	*mtlʾ*, parable[24] (in an evangelical sense; frequently used)
furqān	from	*pwrqnʾ*, salvation[25] (II.50 and passim)
ṭāghūt	from	*ṭʿywt ʾ*, error, infidelity (II.257 passim)
rabbānī	from	*rbnʾ*, perceptor,[26] doctor (III.73; V.48 and 68)
qurbān	from	*qwrbnʾ*, sacrifice (III.179 and passim)
qiyāma	from	*qymtʾ*, resurrection (frequently used)
malakūt	from	*mlkwtʾ*, Kingdom of Heaven (VI.75 and passim)

janna	from	*gnt*ʾ, the Garden, i.e., *Heaven* (frequently used)
malāk/malak	from	*mlʾk*ʾ, angel, frequently used in the singular and plural
rūḥ al-qudus	from	*rwḥ qwdš*ʾ, the Spirit of Holiness (Holy Spirit) (XVI.104)
nafs	from	*npš* ʾ, the spiritual soul (frequently used)
waqqara	from	*yqr*, to glorify God (XLVIII.9)
āya	from	*ʾt* ʾ, sign, verse (frequently used)
Allāh	from	*ʾlh* ʾ (ancient Nestorian pronunciation *Allāha)*, God. The pre-Islamic word for deity seems to be represented by the form *Ilāh*
ṣallā	from	*ṣly*, he prayed, and its derivative *ṣalāt* [*ṣalwah*] (Arabic), from *ṣ lwto*ʾ (Syriac), prayer
ṣāma	from	*ṣm*, he fasted, and its derivative *ṣaruma*, from *ṣwm*ʾ, fast
khaṭ i ʾa	from	*ḥṭ*ʾ, he sinned, and its derivative *khaṭīʾa*, from *ḥṭyṭ*ʾ (Syriac), sin
kafara	from	*kpr*, he denied the faith
dhabaḥa	from	*dbḥ*ʾ, sacrifice (XXXVII.107)
tajallā	from	*ʾtgly*, to reveal oneself (said of God), VII.139
sabbaḥa	from	*šbḥ*, he glorified God, and all its derivatives
qaddasa	from	*qdš*, he glorified God (II.28)
ḥū b	from	*ḥwb* ʾ, crime (IV.2)
ṭūbā	from	*ṭwb*ʾ, blessed be! beatitude (XIII.28)

This dependence of the Qurʾān upon Syriac religious terms is also visible in the theological expressions, such as *light upon light* (= light from light), of XXIV.35 (where *nūr* from *nwhr*ʾ*)*, and in all semibiblical quotations or inspirations, such as the story of the camel and the eye of the needle (VII.39), where *jamal* like *gml*ʾ in Matt. 19:24, and the idea of

God causing to die and to live (LIII.45), where *ʾamāta* and *ʾaḥyā*, like *ʾmyt* and *ʾḥy* in 1 Sam. 2:6, where the Hebrew is in the second form.

The same applies to biblical events and facts, such as *ṭūfān* (VII.130; XXIX.13), *flood*, from *ṭwpnʾ*, and *ṣalaba* from *ṣlb*, *to crucify*, as applied to Christ (IV.156). As such we will also count, *manna*, from *mnʾ*[27] (II.54; VII.160; XX.82), *salwā*, *quail*, from *slwy* (ibid.), *ʾasbāṭ*, *tribes*, from *šbṭʾ*. Another category of verbal Syriacisms is to be found in the literally translated Syriac words; as such we will count the frequently used *rasūl*, *Apostle*, from *šlyḥʾ*, and, *kalima*, *Word* (of God) from *mltʾ* (IV.169 and passim).

I believe that in the above list, the words, the Syriac origin of which could be denied, are very few. The list could be increased by scores of other words, but the above vocables are sufficient for the purpose of this first list. The only Qurʾānic religious terms that betray Hebraic influence are the two technical terms of *taurāt*—Torah, and *Tābūt*, "ark" (II.49; XX.39).[28] The same may to some extent be said of the late Aramaic, *Jahannam*, "hell," which lacks a *mīm* in Classical Syriac. The word *Mathāni*, in XV.87 and XXXIX.24, is obscure, and its connection with the technical word *mishnah* is quite possible but not certain. On the other hand, *ḥabr*, "doctor," is both Syriac and Hebrew, with a slight change in the meaning.

The Jewish influence on the religious vocabulary of the Qurʾān is indeed negligible.

In spite of the close and intimate relations that existed between Ḥijāz and Abyssinia, relations that were strengthened (if we are to believe the Muslim historians on this subject) by the fact that the early Muslims took refuge with Najāshi, the King of Abyssinia, the only Ethiopic religious influence on the style of the Qurʾān, is in the word *ḥawāriyūn*, "Apostles." It is also possible that the word *ṣuḥuf*, "leaves, sheets," may have been inspired by the corresponding Ethiopic word.

Here also we must remark, as we did in the case of the Qurʾānic proper names, that the pronunciation of the above Syriac religious terms is that in use among the Nestorians and not the Jacobites. The latter say *furqōn* and not *furqān*, *qurbōn* and not *qurbān*, *qashīsh* and not *qashshīsh* (with a *shaddah*), and so on.

III. COMMON WORDS

There are words in the Qur'ān that are somewhat uncommon in Arabic but quite common in Syriac. As such we will count:

Arabic		*Syriac*
Qur'ān[29]	from	*qryn'* (Qur'ān), a technical Syriac word to mean *scriptural lesson*, or *reading*
ḥusbān	from	*ḥwšbn'*, numbering (VI.96;XVIII.38; LV.4)
muhaymin	from	*mhymn'*, faithful (V.52; LIX.25)
nūn	from	*nwn'*, fish (XXI.87)
ṭūr	from	*ṭwr'*, mountain (XX.82 and passim)
tabara	from	*tbr*, he defeated, destroyed (XXV.41 and passim)
shāni'a	from	*sn''*, hater (CVIII.3; cf. also V.3, 11)
bariyya	(in the sense of)	*creation* from *bryt'* (XCVIII.5–6)
'aqnā	from	*'qny*, to cause to possess (LIII.49)
ḥanān	from	*ḥnn'*, grace (XIX.14)
'umm	(in the sense of)	*metropolis*, from *'m'* (VI.92, etc.)
abb	from	*ibba* or *abba*, fruit (LXXX.31)
misk	from	*mushk*, musk (LXXXIII.26) [The word is possibly of Persian origin, but it passed into the Qur'ān through Syriac.]
maqālīd	from	*qelīd*, key (XXXIX.63; XLII.10). [The word is of Persian origin, but it passed into the Qur'ān through Syriac. The proof is in the letter Qāf.]
istabraq	from	*istabarg*, silk brocade (LXXVI.21). [The word appears to be of doubtful origin, but it passed into the Qur'ān through Syriac.][30]

Many of the above words are wholly Syriac, and no amount of lexicographical and grammatical subtlety will, in our judgment, succeed in

Arabicizing *nūn, Ṭū r*, or *muhaymin*, and the like. I believe also with Fraenkel[31] that the word *asāṭīr* in VI.25, etc., is the Syriac *ʾšṭrʾ*, "writing, archives, any written thing." The meaning of "legends, stories," given to the word by the Muslim commentators, is arbitrary, a device to give a sense to a sentence that they could not understand, and is not warranted either by the etymological meaning of the root, or by its comparison with the other Semitic languages.[32]

Another Syriac word in the Qurʾān is *raḥmān, compassionate*, from *rḥmnʾ*, and the recently discovered *Book of the Ḥimyarites*[33] shows that the word was used in Yaman before the time of the Prophet.

The Palestinian form of Syriac is represented in the Qurʾān by the word *ṣadīq, ṣdyq, a just man*, and its derivatives. In Classical Syriac the first letter is a *Zayn* [z] but in Hebrew a *Ṣādhé* [ṣ].

The Greco-Roman world is indirectly represented by the three following words, which refer to the state technicalities of currency, weight, and measure: *denarius* (III.36), *drachm* (XII.20), and, *Qinṭār* (III.68, etc.). These are of no importance, and it is highly probable that *dīnār* and *Qinṭār* have passed into the Qurʾān through the intermediary of the Syriac *dynrʾ* and *qnṭrʾ*. This has actually taken place with *qirṭās* χάρης (VI.7 and 91), which has almost certainly passed into the Qurʾān through the Syriac *qrṭysʾ*. The same may possibly be said of *qisṭās* (XVII.37; XXVI.182), *balance, measure*. The spelling ξέστης, however, is nearer to the Arabic form with a final *sīn* (*s*) than the corresponding Syriac *qsṭʾ*; on the other hand, what about the first *Qāf* [q], which is decidedly Syriac? The word, however, represents a technical term of weight as used in the Near and Middle East, and the editor of the Qurʾān wrote it as it was pronounced in his day probably by the Palestinian Syrians. Can the same be said of *sundus*, from σάνδυξ, *red colored* cloth (XVIII.30)?

We believe it to be quite possible that the word *ʾiblīs*, "the evil one," is derived from *diabolus*, through a confusion of the initial *dāl* [d] with an *aliph* by an early qāri, or the first editor of the Qurʾān. This is not absolutely impossible with some ancient forms of the above two letters. The connection of the word with the verb *balasa* is artificial, and, if accepted, would throw us into a non-Arabic and an altogether non-Semitic form of substantives that would baffle a critic. Still more remarkable is the frequently used word *jinn, Jinns*, which is closely associated with the Latin *genii*; and equally remarkable are the words *qalam, pen*, which is reminiscent of κάλαμος, *calamus*, and the word *sijill* (XXI. 104), which is undoubtedly taken from σιγίλλιον, *sigillum*, through the Syriac *sygylywn*. The words used to express precious stones such as *marjān* (LV.22), and *yāqūt* (LV.58), are cosmopolitan, and may have been taken either from Syriac or from Greek, but more probably from Syriac.

As an instance of the curious relation that often exists between the Semitic languages, we may remark that it is possible that *sauṭ* (LXXXIX. 12)—if it can be taken in the sense of "outpour, flood"—has some connection with the Ethiopic *sōṭa*.[34] The commentators, however, give to the word the sense of "lashes, strokes of a whip" from the Syriac (Nestorian) *Shauṭa*. Perhaps the word may also be compared with the Syriac *Shubṭa* (Nestorian pronunciation: Shūṭa), "molten metal."

Another instance of the curious results that arise from a linguistic comparison of the Semitic languages with one another is to be found in the root *fataḥa* (XXVI.118; XXXII.28), which seems to require in the context the sense of "to judge between, judgment"; a meaning that the word possesses in Ethiopic.[35]

As in the case of religious terms, the list of Arabic common words represented in, or derived from, Syriac could be increased literally by scores of others.

No other language is represented in the Qur'ān. Here as in the two previous categories the pronunciation of all the above Syriac words is Nestorian and not Jacobite.

IV. ORTHOGRAPHY

There are numerous words in the Qur'ān that by their orthography betray Syriac influence. The following grammatical features will be sufficient for our purpose.

(a) *ḥayawa*, "life," from *ḥywt'*; *ṣalawat*, "prayer," from *ṣlwt'*; and so on.

(b) The elimination of the *aliph* of prolongation, answering to the Syriac vowel *Zaqāpha*, for example, *bint*, "daughters," for *banāt* under the influence of the Syriac *bnt*. All such plural words are written without *aliph* in the ancient manuscripts of the Qur'ān.

(c) The retention of the *yā'* [y] in the defective verbs when joined to pronouns, for example, *'ajtabiyah* (however, in Egyptian Standard text = verse 122 [Flügel]/121 =*'ajtabāhu*) (XVI.122), "he chose him," for *'ajtabāh* (Syriac *gbyhy*). The *yā'* [y] as a substitute for the *aliph* is written in all the ancient manuscripts of the Qur'ān in the cases under consideration, and is undoubtedly under Syriac influence.

(d) We all know that in the oldest manuscripts of the Qur'ān, thick dots take the place of the short (and occasionally of the long) vowels. I believe that these dots are almost certainly derived from the Syriac Massoretic *puḥḥā més* or *nūqzé*, which fill the same purpose in difficult or ambiguous words.

V. CONSTRUCTION OF SENTENCES

(a) There is a sentence in which the use of *kull* denotes a well-known Syriac expression by means of the corresponding *kl*, an expression absolutely foreign to the Arabic language.

Sura XI.121 says: *wakullan naquṣṣu 'alayka min 'anbā'i-r-rusuli mā nuthabbitu bihī fu'daka*, which translated literally means: "All we relate to thee from the stories of the Apostles is to confirm thy heart thereby." This *kull* betrays the Syriac *kull* used in phrases with the above Qur'ānic meaning and construction, for example, *klh gyr dnḥt lšywly dnḥ' myt'*.[36] To explain away the difficulty the commentators resort to absolutely useless compromises.

Ṭabarī (*Tafsīr*, XII.87) says that the baṣriyūn think that *kull* is in the accusative because it is a *maṣdar* to *naquṣṣu*, (a queer *maṣdar*!), but he prefers the opinion that the word is an *iḍāfah*,[37] which is obviously inaccurate. The same thing may be said of Zamakhsharī's opinion (*Kashshāf*, p. 637) that the word *nab'* is understood after *kull*. The same is asserted by Nīsābūri (*Gharā'ib*, XII.90) and by Bayḍāwī (*Anwār*, I.582), edit. Bulak, 1296 A.H.). That the resort to *iḍāfah* is a worthless compromise is borne out by the fact (a) that there is no second term of *iḍāfah*, (b) that the *aliph* and *tanwīn* of *kull* render the existence of any *iḍāfah* almost out of the question.

(b) There is a sentence in which the demonstrative pronouns are used immediately after the personal pronouns, in the same way as they are used in Syriac, but not in Arabic

Sura II.79 has: *thumma'antum hā'ūlā'i taqtulūna 'anfusakum.* "Then are you the very persons who kill yourselves." The use of *hawilā'* is here very peculiar and denotes the Syriac *hālain.* The use of demonstrative pronouns without the relative pronouns, when followed by a verb the action of which they tend to corroborate, is Syriac and not Arabic.

Zamakhsharī (*Kashshāf*, p. 87) has no good reason to offer for the anomaly. Bayḍāwī (*Anwār*, i., 95) evades the difficulty by giving an example of a demonstrative pronoun *(anta dhaka)*, which is obviously irrelevant. Ṭabarī (*Tafsīr*, I.314) quotes Abū Ja'far, to the effect that a vocative *yā* or such word as *qaum* are understood after *antum*, and refers to some other devices which are really useless. Nīsābūrī (*Gharā'ib* i., 328) believes that *antum* is a "mubtada'," and "hawilā' " its "khabar," by inserting between the two some such words as *ba'da dhālika*, and quotes also the Kūfiyūn to the effect that the demonstrative pronoun has replaced here the relative in a way that they cannot understand.

(c) There is a sentence in which the word *shay'*, "something," is under the influence of the Syriac *mdm*, *something*, used in a meaning not sanctioned by the genius of the Arabic language.

Sura LX.11 says: *wa 'in fātakum shay'um min 'azwājikum 'lā-l-kuffāri.* "And if any of your wives escape from you to the unbelievers." I believe that the word *shai'* applied to a human being is not Arabic at all, and betrays the Syriac *middaim*, which is applied to reasonable beings (*n š'mdm*).

This *shai'* is an unsurmountable difficulty to the commentators, who resort in it to worthless compromises. To avoid the difficulty Ibn Mas'ūd (in Zamakhsharī's *Kashshāf,* p. 1475) changed *shai* into *aḥad.* Bayḍāwī (*Anwār*, II.516) believes that it refers to the dowry of the wives (*shai'un min muhūrihinna*), which is obviously against the context. Ṭabarī (XXVIII.49) evades the difficulty and speaks only of the dowry. Nīsābūrī (*Gharā'ib*, XXVIII.45) says that *shai* ' means here *aḥad*, but like Bayḍāwī makes also mention of the fact that it may refer to the dowry of the wives, and he finally registers the opinion of some linguists that *shai'* is here used for "emphasis" or "derision." This uncommon interpretation is also found in Zamakhsharī and Bayḍāwī *(in loc.).*

(d) There are in the Qurʾān many sentences in which the Arabic word used does not fit in with the meaning required by the context, but when compared with its Syriac equivalent its right meaning becomes clear; for example:

Sura XLVIII.12 says: *wa ẓanantum ẓanna –s-sawʾi wa kuntum qawman būran.* "(But you believed that the Apostle and the believers would not come back to their families, and this appeared pleasing in your hearts), and you believed wrongly and you were ill advised people."

The word *būr* has been translated as meaning "worthless, rogue" or "an undone people," which does not suit the context. Is it not the transliteration of the Syriac *būr* that means "ignorant, ill advised"? The same meaning seems also to be more suitable in XXV.19.

In Sura XXXVIII.2, occurs the sentence: *fanādū wa lāta ḥīna manāṣin.* "And they cried but no time was it of escape." Let us admit frankly that this *lāt* is a barbarous anomaly in the Arabic language, and scores of pages have been written about it by Muslim commentators and grammarians without advancing our knowledge one iota. I believe that it is almost certainly the Syriac, *lyt*, "there is not, there was not," a contraction of *lʾ ʾyt*. This is also the opinion of Suyūṭī (*Mutawakkili*, p. 54) and of some other Muslim writers.[38] In many ancient manuscripts of the Qurʾān, the word is spelt *lat* or *layt*, and the *aliph* of prolongation has been added or substituted for the *yāʾ* by later *qurrāʾ*, as they have done for thousands of other words with a medial *yāʾ*. See above the mark (c) in section 4, "orthography" (p. 184).

VI. FOREIGN HISTORICAL REFERENCES

(a) In Sura XVIII.82 sqq., there is an account of the well-known legend of Alexander the Great. The Macedonian conqueror first went westward and found the sun setting in a black muddy spring, and then he journeyed eastward and discovered that below the two mountains between which he was standing lived people who could scarcely understand speech. They implored Alexander to set a rampart between them and a wicked people called *Yājūj* and *Mājūj*. Yielding to their entreaties, Alexander erected a wall of pig iron across the opening between the two mountains, fused it into a solid mass of metal, and strengthened it by pouring molten brass over the whole.

The Romance of Alexander is found in many languages; in Greek (that of Pseudo-Callisthenes, about 200 C.E.); in Latin (that of Julerius Valerius, about 340 C.E., and of Leo the Archpresbyter, eleventh century); in Armenian (unknown date, but probably from the Greek); in Syriac (written about the beginning of the seventh, but known at the beginning of the sixth century); in Ethiopic (unknown date, but centuries after the Arab invasion); and in Coptic (about the ninth century). Later versions include the Persian, the Turkish and, *mirabile dictu*, the Malay and the Siamese.

The best study of the Romance is to our knowledge that of Nöldeke,[39] who wrote after the publication of the Syriac text of the story by Budge.[40] From the works of Jacob of Serug we know, however, that the story was well known in Syriac circles prior to 520 C.E. Of all the above peoples to whom the Romance was known in one form or another, the only ones who could have influenced the Qur'ān were the Syrians and the Ethiopians; but since we have no evidence that the Ethiopians knew anything of the story in the Prophet's lifetime,[41] we have only the Syrians left from whom the Prophet, or the editor of the Qur'ān, could have derived his information. This may be corroborated by the following considerations:

(1) All the early versions write the word "Gog" only as *Gog*, while the Qur'ān writes it as *Agog*[41] or, more generally, *yā-gōg* (with an *aliph* or with a *yā'* and an *aliph* at the beginning). In a poem by Jacob of Serug written toward the beginning of the sixth Christian century on the Romance of Alexander and Gog and Magog, the word constantly occurs with an initial *alaph* as *A-gog*.[43] This Syriac spelling has probably influenced the Arabic form of the word as used in the Qur'ān. There is even a verse in the Syriac text[44] in which the author seems to derive *A-gog* from *Agoga* = ἀγωγός, "stream, aqueduct."

(2) In the Greek of Pseudo-Callisthenes, Alexander is a pagan king. In the Qur'ān Alexander becomes a pious man and a messenger of Allah. This idea could have emanated only from Syrians, with whom, I do not know for what reason, the Macedonian *jahān-gushā* had become a messenger and a prophet of God. All the poem of Jacob of Serug mentioned above is based on such an assumption.[45]

(b) In Sura XXII.17, occurs the word *majūs*, *Magians*. I believe that this word is from Syriac *mgwš'*[46] and that the Prophet or the editor of the Qur'ān had heard of Magians only from Syrians and not from Greeks, Persians, or any other people, because curiously enough the word is meant in the Qur'ānic text to be in the plural form from an hypothetical singular, the nature of which we cannot guess with certitude. Now in Syriac, contrary to Greek and Persian, the form of the word does not change in its consonants when passing from singular into plural, and the Prophet or the editor of the Qur'ān used the term in the plural of Syriac and not that of Arabic, as he heard it pronounced in his time. This difficulty was so keenly felt by post-Qur'ānic Muslim authors that from the plural form of the word as used in the Qur'ān they created (as if it was a gentilic and ethnic vocable) a singular form, *majūsī*.

Etymologically, the Syriac word itself is derived from the Persian *mugh* (in Zend Moghu), "a fire worshipper."

(c) The Christians are called in the Qur'ān *naṣārā*, which I take to be from the Syriac *nṣry'*. Indeed there is no other language besides Syriac in which the word "Christians" is expressed by the word *naṣāra* or anything near it. Further, in many ancient documents, the Syriac word *naṣrāya* is applied exclusively to Christians without any reference at all to the "Nazarenes." The Martyr, Simon bar Ṣabbā'é, the great Patriarch of the East, is in 341 C.E. called the "head of the *Naṣrāyé*,"[47] that is, of the Christians. All Christians are called *naṣrāyé* in the life of the same saint written about the end of the fourth century.[48] The same name is also applied to them in more than one hagiographical piece emanating from writers whose country was situated within the boundaries of the Sassanian Empire. Saint Pethion was asked in 447 C.E.: "Which benefits have accrued to thee from thy connection with the *Naṣrāyé*?"[49] that is, Christians. A Zoroastrian Persian general living before the Arab invasion sends a word to his Byzantine Christian opponent to observe a certain feast "because of the Jews and *Naṣrāyé* (i.e., Christians) that are found in my army."[50] There is no need to give more examples, but we will allude to the fact that in the Romance of Julian the Apostate alone *Naṣrāya* is used several times to express a Christian.[51]

There is no doubt whatever that in the Persian Empire, and to some extent also in the Roman Empire, the Christians were called by non-Christians *naṣrāyé* (the *Naṣāra* of the Qur'ān), and that the Prophet took the word from the Syrians.

(d) In XI.46, mention is made of the fact that the ark of Noah stood on a mountain called *jūdī*. Few scholars will be inclined to deny the fact that this queer word is the Syriac *qrdw*, the mountain on which according to the

Peshiṭta Version (Gen. 8:4) and the Targum (contrary to all the other versions of the Bible which call the mountain *Ararat*) the ark of Noah stood above water. The Prophet or the editor of the Qur'ān had heard, therefore, the story of Noah and his flood only from Syrians. The reading of a *wāw* for a *ra'* (the difference between the two letters is very slight in Arabic script) may be ascribed to an early kari or to the editor of the Qur'ān himself. The pronunciation of the initial *Qāf* as *Gāf* is used even in our days by almost all the Arabs of the desert, with whom every *Qāf* is invariably a *gāf*. No other explanation of the word *Jūdi* seems to me worth mentioning.

(e) Frequent use is made in the Qur'ān of the word *ḥanīf*, which I take to be derived from the Syriac *ḥnp'*, *pagan*. This is also the opinion of some Muslim writers themselves.[52] In its singular form the word is used as follows: in II.129; III.89; VI.79 and 162, XVI.121 and 124, all in connection with Abraham being a *ḥanīf* and not a *mushrik*; in III.60 in connection with Abraham being neither a Jew nor a Christian, nor a *mushrik*, but a *ḥanīf*. In IV.124 Abraham is a *ḥanīf*. In X.105 and XXX.29 the Prophet himself is ordered to be a *ḥanīf*. In its plural form the word is used in XXII.32, where the faithful are ordered to be *ḥanīfs* but not *mushriks*, and in XCVIII.4, where they are ordered to be *ḥanīfs* and pray and give alms.

The Syriac derivation of the word offers to my mind no difficulty at all. The real difficulty lies in the fact that the word is used in a good sense in the Qur'ān wherein it is almost synonymous with "Muslim." To this difficulty I can offer no decisive solution, but I will tentatively propose the following considerations:

(1) On the one hand, the Prophet must have heard many Christians say of him that since he was neither a Jew nor a Christian, he was by necessity a *ḥanfa*; on the other hand, he must have also heard from them that Abraham was likewise a *ḥanfa*: a perfectly true assertion. By its association with the great Patriarch Abraham, revered and respected by both Christians and Jews, the word *ḥanfa* came to acquire with Muhammad a good and praiseworthy meaning. This is the reason why the Prophet is at some pains to emphasize the fact that Abraham was neither a Jew nor a Christian, but a *ḥanfa*, and wishes also his own religion to be *ḥanfūtha*.

(2) To express "idolatry" and "idolater," the Qur'ān uses some forms of the root *sharaka*, which means "to associate." Now this "association" is always meant an association or a partnership of other beings with

Allah, the true God, and never with any pagan deity, and this in spite of the fact that to express "idols" the Qur'ān knows of *authān* (XXII.31; XXIX.16 and 24), *aṣnām* (passim), and *tamāthīl* (XXI.53; XXXIV.12). This bad meaning of the root *sharaka* is naturally held to be as unworthy of Muhammad as it is of Abraham, and this is the reason why so much stress is laid on the fact that Abraham was not a *muskrik.*

No solution of the difficulty offered by Muslim commentators or historians is worth mentioning. All their stories concerning a class of *ḥanīf*s and the good works of the so-called *taḥannuf* appear to me to be unhistorical and purposely invented to explain the difficulty created by the Qur'ānic verses under consideration.

(f) In XXX.10 the word *Rūm* is used to express the Byzantines, the Greeks of Constantinople, the "New Rome" (Ῥώμη νέα). Whatever our views may be as to the linguistic peculiarities of the word, we are not at liberty to deny that it is derived from the Syriac *Rūmāya.* Indeed the Syrians went so far in their application of the word to Byzantines that they often called simple "soldiers" *Rūmāyé,*[53] as if the only soldiers they knew were Byzantine soldiers.

NOTES

1. T. Nöldeke, *Neue Beiträge zur semitischen Sprachwissenschaft* (Srassburg, 1910).
2. J. Horovitz, *Koranische Untersuchungen* (Berlin, 1926).
3. D. Margoliouth, "The Origins of Arabic Poetry." *JRAS* (1925): 415–49.
4. A. Mingana, *Odes and Psalms of Solomon* (1920), ii.125.
5. The Qur'ān itself testifies to this with emphasis in XLVI.8; LXVIII.37 LII.41; LXII.2; XXXIV.43; XXXV.38; XXXVII.156.
6. S. Fraenkel, *De Vocabulis in ant. Arab. carm. et in Corano peregrinis* (Leiden, 1880).
7. Dvorak, *Ueber die Fremdwörter im Korân*, in the publications of the Vienna Academy.
8. Jalāl ad-Dīn Suyūṭī, *Itqān* (Calcutta, 1856), pp. 314–27.
9. Jalāl ad-Dīn Suyūṭī, *Mutawakkili*, ed. W. Y. Bell (N.p.: Nile Mission Press, 1924).
10. The official text of the Bible in Syriac-speaking Christian lands from the early fifth century C.E.

11. We can, however, assure the benevolent reader that no Qur'ānic word has been asserted as derived from Syriac, Hebrew, Ethiopic, Greek, Latin, or Persian except after deep thought and consideration.

12. Pp. 709 and 714 in Wright's catalogue. On the gods *Shalman* and *Solomon* see Clay, *The Empire of Amorites,* pp. 91, 156, and Meyer, *Die Israeliten,* p. 295.

13. See Fraenkel, *ZA*, xv., 394.

14. Ed. Berliner, 1875.

15. *Kitāb ad-Dīn wad-Daulah*, p. 157 of my translation.

16. *Palestinian Syriac Lectionary*, p. 289 (ed. Mrs. Lewis and Mrs. Gibson).

17. Ibid., p. 24.

18. *Moslem World* (1925): 343.

19. *Johannesbuch*, ii., 73: cf. also Nöldeke in *Z.A.*, xxx., 158 sq.

20. P. 714 in Wright's catalogue.

21. Nöldeke's *Mand. Grammar*, xxix and 55; Lidzbarski, *Mand. Liturgien*, 191.

22. Mitchell's *St. Ephraim's Prose Refutation of Mani, Marcion, and Bardaisan*, vols. 1–2 (1912–21) (as in index), and see my study on same in *JRAS* (1922): 530.

23. It is in place here to remark that the Syriac word *Qashshīsh* was used as a proper name by many Ghassanid Arabs of South Syria. See "Mar Qashshīh, the Arab," in Brit. Mus. Syr. MS. Add., 14, 458, p.48, in Wright's catalogue. The manuscript was copied before the death of Muhammad.

24. Many worthless conjectures have been put forward concerning this word by Muslim commentators who knew no other Semitic language besides Arabic.

25. Ibid.

26. Ibid.

27. It could not have been taken from Hebrew because of its mention with *Salwa*. See Fraenkel, *De Vocabulis*, p. 24. With this scholar I am in perfect agreement concerning some other words in this section.

28. The word *Sūrah* is of unknown origin, and its right etymology is in our judgment still obscure.

29. There is not much doubt in my mind that the word Qur'ān is imitated from the Syriac *Qiryān*. All the biblical lessons to be read in the churches are called by the Syrians *Qiryāns*. The Prophet called simply his book by the word that was used to name the pericopes of the Revelation in the Christian churches of his day. We should also remember that in the oldest manuscripts of the Qur'ān, the word is simply written *qrn* which may be, and has already been, read *Qur'ān* or *Qurān* without *hamzah*. I suspect that this reading of the word without *hamzah*

is reminiscent of an earlier pronunciation, *Quryān* or *Qiryān* (with a *yā*ʾ), and that the *hamzah* pronunciation is a late reading adopted to make the word more Arabic and in harmony with the root of the verb *Qaraʾa*.

30. Ibid., p. 250.

31. See Fraenkel, *De vocabulis*, p. 25, who refers to Lagarde's *Gesammelte Abhandlungen*, p. 13. So also Siddiki, *Studien*, p. 8.

32. Cf. Nöldeke-Schwally, *Ges. d. Qor.*, i., 16, and especially the references given by Horovitz, *Koranische*, p. 70, to the South Arabian inscriptions.

33. A. Moberg, ed., *Book of the Hymyarites* (Lund, 1924), p. 10.

34. Barth, *Etymologische Studien*, p. 14; Horovitz, *Koranische*, p. 13.

35. Cf. Horovitz, *Koranische*, p. 18; Nöldeke-Schwally, *Geschichte*, i., 219.

36. *Breviarium Chaldaicum*, i., 383.

37. See W. Wright, *A Grammar of the Arabic Language*, 3d ed. (Cambridge, 1967), vol. 2, p. 198 C: *iḍāfah* is essentially the relation subsisting between a determined noun and a determining noun.

38. On the expression *haita la-ka*, "come hither," in XII.23, see Suyūṭī, *Mutawakkili*, p. 54, and *Itqān*, p. 325. He believes the phrase to be Syriac, which is perfectly true so far as *la-ka* is concerned.

39. *Beiträge zur Gesch. des Alexanderromans* in the Vienna Academy's publications of 1890.

40. *The History of Alexander the Great* (1889).

41. The Ethiopic story published by Budge in 1896 under the title of *The Life and Exploits of Alexander the Great* is clearly a post-Islamic production and is undoubtedly under the influence of the Qurʾān and of late Muslim writers.

42. See examples in Nöldeke's *Geschichte des Qorans*, p. 270.

43. Ibid., p. 378.

44. Edit. of Budge in *Zeitsch. f. Assyriologie*, vi., pp. 376, 382, 389, 391, 393, 398, 400–401, and 403.

45. About Alexander's wall see the *Chronicle of Dionysius of Tellmahre*, ed. Chabot, p. 24 sq.

46. Cf. Nöldeke, *Persische Studien*, ii., 37.

47. *Pat. Syr.*, ii., 792, 818, and 867.

48. Ibid., ii., 799. Cf. Horovitz, *Koranische*, p. 145.

49. *Acta Martyrum et Sanctorum* (ed. Bedjan), ii., 576.

50. Land's *Anecdota Syriaca*, iii., 258.

51. See the index of Hoffmann's edition, *Julianos der Abtruennige*, p. xiv.

52. Masʿūdi's, *Tanbīh*, in *Bibl. Georg. Arab.* (ed. De Goeje), viii., 6, 90, 122, 136; cf. *Encyclopaedia of Islam*, ii., 259–61.

53. See the remark of Wright in *Chronicle of Joshua the Stylite*, p. 30.

3.2

Some Additions to Professor Jeffery's *Foreign Vocabulary of the Qur'an*

D. S. Margoliouth

In the thirty-eighth section of his *Itqān*, the polygraph Suyūṭī furnishes a summary of a monograph called *al-Muhadhdhab fī mā waqaʿa fiʾl-Qurʾān min al-muʿarrab*, in which he dealt with the question whether the Qurʾan contained any foreign words, and if so, to what language they belonged. The orthodox felt some difficulty about admitting the existence of such an element in the language of the Sacred Book, which claims to be in perspicuous Arabic; it was, however, difficult to maintain that the proper names that occur in the volume were all of Arabic origin, and certain other words have an obviously foreign appearance. Suyūṭī himself compromises by admitting in such cases the foreign etymology, but maintaining that the words had received Arabic naturalization.

Professor Jeffery's work, forming volume 79 of the Gaekwar of Baroda's Oriental Series, and dated 1938, is practically an exhaustive treatment of the subject, based on extraordinarily wide linguistic knowledge and no less wide acquaintance with what has been previously written about the words in question. The soundness of his judgment is throughout conspicuous. A good many puzzles indeed remain, for example, the connection of the word *Ḥanīf* with natural religion and in particular with Abraham. We are scarcely better off in the case of *Nazoraios* in the New Testament.

I propose to suggest a few additions to Professor Jeffery's list.

D. S. Margoliouth, "Some Additions to Professor Jeffery's *Foreign Vocabulary of the Qurʾan*," *JRAS* (1939): 53–61. Reprinted with the permission of the Royal Asiatic Society.

(1) In Sura XXXIV.13 the Jinn learn that Solomon is dead because of a termite gnawing his *minsa'at*; in consequence of which Solomon collapsed. This word has occasioned difficulty: certainly the Prophet's uncle and protector is quoted for the word, and indeed according to Lisān al-ʿArab by the grammarian al-Farrā, though whence he got the line is not clear; it is not to be found in the odes ascribed to Abū Ṭālib in the *Sīrah*, which are certainly spurious. According to an authority quoted by Tāj al-ʿArūs al-Farrā even suggested an emendation, *min sa'atihi*, supposing that *si'at* here stood for *siyat*, the curved end of a bow. To this there was the objection that Solomon was unlikely to be leaning on a bow. The verb whence *minsa'at* is said to be derived is given the sense "to drive" cattle, but whether a stick used for this purpose would suit the luxurious Solomon may be doubted.

I do not remember to have seen it suggested, though I think it must have been, that the Arabic word is a transformation of the Hebrew משענת (*mišʿnt*) to which Mandelkern assigns the meanings *fulcrum*, *scipio*, *baculus*, *sceptrum*. The verb whence it is derived means "to lean"; and doubtless the sense required in the Qur'anic verse is "scepter." Solomon's connection with the Jinn goes back to the difficult words in Eccles. 2:8, where the author among his acquisitions enumerates שדה ושדות (*śdh wśdwt* meaning "field" and "fields.").[1]* By the time of Josephus his relations with the demons had assumed serious proportions. The *Aggadah* does not appear to have preserved anything analogous to the Qur'anic narrative; the Hebrew word for "scepter," meaning something to lean upon, is likely to have been used in it.

(2) In Sura II.261, there is a story of a man who was put to death by Allah for a hundred years, after which he was resuscitated. Asked how long he had remained (unconscious), he replied: a day or part of one. No, he was told, a hundred years; so look at your food and drink *lam yatasannah*. The note of Ṭabarī (Comm. iii, 24) on this passage is unusually interesting, since it records how one Hānī', client of the Caliph ʿUthmān, with *nisbah* al-Barbarī, acted as intermediary between the

---

*Prof. Margoliouth seems to have interpreted Eccles. 2: 8 in his own fashion, for the Hebrew Bible (*Biblia Hebraica*, Stuttgart, 1952, p. 1213) reads *šrym wšrwt*. This is a difficult passage, which has been variously interpreted; the older interpretation gives: *sommelière and sommelières* (wine waitresses?). Modern editors of the *Biblia Hebraica* propose the reading: śrh wśrwt, meaning: *prince and princes*. The King James Version has *men and women singers*.—Ed.

Caliph and the editor of the Qur'an, Zaid b. Thābit: he was sent by the latter to ask which was right *lam yatasannan* or *lam yatasannah* and the Caliph chose the latter. Ṭabarī records variations as to the person consulted. He also mentions a third reading *lam yatasanna*. It seems to be agreed that the sense of the word is *changed*, that is, neither food nor drink has gone bad; this gloss is traced to Wahb b. Munabbih, and scarcely differs from the rendering "does not stink," which derives the form from the group *'sn* or *sn*. The sense *changed* is obtained indirectly from the word *sanatun* "year," on the assumption that a verb "to year" might mean "to be affected by the passing of the years."

I would suggest that we have here a Hebraism, the word being referable to the Hebrew שנה (*šnh*) "to be changed," Piel שִׁנָּה (*šinnāh*) "to change" (transitively), both of which have a tendency to imply a change for the worse. Since the person who underwent this experience might have found the corruption of his food and drink a more convincing proof that he had been dead a hundred years than their preservation, this detail occasions some surprise. It would, however, seem clear that their preservation is meant.

(3) Where Arabic words are practically identical with such as are found in other Semitic languages of which we possess earlier monuments, it is at times difficult to decide whether they are *ursemitisch* or borrowed: even *Lautverschiebung*, where it occurs, is not always a safe guide. It is a great merit of the Qur'an that it taught the Arabs their language, and where there is reason for thinking that the sense of a word was inferred from its usage in that book, there is a probability in favor of its having been introduced into the language therein.

The word that suggests this consideration is *nataqnā* in Sura VII.170, *wa 'idh nataqnā l-jabala fawqahum Ka- annahu ẓullatun*: "and when We . . . the mountain over them as though it were an umbrella." In parallel passages recording how a mountain was raised over the beads of the Israelites (II.60 and 87; IV.153), the verb corresponding with that which has been left untranslated is *raf'nā*: "We raised." What, then, is the exact sense of *nataqnā*? If Ibn al-Athīr in his *Nihāyah* is right, the word was extraordinarily appropriate to the operation described: it means, he says, *in taqla' u sh -shai'a fa-tarfa'uhu min makānihi li-tarmiya bihi*: "your uprooting a thing and raising it from its place in order to fling it." Since the Israelites (as the Surah proceeds to assert) were afraid the mountain would fall upon them, the verb that contains the three ideas of uprooting, raising, and flinging suits the situation exactly. Only it seems more probable that the sense was inferred from the Qur'anic passage than that the language had a verb involving all three notions. Hence it is permissible to suggest that the Arabic verb is borrowed from the Hebrew and Aramaic נתק (*ntq*). Mountains, according to Job 28:9, have "roots"; and this verb is applied to the pulling up of roots in Ezek. 17:9. For its employment in the later literature Levy gives it the sense *losreissen, ausreissen.*

Ibn Duraid in his *Jamharah* (ed. Krenkow, ii, 26) gives as the meaning of the Arabic verb *nafaḍa* "to shake out," as when you shake out the contents of a vessel; he quotes for it a verse of the Rajaz writer ʿAjjāj (found, but corrupt, in Ahlwardt's edition xxiii, 3), where it is used of a camel shaking vermin out of the rider's cloak. It would seem then that Ṭabarī's rendering *ʾiqtalaʿa*, "uproot," goes back to someone who was acquainted with the Hebrew and Aramaic sense of the group.

(4) A similar doubt, as to whether the word is *ursemitisch* or borrowed, occurs in the case of *ḥusbān*, which is identical with the Hebrew חשבון (*ḥišbōn*), Aramaic חושבן (*ḥušbān*). This word occurs VI.96, in the Hebrew Aramaic sense "reckoning": "He made . . . the sun and the moon *ḥusbānan*," meaning doubtless a means of reckoning dates. In LV.4, *bi-ḥusbān ash-shamsu wa-l-qamaru* seems similar, though the word looks like a misreading of *yasbaḥā n* "they twain give praise," since what follows is "the star and the trees prostrate themselves." But in a third place the rendering "reckoning" seems inappropriate. This is XVIII.38, where the speaker says: "Peradventure my Lord will give me something better than thy garden, and send thereon a *ḥusbān* from heaven, and it shall become slippery soil." Ṭabarī cites authorities who gave it the sense "punishment," which indeed might be a synonym of "reckoning," but what is wanted is something more material, having the effect of doing away with all the vegetation. Hence, numerous guesses were offered for the interpretation: Ibn Kathīr thinks violent rain must be meant; other suggestions are lightning, fire, and hail. Now the word in its Syriac form has some material sense, of which Payne Smith cites two examples from a pre-Islamic writer, John of Ephesus: only in both cases it is some personal possession, apparently an article of wearing apparel, as in the first example it is one of the things *on* a person who is stripped by robbers; in the second it comes between books and vessels. Payne Smith, who trans-

lated the Syriac text, gave the word the sense "pillow," which is one of the meanings given the Arabic word: and that in this sense it is an Arabic borrowing from Syriac may be assumed. There would be little difficulty about supposing a cushion to be sent down from heaven, only the result stated in the verse, the levelling of the ground, would be surprising. If the word in this sense is really derived from *ḥšb*, and not altered from some foreign word, it may be suggested that it is specialization of the Hebrew or Syriac in the sense of "a device," a usage found twice in the Old Testament, once indeed in the sense of "engine" (2 Chron. 26:15), such as is used in war. I should be inclined to render the word in the text of the Qur'an by "device," meaning some means whereby the leveling of the soil would be effected, the speaker not specifying further.

(5, 6) The following two words are dealt with by Professor Jeffery, but I venture to disagree with his conclusions. In Sura LXXXIII.18, "the book of the virtuous" is said to be in *ʿilliyyīna*, which is then glossed as "written book." In verse 7, "the book of the evildoers" is said to be in *sijjīnin* to which the same gloss "written book" is attached. These glosses are dismissed as worthless by Ṭabarī and his successors. For *ʿlywn*, Professor Jeffery accepts the view of Fränkel, who identifies it with עליון (*ʿlywn*), a divine name found in the Old Testament and elsewhere. If this were right, there would be no occasion to regard the Arabic word as foreign. It may be suggested that the first letter should have a point, and that it is the Syriac *gelāyūnā*, the גליון (*glywn*) of Isa. 8:1, where it is some sort of tablet on which something was to be written. The words that follow in the Qur'an (verse 21) *yashhaduhu l-muqarrabūna*, "to be witnessed by high officials" remind one of what follows in Isaiah: "and I took unto me faithful witnesses." The gloss of Bar Bahlul on the Syriac word is *sijjil ṭūmār*, which justifies us in identifying the other word *sijjīn* with the Syriac *sygylywn*.

The substitution of *N* for *L* in *sijjīn* for the sake of the rhyme is parallel to *Jibrīn* for *Jibrīl* (Gabriel). The use of the *gh* to represent ג (*g*) at this period might be harder to illustrate; it is to be observed, however, that the letter in both Hebrew and Aramaic had two pronunciations.

The glosses in the Qur'an are therefore correct, though it is noticeable that in Rabbinic usage the *gillayon* was *ein noch unbeschriebenes Schreibmaterial* (Levy). The difference between the two "books" would seem to be that the one containing the record of the evildoers is closed, that of the virtuous open.

The following words may be explained from Ethiopic.

(7) In XL.38 Pharaoh says to Haman, "Build me a tower peradventure I shall reach," *al-ʾasbāba ʾasbāba* "of the heavens and come in sight of the god of Moses." The word left untranslated is used elsewhere in the Qurʾan in the sense of "rope"; this does not seem appropriate here, and Ṭabarī reports various suggestions, "roads," "gates," "dwellings." These are all guesses, none of them felicitous. Dillmann gives examples of the Ethiopic *ʾasbāb* in the sense *excubiae*, *excubitores*, *stationes*, and the supposition that the Arabic word which is identical has the meaning "guardhouses" in the Qurʾanic verse seems to be rather plausible. In Isa. 21:8 the word משמרת (*mišmeret*), properly "guardhouse," is rendered by Gesenius *specula*, "watchtower," an elevated place whence objects at a distance could be seen. What Pharaoh wishes is to get a sight of the god of Moses, if such a being is really in heaven, and if Haman will build him a tower reaching the level of the watchtowers of heaven he will compass this object. In the book of Esther, Haman builds a gallows fifty cubits high; in Gen. 11 the builders of Babylon say, "let us build us a city and a tower, whose top may reach unto heaven." This passage is somewhat nearer the narrative in Sura XXVIII.38, where Haman is told to "kindle for me upon the clay and make for me a tower, peradventure I shall come in sight of the god of Moses"; since the builders of Babylon say, "Go to, let us make brick and burn them thoroughly." Since the first meaning assigned to the verb *farʿa* is *ascendit montem*, it might seem that Pharaoh by this project was justifying his name.

(8) In Sura XLIV.23, where the crossing of the Red Sea by the Israelites is described, Moses is given the order *wa-truk il-baḥra rahwan*, "Leave the sea . . . verily they are a host that shall be drowned." This is the only place in the Qurʾān in which the word *rahwun* occurs, and it is clear from Ṭabarī's note that its signification was unknown, and had to be guessed from the context. Ḥarīrī supposed it to mean "tranquil," as he writes (Maq. xxxix, ed. de Sacy, p. 432), *lam nazal nasīru wa l-baḥru rahwun wa l-jawwu ṣaḥwun*, "we ceased not travelling with the sea calm and the weather fine," but this sense does not suit the Qurʾanic passage, since the sea was neither calm nor stormy, a passage having been hollowed out, the water on each side being like a great mountain (XXVI.62). Hence for "calm" authorities cited by Ṭabarī substitute "undisturbed," that is, leave the sea as it is, do not restore it to its previous condition. I

am inclined to regard the word here as the Ethiopic *rekhewe*, "open," of which Dillmann gives several examples: thus Acts 10:11, "he saw the heaven opened," XVI.27, "seeing the prison doors open," and many other passages. This sense suits the scene with which the text of the Qur'an is dealing, in which a way has been left open in the sea through which the Israelites passed: Moses is commanded not to close it, but leave it open for the Egyptians, on whom it will close, so that they will be drowned. Dillmann's statement about the letter *kh* is "the old pronunciation would sound like the Arabic *kh*, later confused with *ḥ* and *h* (Ethiopic letters)." The words *antiquitus* and *posthac* give little clue to the time at which the confusion began.

(9) In Sura XLIV.18, we read that among the injunctions of Moses to the people of Pharaoh was *wa ʾan lā taʿlū ʿalā -l- lāhi*. This is ordinarily rendered *and exalt not yourselves against Allah*. This may be right; but we seem to obtain a more natural sense from the Ethiopic usage of the same group, *ʿaläwä* which is familiar in the sense of "rebel." Dillmann's renderings include "rebel or be refractory, to separate oneself from, to abandon," *rebellem vel refractarium esse, desciscere, deficere*, and he furnishes numerous examples; in historical texts the word is used for "to revolt." The same usage is found in XXVII.31, where a letter of king Solomon to the people of Saba is reproduced, beginning *ʾallā taʿlū ʿalā wa ʾatūnī muslimīna*, where the meaning is clearly "disobey me not, but come to me submissively." We are, I think, justified in regarding this usage as an Ethiopism.

(10) In XXXIII.19 there occurs the phrase *ʾidhā dhahaba l-khawfu salaqūkum bi-alsinatin ḥidādin*, evidently meaning "when their fear has departed, they abuse you with sharp tongues." The verb *salaqa* is given no fewer than eleven senses by Freytag, and it evidently has several sources. One of them is to be found in *istalaqā*, "to lie on one's back," to the stem of which its relation is similar to that of *sabaqa* to *baqā*. Another is a stem found also in Aramaic, meaning "to ascend." The most common sense of the word, "to boil," is that of the Aramaic and late Hebrew שלק (*šlq*), whereas "ascend" is that of סלק (*slq*). For the sense "abuse" we must go to Ethiopic, where the derived form *tasālaqa* has the sense "to play with, to mock" *illudere, ludibrio habere*. Of this Dillmann gives numerous examples. Perhaps the Qurʾanic usage may be regarded as an Ethiopism.

(11) The two angels of II.96 who taught people spells destructive of connubial happiness, Harut and Marut, have been the subject of many conjectures. The second of these names seems to be identical with the Ethiopic *mārīt Mārīt*, rendered by Dillmann "soothsayer, prophetic" *divina, fatidica*. The masculine form, *Mārī*, is given the additional meaning *magus*; it seems to be likely that this Ethiopic word is the source of this angel's connection with magic; and Babylon, where the two angels are located, is the home of magic.

Tunc Babylon Persea licet secretaque Memphis
Omne vetustorum solvat penetrale Magorum

(Lucan, *Pharsalia*, vi, 150)

The Qurʾan favors the form *qātūl* for foreign names, giving *Yājūj* and *Mājūj* for Gog and Magog, *Qārūn* for Corah, *Hārūn* for Aaron, *Jālūt* for Goliath, and so on. Both these angels' names are accommodated to this scheme, and Hārūt is to the Syriac *Herta*, "strife," what *Jālūt* is to Goliath. Possibly Lagarde's etymology may explain why these beings became angels, though the tracing of Qurʾanic matter to Old Persian mythology seems hazardous: the etymologies given above explain their connection with magic and strife.

I must in finishing once more express my admiration for Professor Jeffery's work.

3.3

The Arabic Readers of the Koran

Paul E. Kahle

By studying problems connected with the Masoretic text of the Hebrew Bible, I came across an Arabic manuscript belonging to the collection of rare Arabic texts of Mr. A. Chester Beatty, of which I was preparing a catalogue at that time. The manuscript deals with the reading of the Koran and seemed to me to be of a certain importance as it offered some striking parallels to the development of the Hebrew Masora. So I published the text with the translation in my Schweich Lectures on the Cairo Geniza and discussed the problems connected with the text.[1] Later on I came across a second manuscript confirming in several directions the results I had found. I have dealt with this text in an article, "The Qurʾān and the ʿArabīya," which I wrote as a contribution for the Goldziher memorial volume (pp. 163–82), which as I hear will be published in the near future. But since writing this article, new problems have arisen, especially in connection with the correspondence with Professor Johannes Fück of Halle University, a great authority on Islamic tradition, and I believe it advisable to discuss here the whole problem again.

At the International Congress of Orientalists held in 1905 in Algiers, Carl Vollers, an expert not only on classical Arabic but also on the Arabic spoken in Egypt, where he had been for many years the director of the Khedivial Library, tried to show that the Koran was read by the Prophet in a language in which many of the rules of classical Arabic were not

Paul E. Kahle, "The Arabic Readers of the Koran," *Journal of Near Eastern Studies* 8, no. 2 (April 1949): 65–71. Reprinted with the permission of the University of Chicago Press.

observed; that this language, therefore, differed clearly from the classical Arabic in which the Arabs are accustomed to read the Koran. The classical language was developed in the century after the Prophet on the basis of Bedouin poetry by early grammarians and readers of the Koran, and to this language the consonantal text of the Koran was adapted.

The reading of this lecture in an Islamic country gave rise to a real revolt among the Muslim members of the Congress. Vollers then developed his theory in his book *Volkssprache und Schriftsprache im alten Arabien.*[2] He attempted here to characterize the language spoken in Mecca at the time of the Prophet on the basis of variant readings in the Koran that he collected from various sources. He presumed these to be *unofficial* readings, rejected in general by the authorities, and he attributed their great importance to the fact that their mode of transmission gives every guarantee that they belong to the time of the Prophet, his contemporaries, or the succeeding generations. Thus he arrives at the conclusion that these readings belong to the language actually spoken in the seventh century in Mecca. He describes this language in his book. The last paragraph is devoted to the *Iʿrāb*, the vocalic endings of Arabic words according to the rules of the classical language. He is convinced that, besides this official language, a more simple language existed in Mecca at that time that was more in accordance with Arabic dialects and with other Semitic languages. A chief characteristic of that language was that the *Iʿrāb* was not generally observed in it. It might have been used by certain tribes of the Bedouins, but even there it was only the privilege of the higher language, in the main restricted to metrical poetry.

From this statement Vollers draws the conclusion that the language of the Koran had been transformed on the whole in accordance with the poetry of the Nejd Bedouins. This transformed language had been victorious and had destroyed or driven aside the local and individual shape of the original language. For more than twelve hundred years this language had been regarded as the original, genuine, and undisputed language of the Holy Book.

It is well known that serious objections were raised to the whole theory of Vollers, especially by an authority like Theodor Nöldeke. He pointed out several misunderstandings and shortcomings in Vollers's deductions. The material with which he argues is really very insufficient. Nöldeke's chief objection against the theory was: *if the Prophet and his faithful companions had read the Koran without* Iʿrāb, *the tradition of it would not have been lost without a trace.*

Traditions that the Koran was read sometimes without *Iʿrāb* have not been generally known so far. Vollers refers to two traditions reported by as-Suyūṭī (d. 911 A.H.), but he correctly remarks that, for so late an authority as as-Suyūṭī, it was unthinkable that the Koran should ever have been read without *Iʿrāb*. As-Suyūṭī tries to understand these traditions as referring to stylistic and rhetorical elegancies.

When Gotthelf Bergsträsser was writing the new edition of the third part of Nöldeke's *Geschichte des Qorāns*,[3] he passed over Vollers's arguments in silence. For him the chief source of information on the reading of the Koran is the introduction to the book on the Ten Readers composed by Ibn al-Jazarī (d. 833 A.H.) under the title *An-nashr fi'l-ḳirā'āt al-ʿashr*. This introduction is of value for him especially from the historical point of view, because it is rich in quotations from earlier books on this matter. Nobody will deny the great value of that book. But I think that Bergsträsser did not reckon with the possibility that in the historical retrospect of such a leading handbook only such problems were reported and discussed as were not in conflict with the generally accepted views of later times. Bergsträsser is not aware that the sources used by him do not help us to understand the real conditions in the beginnings of Islam. He discussed the two conditions that had been stipulated by Ibn Miḳsam (d. 354 A.H.)—correctness of the language and conformity with the text of ʿOthmān—and declares that the first condition was of no great importance. He tries to explain it by referring to the fact that a great number of clients (*mawālī*) who entered Islam often caused incorrectness in reading the Koran, but they were of no importance, as too many genuine Arabs participated in these readings who had a strong feeling for the correct language.

This is hardly right for the beginning of Islam. As far as we know, one of the reproaches against Ibn Miḳsam was that points and vowels were added by him to the ʿOthmānic text on the only condition that the readings were justified by the rules of Arabic grammar. According to Ibn Mujāhid, his opponent, every reader had to conform to one of the Seven Readers. When in 322 A.H. Ibn Miḳsam's practice was condemned by a court of lawyers and readers, before which he had to appear, summoned by the Sultan, he had to recant and his books were burned, and we know of them only from occasional quotations. If these books had been preserved, we might find in them several things that could help us to understand the conditions of earlier times. The same may be said about many books now lost to us.

Even Otto Pretzl did not see clearly the problems which exist here. In his learned article "Die Wissenschaft der Koranlesung,"[4] he describes a number of texts dealing with the reading of the Koran. Many of these books were hitherto unknown. Pretzl refers to the fact that books on the reading of the Koran are generally of much later origin than books dealing with more profane matters, such as, for instance, grammar, and he suggests that books devoted to religious problems were submitted to a sharper scrutiny. The fact that on the whole only late commentaries or comparatively recent books were available to us was the reason that no special attention was devoted to these studies in the West. He hopes that on the basis of the material made available by him, new results for the history of the language and the religion may be obtained by these studies.

When he himself, however, would review these problems, he confined himself to reproducing the ideas of ad-Dānī, one of the chief authorities for the later orthodox practice. But in the books composed by that authority we rarely find any new light shed on the early period of Islam. The reason why earlier books have disappeared may be that the problems discussed in them were uncongenial to later times. The Muslims themselves hesitated to propagate books of that kind.

Nevertheless, the tradition that the Koran was read sometime without *Iʿrāb* was not altogether lost without trace, as Nöldeke supposed. I have already referred to the two texts that I have found among the manuscripts of Mr. Chester Beatty. With the text of al-Farrāʾ, published in my Schweich Lectures on the Cairo Geniza, I will deal later on. First I have something to say on the other text. It is the book *At-tamhīd fī maʿrifat at-tajwīd*, composed by al-Mālikī (d. 438/1046), where these problems are discussed in full. The first part of this book contains sayings exhorting the people to read the Koran in a dignified and beautiful manner. It is of a more general character, interesting too, but not of special importance. The second part contains ten chapters of which the long chapter 6 deals with the problems discussed here. It has the heading "On Urging the Readers to Make Effort of Seeking the *Iʿrāb*" and contains more than 120 exhortations admonishing people to use the *Iʿrāb* in reading the Koran. The first thirty-one traditions are attributed to the Prophet, the next thirty-six (nos. 32–67) to his companions, the rest (nos. 68–122) to the followers and to the followers of followers. The most important of these traditions are those attributed to the Prophet and his companions. I have published a translation of these sixty-seven exhortations in my contribution to the Goldziher memorial volume. The following specimens may give an impression of the kind of exhortations contained in these traditions.

(1) The Prophet said: Whoever recites the Koran and reads with *Iʿrāb* the whole of it, shall have for every letter forty recompenses. Whoever reads with *Iʿrāb* a part of it and uses *laḥn* in a part, shall have for every letter twenty recompenses. Whoever does not read anything with *Iʿrāb*, shall have for every letter ten recompenses.

(2) Whoever learns the Koran and reads it with *Iʿrāb*, shall have the reward of the veracious (*ṣiddīḳ*), the martyr (*shahīd*).

(3) Whoever recites the Koran and does not read it with *Iʿrāb*, for him God has appointed an angel who writes it down for him (correctly) as it was revealed, and he has for every letter ten recompenses. When he reads a part of it with *Iʿrāb* and a part without *Iʿrāb*, for him God has appointed two angels who write for every letter twenty recompenses. And when he reads the whole with *Iʿrāb*, God has appointed for him four angels who write down for him for every letter seventy recompenses.

(6) Whoever recites the Koran according to any method, for him God has written ten recompenses and canceled ten evil acts and elevated ten degrees. Whoever reads a part with *Iʿrāb* and a part with *laḥn*, for him twenty recompenses are written, twenty evil acts are canceled, and twenty degrees are elevated. Whoever recites the whole of it with *Iʿrāb*, for him forty recompenses are written, forty evil acts are canceled, and forty degrees are elevated.

(7) Whoever recites the Koran and reads it with *Iʿrāb*, he has a favor with God which is granted to him, if he desires he hastens it for him in this world, if he desires, he reserves it for him in the other world.

(8) Whoever learns the Koran with *Iʿrāb*, he is like the warrior on the path of Allāh (*mujāhid fī sabīli-llāh*).

(30) Behold, some of the poetry is wisdom, and if anything from the Koran is dubious to you, look for it in the poetry, for it is the Dīwān of the Arabs.

(32) Abū Bekr: I would prefer to read with *Iʿrāb* a verse from the Koran than memorize a verse.

(46) ʿAbdallah b. Masʿūd: Read with *Iʿrāb* the Koran, for it is Arabic. There will come a people who would like to correct it, but they are not the best of you.

(67) ʿĀisha from her father: Learn the poetry, for it brings the *Iʿrāb* onto your tongues.

These few specimens—ten of more than 120—may be considered sufficient. The rich material preserved by al-Mālikī shows clearly that correctness of language in reading the Koran was of real importance. Offenses against the *Iʿrāb*, the vocalic endings of grammatical forms, were much more frequent than scholars like Bergsträsser and Pretzl were willing to admit. Professor Johannes Fück, with whom I had a long correspondence on this problem, pointed out that a great number of these traditions collected by al-Mālikī could have been known before. Of the sixty-seven exhortations translated by me, he has found nearly forty in the great Thesaurus of traditions collected by al-Muttaḳī al-Hindī (d. 975/1567) in his *Kanz al ʿummāl*, published in eight volumes in Hyderabad in 1312–14 /1894–96, half a century ago. It is true that in this vast collection these traditions are distributed among different chapters and are not easily found. Al-Mālikī brought them together in a very convenient and impressive way on about fifty pages of his book.

Have we any possibility of dating the traditions collected by al-Mālikī? From the fact that they were attributed to the Prophet and his companions we cannot necessarily conclude that they really go back to these authorities. Such texts are, however, of great value for studying the ideas of the people of that time. As al-Mālikī composed his book at a comparatively late time (400/1010), it is very likely that not all these traditions are from the same time and origin. Fück pointed out that none of these traditions are mentioned by al-Bukhārī or Muslim or the other canonical collectors of Ḥadīth, and he concludes that these authorities may have had the impression that these traditions did not belong to the first century A.H. That is really not very likely, as, for instance, the grammatical terms and other items occurring in some of these traditions reflect problems in which people were interested from the second century onward. On the other hand, traditions of that kind cannot be later than the second century, as al-Farrāʾ, who was living in the second half of the century, knows of them.

The traditions collected by al-Mālikī show, therefore, that, let us say, in the second century the classical Arabic language was not generally used for reading Koran—that it certainly did not dominate in such a way as was supposed by Bergsträsser, for whom, as we have seen, correctness of language, one of the conditions stipulated by Ibn Miḳsam, seemed to be of no importance. What were the conditions in the time before?

There are two alternatives. First, the Prophet and his companions read the Koran according to the rules of classical Arabic. In this case we have to suppose that the language spoken by the Ḳuraish in Mecca, to whom the Prophet belonged, was in the main identical with it. The incorrectness in reading the Koran that existed in the second century was caused by the Mawālī, the non-Arabic clients who had entered Islam in great numbers. That was the supposition of Bergstässer, who, however, did not realize that the incorrectness in reading the Koran had spread in such a way that in about 400 an author like al-Mālikī was able to collect more than 120 exhortations to read the Koran correctly. The other alternative is that, in the language spoken by the Ḳuraish in Mecca, the rules of classical Arabic were not observed; that the Prophet and his companions did not use classical Arabic in reading the Koran, the language now connected with the Holy Book. Then we have to suppose that this model language was worked out on the basis of Bedouin poetry by the early readers and grammarians. To this model language the text of the Koran was adapted by a system of vowels and signs added to the consonantal text. This adaptation was finished in the second century. By that time people had to be admonished to use the *I'rāb* and to observe all the rules of classical Arabic in reading the Koran that had not been observed before. That is in the main the theory of Karl Vollers.

I think that the text of al-Farrā' published and discussed by me in the Schweich Lectures on the Cairo Geniza brings a clear solution of this problem. Al-Farrā' says:

> We have seen that the readers who know the book and the practice and are authorities on correct speech are agreed that it came down in the most correct forms of speech. This was opposed by some of those who investigated the poetry and "the days of the Arabs." They said: Those who claimed the excellence of the Koran have merely done so in accordance with what God made obligatory for honoring the Koran but when we look for correctness of speech, we find it among the Bedouins.

But in this they disagreed. The people of Kufa said: *Correctness is to be found among the Asad*, because of their vicinity to them. The people of Basra said: *Correctness is to be found among the upper Tamīm and the lower Ḳais from ʿUkl and ʿUḳail.* The people of Medīna said: *Correctness is to be found among the Ghaṭafān*, because they are their neighbours. The people of Mecca said: *Correctness is to be found among Kināna b. Saʿd b. Bekr and Thaḳīf.*

We wished to refer them through tradition, analogy and example to the superiority of the speech of the Ḳuraish over all other languages. So we said: Do not the Ḳuraish surpass the people in the beauty of their statures, in the sagacity of their minds, in the fullness of their bodies? They answered: We know this as well as anyone. But sagacity and beauty came to them merely because the Arabs were accustomed to come to the sanctuary for Ḥajj and ʿUmra, both their women and their men. The women made the circuit round the House unveiled and performed the ceremonies with uncovered faces. So they selected them by sight and thought after dignity and beauty. By this they gained superiority besides those qualities by which they were particularly distinguished. We said: In the same way they were accustomed to hear from the tribes of the Arabs their dialects; so they could choose from every dialect that which was the best in it. So their speech became elegant and nothing of the more vulgar forms of speech was mixed up with it. . . .

Al-Farrāʾ refers then to the fact that in the language of the Ḳuraish, which he takes as identical with the official language of the Koran, certain irregularities are not to be found that occur in the language spoken by the Bedouins, and he continues: "Correctness came to them from their selection of pronunciation just as they selected their wives. And by this we refuted their arguments and reverted to the arguments of those who know the Koran better than they."

Al-Farrāʾ then quotes a number of traditions dealing with the correct reading of the Koran and exhorting people to use the *Iʿrāb* in reading it, quite similar to those collected by al-Mālikī. Some of al-Mālikīʾs traditions are quoted by al-Farrāʾ also.

Al-Farrāʾ admits that the statement that the Koran came down in the most correct form of speech was a dogma that had validity only for a convinced Muslim. There was no doubt that correctness of language was to be found among the Bedouins. From the words of al-Farrāʾ we learn that in the chief centers of early Islam, the early readers of the Koran went out to the Bedouins in their neighborhood in order to study their poetry. So far this poetry had been orally transmitted only. The early readers needed this poetry as a model for the language in which the Koran had to be read. The practical need of readers and grammarians seems to have given the impetus for collecting and recording pre-Islamic poetry at the beginning of Islam. On the basis of this material a model language was established. One of the characteristics of this model language was that the rules of *Iʿrāb* were carefully observed. When the Muslims were admonished again and again to use the *Iʿrāb* in reading the Koran, when they were told that reading the Koran with *Iʿrāb* was much more valuable than reading it without *Iʿrāb*, we have to draw the conclusion that the people admonished in this way had not been accustomed to read the *Iʿrāb* in their language. "Learn the poetry, for it brings the *Iʿrāb* onto your tongues," ʿĀisha is reported to have said.

Al-Farrāʾ was in a difficult position. As a *grammarian* he could not deny that correct Arabic was to be found in Bedouin poetry. As a good *Muslim* he had to believe that the word of God had been revealed to the Prophet in the most correct language. As a *theologian* he was not allowed to admit any alterations in the language of the Holy Book. So he had to find a compromise. He found it by declaring that the influence of Bedouin language on the language in Mecca had taken place long before the time of the Prophet. From the different tribes of the Arabs who had come on pilgrimage to Mecca, the Ḳuraish had been able to hear all kinds of Arabic. So they had been able to select from the different forms of Arabic the best of each, just as they had selected their wives. In this manner their language had become superior to all the languages spoken by Arabs, superior also to the language spoken by the Bedouins, since certain inaccuracies that are to be found in the language spoken by the Bedouins had not been taken over by the Ḳuraish and were not to be found in the language spoken by the people of Mecca. In such a way the model Arabic that was used for reading the Koran from the end of the first century onward was identified by al-Farrāʾ with the language spoken by the Ḳuraish in the time of the Prophet.

But the real conditions can easily be recognized. Al-Farrāʾ would certainly not have reported that the early readers went out to the Bedouins in order to study their language, when they had not really done so. Why did they go? They went out in order to study correct Arabic. This correct Arabic was found among the Bedouins. If the people of Mecca were accustomed to hearing correct Arabic spoken at home by the Ḳuraish, there was no need for them to go to the Bedouins. What could they have learned from the Bedouins under these circumstances?

The traditions preserved in these two manuscripts are really of importance. They not only show something of the real conditions of reading the Koran in the early times of Islam, they also give us an impression to what degree texts on reading the Koran have been corrected, revised, and purged. If neither Nöldeke nor Pretzl nor Bergsträsser had been able to discover hints of these problems in all the texts available to them, it does not prove that these problems did not exist. We can only conclude, on the evidence of these two manuscripts, that the texts available to them had been brought into accordance with the later adopted practice.

NOTES

1. Paul E. Kahle, "The Cairo Geniza," in *The Schweich Lectures of the British Academy, 1941* (London, 1947).

2. Carl Vollers, *Volkssprache und Schriftsprache im alten Arabien* (Strassburg, 1906).

3. Theodor Nöldeke, *Geschichte des Qorāns*, 2d ed., Vol. 3: Die Geschichte des Qorānstexts (Leipzig, 1938).

4. *Islamica* 6 (1934): 1–47, 230–46, 290–331.

3.4

The Beginnings of Classical Arabic

C. Rabin

Our knowledge of the structure of the Arabic language is only to a small extent due to modern research: For most of it we have to thank the Moslem medieval philologists of the three centuries preceding az-Zamakhsharī (1075–1143 C.E.). The grammar most widely used today, W. Wright's *Arabic Grammar*, goes back to C. P. Caspari's *Grammatica arabica* of 1848, which was based principally on Zamakhsharī, with some slight modifications due to the observations of H. L. Fleischer. In twice revising the work, Wright used extensively both the Muslim philologists and the work of European scholars based upon them. The revision by R. Smith and M. J. de Goeje for the third edition left the framework intact, so that we may without exaggeration say that the university student of our days is essentially offered the same course in Arabic grammar as the student of a late Abbasid *madrasa.*

The treatises on Arabic syntax by C. Brockelmann,[1] H. Reckendorf,[2] and R. Blachère[3] depart a good deal farther from the medieval system, without, however, breaking with it. If one considers how radically modern linguistics has abandoned the traditional approach to the grammar of European languages, we cannot fail to be struck by the extent to which the categories established by Sībawaihi and his predecessors in the ninth century C.E. are still felt to be serviceable.

In fact, upon closer examination it appears that the result of the exten-

C. Rabin, "The Beginnings of Classical Arabic," *Studia Islamica* 4 (1955): 19–37. Reprinted with permission.

sive modern research has been mainly to show certain deviations from the norms set up by the Arab grammarians, grouped around the traditional rules somewhat like the deviations around a statistical curve.

This is not accidental, nor is it entirely due to the thoroughness and acumen of the Arab philologists. It is due to the prominent place the study of the works of these philologists held in the education of those who wrote Arabic, combined with the constant reading of those very texts upon which the philologists had based their analysis: the Koran and the ancient poetry. At least since the end of the Umayyad period, Classical Arabic was not a spoken language, and like all purely literary idioms, naturally conservative, but the place occupied in its acquisition by systematic grammar is, as far as I know, unique among languages. In modern linguistics the question has been much debated by which psychological processes the *langue*, the system of language which lies behind our individual speech-acts, or *langage*, functions within our minds. With regard to Arabic there can be little doubt that the *langue* consisted principally of an articulate set of scientific statements, inculcated in one's youth. Reckendorf observed[4] that progress in the study of Arabic syntax was unlikely as long as it produced only average views ("Durchschnittsbilder"), not studies of individual periods or authors. The fact is that the average view is identical with the philologists' system, while the detailed studies provide systems that will always largely cover it, but where certain sets of deviations may in fact give the whole a markedly different structure. Since, however, the *langue* remains the same throughout, and does not allow any such deviations to become part of itself, a true diachronic treatment of Arabic grammar appears to be an impossibility. Vocabulary and style, on the other hand, though also extensively studied by the philologists, were not fixed by them with the same rigidity. A continuous development is therefore observable, and one hopes that the sound foundations laid for this study in J. Fück's *Arabiya*[5] will lead to a rapid development of research in this field.

Where structure is concerned, research can hope to reach results independent of the Arab philologists only in the study of that period of the language before their influence became decisive, a period which is, of course, also of particular interest as being the formative stage of the literary idiom. At first sight this seems a manageable task, since we possess literary remains of that period (sixth–eighth century C.E.) that are extensive enough to allow us to examine all aspects of the language and yet not too large to permit a total examination. As soon, however, as we look more closely into these sources, the question arises: What is it that we are investigating?

The material falls into four groups:

(1) Pre-Islamic and early Islamic poetry. With regard to the former, doubts have been raised as to authenticity, and we must, even if we consider the corpus as a whole authentic, reckon with the possibility of any individual verse or poem being a later forgery. Both pre-Islamic and early Islamic poems have been revised by editors, as can be seen not only from the extensive variants, but also from the not infrequent cases where verses are quoted by grammarians for some linguistic oddity, while on looking up the *Dīwān* we find the same line slightly reshaped so that the oddity is eliminated. Nevertheless, we possess here a first-class source for the study of the pre-Islamic language.

(2) The Koran. Here again, variants affecting grammar are frequent, and a certain amount of working-over by philologists is admitted, for example, in the introduction of the *hamza*-sign into an orthography representing a pronunciation that had eliminated the *hamza*. On the other hand, variants affect only circumscribed aspects, as the consonant skeleton has, at least since the Othmanic revision in ca. 650 C.E., been carefully guarded from alteration.

(3) The Traditions (*ḥadīth*). These have been extensively used as a source for syntactic phenomena by Reckendorf, and recently by Bloch,[6] who employed mainly examples drawn from this category to represent prose as opposed to poetry. Here the problem of authenticity, raised first by Goldziher, is nowadays generally answered in the negative.[7] Although even on these modern assumptions many traditions go back to the beginning of the second Islamic century, that is, before the development of philology, an investigation by an Oxford research student, J. L. Pollard—whose untimely death is a great loss to our studies—shows that in the form in which we get them in Bukhārī and Muslim, they are considerably changed by the introduction of archaizing and pseudodialectal elements, some taken from poetry, which are still absent from the older versions of the same traditions.

(4) A small number of first-century papyri and documents handed down in works on history. These include treaties and letters said to have

issued from the secretariat of the Prophet[8] which, if genuine, would be extremely valuable evidence for the language used in writing at the time the Koran was revealed.

Medieval Muslim writers were generally agreed on two points: (1) that the language in which the poems were composed was identical with the spoken language of the bedouins of central and eastern Arabia; and (2) that the language of the Koran was the spoken language of the Prophet, that is, the dialect of Quraish. Since they also held that the language of the Koran was essentially the same as that of the poems, and that it represents Arabic at its best and purest, some[9] drew the conclusion that the dialect of Quraish was the most correct of all Arabic dialects. At the same time, the philologists did not obscure the fact that considerable differences were known to have existed between the different dialects; on the contrary, they collected them assiduously, so much so that it has been possible to achieve at least a partial reconstruction of those dialects.

In modern times these statements have been felt to be incompatible, though by no means by all scholars.[10] In some cases statement 1 or 2 was accepted at its face value and the other rejected. Thus Ṭā hā Ḥusain[11] drew from his acceptance of the identity of Classical Arabic and the dialect of Quraish the conclusion that all pre-Islamic Arabic poetry, except that attributed to Hijazi poets, must be forged. K. Vollers,[12] on the other hand, accepted the view that the bedouins of Nejd and Yamāma spoke a form of Classical Arabic, and concluded that the Koran could not have been conceived in this language, but was only made to conform with it by an extensive process of revision. Its original form Vollers sought to find in the noncanonical readings, which provided a composite picture of a "vulgar tongue" that structurally belonged to the colloquials, not the old dialects, and in particular had lost the case endings (*iʿrāb*).

It is interesting to note that both Vollers and Ṭāhā Ḥusain include in their treatment of the question lengthy chapters on the ancient dialects of Arabia, for it is the relation of the classical language to the dialects that really provides the key to the question.

I believe J. G. Wetzstein was the first to claim that Classical Arabic was not the spoken language of the poets who used it for their poetry. This view has been accepted by practically all more recent European writers who discussed the matter at all, whether they believed, with Wetzstein, the classical language to be different from all ancient dialects, or to be based on one or several actual dialects.[13] In recent years it has become usual to call it the "poetic *koinē*"—not an entirely happy term, since the Greek *koinē* was, after all, a spoken language, and Classical Arabic, on this view, resembles more closely the status of Homeric Greek. This language is discussed at length in R. Blachère's *Histoire de la littérature arabe*,[14] which also adduces numerous examples of such separate poetic idioms in other societies.[15]

Apparently independently, H. Fleisch,[16] R. Blachère,[17] and C. Rabin[18] arrived in the forties at the conclusion that the language of the Koran, far from being pure Meccan either subsequently revised (Vollers) or slightly adapted to the poetic idiom,[19] was none other than the poetic *koinē*.[20] The deviations from the usage of the poems were seen to be due to unconscious backsliding into the Meccan dialect. Some of them may, as Fück has pointed out,[21] be explained as due to the novelty and difficulty of its thought, as well as to the fact that it was perhaps the first attempt to write Arabic prose. Indeed, the latter aspect is put forward with much force, and with apposite parallels from the history of Hebrew, by H. Birkeland,[22] whose discussion, though not touching upon the question of idiom, lends much support to the theory just mentioned.

As against this, P. Kahle[23] about the same time went in for a spirited revival of Vollers's theory. Nöldeke[24] had adduced against it that, if the Prophet and his contemporaries had recited the Koran without *iʿrāb*, the tradition of it would not have been lost without a trace. Kahle—whose merit in Hebrew studies is to have led research from late and harmonizing sources back to the genuine old traditions—claims that this impression was due to Nöldeke's ignorance of certain old sources. He adduces numerous traditions from a *tajwīd* work of about 400 A.H.[25]—many of them traceable in earlier collections—exhorting people to read the Koran with *iʿrāb*, and statements in a fragment by al-Farrāʾ, a Kufan grammarian who died in 207 A.H., to the same effect. Thus he comes to the quite correct conclusion that in the second Islamic century the Koran was frequently read without *iʿrāb*. It is less easy to follow him in the further conclusion that this proves the Koran to have been recited from the beginning in this manner, and the case endings to have been introduced only by Koran readers who had studied Classical Arabic from poetry and by contact with Bedouin tribes.

The tenor of the traditions quoted, which promise heavenly rewards for reading the Koran with full or even partial *iʿrāb*,[26] shows clearly that private recitation by the uneducated is intended, not that by trained readers. The opposite of *iʿrāb* is called *laḥn*; hence, we may conclude that the injunctions do not necessarily refer to complete omission of the case endings, but to their wrong use. We have numerous anecdotes proving that even noble Arabs frequently erred in this matter, and that it was the fear of blasphemous meanings by misplaced case endings that caused the insistence on correct *iʿrāb* as much as the desire to have the Koran recited beautifully. Indeed, it would matter little if these traditions, instead of being probably invented in the second century, really went back to the time of the Prophet, for there must have been many among his followers whose divergent linguistic background caused them to commit solecisms.

It is even possible that the habit of *reading* without vowel endings is old. As is well known, the case endings are omitted in Arabic spelling, which writes all words as if they stood in absolute initial and pausal position. This, of course, is due to the habit of dictating slowly, with automatic pausal pronunciation. But if writing was slow, reading of the Kufic polyphonous script cannot have been fast, and the same adaptations may well have been made. While they did not matter in private letters or books, they were naturally discouraged in reading Koran or poetry. In ordinary prose, sentences were generally turned in such a way that no misunderstanding could arise by the omission of the case endings, which thus became something of a luxury.[27] Poetry, on the other hand, could permit itself certain types of tmesis ("Sperrung") that depended for their effect entirely upon the presence of case-signs.[28] The Koran, too, contains quite a number of phrases that do not make sense unless they were conceived with case-vowels.

The insistence on the presence or absence of case endings ignores the fact that the dialect of Quraish was not simply Classical Arabic minus the *iʿrāb*. It is not possible today to turn a piece of colloquial Arabic into literary by adding case endings. If anything, the dialect of Quraish must have been more unlike the classical than the present-day colloquials, which, after all, are derived from Classical Arabic or from a *Vulgärarabisch* closely related to it. Had the Koran been composed in either the dialect of Quraish or in a "vulgar tongue," no amount of revision without altering the consonant outlines could have made it as similar to classical as it is. One need only consider the havoc the one consistent Quraishism, the omission of *hamza*, has played with the spelling. If, however, the language of the Koran made concessions to the literary *koinē*, the *ʿArabiyya*, then it must needs have accepted also the case endings, that feature which was felt to be so essential that it was called by the same word as the use of that language itself, *iʿrāb*. Fück[29] may well be right in seeing in the words Sura XVI.103/5 *wa-hādhā lisānun ʿarabiyyun mubīnun* evidence that Muhammad himself was conscious of using the Bedouin *ʿArabiyya*, since elsewhere in the Koran *ʿarab* means "Bedouins."

A question that strangely enough no one seems yet to have asked is this: What reasons caused Muhammad to address his fellow townsmen in a language that originated, and was at the time used, for narrowly circumscribed purposes in Bedouin society, and that mainly in regions fairly remote from Mecca? It has, of course, been long recognized that the acceptance of a standard language has nothing to do with the intrinsic merits of the dialect chosen, but is mainly determined by the social prestige of the group from which the dialect emanates, or, in some cases, by spiritual forces using the dialect for their expression. The biography of the Prophet suggests in some of its episodes that the Quraish valued their genealogical connections with Bedouin tribes, and were in any case interested in attracting Bedouins to their fairs and religious ceremonies. It is possible, therefore, that the self-valuation of the nomad aristocracy was accepted by the townspeople to such an extent that they adopted also the language and the poetry that were the cultural badge of honor in that society. Muhammad's attitude to Ḥassān b. Thābit and Kaʿb b. Zuhair rather supports this, though we must remember that both belong to the Medinean period, when the Prophet was interested in extending his sway over Bedouin tribes. Another possibility is that Christian missionaries, starting from Hira, had picked upon the language of the poets, so highly valued at that court, as the vehicle for carrying the Gospel through Arabia. It would be a natural choice, because it was a dialect already widely understood and respected. If indeed these missionaries used a pre-Islamic translation of the Gospels into Classical Arabic[30]—and they must have had *some* written material—then the mere existence of a literature written in it would have lent it immense prestige and encouraged those who, like the Quraish merchants, recognized the usefulness of writing to employ the same language. Besides, there can be no doubt of the presence of some

Christians at Mecca. The documents handed down as Muhammad's letters and treaties may well have undergone some alterations, but it seems that they provide fairly strong evidence that the use of Classical Arabic in documents was already established in Mecca at the time. However strange the materials on which the Companions had written down the revelations,[31] the fact that they were written down shows that here was a society where people already placed more reliance on writing than on their memory, and that the language of the revelations was a recognized written idiom with a more or less established spelling. We may speak of a Meccan "office" language, which was there to be used for the new literary purposes.

This theory would also explain how Muhammad could so violently reject the poets while at the same time using their language: If he received the poetic *koinē*, so to speak, at one remove, he might not have been conscious of the connection. Finally, there may be some kernel of truth in the assertion of the superiority of the language of Quraish, and that it contained all that was best in the other dialects, if these statements refer to the written "dialect," not to their spoken language. After all, a great deal of what we are told about other tribal dialects refers to the special nuances of that tribe's literary usage rather than to their spoken dialect. If this theory is accepted, it would also affect our view of the Hijazi features in the style of the Koran. Many of them might not be due at all to the Prophet's imperfect command of the *ʿArabiyya*, but might have been taken over by him as recognized features of a local linguistic tradition.

I would hasten to add that this suggestion still leaves a large number of loose threads. The theory of Vollers and Kahle, on the other hand, seems to me to founder completely on this very problem. If both Muhammad and the Meccan aristocracy were using their own colloquial exclusively, and if the semi-Bedouin inhabitants of Medina saw nothing wrong in divine revelations being delivered in a "vulgar tongue," what were the reasons for accepting the Bedouin language as an absolute authority in the first and second Islamic centuries, when that Meccan aristocracy was all-powerful and the star of the Bedouins in the descendant? If in the century before Muhammad we are entitled to surmise the working of social forces of which we have no clear record, we have no right to do so in a period fully in the light of history. Unless the prestige of the *koinē* had been securely established before the conquests, I cannot see any way of it having become so established afterward. If, on the other hand, the respect for the *rāwī*, the guardian of correct usage in the accepted literary language, was transmitted by the Arab ruling class to the *Māwalī*, we can understand that the latter turned to people like Khalīl b. Ahmed in order to perfect their knowledge of the language, and finally to Bedouins as informants for their incipient philological studies.

Bloch's researches[32] throw some additional light on our problem. Though restricting himself on the whole to the order of words, he appears to have established the point that the language of poetry does not, within Classical Arabic, constitute a special poetic variety, in the way, say, that the language of poetry does within biblical Hebrew.[33] He shows, however, that a number of words and forms are preferred because they go more easily into meters,[34] and that in general poetry freely uses constructions that are distinctly rare in prose. Bloch himself quotes G. Bergsträsser's dictum that the chief characteristic of Arabic syntax is the restriction of the large choice of proto-Semitic constructions to a few standardized types.[35] This tendency of development is thus shown to continue into the development of Arabic prose out of the poetic *koinē*. It is obvious that we have to reverse Bloch's approach, and not to treat poetry as a special case of a language principally used as prose but, on the contrary, prose—in Arabic at least—as a special use of an idiom normally associated with poetry. The freer syntax of the poems and of the Koran—and this is likely to apply to most of the Koranic particularities noted by Nöldeke[36]—is the original state of affairs, while the more regularized constructions of prose style are peculiar to the latter. The only construction Bloch found to be unparalleled in prose, *idhā* clauses with the subject following immediately upon the conjunction,[37] appears to be an archaism preserving the emphatic-demonstrative character of the particle.[38]

Another possible archaism of the poetic language is stated by W. Caskel,[39] namely, that in pre-Islamic poetry diptotes and triptotes "are not yet strictly distinguished."[40] This would be a difference of great interest if it were quite sure that the distinction between diptotes and triptotes developed only within Arabic, or, according to this view, within the *ʿArabiyya*. However, it has been suggested that diptosy existed in Ugaritic;[41] and Old-Accadian, in denying case inflection to proper names,[42] seems to have a similar phenomenon. It may thus be preferable to follow for once the Arab philologists in treating this confusion as a poetic license. It may well owe its wide extension to different usages in this respect in the home dialects of the poets, a factor that is perhaps also responsible for the bewildering variety of case usage in coordinated phrases.[43]

An interesting problem is raised by Bloch's list of common forms and constructions unsuitable for poetry because they contain sequences of three short syllables that fit into few metres, and of four short syllabes that fit into none, for example, *faʿala, faʿalatā, malikuka, fafaʿalahū*.[44] The existence of such forms seems to be a forceful argument against the theory that the language was largely created by the poets;[45] the syllabic structure must have existed in the dialect or dialects on which the *koinē* was based, and which the poets did not feel entitled to alter. Even if such forms were never used in a line of verse, they existed virtually in the system, and were at hand when a prose emerged that was not bound to certain rhythmic sequences.

No progress seems to have been made in recent years in solving the problem of the place of origin of the poetic *koinē*. We have still no data to place it any more exactly than in the general region of Nejd, Yamāma, and the Euphrates. The position of Hira as an early center of poetry, and the fact that the earliest cycle of poems is connected with the War of Basūs, which took place in the Euphrates region, would give a certain preference to that part of the area. As against this, Imruʾul-qais, one of the earliest great poets, was of Kinda, and the Kinda empire somehow seems to provide the natural background for the emergence of an Arab national art.

The real clue should, of course, be provided by comparison with the ancient, pre-*ʿArabiyya*, dialects. Interest in these dialects has become widespread in recent years, and between 1940 and 1951 not less than four full-sized studies dealing with the subject have appeared: by H. Kofler,[46] I. Anīs,[47] A. Ḥammūda,[48] and C. Rabin.[49] Kofler's is the most complete collection of material and references, though without an attempt at geographical evaluation.[50] Anīs concentrates on phonetic matters, trying to provide something like an Arabic comparative phonology. Ḥammūda draws upon an important source not used by the others, the Koran commentary by Muḥammad b. Yūsuf Abū Hayyān.[51] My own treatment, along the lines of geographical linguistics, is an attempt to recognize the common features of a group of dialects, those along the Western highlands, with particular stress upon the Hijazi dialect.

Between them these four works exhaust pretty well the information that is to be gotten out of Arab philologists concerning the grammar and syntax of the dialects. A good deal of work still remains to be done on their vocabulary, and is likely, as in the case of European studies in geographical linguistics, to provide us with better criteria for dialect geography than is done by grammar. It is disappointing, however, that all this work has brought us no nearer to a solution of the problem of the *koinē*. No dialect or group of dialects within the above-mentioned wide area has emerged with a special claim to be the cradle of the *ʿArabiyya*. On the contrary, precisely those regions in which poetry was cultivated most—the Euphrates region, Tamīm, the areas of Nejd bordering on the Hijaz—have turned out to have spoken dialects rather distinct from the poetic idiom. It is unlikely that a study of the vocabulary will give clearer results, for vocabulary is easily borrowed, and it has long been recognized that the poetic idiom has widely borrowed from different dialects.

The mystery is deepened by the epigraphic languages of Arabia. After the systematic presentation of the grammar of South-Arabian by M. Höfner[52] there can be no possible doubt that we have here a language completely distinct from Arabic, and the researches of W. Leslau[53] show that it forms a group together with Ethiopic and possibly Accadian, so that any genetic connection with Arabic is becoming increasingly unlikely. Some of the results of Rabin,[54] as well as a recent study by I. Al-Yasin,[55] suggest connections of Arabic with Northwest Semitic. Arabic has generally been considered to form part of a separate branch of the Semitic languages called South Semitic or Southwest Semitic. Among the features distinguishing this branch are the preservation of a wider range of dental consonants and the broken plurals. The first feature is now known also to have distinguished Ugaritic, a Northwest Semitic language known since 1929, and the broken plurals are almost certain to be a late development, which has little value as a genetic criterion. It is, of course, an entirely different question to what extent Classical Arabic contains South Arabian loanwords, or was influenced in its style by South Arabian.

While thus the various South Arabian dialects are not very closely connected with Arabic, there is every likelihood of a close connection between Arabic and several languages known to us only through short inscriptions and graffiti in the northwest of the peninsula and to a smaller extent in the neighborhood of the Persian Gulf. These "proto-Arabic" languages are distinguished as Thamūdic, Liḥyānic, and Ṣafāitic. In recent years the number of known graffiti has much increased, and grammatical research has been pushed forward.[56] From references to various events it has been concluded that graffiti in these languages continued to be incised until well into the third century C.E.,[57] perhaps even up to the lifetime of the Prophet.[58] They are thus not far removed from the time to which we can ascribe the data recorded as referring to the ancient dialects or the period generally considered to be that of the beginning of Arabic poetry.

These languages resemble Arabic closely in their phonological system. Their vocabulary is similar but distinct. Because of the briefness and stylistic monotony of the texts their grammar is imperfectly known, but it shows some striking differences from Arabic, for example, a definite article *h-* (sometimes *hn-*) resembling Hebrew. The cultural connection between them and the later bearers of Arabic poetry is amply demonstrated by the large common fund of proper names, some of which can be traced back as far as Assyrian inscriptions about fights with "Aribi" of the ninth and eighth centuries B.C.E., while some are still borne by present-day Bedouins in Arabia and North Africa.

The strange thing is that these languages or dialects throw no light upon the linguistic development of Arabic. They are a group quite distinct from the dialects mentioned by the Arab philologists, and none of their distinctive traits can be traced among data about those dialects. The reason for this seems to be, partly, that the area covered by them, later called that of the Quḍāʿa tribes, took no part in the poetic activities of the sixth century,[59] and was not reckoned as part of the region whose Arabic was correct. Yet there are some data available concerning Quḍāʿa dialects, and none of these fit in with what we know about the three proto-Arabic languages. As is well known, Arab historical tradition has much to tell about *al-ʿarab al-bāʾida*, lost tribes without genealogical connection with those of historical times. Some such tribes were actually still in existence, such as the Jurhum, from whose language a second-century authority[60] purports to give twenty-four words. Some of the dialects dealt with by the philologists differ so strongly as to suggest that they belong to an older layer. Indeed, for the Ḥimyar dialect spoken in the uplands of Yemen and the Azd dialect of the isolated coastal areas of Oman in the east and Asir in the south,[61] the map suggests that they were remnants of earlier North Arabian expansions surrounded by seas of later, more "Arabic" arrivals.

At one time it was generally assumed that Arabia was the home of the Semitic peoples. The Arabic language, that is Classical Arabic, was likewise assumed to differ but little from the proto-Semitic parent language. It appeared as a quiet pool, opposed to the stormy development of the other Semitic languages. The realization that the camel was domesticated only around the beginning of the first millennium B.C.E., and that human settlement in Arabia is likely to date from that event, is now leading ever wider circles to a view of that country as an area of immigration as well as emigration, a meeting place of ethnic elements coming from various directions. These movements produced language mixtures[62] and a checkered map of linguistic boundaries, islets, and isolated remnants of earlier migrations. I have tried to explain the chief linguistic cleavage of pre-Islamic Arabia, that of West Arabian and the eastern dialects, as being due to the meeting of genetically disparate linguistic groups.[63]

Classical Arabic is seen to stand at the end of a development, not at its beginning. When this development becomes clearer, as one hopes it will now that the archaeological reconnaissance of the peninsula has begun, its ancestry may well turn out to be a highly complicated one.

POSTSCRIPT

The important study "Stress Patterns in Arabic" by H. Birkeland[64]—which I saw only after the completion of this article—introduces a new problem into the question of the relation between the ancient dialects and the *ʿArabiyya*. The author shows (p. 12) that the fixed expiratory stress of the modern colloquials of Syria, Iraq, and Egypt was superimposed on a state of language that had long and short vowels where Classical Arabic has them, but had at that time already lost the *hamza* of words ending in *-āʾ*. He further comes to the conclusion that this older state of the language had no fixed expiratory stress at all. Both the absence of such a fixed stress and the loss of *hamza*, however, are features of West Arabian. On the other hand, we find that the ancient East Arabian dialects had a strong fixed expiratory stress, and that the reductions caused by it show it to have been just in the places where it is in the above-mentioned colloquials. It is reasonably certain that the eastern dialects had preserved the *hamza* of *-āʾ*, especially as they are said to have had in a few cases *-āʾ* as against Hijazi -*ā*;[65] since the Arab grammarians do not know the concept of stress, and the structure of -*ā'* nouns is such that tell-tale contractions cannot occur, we shall never know how these words were stressed in the ancient eastern dialects.

In any case, the colloquial situation presents a curious mixture of eastern and western features. One explanation might be that fixed stress spread in a "wave" movement from the Persian Gulf area, that it reached the home of the standard *ʿArabiyya* too late to affect its vocalism, and affected the Fertile Crescent and Egypt only after their spoken dialects had lost the final *hamza*. This theory fits in with Birkeland's discovery that in the Maghribine colloquials the same fixed-stress pattern is superimposed on another fixed-stress pattern, or, in other words, that it reached those colloquials only after a lengthy development bad taken place (p. 28). The situation in the ancient eastern dialects is, as far as I can see, fully consistent with the assumption that fixed expiratory stress was a fairly recent innovation. It may even have been due to contact with speakers of Aramaic, a language in which the effects of stress play a prominent role.

NOTES

1. C. Brockelmann, *Grundriss der vergleichenden Grammatik der semitischen Sprachen*, vol. 2 (1908).

2. H. Reckendorf, *Die syntaktischen Verhältnisse des Arabischen* (1895–98); *Arabische Syntax* (1921).

3. In M. Gaudefroy-Demombynes and R. Blachère, *Grammaire de l'arabe classique* (1937).

4. Reckendorf, *Arabische Syntax*, p. iii.

5. J. Fück, *ʿArabiya* (Berlin, 1950).

6. Bloch, *Vers und Sprache im Altarabischen* (Basel, 1946), *Acta Tropica*, Suppl. 5.

7. See especially J. Schacht, *Origins of Muhammadan Jurisprudence* (Oxford, 1950).

8. Collected by M. Hamidullah, *Documents sur la diplomatie musulmane*, etc. (Paris, 1934).

9. Cf. C. Rabin, *Ancient West-Arabian* (London, 1951), pp. 21–23. The theoretical foundation of this view, said ibid., p. 22, to emanate from Ibn Fāris, seems in fact to be due to al-Farrā', cf. P. Kahle, *JNES* 8 (1949): 70 col. 1.

10. For instance, P. Dhorme, *Langues et écritures sémitiques* (1930), p. 53, and L. H. Gray, *Introduction to Semitic Comparative Linguistics* (1934), p. 5, accept unquestioningly the identity of Classical Arabic with the Meccan dialect. Even Fück, *Arabiya*, pp. 2–3, is rather vague on this point, though he admits that the Meccan dialect may have differed from the Bedouin dialects as much as these last did between themselves.

11. Ṭāhā Ḥusain, *Al-Adab al-jāhilī* (Cairo, 1927).

12. K. Vollers, *Volkssprache und Schriftsprache im alten Arabien* (1906).

13. A list of views in Rabin, *Ancient West-Arabian*, p. 17. An interesting new suggestion is that of W. Caskel, that the *ʿArabiyya* originated among the settled populations of NW Arabia and was transported into Central Arabia as part of the process of Bedouinization (*ZDMG* 103 (1953) p. 34; trans. in "Studies in Islamic Cultural History," *American Anthropological Association Memoir* 76 (April 1954): 43.

14. R. Blachère, *Histoire de la Litterature arabe* (Paris, 1952), vol. 1, pp. 66–82.

15. Ibid., pp. 80–81.

16. H. Fleisch, *Introduction à l'étude des langues sémitiques* (Paris, 1947), pp. 97–101.

17. R. Blachère, *Introduction au Coran* (Paris, 1947), pp. 156–69.

18. Fück, *ʿArabiya*, pp. 3–4 (the manuscript was sent to the publisher in 1947).

19. So Brockelmann in *Grundriss*, vol. 1 (1908), p. 25.

20. This was also the view of Brockelmann in 1947, according to a note in Fleisch, *Introduction à l'étude des langues sémitiques*, p. 100.

21. Fück, *ʿArabiya*, p. 3.

22. H. Birkeland, *Språk og religion hos Jøder og Arabere* (Oslo, 1949), pp. 35–41. See, however, below.

23. P. Kahle, *The Cairo Geniza* (London, 1947), pp. 78–84; *Goldziher Memorial Volume I* (Budapest, 1948), pp. 163–82; *JNES* 8 (1949): 65–71.

24. F. Nöldeke, *Neue Beiträge zur sem. Sprachwissenschaft* (1910), p. 2.

25. Al-Ḥasan b. Muḥammad al-Mālikī, *At-tamhīd fī maʿrifat at-tajwīd* (Chester Beatty MS. no. J. 152).

26. So, and not, as Kahle has it, "whoever reads a part with *iʿrāb* and a part with *laḥn*."

27. Cf. O. E. Ravn, *Om nominernes bøjning*, etc. (1909), p. 21.

28. Ibid., p. 117.

29. Fück, *ʿArabiya*, p. 2.

30. Cf. Violet, *OLZ* 4 (1901) 384–403; A. Baumstark, *Oriens Christianus*

18 (1934): 55–66; B. Levin, *Die griechisch-arabische Evangelien-Uebersetzung* (1938). The numerous reminiscences of the New Testament discovered in the Koran by W. Rudolph (*Abhängigkeit d. K. von Judentium und Christentum* [Stuttgart, 1922]) and K. Ahrens ("Christliches im Q.," *ZDMG* 84 [1930]: 15–68, 148–90) really presuppose an Arabic written source, not mere oral preaching. Wellhausen also believed that Christians were the first to use Arabic as a literary language (*Reste arabischen Heidentums*, p. 232).

31. Papyrus scraps, stones, palm leaves, bones, pieces of leather, and pieces of wood; cf. Nöldeke, *Geschichte des Qorâns*, 2d ed., vol. 2, p. 13.

32. See above, n. 6.

33. Cf. G. R. Driver, *Hebrew Poetic Diction*, Supplements to *Vetus Testamentum* (1953), vol. 1, pp. 26–39.

34. Pp. 7–10.

35. Bloch, *Einleitung in die semitischen Sprachen* (1928), p. 135.

36. Nöldeke, *Neue Beiträge zur semit. Sprachwissenschaft*, pp. 5–23; French translation by G. H. Bousquet, *Remarques critiques sur le style et la syntaxe du Coran* (Paris, 1954).

37. P. 105.

38. Cf., for instance, Rabin, *Ancient West-Arabian*, p. 38.

39. In the lecture quoted above, n. 13; p. 37 of the English, p. 29 of the German version.

40. For examples, cf. Wright II, pp. 387–88.

41. C. H. Gordon, *Ugaritic Grammar*, 2d ed. (1947), p. 43.

42. W. von Soden, *Grundriss d. Akkadischen Gramm.* (1952), p. 81, par. 63 f.

43. E. g., Wright, II, 40C, 97A.

44. Pp. 7–10.

45. This seems to be, among others, the opinion of Brockelmann in *EI*, I, 408b.

46. "Reste altarabischer Dialekte," *WZKM* 47 (1940)–49 (1942), altogether 188 pp.

47. *Al-lahajāt al-ʿarabiyya* (Cairo, ca. 1946), 183 pp.

48. *Al-qirāʾāt wal-lahajāt* (Cairo, 1948), 226 pp.

49. See n. 9.

50. A briefer treatment, partly along geographical lines, based upon Kofler's material was undertaken by E. Littmann in his article, *Bāqayā l-lahajat alʿarabiyya fī ʾl-adab al-ʾarabī, Majallat Kulliyyat al-Ādāb*, 10, no, 1 (May 1948): 1–44. Another interesting attempt to work out features of a single local dialect is by K. Petráček, "Material zum altarabischen Dialekt von al-Madīna," *Archiv Orientálni* 22 (1954): 460–66.

51. See Nöldeke, *Geschichte des Qorâns*, 2d ed., vol. 3, p. 243.

52. M. Höfner, *Altsüdarabische Grammatik* (Leipzig, 1943).

53. "South-East Semitic," *JOAS* 63 (4–14); "Vocabulary Common to Accadian and S.-E. Semitic," *South-East Semitic* 64 (1944): 53–58.

54. Cf., e.g., Rabin, "Archaic Vocalization in Some Biblical Hebrew Names," *Journal of Jewish Studies* 1 (1948): 22–26; "The Ancient Arabic Dialects and Their Relationship to Hebrew," *Melilah* 2 (1946): 243–55 (in Hebrew); *Ancient West-Arabian*, pp. 196–69.

55. I. Al-Yasin, *The Lexical Relation between Ugaritic and Arabic* (New York, 1952), providing 660 equations, not all of them equally certain.

56. Bibliography by G. Ryckmans, *Le Muséon* 61 (1948): 137–213. A. v. d. Branden, *Les inscriptions thamoudéennes* (1950). Good introduction in E. Littmann, *Thamūd und Ṣafā* (1943).

57. Cf. Rodinson, *Sumer* 2 (1946): 137–55; a line in Thamudic appears on a Nabataean stela of 267 C.E.

58. F. V. Winnett, *JAOS* 73 (1953): 41, dates a Ṣafāitic graffito in 614 C.E.

59. Cf. Lammens, *L'Arabie Occidentale*, p. 308.

60. Cf. Rabin, *Ancient West-Arabian*, p. 7.

61. Ibid., pp. 42–63.

62. The Tayyiʾ are said to have adopted the language of the Suhār, whom they had overcome, according to Yāqūt, *Muʿjam al-buldān*, vol. 1, p. 127; the Hudhail dialect betrays strong Eastern Arabic influence, cf. Rabin, *Ancient West-Arabian*, p. 79.

63. Rabin, *Ancient West-Arabian*, pp. 1–2.

64. *Avhandlinger utgitt au det Norske Videnskaps-Akademi i Oslo*, II, Hist.-Filos. Kl. 1954, No. 3; Oslo, 1954.

65. Cf. my *Ancient West-Arabian*, p. 141.

3.5

The Role of the Bedouins as Arbiters in Linguistic Questions and the *Mas'ala Az-Zunburiyya*

Joshua Blau

The Arabic sources appear to be unanimous about the outstanding role played by Bedouins in the development of Classical Arabic. For them, Classical Arabic is identical with the spoken language of the Bedouins. Whereas the Arabs dwelling in towns came in contact with the indigenous population, so that their language deteriorated, the Bedouins, it is claimed, preserved their speech free from contamination and continued to speak pure Classical Arabic, just as they had done in the days of the *djāhiliyya*. Not only did a real Bedouin not understand the gibbering of the lower strata of the settled population,[1] he could not even constrain himself to utter any locution offending the rules of Classical Arabic. The Arabic sources bristle with anecdotes that show how much the linguists of the first Islamic centuries depended on Bedouins in ascertaining the proper rules of Classical Arabic.[2]

Modern scholars have realized for some time that this is not borne out by the facts as related by the same Arabic sources. These tell us expressly that considerable differences separated the tribal languages from one another and thus confirm our a priori assumptions about dialects scattered over such a wide area as the Arabian peninsula. These various dialectal features were assembled in a comprehensive paper by H. Köfler[3] and independently collected again and evaluated for the West Arabian language area by C. Rabin, who applied the criteria of dialectal geography.[4] These

---

Joshua Blau, "The Role of the Bedouins as Arbiters in Linguistic Questions and the *Mas'ala Az-Zunburiyya*," *Journal of Semitics* 8 (1963): 42–51. Reprinted with the permission of Oxford University Press.

works clearly prove that the dialectal differences were so considerable that the various tribal languages must, to some extent at least, be considered as different idioms. Consequently, it cannot be maintained any longer that Classical Arabic is identical with the "Common Bedouin Language," simply because no such common Bedouin language existed, and, as is borne out both by general considerations and by the traditions transmitted by Arabic sources, the Bedouin local dialects differed from one another. Hence, there is substantial agreement among modern scholars[5] that to most or all of those who employed Classical Arabic for writing poetry it was to some extent a foreign idiom which had to be acquired. We may in this connection disregard the hackneyed question whether or not Classical Arabic emerged from the dialect of a single tribe. For our purpose it is enough to state that as early as the second half of the sixth century C.E., Classical Arabic showed every sign of being a common tribal language, being open to (i.e., freely borrowing from) the various Bedouin dialects in lexicography, and, as it seems, even in phonology, morphology, and syntax. Thus, it necessarily became something quite different from the everyday language of one tribe. Moreover, the elevated nature of poetic language and the subject matter of pre-Islamic poetry inevitably resulted in a language rather different from everyday speech. Typologically, however, Classical Arabic and the various ancient Arabic dialects were closely akin, being all of them languages of the synthetic type, that is, tending to express several notions by the same word, so that the need to change over from the dialects to Classical Arabic caused no real difficulties.

It is somewhat surprising that although modern research almost unanimously agrees about the differences between Classical Arabic and the individual Bedouin dialects before Islam, scholars continue to accept stories that presuppose a common spoken Bedouin language identical with Classical Arabic in the first Islamic centuries. Rabin, it is true, has stated his disbelief in clear terms,[6] but generally European scholars accept such stories. Even the most important recent publication on the development of Classical Arabic, J. Fück's *Arabiya*,[7] wholeheartedly accepts the thesis of a common Bedouin language, for all practical purposes identical with Classical Arabic. Being well aware of the dialectal differences between the Arab tribes before Mohammad, he arrives at the ingenious solution that this diversity was blurred during military expeditions and by the common life in the camps. Here the various Bedouin dialects intermingled and a common Bedouin language arose, which in the first centuries of Islam constituted the basis of Classical Arabic. Thus, though in the pre-Islamic centuries dialectal differences had occurred and no common spoken Bedouin language had existed, a common spoken Bedouin language emerged from the military camps. Consequently, it is suggested, we have no reason to doubt the reliability of stories depicting the dependence of the grammarians on the Bedouins, who, according to this view, were the arbiters in linguistic questions.

Despite its ingenuity, however, Fück's solution seems to us contrary both to the general trend of linguistic development and the express statements of our sources. It is clear that the centrifugal forces exceeded the centripetal. There was, no doubt, some general leveling of the dialects in the military camps, but this was only ephemeral. New dialects arose everywhere, the determining factor in each instance being the ancient dialect that happened to be prevalent.[8]

We have to assume that the great conquests and migrations affected the ancient Arabic dialects, but they resulted only in a variety of dialects and did not produce any common spoken Bedouin language. This is attested by the contemporary sources: Fück himself quotes Hamdānī's description of the complicated linguistic situation in South Arabic—already, it is true, in the tenth century—but we possess also an express statement of al-Djāḥiẓ[9] that in every province the dialect of the tribe that had settled there prevailed. According to al-Djāḥiẓ, this accounted for the difference between the dialects of Kufa, Basra, Syria, and Egypt. Furthermore, even the great variety of traditions about the most correct tribal language assume that the dialects were different from one another. So our contention that no common Bedouin language existed either before or after the Islam is corroborated both by general considerations and express attestation.[10]

Since no common Bedouin language existed, the stories in which every ordinary Bedouin poses as an expert in every fine shade of Classical Arabic must be considered as apocryphal. But how, then, did these apocryphal stories arise? There must have been a background favorable for them. Rabin, in our opinion, goes too far in maintaining that these stories were only "justified by the rich speech of the Bedouins and his natural rhetorical ability and by the fact that a tradition of Classical Arabic poetry still continued among the tribes for some centuries, as proved by the Diwan of Hudhail." Of these points, only the last is of real importance. It seems evident that the tradition of Classical Arabic poetry continued among the Bedouins largely because their conditions of life, in contradistinction to those of the settled population, had not changed, and still, as before Islam, constituted the background to Bedouin poetry. Another important point, adduced by Rabin, is that the native assistants of the schools were probably *ruwāt*.[11] These *ruwāt*, we may add, were experts in Classical Arabic poetry, as they continued to live among the same conditions as their ancestors and, therefore, were inclined to write in the same way. But besides these sociological reasons there was also a linguistic consideration that not only facilitated the survival of Classical Arabic poetry among the Bedouins, but, in our opinion, also contributed to the emergence of these apocryphal stories. This was the dichotomy of the Islamic Arabic dialects, divided into Bedouin and urban vernaculars. In an analysis of early Islamic papyri, the author has attempted[12] to prove that immediately after the great conquests the dialects of the settled population, which came in contact with foreign elements, became contaminated, so that vernaculars arose that may already be justly considered Middle Arabic dialects. These Middle Arabic dialects, though separated from one another by many dialectal differences, emerging, developing, and disappearing again in the way envisaged by the wave hypothesis, nevertheless exhibit a certain unity when compared with Classical Arabic and the Bedouin dialects. If we may reduce the different and intricate features that typify these dialects to a common denominator, the most conspicuous feature that characterizes them is that they diverge from the synthetic type, that is, they do not tend any more, like Classical Arabic and Bedouin dialects, to express several notions by one word, and instead approximate to the analytic type, generally expressing each notion by a separate word. The most obvious sign of this phenomenon is the disappearance of the cases and moods. Because of the chasm between Middle Arabic dialects and Classical Arabic, the urban speakers had to overcome considerable difficulties when they tried to use Classical Arabic, whereas even ordinary Bedouins, speaking, as in the *Djāhiliyya*, synthetic dialects closely akin to Classical Arabic, could do so relatively easily and were less apt than the urban population to make mistakes. It was therefore much easier for a *rāwī* of Bedouin stock to transmit Classical Arab poetry. Moreover, even an ordinary Bedouin, speaking his own dialect, may have appeared to speakers of Middle Arabic vernaculars of the lower strata of the town population to be speaking some kind of Classical Arabic, since he used case endings, the most conspicuous outward sign of the literary language. Against this background, the emergence of stories extolling the linguistic faculties of Bedouins becomes quite understandable. Sometimes we may assume that the heroes of these stories were not ordinary Bedouins, but *ruwāt*, referred to, as it seems, by expressions like *ʿarabun turḍā ʿarabiyyatuhum* ("Bedouins whose Arabic is agreeable"), *al-ʿarabu al-mawthūqu bihim* ("reliable Bedouins"), *fuṣaḥāʾ u-l-ʿarabi* ("correctly speaking Bedouins"),[13] *al-ʿarabu al-fuṣaḥāʾu al-ʿuqalāʾu* ("correctly speaking and intelligent Bedouins").[14] Other stories, however, illustrating the linguistic faculties of ordinary Bedouins, must be considered apocryphal, arising against the background of the somewhat paradoxical Bedouin superiority in linguistic matters, which depended on Bedouin *ruwāt* and the kindred character of Bedouin dialects and Classical Arabic. The Bedouins were also extolled, as Rabin his pointed out, as a part of the general idealization of early Islamic society and in accordance with the romantic hankering after the primitive in other urban societies, and, we may add, sometimes also from a taste for paradox, since the superiority of a common Bedouin to the refined citizen was not without a paradoxical touch. In some cases, too, Bedouin boasting has to be taken into consideration. Only in one field does the early Arab philologist seem to have relied on the ordinary Bedouin, that is, in lexicography. Apparently, in the early period the Arab philologists excelled each other in collecting every lexical detail from every source available, that is to say, Classical Arabic remained at this time lexicographically "open" to the Bedouin dialects, just as it had done before Islam, for this fitted well the Arab flair for *rariora* (*nawādir*).[15] On the other hand, the earliest philologists already seem to have restricted the range of "correct" orthographical, morphological, and syntactical usage, apparently adjusting the sources transmitted by them to the patterns they demanded. The fact that Koranic orthography was revised in accordance with the rules of Classical Arabic and that features like the omission of the glottal stop were excised,[16] presupposes a language with fixed rules already firmly established. The result is that Classical Arabic, as transmitted by the early philologists, is rich in vocabulary, but much more restricted in orthography, morphology, and syntax than one would have expected of a language "open" to a great number of tribal dialects.

We thus acquire new criteria for examining the reliability of stories about the linguistic superiority of the Bedouins. Some of these stories are, in our opinion, historical, since they refer to Bedouins who acted as *ruwāt* and were therefore masters of Classical Arabic. Sometimes even ordinary Bedouins were questioned on matters of lexicography. On the other hand, in matters of phonology, morphology, and syntax the ancient philologists were much stricter and appear to have restricted the old usages more and more; it is therefore unlikely that they relied on ordinary Bedouins in these fields. It must always be borne in mind that even the *ruwāt* did not generally speak Classical Arabic as their natural language. Thus, all the stories about Bedouins who simply could not speak anything but "correct" Arabic are to be regarded as apocryphal.

In the light of these criteria, it will be worthwhile to analyze an account of one of the most famous linguistic disputes, the so-called *masʾala az-zunbūriyya*. This story exists in several different versions. According to all of them,[17] the dispute took place in Baghdad between the famous grammarians al-Kisāʾī and Sībawayhi about the use of the accusative in two expressions. In the first, the problem was whether the continuation of the sentence *kuntu aẓunnu anna -l-ʿaqraba ashaddu lasʿatan mina -z-zunbūri* ("I thought that the scorpion stung more severely than the wasp" [*az-zunbūr*, whence the name of the dispute, "the question concerning the wasp"])—should be only *faʾidhā huwa hiya* or also *faʾidhā huwa ʾiyyāhā* ("And behold, the one is [like] the other"). The other problem concerned the sentence *kharajtu faʾidhā ʿAbdu -llāhi -l-qāʾimu/a* ("I went out, and behold, there was A., who was standing"), and whether it was correct to use *al-qāʾima* as well as *al-qāʾimu*. Whereas al-Kisāʾī considered the use of both nominative and accusative in each case as correct, Sībawayhi would only approve of the use of the nominative. It was agreed to refer the question to Bedouins,[18] who decided in favor of al-Kisāʾī. There were rumors that this decision had been brought about by bribery.

The grammatical issue in the dispute was thoroughly analyzed by A. Fischer. In the wake of H. L. Fleischer, Fischer demonstrated that the use of *ʾiyyā* in a phrase like *faʾ idhā huwa ʾiyyāhā* is attested and may be regarded as correct. The second accusative, however, in a phrase like *faʾidhā ʿAbdu-llāhi al-qāʾima*,[19] is, according to Fischer, rather harsh, being used on the assumption of the Kufic grammarians that a circumstantial phrase may also be definite.

The historicity of this story is generally asserted. Fischer, while taking account of the different versions, nevertheless inclines to regard the dispute as historical. Fück, who assumes the existence of a common Bedouin language that provided the basis of later Classical Arabic, and who therefore accepts the traditional view of the unlimited linguistic superiority of the Bedouins, adduces our story as proof that Bedouins acted as arbiters in linguistic questions.[20] Blachère apparently regards even the rumors about the bribe as historical, accepting them as proof of the low moral standards prevailing among Bedouins.[21] However, this last point, at least, seems to be apocryphal;[22] this part of the story is always attached to the main body rather as an afterthought. It is generally only connected by *wayuqālu* ("and it is said"), and the like, as, for example, in the *Mughni-l-labīb* of Ibn Hishām.[23] Very interesting is the passage quoted by Ibn al-ʿAnbārī[24] in the name of Basran authorities: *ʾammā mā rawauhu ʿani -l-ʿarabi . . . famina -sh-shādhdhi -lladhī lā yuʿbaʾu bihi . . . ʿalā ʾannahu qad ruwiya ʾannahum ʾuʿṭū ʿalā mutābaʿati -l-Kisāʾiyyi djuʿlan falā takūnu fī qaulihim ḥudjdjatun litaṭarruqi -t-tuhmati fi-l-muwā-faqati* ("And the traditions of the Bedouins [permitting the use of the accusative in the above-mentioned expressions] . . . are so isolated that one must not take them into account. And there is a tradition that they received a bribe in order to agree to the opinion of al-Kisāʾī, and if so, there is no proof to be adduced from their judgment, as it may be mistrusted.") This passage deserves special attention, as it proves that even in Basran circles the tradition concerning the bribe was not well founded. It is therefore not surprising that in some versions the bribe is omitted altogether, as by Suyūtī. In other sources, for instance one source in the *Mughni -l-labīb* and especially Ibn Khallikān,[25] the traditions concerning the bribing of the Bedouins are apocryphal when they depict the Bedouins as unable to utter an incorrect sentence and therefore forced to say only "al-Kisāʾī is right," instead of repeating the "incorrect" phrases approved by him. So one may claim that the acceptance of bribes was quite common among the *ruwāt* and, as Blachère himself perhaps intended to do, regard this part of our story as typical rather than historical.

Even the gist of our story, concerning the role of the Bedouins, seems to us unhistorical. It is so, no doubt, according to the version of Ibn Khallikān, which maintains that a single Bedouin acted as umpire. Certainly, Bedouin dialects were different from one another so that an expression like *faʾidhā huwa ʾiyyāhā* may have been familiar in one, but relatively unknown in another vernacular. Therefore, to apply to an unknown Bedouin, whose only qualification was his pure Bedouin speech, is rather like casting lots, since by chance this man may or may not have known the construction in question. Men like al-Kisāʾī and Sībawayhi, no doubt, were well aware of this fact and it is unlikely that they would have agreed to such a way of deciding the dispute. Even the tradition that several Bedouins acted as arbiters is not well founded. According to the tradition preserved by Ibn al-Anbārī,[26] it seems that all the Bedouins, of whom four are known by name, agreed with al-Kisāʾī, though it is not probable that Sībawayhi did not know a turn of phrase known to all or almost all the Bedouins. The tradition in *Taʾrīkh Baghdād*,[27] the smoothest and so, in our opinion, the latest version, relates that some of the Bedouins supported Sībawayhi, but eventually the majority decided in favor of al-Kisāʾī. This may have worked well, theoretically, in the case of *faʾidhā huwa ʾiyyāhā*, which is attested in Classical and Middle Arabic, but this version fails to explain how the majority of the Bedouins decided in favor of *faʾidhā ʿAbdu -llāhi -l-qāʾima*, which is described by Fischer as rather harsh and based only upon the theory of the Kufan grammarians that a circumstantial phrase may be definite as well. Could it, then, be imagined that the *majority* of the Bedouins would have supported the possibility of using such a construction, which, except in rhyme, could not be demanded even by *ḍarūrat ash-shiʿr*? It seems, therefore, that the whole story that the *masʾala az-zunbūriyya* was decided by Bedouins is apocryphal.

We have accordingly reached the conclusion that stories enhancing the role of Bedouins as arbiters in linguistic questions must be taken with a grain of salt. It was the dichotomy of the Arabic language as it emerged after the great conquests that produced these stories. On the one hand, there existed the Middle Arabic dialects of the urban population, analytic in type and typologically closely akin to the modern Arabic dialects, and on the other hand, the local Bedouin tongues, which had remained unchanged in their main features, and which were thus still close to Classical Arabic so that their speakers could readily change to speaking Classical Arabic. Since these dialects preserved, in contradistinction to the urban vernaculars, the most conspicuous outward sign of the synthetic trend, the case endings, townsmen listening to them might have been given the superficial impression that they were hearing Classical Arabic. If we also remember the fact that Classical Arabic poetry continued among the

Bedouins for both linguistic and sociological reasons, the general idealization of early Islamic society, the romantic hankering after the primitive, the delight taken in the paradox that the Bedouins excelled the cultivated urban population, and also Bedouin boasting, we shall understand how these stories developed. When examining them, one has to bear in mind the basic fact that Bedouin dialects, however close to each other and to Classical Arabic, differed from one another and from Classical Arabic in many respects, so that unknown Bedouins, as distinguished from *ruwāt*, could not be asked questions concerning morphology and syntax, whereas in the field of lexicography Classical Arabic remained open to Bedouin speech for a long while. The linguistic situation of the first centuries of the Islam, thus revealed to us, is complicated, as Middle Arabic and Bedouin dialects, which had developed along complex lines, mingled, absorbed each other and often converged, whereas Classical Arabic, typologically akin to the Bedouin dialects, served as the literary language.

NOTES

1. See Djāḥiẓ, quoted by J. Fück, *ʿArabiya* (Berlin, 1950), p. 66 n. 8.

2. See, for example, R. Blachére, "Les savants iraquiens aux IIᵉ–IVᵉ siècles de l'Hégire," *Mélanges . . . W. Marçais* (Paris, 1950), pp. 37–48, and Fück, *ʿArabiya*, pp. 29 ff., 66 ff.

3. "Reste altarabischer Dialekte," *WZKM* 47–49 (1940–42).

4. In his important work, *Ancient West-Arabian* (London, 1951).

5. See Rabin, ibid., p. 17; *Studia Islamica* 4 (1955): 19 ff.; *EI,* 2d ed., vol. 1, p. 565*a*.

6. Rabin, *Ancient West-Arabian*, pp. 17 ff.; it seems to us that he went too far in his skepticism.

7. Fück, *ʿArabiya*.

8. See W. Fischer, *Die demonstrativen Bildungen der neuarbischen Dialekte* ('s-Gravenhage, 1959), p. vii; see also the balanced judgement of C. Pellat, *Le milieu baṣrien et la formation Ǧāḥiẓ* (Paris, 1953), p. 125, on the formative factors of the dialect of Basra. Though allowing for the general leveling influence of the *koine* in the use of the troops in the military expeditions, he rightly takes into consideration the dialects of the principal tribes of Basra in the formation of a special dialect.

9. Ed. Sandūbi, 1926/7, I, 33, quoted by Fück, *ʿArabiya*, p. 65, and Pellat,

Le milieu baṣrien et la formation Ğāḥiẓ, p. 125, where the page quoted is mistaken.

10. For similar reasons Ferguson's (*Language* 35 [1959]: 616 ff.) contention that the modern Arabic dialects emerged from a *koine*, has to be rejected. In a Hebrew paper, published in *Tarbiẓ* 30 (1961), the author has dealt briefly (pp. 133–35) with the features claimed by Ferguson to represent this *koine*. A special paper devoted to this subject is still unpublished.

11. Blachère, "Les savants iraquiens aux IIe–IVe siècles de l'Hégire," p. 39, maintains that most of the Bedouins mentioned in the sources were also poets.

12. In his paper "The Importance of Middle Arabic Dialects for the History of Arabic," in *Scripta Hierosolymitana of the School of Oriental Studies* (Jerusalem, 1961).

13. Used by Sībawayhi, see Fück, *ʿArabiya,* pp., 29–30.

14. Used by Djāḥiẓ, see ibid., p. 66.

15. Cf., for example, the story quoted ibid., p. 69 n. 1, which is, in our opinion, applicable to such *rariora*.

16. For details see C. Vollers, *Volkssprache und Schriftsprache im alten Arabien* (Strasburg, 1906), without accepting his theory that variants in the Koran necessarily reflect ancient features. See also Rabin, *Ancient West-Arabian*, p. 9.

17. Deviations from this, it seems, have to be regarded as mere mistakes, see Fischer, *Die demonstrativen Bildungen der neuarbischen Dialekte.* See Fischer's account in *A Volume of Oriental Studies presented to E. G. Browne* (Cambridge, 1922), pp. 150 ff.; see also Fück, *ʿArabiya*, p. 30 n. 11.

18. See below on these *variae lectiones*.

19. Fischer, *A Volume of Oriental Studies*, p. 155, rightly rejects the view that Sībawayhi disapproved even of a phrase like *faʾidhā ʿAbdu -llāhi qāʾiman, qāʾiman* being indefinite.

20. Fück, *ʿArabiya*, p. 30.

21. Blachère, "Les savants iraquiens aux IIe–IVe siècles de l'Hégire," p. 48.

22. We do not even deal here with a source like *Taʾrīkh Baghdād*, which, being in favor of al-Kisāʾī, of course rejects the mere possibility of bribery.

23. Quoted by de Sacy, *Anthol. gram. arab.*, pp. 199–201.

24. Ibn al-ʾAnbārī, *Die grammatischen Streitfragen der Basrer und Kufer*, ed. G. Weil (Leiden, 1913), p. 294.

25. Ed. Bulāq (1299 A.H.), I, 487.

26. Apparently, Suyūṭī's version, and even that of Ibn Hishām, *Mughni -l-labīb*, are abridgements of Ibn al-ʾAnbārī, though it may be claimed that Ibn al-ʾAnbārī's version, which contains so much detail, is complementary to the shorter tradition, as preserved by Suyūṭī and Ibn Hishām.

27. Khaṭīb (Cairo, 1349 A.H.), XII, 105.

3.6

SOME SUGGESTIONS TO QUR'ĀN TRANSLATORS

A. Ben-Shemesh

I. THE MEANING OF "AL-RAḤĪM" IN THE QUR'ĀN

Two of God's ninety-nine "Most Beautiful Names," namely, *al-Raḥmān* and *al-Raḥīm*, are the most frequently mentioned in the Qur'ān. Apart from several instances in the text, we find them joined together in the "Opening" (B 'Sūrah I)[1] and in the first verse of all *B 'Sūrahs*, but one. Macdonald renders them as: "The Compassionate Compassionator."[2] As the Arabic root of both these epithets is *r ḥ m*, this rendering may be accepted as a correct literal translation. In B 'Sūrah XII.64, 92, however, this meaning is expressed by the words: *Arḥam al-Rāḥimīn*.

The English, French, and German translators seem reluctant to accept the notion that because these two attributes have the same root in Arabic, they are merely a repetition. They translate, therefore, both words differently.

For the purpose of this paper I shall quote a few divergent translations as follows:

"The most merciful God" (Sale), "The merciful the compassionate" (Arberry, Bell, Palmer), "The compassionate the merciful" (Rodwell, Dawood), "The Beneficient the Merciful" (Pickthall, Muhammad Ali). Blachère translates in French: "Le Bienfaiteur Miséricordieux," and Masson: "Celui qui fait miséricorde, le miséricordieux," while the Germans render them as: "Des Erbarmers, des Barmherzigen" (Henning and

A. Ben-Shemesh, "Some Suggestions to Qur'ān Translators," *Arabica* 16 (1969): 83. Reprinted with the permission of Brill Academic Publishers.

Paret in 1950) and "Des Barmherzigen und Gütigen" (Paret in 1966).[3] "Des Gnädigen des Barmherzigen" (Mahmud Ahmad, Pakistan 1959), "Des allbarmherzigen Gottes" (Grigull), "Des Allbarmherzigen" (Ullmann-Winter, 1964).

These various efforts to avoid repetition, together with the fact that among the ninety-nine names we find another attribute—*al-Ra'ūf*—that also connotes "the merciful" or "the compassionate," make *al-Raḥīm* look really repetitious and superfluous.

To avoid this, I humbly suggest, in my translation of the Qur'ān into modern Hebrew, which I am now preparing, to interpret *al-Raḥīm* as "the Beloved." I base my proposition on the following grounds:

(1) The Arabic and Hebrew root *r ḥ m* denotes two main emotions: love and compassion. They seem to be strongly related to the name *r ḥ m* in both languages, which denotes, according to the dictionaries, "womb," but originally meant "a female," a "mother." A relic with such a meaning is found in Judg. 5:30, where *Reḥem Raḥamatayim* means "a female or two." The ancient man, observing the natural love and compassion in the behavior of a mother toward the offsprings of her womb, called these emotions by the name the mother was known to him, that is, *r ḥ m.*

(2) However, these two names for the emotions of a mother did not enjoy an equal development. In Arabic and Hebrew the root was mainly used to denote "compassion," although we find a trace for its use for "love" in verse 2 of Psalm 18, where the words *Erḥamḥa Adonay* mean: "I love thee my Lord." In Aramaic, another sister language, the root *r ḥ m* was used to denote only "love" and not "compassion." In the Aramaic translations of the Bible, wherever the Hebrew root *a h b* ("to love") appears, it is translated by the root *r ḥ m*. The use of *raḥīm* denoting "beloved" must have been well known amongst the Jews in the centuries preceding Islam, like its twin, *raḥūm*. Even in modern Hebrew, Aramaic phrases with such meanings are used, for example, *Aḥī Raḥimā'ī* for "my beloved brother." Consequently, the Aramaic translation of the word *Erḥamaḥa* (Ps. 18:2) is given as *Aḥabbinak* from a root similar to the Hebrew *a h b* and the Arabic *Ḥabba* ("love"), which is used in the Qur'ān in the verses dealing with the love for God, as follows:

(a) In B' Sūrah II.160 (Per Bell's translation) a warning is given to the pagans "who love their idols with a love like that given to Allāh."

(b) In B' Sūrah III.29 it is said: " If you love Allāh follow me and Allāh will love you." This is repeated also in B' Sūrah v. 59.

(3) The love *for* God is therefore an essential element in the relation between Allāh and his creatures. In the ninety-nine attributes, however, we find only one epithet describing God's love, namely, *al-Wadūd*, that is, "the very loving," and nothing about God *being* loved. We have to remember that the love *for* God forms a most important part of the Jewish faith. In the *Shemà*, the children of Israel are ordered: "You shall love the Lord your God with all your heart and with all your soul and with all your might" (Deut. 6:5). Muḥammad repeatedly declares in the Qur'ān that he came to confirm the Bible. He makes several allusions to the *Shemà* and accuses the children of Israel of not complying with its contents (e.g., Qur'ān II.87, IV.48, VIII.21).

(4) The resemblance of the Aramaic attribute *al-Raḥīm* to the Arabic root *r ḥ m* caused one of the most important precepts of the faith, "to love God," to be overlooked. It can easily be rectified by interpreting *al-Raḥīm* to mean "the Beloved." This will restore it to its appropriate meaningful position as the third one amongst God's other attributes.

My proposition to place the epithet *al-Raḥīm* in its rightful dignified position does not preclude the use of it as an adjective in its "compassionate" sense. In all verses in which it is joined to a different root where an allegation of repetition is excluded, it certainly can be translated "the compassionate," and so in many other instances where the context so requires, for example, *al-Tawwāb al-Raḥīm, Ra'ūf Raḥīm.*

The *Basmallah* should therefore be translated: "In the name of God the compassionate the beloved."

II. THE MEANING OF FIR'AWN D̲Ū AL-AWTĀD

The name Fir'own (Pharaoh) appears several times in the Qur'ān but only in two verses with the epithet: D̲ū al-Awtād (Q. XXXVIII.2 and LXXXIX.9). The following different translations were given to this adjective:

"Pharaoh the contriver of the stakes." (Sale)
"Pharaoh the impaler." (Rodwell, Dawood)
"Pharaoh the lord of the hosts." (Muhamad Ali)
"Pharaoh of the Stakes." (Bell)
"Pharaoh, he of the tent-pegs." (Arberry)

The German and French translation adopt similar renderings, which make no sense and have no basis whatsoever. Now, the word *awtād* appears only three times in the Qur'ān: twice in the above-mentioned verses and once again in LXXVIII.7, where mountains are described as *awtād*. Relying on this passage it should be translated, "Pharaoh of the mountains." However, the only mountains a Bedouin could see in Egypt were the Pyramids, which look from far away like pointed tent-pegs, that is, *awtād*.

I therefore suggest that *Fir'own ḏū al-Awtād* should be translated as: "Pharaoh of the Pyramids," which is a most fitting and sensible translation based on the Qur'ān itself.

NOTES

1. My contention is that "Surah" is an arabicized form of the Hebrew name בשורה B' surah, that is, Gospel, given to the Christian Gospels during the early centuries of Christianity and adopted in the Qur'ān for "revelation."
2. *Short Enc. of Islam*, p. 34.
3. Paret explains this change "aus rein stilistischen grunden."

Part 4

Sources of the Koran: Essenian, Christian, Coptic

4.1

Introduction to the Dead Sea Scrolls

Ibn Warraq

Hundreds of Hebrew and Aramaic scrolls have been discovered in eleven caves near the Dead Sea since 1947. These documents, scrolls written on leather, one embossed on copper, thousands of fragments on papyrus or leather, have been dated to roughly between 200 B.C.E. and 70 C.E., with a small portion of the texts perhaps going back to the third century B.C.E., and the bulk of the extant material dating to the first century B.C.E.[1]

The caves in which the scrolls were found are located near a complex of ruins known as Khirbet Qumran, near the Dead Sea. Excavations revealed the existence of various buildings showing evidence of a community, which has since been identified as that of the Essenians, described by Josephus, Philo, and Pliny the Elder. It is also now recognized that the scrolls found in the caves must have come from this settlement of the Essenes. However, not all scholars are happy about identifying the Qumran settlement with the Essenes.[2]

In cave 11 were found eight[3] noncanonical psalms, of which four were known, prior to the recovery of the scroll from Qumran, in ancient translations. The scroll now reveals to us the Hebrew text on which these translations were based. All four poems were originally composed in Hebrew. None of them was written in the first century C.E., the date of the scroll itself; the youngest of the four may have been written as many as two centuries or more before the scroll was written. The so-called Psalm 151, which is in two sections, 151A and 151B, was excluded from the

Masoretic Bible (the standard Hebrew Bible) but was known through various manuscripts like the Septuagint, the Greek translation of the Old Testament made in Alexandria, which does not always correspond with the Hebrew Bible; in Latin through the Vetus Latina;[4] and in Syriac through the Syro-Hexaplaire (a Syriac collection of five noncanonical psalms). The Syriac and Latin translations were very probably made from the Greek translation.[5]

Edmund Wilson takes up the story:

> This 151st Pslam of the Septuagint now turns up in the new text as two separate pieces, which have evidently been combined in the Greek and Syriac versions and to some extent censored. This censoring is thought to be significant, because in this new Hebrew version [from cave 11 at Qumran] the flocks and the trees are made to respond to the music of David's lyre as they are not in the other versions. Now, the influence of the Greek cult of Orpheus, whose music was supposed to have enchanted its animal and vegetable hearers, is clearly traceable both in Jewish and Christian art, in the former of which Orpheus merges with David and in the latter of which with Christ. The animals and trees charmed by Orpheus are transformed into the sheep watched by David and the flock of that other good shpeherd, Christ. Among the frescoes of a third-century synagogue discovered at Dura-Europus on the Upper Euphrates, is one of Orpheus in a Phrygian cap playing his cithern to a monkey and a lion.[6]

Philonenko gives Dupont-Sommer's translation. But there was a certain amount of controversy about this translation. I give Edmund Wilson's summary of the issues:

> The scholars who have translated this psalm (151) have differed from one another in emphasizing or minimizing the supposed Orphic influence to be seen in it. Almost all of them, like Mr. Sanders, translate the words that precede the statement that the trees and the flocks respond to David's music as a statement that the mountains do NOT bear witness to the Lord nor do the hills proclaim Him. The Hebrew negative is certainly there, but M. Dupont-Sommer, in a paper called *David et Orphée* [Institut de France annual public session of Cinq Académies, Monday, 26 October 1964, Paris, plaquette no. 20, 11 pages], avoids these apparently

contradictory statements by interpreting these lines as questions: "Do the mountains not bear witness ?" etc. He regards the lines that follow as also betraying Greek influence—in this case, Pythagoreanism, a conception of the harmony of the world, the music of the spheres, which the pious musician imitates and reproduces on his lyre in homage to the supreme God. "For who will proclaim and who will recount the works of the Lord ? God sees the universe; God hears the universe, and he gives ear." The Hebrew phrase for *the all* J. A. Sanders simply renders as everything; Dupont-Sommer translates "l'univers" as I have left it above. . . . The Jews, in their reaction against the Greeks, would have eliminated any trace of Orphism of Pythagoreanism, hence the abridged version in the Septuagint and the Syriac texts of this Hellenistic psalm.[7]

I give Geza Vermes's English translation of Psalm 151A for comparison.

Hallelujah. Of David, son of Jesse

1. I was smaller than my brothers, and younger than the sons of my father.
   He made me shepherd of his flock, and a ruler over his kids.
2. My hands have made a pipe and my fingers a lyre.
   I have rendered glory to the Lord ; I have said so in my soul.
3. The mountains do not testify to him, and the hills do not tell (of him).
   The trees praise my words and the flocks my deeds.
4. For who can tell and speak of and recount the works of the Lord?
   God has seen all, he has heard all, and he listens to all.
5. He sent his prophet to anoint me, Samuel to magnify me.
   My brothers went out to meet him, beautiful of figure, beautiful of appearance.
6. They were tall of stature with beautiful hair, yet the Lord did not choose them.
7. He sent and took me from behind the flock, and anointed me with holy oil.
   As a prince of his people, and a ruler among the sons of his Covenant.[8]

151B in J. A. Sanders's translation:

At the beginning of David's power after the prophet of God had anointed him.

Then (I saw) a Philistine
Uttering defiances from the r[anks of the enemy]
. . . I . . . the . . .
. . .[9]

I now give Dupont-Sommers's French translation of 151A and B:

Alleluia! De David, fils de Jessé.
J'étais le cadet de mes frères
Et le plus jeune des fils de mon père.
At (celui-ci) fit de moi le pasteur de son troupeau
Et le chef de ses chevrettes.
Mes mains fabriquèrent un instrument de musique
et mes doigts, un lyre;
et je rendis gloire a Iahvé,
m'etant dit, moi, en moi-même:
"Les montagnes ne Lui rendent-elles pas témoignage ?
Et les collines ne (Le) proclament-elles pas?"
Les arbres prisèrent mes paroles
et le troupeau, mes poèmes.
Car qui proclamera et qui célébrera
et qui racontera les œuvres du Seigneur?
L'univers, Eloah, le voit;
l'univers, Lui l'entend, et Lui prête l'oreille.

Il envoya Son prophète pour m'oindre,
Samuel pour me grandir.
Mes frères sortirent à sa rencontre,
eux qui avaient belle forme et bel aspect,
qui étaient de haute taille,
qui avaient de beaux cheveux:
Iahvé Dieu ne les choisit point.
Mais Il envoya me prendre de derrière le troupeau,
et Il m'oignit de huile sainte,
et I fir de moi le prince de Son peuple
et le chef des fils de Son Alliance.

151B:

Commencement des hauts [fa]its de David, après
que le prophète de Dieu l'eut oint.
Alors j'[entend]is un Philistin qui défiait les
Li[gnes d 'Israel]
. . .[10]

Psalm 151A "is made up of seven pairs, or couplets, of bi-colons preceded by a short title. Hebrew poetry can be measured in sense-accented feet, or stresses ; the bi-colons in our psalm generally have the 3/2 metre save for verses 4 and 7, which have bicolons in 3 /3. . . . Psalm 151 A has two strophes clearly indicated by the slightly longer verses of 4 and 7, each of which closes a strophe."[11]

To end, I give Psalm 151 from the Septuagint:

This Psalm is a genuine one of David, though supernumerary, composed when he fought in single combat with Goliad.

I was small among my brethren, and youngest in my father's house: I tended my father's sheep. My hands formed a musical intsrument and my fingers tuned a psaltery. And who shall tell my Lord? the Lord himself, he himself hears. He sent forth his angel, and took me from my father's sheep, and he anointed me with the oil of his anointing. My brothers were handsome and tall; but the Lord did not take pleasure in them. I went forth to meet the Philistine; and he cursed me by his idols. But I drew his own sword, and beheaded him, and removed reproach from the children of Israel.[12]

NOTES

1. Geza Vermes, *The Complete Dead Sea Scrolls in English*, (Harmondsworth: Penquin, 1998), pp. 13-14.

2. Others associate the Qumran sect with the Pharisees, Sadducees, Zealots, or Jewish-Christians: see R. Eisenbaum and Michael Wise, *Dead Sea Scrolls Uncovered* (Harmondsworth: Penguin, 1992), pp. 5, 11.

3. Scholars do not always seem to agree: Vermes says there were seven noncanonical psalms found, *The Complete Dead Sea Scrolls*, p. 301, while Dupont-Sommer insists on eight: *La Bible: Ecrits Intertestamentaires*, ed. Dupont and M. Philonenko (Paris: Gallimard, 1987), p. 303.

4. Vetus Latina is a general term for all Latin translations of the scriptures prior to Saint Jerome's Vulgate (Saint Jerome 342 B.C.E.–420 C.E.). They show considerable variations since they were not the product of one translator, and they were translated from the Greek of the Septuagint, unlike Jerome's Vulgate, which was translated from the original Hebrew.

5. Most of the information in this paragraph, and the rest of this introduction,comes from J. A. Sanders, *The Dead Sea Psalms Scroll* (Ithaca, N.Y.: Cornell University Press, 1967), pp. 93–103.

6. E.Wilson, The *Dead Sea Scrolls, 1947-1969* (New York, 1969), pp. 145–47.

7. Ibid.

8. Vermes, *The Complete Dead Sea Scrolls*, p. 302.

9. Sanders, *The Dead Sea Psalms Scroll.*

10. Dupon-Sommer, *La Bible.*

11. J. A. Sanders, *The Dead Sea Psalms Scroll*, p. 94.

12. *The Septuagint Version of the Old Testament and Apocrypha*, with English translation by Sir Launcelot Lee Brenton (London, 1976), p. 787.

4.2

THE QUMRĀN SCROLLS AND THE QUR'ĀN

Eric R. Bishop

Rather more than ten years ago the first cave containing the Dead Sea Scrolls was discovered. Since then, besides the uncovering of the monastery of the Qumrān sectarians, other caves have yielded their literary treasures. According to computations, the books and pamphlets dealing with the "finds" run into hundreds. "The literature on the Scrolls," wrote Professor Rowley in September 1957, "is so enormous that any full reference to the discussions on the various points is impossible."[1] Whether or not there has been much reference in this accumulation to possible contacts in thought or diction as between Qumrān and the Qur'ān, which of course must mean the contemporary Arabian scene at the rise of Islam, is an equally unknown factor for the paragraphs that follow. In six or seven books that have been read, whether by Jewish, Christian, or secular writers (some books with indexes, some without), there would not appear to occur very much in the nature of cross-references to Islamic beginnings.[2] This is equally true of pamphlets and articles, including that in Arabic by Dr. Anis Frayha, whose discussion appears in the annual publication of essays by Near Eastern scholars, *Egyptian and Lebanese*.[3] It may be that it is still too early to look for anything definite or constructive. This must wait till the more important Qumrān documents have been translated into Arabic. Even the "Zadokite Work" from the Cairo Genizah, though known to Western learning for half a century, has not yet been done into Arabic.

Eric R. Bishop, "The Qumrān Scrolls and the Qur'ān," *Muslim World* 48 (1958): 223–36.

It may, therefore, be considered somewhat presumptuous at this stage to suggest possible affinities between the ideas of this monastic or largely monastic Dead Sea Community, now fairly certainly dated in the era immediately preceding and succeeding the Christian Dispensation, and the Semitic developments in Northern Arabia half a millennium and more later. Yet there can be little doubt that some time before Islam the knowledge of Old Testament personalities, accruing from Arabian contacts with the Jewish settlements in Yathrib, Khaibar, and elsewhere, would have been substantiated by the merchants who frequented the Great Incense Road on their travels from the Ḥijāz or Ḥaḍramaut en route to Egyptian Temples or eastern Mediterranean ports. Such merchants would become doubly familiar with the story of Lot and the cities of the Plain—after all, the Dead Sea is still known by Arabic-speaking people as Baḥr Lūt. The Qur'ān has some twenty-five verses in which Lot is mentioned, including those in Surat Hūd—a sura which deals with the attitude and fate of unbelievers in familiar Near Eastern localities. The discovery, too, of Abraham and Ishmael in pre-Islamic times in some sense must have helped to pave the way for the importance the pair came to occupy in the unfolding religion, as in its two monotheistic precursors. Furthermore, we have come to recognize an affinity, through this relationship, in the ideas and even canonical pronouncements of the Prophet, enshrined in the Qur'ān, which are today the treasured inheritance of so many millions across the heat belt of our world.

There is surely ample research, in this field of possible affinity between the Qur'ān and Qumrān, awaiting doctoral theses for the rest of this century. More important, it should also provide scope for sorely needed cooperative effort among Jewish, Muslim, and Christian scholars. For an inquiry of this nature, the student will be absolved from the consideration of questions involving the identification of personalities, whether Kittians, Wicked Priests, or different Messiahs. The research should only be directed toward common ideas and the forms in which they are clothed. Without being more imaginative, may it be permitted here merely to touch the fringe of this subject of tentative comparisons between Qumrān and the Qur'ān. Their general Semitic outlook would seem to invite closer investigation. It is for affinities, not for Qur'ānic dependence on or borrowings from Qumrān, that we are looking. As there are similarities in thought and language between Qumrān and the New Testament, these may also be found, if less distinctly, when adopted or adapted by Muḥammad.

A. "THE ANGEL OF TRUTH"

In the *Manual of Discipline* there is allusion to the "spirits of truth and error," followed by a reference to the "angel of darkness" and all the "spirits of his lot," who try to make the sons of light stumble; but "the God of Israel and His *angel of Truth* have helped all the sons of light."[4] If here there is some linguistic resemblance to the Johannine expression: "By this we know the spirit of truth and the spirit of error," attention must also be called to the phrase "His angel of truth." Both Stephen and Paul make reference to the service rendered by angels in the giving of the Law. "Ye who received law by the disposition of angels and have not kept it."[5] "The law was ordained through angels by the hand of a mediator."[6] What is plural in the New Testament, however, becomes singular in the Qur'ān. It is true that in the Meccan suras (as Dr. Watt and others have pointed out)[7] there is no reference to Gabriel, though the revelations during that period were mediated through Gabriel, since this archangel is generally regarded in Islam as the channel of inspiration. He is referred to as "the Spirit" along with angels in three Qur'ānic contexts.[8]

There is the expression in Surah LIII. *shadīd al-quwwā*,[9] as one who taught the revelation. Is it possible that, in the traditional account of the experiences of the Prophet at Mount Hirā', the phrase "the Truth came to him," with the "annunciation" that he was the Messenger of God, *could mean Gabriel*, comparing the statement in the *Manual of Discipline* concerning God's "angel of Truth"? It has often been suggested that, as his career progressed, Muhammad seems to have ceased differentiating between Gabriel and the Holy Spirit. There would appear a somewhat similar confusion between the "Angel of Truth" and the "Spirit" in the scroll. Anyhow we are confronted by people in the same circle of ideas; while in assessment the *Manual* is nearer to the agent in *inspiritation* according to Qur'ānic presentation than it is to the allusions in the New Testament. But there is a further point of affinity in the word for "Truth," which occurs so frequently in the scrolls and which is used (according to Dr. Gaster) "in the specific sense of the Mosaic Law."[10] Gaster says the Samaritans refer to this as *Qushta* or "the Verity." The sisterword in Arabic is *al-qisṭ* is the one employed in the passage in Ibn Hishām, where the biographer gives a version of the closing verses of Saint John 15, where our Lord is quoted as using the phrase *rūḥ al-qisṭ*—"Spirit of Truth," or perhaps "Justice" or 'Equity."[11] ("Justice" is how Arberry renders the word in his translation of the fourteen occurrences in the Qur'ān).[12] *Al-qisṭ* and *al-quds* are not dissimilar in sound.

B. "THE FRIEND OF GOD"

Abraham, in the Islamic form of Ibrahim, probably occurs more often in the Qur'ān (sixty-nine times) than the name of any other character.[13] In Surat al-Nisa' he is described in the same way as in the Epistle of Saint James[14] as "the Friend of God" *Khalīl Allāh* the phrase coming at the conclusion of a description of the well-doer:

> Who is there that has a fairer religion
> Than he who submits his will to God
> Being a good doer, and who follows
> The Creed of Abraham, a man of pure faith?
> And God took Abraham for a friend.[15]

Thus the Qur'ān; while the *Zadokite Document* states:

> Abraham, however, did not walk in this way (that of the sons of Noah who went astray). Therefore because he kept the commandments of God and did not prefer the desires of his own spirit, be was accounted the Friend of God and transmitted this status in turn to Isaac and Jacob."[16]

The word translated "Creed" by Arberry is *milla*, which has come to include much more than belief—it was more than this that Abraham transmitted to his posterity. There is an echo of this "cultural continuance" of the *milla* in Joseph's remark to the imprisoned baker and butler—that he was a follower of the *milla* of his fathers Abraham, Isaac, and Jacob.[17] One way or another, Qumrān and Qur'ān recognize, with Saint Paul, those who walk in the steps—follow the *milla* of our Father Abraham, the steps of that faith which he had in uncircumcision.[18]

C. "RIGHTEOUSNESS"

One thing leads on to another. With Abraham the whole relevance of "righteousness" and "piety"—*birr* and *taqwā*—is involved. While it is true that the adjective *birr* only occurs three times in the Qur'ān—of God where it is rendered "benign" or "beneficent," and of Yaḥyā and 'Īsā, when it is usually translated "dutiful," there are two occasions where the corresponding verb appears, in each case in company with another from a sister root.[19] The context is implicative of an attitude to life and society. There are references too to the abstract noun: "Help one another in piety and godliness." "Conspire not in sin and enmity . . . but conspire in piety and godliness."

The prayer toward the close of Surat Āl-Imrān: "O Lord, forgive Thou our sins and acquit us of our evil deeds, and take us to Thee with the pious,"[20] has the same kind of ring about it as the request put into the mouth of Balaam the son of Beor: "Lord let me die the death of the righteous, and let my last end be like his."[21] There is no need to labor the Old Testament emphasis on this characteristic, particularly in the Psalms and Proverbs, or the Pauline interpretation of righteousness in respect of Abraham, the paragon of piety for the three monotheistic faiths. But the issue is that, when the time comes for a fresh examination of the relationship of what is being called "biblical theology" with that of the Qur'ān, the Dead Sea Scrolls must not be left out in the caves of the wilderness of Judaea. One of the early adjudications of Dr. Brownlee, quoted by Professor Millar Burrows, has relevance in this connection—"The Sect had its birth in Biblical interpretation."[22]

> "Even those who practice righteousness are made liable to error."
> "All the ways of righteousness and truth."
> "A zeal for righteous government."
> "If a man casts his portion with truth, he does righteously."

Thus the *Manual*, where it is also stated that the duty of the Community shall be "to set the standard for the practice of truth, righteousness and justice." This is taken up again in the *Zadokite Document*, the moralizing being based on the words of Moses: "Not for thy righteousness nor for the uprightness of thy heart art thou going in to possess these nations, but because of His love wherewith He loved thy fore-fathers and because He would keep the oath."[23]

For the inheritance of the ancestral covenant applied to those who entered the "new covenant in the Land of Damascus"; but for those who lapsed from the proper observance of the rules there would be the visitation of Divine judgment. But when they have repented "they shall speak each to his neighbour to bring him to righteousness. . . ." "Then shall ye distinguish (again) the righteous from the wicked."

Similarly the formula for the blessing of the president of the Community, whom God "has appointed to judge the needy in righteousness." The *Book of Hymns* breathes much the same atmosphere: "For none can prove himself righteous when Thou bringest him into judgment. Though man may prove more righteous than man, none can contend (with 'Thee')."[24]

There is the same milieu of ideas, the same Semitic outlook. When even in these days there is in the Near East evidence of the inherent Semitic sense of the meaning of justice, piety, and righteousness, pervading a sequence of thought through the centuries, we should surely recognize an affinity derived from a shared ancestry; though at different stages the fuller implications, as we might acknowledge them in Saint Paul, may be reckoned insular or exclusive or undeveloped. The final verdict of the first Christians that their interest was not so much in a Teacher of Righteousness as in a Righteous Teacher sui generis, could never have reached Islamic thinkers in its simplicity or the Qur'ānic doctrine of *birr* would have approximated to the New Testament rather than Qumrān.

D. "ANCIENT SINNERS"

In the *Zadokite Document*, what leads to the discussion of "Millat Ibrahim" is the mention of the "Ancient sinners" who "fell" under the Divine wrath. Here is surely the correct Qur'ānic tradition of later times. Interestingly there is natural reference to the contemporaries of Noah. For Qumrān, those who went astray included members of his immediate family. This is again common ground with the Qur'ān, though a divergence is noticeable in the actual personalities who suffered from the cataclysm.[25] The previous notices of the "Watchers of Heaven" or "their sons whose height was like the lofty cedar" have their parallels in *'Ād and*

Thamūd, so far as Arabian folklore is concerned. For Qumrān and the Qur'ān, God's anger was kindled against such evildoers. Here the Dead Sea Scrolls would seem to emphasize the ultimate debt of much Islamic thinking to contemporary Arabian Judaism. When the Community was scattered by the Roman extirpation of so many thousands of Jews, it is tempting to suggest that some of the Qumrān adherents, rather than "members," may have found their way to the already established Jewish settlements in the Ḥijāz, to the permanent enrichment of the latter.

E. "QUMRĀN, THE QUR'ĀN AND THE ANGELS"

Then there is the whole question of Comparative Angelology. Belief in the angels is fundamental in the Creed of Islam.[26] There are the Four Archangels, two of whom figure in the New Testament, and to one of these reference has already been made. On the whole, however, they do not figure in Christian thought as in Islamic and Qumrānic. In the heavenly hierarchy in Islam, the archangels are supplemented by the Guardian Angels, the Recording Angels, the "Throne Bearers"; while there is Ridwan in charge of heaven; Malik, who presides over hell; Munkar and Nakīr, who visit the graves of the dead. There is some parallel here with scattered passages in the New Testament, the majority of the allusions (the Apocalypse apart) being perhaps to ministering angels. The more developed angelology of the Qur'ān is also found in the scrolls. The *Manual of Discipline*, the *Zadokite Document*, the *War Scroll*, and the *Hymns* have a full quota of references to angelic beings. Gaster enumerates five groups, three of them with considerable subdivisions. Besides the archangels, whom he designates "Protective," there are "Guardian Angels" (somewhat like the "Ministering"), and certain "Particular" angels possessed of special commissions. Then there are the angels described by another name—"Host of Heaven" or "of the Holy Ones," "Stalwarts" or "Glorious Ones"; and last, but not least, those who participate in the final eschatological war.[27] In this analysis there would appear some crisscrossing. But the total list is as impressive as that of Islam; while both Qumrān and Islām may be in debt to Persian thought. Millar Burrows in the "angelic" paragraphs in his chapter on Qumranic belief, notes a spiritual kinship with apocalyptic literature, agreeing that "sons of heaven" and "holy ones" are probably expressions that refer to angels.[28] In the *Manual of Discipline* he finds only one occasion where "angel" is used for a good spirit—"the angel of God's Truth." He refers, perhaps incidentally, to the curiously interesting coincidence with later Islamic history. The *War Scroll* tells how there are "holy angels with the army of the righteous." We cannot but be reminded of the Qur'ānic account of the Battle of Badr, which probably more than any other was the "Hastings" of nascent Islam, and the "Bannockburn" of Arabian paganism! In Surat Āl-Imrān is the following allusion:

> When thou wentest forth at dawn from thy people to lodge the believers in their pitches for the battle—God is All-hearing, All-knowing—when two parties of you were about to lose heart, though God was their Protector—and in God let all the believers put all their trust—and God most surely helped you at Badr, when you were utterly abject. So fear God, and haply you will be thankful. When thou saidst to the believers; "Is it not enough for you that your Lord should reinforce you with three thousand angels sent down upon you? Yea, if you are patient and godfearing, and the foe come against you instantly, your Lord will reinforce with five thousand swooping angels."[29]

Muhammad was, of course, looking back to an event in recent history, and in part accounting for the Muslim victory. But the *War Scroll* is more interested in eschatological warfare:

> Be of good courage for the battle of God; for this day has been determined as the day of battle—as the day of combat against all flesh. The God of Israel lifts up His hand with wondrous power against all the spirits of wickedness. And the Warrior angels gird themselves for battle; they are marshalled in serried ranks (and mustered for the day of combat).[30]

Two of the Qumrāni hymns have something of the same conception:

> . . . the hosts of heaven give forth their voice, and the world's foundations rock and reel; when warfare waged by the soldiers of heaven sweeps through the world.[31]
>
> His legions shall go marching from end to end of the earth.

Or once again in the War Scroll:

Warrior angels are in our muster.[32]

There is one difference in this attitude to angels as between the Qumrān sectaries and some at least of the more orthodox thinkers in Islam. The sectaries seem to have regarded the possibility of angels being sinful or good, much as in the Epistle of Jude.[33] The Qur'ān, moreover, refers to two such, *Hārūt* and *Mārūt*, as well as to the refusal of *Iblīs* to worship Adam. In the latter case Al-Taftazānī (for instance) claims that *Iblīs* was the exception who proved the rule of angels being usually good. He was "a lone Jinnī inexperienced in worship in the midst of the angels."[34] *Hārūt* and *Mārūt* on their part were, in his view, "uncommitted" angels, neither responsible for unbelief nor guilty of a great sin. They were rebuked like the prophets for inadvertence; they may have taught people magic, but it is not unbelief to teach magic. They failed to appreciate the failings of human beings, so were sent to earth for their testing. This difference, if such it be, should not deter us from recognizing some affinity in the general Qur'ānic attitude to celestial beings with that of the Qumrān sectaries. Professor Jeffery says that Muslim authorities are unanimous in regarding *malāk* as Arabic. But (he adds) there can be little doubt that the source of the word is Ethiopic, in which language the word bears the twin meanings of *angelus* and *nuntius*, thus making it correspond exactly with the Hebrew. His conclusion is that the "word seems to have been borrowed into Arabic long before the time of Muhammad, for the Qur'ān assumes that Arabian audiences are well acquainted with angels and their powers, and the form indeed occurs in the North Arabian Inscriptions."[35] There seems enough affinity in the Qumrānic and Qur'ānic systems of angelology to suggest the need for more detailed investigation.

F. "FIGHTING IN GOD'S WAY"

The Eschatological War naturally invites comparison with the Qur'ānic conception of the ideals and purposes of *Jihād*. The very title awarded to the scroll of the "War of the Sons of Light with the Sons of Darkness" brings to mind the "great divide" in early Islam, when the world around was either "*Dār al-Islam* or *Dār al-Harb*."[36] It is true that the *War Scroll*, as it progresses, seems to visualize the consummation of the world. But at the start there is direction for the extermination of opposing nations. There is a sequence in campaigning, a full nineteen years being devoted to warring against Near Easterners from Syria to Persia, from Lydia to Southern Arabia. It is quite obvious who, respectively, are sons of light and sons of darkness.[37] It is just as obvious who belong to *Dār al-Islām* and who to *Dār al-Harb*. For the *War Scroll* the inscriptions on the standards are proof enough. The warriors are to be "felling the slain to the judgment of God" or "subduing the enemy" by His might: or through pursuit to annihilate him in the Battle of God unto his eternal extinction,

> Thou art He that told us aforetime that Thou wouldst be in our midst, a great and awful God to make spoil of our enemies before us. . . . Your God is marching with you to do battle for you against your foemen to the end that He may save you.[38]

Though in the same Semitic realm of ideas, there are differences to note in this call to *Jihād*. For the Qumrāni and the Muslim alike *Jihād* was incumbent on the nation rather than the individual as such; but for the Muslim the extermination of opposing forces would not seem to have been primary, since the main object was winning these opponents over to Islam. The Qur'ān can speak for itself: "The believers fight in the way of God, the unbelievers fight in the idols' way. Fight you, therefore, against the friends of Satan; surely the guile of Satan is ever feeble."[39]

There was probably not much to choose between Satan and Belial. The Qumrāni, however, rather tended to regard his case as resting for justification on the past, something to which the first Muslims could hardly refer. Albeit it is a Semitic tendency to which later generations have too easily succumbed. Instead, in the Qur'ān the believer is urged to participation in *Jihād* by current considerations and future rewards for himself and others. The purpose is the spread of Islam. "And fight in the way of God with those who fight with you, but aggress not: for God loves not the aggressors."[40] Here however, we come against a contradiction with the famous verses at the outset of Sura IX.

> A proclamation from God and His messenger unto mankind on the day of the Greater Pilgrimage: "God is quit, and His messenger, of the idolaters." So if you repent that will be better for you; but if you turn your back; know that you cannot frustrate the Will of God. And give thou

> good tidings to the unbelievers of a painful chastisement: excepting those of the idolaters with whom you made covenant; then they failed you nought neither lent support to any man against you. With them fulfil your covenant till their term; surely God loves the God-fearing. Then when the sacred months are drawn away, slay the idolaters wherever you find them, and take them and confine them, and lie in wait for them at every place of ambush. . . ."[41]

These opening phrases are, as it were, in the best tradition of *Jihād*, an echo of the trumpets of carnage and the trumpets of ambush in the battles waged against the troops of Belial, when the Qumrāni would probably have refused quarter to the repentant, unlike the Quranic reservation. Then comes the paradox. The sectarians visualized a campaign of twenty-nine years or more, after six for mobilization, but every seventh year the recruitment of fresh soldiery is to cease and the sabbatical rest for Israel be observed. If in this latter phenomenon there is some parallel with the pre-Islamic custom prevalent in Arabia of maintaining guerilla warfare two-thirds of the year—with the remaining four months reckoned "sacred," when fighting was banned—the parallel is with a ruling that the Qur'ān abrogated. The Qumrānic prohibition was Semitic but not Qur'ānic. There came a time when the *ashhur al-ḥurum* would have to be disregarded. This verse in Surat al-Taubah was probably first invoked when Abū Bakr was faced with the reconquest of recalcitrant tribes, who were threatening to relapse into darkness after being sons of light. For his Khalīfah, as for the Prophet, *Jihād* had become a matter of military necessity; for the Qumrāni down by the Dead Sea wastes, the extermination of the anclent enemies, starting with Edom, Moab, and Ammon, just across the Sea of Lot, can never have reached much beyond the range of wishful thinking. There were always more Kittians in expanding circles. The Muslims in real life were to discover this as the seventh century merged into the eighth and *Jihād* itself took a different turn.

G. "THE PROPHET"

About two-thirds of the way through the *War Scroll*, before the High-priestly Benediction, there is inset a hymn, looking forward to the consummation of the Campaign, when Jerusalem shall have come into her own again. The verses have a Messianic ring about them.[42] One of the Dead Sea Scroll discussions has centered round the Messianic idea or ideal. The general consensus of opinion points to "Messiah" having been capable of both political and religious connotation—for both king and priest were anointed. Professor Bruce has pointed out that the New Testament with the addition of "Prophet" attributes the combination of the three titles with their implications to Jesus Christ. It is, however, the "Prophet" per se that constitutes a parallel with Qur'ānic thinking.[43] Qumrān would appear to have some light to throw on a controversy of important identification, involving Judaism, Christianity, and Samaritanism as well as Islam. The *Manual of Discipline* or *Rule of the Community* (Bruce) has the very vital sentence that "until the coming of the Prophet and of both the Priestly and Lay Messiah" the Community "is not to depart from the clear intent of the Law to walk in any way in the stubbornness of their own hearts." So far as the Qur'ān and the "use" of "Messiah" is concerned, there is little doubt that Muḥammad neither regarded *al-masīḥ* as anything else but an alternate way of referring to Jesus—sometimes uniting the words in a single phrase as in the New Testament and throughout Christian history—nor did he ever suggest himself as being Messiah of the Jews (in Arabia). If Qumrān was satisfied with two Messiahs, respectively Aaronic and Davidic (Israelite), Muḥammad lived at a period in Near Eastern history when the Christian evangelistic conviction that Jesus was proved the only Messiah had been accepted as decisive—had in point of fact become part of the normal way of alluding to him. But it was not quite the same with regard to the term "Prophet." Muḥammad's claim was that God had sent him with a message to the Arabs. Added to this was a confident assurance that the Jewish Scriptures supported his "prophethood" through a fresh application of the text in Deuteronomy, which had proved so controversial in the early days of Christianity, being quoted both by Peter and Stephen: "I will raise them up a prophet from among their brethren, like unto thee."[44]

This quotation has turned up again in the fragment from Cave 4, which seems to be a list of proof texts for the Messianic era.[45] Starting with this quotation from the Lord's world to Moses dealing with the "Prophet" like him, the subsequent "proof text" is from Balaam's prophecy of the "Star of Jacob." Here the implication is of the *military* prowess of the king, who "would smite the brow of Moab." The third consists of the Mosaic blessing of Levi, and is consequently *priestly* in character. These three traits are united according to Christian interpretation in the person of Christ. Whether or not prophets were regularly anointed (as seems inferentially likely from the use of the Isaiah passage by Jesus in the synagogue at Nazareth), the two more Messianic qualities merge in sublimation when used of Jesus as the *Christ*. This Christian nomenclature would seem to have established itself in pre-Islamic Arabia, despite any meaning that the Jewish settlements in contact with Muḥammad may have given the term. The Messenger of God in Arabia made no attempt to prove any "Messianic" connection with himself; but he does not seem to have realized that for Christian tribes, taking for granted the use of *al-masīḥ*, "Prophethood" par excellence was as much wrapped up in the person of Jesus as the other two more generally conceded qualities of Messiahship. But presumably, Jewish thought in Arabia remained as pigeonholed as in Qumrān, or as in the relevant parts of the Old Testament as interpreted by Judaeans or Samaritans. Muḥammad was in consequence, then, enabled to regard himself as "the Prophet," whom, in accordance with Mosaic expectation, Jahveh would "raise." To this the Samaritan passage mentioned in Saint John 4 lends considerable support. Qumrān certainly left the loophole open. There is no parallel in the Qur'ānic use of "Messiah" with that of Qumrān. There is a parallel in the construction put on the Deuteronomic context in Qumrān and the Qur'ān. "The Prophet was raised" wistfully for the Qumrāni, factually for the Muslim.

H. "WHAT ABOUT ISRAEL?"

There is still another point in this context that brings the Qumrān sectarians up to date; while there are passages in the Qur'ān that come to much the same thing. It has been noted, as by Millar Burrows, that the Royal Messiah was normally expected to arise from the tribe of Judah, as in the Matthean explication of Micah in the Nativity story. This was also in conformity with the prophecy of Balaam, who like Micah after him associates this question of royal rule with "Israel" rather than Judah.[46] It would appear that *Israel* is employed in this Qumrānic list of proof texts in its more comprehensive connotation, as in the mocking of the priests at the time of the Crucifixion: "Let Christ (Messiah) the King of Israel come down from the Cross."[47] There are more than forty occurrences of Israel in the Qurʾān (two of them being alternate to "Jacob"). Jeffery contends for a Christian origin for the name—probably Syriac.[48] This might mean that Muḥammad regarded the "Banū Isrāʾīl" as the ancestors of the Jews (Yahud) in a sense wider than that of pure consanguinity. It was from the Jews of his time that he gathered his information with regard to past; they were the representatives of Israel spiritually and historically. "Israel" is about as synonymous for "Jews" as "Messiah" for "Jesus." If the identification of the "Prophet" is still a moot point as between the followers of the three monotheistic faiths, there remains the resuscitated question as to the real meaning of "Israel" today—is it geographical, political, spiritual, or what? Can Qumrān and Qurʾān help to unravel the tangled skein of rival Semitic interpretations? The problem is not merely antiquarian.

I. "FRAGMENTS"

Throughout the literary material from the Dead Sea Caves so far made available, there is scattered phraseology of a Semitic nature reminiscent of similar phraseology in the Qurʾān—though there may be a somewhat different slant in some cases. If we leave the respective references to Gog to modern commentary (whether in Ezekiel, Qumrān, Apocalypse, or the Qurʾān) there are detailed similarities more rewarding that bespeak a common background. The "Most High God" in the Seventh Thanksgiving Psalm is equally Semitic as El-Elyon on the lips of Old Testament worthies and as Allāhu Taʿālā in Qurʾānic Arabia or even the modern Near East. Qumrāni and Muslim are equally emphatic on the prerogative of Divine Creation. "It is He that hath made us and we are His" is Qurʾānic and Qumranic. There is the repeated emphasis on the equally Divine prerogative of "mercy." The use of the term "Blessed" in respect of God comes into the same category. Qumrān and ʿArafāt unite in a chorus of "praise to the Holiest in the height."

Both scrolls and fragments imply the provenance and popularity of the work of Isaiah, a popularity substantiated in the Gospels, in particular the command to "prepare the way of the Lord in the wilderness." It was this Isaianic vision that was as responsible as anything else for the early prayer in Islam that came to occupy the place of preeminence at the outset of the Qur'ānic suras. It was always difficult through thirty years in Palestine not to feel *ihdinā al-ṣirāṭ al-mustaqīm* had roots in the previous experience of Judaism and Christianity. For this pregnant phrase Gaster even suggests that "the Figure of the Teacher of Righteousness was the prototype for the Islamic development of the *Mahdī*"[49]—if so, it brings Qumrān to Omdurman in nineteenth-century Africa. But being guided along the "straight path" mostly meant for the Qumrāni that study of the Law "that all things may be done in accordance with what is revealed therein."[50] For the Christian greater attention is paid to the fact that the wilderness is not out of date in the call to preparation for the teachings of Christ. The Muslim may feel that God alone can guide along this straight path and be inclined at times to "leave it at that."

But the common idea derives from an Old Covenanting Prophet who knew the highways and byways of his Palestine so well as to realize that it would give his world a picture of what was and what might be. After all, this petition is the central plea of the Fātiḥah, and it would be entirely possible to rewrite this little sura in Qumrānic language with comparatively little change in wording. Mutatis mutandis sentences in the closing paragraphs of Millar Burrows's chapter on the beliefs of the Dead Sea sectaries might well stand as true of much of the attitude to life and thought bequeathed by the Qur'ān to the immediate followers of Muḥammad in the seventh century.

Here in future "Elysian Fields" are possible parallels between Pharisaic, Qumrānic and Qur'ānic conceptions of the Resurrection of the Body. Here, too, we note the same heedless way in which Divine warnings were disregarded by those of ancient times. But more, both Dead Sea and desert alike inculcated or emphasised a domestic and personal involvement.

> Unlike most other Jewish groups" the Qumrān sectaries "even believed that they had been granted a new revelation that made clear the true meaning of the Scripture. In the prophets they found their own past and future prefigured. . . . They believed that all things were ordained of God. Even the existence of evil and the struggle between good and evil in human society and in the individual soul were part and parcel of the divine plan. At the end of the appointed time God would deliver His elect and destroy the hosts of wickedness. . . . The Covenanters firmly

> believed that they were God's elect, not only as members of the chosen people but also individually as sons of light, the men of God's lot. . . . They confidently expected the judgment and eternal punishment of the sons of darkness . . . they fervently hoped to enjoy eternal felicity in the presence of God. . . ."[57]

May it not be that there is enough affinity here between Qumrān and the Qur'ānic scheme of life and death, to warrant further research into the comparative thinking of the desert and the Dead Sea? Writers who deal with this growingly vast subject refer to the tenth-century Qaraite Al-Qirqisānī, who, among others before and after him, mentions a cave-sect, so named because their literature came to light in a cave—hence the Arabic form "Maghārians." There are reasons for thinking that these "Adullamites" might be the Qumrānis, flowering each side of the Christian era. If Jewish and Christian scholars in diverse languages have been contrasting and comparing the tenets of these Maghārians with contemporary Judaism, or examining the relationship of their thought forms with New Testament literary expression, we must ask Islamic scholarship as well to make research into the treasures hidden within the caves.

NOTES

1. *Bulletin of the John Rylands Library* 40 no. 1:114.
2. For the only one (so far), see Gaster, *The Scriptures of the Dead Sea Sect*, p. 105 n. 30.
3. Vol. 58 ff.
4. Gaster, *The Scriptures of the Dead Sea Sect,* p. 53. Cf. Millar Burrows, *The Dead Sea Scrolls*, p. 261.
5. Acts 7:53.
6. Gal. 3:19.
7. Wolf, *Muhammad at Mecca*, pp. 43 f.
8. Suras LXX.4, XCVII.4, XVI.2.
9. Sura LIII.5.
10. Gaster, *The Scriptures of the Dead Sea Sect*, p. 103.
11. See *Muslim World* (October 1951): 251–56.
12. E.g., Sura III.18, 21.
13. Jeffery, *Foreign Vocabulary of the Qur'ān*, pp. 44–46.
14. James 2:23.

15. Arberry, vol. 1, p. 119.

16. Gaster, *The Scriptures of the Dead Sea Sect*, p. 73.

17. Sura XII.38.

18. Rom. 4:12.

19. Sura II.224, LX.8.

20. Arberry, vol. 1, p. 98.

21. Num. 32:10.

22. Burrows, *The Dead Sea Scrolls*, p. 247.

23. Gaster, *The Scriptures of the Dead Sea Sect*, p. 81.

24. Ibid., p. 63. Cf. Burrows, *The Dead Sea Scrolls*, p. 407.

25. Gaster, *The Scriptures of the Dead Sea Sect*, pp. 73, 109 n. 2. The Qur'ān says Noah's wife; see Hanauer, *Folklore of the Holy Land*, pp. 13, 66.

26. See, e.g., Klein, *The Religion of Islam*, pp. 65 f.

27. Gaster, *The Scriptures of the Dead Sea Sect*, pp. 316, 317.

28. Burrows, *The Dead Sea Scrolls*, p. 261.

29. Arberry, vol. 1, p. 89.

30. Gaster, *The Scriptures of the Dead Sea Sect*, p. 280.

31. Ibid., p. 143 et passim.

32. Ibid.

33. Verse 6.

34. Elder, *Commentary of Al-Taftazānī*, pp. 134, 135.

35. Jeffery, *Foreign Vocabulary of the Qur'an*, p. 269 ff.

36. Klein, *The Religion of Islam*, p. 73 ff.

37. Gaster, *The Scriptures of the Dead Sea Sect*, pp. 261–62.

38. Ibid., pp. 272–73.

39. Sura IV.16.

40. Arberry, vol. 1, p. 57.

41. Ibid., p. 207.

42. Gaster, *The Scriptures of the Dead Sea Sect*, p. 276.

43. *Second Thoughts on the Dead Sea Scrolls*, pp. 77 ff.

44. Deut. 18:18, 19.

45. Bruce, op. cit. ad. loc., Gaster, *The Scriptures of the Dead Sea Sect*, pp. 353–54.

46. Num. 24:15–17, Mic. 5:2, Matt. 2:5.

47. Mark 15:32.

48. Jeffery, *Foreign Vocabulary of the Qur'an*, pp. 60, 61.

49. Gaster, *The Scriptures of the Dead Sea Sect*, p. 36.

50. *Manual of Discipline in the Rules of the Order*. See Burrows, *The Dead Sea Scrolls*, p. 382.

51. Ibid., pp. 271–72.

4.3

An Essenian Tradition in the Koran

Marc Philonenko

Translated by Ibn Warraq

The question that I propose to address is undoubtedly rather new. The question of the Jewish influence on nascent Islam is not. As early as 1833 Abraham Geiger[1] posed it dramatically in a small book, very remarkable for the period and, since then, it has been taken up again so many times. Suffice it to cite here the works of Hirschfeld,[2] of Speyer[3] or of Torrey.[4] The author of a relatively recent study does not hesitate in concluding: "the influence of Judaism on Early Islam must have been very considerable, if not decisive."[5] Our study thus rejoins all a line of research that goes way back.

One may remark nevertheless: Essenians have scarcely been touched on in this discussion. More precisely, they have been referred to by fluke, to the extent that one is believed to have revealed the influence of Judeo-Christian sects on Islam in its early stages. Thus Renan believed that by its doctrine of the true prophet, Islam was connected to "Esseno-ebionism."[6] It is thus through this channel of Judeo-Christianity that one imagined that the Essenians could have exerted their influence over Islam. We are not in any way thinking of excluding this possibility. Judeo-Christianity is one of the legitimate heirs of the Essenes. It could very well have played here this role of an intermediary. It is nonetheless true that, as far as the origins of Islam are concerned, one has scarcely thought of the Essenes as such. Without doubt, in the time of Renan, it would have been rash to conjecture

From *Revue de l'Histoire des Religions* 170 (1966): 143–57. This paper was originally presented at the Ernest Renan Society, February 26, 1966. Reprinted with permission.

direct relations between Islam and the Essenes, while the sources of information on the Jewish sect amounted to, essentially, the brief accounts in Philo and Josephus.[7] Now that, through the discoveries of the Dead Sea, our knowledge of the Essenes has been totally revitalized, new possbilities present themselves to the critic. As early as 1950, Father Roland de Vaux noted in various Arab writers traces of the Essenians hidden under the name of Magharia.[8] This lead has been followed since by several others.[9] But it is possible, it is useful, it is, we believe, necessary to go further back. Can one see in the Koran itself some traces of strictly Essenian influence ? Certain preliminary probes give a glimpse of the riches of the terrain whose exploration should be carried out on an equal footing by a specialist in Qumrān studies and an informed Islamologist.[10]

We shall deliberately limit ourselves here to one Essenian tradition that we should like to show was taken up again by the Prophet.

* * *

The point of departure for this research was provided by Psalm 151. Everyone is aware that the Hebrew Psalter comprises 150 psalms. The Greek version, called the Septuagint, has 151. This Psalm 151 is also found to be the first psalm of a collection of five psalms preserved in Syriac and attributed to David. M. Dupont-Sommer was so kind as to suggest, in 1958, that I study them. The Essenian character of the collection struck me immediately. In an article published some months later, I gave evidence of the Esssenian origins of these pslams from which I noted down the typical Qumrānian expressions.[11] In 1963 a young American scholar, J. A. Sanders, published the Hebrew text of Psalm 151,[12] then, the following year, published the Hebrew text of the second and third psalms of the Syriac collection, all found in Cave 11 at Qumrān.[13] This discovery brought to bear an unexpected confirmation of the thesis I had maintained some years earlier. It goes without saying, however, that the original of the first three psalms being now known, my article needs several revisions and corrections.

Psalm 151 posed a special problem. On reading it attentively, such as it had been transmitted to us in Greek and Syriac, one noticed nothing there, in contrast to the four others, that reflected the mystical conceptions of the sect and its own particular vocabulary. I concluded: "This psalm contains nothing typically Essenian."[14] This conclusion, perfectly legitimate when only considering the Greek and Syriac texts, must now, however, be abandoned. The original Hebrew of Psalm 151 comprises, in effect, a certain number of phrases that are absent in the Greek and Syriac versions, without doubt because they had been deliberately edited out from the original Hebrew by a copyist, who had acted as a censor. These sentences find their best explanation in the Essenian origin of the psalm.[15]

Let us to quote this fundamental text:[16] Psalm 151.

A Hallelujah of David, son of Jesse.

Smaller was I than my brothers
And the youngest of the sons of my father,
So he made me shepherd of his flock and ruler over his kids.

My hands have made an instrument of music
And my fingers a lyre;
And I rendered glory to the Lord,
I, having said, within myself:

"The mountains, do they not render witness to Him?
And the hills, do they not proclaim Him?"
The trees appreciated my words,
And the herd, my poems.

For who will proclaim and who will celebrate
And who will recount the works of the Lord?
The universe, God sees it;
The universe, He hears it, and He listens to.

He sent His prophet to anoint me,
Samuel to exalt me.
My brothers went out to meet him,
They who were handsome of figure and appearance,

Who were tall of stature
And who had beautiful hair:
The Lord God did not choose them.

But He sent and took me from behind the flock
And anointed me with holy oil,
And made me the Prince of His people
And leader of the sons of His covenant.[17]

Mountains and hills, trees and herds! The author of the Qumran psalm took his inspiration here undoubtedly from a canonical psalm, Ps. 148:7–8:

> Praise the Lord from the earth . . .
> Mountains and all hills; fruitful trees, and all cedars:
> Beasts and all cattle; creeping things, and flying fowl.

It is important to recognize the biblical source of the Qumrānian psalm, but the essential is elsewhere. As Sanders saw perfectly well and as Dupont-Sommer has magisterially demonstrated, there is in these lines—*the trees appreciated my words and the herd my poems*—a clear allusion to the legend of Orpheus charming the trees and the herds[18] with songs from his lyre. It is this David-Orpheus that we meet again on the frescoes of the synagogue of Doura[19] and in the miniatures of numerous Christian psalters.[20]

Perhaps we should even ask in the future if the use of the Orphic myth among the Essenians is limited to the revival of a single theme: that of "Orpheus among the animals."[21]

* * *

We can now open the Koran.[22] David has an important place in it. He appears in the procession of the servants of God,[23] and is, most often, accompanied by Solomon.[24] It is true that the father and the son are united to one another by a common wisdom. David, for the Koran, is first of all a man of wisdom. Thus we read in Sura XXXVIII.20: "We made his kingdom strong, and gave him wisdom (*ḥikma*), and discriminating judgment." Similarly, in Sura XXI.79: "We made Solomon understand the case, and to each of them We gave judgment and knowledge."

This continuous underlining of the wisdom of David is a little surprising. According to rabbinical literature, in fact, the wisdom of David was decidedly inferior to that of his son. Let us note, nonetheless, that in the psalm scroll discovered at Qumrān, David comes through as being a sage [HKM:] to whom God has given "a mind of intelligence and judgment."[25] This initial encounter of the Koranic text and the text from Qumran is certainly not fortuitous.

Another important trait is retained in the Koran: David, adversary of Goliath. [26]

Evidently, in the Koran, David also appears as the bard of God, someone to whom God has given the Psalms.[27] A sura of the second Meccan period deserves to hold our special attention: XXXVIII.18–20:

> Bear with what they say, and remember our servant David so full of power and ever penitent.
>
> We made the mountains subject to him, glorifying with him the Lord evening and morning,
>
> And the birds gathered together around him, all were obedient to him.

This theme is taken up again in Sura XXI.79:

> We made Solomon understand the case, and to each of them we gave judgment and knowledge. We caused the birds and the mountains to exalt us, along with David, and We were doers.

Likewise, in Sura XXXIV.10:

> Assuredly, We gave David grace from Us. "O Mountains and birds, echo his psalms of praise!"

The allusion to Psalm 148 is undeniable:

> Praise the Lord from the earth . . .
> Mountains and all hills; fruitful trees, and all cedars:
> Beasts and all cattle; creeping things, and flying fowl".

The scholars, moreover, did not miss this allusion.[28] But there is more in the Koranic text than a simple allusion to Psalm 148. The idea is that all of creation, subjected to David, with him give glory to the Lord. This interpretation so unusual—and which seems unknown in the rabbinical tradition—is the one that, without any doubt, appears for the first time in the Qumrān psalm. The mountains that sing with David, these are the mountains attracted by Orpheus, and these birds gathered around David, these are the ones which charmed the son of Calliope.

Thus, as in the Qumrān psalter, it is David-Orpheus who sings in the Koran.

* * *

Our exegesis finds astonishing confirmation in Islamic tradition. The features of David-Orpheus are going to appear, in very pronounced relief, in certain texts inspired by the Koranic passages that we have pointed out.

In the ninth century C.E., Ṭabarī, the great Arab historian, commenting on Sura XXXIV, writes:

> When the sons of Israel rallied round David, God revealed the Psalms to him, taught him ironwork and softened the iron for him, and ordered the mountains and the birds to sing along with him when he sang.
>
> They say that God did not give to any of his other creatures a voice comparable to his. When he recited the Psalms—they say—the wild beasts came so close to him that one could take them by the neck; they listened with rapt attention to his voice. The devils have only fashioned flutes, luths and harps based on the diverse tonalities of his voice.[29]

Do we not find there Orpheus, the divine bard, such as Virgil describes, "charming the tigers,"[30] or such as Ovid shows him, "seated in the middle of a circle of wild beasts and a multitude of birds"?[31] There are numerous monuments decorated with figures that represent Orpheus playing the lyre. Around him are assembled the most diverse kind of animals, the lion, the tiger, the serpent; birds among which we recognize the peacock, the eagle, the dove.[32] Should we perhaps point out that in the Arabic text of Ṭabarī there is no mention of birds? They are found, however, in the Persian version of his chronicle: "God had given David a beautiful voice, so that he sang the psalms with melodies of such beauty, that no one had ever heard its like. Now, when David began singing the praises, the birds of the sky would come and place themselves around his head and listen."[33]

The person of David-Orpheus is found again even in Sufism. In the eleventh century Hujwīrī, a Persian author, treating the principles of hearing, wrote in his Kashf al-Maḥjūb:[34]

> You must know that the principles of audition vary with the variety of temperaments, just as there are different desires in various hearts, and it is tyranny to lay down one law for all. Auditors (*mustamiʿān*) may be divided into two classes: (1) those who hear the spiritual meaning, (2) those hear the material sound. There are good and evil results in each

case. Listening to sweet sounds produces an effervescence (*ghalayān*) of the subtance moulded in Man: true (*ḥaqq)* if the substance be true, false (*bāṭil*) if the substance be false. When the stuff of the man's temperament is evil, that which he hears will be evil too. The whole of this topic is illustrated by the story of David, whom God made His viceregent and gave him a sweet voice and caused his throat to be a melodious pipe, so that wild beasts and birds came from mountain and plain to hear him, and the water ceased to flow and the birds fell from the air. It is related that during a month's space the people who were gathered round him in the desert ate no food, and the children neither wept nor asked for milk; and whenever the folk departed it was found that many had died of the rapture that seized them as they listened to his voice: one time, it is said, the tale of the dead amounted to seven hundred maidens and twelve thousand old men. Then God, wishing to separate those who listened to the voice and followed their temperament from the followers of the truth (*ahl-i ḥaqq*) who listened to the spiritual reality, permitted Iblis to work his will and display his wiles. Iblis fashioned a mandoline and a flute and took up station opposite to the place where David was singing. David's audience became divided into two parties: the blest and the damned. Those whe were destined to damnation lent ear to the music of Iblis, while those who were destined to felicity remained listening to the voice of David. The spiritualists (*ahl-i maʿnī*) were conscious of nothing except David's voice, for they saw God alone; if they heard the Devil's music, they regarded it as a temptation proceeding from God, and if they heard David's voice, they recognized it as being a direction from God. . . .[35]

So, then, from the mountains and the plains the wild beasts and birds came to listen to David, and at the sound of his voice the water ceased to flow, and the birds fell from the sky. Under the features of this David, is it not Orpheus who is once again revealed to us? For proof I only want the text of Seneca:

At the sound of the voice of this poet the roar of the rapid torrent stopped, and forgetting to follow its course, the water lost its impetuous spring; when the rivers stopped thus the distant Bistonians thought the river Hebrus had dried up at the home of the Getes. The forest itself brought to him its birds and the dwellers of the wood came to him: those who were flying about in the air, on hearing his melodies, fell betrayed by their force.[36]

All the traits applied by Seneca to Orpheus in Hujwīrī are attributed to David. Not only are the wild beasts and the birds charmed by the words of one (David) and the other (Orpheus), not only do the rivers stop flowing for one (David) and the other (Orpheus), but further still the birds fall from the sky at the feet of David and Orpheus, who, here, are but one.

Not only do Ṭabarī and Hujwīrī reproduce the portrait of David-Orpheus, but on one point they have even modified it. It is just that all borrowing is never mechanical and implies appropriation and transformation. While there was not the slightest allusion in the suras from which they drew their inspiration to an instrument of music, the one and the other mention one. They attribute to the devils the invention of the flute, the harp and the lute. The explanation for it is no doubt to be found in a certain austerity that rejects the instrument in order to keep just the human voice. But, in our context, this explanation is not entirely satisfactory. The Arab and Persian authors must have known of a tradition that attributes the gift of the harp or the cither to the divine bard. In fact, we know that Orpheus, without having invented the harp, had perfected it in adding to it one or two cords, taking thus in any case the number of the latter to nine, in harmony with the number of Muses.[37] Perhaps even the author of Psalm 151 made of David the inventor of the harp, when he shows David fashioning with his own hands his instrument.

The fact that the allusions to the legend of Orpheus are even more clear and precise in the tradition than in the Koran poses a very delicate problem. One could admittedly think that the commentators, having recognized in David the Thracian poet, had added to the portrait of the Koranic David-Orpheus. This explanation cannot be rejected outright, but it remains insufficient. To take here only the case of Ṭabarī, we could show that this compiler had access to truly Essenian sources and that he had very likely known Pslam 151.

This psalm, let us recall, consists of two parts. The first is perfectly perserved: We quoted it earlier. Of the second part, we only possess fragments of the first two lines:

> Beginning of the great [de]eds [?] of David, after the prophet of God had anointed him.
>
> While I [heard] a Philistine who defied the [Israeli lines . . .].

The subject of this second part of the psalm is thus the battle between David and Goliath. So, in the same psalm, David appears under the features of the poet of Greek mythology and those of the adversary of Goliath. If the original Hebrew of this second part of the psalm is unfortunately lost, the version of the Septuagint, the Syriac version, and the Vetus latina allows us to restore it in part. The text of the *Vetus latina* is particularly interesting. One reads (Ps. 151:6–7):

I went out to meet the stranger
And he cursed me with his idols
But I, he having drawn his sword, cut his head off
And I lifted the shame from the sons of Israel.

In a manuscript in Augsbourg to which Dupont-Sommer has drawn attention with his usual perspicacity, we find after: "I went to meet the stranger, and he cursed me with his idols"—that is to say after verse 6—a verse that does not figure either in the Septuagint version or the Syriac one, or in the other manuscripts of the *Vetus latina*: "And I hurled against his forehead three stones, by the strength of the Lord, and I felled him."[38] This sentence is obviously inspired by the account in 1 Samuel 17; it is evident that it is well placed in the psalm between verse 6, which shows David advancing to meet the Philistine, and verse 7, which shows him severing the head of his adversary: between these two actions, the psalmist could hardly avoid showing David striking Goliath from his sling. Dupont-Sommer rightly concludes then that "the manuscript of Augsbourg restores to us, here, it seems, something of the original Hebrew."[39]

One point to note: the book of Samuel talks of five stones that David gathered in a torrent, and it was with only one stone that he killed the Philistine. According to rabbinical tradition, these five stones were amalgamated into one.[40] According to the tradition retained in the Augsbourg manuscript, and thus without doubt the original Hebrew of Psalm 151, it is with three stones this time that David killed Goliath. Now, this Midrashic Essenian tradition is the same one that Ṭabarī knew and which he refers to and explains in his commentary on the Koran for the battle of David and Goliath (Sura II.252). Let us note at once that in his commentary, Ṭabarī, just like the author of Psalm 151, makes of David-Orpheus the adversary of the Philistine: "David said to his father: . . . I do not hurl stones from my sling against something without bringing it down; . . . I penetrated between the mountains and I found a lion lying down; I mounted it and I held it by its ears; it did not get up; . . . I walk between the mountains and I sing; then there does not remain one mountain that doesnot sing with me."[41] Ṭabarī presents David in this way: "David was a stocky man, of pale complexion, with sparse hair. He had a pure heart. His father said to him: 'My child, we have prepared a meal for your three brothers, so that they can find the (necessary) strength to fight the enemy; take it to them. As soon as you have taken it to them, come back to me quickly.' He said, 'Yes.' Then he left carrying the meal of his brothers, his sack, in which he put stones and his sling which he used to defend his herd of sheep, slung over his shoulders. On the way, a stone said to him: 'O David, take me, put me in your sack; you will kill Goliath through me; for I am the stone of Jacob.' He picked it up and put it in his sack and continued walking.; another stone said to him: 'O David, take me, put me in your sack; you will kill Goliath through me; for I am the stone of Isaac.' He picked it up and put it in his sack and continued walking; a third stone said to him: 'O David, take me, put me in your sack; you will kill Goliath through me; for I am the stone of Abraham.' He picked it up and put it in his sack and continued walking."[42] The time for the combat came: "David put the three stones in his sling. He said in putting the first: 'In the name of my father Abraham'; the second: 'In the name of my father Isaac'; the third: 'In the name of my father Israel.' After having whirled the sling round, the stones became just one."[43]

* * *

But let us leave Ṭabarī and Hujwīrī there. Their testimony confirms our exegesis, which discovers a David-Orpheus in the Koran. How do we account for this strange presence in the holy book?

"We made the mountains and the birds exalt us with David." It is right that we recognized there an echo of Psalm 148. But there is more here, as we have seen, than a simple recollection of the biblical text, however clear-cut it may be. The Koranic texts take up again the Qumranian interpretation of Psalm 148—interpretation confirmed in Psalm 151: all of creation glorifies the Lord with David, the new Orpheus. That is to say that the Prophet [Muhammad] had known Psalm 148 elucidated by an Essenian exegetical tradition. This does not necessarily imply—but does not exclude either—that he had knowledge of Psalm 151 itself. We are thus led to inquire into the character of the Psalter that Muhammad could have known.

In the Koran, the only specific quotation from the Psalter indeed of the entire Old Testament is found to be a quote from Ps. 37:29. One reads, in effect, in a sura of the second Meccan period (XXI.105): "Our righteous servants shall inherit the earth." The verse from the psalm is taken up again in VII.128 "Moses said to his people: 'Ask for help from God and be patient! The earth is God's, and He gives it to those of His servants whom He chooses. The issue ultimate is to the godfearing.' But this verse of Psalm 37 has scarcely occupied the attention of the rabbis, who cite it rarely.[44] On the other hand, it had certainly received in the Essenian milieu a special interpretation. Already, the verse of the psalm is cited in the book of Enoch (5:7): "And for the chosen, there will be light, and joy and peace, and they will inherit the earth."[45] But there is more. The discoveries at Qumrān have given us a *Commentary on Psalm 37*. Verse 29, quoted in the Koran, falls unfortunately in a gap. Fortunately, verses 9b and 11, with a very similar meaning, have been preserved for us, as well as their commentary. Here is the text:

> *But those put their hope in God, those are the ones who will inherit the earth* (v. 9b). The explanation of the latter is that *those* are the Congregation of His chosen ones, who carry out His will . . . *But the humble will possess the earth and rejoice in a perfect happiness* (v.11). The explanation of this verse concerns the Congregation of the Poor, who accept the time of affliction and will be delivered from all the snares of Belial, and then they will rejoice in all the pleasures of the earth, and all affliction will be expelled from the flesh.[46]

The communal and eschatological interpretation of Psalm 37 given by the Qumrānian *Commentary* thus prefigures and prepares that held by the Koranic text.

Would Muhammad have gotten these traditions, and others still, from a group of Jews, precisely—in a word, let us admit it—from the Essenians, in Mecca first, perhaps in Medina afterward?

The hypothesis is permissable. We have been inquiring for a long time into the origins of the Jews that Muhammad had met in Arabia. Who were they? Where did they come from? When they did they arrive? This immigration undoubtedly stretched out over the course of centuries. Some Jews could have settled in Arabia early on, right from sixth century B.C.E.[47] Others, and the idea is Nöldeke's, would have arrived much later, fleeing the Roman legions, which in 70 C.E., under the command of Titus, were to take possession of Jerusalem.[48] Among these refugees, there were certainly some Essenians who had abandoned the site of Qumrān. Certain others fled into Transjordan and mixed with the Judeo-Christians,[49] others emigrated to Arabia. Up to the 7th century C.E., they kept their traditions alive, and were able to exercise an influence over nascent Islam.

Thus, we are faced with a problem whose elements are totally new: what is the part of the Essenians in the origins of Islam? Here again, the manuscripts of Qumrān will thoroughly disperse the obscurities and will decidedly bring some illumination.

NOTES

1. A. Geiger, *Was hat Mohammed aus dem Judenthume aufgenommen?* (Bonn, 1833), reprinted in *The Origins of the Koran*, ed. Ibn Warraq (Amherst, N.Y.: Prometheus Books, 1998).

2. H. Hirschfeld, *Judische Elemente im Koran* (Berlin, 1878); *Beitrage zur Erklarung des Koran* (Leipzig, 1886); *New Researches into the Composition and Exegesis of the Koran* (London, 1901). [See also: A. Katsch, *Judaism in Islam* (New York, 1954); D.Sidersky, *Les Origines des légendes musulmanes dans le Coran* (Paris, 1933); H. Speyer, *Die Biblischen Erzahlungen im Qoran* (Hildesheim, 1961); B.Heller, "Récits et personnages bibliques dans la légende mahométane," *REJ* 85 (1928): 113–36; "La légende biblique dans I'Islam," *REJ* 98 (1934): 1–18; P. Jensen, "Das Leben Muhammeds und die David –Sage," *Der Islam* 12 (1922): 84–97; I. Schapiro, *Die haggadischen Elemente im erzalenden Teil des Korans*, vol. 1 (Leipzig, 1907); H. Schwarzbaum, "The Jewish and Moslem Versions of Some Theodicy Legends," *Fabula* 3 (1959–60): 119–69; C. Gilliot, "Les "informateurs" juifs et chrétiens de Muhammad. Reprise d'un problème traité par Aloys Sprenger et Theodor Noldeke, " *JSAI* 22 (1998): 84–126.]

3. H. Speyer, *Die Biblischen Erzahlungen im Qoran* (Hildesheim, 1961).

4. C. C. Torrey, *The Jewish Foundation of Islam* (New York, 1933), reprinted in *The Origins of the Koran*, ed. Ibn Warraq (Amherst, N.Y.: Prometheus Books, 1998).

5. S. D. Goitein, *Jews and Arabs* (New York, 1955), pp. 60–61.

6. E. Renan, *Marc-Aurèle* (Paris, 1899), p. 83 n. 1.

7. See however, A. Sprenger, *Das Leben und die Lehre des Mohammad*, 2 (Berlin 1869),vol. 1, p. 18–21 [Josephus, (*War* 2.8.119–61; *Antiquities,* 13.5171–2; 15.10.371–9; 18.1.11, 18–22); Philo (*Quod omnis probus* 12–13 [75–91]; *Hypothetica*, in Eusebius, *Praeparatio evangelica* 11.1–18); Pliny the Elder (*Natural History* 5.15.73); C. Julius Solinus, *Collectanea Rerum Memorabilium* (for the latter see, C. Burchard, Revue Biblique, July, 1967]

8. R. de Vaux, "A Propos des manuscrits de la mer Morte," *Revue biblique*, 57 (1950): 417–29.

9. E. Bammel, "Hohlenmenschen" *Zeitschrift fur die neutestamentliche Wissenschaft* 49 (1958) 77–88; P. Kahle, *The Cairo Geniza* (Oxford, 1959), pp. 24–25; N. Golb, "Who Eere the Magariya?" *JAOS* 80 (1960): 347–59; "The Qumran Covenanters and the Later Jewish Sects," *JR* 41 (1961): 38–50. On another point see H. Nibley, "Qumrān and "The Companions of the Cave"," *Revue de Qumran* 5 (1965): 177–98.

10. I intend to carry out this research in collaboration with my colleague from Strasburg, T. Fahd. Let me point out two articles by E. F. F. Bishop, "The Qumran Scrolls and the Qur'ān," *Muslim World* 48 (1958): 223–36; "Qumrān and the Preserved Tablet (s)," *Revue de Qumran* 5 (1965): 253–56. The force of C. Rabin's remarks in *Qumran Studies* (Oxford, 1957), pp. 112–30, is diminished by his paradoxal hypothesis of the Phariseean origin of the Qumrān texts.

11. M. Philonenko, "L'origine essénienne des cinq psaumes syriaques de David," *Semitica* 9 (1959): 35–48.

12. J. A. Sanders, "Ps.151 in 11 QPSS," *ZATW* 75 (1963): 73–86.

13. J. A. Sanders, "Two Non-Canonical Psalms in 11 QPs," *ZATW* 76 (1964): 57–75. One can now read the original Hebrew of the three psalms in the definitive edition of J. A. Sanders, *The Psalms Scrolls of Qumran Cave 11* (Oxford, 1965). The publication of the Hebrew text of Psalm 151 has given rise to quiet a number of studies. Let us cite, among others, J. Carmignac, "La forme poètique du Psaume 151 de la grotte 11," *Revue de Qumran* 4 (1963): 371–78; W. H. Brownlee, "The 11 Q Counterpart to Psalm 151, 1–5," *Revue de Qumran* 4 (1963): 379–87; I. Rabinowitz, "The Alleged Orphism of 11 QPss 28, 3–12," *ZATW* 76 (1964): 193–200. The most important is that of A. Dupont-Sommer, "Le Psaume CLI dans II QPs a et le problème de son origine essénienne," *Semitica* 14 (1964): 25–62. We shall quote Psalm 151 in this scholar's translation.

14. Philonenko, "L'origine essénienne des cinq psaumes syriaques de David," p. 37.

15. See Dupont-Sommer, "Le Psaume CLI dans II QPs a et le problème de son origine essénienne," p. 29

16. [Philonenko gives Dupont-Sommer's translation. But there was a certain amount of controversy about this translation; see introduction for the details.]

17. [Cf. Geza Vermes's English translation: Psalm 151 A: Hallelujah. Of David, son of Jesse.]

18. Sanders, "Ps. 151 in QPSS," pp. 82–84; *The Psalms Scroll of Qumran Cave 11*, pp. 61–63; Dupont-Sommer, "Le Psaume CLI dans II QPs a et le problème de son origine essénienne," pp. 37–40, 42–43, 56–61; *David-Orphée* (Paris, 1964).

19. E. R. Goodenough, *Jewish Symbols in the Greco-Roman Period* (New York, 1964), vol. 9, pp. 89–104.

20. See for example, L. Réau, *Iconographie de l'art chrétien* (Paris, 1956), vol. 2, p. 55. Note the strange miniature of the Stuttgart Psalter reproduced in G. Bandmann, *Melancholie und Musik* (Koln-Opladen, 1960), p. 143.

21. Here, I must draw attention to a hymn attributed to David and preserved in the *Liber Antiquitatum Biblicarum* of Pseudo-Philo. I have tried to show the Essenian origin of this text in an article entitled: "Remarques sur un hymne essénienne de charactère gnostique," *Semitica* 11 (1961): 43–54. In this hymn, David, through the song of his harp, overcomes the evil spirit, come from Tartarus, who was tormenting Saul. The allusion to Orpheus, conqueror by his lyre of the masters of hell, is evident. One can find there a supplementary confirmation of the Essenian origin of the hymn.

22. [M. Philonenko uses R. Blachère's French translation for his Koranic quotes (*Le Coran* [Paris, 1957]). I have used the translations of Dawood, Rodwell, Pickthall, Arberry, Yusuf Ali; for bibliographic details on these translation see the introduction.]

23. Suras IV.161; VI.84

24. Suras XXI.79; XXVII.15; XXXIV.10–11.

25. *11 QPs a 27*, p. 4.

26. Sura II.252

27. Suras XVII.57; IV.161

28. Cf. R. Bell, *The Qur'ān* (Edinburgh, 1937), vol. 1, p. 311 n. 3.

29. Ṭabarī, *Tarikh,* ed. M. J. de Goeje (Leiden, 1881–1882), I2, p. 562. I owe this translation of Ṭabarī as well as the passage cited further down to my colleague and friend T. Fahd.

30. Virgil, *Georgics,* 4, 510.

31. Ovid, *Metamorphosis*, 10, 143-144.

32. Cf. A. Boulanger, *Orphée* (Paris), pp.149–55.

33. Ṭabarī, *Chronique,* I, 91, ed. H. Zotenberg (Paris, 1867), vol. 1, p. 426.

34. [I have used R. A. Nicholson's English translation of Alī b. ʿUthmān al-Jullābī al-Hujwīrī, *Kashf al-Maḥjūb* (London 1967) pp. 402–403.]

35. Hujwīrī, *Kashf al-Maḥjūb*, ed. Zukovski (Leningrad, 1926), pp. 524–25. M. G. Lazard, professor at the School of Oriental Languages, Paris, willingly translated this Persian text for me. I thank him heartily here.

36. Seneca, *Hercule sur l'Oeta 1036–1047*, trans. L. Hermann, ed. Guillaume Budé.

37. Cf. J. Coman, *Orphée, civilisateur de l'humanité* (Paris, 1939), p. 27.

38. See Dupont-Sommer, "Le Psaume CLI dans II QPs a et le problème de son origine essénienne," pp. 52–53.

39. Ibid., p.53

40. Cf. M. Grunbaum, *Neue Beitrage zur semitischen Sagenkunde* (Leiden, 1893), p. 192.

41. Ṭabarī, II, p. 278, I.12 sqq.

42. Ṭabarī, II, p. 275-276, I.22 sqq.

43. Ṭabarī, II p. 278, I.23 sqq.

44 See Strack-Billerbeck, *Kommentar zum Neuen Testament aus Talmud und Midrasch* (Munich, 1956), vol. 1, p. 199.

45. Cf also Matt., 5:5.

46. Translation by A. Dupont-Sommer.

47. Cf. Ben-Zvi, "Les origines de l'établissement des tribus d'Israel en Arabie," *Le Muséon* 74 (1961): 143–90.

48. T. Nöldeke, *Beitrage zur Kenninis der Poesie der alten Araber* (Hanover, 1864), pp. 52–53; cf. C. A. Nallino, "Ebrei e Cristiani nell' Arabia preislamica," in *Raccolta di scritti editi e inediti* (Rome, 1941), vol. 3, p. 101.

49. Cf. O. Cullmann, *The Significance of the Qumran Texts for Research into the Beginnings of Christianity*, in K.Stendhal, *The Scrolls and the New Testament* (London, 1958), p. 282 n. 32.

4.4

A Qumrānian Expression in the Koran

Marc Philonenko

Translated by Ibn Warraq

In the name of God, the Compassionate, the Merciful.

By the heaven with its constellations
By the Promised day
By the witness and the witnessed
Killed were the men of the trench
The fire abounding in fuel
When they sat by it,
And were themselves witnesses of what they did with the believers
They took revenge on them only because they believed in God,
the Almighty, the all-laudable. . . .[1]

Sura LXXXV has always disconcerted translators and commentators. The whole interpretation of the text is in fact dictated by the reply to the question: Who are "the men of the trench [or ditch or the Pit]"[2] that curse the Prophet?

Three major solutions have been suggested, which we shall make a note of here. The most widespread solution sees in the sura an evocation of the persecution of the Christians of Najran by the Jewish king Dhū Nuwās in 523.[3] The persecuting king would have had an immense trench dug that would have been filled with combustible material. A great number of martyrs must have been hurled on the brazier.

From *Atti del Terzo Congresso di Studi Arabi e Islamici, Ravello, 1–6 September* (Naples: Instituto Universitario Orientale 1967), pp. 553–56. Reprinted with permission.

Other scholars, from Geiger[4] and Loth[5] up to Blachère[6] see in our sura rather an allusion to the history of the Three Young Men in the furnace (Dan. 3:19–20).[7]

These two interpretations come up against some difficulties that J. Horovitz has highlighted. The imprecations in verses 1 to 3 could scarcely apply to past events, but presuppose, on the contrary, a judgement to come. Taking up again a suggestion of H. Grimme,[8] Horovitz sees in "the men of the trench" the impious thrown into the fire of hell and who, on the Day of Judgement, would have to give an account of the crimes they had perpetrated against the believers.[9] Let us note nonetheless that just one example has been produced where the word "trench" (*ʾukhdūd*[10] in Arabic) could designate hell in the grip of flames.[11] The verse in question is IV Esdras[12] (7, 36): Then the place [French, *Fosse*] of torment shall appear, and over against it the place of rest; the furnace of hell shall be displayed, and on the opposite side the paradise of delight."[13]

Such, then, is the state of a question that the manuscripts discovered near the Dead Sea have entirely revived.[14] Hell, the Sheol,[15] is constantly designated there by the Hebrew *šaḥaṯ,* 'trench," which already in the Old Testament designates the abode of the dead.[16] Thus, we read in "The Teaching on the Two Spirits" (Rule 4, 11–13): "And the visitation of all who walk in this spirit shall be a mulititude of plagues by the hand of all the destroying angels, everlasting damnation by the avenging wrath of the fury of God, eternal torment and endless disgrace together with shameful extinction in the fire of the dark regions."[17]

The passage is important for the exegesis of the sura. The Qumrān text describes, in effect, the torments of the damned in the hereafter on the Day of Judgement: in "the eternal trench," they will be burned by "the fire of the gloomy regions."[18]

The Book of Hymns repeatedly describes in some visions of the Apocalypse the forces of the Trench that sweep through the world at the end of time. "The wombs of the Pit shall be prey to all the works of horror,"[19] "the arrows of the Trench"[20] fly in the sky; "the doors of the Pit shall close,"[21] while "all the snares of the Pit were opened."[22]

There is more. The Qumrān texts expressly call the impious by the name of *benē haš-šaḥaṯ*, "sons of the Trench,"[23] or better still, *anešē haš-*

šaḥat̲ "men of the Trench," meaning the damned, those who are destined for the infernal Trench.[24] One thus reads in the Rule (9, 16): "And let him not reprimand the men of the Trench nor dispute with them"; or, in 9, 22, "eternal hate toward the men of the Trench because of their spirit of hoarding money!"[25] or, better still, in 10, 19–20:

> I will not grapple with the men of perdition [the men of the Trench] until the Day of Revenge, but my wrath shall not turn from the men of falsehood and I will not rejoice until judgement is made.[26]

The latter text is particularly interesting, for "the men of the Trench" [the men of perdition] here they are truly the ones on whom the punishments of the Day of Judgement will be exercised.

The origin of the Koranic formula *aṣḥāb al-ʾukhdūd* is thus established. It is a simple transposition of the Qumranian expression *anešē haš-šaḥat̲*. The general sense of the sura is assured as a consequence. It is the scene of the Last Judgement. The impious shall be thrown in the trench set alight by hell, where they will burn on a low flame, in punishment for the crimes that they have committed against the righteous.

Verse 10 corroborates our interpretation: "In truth, they who persecute the believing men and women, and do not repent, theirs will be the torment of hell, and theirs the doom of burning."[27] Admittedly, a number of scholars have there detected a later addition, but this interpolation was not made at random. It reveals an intimate and reliable understanding of the sura, for which it provided, so to speak, the oldest and most profound commentary.

The presence in the Koran of a Qumrānian expression as technical as "men of the Trench" suggests in the most precise manner that the Prophet had had knowledge of typically Essenian ideas and formulas.[28] It is an earnest invitation to take up again the study of Koranic eschatology in the light of Qumrān texts.

NOTES

1. I was able to discuss this text with my colleague at Strasbourg, T.Fahd. The translation [in French in the original article] that you have just read is the

fruit of this discussion. [I have used various English translations, including those of Arberry, Dawood, Yusuf Ali, and Pickthall—Ed.] Sura LXXXV.1–8.

2. [Cf. other translations: Dawood: "Diggers of the trench"; Arberry: "Men of the Pit"; Pickthall: "Owners of the ditch"; Bell: "fellows of the Pit."]

3. See for example: A. P. Caussin de Perceval, *Essai sur l'histoire des Arabes* (Paris, 1847), vol. 1, p. 129 n. 2; T. Nöldeke, *Geschichte der Perser und Araber zur Zeit der Sassaniden* (Leiden, 1879), p. 186; I. Guidi, *L'Arabie antéislamique* (Paris, 1921), pp. 73–74; T. Andrae, *Les origines de l'Islam et le Christianisme* (Paris, 1955), pp. 18–20.

4. A. Geiger, *Was hat Mohammed aus dem Judenthum aufgenommen?* (Bonn, 1833), p. 192

5. O. Loth, "Die Leute der Grube," *ZDMG* 35 (1881): 610–22.

6. R. Blachère, *Le Coran* (Paris, 1957).

7. [Dan. 3:20: "And he [Nebuchadnezzar] commanded the most mighty men that were in his army to bind Shadrach, Meshach, and Abednego, and to cast them into the burning fiery furnace."]

8. H. Grimme, *Mohammed* (Munster, 1895), vol. 2, p. 77 n. 4.

9. See also R. Paret, EI2, vol. 1, p. 713.

10. [Cf. E. W. Lane, *An Arabic-English Lexicon* (Beirut, 1968), part 2, pp. 705–706: *khadda* = to make a trench; *ʾukhdud* = furrow, trench, or channel in the ground.]

11. H. Speyer, *Die biblischen Erzahlungen im Qoran* (Hildesheim, 1961), vol. 2, p. 424.

12. [IV Esdras = The Second Book of Esdras of the Apocrypha.]

13. [*New English Bible with Apocrypha* (Oxford, 1970), p. 32 of the section 'The Apocrypha.']

14. We shall quote the Qumrān texts in the translations of A. Dupont-Sommer, *Les écrits esséniens découverts près de la mer Morte* (Paris, 1964).

15. [In the Old Testament, *Sheol* has the meaning of the underworld, the place of departed souls. It is usually translated in the Authorized Version as "hell," "grave," or "pit."]

16. See, for example, Ps. 16:10 ["For thou wilt not leave my soul in hell," King James Version; "For thou wilt not abandon me to Sheol," The New English Bible.]; 30:10; 55:24; Job 33:24, 28, 30.

17. [I have used Geza Vermes's translation: *The Complete Dead Sea Scrolls in English* (Harmondsworth, 1998), The Community Rule, p. 102] Dupont-Sommer's French translation:

Et quant à la Visite de tous ceux qui marchent en cet (Esprit), elle consiste en l 'abondance des coups qu'administrent tous les Anges de destruction en la Fosse éternelle par la furieuse colère du Dieu des vengeances, en l' effroi éternel et la honte sans fin, ainsi qu'en l'opprobre de l "extermination par le feu des régions ténébreuses.

18. Compare what Josephus says of the Essenians in his *De Bello Judaico*, II, § 155: ". . . while the evil souls, they relegate them to a gloomy hollow. . . ." See also I *Enoch* 103, 8; *Liber Antiquitatum Biblicarum* 63, 4.

19. Hymns 3:12 [Vermes, *The Complete Dead Sea Scrolls*, p. 260]; Dupont-Sommer's translation: "Les flots de la Fosse (se déchaînent) pour toutes les œuvres d'épouvante."

20. Hymns 3:27.

21. Hymns 3:18 [Vermes,*The Complete Dead Sea Scrolls*, p. 260]; Dupont-Sommer: "les battants de la Fosse se referment."

22. Hymns 3:26 [Vermes, *The Complete Dead Sea Scrolls*, p. 261]; Dupont-Sommer: "toutes les trappes de la Fosse."

23. Ecrit de Damas [Damascus Covenant or Damascus Document], 6, 15; 13, 14; cf; Book of Jubilees 10:3; 15:26.

24. Cf. Dupont-Sommer, *Les écrits esséniens découverts près de la mer Morte*, p. 96, n. 1 and 115 n. 2.

25. Dupont-Sommer's translation: "haine éternelle envers les hommes de la Fosse à cause de (leur) esprit de thésaurisation!" But cf. Vermes, *The Complete Dead Sea Scrolls*, p. 111: "Everlasting hatred in a spirit of secrecy for the men of perdition!"

26. Ibid., p. 113–14]

27. [Essentially, Pickthall's translation. Our author used Blachère's French translation.]

28. See other examples of it in the author's "An Essenian Tradition in the Koran," *RHR* 170 (1966): 143–57; chap. 4.3 of this volume.

4.5

A Possible Coptic Source for a Qur'ānic Text

Wilson B. Bishai

The Qur'ān includes certain statements about the creation of Adam and the fall of Satan that are so different from the biblical record as to pose certain problems regarding their possible origins and relationships. These statements are recorded in several suras, of which Suras VII.7–18 and XXXVIII.72–79 are the most prominent.[1] The following text in Sura XXXVIII includes most of the details of this account:

72 When thy Lord said unto the angels: lo! I am about to create a mortal out of mire,
73 And when I have fashioned him and breathed into him of My Spirit, then fall down before him prostrate,
74 The angels fell down prostrate, every one,
75 Saving Iblīs; he was scornful and became one of the disbelievers.
76 He [God] said: O Iblīs! What hindereth thee from falling prostrate before that which I have created with both My hands? Art thou too proud or art thou of the high exalted?
77 He [Iblīs] said: I am better than him. Thou createdest me of fire, whilst him Thou didst create of clay.
78 He [God] said: Go forth from hence, for lo! thou art outcast,
79 And lo! My curse is on thee till the Day of Judgment.
80 He [Iblīs] said: My Lord! Reprieve me till the day when they are raised.

Wilson B. Bishai, "A Possible Coptic Source for a Qur'ānic Text," *JAOS* 91, no. 1 (1971): 125–28. Reprinted with permission.

81 He [God] said: Lo! thou art of those reprieved
82 Until the day of the time appointed.
83 He [Iblīs] said: Then, by Thy might, I surely will beguile them every one,
84 Save Thy single-minded slaves among them.

Sura VII.10 and 16 add to the above account the following statements:

10 And We have given you [mankind] power in the earth, . . .
16 He [Iblīs] said: Now, because Thou hast sent me astray, verily I shall lurk in ambush for them on Thy Right Path.[2]

Referring to these passages in the Qur'ān, A. Guillaume stated that such a story about angels being ordered to worship man cannot be of Jewish origin, since man in Judaism is made a little lower than angels. Accordingly, another source, possibly Christian or gnostic Christian, is to be sought.[3]

In 1926 Rabbi Leo Jung published an excellent study dedicated wholly to *Fallen Angels in Jewish, Christian, and Mohammedan Literature*. He cites many accounts of the creation of man and the fall of Satan from Jewish, Christian, and Islamic sources; but he makes clear that the original source of these accounts must have developed from two separate stories—one involving Satan's objection to Adam's creation and the other dealing with Satan's refusal to worship Adam after his creation.[4] Jung stipulates that the origin of the first story of Satan's objection to man's creation was Jewish and cites some samples for it.[5] However, he maintains that the origin of the other story of Satan's refusal to worship Adam was basically Christian and non-Jewish. He asserts that in Islam, Muḥammad, and those whom he calls "the fathers of Moslem traditions" confused the two accounts, and put emphasis on the idea that revenge was the reason why the devil lurked for man and sought to beguile him.[6] Jung also cites translations of pertinent portions in the Syriac book *The Cave of Treasures* and of the pseudepigraphic books of *Adam and Eve*.[7]

The Syriac book *The Cave of Treasures* was edited, translated into German, and published by Carl Bezold in 1883.[8] In 1927 E. A. Wallis Budge published a translation of it in English with ample notes and comments.[9] Wallis Budge wanted to consider as its author Ephraim, the Syrian, himself, who died in 373 C.E. However, he finally agreed with Bezold that it was perhaps first written in the sixth century by a Syriac scribe belonging to the Ephraim school of Syriac apocryphal authors, who, due to great demand by the Christian communities of the early Christian centuries, borrowed, wrote and circulated many nonbiblical stories about the patriarchs, the prophets, Christ, and the apostles.[10]

The particular book in the group of pseudepigraphic books entitled *Adam and Eve*, which records an account of the fall of Satan parallel to the Qurʾānic text, is the one entitled *Vita Adae et Evae*. It is well edited and translated in R. H. Charles's *Apocrypha and Pseudepigrapha*. In his introduction to these books, Charles asserts that the main bulk of the stories included are essentially Jewish, and some of them could be traced back to pre-Christian times.[11] However, Charles maintains that during the early Christian centuries, many Christians and gnostics did borrow these stories and embellish them with several other clearly Christian and gnostic ideas, which were later translated into Latin and Greek.[12] A clear sample of such embellishments can be detected in the portion in *Vita Adae et Evae*, which narrates the story of Satan's refusal to worship Adam and his subsequent fall from heaven. Both Charles and Jung tend to believe that the Syriac book of *The Cave of Treasures* was one of the background sources associated with such embellishments in the *Vita*.[13]

The third and most neglected account of the fall of Satan is included in the *Encomium* of Theodosius, Archbishop of Alexandria, on Saint Michael, the Archangel. E. A. Wallis Budge translated it among other miscellaneous texts in 1915 and used for his translation two Coptic manuscripts dated in 983 and 987 C.E.[14] When I examined this document in Coptic and as Budge had translated it, I observed that the account of the fall of Satan in it was quite elaborate and by far the closest to the Qurʾānic account. There is no reason to reject the claims of the two Coptic manuscripts attributing the arrangement of the *Encomium* to Theodosius, Archbishop of Alexandria, who died in 567 C.E.[15] This should not exclude the possibility that the ideas expressed in this *Encomium* were in circulation in Egypt before Theodosius's time. Since the account of Satan's refusal to worship Adam and his subsequent fall is recorded in some detail in the Coptic text, I shall quote from Budge's translation only the pertinent statements that reveal close similarities to the Qurʾānic text.

> Adam saith, . . . He [God] breathed into my face a breath of life, He set me upon an exceedingly glorious throne, and He commanded all the hosts

> of heaven who were in truth under His power, saying, "Come ye, and worship the work of My Hands, My likeness and My image." And there was there [a hateful being], who was of the earlier creation, that is to say, Satanael, who is called the Devil, and he was an Archangel. Furthermore, when the command had issued from the mouth of God, Michael, the Archangel, . . . and his host came and worshipped. . . . And afterwards, Gabriel the Archangel and his host came, and they bowed low in homage even as did Michael, and so likewise did all the hosts of angels, each rank in its proper order. Finally, the Master said unto that Mastema, the interpretation of which is "hater," Come thou also, and worship the work of My hands. . . ." And Satanael answered boldly and said, ". . . Far be it from Thee to make me worship this thing (of earth)! . . ."
>
> And the compassionate God said unto him, "Satanael, hearken unto me! . . ." And the Mastema said, ". . . Far be it from us to worship that which is inferior to us! Moreover, we are beings of spirit, but this creature is of the earth, . . ."
>
> And straightway God was angry, and He commanded a mighty cherubim [*sic*], who smote him and reduced him to helplessness, . . . and he cast him and all those who were with him forth from heaven. And the Good God cried out unto Michael ". . . I know that the Mastema will fight against My created being, wishing to cast him away from Me even as I cast Mastema forth from My kingdom. But behold, I entrust My created beings unto thee. . . ."[16]

It is very clear from this Coptic account that, with the exclusion of the references to Michael and Gabriel, it runs quite parallel to the Qur'ānic rendition. Content analysis of both the Coptic and the Qur'ānic texts reveals that the following eight points stand out clearly in common:

(1). God created Adam and breathed in him the breath of life.
(2). God exalted Adam with glory.
(3). God ordered all angels to worship him.
(4). All angels obeyed except Satan and his hosts.
(5). God entered into a conversation or an argument with Satan about the latter's refusal to obey.
(6). Satan's excuse was his being created of spirit or fire while Adam was created from earth.
(7). Satan and his hosts were cast out of heaven.
(8). Satan threatened to lurk for and tempt Adam in revenge.

The account in *The Cave of Treasures* is quoted here in its entirety as translated by Wallis Budge:

> And when the prince of the lower order of angels saw what great majesty had been given unto Adam, he was jealous of him from that day, and he did not wish to worship him. And he said unto his hosts, "Ye shall not worship him, and ye shall not praise him with the angels. It is meet that ye should worship me, because I am fire and spirit; and not that I should worship a thing of dust, which has been fashioned of fine dust." And the Rebel meditating these things would not render obedience to God, and of his own free will he asserted his independence and separated himself from God. But he was swept away out of heaven and fell.[17]

It is obvious that in contrast to the contents of the Coptic and Qurʾānic texts, the account in *The Cave of Treasures* fails to record any direct conversation or argument between God and Satan, and instead records a conversation between Satan and his own angels in which Satan asked his angels to worship him. Moreover, it also fails to portray the revengeful attitude of Satan against Adam after Satan had been cast out.

The account of Satan's refusal to worship Adam in *Vita Adae et Evae* is also quoted here in its entirety as translated by R. H. Charles:

> And Michael went out and called the angels saying:
>
> "Worship the image of God as the Lord God hath commanded."
>
> And Michael himself worshipped first; then he called me and said: "Worship the image of God the Lord." And I answered, "I have no [need] to worship Adam." And since Michael kept urging me to worship, I said to him, "Why dost thou urge me? I will not worship an inferior and younger being [than I]. I am his senior in the Creation, before he was made was I already made. It is his duty to worship me."
>
> When the angels, who were under me, heard this, they refused to worship him. And Michael saith, "Worship the image of God, but if thou wilt not worship him, the Lord God will be wrath with thee." And I said, "If He be wrath with me, I will set my seat above the stars of heaven, and will be like the Highest."[18]

Although this account is more elaborate than the one in *The Cave of Treasures*, it does not record any conversation between God and Satan. On the contrary, it contains a dialogue between Satan and Adam, in which

Satan was telling Adam the background of why he (Satan) had been tempting Eve. During this conversation, Satan quotes a dialogue between himself and Michael—not God—in which Michael was the one who asked Satan to worship Adam.

From the above comparisons, it becomes quite clear that the Qur'ānic text concerning the fall of Satan bears more resemblance to the Coptic account than either *The Cave of Treasures* or *Vita Adae et Evae*, giving rise to the assertion that the Coptic account constitutes a very likely source for the Qur'ānic text. This assertion is strengthened by the fact that the Copts of Egypt during the early Christian centuries were known for their massive production of Apocrypha and pseudepigrapha.[19] This characteristic of the early Copts should not be surprising to us in the light of the evidence of gnostic influence on the early Coptic Christian thought. The gnostics were literate people and well acquainted with ancient religions and mythology. As Christianity was spreading in Egypt, a group of these gnostic Christians apparently made an effort to tie old Egyptian myths to Christian beliefs. In this respect C. J. Bleeker mentions the following:

> It can be proved that a number of gnostic conceptions go back to ancient Egyptian religious thoughts. What is even more important, there is some evidence that to a certain extent there existed a typological affinity between the ancient religion of the valley of the Nile on the one hand and gnosticians at the other side.[20]

A very plausible story of ancient Egypt that fitted very well into the biblical record of creation was the legend of the rebellion of Seth against Horus. Seth, a synonym of hatred and disobedience in Egyptian mythology, caused all sorts of troubles to befall man in revenge for his banishment by Horus and the rest of the Egyptian Ennead.[21] In the minds of the early Egyptian Christians, Satan, as a parallel to Seth, became the rebel and the enemy of man, who began to lurk in ambush in order to drag him (man) into disobedience. As a matter of fact, Wallis Budge himself, commenting on the story of the fall of Satan in *The Cave of Treasures*, recognized its possible Coptic origin and remarked that the early Egyptian Christians were known for compiling various apocryphal stories, drawn mainly from ancient Egyptian legend. He even mentioned the story of the struggle of Seth against Horus as a possible source for the account of the fall of Satan in *The Cave of Treasures*.[22]

Since the early Coptic Church (at least until the fifth century) was among the leading churches in early Christendom, it is not surprising to find that many of its apocryphal stories spread throughout the Christian Middle East. By way of Abyssinia, Coptic ideas could have spread into Arabia, at least during the Abyssinian occupation of Yemen between 525 and 571 C.E., if not before, due to trade and religious persecution. In pre-Islamic times, Arabia was a haven of refuge to all dissatisfied and persecuted Christians, especially the Copts after the Council of Chalcedon had ruled against them in 451 C.E. Muḥammad must have come in contact with many of these Copts and listened to their stories. Muḥammad's friendship to Christians of Coptic faith is reflected in many aspects of his life. He is known to have had cordial relations with the Negus of Abyssinia, as indicated by the fact that he advised his followers at a time of persecution to flee there. He married a Coptic wife named Mariya, and he is reported to have advised his followers to be especially kind to the Copts of Egypt, considering them his in-laws.[23] Such friendly gestures to the Copts add more credence to the possibility that Coptic was the most likely source of the Qur'anic account of the fall of Satan.[24]

NOTES

1. Other accounts occur in Suras XV.26, XVII.61, XVIII.51, and XX.116.
2. Quoted from M. M. Pickthall, *The Meaning of the Glorious Koran.*
3. Alfred Guillaume, "The Influence of Judaism on Islam," in *The Legacy of Israel*, ed. E. R. Bevan and Charles Singer (Oxford, 1927), p. 139.
4. Rabbi Leo Jung, *Fallen Angels in Jewish, Christian, and Mohammedan Literature* (Philadelphia, 1926), p. 53.
5. Ibid., p. 47.
6. Ibid., pp. 53–56.
7. Ibid., pp. 57–59.
8. Carl Bezold, *Die Schatzhöhle I* (Leipzig, 1883).
9. E. A. Wallis Budge, *The Book of the Cave of Treasures* (London, 1927).
10. Bezold, *Die Schatzhöle I*, p. 4, and Budge, *The Book of the Cave of Treasures*, pp. 6, 21, 22. Syriac and Arabic Texts.
11. R. H. Charles, *The Apocrypha and Pseudepigrapha of the Old Testament* (Oxford, 1963), vol. 2, pp. 123, 126.
12. Ibid., pp. 125, 126.

13. Ibid., pp. 128, 131. See also Jung, *Fallen Angels in Jewish, Christian, and Mohammedan Literature*, p. 53.

14. E. A. Wallis Budge, *Miscellaneous Coptic Texts* (Oxford, 1915), pp. liii, lvi.

15. E. L. Butcher, *The Story of the Church of Egypt* (London, 1897), pp. xiii, 330.

16. Budge, *Miscellaneous Coptic Texts*, pp. 904–906.

17. Budge, *The Book of the Cave of Treasures*, p. 55.

18. Charles, *The Apocrypha and Pseudepigrapha of the Old Testament*, p. 137.

19. Compare W. H. P. Hatch, "Three Leaves from a MS. of the *Acta Apostolorum*," in *Coptic Studies in Honor of Walter Ewig* (Boston, 1950), p. 310.

20. C. J. Bleeker, "The Egyptian Background of Gnosticism," in *Le Origini dello Gnosticismo* ed. Ugo Bianchi (Leiden, 1967), p. 231. The entire article as well as other related articles in the same work contain useful remarks and footnotes about the subject.

21. The struggle between Seth and Horus is very well discussed in J. H. Breasted, *Development of Religion and Thought in Ancient Egypt* (New York, 1912), pp. 31–65. See also H. Te Velde, *Seth, God of Confusions* (Leiden, 1967).

22. Budge, *The Book of the Cave of Treasures*, pp. 56–8. Surprisingly enough, Budge failed to associate the vividly related account about Satan in the *Encomium* with that in *The Cave of Treasures*. Apparently, the years that had lapsed between 1915 and 1927 caused him to neglect to connect the two accounts.

23. See Wilson B. Bishai, *Islamic History of the Middle East* (Boston, 1968), p. 147.

24. This conclusion adds more support to Ilse Lichtenstadter's contention that certain Qur'ānic interpretations and symbols can be better understood in the light of ancient Egyptian history. Needless to say, ancient Egyptian religious symbols could never have reached pre-Islamic Arabia without the Coptic intermediate stage.

See Ilse Lichtenstadter, "Origin and Interpretation of some Koranic Symbols," in *Arabic and Islamic Studies in Honor of Hamilton A. R. Gibb,* ed. George Makdisi (Leiden, 1965), pp. 426–36.

4.6

Introduction to Raimund Kobert

Ibn Warraq

Koran XXII.30: *dhālika wa man yuʿaẓẓim ḥurumāti—l-lāhi fahuwa khayrū-l-lahū ʿinda rabbihī wa ʾuḥillat lakumu-l-ʾanʿāmu ʾillā mā yutlā ʿalaykum fajtanibū -r- rijsa mina-l-ʾawthāni wa—jtanibū qawla-ẓ-ẓū ri*

31: *ḥunafāʾa lil-l- lāhi ghayra mushrikīna bihī wa man-yshrik bi-l-lāhi fakaʾannamā kharra mina-s- samāʾi fatakhafuhu- ṭ-ṭayru ʾaw tahwi bihi-r-rīḥu fī makānin saḥīqin*

30: That (is the command) And whoso magnifies the sacred things of Allah, it will be well for him in the sight of his Lord. The cattle are lawful unto you save that which hath been told you. So shun the filth of idols, and shun lying speech [false words, *qawla-ẓ-ẓū r*].

31: Turning unto Allah [only], not ascribing partners unto Him [*mushrikīna bihī*]; for whoso ascribes partners [*yshrik*] unto Allah, it is as if he has fallen from the sky and the birds had snatched him or the wind had blown him to a far-off place.

A number of scholars have argued that the *mushrikūn* mentioned in the Koran are to be taken as referring to "Christians." Gunter Luling, for instance, has put forward the thesis that the Koran that we know today contains within it a pre-Islamic Christian text. The transmitted Islamic Koran text is the end result of several successive editorial revisions, which must be seen against the background of polemics against the Trinitarian Christians of Mecca, who associated Jesus to God (*mushrikūn* = "associators"), thus deifying him. According to Luling, there is "a massive number of references in the writings of early Muslim scholars which plainly show that they took *mushrikūn* and the synonyms of this word as 'Christians' of the trinitarian creed."[1] For Luling, these references to Christians reflect a real historical situation in Mecca just before the rise of Islam.

Hawting, on the other hand, wants to argue that "material in Muslim tradition that has been understood as informing us about religious conditions in and around Mecca in the time of the Prophet should not be understood primarily as a reflexion of real historical conditions. Rather it reflects two fundamental Muslim beliefs: that Islam is identical with the religion of Abraham (dīn Ibrāhīm), and that the Koran is revelation made in Mecca and Medina. The former belief is mirrored in reports documenting the persistence of elements of Abrahamic religion in inner Arabia in spite of its degradation by the idolatrous Arabs; the latter leads to the view that the opponents called *mushrikūn* in the Koran must be the Arab contemporaries and neighbours of Muhammad."[2]

Though Muslim tradition does talk about pre-Islamic Mecca and Medina as societies dominated by polytheism and idolatry, it also suggests that the Arabs had some sort of an idea of a supreme god, over and above their local idols, called Allah, who was especially associated with the sanctuary called Kaʿba. The latter was the locus of an annual pilgrimage (ḥajj).

Hawting continues:

> It is against this background that the traditional charge of *shirk* is usually understood. That Arabic noun (to which are related the verbal form ashraka and the active participle mushrik), is, . . . frequently understood as "idolatry" or "polytheism" but in a basic, non-religious sense it refers to the idea of "making someone or something a partner, or associate, of someone else or something else." . . . According to the traditional material, the *mushrikūn* were not simple polytheists who were ignorant of the existence of God: they knew of Allah and on occasion prayed to and worshipped Him, but generally they associated other beings with Him and thus dishonoured Him.[3]

Muslim tradition also tells us of the *talbiya*, "the invocation made in a loud voice and repeatedly by the pilgrim when he enters the state of ritual taboo (iḥrām) for the Pilgrimage at Mecca."[4] This verbal formula is called the *talbiya* because it begins with the words *labbayka Allāhumma labbayka* ("at your service, O god, at your service"). As Hawting adds, "In a completely monotheist version it is an important part of the Muslim ḥajj rituals, but tradition tells us that before Islam many tribes had their own versions which exhibited the distinctive mixture of polytheism and monotheism that characterised *shirk.*"

The talbiya of the Quraysh goes: *labbayka Allāhumma labbayka lā sharīka laka illā sharīkun huwa laka tamlikuhu wa-mā malaka* ("at your service, O God, at your service; you who have no associate apart from an associate which you have; you who have power over him and that over which he has power").[5] Muqātil b. Sulaymān (died 767 C.E.) in his *Tafsīr* gives a list of fifty-six talbiyas. "Kister[6] makes it clear that for . . . Muqātil the various talbiyas of pre-Islamic Arabia were evidence of the way in which the pure monotheism brought to Arabia by Abraham had been corrupted in the generations that followed him. Commenting on Koran XXII.30, Muqātil identifies the 'false speech' (*qawl aẓ-ẓūr*) that we are there commanded to shun as that contained in the talbiyas of the pre-Islamic Arabs. What we must avoid, he says, is attributing a partner to God in the wording of the *talbiya* (*al-shirk fī'l-talbiya*)."[7]

For Hawting,

> the identification of the *mushrikūn* as pre-Islamic idolatrous Arabs is dependent upon Muslim tradition and is not made by the Koran itself; the nature of the Koranic polemic against the *mushrikūn* does not fit well with the image of pre-Islamic Arab idolatry and polytheism provided by Muslim tradition; the imputation of one's opponents of "idolatry"—of which *shirk* functions as an equivalent in Islam—is a recurrent motif in monotheist polemic [e.g., in Reformation Europe] and is frequently directed against opponents who consider themselves to be monotheists; the traditional Muslim literature which gives us details about idolatry and polytheism of the pre-Islamic Arabs of the *jāhiliyya* is largely stereotypical and formulaic and its value as evidence about religious ideas and practices of the Arabs before Islam is questionable. . . .[8]

For Hawting, the rise of Islam can only be understood against a monotheist background; Islam was born as a result of disputes among monotheists, not from a confrontation with real idolaters. Nor was it born in a remote area of western Arabia but probably in Palestine, Syria, and Iraq, where the monotheist tradition was already firmly established.

Luling and Kobert, on the other hand, accept the traditional Muslim framework, both the geography and chronology. They point to various accounts that seem to attest to the presence of monotheism of various sorts in the Hijaz and even in Mecca, where the Kaʿba is said to have contained a picture of Jesus and Mary. Indeed for Luling, the Kaʿba had been a Christian church.[9] However, Luling, like Hawting, also believes Islam was born out of the discord between the different factions and confessions of Christendom. But unlike Hawting, Luling believes all this took place in Mecca and its environs. Luling and Kobert see their task as uncovering the Christian layers that have lain hidden, indeed deliberately disguised by Muslim editors, in the Koran and Muslim tradition.

Thus Kobert tries to show that the words in sura XXII.30: *ijtanibū qawlāẓ-ẓūri* ("shun lying words" or "shun lying speech") are not just about lying but more to do with avoiding *shirk*, that is associating or attributing a partner to God.

More specifically, Kobert believes that there was a *talbiya,* the verbal formula frequently repeated during the rituals connected with the hajj, which was influenced by Christianity but one which the Prophet rejected as *false words*.

Early Muslim tradition recognized that *mushrikūn* referred to Christians, but this was gradually forgotten as the final form of the Muslim dogma took shape.

Kobert then tries to show the presence of Christianity in the Hijaz, giving linguistic and biographical evidence.

NOTES

1. Gunter Luling, *On the Pre-Islamic Christian Strophe Poetical Texts in the Koran* (forthcoming), p. 21, n. 15

2. G. R. Hawting, *The Idea of Idolatry and the Emergence of Islam. From Polemic to History* (Cambridge, 1999), p. 20.

3. Ibid., p. 21

4. EI2 s.v. Talbiya.

5. Hawting, *The Idea of Idolatry and the Emergence of Islam*, p.22.

6. M. J. Kister, "Labbayka, Allāhumma, Labbayka . . . ," *JSAI* 2 (1980): 33–57.

7. Hawting, *The Idea of Idolatry and the Emergence of Islam*, p.32

8. Ibid., p.5

9. G. Luling, *Der christliche Kult an der vorislamischen Kaaba als Problem der Islamwissenschaft und christlichen Theologie* (Erlangen, 1977, 1992); *Die Wiederentdeckung des Propheten Muhammad* (Erlangen 1981), esp. chap. II.2.a.

4.7

The Shahādat aẓ-ẓūr: The False Witness

Raimund Köbert

Translated by G. A. Wells

A few years ago in another publication[1] it was shown that a formulation of the *talbiya*, the *ḥajj*-festive cry, had existed that had been subjected to Christian influence, and had been rejected by Muhammad. At that time the present writer was not aware that tradition linked Koran XXII.30/31 with this very *talbiya* and that it may well be the *qawla-ẓ-ẓūr* named there.

Traces of the correct state of affairs remain in most of the commentators (Ṭabarī, Zamakhsharī, Nasafī, Nīsābūrī). But to my knowledge al Khāzin gives what is most complete. Hence I give what he says verbatim:

> [On the Koranic text:] Keep away from false words (*qawla-ẓ-ẓūr*), observes Ibn Abbas: "It is a question of the *shahādat aẓ-ẓūr* (the false *shahādat* or witness)." According to Aiman b. Khuraim,[2] there is a tradition that the Prophet rose for the *khuṭba* and said: "O ye people, the false *shahāda* (witness), and likewise giving God a companion, is mistaken!" Thereupon he recited the verse: "Keep away from the dirt of the idols and keep away from false words." Tirmidhī quotes these words and comments on them: "There are differences of opinion about what Aiman says, and we do not know whether in fact he heard the Prophet." Abu Dā'ūd quotes the same passage, but from Khuraim b. Fātik. It sup-

Raimund Kobert, "Die Shahādat aẓ-ẓūr," *Der Islam* 34 (1959): 194–95.

posedly means that the *mushrikūn* said in their *talbiya*: "*Labbayka*, thou hast no companion other than a companion who is yours, over whom, and over the area he rules, thou rulest." [cf. 1 Cor. 15:27: " For he hath put all things under his feet. But when he saith, all things are put under him, it is manifest that he is excepted, which did put all things under him. 28: And when all things shall be subdued unto him, then shall the Son also himself be subject unto him that put all things under him, that God may be all in all. "]

A. Khuraim b.Fātik is attested in Ibn Saʿd (6, 24, 22) as a contemporary of Muhammad. There can hardly be any doubt that by *qawla-ẓ-ẓūr* the *shahādat aẓ-ẓūr* is meant, and with it that *talbiya.* For if, as is usually done, one takes *qawla-ẓ-ẓūr* as meaning "lie and slander" (*kadhib wabuhtān*), it is strange that this prohibition should come in the middle of a coherent passage about the *ḥajj* and interrupt it. That the expression, as it is to be understood in the Koran, means a perverse cult action, that is, the false *talbiya*, and *shahāda* is also clear from the words that immediately follow: "faithful (*ḥunafāʾa* = *mukhliṣīna*) to God, without giving him a companion." On this, the commentator notes: "These words draw attention to the fact that someone who takes upon himself a task of honoring God intends with the devotion he performs thereby to serve God honestly and no other."

NOTES

1. *Biblica* 35 (1954): 405 f.
2. Cf. Ibn Saʾd, 6, 25, 2.

4.8

On the Meaning of the Three Final Words of Sura XXII.30–31

Raimund Köbert

Translated by G. A. Wells

Rudi Paret's new translation of the Koran[1] has drawn attention to the possibility that the words *ijtanibū qawla-ẓ-ẓūri* of Sura XXII, which are in the midst of stipulations about the *ḥajj* (XXII.27/28–33/34), may not mean the simple avoidance of false statements. Nor, as an account widely diffused in the West, and perhaps in Islam, too, will have it, might they be a statement prohibiting lying.[2]

In the first instance it seems that the plural in the translation "Avoid false statements" is particularly apposite if the words are taken as equivalent to "Avoid lies." Otherwise it is more difficult to justify and in any case leaves open the possibility of a singular. The lexical identification of *qawla-ẓ-ẓūr* with *kadhib,buhtān* (lie and slander) is already registered after Ṭabarī, by Mujāhid.[3] From him it passes through the commentaries of Baghawī, Zamakhsharī, Nīsābūrī,[4] Khāzin, Maḥallī, admittedly never as an ordinary prohibition of lying, which would be simple, relevant for all times, and even expected if one ignores the context. Rather it is a linkage always forged in often forced way with the prohibition of *shirk*, of the doctrine that God has an equal. For instance, in Zamakhsharī:

> After (the holy text) has urged that [God's] sacred things be honored and has found him who does so worthy of praise, it follows this with the command to avoid idols and lies. For to acknowledge God's unity, to deny that he has his equal, and to be honest in speaking are the highest

Raimund Köbert, "Zur Bedeutung der drei letzen Worte von Sure 22.30–31," *Orientalia* 35 (1966): 28–32.

> and the first sacred things [of God]. The [text] brings *shirk* and lying together in a single Koran verse. For *shirk* belongs in the category of lies because its devotees allege that an idol is worthy of adoration. The [text] therefore says, in effect, "Avoid therefore the service of idols, which is the source of lies, and avoid every lie. Have nothing to do with any of this, because [thereby] one remains long in baseness and disgrace and above all because it is a sort of idolatry (literally: and what is one to think of something the nature of which is idolatry?)"[5]

Maḥallī, writing late and striving for brevity, is the least forced. He restricts himself to saying: " 'Therefore avoid the dirt of idols'; explicatory [genitive], the [dirt] which are idols. 'Avoid false words.' "—with Maḥallī the thought of the lie recedes—"that is to say, [the doctrine] that God has a companion, the doctrine which is expressed in the *hajj* festive call of the *mushrikūn*, or 'avoid false witness (*shahādat aẓ-ẓūr*).' " Here there is a new factor, the *talbiyat al-mushrikūn*, which is lacking in Ṭabarī. Most of our ancient sources for the tafsīr are accessible in Ṭabarī and only in him. Yet he surely does not comprise all that is relevant, either because everything was not available to him, or because he passed over much as of little importance, so that such items were preserved only in later writers. Just as he is selective in his *Annals*, so in his commentary on the Koran his prime purpose is not to put together all that there is, but to orientate and point out a direction to his contemporaries. Merely to record that there was, at the time of the Prophet, a *talbiya* influenced by Christianity, one which the prophet rejected as *qawla-ẓ-ẓūr*, was, already in Mujāhid's time, insignificant and no longer necessary for the exegesis of the Koran.

The verse to be explained stands in Ṭabarī, as is natural, in the context of the *ḥajj* stipulations. His interpretation, which, as always, he puts first, leads him back to ʿĪsā (Baṣra c. 149 A.H.) as also, via Ibn Abī Najīḥ (Mecca, c. 132 A.H.) and Ibn Jurayj (died 149 or 151), to Mujāhid, and finally via Muhammad b.Saʿd and his authorities, to Ibn ʿAbbās himself, the father of Koranic exegesis. According to him, [the text] says:

> Avoid the *qawla-ẓ-ẓūr* [and] means [thereby]: Be careful not [to propound] lies and untruths against God by saying, with reference to the gods: 'We serve them only so that they bring us close to God' (Koran XXXIX.3/3), and, with reference to the angels [says]: "They are daughters of Allah."

If one takes into consideration the religious situation of Arabia in the sixth and seventh centuries,[6] one has to say a word that sounded approximately like Koran XXXIX.3/3—of course without the plural "gods," which can hardly have been spoken other than by Christians. These would accordingly be here the opponents of the Prophet. The designation *mushrikūn* soon admitted more than one interpretation, and could mean "Christians" and "polytheists," although *sharīk* would not be an obvious term for a god of polytheists. The phrase "your, their *shurakāʾ* for "your, their gods"—where one really has to envisage *shurakāʾ* in quotation marks as if it were a phrase taken over from an opponent—is quite common in the Koran (e.g., VI.22/22; X.28/29; XVI.86/88; XXVIII.64/64; XXXV.40/38). From the context it stands for *shufaʿāʾ*,[7] "advocate, mediator, helper." *Shafīʿ*, too, notably in connection with the Judgement Day, takes up Christian ideas. The clause in the Epistle to the Hebrews 7:25: "Wherefore he is able to save them to the uttermost that come unto God by him, seeing he ever liveth to make intercession for them," has had a profound effect on Christian thinking and feeling throughout the centuries. In the Egyptian koine and elsewhere it is rendered: *liʾannahū ḥaiyun fī kulli ḥīnin wa-yashfaʿu ʿanhum.* Unfortunately, its first appearance in Arabic cannot be ascertained.[8] *Sharīk* in the singular could have been an attempt to reproduce *homoousios* in pure Arabic. But the testimonies for that are not extant. One may further ask whether *shabaḥ*—which in the *tawḥīd* definition of Junayd means, according to al-Anṣāri, "person"[9] and which, according to the Muʿtazila, may not be said of God[10]—may also belong in this ancient layer of Christian terms in Arabic. In *Orientalia Christiana Periodica,* Rome 29 (1963), 480–481, one was referred to another stratum, the date of which likewise cannot be determined.

But is it not altogether wrongheaded to believe that Muhammad was in touch with the details and niceties of Christian theology that have been mentioned? Is it not better to assume, with W. Rudolph, K. Ahrens[11] and others, that the rejection of sonship of God is due to Muhammad's having always thought merely of physical sonship, and the like? Crude misunderstandings and distortions of each other's doctrines arise principally when religious communities are firmly entrenched and live separately from each other, not so long as they are in touch with each other. In the case in question, that is at a relatively late period, if one discounts the effects of the polemics of the Koran, which does not distinguish between

Christianity and polytheism. The beginning of Simeon of Bet-Arsam's letter of 524, the original form of which T. Nöldeke (Ṭabarī, 185) justly called "positively genuine," shows that already at that time, the Maʿadd[12] understood the differences between Melchites, Monophysites, and Nestorians well enough to exploit them in diplomacy. Muhammad also met men such as Haudha b. Alī al-Ḥanafī,[13] and the influence of Ḥīra was extensive. Public life itself there had, from the court downward, a Christian aspect.[14] ʿAdī b. Zayd woos Hind bint Nuʿmān "three days after Easter," that is, after our Maundy Thursday on Easter Monday, on which even now the time of marriage solemnizations begins (CIC § 1108). He first saw the girl in the Church of Dair Tūmā, likewise on a Maundy Thursday, "which falls three days after Palm Sunday," when one went to the celebration of the Eucharist. On this occasion in Muhammad's time, Haudha (already mentioned) successfully petitioned for the release of the Tamim held captive by the Persians in Bahrain, and himself, with those he had liberated, took part in the Eucharist.[15] About the middle of the sixth century, Kyros of Edessa held his Aramaic *ʿellātā* in the theological school of Ḥīra, which he had founded. These *ʿellātā* are lectures on the subject (*ʿeliĕtâ*) of the festivals of the ecclesiastical year, and they have come down to us in the tract of East Syrian theology that has been most fully preserved.[16] In the creed of the Muʿtazila the relevant clause *taqaddasa [illāhu] ʿan mulāmassati n-nisāʾ* also stands at the end like an afterthought, whereas with the Sunnis *lam yattakhid ṣāḥibatan*, in more cautious wording that strictly keeps to the Koran (72.3/3) is brought to the front.[17] K. Ahrens and W. Rudolph regard it as certain that Sura 112 is directed against the Nicene formula *γεννηθεντα, oύ ποιηθέντα* [*begotten not made*]. Since this formula is included in the baptism symbol,[18] it must have spread in Aramaic, and will hardly have been unrepresented in Arabic. If it may no more be said that the angels are the daughters of Allah, then the Koran is not here quoted verbally (XLIII.19/18; XVI.57/59, etc.), and that is striking. The difficulty of doing justice to the quotation is partly due to the fact that ʿUzza, Allāt, and Manāt are named daughters of Allah, yet the term for them, *jarāniqa*, does not denote female beings.[19] The difficulty is also due in part to the fact that angels are cosmic intelligences; the most supreme of which was sometimes addressed as the Logos. These questions have as yet produced no answer and must be left aside.

The Prophet's equating of *shahādat aẓ-ẓūr* [false witness] with *shirk* we find in a hadith traced back to Wā'il b. Rabī 'a.[20] Tirmidhi [21] and Abū Dāwūd[22] name a different *tābiʿī*. Returning now with a correction to what I wrote in *Der Islam* 34 (1959): 195, let me repeat here the form of the tradition in Khazin. The hadith recurs in similar form in Zamakhsharī, Nīsābūrī,[23] and Maḥallī.

Khāzin has the following:

> "Avoid the *qawla-ẓ-ẓūr,* that is, lie and untruth. Ibn ʿAbbās (in Baghawī: Ibn Masʿūd) said: "What is meant is the *shahādat aẓ-ẓūr*. According to Aiman b. Khuraim, there is a tradition that the Prophet rose to the *khuṭba* and said: 'Ye people, I regard the *shahādat aẓ-ẓūr* as the same as *ishrāk bi-llāh.*' He then quoted the verse: 'Avoid therefore the dirt of idols and avoid the *qawla-ẓ-ẓūr*.'" Tirmidhi quotes [the hadith] and observes: "Concerning the handing down of it there are differences of opinion. We do not know that Aiman had [heard] a word directly (*samāʿ*) from the Prophet." Abū Dāwūd quotes the same hadith: but from Khuraim b. Fātik.

Khuraim is the father of Aiman.[24] There it is said of the father that he was among the Prophet's Companions and passed on immediate traditions from him. If a manuscript states the first of two, and reads *ṣaḥiba huwa wa-abūhu bi-rasūli-llāh* instead of *li-abīhi subḥa bi-rasūli-llāh,* that may be an ancient version, perhaps the original, inexact one, which was corrected. Directly or indirectly, it will have occasioned the observation of Tirmidhi that I have mentioned. According to the stories in the *Kitab al-Aghāni*, Aiman was still alive in the latter years of Abd ul-Malik b. Marwān. The allegation that Fātik had been *ṣaḥābī*, and died in the time of Muʿawiya is found also in the *Khulāṣa*.[25] There, Aiman is called *tābiʿī*. In the worst case we are dealing with a *ḥadīth mursal bihī* with an incomplete chain of tradition, which goes back to a court poet in matters that link up less with his sphere. If we believe J. Schacht, this state of affairs does not impugn the credibility of the tradition, since no one exerted himself afterward to produce a complete *isnād*, such as was later demanded.

If we may return to Khāzin, he appends a further explanation with *qīla* which, in Maḥallī, we found taken into the overall account of the verse's ending. The words are: It is also said that (with *qawla-ẓ-ẓūr*) the words of the *mushrikūn* in their *talbiya* are meant: Labbayka, you have no companion other than a companion who is yours, over whom and over whose realm you rule. Instead of *qawl al-mushrikīn*, Zamakhsharī and Rāzī[26] say *ahl al-jahilīya*. Abu Ḥaiyan[27] names in *Baḥr al-muḥīṭ* 5:351 Mujāhid, ʿIkrima, ash-Shabʾī, and Qatāda as the source; men from the first generation after Ibn ʿAbbās. The *talbiya* itself is preserved early in the *Kitāb al-aṣnām*[28] (of Ibn al-Kalbī) where it is said that it is a *ḥajj* festive cry distorted by additions, and used by the Nizār at the *ihlāl*. The Nizār[29] and all the Banū Ismāʿil

> did [indeed] confess with their *talbiya* the one God, [but] they placed him beside their gods and gave the kingdom of these gods (according to XVII.111/111; XXV.2/2; Ashʿarī *Maqālāt*, 156,8) into his hand; this is why God has said to his Prophet: "Most [people] do not believe in God, without associating with him other gods (XII.106/106)"; that is, notwithstanding the recognition of what I really am, they confess me as one, not without having given me a companion from among my own creatures.

A little later than Ibn al Kalbī, Ibn Ḥabib[30] gave in *Muḥabbar* 311,11–13 the wording of the festive cry. Significantly, it is still said by Suyūṭī in *Tafsīr al-Jalālain* on XII.100/106, that, by the *sharīk* (singular), the *mushrikūn* meant their idols (plural: *aṣnām*).

From what I have said it is certain that the formula given in authentic *sajʿ* existed in early Islam. It can also be said that its content is clearly reminiscent of 1 Cor. 15:27. There is less to be said for the view that here the rhyme, in unity with the thrust of the metre, was father to the thought.: *labbayka Allāhumma labbayka lā sharīka laka illā sharīkun huwa laka tamlikuhū wa-mā malaka* ("at your service, O God, at your service; you who have no associate apart from an associate which you have; you who have power over him and that over which he has power"). If the testimony of Ibn al-Kalbī rules out the assumption that the *talbiyat al-mushrikīn* arose only in Muhammad's time as a Christian compromise formula, and was rejected by him, then one is led to the position that *sharīku-llāh* was earlier already a technical term, perhaps in the sense of what has been indicated above. Be that as it may, in connection with the pilgrimage stipulations of the sura, the rejection of this *talbiya* is the most immediately obvious sense of the final words of verse 30/31, as the forced nature of the other explanations shows.

NOTES

1. See final footnote of the first side of the third installment, p. 273, n. 38

2. Here I am repeating, supplementing, and improving what is said of this passage in *Biblica* 35 (1954): 405 f. and *Der Islam* 34 (1959): 195 f. In doing this, I can make grateful use of observations and corrections with which a number of scholars—Professors J. Fück, G. Levi Della Vida, and especially A. Spitaler—have supplied me. I have also used reliable secondary information when the literature it referred to was not accessible and so could not be fully exploited. I hope that this has not resulted in any substantial distortion of what the facts are.

3. Ca. 102/4 A.H. in Mecca

4. Eighth to twelfth centuries GAL S 2: 273

5. *Kashshāf* [Egypt 1354 A.H.]:

6. Cf., for example, G. Graf, *GCAL* 1 (= *SeT* 118 Rome 1944): 15-27; J. Wellhausen, *Reste* (Berlin 1897; 1964), p. 217; Ṭabarī, *Ta'rīkh*, I: 1723

7. Wellhausen, *Reste* 219 n. 2—Koran VI.64/64

8. 10 On the influence of the New Testament epistles, cf. K. Ahrens in *ZDMG* 84 (1930): 169–71.

9. R. Hartmann, *Kuschairi* (Berlin, 1914), p. 50

10. *Ashʿarī*-Ritter, *Maqālāt*, p. 155.

11. K.Ahrens, *M. als Religionsstifter* (Leipzig1935), p. 85.200

12. [Maʿadd: a collective name for certain Arab tribes, in the traditional usage for those of N. Arabian origin in contrast to the Yemen tribes. Ed.]

13. *Orientalia* 25 (1956): 307; in line 17 *yqrb* instead of *ygrb* is to be read.

14. See *Kitāb al-Aghānī*, 2:131, 4–5; 129, 3–6.

15. de Goeje, Ṭabarī, *Ta'rīkh*, I:987.19; A'shā Maimūn, *Dīwān* 13:69.

16. See on this Willian F. Macomber, S.J. in *OCP* 30 (1960): 5–38; 365–84; particularly 7–9.

17. Ashʿarī-Ritter, *Maqālāt*, 156,13; 290,5.

18. C. P. Caspari, *Quellen* (Christiania), 1,116.

19. *GdK*2 I 100; otherwise J.Wellhausen, *Reste* 24; F. Schwally, *GdK*^{2} I, 71; K. Ahrens, *ZDMG* 84, 151.

20. Died at the time of Muʿāwiya; Ibn Saʿd 6:146, Ibn Ḥajar, *Iṣāba* Nr. 9100.

21. Book 33, [*abwāb ash-shahādāt*] chap. 3 (*mā jā a fī shahādat aẓ-ẓūr).*

22. Book 23, [*kitab-aqdiya*, bāb 15, *fī shahādat aẓ-ẓūr*].

23. Eighth to twelfth centuries GAL S 2: 273.

24. *Kitāb al-Aghānī*^{2} 21:7-12.

25. Cairo, 1322 A.H. 36:16 of the Khazrajī (died 923/1517; *GAL S* 1:606).

26. Died 606/1209; *GAL S* 1:506.

27. Died 744/1345; *GAL S* 2:136. GdK2 3:243.

28. R. Klinke-Rosenberger (Leipzig, 1941), p. 4; Ibn al Kalbī: died 204/819 or 206.

29. R. Klinke-R, 75.

30. Died 245/860; *GAL S* 1:166.

4.9

Early and Later Exegesis of the Koran: A Supplement to Or 35

Raimund Köbert

Translated by G. A. Wells

Dies diem docet, the day teaches the day, and that over many a long year. There is Ṭabarī's explanation of XXVII.91 ("I am commanded only to serve the Lord of this city, Who has made it sacred, and His are all things, and I am commanded to be of those who submit.") and then the explanation of Qatāda,[1] which he quotes under the usual *qāla ahl at-taʾwīl*—an explanation which is designated, with the usual *binaḥwi lladī qulnā, qāla ahlu t-taʾ wīl*, as on the whole concordant with his own. Whoever reads and ponders these will not overlook the differences that make clear to us of the present day the change that has occurred when, at different times, the question was put: From whom did Muhammad distance himself with this verse, or who are the people whom both call *mushrikūn*? For Ṭabarī they are clearly, such as were quite generally until recently called, "heathen idolaters." Information about their gods in Arabian prehistory has been preserved for posterity by Ibn al-Kalbī. With Qatāda it is different. His *mushrikūn*, let it be said straightaway, are the Christians of Mecca,[2] who in the *ḥajj* of pre-Islam had their *wuqūf* (statio)[3] in the Wādī Muḥassir[4] and in Muhammad's time chose the *ḥajj* festive cry:, *labbayka lā sharīka laka illā sharīkun*[5] *huwa laka tamlikuhū wa-mā malaka*, "Thou, O God, hast no one who shares [in your power, or, as the case may be, in your divine being] except one, over whom and whose orbit thou art Lord"; this clearly following 1 Cor. 15:26.

Raimund Köbert, "Fruhe und spatere Koranexegese Eine Erganzung zu *Or 35*," *Orientalia* (1986): 174–76.

Simple reading of Ṭabarī's text suffices to prove what has been said. He states, explaining the Koran's words (XXVII.91): "I was given no instruction except to worship the Lord of this place, which he has placed under a prohibition. To him everything belongs, and I was ordered to be one of the Muslims." Thereby God says to his Prophet: Muhammad say: I was given no other instruction but to worship the Lord of this place, namely Mecca, the Lord who has, in consideration of it, strictly forbidden his creatures to shed blood illicitly in it, to wrong some one in it, to hunt game in his name, or to soil it (*aw yukhtalā khalāhā*), except the idols which you *mushrikūn* worship.

The exegetes of earlier days are, on the whole, in agreement with what we have said. So, for instance, Bishr, according to Yazīd, according to Saʿīd, according to Qatāda:

> The words of the Koran: "I was given no other instruction than that I worship the Lord of this place, which he has placed under prohibition (or declared holy and inviolable)," means Mecca. And the words "to him everything belongs" means: "All things belong to the Lord of this place as property (*mulkan*). I have been instructed to worship him, not one who possesses nothing (*lā man lā yamliku shay'an*).

Qatāda continues:

> He whose praise is sublime, the Lord of this place which he has made holy (*ḥarramahā*) which he has [here] especially chosen in distinction from all other lands, although he is Lord of all lands, [did that] because in his grace and condescension he thereby wished to teach the *mushrikūn* about the nation of God's messengers, who are Meccan. Whoever finds it appropriate to worship him (that is the *sharīk* of the rejected *talbiya*) is denied their land, and the people are kept [by his supporters] at a distance. These devour each other in all countries and kill each other. [To be worshipped] [is] not someone who has obtained no grace for them and who can neither help nor harm them.
>
> The words of the Koran: "and I was ordered to be one of the *muslimūn*" means: [God] has ordered me to make myself over to him as a man of proper devotion to God (*ḥanīfan*) and to be one of those devoted to God (*muslimūn*) who follow the religion of Ibrahim, the friend of God, your

ancestor, ye *mushrikūn*, not one who is in conflict with the religion of his proper ancestor and who follows the religion of the Devil, God's enemy.

A few words are needed to make the reading of the Qatāda text precise. The catchword *mulk*, absent in the Koran and in Ṭabarī, together with the pointed expression *lā man lā yamliku shay'an*, lead directly to the *shahādat aẓ-ẓūr*, except that from the latter the consequence is derived that this *sharīk* of the Christians has neither possessions nor power. If he is worshiped, he can neither harm nor profit those who honor him, and so likewise falls under the verdict of XX.89. Grace for his devotees is not given him. And that these are divided among themselves—it follows that the Christians are meant—is pilloried with the sharpest of language.

The catchword *mulk*, missing from XXVII.91 can, however, be found in XXV.1–4 and correspondingly in Ṭabarī. Here is said: "Praise be to him . . . who has the lordship of heaven and earth, who gave himself no son (or no child), who has no one sharing ("no associate" = *lahu sharīk*) the dominion (*mulk*). . . ." Among those who are turned away with these words Ṭabarī includes those of his numerous *mushriqī al-ʿarab*, who use the *talbiya* of the Christians. It is quoted word for word.

At this point, namely in the face of Qatāda's rejection of worship of a *man lā yamliku shay'an*, the two verses ʿAdī b. Zayd of Ḥīra wrote, c. 600 C.E., to his jailer Nuʿmān b. Mundhir, gain especial significance. They read: "The enemies have exerted themselves not to leave undone any evil against you, by the lord of Mecca and the Cross. They wish you to take time over ʿAdī so that he remains imprisoned or goes into the pit."[6] According to this, Christ (Messiah), the crucified God, would have been, for Arabic Christians, the lord of Mecca.

As for the term *sharīk*, it was already said earlier, and endorsed (e.g., by G. Luling) that, since it means "sharer" (in power or, as the case may be, in divine being), it is hardly imaginable in the sphere of polytheism, and is very unlikely to be found as the designation of a deity. Rather does it derive from the sphere of Christological discussions. Those who wish to regard it as an attempt to find an Arabic equivalent for *ομοουσιος*, Aramaic *shweʾ qyāmā*, could perhaps point to the not inconsiderable number of Christian expressions in good Arabic of pre-Islamic times, for example *ṣibgha* = "baptism," with which *ṣibghat Allah* is contrasted in II.138, *shiqāq* = σχισμα (II.137), and others in addition. In this way we would come to sharing (in power or in the being of God) as the basic meaning of *shirk*; *mushrik* would be someone who believes in the *sharik*. For Muhammad this latter would be an additional God, *shirk* is therefore polytheism and a *mushrik* is a polytheist. The same is true for the whole of Islam, more so as time passed. Only scholars knew of the rejected *talbiya*, but without clarity as to what it meant.

The original sense of *mushrik* seems to me to be still discernible also in the V.82 (Ṭabarī, *Tafsir*, 7:2) which exegetes link with the migration, dated in year 5 of the call, of the two oppressed believers to Ethiopia and their friendly reception there. (The Negus is said to have been rewarded for this with the privilege of becoming a Muslim, either on the occasion of a personal meeting with Muhammad in Medina; or perhaps he began the journey but died on the way.) What I have in mind is the contrasting pair *alladhīna ashrakū* and *alladhīna qālū: innanā naṣārā.* These, the Ethiopians, have shown themselves, by their behavior in receiving the oppressed ones, to be true Christians, and justly call themselves this; while those other ones, the Meccan *mushrikūn* and oppressors, are Christians merely in name.

Concering the *jāhilūn* of XXXIX.64, the exegetes have thought of the people of the *ʿibādat al-awtān* and of the *jahilīya* (*agnoia*), who are fools—this is not about *mushrikūn*. There may well still have been those who honored the *dīn al-ābāʾ*. But this interpretation is not compelling.

Finally, as a summary of what I have said: An early stage of Koranic exegesis is visible: XXII.30 in the hadith of Aimān b. Khuraim b. Fātik concerning the Prophet, in Qatāda on XXVII.91, and even in Ṭabarī on XXV.2. This early stage was later no longer relevant and disappeared, whereas there was agreement on how Islamic fundamentals were to be understood.

NOTES

1. Qatāda was a *muqriʿ* in Basra in 170 A.H.

2. Cf. G. Luling, *Kritisch-exegetische Untersuchung des Qurʾantextes* (Warna Diss., 1970): xii and n. 21.

3. The liturgical expression *statio* (goal of the pilgrim procession and fes-

tival celebration on a specific day of the year) is found for instance in "*statio ad sanctam crucem in Jerusalem.*" The celebration took place in the statio-church Santa Croce in Gerusalemme at Rome on the fourth Sunday in Lent. The mystery of the cross was celebrated in their own territory at a place they called Jerusalem. Thereby the relevant place would be regarded as the location of the mystery itself.

4. *GdK*2 (Leipzig, 1909), p. 147, 3

5. Text variant: *sharīkan* in Ṭabarī, *Tafsīr*, 18: 123 Koran XXV.3.

6. L. Cheikho, *Kitāb ash-shu'arā' an-naṣrānīya* (Beirut, 1890): pp. 451, 13 f.; *Kitāb al-Aghānī* 2 (Cairo, 1346/1928), p. 111, 5. Other oath formulas from Ḥīra c. 600 C.E. are: *wallāhi* ('Adi b. Zayd) *Kitāb al-Aghānī* 2, p. 113, 5; *waṣ-ṣalībi wa-l-ma'mudīya* ('Adi b. Marīna) 2: 107, 3 f.; *wa-yamīni l-'ilāhi* (Ubai b. Zayd) 2: 113, 5; *la 'amrī* (ibid.) 2:120, 3; *wal-lāti wal-'uzzā* (the Lakhmid Mundhir b. Mundhir died 580).

Part 5

SURAS, SURAS, SURAS

5.1

INTRODUCTION TO SURA IX.29

Ibn Warraq

qātilū -l-ladhīna lā yu'minūna bi-l-lāhi walā bi-l-yawmi-l-'ākhiri walā yuḥarrimūna mā ḥarrama-l-lāhu wa rasūluhū walā yadīnū-na dīna-l-ḥaqqi min alladhīna 'ūtū l-kitāba ḥattā yu'ṭū-l-jizyata 'an yadin wa hum ṣāghirūna.

Al-Bayḍāwī (thirteenth century C.E.) on IX.29:

'an yad, out of hand: indicating the condition of those who pay the tribute. Out of a hand that gives willingly, in this way indicating that they submit obediently; or out of their hand, meaning that they pay the tribute with their own hands, instead of sending it through others; no one is allowed to use a proxy in this case. Or again: out of abundance (*'an ghinā*); thus some claim that the tribute should not be demanded of the poor. Or still: by a hand which has power over them, hence indicating that they are humbled and powerless. "Out of hand" could also refer to the condition of the tribute. Meaning: paying the tribute in ready cash which is handed over from hand to hand.; or, as a charity, allowed to the one who is obliged to pay tribute. It is thus a great charity that they are spared from the tribute.

And have been humbled: brought low. According to Ibn 'Abbās the dhimmī is struck on the neck (with the hand) when the tribute is collected from him.

. . . The tribute is only demanded of the People of the Book [which includes the Zoroastrians]. . . . But tribute may be not be collected from

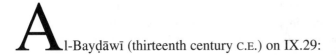

> other unbelievers. However Abū Ḥanīfa says it should be collected from them . . . Mālik (ibn Anas) says the tribute should be collected from all unbelievers except the apostates. . . .[1]

Ibn Kathīr (fourteenth century C.E.]: " 'Until they pay the tribute out of their own hands; plainly humiliated.' The believers should then fight the People of the Book until they pay the required tax, and cower. Those who live in a Muslim country in total security, enjoying the protection of the believers ought to be found in this state: humiliated and submitted to the tax."[2]

Bell:

> *Jizya*, only here, in later Muslim law was the special poll-tax levied upon non-Muslims living under Muslim rule, and was distinguished from the *kharāj* which rested on land. But it is doubtful if this distinction was introduced before the second [Muslim] century; and probably the word here is equivalent to "tribute" in general.
>
> *An yad*, the exact meaning of the phrase is uncertain *Bayḍāwī* gives "submissively" or "in person"; the latter is adopted by Becker (EI art. *Djizya*) Another possible sense is "out of hand," i.e. at once, on the spot, in ready money.[3]

Dozy: *ʿan yadin* in Sura IX.29, where we find the order to fight the Christians and Jews *ḥattā yuʿṭū-l-jizyata ʿan yadin*. This expression is explained by the commentators, as we can see in Bayḍāwī, in so many discordant ways, that one would be tempted to say that they would be better off in confessing that they did not understand it."[4]

E. W. Lane: "*ʿan yadin* as occurring in the Koran IX.29, He gave it in acknowledgement of the superiority of the receiver; that the power (*yad*) of the latter was superior to that of the giver: or, because of favour received; or, from subjection and abasement: (M:)[5] or from compulsion: (Abū ʿUbayd, T.)[6] or, obediently: or, in ready money. (TA)[7]"[8]

NOTES

1. al-Bayḍāwī, *Anwār al-tanzīl wa-asrār al taʾwīl*, ed. H. O. Fleischer, 2 vols. (Leiden, 1846–1848). No one seems certain of the date of his death; four dates have been proposed: 1286, 1292, 1293, and 1316.

2. Ibn Kathīr (died 1373 C.E.): *Tafsīr al-Qur'ān al-'aẓīm* (Beirut, 1385/1966).

3. R. Bell, *A Commentary on the Qur'an* (Manchester, 1991), vol.1, p. 299.

4. R. Dozy, *Supplément aux Dictionnaires Arabes* (1881, 1st ed.), Beyrouth, 1981), vol. 2, p. 857.

5. Ibn Sīda, *al-Muḥkam*. Ibn Sīda was an Andulasian philologist and lexicographer; compiled two dictionaries *al-Mukhaṣṣaṣ* and *al-Muḥkam*. Died 458/1066.

6. al-Azharī, Arab lexicographer, born and died in Harat 284/895: 370/980. Compiled dictionary *Tahdhib al-Lugha*.

7. Ibn Murtaḍā, *Tāj al-'Arūs*. Murtaḍā died in 1205 A.H.

8. E. W. Lane *An Arabic-English Lexicon* (Beirut [1863–1893], 1968), vol. 8, p. 3063.

5.2

Some Minor Problems in the Qur'ān

Franz Rosenthal

The basic problem involved in the following discussion is whether we are permitted to doubt the traditional understanding of the Qur'ān. It is the same basic problem that, raised in connection with the Bible and answered in the affirmative, constituted the starting point of biblical criticism. In the case of the Bible, there can be no doubt in the philological mind that there is ample reason to be skeptical with regard to the tradition upon which our interpretation of the Bible depends almost completely. The astonishing discovery of the last few decades has been that that tradition has so often been proved to be reliable. Nevertheless, this fact ought to serve only to sharpen our critical faculties but not to assuage them.

In the case of the Qur'ān, the situation is very different. The authorship of the Qur'ān is a uniform one. The scholarly occupation with it goes back almost to the time of its author. The milieu and linguistic environment in which it originated were quite familiar to the early interpreters. Therefore, it is, indeed, permissible to question the legitimacy of any departure from the traditional understanding. One may add that the amount of independent material for purposes of control is much smaller in the case of the Qur'ān than it is in that of the Bible. Furthermore, the pre-Islamic history of Arabia is much less known than the ancient oriental

Franz Rosenthal, "Some Minor Problems in the Qur'ān," *The Joshua Starr Memorial Volume* (New York, 1953), pp. 68 f. Reprinted with permission.

setting of the Bible, so that there will always be missing links between the statements of the Qur'ān and their supposed sources.

Yet, few scholars would deny that the traditional Qur'ān interpretation can and should be subjected to all the known rules of philological criticism. If the situation should require it, the traditional interpretation may, and ought to be, dispensed with. It may then be replaced by hypotheses of our own. Those hypotheses might, of course, often be as far from the mark as the rejected traditional interpretation. Still, they will have their rightful place and fulfill a useful purpose in the trial-and-error method, which alone can be expected to throw light into the dark corners of scholarship: *al-ẓann miftāḥ l-yaqīn* [conjecture is the key to certainty].

There are a number of reasons that show the possible fallibility of the traditional interpretation of the Qur'ān. It might seem an all too obvious and unconvincing argument to point to the constant differences of the interpreters and conclude from their disagreement that none of them is right. However, there is something to such an argument. Although most of the commentators have their special ax to grind, one should think, at least in a number of instances, that if an evident and simple explanation existed, there would have been much less obstinate disagreement.

The existence of words and topics in the Qur'ān that clearly are of foreign origin offers a better argument. Muḥammad himself might have been acquainted with their correct interpretation (though, admittedly, this is an assumption that can hardly be proved). But it is certain that their correct interpretation often eluded the commentators.

One may also refer to the tradition according to which the Prophet did not like to be questioned about religious matters, including, probably, the interpretation of the Qur'ān.[1] It would seem very plausible that when he was developing into the important political leader that he became in Medina, Muḥammad was hesitant to let himself be forced into giving explanations concerning a great many points of the early revelation.

Then, there is the fact that the pagan environment in which Muḥammad grew up began to shrink—through his efforts—already during his lifetime. The early Muslims, who must have possessed a good knowledge of it, can be certain to have done all in their power to repress that knowledge.

Finally, idioms change rapidly. In addition, all the efforts the commentators made, in order to gain authentic information on linguistic points, may have greatly suffered from the power of suggestion, which only the most highly trained and experienced researcher can avoid in dealing with linguistic informants.

Three well-known problems in the Qur'ān have been here selected as illustrations of the preceding remarks. The solutions proffered are in no way considered final, but it is hoped that it will be considered legitimate to seek solutions along the lines here suggested.

(1) QUR'ĀN IX.29 (29): AL-JIZYATA 'AN YADIN

The famous verse IX.29 has been of tremendous practical significance in the lives of millions of people. It reads: "Fight those who do not believe in God and in the Last Day and who do not consider forbidden what God and His Messenger have forbidden, and who do not take as their religious norm the true religious norm, of those who have been given the Book, until they give *al-jizyata 'an yadin wa-hum ṣāġirūn*."

Ṣāġirūn occurs elsewhere in the Qur'ān. It means "humble, lowly." *Al-jizyah* and *'an yadin*, however, have no parallel in the Qur'ān. The phrase *'an yadin* has so far completely defied interpretation. All post-Qur'ānic occurrences of it are based upon the Qur'ān.[2]

For the commentators, especially those who were interested in the legal aspects of Qur'ān interpretation, it was very natural to try to find some details about poll tax collection in the difficult phrases, some evidence of how it should be collected, since there was so very little they had to base their poll tax theories on. Therefore, they were eager to interpret the words *'an yadin wa-hum ṣāġirūn* in a way that would give them some authoritative hint concerning the collection of the poll tax.

On the other hand, it is extremely unlikely that Muḥammad himself should have bothered with such details. The practical side of poll tax collection must have been entirely uninteresting for him in the historical situation in which the Qur'ānic verse was revealed. There was no need for him to state anything else except that the People of the Book should pay something. Consequently, we cannot expect to find in the verse the details the commentators were inclined to find in it.

The objection may here be raised that the phrase *wa-hum ṣāġirūn* actually seems to indicate some aspect of poll tax collection. This could be the case, if the phrase is understood as it sometimes is, but in order to achieve a correct understanding of it, we have to pay attention to a subtle nuance in meaning that, at times, was rather cavalierly disregarded by Qur'ān commentators and translators.[3] It is, indeed, grammatically possible to interpret the *ḥāl* sentence as referring to the mode of giving the *jizyah*: "being humble, while paying the *jizyah*" = "paying it humbly." However, the *ḥāl* sentence may refer to the status of the People of the Book at the time when they make their payment: "paying the *jizyah* while [since] they are in a state of humiliation." Both interpretations are possible, but the latter alternative is the more natural one of the two (cf. also Qur'ān XXVII.37/37). Consequently, *wa-hum ṣāġirūn* does not refer to the mode of payment, but to the general condition in which the people who make the payment find themselves.

The phrase, therefore, would not support any interpretation of *ʿan yadin* as referring to a detail of the manner of poll tax collection, and the general tenor of the revelation militates against it. Thus, all those interpretations that find such a reference in *ʿan yadin* have very little in their favor. This does away with such interpretations—all of them conveniently summarized by al-Bayḍāwī, who, in turn, was already quoted by G. Sale in his translation of the Qur'ān[4]—as *munqādīn*, "being docile"; *ʿan ġinā*, "from wealth"; *naqd*[an] *musallamah ʿan yad ilā yad*, "in currency, being handed from one hand to the other"; *musallimīn bi-aydīhim ġayr bāʿiṯīn*, "handing it over personally, not sending it."

The last mentioned interpretation has been adopted by legal theorists. It found wide acceptance, especially with the translators. It occurs, for instance, in the translations of Marracci (Latin), Henning (German), C. H. Becker (in *EI, s. v. Djizya*), N. P. Aghnides,[5] and T. Sabbagh.[6] It also has important philological support. In his *Tafsīr*, aṭ-Ṭabarī says: "*ʿAn yadin*: from his hand to the hand of the one to whom he pays it. Thus, the Arabs (Bedouins) say to anyone who gives something to someone who has control over him: He gave it *ʿan yadihī*, or *ʿan yad*."[7]

This statement of aṭ-Ṭabarī could well be decisive. It is certainly possible that a phrase such as *ʿan yadin* acquired some such special meaning in idiomatic usage. R. Bell, in his translation of the Qur'ān, ingeniously translates *ʿan yadin* through "offhand." In a footnote to the translation, he states that the exact meaning of the phrase is uncertain. In fact, "offhand" would be quite meaningless in the context. It is, however, a good reminder of the fact that exactly the same elements that we find in Arabic

ʿan (off) *yadin* (hand) are combined in English in an idiomatic expression with a meaning that could hardly be guessed from its component elements.[8] The same could have been the case with Arabic *ʿan yadin*, and the problem would be largely solved—if we could be convinced that aṭ-Ṭabarī has here preserved some genuine linguistic information. Unfortunately, there is nothing to prove that this was the case. There is no independent information to support aṭ-Ṭabarī's statement. It also did not find the general acceptance by Qurʾān commentators, which, we should think, it would have found if they had considered it reliable. It seems, therefore, not necessary for us to abide by aṭ-Ṭabarī's dictum.

Yad has very many derived meanings in Arabic. The Qurʾān commentators naturally thought of that, not only when they were interested in finding details of the manner of poll tax collection (as in the case of *ġinā*, above), but apparently also when they had no such thought in mind. We thus find in al-Bayḍāwī: *ʿAn yad qāhirah ʿalayhim bi-maʿnā ʿājizīn*, "from a hand that has power over them, in the sense of being impotent"; further: *ʿAn inʿām ʿalayhim*, "from [here, apparently, in the sense of 'for'][9] being shown kindness." These interpretations, especially the last one, seem to be on the right track. They render, however, no account of the meaning of *ʿan* in the context, and, of course, they do not consider the possibility that *jizyah*, in this verse of the Qurʾān, could be anything but the technical term for poll tax.

In fact, it would seem possible that *jizyah* (whatever its origin) was assimilated here in Muḥammad's mind[10] to the Arabic verb *jazā*, "to recompensate" and that the preposition *ʿan* depends on the noun *jizyah*, which retains part of its verbal force. *Jizyah ʿan* would thus mean "recompensation for." Such combination of a noun (with article or another form of determination) and depending preposition is not infrequently found in Arabic; cf., for instance, Qurʾān V.7 (10), etc.: *niʿmata llāhi ʿalaykum*, and XII.6 (6): *niʿmatahū ʿalayka*; XXII.30 (31): *ar-rijsa min al-awṯān*; XXI.18 (18): *al-waylu mim-mā taṣifūn*; XXXIII.38 (38), 62 (62): *sunnata llāhi fī l-laḏīna*; . . . and XCVII.4 (4): *bi-iḏni rabbihim min kulli amrin*, if this verse must be understood to mean "with the permission of their Lord for everything."[11] A minor difficulty is the fact that the preposition depending on *jizyah* would be *ʿan* while, in the required meaning, *jazā* is construed with *bi*, cf. Qurʾān XXXIII.24. Elsewhere, however, *ʿan* is also found in connection with the verb.[12]

What, then, would be the particular meaning of *yad* that would best fit in with the suggestion just made? It might be "kind treatment."[11] More fitting, however, would be the meaning of "solidarity, support coming from solidarity shown to someone," as we find it, for instance, in the story of Ḥāṭib b. Abī Baltaʿah.[14] The meaning of the whole doubtful phrase would thus be:

> Until they give recompensation [tax] for support from solidarity [shown by us to them], while they are in a state of lowliness.

(2) QUR'ÂN CXII.2 (2): AṢ-ṢAMAD

The hapax legomenon *aṣ-ṣamad* occurs in one of the most prominent suras of the Qur'ān, the famous *Sūrat al-Iḫlāṣ* which, according to the tradition, equals one-third of the whole book. It has a long and varied history behind itself both in Islam and in Western scholarship, but its meaning has not yet been fixed with any certainty.

The treatment that the word has received in Western scholarship can by no means be considered an exemplary one. As a rule, it is translated by "eternal," a meaning of *aṣ-ṣamad* which is indicated by some Arabic sources, but which, though old,[15] has never been credited with much authority. As far back as I was able to follow up the occurrence of "eternal" for *aṣ-ṣamad* in the West, the first scholar to have it, among other meanings, is A. Giggei in his *Thesaurus linguae Arabicae*.[16] However, for the Qur'ānic passage, Giggei has: *Deus ad quem omnia nostra diriguntur. Perfectissimus.* It might be noted that Giggei's predecessor, Fr. Raphelengius, in his *Lexicon Arabicum*,[17] renders *ṣamad* with *indesecabilis, incorporeus*. Before that, there could be no question of adopting the translation of "eternal," except, perhaps, in the thirteenth-century Spanish translation of al-Mubaššir b. Fātik's *Muḫtār al-ḥikam* where *aṣ-ṣamad* appears to have been rendered through *el durable*.[18] The Qur'ān translation produced for Peter of Cluny in 1143, which has been unjustly maligned as being of a poor quality since the days of the great Scaliger,[19] has *necessarium omnibus et incorporeum*.[20] The *Vocabulista in Arabico* misunderstood the Arabic tradition and thus thought that *aṣ-ṣamad* meant *venter*.[21] The ninth-century Theodor Abū Qurrah renders *aṣ-ṣamad* by σφυρόπηκτος "hammered together, solid."[22]

With the publication of A. du Ryer's French translation of the Qur'ān in 1647, the translation of *aṣ-ṣamad* through "eternal" found universal acceptance. It was promoted by J. Golius's *Lexicon Arabico-Latinum*, which featured *perpetuus, permanens* among other significations of *ṣamad*.

A brief survey of a number of translations of the Qur'ān into various languages presents the following picture:[23]

G. Arrivabene (Venice 1547, from Bibliander): necessario à tutti, & incorporeo.

S. Schweigger (Nürnberg 1616, 1623, from Arrivabene) not available, but the Dutch translation following Schweigger (Hamburg 1641) has: een eenich God(!).

A. du Ryer (Paris 1647, 1649, 1672; Den Haag 1683, 1685; English translation London 1649, in 8° and 12°, 1688); éternal, eternell.

I. H. Glazemaker (Amsterdam 1696, Leiden 1721, from Du Ryer): eeuwig.

L. Marracci (*Refutatio Alcorani*, Padova 1698): Deus sempiternus.

D. Nerreter (*Neu eröffnete Mahometanische Moschea*, Nürnberg 1703, following Marracci): der ewige Gott.

M. Chr. Reinecke (Leipzig 1721, following Marracci): Deus sempiternus.

G. Sale (London 1734, and numerous later editions): the eternal God.

M. D. Fr. Megerlin (Frankfurt 1772): Der ewige Gott.

Fr. E. Boysen (Halle 1773, 1775) not available, but S. Fr. G. Wahl (Halle 1828) who follows Boysen has: Der ewige Gott.

M. Savary (Paris 11–83), not available, but the editions Paris 1821, 1826, 1829 have: Il est éternal. However, an undated Paris edition has: C'est le Dieu à qui tous les êtres s'adressent dans leurs coeurs (cf. Kasimirski, below).

L. Ullmann (Crefeld 1840, 1842; Bielefeld 1857, 1872; Bielefeld-Leipzig 1881): (der einzige und) ewige Gott.

M. Kasimirski (Paris 1841, in G. Pauthier, *Les livres sacrés de l'Orient*; Paris 1847): C'est le dieu éternal. However, apparently under the influence of al-Bayḍāwī, who was published in 1846-48, the editions Paris 1857, 1859, 1865, 1869, 1891, and probably many other editions (cf. also J. La Beaume, *Le Koran analysé*, Paris 1878, p. 250) have: C'est le Dieu à qui tous les êtres s'adressent dans leurs besoins.

Fr. Crusenstolpe (Stockholm 1843): Gud den Evige.

L. J. A. Tollens (Batavia 1859, following Kasimirski and others): Hij is de God, tot wien alle wezens zich in hun behoeften wenden.

J. M. Rodwell (London 1861) not available, but London 1876 has: God the everlasting. London–New York 1908, 1937 (*Everyman's Library*, p. 29): God the eternal.

J. Penrice (*A dictionary and glossary of the Ḳor-ân*, London 1873, s. v. ṣamad): A Lord, one to whom reference is made in matters of importance; as an adjective it means, sublime, everlasting.

E. W. Lane (*Selections from the Ḳur-án*, new edition, Boston 1879, p. 5): God, the Eternal.

E. H. Palmer (Oxford 1880, Oxford-London 1928): God the Eternal.

Anonymous (Milan 1882, 1912, from Savary): è eterno.

Th. P. Hughes (*A dictionary of Islam*, New York-London 1885 , *s. v. aṣ-Ṣamad*): The Eternal (followed by some reference to the original meaning of the word).

E. M. Wherry (*A comprehensive commentary on the* Qur'an, Vol. 4, Boston 1886, London 1886): The eternal God.

K. J. Pentakis (Athens 1886, following Kasimirski and others): `ὁ ϑεός ὁ αιωνιος.

Fr. Rückert (ed. by A. Müller, Frankfurt a/M 1888): Ein ewig reiner.

M. Klamroth (Hamburg 1890, p. 86): Allah ist ewig, nach Felsenart.

Persian translation (Tehran 1893; Bombay 1325/1907): *H̱udāy bī-niyāz* (God without need).[24]

C. A. Nallino (*Chrestomathia Qorani Arabica*, Leipzig 1893, glossary, *s. v. ṣamad*): perpetuus, sempiternus.

Th. Fr. Grigull (Halle 1901): Gott ist der Ewige.

M. Henning (Leipzig 1901): Der ewige Gott.

Sablukov (third edition, Kazan 1907):[25] *Krepkiy bog* (The strong [firm][26] God).

Muḥammad ʿAli (Lahore 1908): God is He on Whom all depend. The editions Woking 1917, Lahore 1920, have: Allah is the one on whom all depend followed by a long exegetical note, with references to Qur'ān commentaries).

E. C. Branchi (Rome 1912, from Kasimirski): E' il Dio, al quale tutti gli esseri si rivolgono nei loro bisogni.

Mirza Abu'l-Faḍl (Allahabad 1912): God the eternal.

D. B. Macdonald (*EI, s. v. Allāh*, 1.303a, Leiden 1913): The Eternal (followed by a brief reference to aṭ-Ṭabarī and to the uncertainty of the interpretation of the term).

A. Fracassi (Milan 1914): Dio Eterno.

L. Goldschmidt (Berlin 1916): Der unwandelbare Gott.

K. V. Zetterstêen (Stockholm 1917): Gud, den Evige.

ʿAbdallah Allahdin (*Extracts from the Holy Quran*, Secundarabad 1922, p. 4): Allah is eternel.

H. Grimme (Paderborn 1923): Ein ewig Seiender.

E. Montet (Paris 1925, p. 268): Allāh l'Éternel.

R. Brünnow-A. Fischer (*Arab. Chrestomathie*, fourth ed., Berlin 1928, glossary, p. 70): Fürst, Herr; *c. art.* Beiname Gottes.

L. Bonelli (Milan 1929): Dio l'eterno.

Hafiz Ghulam Sarwar (Singapore-Woking 1930): God Unique.

M. Pickthall (New York 1930): Allah, the eternally Besought of all.

A. Laimèche-B. Ben Daoud (Paris-Oran, n. y. [1932]): Dieu, le Refuge des bons.

Maḥmūd Muḥtār-Kātircioglū (*The wisdom of the Qur'ān*. English translation from the French by J. Naish, Oxford-London 1937, p. 143): God the Unchangeable.

ʿAbdullāh Yūsuf ʿAlī (Lahore 1937-38): God, the Eternal, Absolute. Cf. p. 292: Eternal, Free of all needs; on whom / Depend, to whom go back, all things (with exegetical note).

R. Bell (Ediburgh 1939, Vol. 2): Allah, the Eternal (followed by a footnote which refers to the Arabic commentators, and suggests a connection with Semitic *ṣmd* "to bind together," thus: The Undivided).

As the preceding list shows, quite a number of translations were not available. Moreover, some translations had the good fortune of going through many editions, which at times underwent major or minor changes. Only one or the other of those editions was available, and at times, the first and the last editions were not among those available.

However, the collected evidence makes it sufficiently clear that the fatuous "eternal" has been the favorite of Western translators since the seventeenth century. One of the contributing reason for its persistence probably was the fact that "eternal" was a plain and simple word. Since

Kasimirski, there has been, in addition, a haphazard and arbitrary usage of the meanings suggested by the Arabic commentators. Occasionally, we are treated to a liberal dose of the translator's free imagination. To my knowledge, no one ever attempted to take an independent philological approach to the subject before Bell a few years ago.

The passages in Arabic literature that deal with *aṣ-ṣamad* are very numerous. It would be tempting to trace the history of the word in Muslim dogmatics,[27] philosophy,[28] and mysticism.[29] Though based upon the suggestions of the Qur'ān commentators, the meanings that were attributed to *aṣ-ṣamad* to suit particular trends of thought are, of course, far removed from what could possibly have been the actual meaning of the word. Underneath all the glittering variety and fullness of meaning attributed to *aṣ-ṣamad*, the fact cannot be concealed that the most ancient and prosaic attempts to explain the word were not able to find much variety and meaning in it.

The fundamental text for the interpretation of *aṣ-ṣamad* is aṭ-Ṭabarī's *Tafsīr*. His discussion of *aṣ-ṣamad* will, therefore, be reproduced here in extenso. Aṭ-Ṭabarī says:[30]

> "And His word: *Allāhu ṣ-ṣamad* expresses (the idea): The One who is worshiped, He the *ṣamad*, nobody except Him can be properly worshiped. The Qur'ān commentators disagree as to the meaning of *aṣ-ṣamad*.
>
> (I) Some of them say: He is the one who is not hollow,[31] who does not eat and drink.[32] This opinion is held by the following personalities:
>
> (1) ʿAbd-ar-Raḥmān b. al-Aswad <Muḥammad b. Rabīʿah <Salamah b. Sābūr <ʿAṭīyah <Ibn < ʿAbbās: *Aṣ-ṣamad* is he (that) who (which) is not hollow.
>
> (2) Ibn Baššār <ʿAbd-ar-Raḥmān <Sufyān <Manṣūr <Mujāhid: *Aṣ-ṣamad* is the solid one (*muṣmat*) who has no hollowness.
>
> (3) Abū Kurayb <Wakīʿ <Sufyān <Manṣūr <Mujāhid: ditto.
>
> (4) Al-Ḥāriṯ <al-Ḥasan <Warqā', all together <Ibn Abī Najīḥ <Mujāhid: (ditto).[33]
>
> (5) Ibn Baššār <Abd-ar-Raḥmān and Wakīʿ <Sufyān <Ibn Abī Najīḥ <Mujāhid: *Aṣ-ṣamad* is the one who has no hollowness.
>
> (6) Abū Kurayb <Wakīʿ, also Ibn Ḥumayd <Mihrān, all together <Sufyān <Ibn Abī Najīḥ <Mujāhid: ditto.
>
> (7) Ibn Baššār <ʿAbd-ar-Raḥmān <ar-Rabīʿ b. Muslim <al-Ḥaṣan:

Aṣ-ṣamad is the one who has no hollowness. He said: Ar-Rabīʿ b. a Muslim told us on the authority of lbrāhīm b. Maysarah who said: Mujāhid sent me to Saʿīd b. Jubayr to ask him about *aṣ-ṣamad*. He said: He who has no hollowness.

(8) Ibn Baššār <Yaḥyā <Ismāʿīl b. Abī Ḫālid <aš-Šaʿbī: *Aṣ-ṣamad* is the one who does not taste food.

(9) Yaʿqūb <Hušaym <Ismāʿīl b. Abī Ḫālid <aš-Šaʿbī who said: *Aṣ-ṣamad* is the one who does not eat food and does not drink.

(10) Abū Kurayb and Ibn Baššār <Wakīʿ <Salamah b. Nubayṭ <aḍ-Ḍaḥḥāk: *Aṣ-ṣamad* is the one who has no hollowness.

(11) Abū Kurayb <Ibn Abī Zāʾidah <Ismāʿīl <Âmir: *Aṣ-ṣamad* is the one who does not eat food.

(12) Ibn Baššār and Zayd b. Aḫzam[34] <Ibn Dāwūd <(al-)Mustaqīm b. ʿAbd-al-Malik <Saʿīd b. al-Musayyib: *Aṣ-ṣamad* is the one who has no stuffing (intestines).

(13) I was told on the authority of al-Ḥusayn who said: I heard Abū Muʿāḏ say; ʿUbayd told me: I heard aḍ-Ḍaḥḥāk say concerning His expression *aṣ-ṣamad*: He who has no hollowness.

(14) Al-ʿAbbās b. Abī Ṭālib <ʿUmar b. Rūmī[35] <ʿUbaydallāh b. Saʿīd, the guide of al-Aʿmaš <Ṣāliḥ b. Ḥayyān <ʿAbdallāh b. Buraydah <ʿAbdallāh's father—He said: I do not know (anything about) it (?) except that he led it back to the Prophet—who said: *Aṣ-ṣamad* is the one who has no hollowness.

(15) Ibn ʿAbd-al-Aʿlā <Bišr b. al-Mufaḍḍal <ar-Rabīʿ b. Muslim: I heard al-Ḥasan say: (ditto).

(16) Ibn ʿAbd-al-Aʿlā <Ibn Ṯawr <Muʿammar (Maʿmar) <ʿIkrimah: (ditto).

(II) Others say that he is the one from whom nothing comes out. This opinion is held by the following personalities:

(1) Yaʿqūb <Ibn ʿUlayyah <Abū Rajāʾ: I heard ʿIkrimah say concerning His expression *aṣ-ṣamad*: He from whom nothing comes out and who did not beget and was not begotten.

(2) Ibn Baššār <Muḥammad b. Jaʿfar <Šuʿbah <Abū Rajāʾ Muḥammad b. Yūsuf (*leg.* Sayf)[36] <ʿlkrimah: *Aṣ-ṣamad* is the one from whom nothing comes out.

(III) Others say: He is the one who did not beget and was not begotten.[37] This opinion is held by the following personalities:

(1) Ibn Ḥumayd <Mihrān <Abū Ja'far <ar-Rabīʿ <Abū l-ʿÂliyah: *Aṣ-ṣamad* is the one who did not beget and was not begotten. For nothing begets which is not going to leave an heir. And nothing is begotten which is not going to die. Thus, He informed them that He would not leave an heir and would not die.

(2) Aḥmad b. Manīʿ and Maḥmūd b. Ḫidāš <Abū Saʿīd aṣ-Ṣanʿānī: The polytheists said to the Prophet: Give us the genealogy of your Lord. Whereupon God revealed *Sūrah* 112. . . . For nothing is begotten which is not going to die, and nothing dies which is not going to leave an heir. God does not die and leaves no heir. "And He has no equal." And He has nobody who is like Him or equal to Him, and nothing is comparable to Him.

(3) Abū Kurayb <Wakīʿ <Abū Maʿšar <Muḥammad b. Kaʿb: *Aṣ-ṣamad* is the one who did not beget and was not begotten and did not have an equal.

(IV) Others say: He is the lord (*sayyid*) whose lordship has reached its peak. This opinion is held by the following personalities:

(1) Abū s-Sā'ib <Abū Muʿāwiyah <al-Aʿmaš <Šaqīq: *Aṣ-ṣamad* means the lord whose lordship has reached its peak.

(2) Abū Kurayb, Ibn Baššār, and Ibn ʿAbd-al-Aʿlā <Wakīʿ <al-Aʿmaš <Abū Wā'il: (ditto). Abū Kurayb and Ibn ʿAbd-al-Aʿlā omitted "lordship."

(3) Ibn Ḥumayd <Mihrān <Sufyān <al-Aʿmaš <Abū Wā'il: ditto.

(4) ʿAlī <Abū Ṣāliḥ <Muʿāwiyah <ʿAli <Ibn ʿAbbās, with regard to His expression *aṣ-ṣamad*: It means the lord whose lordship is perfect; the noble one whose nobility is perfect; the great one whose greatness is perfect; the kind one whose kindness is perfect; the rich one whose richness is perfect; the mighty one whose might is perfect; the knowing one whose knowledge is perfect; the wise one whose wisdom is perfect. He is the one who is perfect in every aspect of nobility and lordship. He is God, Praised be He. This is His attribute, applicable only to Him.

(V) Others say: In reality, *aṣ-ṣamad* is the enduring one who does not disappear. This opinion is held by the following personalities:

(1) Bišr <Yazīd <Saʿīd <Qatādah, with regard to *Sūrah* 112: Al-Ḥasan and Qatādah used to say: He who endures after His creation. He said: This is a pure (*ḫāliṣah*) *sūrah*. Nothing is mentioned in it about matters of this world and the other world.

(2) Ibn ʿAbd-al-Aʿlā <Ibn Ṯawr <Muʿammar (Maʿmar) <Qatādah: *Aṣ-ṣamad* is the lasting one.

(VI) Says Abū Jaʿfar (aṭ-Ṭabarī): With the Arabs (Bedouins), *aṣ-ṣamad* means the lord to whom recourse is had[38] and above whom there is nobody. It is used with reference to their noble men. Thus, the poet says:

There came in the morning the herald of the
death of the two best ones of the Banū Asad,
Of ʿAmr b. Masʿūd and the *ṣamad* lord.[39]

And as-Zibriqān says:

There is no guarantee but (better than) a *ṣamad* lord.[40]

(Conclusion) If this is so, the meaning (of *aṣ-ṣamad*) which is known from the speech of those in whose language the Qurʾān was revealed is to be preferred for the interpretation of the word.

If the tradition of Ibn Buraydah on the authority of his father (above I, 14) were sound, it would be the statement most likely to be sound, since the messenger of God was best informed about what God meant and what was revealed to him.

All the other commentaries, as far as they were available, contribute nothing of any importance for the original meaning of *aṣ-ṣamad*. They often refer to all the opinions which are found in aṭ-Ṭabarī; occasionally have some further expansions and additions;[41] or restrict themselves to what they consider the preferable interpretation, which as a rule is (VI) combined with (IV), and, less frequently, (I) in the sense of "solid." It may be added that later authors, such as Ibn Taymīyah,

Faḫr-ad-dīn ar-Rāzī, and as-Suyūṭī,[42] speculate much about the grammatical significance of the appearance of the article in connection with samad.

In examining aṭ-Ṭabarī, we can safely, without any further discussion, rule out (III). We can also say that (II) is nothing but a slightly different interpretation of the same basic concept which is at the bottom of (I). And (IV) is obviously a variant of (VI).

We are thus restricted to only three interpretations. One of them (V)

is very weakly attested and is highly suspect as it seems to be merely a guess at the meaning of *aṣ-ṣamad* under the influence of speculations concerning the divine attributes.

On the other hand, the meaning of "solid," which is suggested by (I) and (II), cannot be discounted on the strength of the fact that this meaning was later twisted to suit dogmatic considerations. The meaning of "solid" is much too peculiar to have been invented by later dogmatists. We are forced to assume that the word *ṣamad* somehow had the meaning of "solid" in Arabic. It is, however, quite a different story whether this meaning was actually intended in the passage of the Qur'ān. Even if *aṣ-ṣamad*, "solid," must be interpreted as one who has no need for food and drink, as the exegetes assert and as it appears to be corroborated by a very obscure verse to this effect quoted by the author of the *Lisān al-ʿArab*,[43] it still would not be clear how a word having such a meaning would fit into the context of Sura 112. Unless a natural application of *ṣamad* in this meaning to the context can be found, we would have to assume that this meaning of *ṣamad* is not the one intended in the Qur'ān.

Thus, there remains the meaning of "paramount lord," or "lord and refuge for those in any need whatever." This meaning would, of course, fit with the greatest ease into the context of Sura 112. Furthermore, some good philological evidence appears to exist for it. It is, therefore, to the credit of the philological acumen of Muslim scholarship that this meaning has in general been the preferred one. The crucial point is the significance and genuineness of the poetic testimonies.[44]

The dubious verse just referred to, the spurious verse attributed to Waraqah,[45] and a verse ascribed to Ḥassān b. Ṯābit that clearly depends on the Qur'ān[46] can be disregarded. The other verses all refer to the combination *as-sayyid aṣ-ṣamad*, or, in one instance, *al-bayt al-karīm al-muṣammad*. The evidence was most fully presented by al-Qālī, who has the following remarks:[47]

> Abū ʿAlī (al-Qālī) said: Abū Bakr b. al-Anbārī told us as follows: There are three interpretations of *aṣ-ṣamad*. A number of lexicographers said: *Aṣ-ṣamad* is the lord above whom there is nobody because the people have recourse to him in their affairs. So, he said and recited to us the following verses:

> Travel ye all 'in the middle of the night and be confident.
> There is no guarantee but (better than) a *ṣamad* lord.[48]

Another poet said:

> I hit him with a sword, then said to him:
> Take it, Ḥuḏayfah, for you are the *ṣamad* lord.

He means Ḥuḏayfah b. Badr.[49]
Another poet said:

> There came in the morning the herald of the death of the
> two best ones of the Banū Asad,
> Of ʿAmr b. Masʿūd and the *ṣamad* lord.[50]

Abū ʿAli said: *yuṣmadu* means the same as *yuqṣadu*. Ṭarafah said:

> And if the whole tribe comes together, you will meet me
> At the summit of the noble *muṣammad* house.[51]

Abū ʿAlī said: This interpretation is the one which is correct according to etymology and idiomatic usage. . . .[52]

The special meaning of *aṣ-ṣamad* as such is not indicated by those verses. It hardly could be "lord" because it is used as an attribute to the word "lord" and, thus, presumably indicates a quality of a noble lord.[53] This quality could be something like "solid," and then, there would be no difference between this interpretation of *aṣ-ṣamad* and the aforementioned one. However, this cannot be proven.

Whether we should stop here with our investigation or not depends largely on our willingness or unwillingness to accept the quoted verses as genuine. That they are more than one does not necessarily speak for their genuineness. I submit that we have no means at our disposal through which we could decide the question. There is enough room for suspicion to permit us having a look at some outside evidence.

There, we encounter a noteworthy phenomenon: the not infrequent religious connotation of the root *ṣmd*.

In Ugaritic, *ṣmd* appears as a stick or club that is wielded by Baʿl. In the Kilammū inscription, line 15, we find *bʿl ṣmd*, apparently, *bʿl* as the owner of his divine club.[54] In the Bible, the adherence of Israel to Baal of Peor is expressed by the nip̄ʿal of the root *ṣmd*. The verb is translated by the Septuagint through ἐτελέσθη (Numeri 25:3, 5; Ps. 106:28). The use of the verb doubtlessly reflects North Canaanite religious terminology.[55]

From Arabic sources, we learn that an idol of the ʿĀd was allegedly called *ṣamūd*,[56] which brings us rather close to the environment of Muḥammad.

The South Arabic evidence unfortunately is not quite clear. It would seem little enlightening to combine a South Arabic proper name *Ṣmd* with Arabic *ṣmd*,[57] and the alleged proper name *ṣmdnʾmr*, in which *ṣmdn* would represent a theophoric element[58] appears to be nonexistent.

It is true that the Canaanite references may belong to the root which in Arabic and South Arabic–Ethiopic[59] appears as *ḍmd* "to bind, yoke." Aramaic, however, still has *ṣmd* in this case (and not the expected **ʿmd*). Thus, if *ṣamad* should be a loan in Arabic, the *ṣ*, instead of the *ḍ*, which appears to be the regular root correspondence in Arabic, would not be surprising.

In view of this material, the suggestion may be made that *aṣ-ṣamad* in the Qurʾān is a survival of an ancient Northwest Semitic religious term, which may no longer have been properly understood by Muḥammad himself, nor by the old poets (*if* the *šawāhid* should be genuine). This suggestion would well account for the presence of the article with the word in the Qurʾān, and it would especially well account for the hesitation of the commentators vis-à-vis so prominent a passage. Such hesitation is what we would expect if we are dealing with a pagan survival from the early period of the revelation.

(3) AŠ-ŠAYṬĀN AR-RAJĪM

In the case of the "stoned Satan," scholars departed long ago from accepting the traditional interpretation as the original one, there is very strong evidence (cf. Sura LXVII.5/5) to show that Muḥammad himself understood the expression in the traditional sense.[60] The combination of *rajīm* with Ethiopic *rᵉgūm*, "accursed," sponsored, among others, by Theodor Nöldeke, is certainly very attractive.

The root *rgm*, to which Ethiopic *ragama*, "to curse," belongs, is becoming constantly better known from the other Semitic languages. Though the fact has occasionally been doubted,[61] it certainly belongs to those verbs that originally meant "to speak," and which took on various specialized meanings in the different languages. Ugaritic *rgm* means "to say." Accadian *rgm* means "to call," "to speak up," and appears to be used preferably in connection with court proceedings where people "speak up" and complain loudly. Hence, derived words mean "noise." The Hebrew cognate is *rgn*. Its precise meaning would be very difficult to discover from the context in which the root occurs in the Bible. Neither the parallelism in Prov. 16:28, nor that in Isa. 29:24 is unequivocal. But the approximate meaning is indicated by a tradition of long-standing and general acceptance. In the Isaiah passage, the meaning would seem to be "those who make only indistinct noises," and in Prov. 16:28, "slanderer" would fit in very well, as it would in the other passages of Proverbs in which the root occurs (18:8 = 26:22, and 26:20). For Deut. 1:27[62] = Ps. 106:25, the meaning of "to grumble" is clearly indicated. The root occurs in the later Hebrew and Aramaic of the Jews but seems always to be conditioned by the for biblical passages. In a Hebrew context, it is in this manner used for the rebellious talk of the snake in Genesis.[63] In an Aramaic context, the root means "to grumble." The Itpaᶜᶜal in the meaning of "to slander," which is indicated by G. Dalman in his *Aramäisch-Neuhebräisches Handwörterbuch*,[64] remains intangible in the absence of any references where the word occurs in that meaning. However, Jewish usage appears to be agreed that that was the approximate meaning of the root.

Rajīm, according to its form, could be active as well as passive. And if, in Arabic, it is an old survival of Jewish (or, perhaps, Christian, though in view of the apparent nonexistence of the root in Aramaic in general, this would be less likely) religious terminology, its meaning could be "talker," or "grumbler." Both those meanings would characterize Satan as well as the adjective "accursed." Or *rajīm* might even be "slanderer = διάβολος."

NOTES

1. Cf., for instance, al-Buḫārī, *Ṣaḥīḥ*, ch. on *iʿtiṣām*, 4.422 ff. (Krehl's ed.)
2. Cf. R. Dozy, *Supplément aux dictionnaires arabes*, 2.849b–850a.

3. The translators often avoided the issue. Thus, C. H. Becker, article *Djizya*, in *EI*, has "in Erniedrigung." R. Bell's translation (Edinburgh, 1937), vol. 1, p. 177, has "being subdued." The wrong side is bravely taken by N. P. Aghnides, "Mohammedan Theories of Finance," *Columbia University Studies in Political Science* 70 (1916): 398, who has: "in order to be humiliated." G. Sale had the same mistake: "until they pay tribute, by right of subjection (=*ʿan yadin*), and they be reduced low." L. Marracci (*Refutatio Alcorani* 305, Padova 1698) had a dubious: "donec persolvant tributum à manu (idest manibus suis) et ipsi sint parvi (idest humiles, ac subjecti)."

4. London, 1734, p. 152.

5. Loc. cit., fn. 3.

6. *La métaphore dans le Coran* (Paris, 1943), p. 133.

7. *Tafsīr* (Cairo, 1321), 10.68.

8. Cf. also the *Reader's Digest*, June 1949, p. 80b: "he confiscates *out of hand* anything the farmer possesses," for a related English idiom.

9. Such a sense of *ʿan* is also implied in the interpretation of the Qurʾānic verse that is given in aṭ-Ṭabarī, *Annales* 1.2657$1_{8}$, cf. H. Reckendorf, *Arabische Syntax* (Heidelberg, 1922), p. 69.

10. As it was by later philologists, cf. *Lisān al-ʿArab* (Būlāq, 1300–8), 18:159_{24}: *wa-hiya fiʿlatun min-a-l-jazāʾi kaʾannahā jazat ʿan qatlihī.*

11. Cf. also H. Reckendorf, *Die syntaktischen Verhältnisse* (Leiden, 1895–98), p. 157, and A. Bloch, *Vers und Sprache im Altarabischen* (Basel, 1946. *Acta Tropica, Suppl.* 5), p. 84 n. 57; further, op. cit. 102: *mā fī l-qurbi lī minki rāḥatun*, where *minki*, according to Bloch, depends on *al-qurb*.

12. Cf. *Lisān al-ʿArab, loc. cit.*

13. Cf. *Lisān al-ʿArab* (Būlāq, 1300–8), 20.304, with reference to a verse by Bišr b. Abī H̱āzim, see G. von Grünebaum, *Journal of the Royal Asiatic Society* (1939): 553.

14. Cf. al-Buḫārī, *Ṣaḥiḥ* 2.268 Krehl.

15. See below, pp. 333–34.

16. 2, col. 1375 (Milan, 1632).

17. 248a (Leiden, 1613).

18. In the life of Socrates.

19. As quoted by Silvestre de Sacy, in *Notices et Extraits* (Paris, 1813), 9.104.

20. Published by T. Bibliander (Basel, 1543; also Basel, 1550), 4.188.

21. Cf. J. Fück, *Die arabischen Studien in Europa*, in *Beiträge zur Arabistik, Semitistik und Islam-wissenschaft* (Leipzig, 1944), p. 108.

22. *Patrologia Graeca* 97.1545. For the derivation of these meanings from the traditional interpretation, cf. pp. 331 f.

23. A bibliography of Qurʾān texts and translations was attempted by Wm. Sage Woolworth, in *Moslem World* 17 (1927): 278–89.

24. The Arabic-Persian dictionary of al-Maydāni (d. 1124), entitled *as-Sāmī fī l-asāmī* (Ms. or. Princeton 274H, fol. 4b), was much closer to the interpretation of the Qurʾān commentators: *Mihtar u-panāh-i-niyāzmandān* (Lord and refuge of the indigent).

25. This was the only one of the translations into Slavonic languages that was available, cf. *The Koran in Slavonic, A list of translations, compiled by the Slavonic Division of the New York Public Library* (New York, 1937, from the *Bulletin of the NYPL*, 1937).

26. *Langenscheidts Taschenwörterbuch* also lists "dauerhaft, haltbar" among the meanings of *krepkiy*.

27. Cf., for instance, al-Ašʿari, *Maqālāt al-Islāmīyīn* 209, 305, 505, 528, ed. Ritter (Leipzig-Istanbul, 1929–30. *Bibliotheca Islamica* vol. 1); al-Isfarāyīnī, *At-Tabṣīr fī d-dīn* (Cairo, 1359/1940), p. 10.

The Qurʾān commentator who dealt with the position of *aṣ-ṣamad* within the doctrine of the divine attributes in the greatest detail is Faḫr-ad-dīn ar-Rāzi, *Mafātīḥ al-ġayb* (Cairo, 1327): 8.534–6.

A verse from a poem attributed to Waraqah b. Nawfal betrays its spuriousness by the fact that it reflects the dogmatic discussion of *ṣamad*. It is, anyhow, said to have been composed in Islamic times. Cf. aš-Šarīšī, *Šarḥ al-Maqāmāt al-Ḥarīrīyah*, 28th *Maqāmah* (Būlāq, 1300), 2.66 f. = 2.57 (Cairo, 1306), following Abū Bakr Ibn al-Anbāri (*GAL* 1.119); al-Baġdādi, Ḫizānah 2.37; 3.250 (Būlāq, 1299).

28. Cf., for instance, Ibn Sīnā, *Tafsīr aṣ-ṣamadīyah*, which forms the basis of the articles *Ṣamad* and *Ṣamadīya* in M.-M. Goichon, *Lexique de la langue philosophique d'Ibn Sinā* (Paris, 1938), pp. 181 f.; Abū l-Barakāt Hibatallāh al-Baġdādī, *Muʿtabar* (Hyderabad, 1357), 3.61.

29. Cf., for instance, A. J. Arberry, *The Mawāqif and Mukḥātabāt of Muḥammad Ibn ʿAbdi ʾl- Jabbār al-Niffari* (Cambridge 1935. *E. J. W. Gibb Mem. Ser. N. S. 9*), pp. 10, 33, 203, and the references indicated by Arberry.

30. *Tafsīr* (Cairo, 1321), 30.196 f.

31. One should keep in mind that the word *jawf* means both hollowness, cavity, and belly, stomach.

32. Cf. also al-Qālī, *Amālī* (Cairo, 1344/1926), 2.288.

33. The brackets indicate that the text of the *Tafsīr* has the full quotation.

34. With *ḫ*, not *ḥ* (cf. Ibn Ḥajar, *Tahḏīb* 3.393, Hyderabad, 1325–57).

35. I. e., Muḥammad b. ʿUmar b. ar-Rūmī, cf. Ibn Ḥajar, *Tahḏīb* 7.16; 9.360; Ibn Taymiyah, *Tafsīr Sūrat* al-Iḫlāṣ (Cairo, 1323), p. 5.

36. Cf. Ibn Ḥajar, *Tahḏīb*, 9.217.

37. For III and IV, cf. al-Buḫārī, *Ṣaḥīḥ*, 3.398 Krehl.

38. Often with the addition: In any need.

39. For the understanding of the verse, cf. *Lisān al-ʿArab* 5.235, *s. v. ḫayr*, and Ibn Hišām, *Sīrah* 401 Wüstenfeld. Cf. below, n. 50.

40. For those verses, cf. p. 336.

41. Al-Qasṭallānī, *Iršād as-sārī* (Būlāq, 1306), 7.440, states on the authority of ʿAbdallāh b. Yazīd that "*aṣ-ṣamad* is a brilliant fire," obviously in invention of Ṣūfī inspiration. A very detailed discussion of *aṣ-ṣamad* appears in the beginning of Ibn Taymiyah's *Tafsīr Sūrat al-Iḫlāṣ*.

42. *Itqān* (Cairo, 1317), chap. 42, 1. 192.

43. 4.246 f. (Būlāq, 1300–8).

44. The alleged occurrence of *ṣamad* in traditions (cf. Ibn al-Aṯir, *Nihāyah* 2.299, Cairo, 1322) can be disregarded as unauthentic.

45. See above, n. 27.

46. Cf. Ibn Hišām, *Sīrah* 738_9 Wüstenfeld; Omar A. Farrukh, *Das Bild des Frühislam in der arabischen Dichtung* (Diss. Erlangen, Leipzig, 1937), p. 31.

47. Amālī 2.291 f. (Būlāq, 1324) = 2.288 (Cairo, 1344). Al-Qālī relied upon Ibn al-Anbārī who, as shown by aš-Šarīšī (above, n. 27), in addition to the other verses, also accepted the verse attributed to Waraqah.

48. Aṭ-Ṭabarī (above, p. 334) ascribes this verse to as-Zibriqān, an early Islamic poet.

49. According to Abū ʿUbayd al-Bakrī, *al-La'ālī fī šarḥ Amālī al-Qālī* (Cairo, 1354, 1916), 1.932 f., this verse has ʿAmr b. al-Aslaʿ al-ʿA bsī (cf. *Aġānī* 16.31 f., Būlāq, 1285) as its author. It is also quoted by al-Jawharī, *Ṣiḥāḥ* (Būlāq, 1282), 1.240, who, in turn, is quoted in the *Lisān al-ʿArab*, 4.246.

50. The authorship of this verse is disputed. A male and a female poet of the sixth century are mentioned, Sabrah b. ʿAmr al-Asadī and Hind bint Maʿbad b. Naḍlah. Cf. A. Fischer-E. Bräunlich, *Schawāhid-Indices* (Leipzig, 1934 ff.), p. 55; Abū ʿUbayd al-Bakri, *loc. cit.*; Ibn Durayd, *Jamharah* (Hyderabad, 1345), pp. 2.274 f. The last mentioned two authors attribute the verse to Sabrah, but a quotation by al-Jāḥiẓ, *Bayān* (Cairo, 1351/1932), pp. 158 f., which is distinguished by the fact that it has two additional verses, ascribes the verse to a woman of the Banū Asad. Cf. also above, n. 39.

51. Cf. Ṭarafah, *Dīwān*, ed. M. Seligsohn (25 Arabic) (Paris, 1901. *Bibliotheque de l'École des Hautes Ét.* 128), p. 34.

Muṣammad here probably means "well joined together, well constructed." It hardly has anything to do with *aṣ-ṣamad*.

52. Al-Qālī then goes on to refer to two other meanings of *aṣ-ṣamad*: "He who does not eat," and "solid."

53. A combination of *ṣamad* in this sense with *ṣīndīd*, "leader," would be possible but is not proved.

54. Cf. C. H. Gordon, *Journal of Near Eastern Studies* 8 (1949): 115b.

55. A disputed magical use of the root in Hebrew (cf. A. Guillaume, *Journal of the Royal Asiatic Society* (1942): 118 f.; G. R. Driver, ibid. (1943: 15) is too uncertain to be adduced here.

56. Cf. aṭ-Ṭabarī, *Annales*, 1.231 and 1.241; al-Masʿūdī, *Murūj aḏ-ḏahab* (Paris, 1861–77), p. 3.295.

57. Cf. G. Ryckmans, *Les noms propres sud-sémitiques* (Louvain, 1934), 1.184. The existence of a meaning of "cette stèle" for an alleged *hṣmd* does not appear to be born out by the reference to H. Grimme, *Texte und Untersuchungen zur ṣafatenisch-arabischen Religion* (Paderborn, 1929), p. 45.

58. Cf. *Corpus Inscriptionum Semiticarum* 4, no. 737; C. Conti Rossini, *Chrestomathia Arabica meridionalis epigraphica* (Rome, 1931), p. 222.

59. In South Arabic, this root also seems to occur in a theophoric name, *ʿmḍmd* (*CIS* 4, no. 973_5), cf. Ryckmans, op. cit., 1. 246: ʿAmm est ami (?).

60. Cf. A. Jeffery, *The Foreign Vocabulary of the Qurʾān* (Baroda, 1938), pp. 138 f.

61. Cf., for instance, F. Praetorius, *Zeitschrift der Deutschen Morgenländischen Gesellschaft* 61 (1907): 620 f. It also would no longer seem advisable to attempt to establish a connection between *rgm* "to stone" and *rgm* "to speak."

62. In this passage, the Targum Onkelos uses a derivation of the root *rʿm*. The translator probably was influenced by etymological considerations of the same sort as we find them in C. Brockelmann, *Lexicon Syriacum*[2] (Halle, 1928), 739a, where Accadian *ragāmu* is compared with *rʿem*, etc.

63. *Genesis rabbā*, section 20.

64. Second edition (Frankfurt a/M, 1922), 398b.

5.3

KORAN IX.29

Claude Cahen

Translated by Ibn Warraq

The traditional interpretation of this passage, which I give in M. Blachère's translation, is: "Fight those who do not believe . . . until they pay the *jizya*, directly,(?)[1] while at the same time they are humiliated."[2] This interpretation is linked to that of the majority of the late commentators (and some of the early ones), which extract from the sacred text the obligation to inflict humiliation upon the *dhimmīs* in the procedure of payment of the *jizya,* that they must in particular carry it out by their own hand, that is to say, in person and in cash.[3] In reality, it is far from the case that all the medieval commentators, not to mention the modern ones, were happy with this interpretation; they proposed several others, which proves above all that none of them understood the text naturally starting only with a knowledge of Arabic.[4] Keeping to the prevailing interpretation for the moment, it presents, it seems, two provisional defects: on the one hand, neither the word *jizya* here, nor the expression *'an yadin*, nor finally the expression *wa-hum ṣāghirūna* possess a perfectly clear and precise meaning; on the other hand, they are translated without bringing out the clear interconnection between the three neighboring expressions. I do not pretend, unfortunately, to provide a totally satisfying solution, either; I should like, however, to request permission to join, very exceptionally, the erudite cohort of *mufassirun* (commentators), to propose reflections, liable perhaps all the same, to direct research in a more rigorous fashion.

Claude Cahen, "Koran IX.29," *Arabica* 9 (1962): 76–79. Reprinted with the permission of Brill Academic Publishers.

We know that the word *jizya*, to which the later usage of the *fiqh* (Islamic jurisprudence) has gradually given the special sense of a personal tax on non-Muslims, in contrast to the land tax *kharāj,* is not always taken, above all not in the early texts, in such a precisely defined *fiscal* sense, since one finds it even sometimes used where one would expect *kharāj.*[5] However there is no doubt that, in all the texts that refer to the conditions of agreement between the conquering Muslims and the conquered non-Muslims, the word *jizya,* which is almost the only name used for the tax, designates, whatever be the the fiscal contents, a payment characteristic of the submission of the conquered to the conqueror.[6] It involves, thus, a certain stigma, the idea of a tax that can only affect men not enjoying to the full their human rights. In Byzantium and among the Sassanians, in the two societies Islam inherited, this stigma was attached to a poll tax in the strict sense of the word;[7] but among the Arabs, who had never paid any tax before Islam, and still only paid an alms tax (*zakāt*) regarded in a different manner, the simple fact of paying a tax strictly speaking seemed to imply a sort of indignity, degradation. For the rest, before the conversions of the indigenous population, the *kharāj* also only afflicted the non-Muslims. Still in the period during which the hadith were developing, several traditions established thus that to put oneself in a situation of having to pay the tax is to confess that one is in or is about to enter into the social class of an inferior, *iqrār bi-l-ṣaghār.*[8] It is for this reason that more specifically the Taghlibites refused to pay the *jizya,* because, although Christian, they had their pride of the Arabs, and that ʿUmar had to impose on them a *zakāt* (alms tax) simply doubled, that is to say, a tax established in another way but above all seen as not really being a tax.[9] It is for the same reason that the prince of the Ghassanids, also an Arab, and prince, was indignant at the thought of paying "the *jizya* of the peasants, *jizyat al- ʿulūj.*"[10] On the other hand, apart from minute textual variants, the treaties of submission of the Christian or Mazdean [Zoroastrian] towns stipulate on their share *iqrār al-jizya wa-l-ṣaghār,* which is obviously a reference to the Koranic text, but all the same must be understood as signifying, with the acceptance of the *jizya,* the recognition of the status of *ṣāghīr.*[11] That does not imply humiliation, I mean to say that it does not add to the recognition of an inferior status some or other humiliating procedure; the authorities reviewed on this subject by Ṭabarī in his *Ikhtilāf*[12] are unanimous on this point, and Shāfiʿī, undoubtedly reacting against the opposite opinion that was emerging, makes the explicit point that the dhimmīs paying the *jizya* were not to be maltreated either by acts or by words, and that the condition of *ṣaghār* signified only that they were entering under the law (*ḥukm*) of Islam.[13] In the light of these explanations, it seems to me that one must translate the Koranic text thus: "(Fight those who do not believe) until they pay the *jizya* as [or: in position of] (or: in recognition of their rank as) inferiors (as subjects?)."[14]

It is now a question, which is more difficult, of finding for the words *ʿan yadin* a meaning that goes well with the above translation. The expression is not met with anywhere else, either in the Koran,[15] or in the ancient literature outside the passages inspired by the Koran, we have no means of cross-checking in order to interpret it, and the solutions proposed all have something gratuitous about them. Without worrying about the late and theoretical explanations of the jurists, keeping to the texts that give an account, authentic or otherwise, of the conditions of capitulation of the conquered, it is clear that the formula was already understood in a varied manner, that is to say, already nobody was any more certain of understanding it.[16] They understood it in the following way: "out of the hand," which is rather feeble as a rendering of the preposition *ʿan*, and as if the word *yad* was accompanied by the article or the possessive; they explain that it means "personally," because the authors were writing at a moment when the differentiation of the personal *jizya* was taking form in the general complex of taxation, and particularly in the face of the tax on land. Naturally, the physical gesture could mean something different, and, although referring to a different rite, another text suggests that it expresses submission, when we are told that the Persian equivalent is *khāk ber ser*, "earth on head."[17] Another gloss on it is "cash,"[18] because the later authors well knew that in their day the *jizya* was characterized as a fixed tax in cash, in contrast to others, variable and sometimes paid in kind; but why would the Koran have insisted on this particular detail, besides contrary to what we had learned of the capitulations of Khaybar or Najrān? Another meaning, which is not explicitly mentioned, I believe, by anyone, but which seems to be implied in certain discussions between jurists is the following: children, women, and monks (this is a controversial point) do not have to pay the *jizya*, since the latter is a redemption of blood, and that these people, in war, should be spared;[19] thus, one must understand the word *jizya* as having a meaning very close to the Arabic root "compensation," and, as in a verbal form, construed normally with *ʿan*, leading to "compensation of hand" (struck on the conquered in order to kill him, or if necessary to reduce him to slavery, like the Latin *manus*). Still others understand by it "according to their means," and it is a fact that in some texts of treaties, next to or in place of the formula *ʿan yadin*, we find: "*ʿalā qadri ṭāqati kulli ḥalimin*" or something close to that, which refers to the discussions as to what is legally required of the non-Muslim subjects.[20] One further finds, "of their work," which technically corresponds however to the prestations of the kind of those of the people of Najrān.[21] Is it necessary to say that all that is equally flimsy and that, historically, it is in any case interesting to note the diverse interpretations that the social climate could have suggested? In the context of the Koran, perhaps we never had, and never shall have any more than our predecessors the true elements for a discussion. Logically, I should simply say that of all these meanings the only one that seemed to me to lead organically to the consequential explanation *wa-hum ṣāghirūn* is that which sees in *ʿan yadin* the indication of a gesture of submission, not understood, as by the later hardliners, as a form of personal, humiliating procedure, but the recognition of the status of *ṣaghār.* Only, to put forward this solution, which has never been done, we would still have to find in the pre- and peri-Islamic Semitic East some trace of such a rite: I am not sure that one can do it; simply, all the same, I should like to verify it, and I pose the question to those who are in a position to respond to it, on the basis of pre-Islamic Arabic inscriptions or some Semitic document or something else ancient.

NOTES

1. [The question mark is Blachère's.]

2. [R.Blachère, *Le Coran* (Paris, 1951), vol. 2, pp. 1082–83: "Combattez ceux qui ne croient point . . . jusqu'à il paient la jizya, directement (?), et alors qu'ils sont humiliés."]

3. A. Fattal, *Le statut légal des non-musulmans en pays d'Islam* (Beyrouth, 1958), pp. 17, 286–88; see below, n. 13.

4. See, for example, Ṭabarī, *Tafsīr*, vol. 10, p. 7; Zamakhsharī, *Kashshāf*, vol. 2, p. 147; Abū ʿUbayd b.Sallām, *Amwāl*, p. 19; Māwardī, *Aḥkām*, p. 247 (trans. Fagnan, p. 300).

5. D. C. Dennett, *Conversion and the Poll Tax* (Harvard, 1950), with the

utilization and discussion of the previous works of Becker etc., Fr. Lokkegaard, *Islamic taxation in the Classic Period* (Copenhagen, 1950), chap. 6; Fattal, *Le statut légal des non-musulmans en pays d'Islam*, p. 265; Claude Cahen, "*Djizya*," in EI2.

6. Besides the Koran itself, see, above all, Balādhurī, *Futūḥ*, ed. de Goeje, passim; for the other references to treaties, see the analysis and notes of Fattal, *Le statut légal des non-musulmans en pays d'Islam*, pp. 34–57.

7. Which only afflicted the socially inferior (smallholders) and perhaps, religiously, in Byzantium (Jews?).

8. Yaḥyā b.Ādam, *K.al-Kharāj*, ed. Juynboll, p. 39 (trans. Ben Shemesh, p. 48); Abū ʿUbayd b.Sallām, *Amwāl*, pp. 77–78. On the contrary, Shāfiʿī, quoted in Ṭabarī, *Ikhtilāf*, ed. J. Schacht, p. 226, if he affirms the *jizya*, denies the *kharāj*, since it is not the substitute for blood shed (see below, n. 18): In fact, in his time, there had been many conversions of men on whom the *kharāj* had been maintained, but who obviously would not have thought that it was, like the *jizya* from which they were exempt, a mark of inferiority.

9. Abū ʿUbayd b. Sallām, *Amwāl*, pp. 28–29, 540–44; cf. Abū Yūsuf, p. 68 (trans. p. 184), Yaḥyā, p. 47, (trans., p. 50).

10. Yaʿqūbī, *Histoire*, vol. 2, p. 161; cf. Balādhurī, *Futūḥ*, p.136. In the version of the letter of the Prophet to Héraclius given by Abū ʿUbayd, *Amwāl*, p. 22, those subjugated to the jizya are called *fallāḥūn* (peasant, farmer), which Abū ʿUbayd explains as comprising in fact all non-Muslims.

11. Esp. Ṭabarī, *History*, vol. 1, p. 2674.

12. Ṭabarī, *Ikhtilāf*, pp. 199, 201, 225–27, 231.

13. Ibid., p. 231.

14. In French: "(Combattez ceux qui ne croient pas) jusqu'à ce qui'ils paient la jizya en qualité (ou: en reconnaissance de leur qualité) d'inférieurs (de sujets)?"

15. In the Koran, the word *yad*, used on its own or with the preposition *bi* is taken in general, either in its real sense or in its current figurative sense, to mean "power."

16. One also finds it in the plural *jizāʾan ʿan aydīhim* (Ṭabarī, *History*, pp. 2044–45).

17. Abū ʿUbayd b.Sallām, *Amwāl*, p. 25, on the faith of Salmān the Persian.

18. Ibid., p. 19.

19. See ibid., p. 31; Shāfiʿī, quoted in Ṭabarī, *Ikhtilāf*, p. 226 (see above, n. 6), then, for example, Zamakhsharī, *Kashshāf*, vol. 2, p. 206.

20. Ṭabarī, *History*, pp. 2655–59; cf. Kister, in *JESHO* 3 (1960): 326 sq.

21. Cf. Hamidullah, *Le Prophète de l'Islam*, vol. 2, p.616, and the lexicon of his *Wathāiq*.

5.4

A Propos de Qur'ān IX.29: Ḥattā Yuʿṭū l-Ǧizyata Wa-Hum Ṣāgirūna

Meïr M. Bravmann and Claude Cahen

This passage has been discussed by C. Cahen in *Arabica*, tome 9, fasc. I, Jan. 1962, pp. 76–79. It is the expression *ʿan yadin* that poses the main difficulty in trying to achieve a satisfactory interpretation of the passage. Cahen mentions several of the explanations of the expression given by the Muslim commentators but finds none of them acceptable. His own conjecture is that the phrase indicates a "gesture of submission": " 'compensation de main' (portée sur le vaincu pour le tuer, ou au besoin pour le réduire en esclavage, comme la *manus* latine)." He notes, however, that no evidence of the existence of such a rite "in the pre- and peri-Islamic Semitic Orient" has come to our knowledge so far.

It is clear that the meaning of *ʿan yadin* must have a close relation to that of *al-ǧizyah*. Lane's explanation of *ǧizyah*, based on the explanation given by indigenous lexicographers, runs as follows: "The tax that is taken from the free non-Muslim subjects of a Muslim government whereby they ratify the compact that ensures them protection [from *ǧazā*]; as though it were a compensation for their not being slain." Cf. *Lisān al-ʿArab* (ed. Bairūt, 1955), 14, 147 a, 3 sqq. = Ibn al-Aṯīr, *al-Nihāyah*, I, 190, 22 sqq.: *al-ǧizyah: . . . wahiya ʿibāratun ʿani l-māli llaḏi yaʿqidu l-kitā-bīyu ʿalaihi ḏ-ḏimmata wahiya fiʿlatun mina l-ǧazāʾi wakaʾannahā ǧazat ʿan qatlihi*. Among the various interpretations of the

Meïr M. Bravmann and Claude Cahen, "A Propos de Qur'ān IX.29: Ḥattā Yuʿṭū L-Gizyata Wa-Hum Ṣāgirūna," *Arabica* 10 (1963): 94–95. Reprinted with the permission of Brill Academic Publishers.

phrase *ʿan yadin* suggested by the Muslim commentators there is one, not mentioned by Cahen, that deserves our attention. We refer to al-Bayḍāwī's commentary (ed. Fleischer, p. 383, 24): . . . *ʿan inʿāmin ʿalaihim faʾinna ibqāʾahum bil-ǧizyati niʿmatun ʿaẓi-matun* "[*ʿan yadin* is also explained as] 'in exchange for a benefaction granted them'; for the sparing of their lifes In exchange for the reward (*ǧizyah*) is an enormous benefaction." That is, *yad*-"hand" is used here in its frequently occurring meaning of "benefaction." Accordingly, the passage should be interpreted as follows: "(Combat the unbelievers . . .) until they give the reward [due] for a benefaction, whilst they are ignominious." The circumstantial clause *wa-hum ṣāġirūna* "whilst they are ignominious" refers to the unbelievers' failure to fight unto death.

We must assume that the clause "until they give the reward [due] for a benefaction" represents a euphemistical paraphrase of what is really meant: "(Combat the unbelievers . . .) until they pay tribute as compensation for their not being killed."

Meïr M. Bravmann

* * *

What seems to me the most important in the explanation of Professor Bravmann is not the meaning of *yad* = generosity—for whether we understand "reward for a benefaction" or "compensation in place of violence" comes to the same thing practically—but the interpretation of *wa-hum ṣāghirūna* as referring to the humiliation in battle. It is certain that following this path leads to a logical and coherent ensemble. I only wonder if, according to the texts of capitulation and others to which I referred, it is really this limited sense that was felt by the Muslims of the conquest; but that, of course, is not an insurmountable objection. While congratulating myself for having furnished the occasion for Professor Bravmann's intervention, I believe that the discussion, even if it has made progress, remains open.

Claude Cahen

5.5

The Ancient Background of the Qur'ānic Concept Al-Ǧizyatu ʿan Yadin

Meïr M. Bravmann

In our note in *Arabica* 10 (1963): 94–95, we interpreted the Qur'ānic verse (Sura IX.29) *qātilū lladina lā yu'minūna bi-llāhi . . . min-a lladina ūtū l-kitāba ḥattā yu'ṭū l-ǧizyata 'an yadin wa-hum ṣāġirūna* as follows: "Combat those nonbelievers who are possessors of a 'book' (i.e., Christians and Jews) until they give the reward due for a benefaction (since their lives are spared), while they are ignominious (namely, for not having fought unto death)." One might be inclined to question why this commandment had not been expressed in a simpler, more explicit manner (without any circumlocution); for instance, as: "Fight the nonbelievers until they (surrender and) pay tribute." Our reply is that the formulation of the commandment in the form in which it exists implies, simultaneously, the legal justification for the payment of the tribute on the part of the vanquished, former enemy and the fact that this justification—and we would like to underscore this point in particular—corresponds to a genuine Arab philosophy of law. According to an ancient Arab concept (quite understandable with archaic, primitive social conditions), the victor in a fight who spare the life of an enemy taken prisoner does actually do the latter a good deed. This "good deed"—and this is highly noteworthy—involves however (and this applies according to the ancient Arab concept to any good deed), simultaneously, a legal claim to a "reward" (a reward

Meïr M. Bravmann, "The Ancient Background of the Qur'ānic Concept Al-Ǧizyatu 'an Yadin," *Arabica* 13 (1966): 307–14; *Arabica* 14 (1967): 90–91. Reprinted with the permission of Brill Academic Publishers.

that—as in the case of any good deed—the "benefactor" could obviously waive of his own free will).

In the reports on Arab intertribal wars (*A yyām al-ʿArab,* "The Days of the Arabs") and related accounts of actual events, we can find a number of references substantiating the above-defined application of the concept "reward for a benefaction."

Aġānī, vol. X, pp. 41, 27 ff. (= *Naqāʾiḍ Ğarīr wa l-Farazdaq*, ed. Bevan, pp. 667, 16 ff.), in the report regarding the Day of Šiʿb Ğabalah (in or about 570 C.E.), it is said: . . . *wa-šadda ʿAwfu bnu l-Aḥwaṣi ʿalā Muʿāwiyata bni l-Ğawni fa-ʾasarahū wa-ğazza nāṣiyatahū wa-ʾaʿtaqahū ʿalā l-ṯawābi,* ". . . and ʿAwf b. al-Aḥwaṣ attacked Muʿāwiyah b. al-Ğawn and took him prisoner and cut off his forelock and set him free on the condition of reward." Moreover, we read in another episode from the same day (*Aġānī*, vol. 10, p. 4 = *Naqāʾiḍ*, pp. 671, 12 ff.): . . . *fa-laḥiqa Qaysu bnu l-Muntafiqi ʿAmra bna ʿAmrin fa-ʾasarahū fa-ʾaqbala l-Ḥāriṯu bnu l-Abraṣi fī saraʿāni l-ḫayli fa-raʾāhu ʿAmrun muqbilan fa-qāla li-Qaysin: in adrakanī l-Ḥāriṯu qatalanī wa-fātaka mā taltamisu ʿindī, fa-hal anta muḥsinun ilayya wa-ʾilā. nafsika tağuzzu nāṣiyatī fa-tağʿaluhā fī -kinānatika wa-laka l-ʿahdu la-ʾafiyanna laka; fa-faʿala . . . fa-laḥiqa ʿAmrun bi-qawmihī, falammā kāna fī l-šahri l-ḥarāmi ḫarağa Qaysun ilā ʿAmrin yastaṯībuhū wa-tabiʿahū l-Ḥāriṯu bnu l-Abraṣi ḥattā qadimā ʿalā ʿAmri bni ʿAmrin . . . ṯumma inna ʿAmran qāla: yā Ḥāri mā llaḏī ğāʾ a bi-ka fa-wallāhi mā la-ka ʿindī min yadin, ṯumma taḏammama minhu fa-ʾaʿṭāhu miʾatan min-a l-ibili . . . ,* ". . . and Qays b. al-Muntafiq joined ʿAmr b. ʿAmr, and this latter took him prisoner; then al-Ḥāriṯ b. al-Muntafiq arrived among the vanguard of the horsemen, and ʿAmr saw him approaching and said to Qays: 'If al-Ḥāriṯ gets to me he will kill me and you will fail to obtain what you expect to get from me; would you like to do me and yourself a favor? Cut off my forelock and put it into your quiver, and I swear to you: I shall recompense you'; and he did it . . . and ʿAmr reached his people. And in the holy month Qays went out to ʿAmr to demand his reward (*ṯawāb*) from him; and al-Ḥāriṯ b. al-Abraṣ followed him until both of them reached ʿAmr b. ʿAmr . . . ; thereupon ʿAmr said [to al-Ḥāriṯ]: 'O Ḥāriṯ!, what brings you to me?, for, by God!, I am under no obligation to you (literally: you have no 'benefaction'—*yad*, as in the Qurʾānic passage—to your credit with me); indeed you had bad intentions with respect to me, you killed my brother and had the intention to kill me'; and he (that is: al-Ḥāriṯ) said: 'Nay, I refrained from you; and if I had wanted—since I reached you—I could have killed you'; and he (i.e., ʿAmr) said: 'I am under no obligation to you'; whereupon he (i.e., ʿAmr) sought to avoid any blame on his (i.e., al-Ḥāriṯ's) part, and gave him hundred camels. . . ."

It is to be noted that in both instances described in these two quotations the ransom money (*fidāʾ*) was not paid prior to the release of the prisoner, but later on only—voluntarily as it were—was granted by the released, former prisoner to his former enemy. Thus, in other words, the *ṯawāb*, the reward, did not represent (in a good many cases) ransom money in its more accepted meaning, but rather a "reward" in its true sense, that is, a compensation resulting from a sense of gratitude so to speak for a good deed, a kind of gift; whereby the payment of this reward is considered however to be a self-evident obligation.[1]

To what extent the concept of law of the ancient Arabs considers it self-evident that the prisoner taken captive in a fight reward his captor who spared his life and released him (instead of killing him, as he could actually have done) is shown by the following account. The poet al-Ḥuṭayʾah, whose poverty prevented him from rewarding by means of a gift (or "reward") in material form the hero Zayd b. al-Muhalhil al-Ṭāʾī, known as Zayd al-Ḫayl, who had released him, was allowed to fulfill his obligation to give thanks by praising Zayd al-Ḫayl in poems; and this was explicitly recognized by the generous captor as having fulfilled the obligation to make a reward. We quote *Aġānī*, vol. 16, p. 56: . . . *fa-ʾaʿṭāhu Kaʿbun farasahū l-kumayta, wa-šakā l-Ḥuṭayʾatu l-ḥāǧata fa-manna ʿalayhi, fa-qāla Zaydun: aqūlu li-ʿabdī Ǧarwalin iḏ asartuhū aṯibnī wa-lā yaġrurka annaka šāʿiru* . . . , ". . . and Kaʿb [b. Zuhayr], gave his red horse to Zayd (as a price of ransom); al-Ḥuṭayʾah, however, pleaded indigence, and Zayd granted him his life and freedom without a price, and Zayd said (in a line of poetry): 'I say to my slave Ǧarwal (i.e., al-Ḥuṭayʾah)—since I took him prisoner—: Reward me! you being a poet should not mislead you. . . .' " After some more lines by Zayd, there follow poems of praise in honor of Zayd by al-Ḥuṭayʾah; whereupon the report says: *fa-raḍiya ʿanhu Zaydun wa-manna ʿalayhi limā qāla hāḏā fīhi wa-ʿadda ḏālika ṯawāban min-a l-Ḥuṭayʾati wa-qabilahū* . . . , "and Zayd was pleased with him (i.e., with al-Ḥuṭayʾah) and granted him his life and freedom, because of what be bad spoken about him (in his poems), and he reckoned that as a reward (*ṯawāb*) on the part of al-Ḥuṭayʾah and accepted it."[2] We quote also al-Ḥuṭayʾah's line (*Dīwān*, ed. Goldziher, no. 52, 1; *ZDMG* 47, p. 61) *illā yakun mālun yuṯābu fa-ʾinnahū sayaʾtī ṯanāʾī Zaydan-i bna Muhalhili*, "since there is no property to given in return [for the favor], my praise will come to Zayd b. al-Muhalhil"[3]

Also the following line of poetry (quoted in the scholion to *al-Mufaḍḍaliyyāt*, ed Lyall, no. 96, 20; p. 642, 20) shows in a very emphatic way how self-understood it was that a benefaction—here called *yad*, as in our Qurʾānic passage—should be rewarded[4]: *raʾaytukumū lā tastaṯībūna niʿmatan wa-ġayrukumū min ḏī yadin yastaṯībuhā* "I saw you never asking reward for a favor, while others than you ask reward from the one to whom a benefaction has been granted," with the remark of the scholiast (ibid., line 12): *hāḏā yaḏummu, yaqūlu: laysa lakum yadun tarǧūna ʿalayhā l-ṯawāba*, "This [line] expresses blame, he says: 'you have no benefaction to your credit, for which you may hope for reward.' " In this last-quoted poetical passage, no specific kind of benefaction is mentioned. But it is quite certain that the intention is directed to the benefaction par excellence, that is: the sparing of the life of a prisoner, as this is expressly stated in the line (*al-Mufaḍḍaliyyāt*, no. 96, 7; p. 642, 12) to which the above line is quoted (in the scholion) as a parallel: *raʾatnī ka-ʾufḥūṣi l-qaṭāti ḏuʾābatī wa-mā massahā min munʿimin yastaṯībuhā*, "She (my she-camel) saw me with my temples bald and smooth as the place where the sand-grouse lays: but their baldness is not due to a captor who—having cut off my forelock-did me a favor for which he could ask reward" (but my baldness is due to the friction of the helmet).[5]

Whereas in the (non-Islamic) examples mentioned by us above the good deed consists in the pardon granted by an individual according to his discretion to an individual who has been vanquished and taken captive by him, in the Qurʾān verse discussed by us the good deed, and hence also the "reward" (*ǧizyah* = *ǧazāʾ* = *ṯawāb*) necessarily following it according to ancient Arab common law have become a practice normally occurring and that must be performed: the life of all prisoners of war belonging to a certain privileged category of nonbelievers must, as a rule, be spared, All must be subject to pardon—provided they grant the "reward" (*ǧizyah*) to be expected for an act of pardon (sparing of life).

Early Islamic tradition expressly states that the *ǧizyah* (which literally certainly means "reward") is to be paid for the sparing of the lifes of the vanquished enemies (ḥaqn al-dimāʾ, cf. n. 2). We refer to Ṭabarī, *Annales*, 1, 2017, 3 ff. (year 12 A.H.): *fa-qabila min-hum Ḫālidun-i l-ǧizyata wa-kataba la-hum kitāban fī-hi: Bi-smi llāhi l-raḥmāni l-raḥīmi. Min Ḫālidi bni l-Walīdi li-bni Ṣalūbā l-Sawādīyi wa-manziluhū bi-šāṭiʾi l-Furāti: Innaka āminun bi-ʾamāni illāhi—iḏ ḥaqana damahū bi-ʾiʿṭāʾi l-ǧizyati—wa-qad aʿṭayta ʿan nafsika wa-ʿan ahli ḫarǧika wa-Ǧazīratika wa-man kāna fī qaryatayka Bāniqyā wa-Bārusmā alfa dirhamin fa-qabiltuhā minka* . . . , "and Ḫālid accepted the *ǧizyah* from them and wrote for them a document concerning this: 'In the name of God, the Merciful, the Compassionate. From Ḫālid b. al-Walīd to Ibn Ṣalūbā, the man of the Sawād, whose residence is on the shore of the Euphrates: You are safe tinder the protection of God'—since he (i.e., Ibn Ṣalūbā) prevented the shedding of his blood (saved his life) by giving the *ǧizyah*—'since you have given for yourself and for your people . . . thousand drachmas, and I have accepted them from you. . . .' "

The following passage (Ṭabarī, *Annales*, 1, 2631, 7 ff.; year 21 A.H.), in which a vanquished enemy offers, in addition to the payment of the *ǧizyah*, a reward for the sparing of his life to the man who captured him, may be compared with the phrase *iḏ ḥaqana damahū bi-ʾiʿṭāʾi l-ǧizyati* in the passage quoted above as well as with the Qurʾānic phrase *al-ǧizyatu ʿan yadin* "the reward for a benefaction": . . . *fa-ʾasarahū wa-ʾaḫaḏa silāḥahū . . . fa-qāla ḏhabū bī ilā amīrikum ḥattā uṣāliḥahū ʿalā hāḏihi l-arḍi wa-ʾuʿaddiya ilayhi l-ǧizyata wa-salnī anta ʿan isārika mā šiʾta wa-qad mananta ʿalayya iḏ lam taqtulnī* . . . , ". . . and he took him prisoner and took his armor . . . and he (i,e., the prisoner) said: 'Go with me to your commander so that I make peace with him by (making him owner of) this land and may (permanently) pay him the *ǧizyah*; and also you, demand of me whatever you want for your taking [me] prisoner; for you have been gracious to me, since you did not kill me. . . .' "

Finally, we note that there are certain hints in ancient Arabic literature that the foreigner under protection of Islam—that is, the Christian or Jew or member of any other privileged group—was marked by the missing forelock, which had been cut off; that means that he was distinguished by that mark, which in early Arab times goes with the obligation of the prisoner of war to pay "reward" for having been freed and not having been killed. We refer to the line of Ǧarīr (*Naqāʾiḍ Ǧarīr wa-l-Farazdaq*, ed. Bevan, no. 50, 43; p. 342, line 3): *wa-tabītu tašrabu ʿinda kulli muqaṣṣaṣin ḫaḍili l-anāmili wakifi l-miʿṣāri*, "And you [o Farazdaq] are wont to spend 'your nights drinking at [the tavern of] every one whose forelock has been cut off, whose finger-tips are moist, and whose wine-press is dripping." The scholion (ibid., p. 342, line 5) remarks on *muqaṣṣaṣ* explicitly: *ay: ḏimmīyun qad quṣṣat nāṣiyatuhū "muqaṣṣaṣ*: i.e., [the] *ḏimmī* (protected foreigner, Jew or Christian) whose forelock has been cut off." Indeed, the reference to the producers and sellers of wine can at this period only relate to the *ahl al-ḏimmah* in the accepted Islamic sense, that is, Jews, Christians, and the like.

* * *

We cannot conclude this note without discussing the interpretation of the Qur'ānic passage under discussion which M. J. Kister has propounded in *Arabica* 11 (1964): 272–78. He translates the verse (p. 278): ". . . fight them . . . until they pay the *ǧizya* out of ability and sufficient means, they (nevertheless) being inferior." He assumes that *yad*, or *ʿan yadin*, means "wealth," or "sufficient resources for spending," or "on the expenses, means, or resources (of someone)," respectively, basing this interpretation of the concept on numerous literary, lexicographical, and exegetical sources, which are only in part available to us. For the sake of clarity we quote some of Kister's statements in extenso (pp. 276 f.): "The expression *ʿan ẓahri yadin* is interpreted by al-Zamaḫšarī in *al-Fā'iq* [III, 228, ed. Cairo 1945–48]: it is explained as *ʿan ẓahri inʿāmin mubtadi'an min ġayri mukāfa'atin ʿalā ṣanīʿin*. The phrase: Aʿṭa l-ǧazīla ʿan *ẓahri yadin* would be rendered thus: he gave plenty, giving it gratuitously, i.e., without any favour being granted to him. . . . Two other expressions are recorded by al-Zamaḫšarī in *Asās* and by Ibn Manẓūr in *L. ʿA.: Fulānun ya'kulu ʿan ẓahri yadi fulānin iḏā kāna huwa yunfiqu ʿalayhi* and *al-fuqarā'u ya'kulūna ʿan ẓahri aydī l-nāsi*. It is evident that the phrase denotes to live on the expenses, means or resources of somebody."

We quote here the entire passage from Al-Zamaḫšarī's *Fā'iq* (III, 248), from which Kister starts in his discussion of the concept *ʿan yadin: Ṭalḥatu (rḍʿh)—gāla Qabīṣatu: mā ra'aytu aḥadan aʿṭā l-ǧazila ʿan ẓahri yadin min Ṭalḥata bni ʿUbaydi-llāhi. Al-yadu: al-niʿmatu; ay: ʿan ẓahri inʿāmin mubtadi'an min ġayri an yakūna mukāfa'atan ʿalā ṣanīʿin*. This must be interpreted as follows: "Ṭalḥah b. ʿUbayd Allāh: Qabīsah said: I have never seen anyone who distinguished himself more in squandering bountiful gifts, out of [pure] charity (*ʿan yadin*, see below), than Ṭalḥah b. ʿUbayd Allāh. *Al-yad*: 'the benefaction,' that is, [*ʿan yadin* means:] out of (pure) charity, spontaneously, not as a reward for a favor (received from the other person)." Similarly, the quotation from Zamaḫšarī's *Asās* and from *Lisān al-ʿArab* is to be interpreted: "A eats (or: lives) on the charity of B, when he (i.e., B) pays his (i.e., A's) living expenses; and: The poor eat (or: live) on the charity of the people."

Moreover, Kister (p. 276, at the bottom) refers to al-Šarif al-Raḍī's explanation of *aʿṭaytu fulānan kaḏā ʿan ẓahri yadin* by *ʿan-imtināʿin wa-qūwatin: lam uʿṭihī ʿan ḫifatin wa-ḏillatin*, using also this definition of the expression as proof for his contention that *yad* in *ʿan* (*ẓahri*) *yadin* means "means or resources (of somebody)." We understand also here *ʿan* (*ẓahri*) *yadin* means "means or resources (of somebody)." We understand also here *ʿan ẓahri yadin* as expressing the idea "I have given someone that and that gift *out of* [*pure*] *charity*," that is, "not out of fear of him, since he did me a favor (e.g., since he spared my life), a favor for which he might exact a reward from me," rather "I have given someone a gift, without owing him anything, that is: out of a position of strength and independence, just because I possess sufficient means (that is, a surplus of possessions), and since I am inclined to be charitable." In this connection we may also refer to the line of Durayd b. al-Ṣimmah (*al-Aṣmaʿiyyāt*, ed. Ahlwardt, no. 24, 3) quoted by Kister (p. 277 at the bottom): *aʿāḏila inna l-ruzʾa fī miṯli Ḫalidin wa-lā ruzʾa fīmā ahlaka l-marʾu ʿan yadi*. Kister interprets this as follows: "O reprover, misfortune is in (the death of a man) like Ḫālid, misfortune is not in what a man squanders (by lavish spending) out of plenty." Kister adds to this interpretation the remark: "*Yad* in this verse explicitly denotes wealth, or sufficient resources for spending (on the poor and needy), or generous distribution (of gifts)." For us the sense of the line is again: ". . . but to spend one's means *in practising* (*genuine*) *charity* cannot be considered a loss."

Also here, *yad* is used in the pregnant sense described above: "charity," that is, "generosity practiced with an entirely altruistic intention, based on social independence and wealth (see below), not caused, for example, by the fact that somebody has laid the other person under obligation."

By the fact that the type of "giving" characterized by the term *ʿan yadin* (or: *'an ẓahri yadin*) is in the philological sources quoted above defined (certainly correctly) as being performed spontaneously (*mubtadi'an*), not representing a compensation (*mukāfa'ah*) for a favor, it is consciously conceived as the contrast of that type of granting money or other valuables to another person in which the benefit granted the other person is granted in discharge of an obligation (and thus, as it were, is granted under duress, *'an ḫīfatin waḏillatin*, see above), namely—in the passages quoted by us—as a reward for the sparing of the life of the person granting the benefit by the person to whom the benefit is granted, that is, in the Qur'ānic passage under discussion: *al-ğizyatu 'an yadin.*

Moreover, in connection herewith, *'an yadin* in the Qur'ānic passage and *'an* (*ẓahri*) *yadin* in the other category of passages (including the line by Durayd b. al-Ṣimmah quoted above) are from the formal-phraseological point of view of a quite different nature. In the Qur'ānic verse, *'an yadin* (*'an ẓahri yadin* here would not be possible) is a necessary complement of the verbal noun *al-ğizyah: ğazāhu 'an yadin*, "he compensated him *for* a favor" (cf., e.g., the sentence *wa-salnī 'an isārika mā ši'ta* in the quotation from Ṭabarī, *Annales*, 1, 2631, 7 ff.). In the other category, *'an* (*ẓahri*) *yadin* is, from the syntactical point of view, a (not absolutely indispensable) complement to the sentence as a whole: "he gave gifts *out of* (or: *as*) charity."

The granting of benefits and favors to another person on the basis of social independence—out of a charitable and gentle attitude toward one's fellowmen, and not in discharge of a duty (as in the Qur'ānic verse and similar passages)—represents a frequent motif of early Arabic sources that appears under a number of variations. Cf., for example, *Ḥamāsah*, p. 516, v. 4: *inna min-a l-ḥilmi ḏullan anta 'ārifuhū wa-l-ḥilmu 'an qudratin faḍlun min al-karami*, in the translation of Rückert (*Die Volkslieder der Araber*, 11, p. 19; no. 418, v. 5): "Eine Schmach ist Lindigkeit, du weisst es wohl; aber Lindigkeit aus Kraft ist ehrenvoll." Furthermore, *Dīwān al-Farazdaq*, ed. Boucher, p. 173, 13: *al-'āṣib*(*u*) *l-ḥarba ḥattā tastaqīda lahū bi-l-mašrafiyyati wa-l-'āfī iḏā qadarā*, which must be interpreted (with Boucher, vol. 11, p. 521, and n. 2, against his alternative interpretation of *qadara* in the text of his translation itself): "Il dompte la guerre et la soumet à son épée, il pardonne lorsqu'il pourrait (punir)." Cf. also, for example, Abū 1-'Atāhiyah, *Dīwān*, p. 58, 4: *wa-'afḍalu l-'afwi 'afwun 'inda maqduratin*, "and the best pardon is the pardon which one grants out of a position of strength"; and so on. Cf. also the saying, frequently occurring in early historical sources: *malakta fa-ʾasǧiḥ*, "you have conquered (or: become possessor), so be forbearing" (frequently used with respect to a vanquished enemy or a prisoner of war). With sayings like these we must also compare the expression *al-ṣadaqatu ʿan ġinan*, to which Kister, *l.c.*, p. 276, ult., refers. This expression represents a well-known *ḥadīṯ: ḫayru l-ṣadaqati ʿan ẓahri ġinan* (see, e.g., Buḫārī, *Ṣaḥīḥ*, ed. Krehl, vol. 1, p. 361, ult.). From the affinity of this saying with the phrase *aʿṭaytu fulānan kaḏā ʿan ẓahri yadin* (see above) one should by no means conclude that *yad* itself (in the contexts under discussion) is synonymous with *ġinan*. The idea implied in *ḫayru l-ṣadaqati ʿan ẓahri ġinan* is that alms should not be given grudgingly—which is possibly the case if the almsgiver possesses only insufficient means, and is not socially independent—but they should preferably be given on the basis of sufficient means, so that an act of genuine charity is performed.

Kister's interpretation of the Qurʾānic passage under discussion—". . . fight them until they pay the *ǧizyah* out of ability and sufficient means, they (nevertheless) being inferior"—is based on his explanation of *yad*, that we are unable to accept (see above). But other objections may be raised against this interpretation of the verse. It is certainly correct, as Kister states, that the amount of the *ǧizyah* to be paid was not to go beyond the payer's economic ability (*ʿalā qadri l-ṭāqah*)—a humane principle which in early Islamic time was generally applied and not only with respect to the *ǧizyah*. It seems, however, strange that this point should have been mentioned—more exactly, implied—in the basic pronouncement itself by which the payment of the *ǧizyah* was imposed on the *ḏimmī*s. We would have expected that this point—if it was altogether found necessary to mention it—would have been added in a second, independent sentence, after the sentence by which the command, that is: the imposition of the *ǧizyah*, was proclaimed.

Also the addition of the clause *wa-hum ṣāġirūna*, "while they are inferior," does not make good sense in the context of Kister's interpretation of the verse as a whole. Kister, indeed, to make the phrase more acceptable, supplies a word: "nevertheless." However, this word does not help remove the incompatibility of the phrase *wa-hum ṣāġirūna* with the preceding phrase ". . . until they pay the *ǧizya* out of ability and sufficient means." Moreover, Kister's interpretation does not take into account the meaning of the word *ǧizya* which after all occurs only in this verse and should be considered as connected with the meaning of the verse as a whole.

* * *

A question necessarily to be treated in connection with the Qur'ānic concept *al-ǧizyatu ʿan yadin* "the reward [due] for a benefaction," is the semantic development of *yad*, literally "hand," into the meaning of "benefaction," and—in its use in the Qur'ānic verse under consideration and in many other passages—more specifically into the meaning of "benefaction constituted by the sparing (saving) of somebody's life." As we already remarked, "the saving (rescuing)—or also: the sparing [by a conqueror]—of somebody's life" is the "benefaction" par excellence in early Arab society and is frequently characterized as such by ordinary terms for "benefaction," as, e.g., *niʿmah, nuʿmā* (cf. also, for example, *Dīwān Imriʾ il-Qays*, ed. Ahlwardt, no. 23, 2).

We quote the following passage from the *Dīwān* of ʿAntarah (ed. Ahlwardt, no. 8, 1–3): (1) *Naḥā fārisu l-šahbāʾi wa-l-ḫaylu ǧunnaḥun ʿalā fārisin bayna l-asinnati muqṣadī* (2) *wa-lau lā yadun nālathu minnā la-aṣbaḥat sibāʿun tahādā šilwahū ġayra musnadī* (3) *falā takfuri l-nuʿmā wa-ʾaṯni bifaḍlihā wa-lā taʾmanan mā yuḥdiṯu llāhu fī ġadī*: "(1) While the horses [were racing along, because of their speed] leaning to one side, the rider of the light-colored mare took the direction toward a horseman who, surrounded by spears, was threatened by outright death. (2) And if a hand of ours had not taken hold of him, it would have happened that beasts would have passed on his limbs one to another, and he would not have been buried. (3) Do not, therefore, deny the benefaction (or: do not be ungrateful for the favor) and acknowledge (or: praise) its excellence and do not feel safe from what God may do tomorrow!"

In our opinion, the phrase (in line 2) *wa-lau lā yadun nālathu minnā* can not only be interpreted, on the basis of the literal meaning of its component elements, by "and if a hand of ours had not taken hold of him," but also by "and if a benefaction of ours had not reached him," or "and were it not for a benefaction granted him by us." That is, the term *yad* (in the phrase *nālathu yadun minnā*, "a hand of ours got hold of him") would be used here synonymously with the term *nuʿmā*, "favor, benefaction," occurring in the subsequent line (line 3) and referring to the action described by the words *nālathu yadun minnā*. We also maintain that what is uppermost in the mind of the poet and what he primarily intends to express, is the idea of "a favor granted," or, more specifically, "the favor granted the horseman in question by rescuing his life." We furthermore assume that the literal sense of the sentence: "a hand of ours reached for him and got hold of him," is likewise expressed by it, but is of minor importance; that is, this literal sense is not primarily intended by the speaker (the poet). What we are dealing with here is "the simultaneous emergence in the mind of two distinct (interrelated) aspects of a notion," a semantic mechanism observed by us and described in our *Studies in Arabic and General Syntax* (*Publications de l'Institut Français d'Archéologie Orientale du Caire. Textes arabes et études islamiques*: XI [Cairo, 1953]), pp. 139–50. In this specific semantic mechanism, the more concrete one of the two distinct aspects of this type of notion, that is—in the case here under discussion—the linguistically expressed idea of "the stretched hand which reaches out for the warrior whose life is threatened," is of minor importance and is apt to get lost completely, so that only the principally intended aspect of the notion, which is not linguistically expressed—that is, the idea of "the benefaction granted the threatened warrior through the rescue of his life"—remains. A result of this development, which can be clearly sensed in ʿAntarah's phrase *wa-lau lā yadun nālathu minnā* (see above), was that the word *yad* ("hand") could now serve also as an expression for the (abstract) concept of "benefaction granted somebody by saving (or: sparing) his life." Finally, *yad* could serve as an expression for "benefaction, favor" generally, regardless of the specific character of the benefaction. This final development in the meaning of *yad* is based on the fact that "the benefaction granted someone by saving (or: sparing) his life" is in early Arab society the "benefaction" par excellence, and, in a sense, corresponds to the sporadic use of *niʾmah*, *nuʿmā* and synonymous words for "benefaction" in the specific meaning of "benefaction granted someone by saving (or: sparing) his life."

The situation described in ʿAntarah's lines quoted above: "someone's hand reaching out for a man surrounded by enemies, in order to save his life," was certainly a frequently occurring event in early Beduin heroic society; and since the term "hand" is the central concept of this process, *yad* was from the outset liable to be associated with the concept of "benefaction granted someone by saving (or: sparing) his life" and thus with the concept of "benefaction, favor" generally.

A parallel to this semantic development (and also based on the semantic mechanism referred to above) we recognize in the development of the term *balā*, as described by us in *Der Islam* 35 (1959): 19 ff. *Balā*$_2$ basically expresses the concept of "exertion (in battle), steadfastness, fortitude." But as part of phrase like *balāʾu fulānin ʿinda fulānin* "A's exertion in battle in the service (or: for the sake) of B," *balāʾ* was apt to acquire the sense of "favor granted someone by another one by his defending him or his fighting for him," and finally *balāʾ* adopted the sense of "benefaction" generally, without the idea of a warlike exertion implied (for details see *l.c.*).

NOTES

1. The same conclusion may be drawn from another episode from the report on the Day of Šiʿb Ǧabalah to which we only refer without quoting it in extenso; see *Naqāʾiḍ*, p. 675, lines 2–3, 5–7, 14–17, p. 676, line 1 ; cf. also p. 675, line 10. A further interesting instance of this type—connected with the Day of Zubālah and involving the famous Bisṭām b. Qays—related in *Naqāʾiḍ*, p. 681, see especially lines 5–8.

2. Cf. also ibid., p. 57, the words ascribed to al-Ḥuṭayʾah: *fa-qad ḥaqana damī waʾaṭlaqanī bi-ġayri fidāʾin fa-lastu bi-kāfirin niʿmatahū abadan* ". . . and he (i.e., Zayd) spared my blood and released me without ransom money, and I shall never forget his good deed." This identification of *ḥaqn al-dimāʾ*, "preventing (or: causing to cease) bloodshed (as a consequence of war or revenge)," as *niʿmat-*, "favor, benefaction," is frequently found; cf. also, e.g., the line of al-Farazdaq in *Naqāʾiḍ*, p. 740, 7: *ḥaqannā dimāʾa l-Muslimīna fa-ʾaṣbaḥat lanā niʿmatun yuṯnā bihā fi l-mawāsimi*, "we took care that the shedding of the blood of the Muslims was stopped, and we were credited with this as a benefaction which was praised at the fairs (taking place at the festival seasons)." This *ḥaqn al-dimāʾ*—in these passages designated as *niʿmat-* (= *yad*), "favor, good deed," which necessitated some reward—was of course the main problem for those non-Muslims who did not adopt Islam but did at the same time (in most cases) not fight unto death (therefore being *dāiġrun*, "ignominious"). Cf., e.g., the following passage referring to the capitulation of the Jews of Ḫaybar arid Fadak, Ibn Hišām, *Sīrah*, p. 764, 5; moreover line 8, which we quote here: . . . *fa-lammā samiʿa bi-him ahlu Fadaka qad ṣanaʿū mā ṣanaʿū baʿaṯū ilā Rasūli-ilāhi ṣlʿm*

yas'alūnahū an yusayyirahum wa'-an yaḥqina dimā'ahum wa-yuḫallū lahū l-amwāla . . . , ". . . and when the people of Fadak heard of them (i.e., of the people of Ḫaybar), what they had done, they (i.e., the people of Fadak) sent to the Messenger of God asking to deport them and to spare their blood, and they would leave to him (as a reward) their possession . . ." (cf. also al-Balāḏurī, *Ansāb al-ašrāf*, vol. 1, ed. M. Ḥamīdullāh [Cairo, 1959], p. 352, 5).

3. In *Aġānī*, vol. 16, p. 56, We find instead of *mālun yūṭābu* the following reading: *mālī bi-'ātin* ("my property is not coming"), which we may consider as a secondary—more readily understood—reading (quasi a *lectio facilior*).

4. How self-understood indeed it was that the "benefaction" (*niʿmat-* or *yad*) effected by freeing a prisoner be rewarded by the latter, we recognize also from the fact that the word for "benefaction" or "doing a benefaction" in this context has almost acquired itself the meaning of "reward" or of "acquiring reward," respectively. This semantic development already perceptible in our above quotations becomes clearly apparent from the following quotation (*Naqā'iḍ*, p. 1063, 10–11): *fa-sa'ala Laqīṭun ʿĀmiran an yuṭliqa lahū aḫāhu fa-qāla Laqīṭun ammā niʿmatī fa-qad wahabtuhā laka wa-lākin arḍi aḫī wa-ḥalīfī llaḏayni štarakā fīhi fa-ǧaʿala Laqīṭun li-kulli wāḥidin mi'atan min-a l-ibili fa-raḍiya* . . . , "and Laqīṭ asked ʿĀmir that he free for him his brother, and Laqīṭ said: 'As to my "benefaction," I give it to you (that is: I waive it), but you should satisfy my brother and my confederate who participated in the matter. . . ." It should be noted that in the parallel tradition of *Aġānī, niʿmatī*, "my benefaction," is replaced by *ḥiṣṣatī*, "my share," which, of course, seems to be far more in agreement with *wahabtuha laka* than *ni ʿmatī*, but is certainly a secondary reading.

5. We quote the following sentences from the commentary to this line, which explain the phrase frequently used in contexts of this kind (See some of the above-quoted passages), *ǧazza nāṣiyatahū* ("he cut off his forelock"): . . . *fa-yaqūla lam yakun ḏahābu šaʿrī li-'anni usirtu fa-ǧuzzat nāṣiyatī ʿalā ṭalabi l-ṯawābi; wa-kaḏālika kānū yafʿalūna: iḏā asara aḥaduhum rağulan šarīfan ǧazza ra'sahū aw fārisan ǧazza nāṣiyatahū ʿalā ṭalabi l-ṯāwābi wa-'aḫaḏa min kinānatihī sahman li-yafḫara bi-ḏālika*, ". . . and he says: The disappearance of my hair was not for the reason that I have been taken prisoner and that my forelock was cut off to enable [the captor] to ask for a reward; one used to do like that: if someone captured a nobleman, he sheared his head; or [if he captured] a horseman, he cut off his forelock and took an arrow from his quiver in order to boast with that" (there follows a line by al-Ḥuṭay'ah as an illustration of the last-mentioned detail). Moreover, we quote the following passage concerning an episode from the year 11 A.H. (Ṭabarī, *Annales*, 1, 2007, 10 ff.): *fa-qālū l-mawtu ḫayrun mimmā antum fī hi ǧuzzū nawāṣiyakum ḥattā ka-'annakum qawmun qad*

wahabtum li-llāhi anfusakum fa-'anʿama ʿalaykum fa-bu'tum bi-niʿamihi (variant: *bi-niʿmati llāhi*) *laʿallahū an yanṣurakum ʿalā hā'ulā'i l-ẓalamati fa-ǧazzū nawāsiyahum wa-taʿāqadu wa-tawāṯaqū an la yafirra baʿḍuhum ʿan baʿḍin*, "and they (i.e., the Kindites in the wars of the *Riddah*, the defection from Islam) said: 'Death is better than your condition. Cut off your forelocks so that you appear like people who have dedicated themselves to God—so He will bestow His grace on you (i.e., will grant you victory and life) and you will acknowledge His favor (or: you will win His favor?); maybe He will grant you victory over these evildoers.' And they cut off their forelocks and obligated themselves mutually not to flee from one another," in this passage the act of the shearing of one's forelock as a symbol of recognition that one's life has been preserved by someone appears very clearly. The passage is moreover interesting through the fact that it is here God—not a human being—to whom one dedicates oneself by means of the act of shearing one's forelocks as a symbol of indebtedness for one's life having been spared.

5.6

"ʿAN YADIN" (QURʾĀN, IX.29): AN ATTEMPT AT INTERPRETATION

M. J. Kister

The crucial passage of Sura IX.29 has been variously interpreted by commentators of the Qurʾān, scholars of Ḥadīṯ and lexicographers. In recent years F. Rosenthal, C. Cahen, and M. M. Bravmann have dealt with this obscure passage.[1] The following lines survey some of the Muslim interpretations of the expression *ʿan yadin* and attempt to arrive at a satisfactory conclusion.

I

Abū ʿUbayda (d. 209 A.H.) explains the expression *ʿan yadin* as yielding on the part of the subdued by payment (scil. of some tax) under compulsion.[2] Al-Kalbī (d. 146 A.H.) is said to have interpreted the expression by *yamšūna bihā*, they are to bring the ǧizya walking.[3] This interpretation is quoted as an anonymous opinion by Abū ʿUbayd.[4] To Abū ʿUbayd (d. 224 A.H.) himself is attributed a similar explanation of *ʿan yadin*: the payer would not come riding, nor would he send the ǧizya by a messenger.[5] Abū ʿUbayd records other interpretations: *ʿan yadin* denotes payment of the ǧizya in cash, or that the payer should stand while the receiver of the ǧizya remains seated.[6] The latter interpretation is recorded by al-Naḥḥās (d. 338 A.H.) as an interpretation of a *ṣaḥābī*, al-Muġīra b. Šuʿba and accepted by

M. J. Kister, "ʿan Yadin" (Qurʾān, IX.29): An Attempt at Interpretation," *Arabica* 11 (1964): 272–78. Reprinted with the permission of Brill Academic Publishers.

ʿIkrima (i.e., the *mawlā* of ʿAbd Allah b. al-ʿAbbās).[7] In fact this interpretation, included in the famous conversation of al-Muġīra with Rustum, is recorded by al-Suyūṭī (d. 911 A.H.),[8] but is given not as an explanation of *ʿan yadin*, but of the following phrase, *wa-hum ṣāġirūna*. Ibn al-ʿArabī (d. 542 A.H.) rightly remarks that this explanation refers to *wa-hum ṣāġirūna*;[9] his gloss is quoted by al-Qurṭubī (d. 671 A.H.).[10] Al-Suyūṭī records interpretations of early scholars. Qatāda (d. 118 A.H.) rendered *ʿan yadin* by *ʿan qahrin*, under compulsion. Sufyān b. ʿUyayna (d. 198 A.H.) explains that it denotes payment of the tribute in person, not through a messenger.[11] Abū Sinān explains *ʿan yadin* by *ʿan qudratin*, ability (i.e., being able to pay or having the ability to collect the tax—the definition is ambiguous).[12] Abū Bakr al-Siğistānī (d. 330 A.H.) records three interpretations: *ʿan qahrin*, by compulsion on the part of the receiver and humbleness on that of the payer, *ʿan maqdiratin minkum ʿalayhim wa-sulṭānin*, strength and power of the receivers of the tribute in relation to the payers, *ʿan inʿāmin*, as recompense for a favor, that is, the acceptance of the ğizya and leaving their life to them is a favor and kindness.[13] Similar explanations are given by Rāġib al-Iṣfahānī.[14] Abū Ḥayyān (d. 754 A.H.) records another explanation of Qatāda: the hands of the payers should be lower than the hands of the receivers of the tax.[15] Two other explanations recorded by Abū Ḥayyān are the interpretation of the recompense for favor and the interpretation of the power of the receivers and the humbleness of the payers.[16]

Three interpretations recorded by Abū Ḥayyān specially deserve to be stressed: the first one renders *ʿan yadin*, *ʿan ğamāʿatin*. This would imply that the ğizya has to be paid for the whole community; no one would be exempted.[17] The second interpretation is that of Ibn Qutayba (d. 276 A.H.): *ʿan yadin* means *mubtadiʾ an ġayra mukāfiʾin*; the ğizya is not a remuneration for a favor.[18] In the third interpretation, *ʿan yadin* does not refer to the receiver, but to the payer of the ğizya. The rendering is: . . . until they pay the ğizya out of (a situation of) ability and (financial) sufficiency (*ʿan ġinan wa-qudratin*); as ğizya is not collected from the poor.[19]

Al-Zamaḫšarī (d. 528 A.H.) explains the expression *ʿan yadin*[20] as referring both to the payer and to the receiver of the tax: referring to the payer it denotes obedience, compliance, and submission; referring to the receiver it denotes a powerful, compelling hand.[21] Other interpretations quoted by al-Zamaḫšarī are payment from hand to hand and payment as recompense for the kindness that their lives (i.e., of the payers) are spared. Bringing the tribute walking (not riding) is mentioned by al-Zamaḫšarī in his description of the humiliation of the payers in connection with the expression *wa-hum ṣāġirūna.*

Ibn al-ʿArabī (d. 542 a.h.) records 15 interpretations of the expression *ʿan-yadin*: 1. the tribute to be given by the payer standing, while the receiver is seated (ʿIkrima); 2.—giving it in person; the tribute is brought walking; 3.—from hand to hand; 4.—out of strength; 5.—openly (*ʿan ẓuhūrin*); 6.—payment is made without acknowledgment (by the receiver) being made (*ġayra maḥmūdīn*); 7.—receiving (scil. the payer) a blow on his neck; 8.—being in a posture of humiliation; 9.—being in a situation of financial sufficiency (the payer); 10.—on the basis of a contract; 11.—paying in cash; 12.—admitting that the hands of the Muslims are above their hands (i.e., admitting the superiority of the Muslims); 13.—by compulsion; 14.—in recompense of a favor received; 15.—payment not being a recompense for a favour or kindness received.[22]

The various definitions recorded by Ibn al-ʿArabī are controversial. Ibn al-ʿArabī is aware of this fact[23] and tries to trace the differences back to various meanings of the word *yad*: whether it is used in the literal sense, a hand, or it is used metaphorically. Literally, it denotes payment from hand to hand in person; metaphorically, it indicates power, prompt payment or favor and kindness.[24]

II

One of the principal difficulties in the understanding of this obscure expression was to determine whether the noun *yad* refers to the receiver of the tribute or to the payer. The expression *ʿan yadin* is defined as *ḥāl*[25] and is interpreted by different commentators as denoting either the payer or the receiver of the tax, according to the suffix added.[26] The interpretations in which two divergent meanings are attached to *ʿan yadin* are an interesting attempt to solve the problem. It is obvious that the interpretations: strength, compulsion, payment from hand to hand, recompense for favor or humbleness of the payer, were the current and prevailing ones. These definitions suited the views of the majority of the *fuqahāʾ*, accorded with the position of the *ahl-al-ḏimma* and the actual tax-collecting procedure.[27]

In order to explain the expression in accordance with some of the interpretations, the preposition *ʿan* had to be glossed by the preposition *bi*.[28] In these interpretations *ʿan yadin* is conveniently complemented by the following circumstantial clause *wa-hum ṣāġirūna*.

But nothing seems to point to the fact that these are the early ones. One may assume that a quite early interpretation was the interpretation of *ʿan yadin* by *ʿan ʿahdin* (no. 10 in the list of Ibn al-ʿArabī). According to this interpretation the phrase would be rendered:

> . . . till they pay the tribute on the basis of a pact (concluded by them with the Muslims) they being inferior (in status).

According to this interpretation the tribute is in fact paid by the *ahl al-ḏimma* in respect of their blood not being shed and their being allowed to reside in the abode of Islam; this is defined by a pact.[29] Ṣaġār is interpreted as compliance with the law of Islam.[30] This interpretation fairly reflects the spirit of the early period of Islam in which the conquering Muslims concluded pacts with the conquered. It does, indeed, seem to be an early interpretation. The problem whether this is in fact the intention of the phrase of the Qurʾān is, however, not solved.

III

The expression *ʿan ẓahri yadin* is interpreted by al-Zamaḫšarī in "al-Fāʾiq":[31] it is explained as *ʿan ẓahri inʿamin mubtadiʾan min ġayri mukāfaʾatin ʿalā ṣanīʾin*. The phrase: Aʿṭāʾ l-ǧazīla ʿan *ẓahri yadin* would be rendered thus: he gave plenty, giving it gratuitously, that is, without any favor being granted to him. *Asās al-balāġa* of al-Zamaḫšarī has the same explanation:[32] *ʿan ẓahri yadin, min ġayri mukāfaʾatin*. Two other expressions are recorded by al-Zamaḫšarī in *Asās* and by Ibn Manẓūr in *L.ʿA.*: *Fulānun yaʾkulu ʿan ẓahri yadi fulānin iḏā kāna huwa yunfiqu ʿalayhi and alfuqarāʾu yaʾkulūna ʿan ẓahri aydī l-nāsi*.[33] It is evident that the phrase denotes to live on the expenses, means, or resources of somebody.

Al-Šarīf al-Raḍiyy (d. 406 A.H.) explains the word *ẓahr* in the saying *al-ṣadaqatu ʿan ẓahri ġinan* as *quwwatun min ġinan*.[34] In this passage al-Šarīf al-Raḍiyy explains the expression *aʿṭaytu fulānan kaḏā ʿan ẓahri yadin* as giving somebody (a gift) out of a position of strength, power of resistance, as opposed to humbleness and fear (*an imtinā ʿin waquwwatin, lam uʿṭihi ʿan ḫīfatin wa-ḏillatin*). "This meaning," says al-Šarīf al-Raḍiyy, "is contrary to the meaning inherent in the words of Allah *ḥattā yuʿṭū l-ǧizyata wa-hum ṣāġirūna*." "It seems," continues al-Raḍiyy, "that the omission of the word *ẓahr* in the phrase of the Qurʾān changed the meaning." Al-Šarīf al-Raḍiyy concludes that *ʿan yadin* in the discussed sentence of the Qurʾān denotes humbleness, submission, fear; the contrary of it is *ʿan ẓahri yadin* denoting strength, free choice and man's own will.[35] In his *Talḫiṣ al-bayān*, al-Šarif al-Raḍiyy explains the expression *ʿan yadin* as a metaphor denoting paying the tribute humbly and submissively (*an ḫušūʿin wa-ḍarāʿatin wa-ḏullin wa-stikānatin*).[36]

He compares this meaning with the idea inherent in the expression *aʿṭā fulānun bi-yadihi* (other explanations—already mentioned—are also quoted).

It is not all the more striking to find al-Zamaḫšarī interpreting *ʿan yadin* in his *Asās al-Balāġa*,[37] as paying the ǧizya in a position of submission and obedience or payment in cash without postponment.

In both interpretations (of al Raḍiyy and of al-Zamaḫšarī) a line is thus drawn between *ʿan yadin* and *ʿan ẓahri yadin*. *ʿAn yadin*, contrary to *ʿan ẓahri yadin*, is explained as submission, obedience, humbleness, and so on.

But the true meaning of *ʿan yadin* can be gauged from the following verse of Durayd b. al-Ṣimma:

> *A-ʿāḏila inna l-ruzʾa fī miṯli Ḫālidin*
> *wa-lā ruzʾa fīmā ahlaka l-marʾu ʿan yadi.*[38]
> "O reprover, misfortune is in (the death of a man) like Ḫālid, misfortune is not in what a man squanders (by lavish spending) out of plenty."

Yad in this verse explicitly denotes wealth, or sufficient resources for spending (on the poor and needy), or generous distribution (of gifts).

That *ʿan yadin* is identical with *an ẓahri yadin* is explicitly stated by Ibn Qutayba.[39] Al-Māwardī records as one of his two interpretations of the discussed expression: *ʿan ġinan wa-qudratin*, paying the ǧizya in a situation of (having) sufficient means and resources and ability to pay.[40]

It is essential to point out that Abū ʿUbayd accepts the idea of the payer's financial ability (*wa-hāḏā ʿindanā maḏhabu l-ǧizyati wa-l-*

ḫarāǧi, innamā humā ʿalā qadri l-ṭāqati min ahli l-ḏimmati) as the basis for fixing the amount of the tax.[41] This passage of Abū ʿUbayd is repeated verbatim by his pupil, Ibn Zanǧawayh.[42]

This seems to have been, in fact, the intention of the discussed phrase in the Qurʾān. The *āya* was revealed on the eve of the expedition of Tabūk.[43] The intention was not to give instructions regarding the ways and procedures governing the collection of taxes;[44] it was an injunction as to the attitude to be adopted by the Muslim warriors towards the *ahl al-ḏimma*. The phrase enjoined the warriors to combat the enemy until they agreed to pay tribute according to their means and capacity. This idea is clearly reflected in the terms of the pacts concluded with the *ahl al-ḏimma*. The pacts concluded with the people of Iṣfahān and Ǧurǧān, for instance, positively state that the amount of the ǧizya would be fixed according to the payer's ability (*ʿalā anna ʿalaykum min al-ǧazāʾi fī kulli sanatin ʿalā qadri ṭāqatikum*).[45] The phrase *wa-hum ṣāǧirūna* is not a complementing phrase for *ʿan yadin*; it constitutes a crucial pronouncement concerning the position of the *ahl al-ḏimma*: but they are inferior in status. The phrase may be rendered:

> . . . fight them . . . until they pay the ǧizya out of ability and sufficient means, they (nevertheless) being inferior.

It is interesting to note that this interpretation is given by the modern Egyptian scholar Rašīd Riḍā. He renders *ʿan yadin* by *ʿan qudratin* wa-saʿatin.[45]

This rendering seems to be faithful to the original intent of the phrase of the Qurʾān.

NOTES

1. Franz Rosenthal, "Some Minor Problems in the Qurʾān," in *The Joshua Starr Memorial Volume* (New York: Jewish Social Studies, Publication no. 5, 1953), pp. 68–72; Claude Cahen, "Coran IX, 29: Ḥattā yuʿṭū l-ǧizyata ʿan yadin wa-hum ṣāǧirūna," in *Arabica* 9:76–79; Meir Bravmann, "A propos de Qurʾān IX, 29. Ḥattā yuʿṭū l-ǧizyata," in *Arabica* 10:94–95. All these articles are to be found in the present volume.

2. Abū ʿUbayda, *Maǧāz al-Qurʾān*, ed. F. Sezgin, 1, 256; and see Al-Ǧaṣṣāṣ, *Aḥkām al-Qurʾān* (Cairo, 1347 A.H.), III, 122: and see *L.ʿA.*, s.v. *ydy* (vol. 15, 424, ed. Beirut).

3. *L.ʿA.*, s.v. *ydy*.

4. *K. al-Amwāl*, p. 54: *qāla baʿḍuhum* (Cairo, 1353 A.H.).

5. *L.ʿA.*, s.v. *ydy*.

6. *al-Amwāl*.

7. *al-Nāsiḫ wa-l-mansūḫ* (ed. Cairo, 1357 A.H.), p. 169.

8. *al-Durr al-manṯūr* (Cairo, 1314 A.H.: reprint offset: Teheran 1377 A.H.), III, 228.

9. *Aḥkām al-Qurʾān* (ed. Cairo 1331 A.H.), I, 378.

10. *al-Ǧāmiʿli-aḥkām al-Qurʾān* (Cairo, 1358 A.H.), VIII, 115; al-Ǧaṣṣāṣ, *Aḥkām al-Qurʾān*; see al-Ṣūlī, *Adab al-kuttāb*, ed. Bahǧat al-Aṯarī (Cairo, 1341 A.H.), p. 215.

11. Recorded by al-Naḥḥā s anonymously, op. cit.; comp. above n. 5.

12. *al-Durr al-manṯūr*.

13. *Ġarīb al-Qurʾān*, ed. Muṣṭafā ʿInān (Cairo, 1355 A.H.), p. 158; see for *ǧizya*: ibid., p. 79.

14. *al-Mufradāt*, s.v. *yad* (Cairo, 1324 A.H.).

15. *al-Baḥr al-muḥīṭ* (ed. Cairo, 1328 A.H.), V, 30.

16. See al-Naḥḥās, op. cit.; *L.ʿA.*, s.v. *ydy*; Niẓām al-dīn al-Nīsābūrī, *Tafsīr ġarāʾib al-Qurʾān* (on margin of the *Tafsīr* of al-Ṭabarī, ed. Būlāq, 1327 A.H.), X, 66; and see al-Ṭabarsī, *Maǧmaʿ al-Bayān* (ed. Beirut), X, 44–45.

17. *Lā yuʿfā ʿan ḏī faḍlin li-faḍlihi.*

18. Abū Ḥayyān quotes Ibn Qutayba: *ʿan yadin* is identical with *ʿan ẓahri yadin*; the interpretation recorded by Abū Ḥayyān is given in Ibn Muṭarrif's *al-Qurṭayn* (Cairo, 1355 A.H.), 1, 193.

19. *Fa-lā tuʾḫaḏu min al-faqīri.*

20. *al-Kaššāf* (ed. Cairo, 1354 A.H.), II, 147–48.

21. Quoted by Abū Ḥayyān; and see the explanation in Ibn al-Aṯīr's *Nihāya*, s.v. *ydy*.

22. *Aḥkām al-Qurʾān* (Cairo, 1331 A.H.), I, 378.

23. *Hāḏihi l-aqwālu minhā mutadāḫilatun wa-minhā mutanāfiratun.*

24. For *yad* explained literally and metaphorically, see Ibn Qutayba, *al-Iḫtilāf fī l-lafẓ*, ed. al-Kawṯarī (Cairo, 1349 A.H.), p. 28; and see al-Bayhaqī, *al-Asmāʾ wa-l-ṣifāt* (ed. Cairo, 1358 A.H.), p. 319; and see al-Šarīf al-Murtaḍā, *Amālī* (ed. Cairo, 1954), II, 3–5.

25. Rāġib al-Iṣfahānī, op. cit.; al-ʿUkbarī, *Imlāʾu mā manna bihi l-raḥmān*, ed. Ibr. ʿAtwa ʿAwad (Cairo, 1961), II, 13: *fī mawḍiʿi i-ḥāli.*

26. *ʿan maqdiratin minkum ʿalayhim* (al-Siğistānī, op. cit.); *ʿan inʿāmin minkum ʿalayhim* (al-Qurṭubī, op. cit.), etc.

27. Comp. the discussion about *itʿāb al-anbāṭ* in Abū ʿUbayd's *Amwāl, ibid.*; See al-Ğaṣṣāṣ, *Aḥkām al-Qurʾān*; see the tradition of Saʿīd B. al-Musayyab in *al-Durr al-manṯūr*; and see A. Fattal, *Le statut légal des non-Musulmans en pays d'Islam*, pp. 286–88.

28. Comp.: *ʿan yadin yaʿnī ʿan naqdin min qawlihim yadan bi-yadin* (al-Ğaṣṣāṣ, *Aḥkām al-Qurʾān*); . . . *aw bi-aydīhim . . . fa-ʿan ʿala hāḏā bi maʿnā l-bāʾ, fa-l-ẓarfu lağwun* (al-Ğamal, *al-Futūḥāt al-Ilāhiyya*, II, 288).

29. See Ibn al-ʿArabī, op. cit., I, 379 sup.: . . . *annahā tağibu bi-l-muʿāqadati wa-l-tarāḍī* . . . ; and see the refutation of this view, ibid., I, 3–4; and comp. al-Ğamal, op. cit., 11, 288: . . . *ka-annahu qīla qātilūhum ḥattā yuʿṭū l-ğizyata an ṭībi nafsin wa-nqiyādin dūna an yukrahū ʿalayhi, fa-iḏā ḥtīğa fī aḫḏihā minhum ilā l-ikrāhi lā yabqā ʿaqdu l-ḏimmati.*

30. See al-Bayhaqī, *Aḥkām al-Qurʾān*, ed. al-Kawṯarī (Cairo, 1952), p. 79.

31. Al-Zamaḫšarī, "al-Fāʾiq," III, 228 ed. ʿAlī Muḥ. al-Biğāwī-Muḥ. Abū l-Faḍl Ibrāhīm (Cairo, 1945–48).

32. Al-Zamaḫšarī, "*Asās al-balāġa*, II, 366, s.v. *ydy*; the same interpretation is recorded in *L.ʿA.*, s.v. *ẓahr*.

33. *Asās al-balāġa*, s.v. *ẓhr*; *L.ʿA.*, s.v. *ẓhr* (vol. 4, p. 521, ed. Beirut).

34. *al-Mağāzāt al-nabawiyya*, no. 44, ed. Maḥmūd Muṣṭafā (Cairo, 1937), p. 66; and comp. the explanation of this expression in *L.ʿA.*, s.v. *ẓhr*.

35. Al-Šarīf al-Raḍiyy, pp. 67 inf.–68 sup.

36. Al-Šarīf al-Raḍiyy, *Talḫīṣ al-bayān* (ed. Baġdād, 1953), p. 59.

37. s.v. *ydy*.

38. *al Aṣmaʿiyyat*, ed. Ahlwardt, XXIV, 3, p. 23.

39. Quoted in *al-Baḥr al-muḥīṭ*, see above n. 17.

40. al-Nuwayrī, *Nihāyat al-arab*, VIII, 235; and see F. Rosenthal, "Some Minor Problems in the Qurʾān," p. 70, quoted from al-Bayḍāwī: *ʿan ġinan*; and see the interpretation in *al-Baḥr al-muḥīṭ*, above n. 17; and see the interpretation no. 9 in the list of Ibn al-ʿArabī.

41. *al-Amwāl*, pp. 41–42 (no. 106–107).

42. *al-Amwāl*, ms. Burdur 183 f. 16a.

43. See Nöldeke-Schwally, *Die Geschichte des Qorans*, I, 224

44. See F. Rosenthal, "Some Minor Problems in the Qurʾān," p. 69.

45. al-Sahmī, *Taʾrīḫ Ğurğān* (ed. Hyderabad, 1950), p. 5; Abū Nuʿaym, *Geschichte Iṣbahans* (ed. S. Dedering), I, 26. I am indebted to Professor Claude Cahen for his kind remarks, which stimulated me to check these sources.

46. *al-Waḥyu l-muḥammadī* (ed. Cairo, 1354 A.H.), p. 278.

5.7

Koran and Tafsīr: The Case of "ʿan Yadin"

Uri Rubin

PREFACE

The *ǧizya* verse (IX.29) is an important part of Koranic law. This verse states that the People of the Book should be fought by the Muslims: *ḥattā yuʿṭū l-ǧizyata ʿan yadin wa-hum ṣāġirūn*. The revelation of this verse is set by Muslim tradition on the eve of the expedition to Tabūk (9 A.H.).[1] The aim of this verse seems to have been to promise the Muslims financial compensation through the *ǧizya*[2] for the loss of income caused by the breaking of commercial relations with non-Muslim traders. The latter are prohibited from approaching Mecca in the previous verse (IX.28).[3]

During the last thirty-five years Western scholars tried to figure out what the Koran expected of the People of the Book in requesting them to pay the *ǧizya ʿan yadin*. In order to elucidate the linguistic meaning of *ʿan yadin* some of them looked for a suitable interpretation in Muslim *tafsīr*. In the present study it will be shown that the various Muslim interpretations of *ʿan yadin* are merely reflections of views of later jurists. It will be demonstrated that the significance of the Koranic *ʿan yadin* is rather preserved in nonexegetical material using the term *yad* in the context of taxation. In general, the present study provides additional evidence that rather than preserve the original meaning of the Koranic legal injunctions, Muslim *tafsīr* reads into the Koran legal procedures that developed much later.

Uri Rubin, "Koran and Tafsīr: The Case of 'an Yadin,' " *Der Islam* 70 (1993). Reprinted with permission.

I

The Muslim interpretations of *ʿan yadin*[4] fall into two main groups: (A) those based on the view that the term *yad* stands for the "hand" of the payer of the *ǧizya*; and (B) those based on the view that the *yad* is that of the receiver.

(A) **yad** *is that of the payer*

In this group we have the following interpretations:

(1) *ʿan yadin* = *ʿan ġinan.*[5] *An ġinan* is actually an abridgment of the phrase *an ẓahri ġinan.* This expression occurs in Muslim traditions stating that charity should only be practiced out of sufficient means.[6] The interpretation taking *ʿan yadin* in the sense of *ʿan ġinan* means that the payment of the *ǧizya* should not affect the economic stability of the payer. It seems to reflect views of Muslim leaders and scholars who tried to fight against overtaxing. Already the Umayyad caliphs were aware of the danger of overtaxing. The caliph Yazīd III undertook in his accession speech (126 A.H.) to destroy nobody's income by overtaxing *ḏimmīs* and thus causing them to flee.[7] In *ḥadīṯ* material, the first caliphs are credited with statements against overtaxing. Many Iraqi *ḥadīṯ*s against overtaxing center around the figure of ʿUmar.[8] There is also one Syrian tradition about ʿUmar's objection to overtaxing.[9] The Kūfans circulated similar traditions about ʿAlī.[10] There is also one prophetic utterance against overtaxing of a Ḥiǧāzī provenance.[11] Notable Iraqi representatives of the Ḥanafī school, like Abū Yūsuf (d. 182 A.H.) and al-Šaybānī (d. 189 A.H.), were very much concerned about overtaxing. Abū Yūsuf stresses[12] that the *ḏimmīs* should be treated with kindness (*rifq*); the Muslims are not to lay upon them rates of taxes that they cannot afford (*fawqa ṭāqatihim*); taxes may be collected from them only according to the obligations of the law (. . . *illā bi-ḥaqqin yaǧibu ʿalayhim*). Al-Šaybānī states that the Muslims may collect taxes from the allied non-Muslims (= the *ḏimmīs*) only with the latter's consent and goodwill (*illā bi-ṭibi anfusihim*). Commenting on this, al-Saraḫsī notes that taking taxes from the *ḏimmīs* without their goodwill (*bi-ġayri ṭībi anfusihim*) means violation of the treaty made with them by the Muslims.[13]

(2) *ʿan yadin* = *ʿan ẓahri yadin.*[14] The expression *ʿan ẓahri yadin* means *mubtadiʾan*, that is, of one's own volition. It occurs in the context of noble gestures, when something is given away not as recompense for a favor, but rather due to one's own benefaction. In this case *yad* means *niʿma; inʿām.*[15] According to this interpretation the *ǧizya* should be paid in the largest possible sums, as if paid due to the payer's own wish to give as much as possible, without holding anything back. This, too, seems to reflect a specific tendency of later Muslim scholars concerning the fixation of the *ǧizya* sums. Some of them were of the opinion that the *ǧizya* should be as high as possible in order to keep the *ḏimmīs* in a state of *ṣaġār* (lowliness), and to force them to embrace Islam. For example, the Šīʿī Imām, Ǧaʿfar al-Ṣādiq, reportedly declared that the *ḏimmīs* should be forced to pay as much as they could afford in order to cause them depression and *ṣaġār*, which is designed to make them prefer being Muslims.[16]

(3) *ʿan yadin* = *ʿanʿahd.* This interpretation[17] means that the *ǧizya* payer must have a treaty in which the rates of the taxes imposed on him are fixed. It is obvious that this interpretation, too, reflects a practice of post-Koranic period. In *ḥadīṯ* material there is often reference to the idea that taxation should be based on mutually agreed treaties. The adherence to treaties which applied mainly to land tax, was attributed by the Iraqis to ʿUmar.[18] *Ḏimmīs* with whom a treaty was made were considered by Sufyān al-Ṯawrī (d. 161 A.H./778) immune against the increase of taxes.[19] The importance of treaties in connection with taxation was also stressed by Meccan authorities.[20] The Prophet himself is said to have uttered admonitions against increasing of taxes that had been fixed in a treaty.[21]

(4) *ʿan yadin* = *ʿan ǧamāʿa.*[22] This interpretation implies that the *ǧizya* is a collective tax imposed on the community as a whole. This interpretation reflects a reality: the entire community had to participate in raising the total sum of the *ǧizya*, as will be shown below.

(5) *ʿan yadin* = "out of one's own hand." This interpretation is represented in a series of variations taking *ʿan yadin* as signifying various aspects of the actual deliverance of the *ǧizya* from the hand of the humble payer to that of the superior receiver. These interpretations reflect the view that the social status of *ḏimmīs* should remain inferior:

a. The *ǧizya* is given in cash (*ʿan naqd*).[23]
b. Payer brings money on foot, with his own hands.[24]

c. Payer gives money directly from his own hand.[25]
d. Payment is made while the hand of the payer is lower than that of the receiver.[26] The idea behind this interpretation becomes clear in view of a *ḥadīṯ* to the effect that the upper hand, that is, the hand that gives, is better than the lower hand, that is, the hand that receives.[27] The intention of this interpretation is, therefore, to maintain the superiority of the Muslims although they are the receiving, not the giving, party.

B. **yad** *is that of the receiver*

All the interpretations in this group reflect the inferior status of the *ḏimmīs*:

(1) *ʿan yadin* = *ʿan niʿma, inʿām.* Payment is made as a favor on the part of the receiver, in agreeing to accept payment.[28] In this interpretation *yad* signifies *niʿma*, as is the case in A(2), above.

(2) *ʿan yadin* = out of power. This view is reflected in a series of interpretations taking *yad* as a metaphorical description of various aspects of the superiority of the Muslims over the *ḏimmīs*:

a. *ʿan qudra*, *ʿan quwwa*[29]—out of ability, or power, of the Muslims to overcome the *ḏimmīs*.
b. *ʿan ẓuhūr*[30]—"out of triumph"
c. *ʿan qahr*[31]—"out of oppression."

There are more interpretations that elaborate on the humbleness of the *ḏimmīs*, but although recorded as *tafsīr* of *ʿan yadin*, they actually pertain to the clause *wa-hum ṣāġirūn*.[32]

II

All the above interpretations are, in fact, retrospective attempts to read into the Koranic text already existing ideas of post Muḥammadan jurists, or existing post-Muḥammadan situations of real life. Most of them evolve round the idea of the lowliness (*ṣaġār*) of the *ḏimmīs*.[33] The wide range of meanings that the word *yad* has in Arabic made it possible to interpret our verse in so many ways. Nevertheless, some Islamicists have been convinced that these interpretations contain a clue to the original meaning of the Koranic *ʿan yadin*. They actually suggested one interpretation or another as the true one, but their suggestions seem quite arbitrary.[34] Most noteworthy are the studies of Bravmann and Kister. Bravmann's translation runs as follows: ". . . until they give the reward due for a benefaction (since their lives are spared)."[35] This is an obvious reflection of the interpretation taking *ʿan yadin* in the sense of *ʿan niʿma* (B[1]). Bravmann's argumentation in favour of his translation is not convincing. He says that *ʿan yadin* "is necessarily complement of the verbal noun *al-ǧizya*: *ǧazāhu ʿan yadin* 'he compensated him for a favour.' " It seems to me, however, that the phrase *ǧazāhu ʿan yadin* is purely hypothetical; it does not occur in practical usage, at least not in the texts adduced by Bravmann himself. In the Koran, *ʿan yadin* is obviously a *ḥāl* of *yuʿṭū*, not a complement of *al-ǧizya*.

Kister, in his study, seems to have chosen more than just one interpretation. He points out as credible the interpretation of *ʿan ġinan* (A[1]) as well as the interpretation of *ʿan ẓahri yadin* (A[2]). Kister's translation is: ". . . until they pay the *ǧizya* out of ability and sufficient means . . ."[38] But as seen above, the two interpretations chosen by Kister are not identical; they reflect two contradictory ideas about how the *ǧizya* ought to have been collected from the *ḏimmīs*. *ʿAn ġinan* means that the *ḏimmīs* are not to be overtaxed, whereas *ʿan ẓahri yadin* means that they have to pay the largest possible sums. In order to uphold his translation, Kister maintains that *wa-hum ṣāġirūn* is not complementary to *ʿan yadin*,[39] and translates it: ". . . they (nevertheless) being inferior." But the *wāw* in *wa-hum ṣāġirūn* is obviously *wāw al-ḥāl*, which means that the *ǧizya* is paid while the payers are being in a state of *ṣaġār*, not in spite of it. In other words, whatever the meaning of *ʿan yadin* may be, the clause *wa-hum ṣāġirūn* is complementing it.

III

If one is still to investigate the significance of the Koranic *ʿan yadin*, one may consult some nonexegetic data preserved in historiographical sources in which the term *yad* is used in the context of taxation. Let us begin with the texts of some early *ǧizya* treaties concluded with the local populations of various places in Iraq and Persia, which are recorded in al-Ṭabarī. Whether authentic or not,[40] the linguistic usage of the term *yad* in these texts is most instructive.

(1) The treaty of al-Ḥīra: This treaty was drawn upon behalf of Ḫālid b. al-Walīd in the year 12 A.H.[41] It is adduced by al-Ṭabarī from Sayf b. ʿUmar (d. 200 A.H.), probably from the latter's *Kitāb al-ridda wa-l-futūḥ*[42] it runs as follows:

> In the name of Allāh, the merciful, the compassionate. This is the treaty made by Ḫālid b. al-Walīd with ʿAdī and ʿAmr, sons of ʿAdī, and with ʿAmr b. ʿAbd al-Masīḥ, and Iyās b. Qabīs and Ḥayri b. Akkāl—ʿUbayd Allāh said: "Jabrī (b. Akkāl)." They represented the people of al-Ḥīra; the people of al-Ḥīra agreed to it and told (the representatives) to (ratify) it (i.e., the treaty). The treaty he made with them stipulated that they should pay 190,000 dirhams per year, as *ǧizya*, out of their 'hands' in this world. [The burden should be shared by] their monks and priests. Exempt are those who have no "hand," who are deprived of temporal (matters), (or) abstain from them. . . .

As we see, the treaty states that the *ǧizya* should be paid out of the "hands" the payers have in this world (*ʿan aydīhim fī l-dunyā*). Exempt are those who have no "hand" (*yad*). It is clear that the term *yad* (and its plural, *aydi*) stands, in this context, for property, possessions. Out of it, a certain amount should be given away as *ǧizya*. It should be observed that among the numerous meanings the lexicons give for *yad*, one is, indeed, *milk*, that is, property, estate.[43] The general rule implicit in this treaty is that the *ǧizya* is only imposed on owners of property to the exclusion of those who have no estate (*yad*) of their own. Although not stated explicitly, it is clear that the individual rates are to be determined by the local leaders themselves according to the extent of property possessed by each payer. The Muslim authorities are only concerned with the total sum.

(2) Lower and Middle Bihqubāḏ (12 A.H.): The treaty made by Ḫā lid with the inhabitants of this region stipulates that the *ǧizya* be paid *ʿan kull ḏī yad*.[44] Here, too, *yad* signifies property: the tax should be paid by the leaders of the community on behalf of every owner of property.

(3) Bāniqya and Basmā (12 A.H.): This treaty[45] stipulates a collective

ǧizya of ten thousand dinars to be (shared by) *kull ḏī yad*: every owner of property. The treaty states also that the individual rates should be proportional to the total amount of one's own property: *al-gawiyyu ʿala qadri quwwatihi, wa-l-muqillu ʿalā qadri iqlālihi*, that is, the rich in proportion to his resources, and the poor in proportion to his limited capability.[46]

(4) Āḏarbīǧān (22 A.H.): The treaty of Āḏarbīǧān[47] stipulates that the *ǧizya* be imposed on every one who is capable of paying, to the exclusion of minors, women, chronically ill people, and pious worshipers; these classes do not have in their "hand" any temporal possessions of their own (. . . *laysa fī yadihi shayʾun min al-dunyā*). *Yad* in this case is not exactly the property itself but rather the hand that "possesses" it.

(5) Qūmis (22 A.H.):[48] The clause containing the term *yad* in this treaty runs as follows: . . . *ʿalā an yuʾaddū l-ǧizyata ʿan yadin, an kulli ḥālimin bi-qadri ṭā-qatihi*—"(they will have protection) on condition that they pay the *ǧizya* out of (their) property (*ʿan yadin*), on behalf of every adult, according to his ability to pay."

Aḫbār *material*

A similar use of the term *yad* in the sense of private property possessed by the taxpayers is made in *aḫbār* material. In a report from Sayf pertaining to 16 A.H., it is related that the peasants of the Sawād were held responsible for the maintenance of roads, bridges, markets, and fields. They were compelled to guide the Muslim troops, as well as to pay *ǧizya* out of their property, and in accordance with what they could possibly afford: *maʿa l-ǧazāʾi ʿan aydīhim ʿalā qadri ṭāqatihim*. The Dihqans, too, had to pay the *ǧizya* out of their property (*ʿan aydīhim*).[49]

In view of the textual evidence of the *ǧizya* treaties and the *aḫbār*,[50] one may assume that the meaning of the same text in the Koranic *ǧizya* verse would not be different. The Koranic *ʿan yadin* may therefore be translated: ". . . (till they pay the *ǧizya*) out of their property. . . ." This means that the tax should be levied on the property possessed by every taxpayer (and be proportional to it).

It should be noted that the Koran could also have used the plural form: *ʿan aydīhim* as is the case in several treaties, but the singular form—*ʿan yadin*—seems to have been preferred as it is more poetic than *ʿan aydīhim*.

The form *ʿan yadin* in the sense of "out of one's property" occurs in classical poetry in the context of noblemen who do not hesitate to spend all their temporal possessions for the sake of the needy.[51] When applied to the Koranic *ǧizya* verse, *ʿan yadin* preserved this very meaning. The People of the Book should readily pay the *ǧizya* out of their own property.

The final clause of the Koranic *ǧizya* verse states that the payers of the *ǧizya* are in a state of *ṣaġār*, that is, lowliness. In fact, taxes were always a sign of lowliness and submission to the authorities. It is a universal phenomenon, in vogue already in the Bible.[52] In the *ǧizya* treaties, too, the lowliness involved in taxpaying is explicit. The treaty of Taflis (22 A.H.) grants *amān* to the population on condition that they consent to *ṣaġār al-ǧizya*, that is, the submission involved in the payment of the *ǧizya*.[53]

IV

In spite of the resemblance between the Koran and the *ǧizya* treaties, the latter do not seem to draw on the former.[54] The Koranic *ǧizya* verse appears in none of the treaties, whereas the Koranic form *ʿan yadin* occurs in only one of them. The non-Koranic nature of the treaties adds considerably to their possible authenticity.[55] It also indicates that at the earliest stages of the development of Muslim law the Koran was not yet effective.[56] A possible source for the *yad* principle of the treaties seems to have been the pre-Islamic Sāsānī taxation policy. It is reported that the Persians imposed a poll tax graded according to the amount of wealth found "in the hands" of the payers (*wa-kāna ḫarāǧ Kisrā ʿalā ruʾūs al-riǧāl ʿalā mā fī aydīhim min al-hiṣṣa wa-l-amwāl*).[57] The Koran itself may reflect the same pre-Islamic Sāsānī model.[58]

Finally, a note on the value of *tafsīr* as a means for unveiling the original significance of the legal parts of the Koran. The significance of *yad* as *milk* is not represented in the *tafsīr*s of the Koranic *ǧizya* verse. It seems to have been eclipsed by other interpretations that seemed to the *mufassirūn* more suitable, The latter, as always, tried to read their own ideas into the Koran. In the case of the *ǧizya* they gave predominance to those interpretations reflecting the social status of the *ḏimmīs* or the procedures of their taxation, as they were known to them from the discussions of the jurists, or as experienced by them in real life. This leads to the conclusion that *tafsīr* in itself is sometimes a very poor tool for elucidating the earliest meaning of the Koranic text, but a very good one for the study of later ideas about the issues treated in the Koran.

REFERENCES

Abd al-Razzaq. *al-Muṣannaf*. Edited by Ḥabīb al-Raḥmān al-Aʿẓamī. Beirut, 1970.

Abū Dāwūd. *Sunan*. Cairo, 1952.

Abū Ḥayyān. *al-Baḥr al-muḥīt*. Cairo, 1328 A.H./1910.

Abū ʿUbayd, al-Qāsim b. Sallām. *Kitāb al-amwāl*. Edited by Muḥammad ʿAmāra. Beirut, 1989.

Abū Yūsuf, Yaʿqūb b. Ibrāhīm. *Kitāb al-ḫarāǧ*. N.p., n.d.

al-ʿAyyāšī, Muḥammad b. Masʿūd. *Tafsīr*. Edited by Hāšim al-Rasūlī al-Maḥallātī. Beirut, 1991.

al-Baġawī, al-Ḥusayn B. Masʿūd. *Maʿālim al-tanzīl*. On margin of al-Khāzin, *Lubāb al-tanzīl*. Cairo, 1381 A.H./1961.

al-Balāḏurī Aḥmad b. Yaḥyā, *Ansāb al-ašrāf*. Vol. 5. Edited by S. D. Goitein. Jerusalem, 1936.

———, *Futūḥ al-Buldān*. Edited by R. M. Riḍwān, Beirut, 1978.

al-Bayḍāwī, *Anwār al-tanzil wa-asrār al-taʾwīl*. Cairo, 1955.

al-Bayhaqī, Aḥmad b. al-Ḥusayn. *al-Sunan al-kubrā*. Hyderabad, 1355 A.H./1936; repr. Beirut, n.d.

Biḥar al-anwār = al-Maǧlisī, Muḥammad Bāqir, *Biḥar al-anwār*. Tehran; repr. Beirut, 1983.

Fatḥ al-bārī = Ibn Ḥağar al-ʿAsqalānī. *Fatḥ al-bārī šarḥ ṣaḥīḥ al-Buḫārī*. Būlāq, 1310 A.H./1892; repr. Beirut, n.d.

al-Ǧaṣṣāṣ, Aḥmad b. ʿAlī. *Aḥkām al-Qurʾān*. Edited by Muḥammad al-Ṣādiq Qamḥāwī. Repr. Beirut, 1985.

Ḥamīdullāh, Muḥammad. *Maǧmūʿat al-waṯāʾiq al-siyāsiyya*. Cairo, 1956.

al-Huwwārī, Hūd b. Muḥakkam. *Tafsīr kitāb Allāh al-ʿAziz*. Edited by Belḥāǧ Šarīfī. Beirut, 1990.

Ibn Abī Šayba, ʿAbdallāh b. Muḥammad, *al-Muṣannaf fī l-aḥādīṯ wa-l-āṯār*, Bombay 1967.

Ibn al-ʾArabī, Muḥammad b. ʿAbdallāh. *Aḥkām al-Qurʾān*. Edited by ʿAlī Muḥammad al-Biǧāwī. Beirut, 1987.

Ibn al-Ǧawzī, ʿAbd al-Raḥmān, *Zād al-masīr fī ʿilm al-tafsīr*. Beirut, 1984.

Ibn Ḥazm, ʿAlī b. Aḥmad, *al-Muḥallā*. Cairo, 1352 A.H./1933.

Ibn Hišām. *al-Sīra al-nabawiyya*. Edited by al-Saqā, al-Abyārī, Šalabī (I–IV). Repr. Beirut, 1971.

Ibn Ḫuzayma, *Ṣaḥıḥ*. Edited by Muḥammad Muṣṭafā al-Aʿẓamī. Beirut, 1975.

Ibn Qutayba. *Tafsīr ġarīb al-Qurʾān*. Edited by Aḥmad Ṣaqar. Beirut, 1978.

Ibn Zamanīn. *Muḫtaṣar tafsīr Yaḥyā b. Salām*. MS, Fas, Qar. 34.

Kanz = al-Muttaqī al-Hindī. *Kanz al-ʿummāl fī sunan al-aqwāl wa-l-afʿāl*. Edited by Ṣafwat al-Saqā, Bakrī al-Ḥayyāni. Beirut, 1979.

al-Kulīnī, Abū Ǧaʿfar. *al-Uṣūl wa-l-furūʿ mina l-Kafī*. Edited by ʿAli Akbar al-Ġaffārī. Beirut, 1980.

Lisān = Ibn Manẓūr. *Lisān al-ʿarab*. Cairo, n.d.

Maǧmaʿ al-zawāʾid = al-Haythamī, Nūr al-Dīn. *Maǧmaʿ al-zawāʾid wa-manbaʿ al-fawāʾid*. Repr. Beirut, 1987.

Mālik/Zurqānī = al-Zurqānī, Muḥammad b. ʿAbd al-Bāqī. *Šarḥ Muwaṭṭaʾ al-imām Mālik*. Cairo, 1961.

Muǧāhid B. Ǧabr. *Tafsīr*. Edited by ʿAbd al-Raḥmān al-Sūratī. Islamabad, n.d.

Muqātil b. Sulaymān. *Tafsīr al-Qurʾān*. MS, Istanbul, Ahmet III, 74.

al-Qummī, ʿAlī b. Ibrāhīm. *al-Tafsīr*. Beirut, 1991.

al-Qurṭubī, Muḥammad B. Aḥmad. *al-Ǧāmiʿ li-aḥkām al-Qurʾān*. Cairo, 1967.

al-Rāzī, Fakhr al-Dīn, *al-Tafsīr al-kabīr*. Cairo, n.d.; repr. Tehran, n.d.

Saʿīd b. Manṣūr, *al-Sunan*. Edited by Ḥabīb al-Raḥmān al-Aʿẓamī. Beirut, 1985.

al-Saraḫsī, Muḥammad b. Aḥmad. *Kitāb al-mabsūṭ*. Repr. Beirut, 1986.

al-Šāfiʿī, Muḥammad b. Idrīs. *al-Umm*. Repr. Beirut, 1983.

al-Šaybānī, Muḥammad B. al-Ḥasan. *al-Siyar al-kabīr—šarḥ Muḥannad b. Aḥmad al-Saraḫsī*. Edited by Ṣalāḥ al-Dīn al-Munaǧǧid. Cairo, 1971.

al-Suyūṭī, Ǧalāl al-Dīn. *al-Durr al-manṯūr fī l-tafsīr bi-l-maʾṯhūr*. Cairo, 1314 A.H./1869; repr. Beirut, n.d.

al-Ṭabarānī, Abū al-Qāsim. *al-Muʿǧam al-kabīr*. Edited by Ḥamdī ʿAbd al-Maǧīd al-Salafī. N.p., 1980–85.

al-Ṭabarī, Muḥammad b. Ǧarīr. *Ǧāmiʿ al-bayān fī tafsīr al-Qurʾān*. Būlāq, 1323 A.H./1905; Repr. Beirut, 1972.

———, *Tahḏīb al-āṯār*. Edited by Maḥmūd Muḥammad Šākir. Cairo, 1982.

———, *Tārīḫ al-umam wa-l-mulūk*. Edited by De Goeje. Leiden, 1879–1901.

al-Ṭabarsī, al-Faḍl b. al-Ḥasan. *Maǧmaʿ al-bayān fī tafsīr al-Qurʾān*. Beirut, 1957.

al-Ṭūsī, Muḥammad b. al-Ḥasan. *al-Tabyān fī tafsīr al-Qurʾān*. Edited by A. H. Q. al-ʿĀmilī. Beirut, n.d.

Yaḥyā b. Ādam. *Kitāb al-Kharāǧ*. Edited by Aḥmad Muḥammad Šākir. Cairo, n.d.

al-Yaʿqūbī, Aḥmad B. Isḥāq, *al-Tārīḫ*. Beirut, 1960.

Yāqūt, *Muʿǧam al-buldān*. Beirut, 1957.

al-Zaǧǧāǧ, Abū Isḥāq, *Maʿānī al-Qurʾān wa-iʿrābuhu*. Edited by ʿAbd al-Ǧalīl Šalabī. Beirut, 1988.

al-Zamaḫšarī, *al-Fāʾiq fī ġarīb al-ḥadīṯ*. Edited by ʿAlī al-Biǧāwī—Abū l-Faḍl Ibrāhīm. Cairo, 1979.

———, *al-Kaššāf ʿan ḥaqāʾiq al-tanzīl*. Cairo, 1966.

NOTES

1. See, e.g., Muǧāhid, *Tafsīr*, I, 276.

2. For the history of the term *ǧizya* see Claude Cahen, s.v. "Ḏjizya," *EI* (see. ed.). For more bibliography, see M. G. Morony, *Iraq after the Muslim Conquest* (Princeton, 1984), pp. 584–88.

3. See Ṭabarī, *Tafsīr*, X, 76–77; Huwwārī, II, 125; Ibn Hišām, IV, 192–3; P. Crone, *Meccan Trade* (Princeton, 1987), p. 172. Both verses seem to form part of the proclamation of the *Barāʾa*, for which see Uri Rubin, "Barāʾa: A Study of Some Quranic Passages," *Jerusalem Studies in Arabic and Islam* 5 (1984): 13–32.

4. The following *tafsīr* compilations are used: Abū Ḥayyān, V, 30; Baġawī, III, 65; Bayḍāwī, I, 196; Ǧaṣṣāṣ, IV, 292–3; Huwwārī, II, 125; Ibn al-ʿArabī, *Aḥkām*, II, 922–23 (the author's numbering of the various interpretations is followed); Ibn al-Ǧawzī, *Zād al-masīr*, III, 420; Ibn Qutayba, *Ġarīb*, 184; Ibn Zamanīn, 125; Muqātil, I, 152 b; Qurṭubī, VIII, 115; Rāzī, XVI, 30; Suyūṭī, *Dur*, III, 228; Ṭabarsī, X, 45; Ṭūsī, *Tabyān*, V, 203; Zaǧǧāǧ, Maʿānī, II, 442; Zamaḫšarī, *Kaššāf*, II, 184.

5. Ibn al-ʿArabi no. 9; Bayḍāwī; Abū Ḥayyān.

6. See *Fatḥ al-bārī*, III, 233 f.

7. See P. Crone and M. Hinds, *God's Caliph* (Cambridge, 1986), p. 68.

8. See, e.g., Abū ʿUbayd, *Amwāl*, no. 106; Yaʿqūbī, II, 152; Yaḥyā b. Ādam, no. 226, 232, 236; Abū Yūsuf, *Ḫarāǧ*, 136. See, also ibid., 14–15; Ṭabarānī, *Kabīr*, XVIII, no. 654; *Maǧmaʿ al-zawāʾid*, VI, 16.

9. See Abū ʿUbayd, *Amwāl*, no. 114; *Kanz*, IV, no. 11478. And see the statement of Ibn ʿAbbās transmitted by Maʿmar b. Rāšid to the effect that the taxes imposed on *ahl al-ḏimma* should be confined to the *ʿafw*, i.e., to their spare property, ʿAbd al-Razzāq, X, no. 19277; VI, no. 10122; Ibn Abī Šayba, XII, no. 12687; Yaḥyā b. Ādam, no. 233; Bayhaqī, *Sunan*, IX, 205. Cf. Abū ʿUbayd, *Amwāl*, no. 253.

10. See Yaḥyā b. Ādam, no. 234, see also, Abū Yūsuf, *Ḫarāǧ*, 16–17; Abū ʿUbayd, *Amwāl*, no. 116; Bayhaqī, *Sunan*, IX, 205; *Kanz*, IV, no. 11488.

11. See Abū Dāwūd, II, 152: . . . *man ẓalama muʿāhadan aw intaqaṣahu aw kallafahu fawqa ṭāqatihi aw aḫaḏa minhu šayʾan bi-ġayri ṭībi nafsin fa-anā ḥaǧīǧuhu yawma l-qiyāma*. See also Bayhaqī, *Sunan*, IX, 205. Cf. also Yaḥyā b. Ādam, no. 235. See also Abū Yūsuf, *Ḫarāǧ*, 135–36.

12. In his *Kitāb al-ḫarāǧ*, 134 f.

13. Šaybānī, *Siyar*, I, 133.

14. Ibn Qutayba, *Ġarīb*; Ibn Zamanīn; Huwwārī; Ibn al-ʿArabī, no. 15; Abū Ḥayyān; Ibn al-Ǧawzi.

15. *Lisān*, "*y.d.y.*" (Aṣmaʿī); Zamaḫšarī, *Fāʾiq*, IV, 126 (= *ʿan ẓahri inʿām*); M. J. Kister, " '*ʿAn yadin*,' (Qurʾān IX/29)," *Arabica* 11 (1964): 276 (chap. 5.6 in this volume); M. M. Bravmann, *The Spiritual Background of Early Islam* (Leiden, 1972), p. 206.

16. See ʿAyyāšī, *Tafsīr*, II, 91, no. 41; Qummi, *Tafsīr*, I, 287–88; Kulīnī, III, 566; *Biḥār*, XCVIII, 63–64. See also the report about the negotiations with the people of al-Ruhā (Edessa), in Abū Yūsuf, *Ḫarāǧ*, 43–44.

17. Ibn al-ʿArabī, no. 10.

18. See ʿAbū al-Razzāq, X, no. 19284; VI, no. 10130. See also Abū ʿUbayd, *Amwāl*, no. 390; Bayhaqī, *Sunan*, IX, 142.

19. See, ʿAbū al-Razzāq, VI, no. 10100. See also X, no. 19270.

20. See ʿAbū al-Razzāq, X, no. 19264; VI, no. 10093.

21. See ʿAbū al-Razzāq, X, no. 19272; VI, no. 10105; Saʿīd b. Manṣūr, II, no. 2603; Abū Dāwūd, II, 152; Yaḥyā b. Ādam, no. 237; Bayhaqī, *Sunan*, IX, 204–205. See also Abū ʿUbayd, *Amwāl*, no. 388–99.

22. Abū Ḥayyān.

23. Ǧaṣṣāṣ; Ibn al-ʿArabī, no. 11; Ṭūsī, *Tabyān*.

24. Ǧaṣṣāṣ (Ibn ʿAbbās); Ibn al-ʿArabī, no. 2.

25. No. 3; Baġawī; Ṭūsī, *Tabyān*; Ṭabarsī; Zamaḫšarī, *Kaššāf*; Rāzī; Qurṭubī; Bayḍāwī; Abū Ḥayyān.

26. Abū Ḥayyān (Qatāda).

27. E.g., Qurṭubī, VIII, 115. See also Ṭabarī, *Tahḏīb*, *Musnad ʿUmar*, I, 26 f.; *Fatḥ al-bārī*, III, 235 f.; Ibn Abī Šayba, III, 211–12; Ibn Ḫuzayma, IV, 98.

28. Zaǧǧāǧ; Ǧaṣṣāṣ; Baġawī; Zamaḫšarī, *Kaššāf*; Ṭūsī, *Tabyān*; Ṭabarsī; Ibn al-Ǧawzī, Rāzī; Qurṭubī; Bayḍāwī; Abū Ḥayyān; Ibn al-ʿArabī, no. 14.

29. Zamaḫšarī, *Kaššāf*; Ṭabarsī; Rāzī; Qurṭubī; Bayḍāwi; Abū Ḥayyān; Ibn al-ʿArabī, no. 4.

30. Ibn al-ʿArabī, no. 5. The phrase *ʿan ẓuhūr* is rendered by Kister (*ʿAn yadin*, 274): "openly." But the correct meaning of *ẓuhūr* is triumph.

31. Ibn al-ʿArabī no. 13; Abū ʿUbayda; Zaǧǧāǧ (*ʿan qahr wa-ḏull*); Ǧaṣṣāṣ (Qatāda); Baġawī; Zamaḫšarī, *Kaššāf*; Rāzī; Bayḍāwī; Ṭūsī, *Tabyān*.

32. E.g., Zaǧǧāǧ; Ibn al-ʿArabī, no. 8: *ʿan ḏull*, out of humbleness. Ibn al-ʿArabī, no. 12: payer recognizes the superiority of the Muslims; no. 7: payer's neck is being struck (i.e., sealed). For this practice, cf. Morony, *Islam after the Muslim Conquest*, pp. 112–13. ʿUmar reportedly used to stamp marks on the necks of the *ḏimmīs* (*yaḫtimu fī aʿnāqihim*). See Ibn Abī Šayba, XII, no. 12682, 12686; ʿAbd al-Razzāq, VI, no. 10090; Bayhaqī, *Sunan*, IX, 195, 198. Another interpretation: payment is made without acknowledgement. See Muqātil; Ǧaṣṣāṣ; Abū Ḥayyān; Suyūṭī, *Durr*; Ibn al-ʿArabī, no. 6. Another one: Payment is made while payer is standing up. See Ǧaṣṣāṣ; Ibn al-ʿArabi, no. 1; Ṭūsī, *Tabyān* (ʿIkrima).

33. The *ṣaġār* became the main message of Koran IX.29 at a relatively early stage of *tafsīr*. Already the Baṣran Qatāda (d. 118 A.H.) adduced this verse to interpret Koran II.114 which speaks about the disgrace (*ḫizyun*) in store for the Jews and the Christians in this world. See ʿAbd al-Razzāq, VI, no. 9879; Ṭabarī, *Tafsīr*, 1, 339.

34. For the various attempts to elucidate the meaning of the Koranic *ʿan yadin*, see R. Paret, *Der Koran, Kommentar und Konkordanz* (Stuttgart, Berlin, Köln, Mainz, 1971), pp. 199–200.

35. Bravmann, *The Spiritual Background of Early Islam*, p. 199.

36. Ibid., p. 207.

37. Kister, *ʿAn yadin*, pp. 277–78.

38. Ibid., p. 278.

39. Ibid.

40. On the problem of the authenticity of these treaties see A. Noth, "Die literarisch überlieferten Verträge der Eroberungszeit als historische Quellen für die Behandlung der unterworfenen nicht-Muslims durch ihre neuen muslimischen Oberherren," in *Studien zu Minderheitenproblemen im Islam*, ed. T. Nagel et al. (Bonn, 1973), pp. 282 f.

41. See Ṭabarī, *Tārīḫ* I, 2044–45; Ḥamīdullāh, no. 290.

42. On Sayf, see E. Landau-Tasseron, "Sayf b. ʿUmar in Medieval and Modern Scholarship," *Der Islam* 67 (1990): 1–26.

43. E.g., *Lisān*, s.v. "*y.d.y.*"

44. Ṭabarī, *Tārīḫ*, I, 2051; Ḥamīdullāh, no. 301. For these districts, see Morony, *Islam after the Muslim Conquest*, pp. 147 f.

45. Ṭabarī, *Tārīḫ*, 1, 2050; Ḥamīdullāh, no. 293.

46. The same idea recurs in many *ǧizya* treaties stating that the people should pay as much as they can afford (*ʿalā qadri ṭāqatihim*). See the treaties of

Māh Bahrādān (19 A.H.): Ṭabarī, *Tārīḫ*, I, 2632–33; Ḥamīdullāh, no. 331. Māh Dīnār: Ṭabarī, *Tārīḫ*, 1, 2633; Ḥamīdullāh, no. 332. Iṣfahān (21 A.H.): Ṭabarī, *Tārīḫ*, I, 2641; Yāqut, I, 209–10; Ḥamīdullāh, no. 333. Cf. Kister, "*ʿAn yadin*," p. 278. Ǧurǧān (22 A.H.): Ṭabarī, *Tārīḫ*, I, 2658; Ḥamīdullāh, no. 337. Cf Kister, "*ʿAn yadin*," 278. Rayy (22 A.H.): Ṭabarī, *Tārīḫ*, 1, 2655; Ḥamīdullāh, no. 334.

47. Ṭabarī, *Tārīḫ* I, 2662; Ḥamīdullāh, no. 339.

48. Ṭabarī, *Tārīḫ,* II, 2657; Ḥamiddullāh, no. 336.

49. Ṭabarī, *Tārīḫ,* I, 2470.

50. The term *yad* occurs in the context of taxation in *ḥadīṯ* as well. It is related that ʿUmar laid a ten dinars tax upon the *Ṣābiʾūn*, but later on he increased the rate according to what was held "in their hands," and according to their occupations (*ṯumma yazīdu ʿalayhim baʿda ḏālika ʿalā qadri mā bi-aydīhim, wa-qadri aʿmālihim*). See *Kanz*, IV, no. 1148 (from Ibn Zanǧawayhi).

51. One such poetic verse of Durayd b. al-Ṣimma is quoted from the *Aṣmaʿiyyāt* by Kister ("*ʿAn yadin*," p. 277): *wa-lā ruzʾa fī mā ahlaka l-maruʾu ʿan yadi*. Kister translates the phrase *ʿan yadin* in this verse: "out of plenty," thus missing the basic idea of the verse. The poet says that unlimited spending out of one's own property (*ʿan yadin*) can not be regarded misfortune. The idea is that one should not hesitate to lose all one's possessions for noble causes like charity. And cf. the analysis of this verse in Bravmann, *The Spiritual Background of Early Islam*, pp. 206 f. For another poetic usage of *ʿan yadin* in the sense of giving away out of one's own possessions, see Balāḏurī, *Ansāb*, V, 197.

52. The Hebrew word for taxes (*missīm*, sing.: *mas*) is used in the Bible in the sense of burdensome tasks (e.g., Exod. 1:11). The singular *mas* denotes submission and slavery (e.g., Deut. 20:11, etc.).

53. Ṭabarī, *Tārīḫ*, I, 2675; Abū ʿUbayd, *Amwāl*, no. 523; Balāḏurī, *Futuḥ*, 204–5; Yāqūt, II, 36; Ḥamīdullāh, no. 348–9. See also D. C. Dennett, *Conversion and poll-tax in early Islam* (Cambridge, 1950), pp. 44 f. The classical law schools paid special attention to the *ṣaġār* of the *ḏimmīs*. Mālik states in his *Muwaṭṭaʾ* (Mālik/Zurqānī, II, 377) that the *ǧizya* was laid upon the People of the Book in order to demonstrate their *ṣaġār*. Mālik holds that the *ǧizya* can be accepted from the People of the Book only on condition that they recognize Muḥammad as the true prophet of the Muslims, and do not speak evil of him and of Islam. Otherwise they must be killed. See Ibn Ḥazm, *Muḥallā*, VII, 317–18 (from Mālik). For al-Šāfiʿī, too, the *ṣaġār* was the basis for the social status of the *ḏimmīs*. Relying on "a number of scholars," he says that the *ṣaġār* of the People of the Book means that they must be subjected to the laws of Islam concerning them (Šāfiʿī, *Umm*, IV, 186). In a special chapter (ibid., 223 f.) he surveys the legal social status of the *ḏimmīs* in the Islamic state. The ẓāhirī Ibn

Ḥazm (d. 456 A.H.), too, states that the *ṣaġār* means that the *ḏimmīs* should be subjected to the laws of Islam, that is to say, to the restrictions ʿUmar laid upon them (Ibn Ḥazm, *Muḥallā*, VII, 346–47).

54. Western scholars seem always to have been of the conviction that the Koran was the source for the *ǧizya* treaties. This seems to have been the conviction of Dennett (*Conversion and Poll-Tax in Early Islam*, 18) who, analyzing Ḫālid's conduct in al-Ḥīra, states that "for legal precedent he had sura 9:29."

55. The *ǧizya* verse appears intact only in much later *aḫbār*. For instance, in the statement allegedly addressed by al-Muġīra b. Šuʿba to the Persian Rustam, as transmitted on the authority of the Kūfan al-Šaʿbī (d. 103 A.H.). See Balāḏurī, *Futūḥ*, 257; Ṭabarī, *Tārīḫ*, I, 2278. The *ǧizya* verse is also included in the speech allegedly addressed by Salmān al-Fārisī to the Persians when he raided their country (Ibn Abī Šayba, XII, no. 12677), as well as in the speech allegedly addressed by Ḫālid b. al-Walīd to the people of al-Ḥīra (Bayhaqī, *Sunan*, IX, 187–88). All these speeches seem to be based an the same literary model. Some apocryphal "letters" of the Prophet and the first caliphs also contain the *ǧizya* verse. For instance, Muḥammad's "letter" to Heraclius (Ḥamīdullāh, no. 27). Abū Bakr's "letter" to al-Yaman (Ḥamīdullāh, no. 302a), and ʿUmar's "letter" to Abū ʿUbayda (Abū Yūsuf, *Ḫarāǧ*, 51–2; Ḥamīdullāh, no. 354–5).

56. Cf. J. Schacht, *The Origins of Muhammadan Jurisprudence* (repr. Oxford, 1979), p. 24.

57. Ṭabarī, *Tārīḫ*, I, 2371. And see also, Claude Cahen, s.v. "*Ḏjizya*," *EI2*, p. 560a: "The Sāsānid empire had possessed a fiscal system which distinguished between a general tax on land and a poll-tax, at rates varying according to the degree of wealth." And see also *Dennett, Conversion and Poll-Tax in Early Islam*, p. 15: "By the fiscal reform of Khusrō I the poll-tax was graded according to each individual's income." See also, ibid., 28. Cf. also, F. Løkkegaard, *Islamic Taxation in the Classic Period* (Copenhagen, 1950), pp. 134, 142 f.

58. The Medinan population paid taxes to the Persians in pre-Islamic times, so that Sāsānī taxation was well known in Medina, where the Koranic *ǧizya* verse was revealed. See, e.g., M. J. Kister, "al-Ḥīra," *Arabica* 15 (1968): 154 f.; Barakat Aḥmad, *Muhammad and the Jews* (New Delhi, 1979), p. 33.

5.8

Koran XXV.1: Al-Furqān and the "Warner"

C. Heger

Sura XXV (*al-furqān*), as it was transmitted, begins with the following verse:

> *tabāraka l-ladhī nazzala l-furqāna ʿalā ʿabdihī*
> *li-yakūna li-l-ʿālamīna nadhīran.*

It is usually translated as:

> Blessed be He who sent down the *furqān* on His servant
> that he might be (or: become) a warner for the worlds,

understanding *al-furqān* as the Koran and the "servant" as Muhammad.

This traditional understanding presupposes the understanding of the word *nadhīr* as "warner." Both suppositions, the identification of *furqān* with the Koran and the understanding of *nadhīr* as "warner," however, are erroneous.

The meaning "criterion" usually maintained for *furqān* results from the attempt to interpret the Syriac *furqān*, which has the meaning of "redemption, salvation," in a way that relates both to the Arabic word *farq*, meaning "separation," and to the contexts in which the word *furqān* is found.[1]

The later and meanwhile traditional identification of *furqān* with the Koran is especially odd in Sura XXV.1. It is highly improbable that in the—according to traditional Islamic scholarship—earliest "revealed" verses the book that allegedly did not yet exist is already being referred to, even by its supposed later name.

The general evaluation of the alleged meaning "the warner" for *nadhīr* is made possible by the etymological circumstances of this word. In all Semitic languages that functioned as vehicles for the transport of the Bible (and other religious material) to Arabia—Hebrew, Aramaic and Syriac—the root *n-dh-r* uniformly has the meaning of "to vow" or "that which is vowed." And so we have also in Arabic for the basic verb *nadhara*, in clear etymological relation to all other Semitic languages, the general and main meaning "to vow."

The noun *nadhīr* on account of its form *faʿīl* is a verbal adjective or noun of predominantly passive participle meaning. The Arabic dictionaries, at least partly, indeed register the primary meaning "vowed," "votive gift," or "consecrated to God";[2] others register "warner," as does the traditional Koran exegesis. This peculiarity is excused with the traditional comment that in this case the word of this pattern *faʿīl* has the meaning as if it were of the pattern *mufʿil* (= *mundhir*, participle active of the IV. form of *nadhara*, which duly has the meaning "warner").[3]

The same lexica, on the other hand, report that the feminine variant of the masculine form *nadhīr,* which reads *nadhīra,* has the meaning "a votive gift": that which he gives who makes a vow, a child appointed by his parents by a vow to become a minister of the Church, and the like (see Lane s.v.) This is quite peculiar: that the masculine noun *nadhīr* for those lexicographers should have a totally different meaning than the feminine noun of the same grammatical structure.

It can be seen from many phrases and examples of the usage of the word, how "to make someone vow" (IV. or causative form *andhara*) could change over to the meaning "to warn someone." Everybody who urges someone into a position where he has to make a vow brings this person into a difficult position and this can be paraphrased as "to warn him." But at the same time it becomes clear that "to warn" is not the real and basic meaning although it can—and this only with the causative (IV.) form *andhara*—get this secondary meaning in some cases.

Since *nadhīr* is a verbal adjective/noun of the basic (I.) form *nadhara*—and not the causative (IV.) form *andhara*—it should originally not have had the meaning "warner," but the same significance as registered for the feminine form *nadhīra* (which can also be understood as a *nomen unitatis* of the masculine noun): namely, "votive gift" or "sacrifice."

In the end we come to the original meaning of XXV.1, namely,

> Blessed be He, who sent down the redemption on His servant
> that he might be (or: become) a sacrifice for the worlds.

Now XXV.1 displays the central Christian teachings on Jesus Christ: "sent down" (John 1), "as votive sacrifice" (Eph. 5:1; Heb. 10:10–14) "for the redemption" (Eph. 1:7 and often) "of the world" (John 3:17 f.).

Additionally, the *rasm* of *ʿālamīna* can be read as dual. And the dual "the two worlds" is theologically precise and correct since Christian theology sees the redemption brought about by Christ extending to the world of the living as well as to the world of the dead. As a corollary we may remark: this verse also displays the signs of the old pre-Islamic parts of the Koran, namely rhyme and metric pattern, as soon as one reads it as vernacular Arabic:

> *tabāraka lladhī nazzala l-furqāna*
> *ʿalā ʿabdah*
> *li-yakūna li-l-ʿālamīna nadhīrā*

> Blessed be He, who sent down the redemption
> on His servant
> that he might become a sacrifice for the (two) worlds.

NOTES

1. For the changing of the meaning from "redemption" through "criterion" to "revelation script" see Theodor Nöldeke, *Geschichte des Qorans* I (Leipzig, 1909), p. 34; *Neue Beiträge zur semitischen Sprachwissenschaft* (Straßburg, 1910), pp. 23 f.; A.J. Wensinck, *Enzyklopädie des Islam (*Leiden-Leipzig, 1913–1938), II, p. 126; Josef Horovitz, *Koranische Untersuchungen* (Berlin-Leipzig, 1926), S. 76; *Jewish Proper Names and Derivatives in the Koran*, Hebrew Union College Annual, vol. II (Ohio, 1925), pp. 145–227; Arthur Jeffery, *The Foreign Vocabulary of the Qurʾan* (Baroda, 1938), pp. 225–29; Richard Bell, *The Origin of Islam in its Christian Environment* (London, 1926), pp. 118–25;

Introduction to the Qur'an (Edinburgh, 1953), pp. 136–38; W. Montgomery Watt, *Muhammad at Medina* (Oxford, 1960), p. 16.

2. See, for instance, P. Bélot, *Al-Faraïd. Arabe-Français*, 17th ed. (Beyrouth, 1955), p. 817, right column

3. See, for instance, E. W. Lane, *An Arabic-English Lexicon* (London-Edinburgh, 1863–1893).

5.9

The Buddha Comes to China

Michael Schub

When the humanistic study of religion succeeds, the alien seems less strange.
—Jacob Neusner[1]

Close reading of Koran verses XXX.15/14:

. . . *Fa-hum fī rawḍatin yuḥbarūna* = ". . . they [viz. those who believe and do good works] will be *yuḥbarūna* in a lovely[2] garden"; and XLIII.70: *ʾudkhulū l-jannata ʾantum wa-ʾ azwāju-kum tuḥbarūna*[3] = "Enter the Garden of Paradise, you [believing Muslims] and your wives, while you are tuḥbarūna" leads us to suspect (as we have previously with (√khld, ZAL 18–88, 95–96) that this expression in its *Qurʾānic* context is a Hebraism; the one here means "congregated together."

The commentators recognized the difficulty: al-Zamakhsharī[4] reports that Mujāhid thought that *yuḥbarūna* means "they are honored"; Qatādah that it means "they are gladdened"; Ibn Kaysān: "they are pleased"; Abū Bakr ibn ʿAyyāsh: "crowns are upon their heads"; and Wakīʿ: "[it refers to] listening to heavenly music in Paradise."

Al-Suyūṭī[5] relegates this term to the "non-Ḥijāzī dialect" of Qays Ghaylān [!], thus betraying his perplexity.

All of the numerous European language translations I have managed to check basically follow the accepted (*mashūr*) "they are happy" theme.

Michael Schub, "The Buddha Comes to China," *Journal of Arabic Linguistics* 29 (1995): 77–78. Reprinted with permission.

The frequently occurring Qurʾānic synonymous passives *yuḥsharūna* and *yuḥḍarūna* for "they are mustered, made to be present, etc." (the latter with a negative connotation) are irrefragably indigenous Arabic.

E. Ullendorf[6] explains the "bi-radical theory":

> There exist certain simple bases which run through a large number of 'roots' common to many Semitic languages, such as *f l* (or *fr*) 'to divide', qt-qḍ 'to cut ', etc. These bases were apt to be expanded, and the third consonant, in initial, medial, or final position, came to act as a modifier . . .

The quotidian Hebraism was employed by the Prophet to complete this morphological and semantic "triplet," a term with a positive connotation for "they are congregated, etc." Its coincidence with the possibly[7] indigenous Arabic root √*ḥbr* for "to be variegated; beautiful, etc." and its similarity in form and intended meaning to the two other Arabic roots catalyzed its infiltration into the Arabic system;[8] it would appeal, at least on a subliminal level, to potential converts in his Jewish audience who would certainly be familiar with this commonplace Hebrew/Aramaic root.[9]

NOTES

1. J. Neusner, *Take Judaism, For Example, Studies toward the Comparison of Religions* (Chicago, 1983), p. xvii.

2. For √rwḍ ~√rḍy vide infra. [√ = triliteral roots . . . , or triliteral radical . . . , or tri-consonantal root . . .]

3. The grammatically "balanced" nature of this verset is a sine qua non for correct Arabicity apud al-Zamakhsharī (J. P. Broch, ed., *Al-Mufaṣṣal* (Christianiae, 1879), § 158, p. 50, in fine) and pace A. A. Bloch, *Studies in Arabic Syntax and Semantics* (Wiesbaden, 1986), pp. 1–13: "A Principle of Balancing." Cf. p. 3 in medio: "We are not, however dealing with a linguistic rule, since the reduplicating pronoun may be absent." [*sic*]—On the concept of "grammaticality" in Arabic, cf. M. G. Carter, " 'Twenty Dirhams' in the Kitāb of Sībawaih," *BSOAS* 35 (1972): 485–96; especially p. 494 in medio. Also see the same author's "An Arab Grammarian of the Eighth Century A.D." in *JAOS* 93 (1973): 146–57; and P. Abboud, "Sībawaih's Notion of Grammaticality," *JAATA* 12 (1979): 58–67.

Cf. also ʾAbū l-Faḍl Ṭabarsī, *Majmaʿ al-Bayān fī Tafsīr al-Qurʾān* [GAL I 405] vol. 9–10 (Tehran, ca. 1965), p. 172 in initio: *qāla z-Zajjāju: w hādhā lā yajūzu ʾillā fī sh-shiʿri li- ʾanna - hum yastaqbiḥūna istaway-tu wa Zaydun.* Al-Zajjāj [the grammarian]: "This is not possible except in poetry: because it is ungrammatical to say: *istaway-tu wa Zaydun = "I and Zayd agree / are equal" [instead of istawaytu-tu ʾanā wā-Zaydun]* Cf. also Z's *Kashshāf* ad loc. Koran III.20: *(wa –mani ttabaʿa- ni) ʿuṭifa ʿalā t-tāʾ i fī "ʾaslam-tu" wa -ḥaṣuna li-l-fāṣili. [Likewise at Koran III.20: ʿanā is omitted after "ʾaslam-tu."]*

4. *Kashshāf* ad.loc. Koran XXX.15[/ 14].

5. *al-ʾ Itqān fī ʿulūm al- Qurʾān* (Cairo, 1951), p. 134 in fine.

6. In C. T. Hodge, ed., *Afro-Asiatic—A Survey* (The Hague, 1971), p. 36.

7. Cf W. Leslau, *Comparative Dictionary of Geʿ ez* (Wiesbaden, 1987), p. 224, col. 2 in medio: "considered by Fraenkel [*Die aramäischen Fremdworter im Arabischen* (Leiden, 1886), p. 247] an Aramaic loanword."

8. "Here we see that the interaction proceeded through a series of linked stages, as an initial period of 'preparation' was followed by the Islamic 'domestication' of Judaism, leading to a period of 'acceptance and independent growth' which in turn gave way to a long era of 'appropriation' in which Jewish ideas became so securely embedded in Islamic thought and practice that their foreign origin and antagonistic premises were substantially obscured, with Judaism becoming an integral part of Islamic philosophical syncretism." —R. M. Somers, ed., in A. F. Wright, *Studies in Chinese Buddhism* (New Haven, 1990), p. x [I have merely substituted "Jewish" for "Buddhist" and "Islamic" for "Chinese" in the above quotation pour épouvanter the tenured and the comatose. (M.S.)]

9. "[They] mocked at etymology and slighted phonology. But what they did was the same as trying to cross the river without a boat and wanting to climb a mountain without ladders." Tai Chen, in A. Chin and M. Freeman, *Tai Chen on Mencius* (New Haven, 1990), p. 30.

5.10

The Secret Identity of Dhū l'Kifl

Michael Schub

A fantastic (in both senses of the word) literature[1] has arisen concerning the origin of Dhū l-Kifl (Koran XXI.85; XXXVIII.48). In all this vastness, however, no one, to the best of my knowledge, has suggested[2] that Dhū l-Kifl is Muhammad's *laqab* (cognomen) for Melchizedeq. Common sense tells us that since Dhū l-Kifl is linked first with Ismāʿ īl and Idrīs (Enoch of Genesis 5.18, etc.) and then with Ismāʿīl and Elisha, he is an important biblical personage.

Melchizedeq is mentioned, in passing, as it were, at Gen. 14.16. The locus of his meeting Abraham is Melchizedeq's valley, named the valley of Shāveh. One is tempted to connect this name (cognate to the Arabic/ musāw in /= "equal [portion]" with /kifl un / (= "one of two equal[3] parts"). At Ps. 110.4[4] Melchizedeq has been made the Israelite king, the legitimate ruler of Israel by the Lord God's covenant. In the Dead Sea Scrolls Melchizedeq is the heavenly high priest; possibly by now this reflects common Jewish and Christian traditions.[5]

Philo of Alexandria, a contemporary of Jesus of Nazareth, noted[6] Melchizedeq "was entitled to a share" of Abraham's booty at Gen. 14.16.

Melchizedeq's stature developed from the original traditum to the point that in early Christianity at Heb. 5:6–11, he has become the very paragon of priesthood and an exemplar for Jesus himself. And in the same Epistle (Heb. 11:5), Enoch is mentioned as an immortal.

The plain sense of the name Dhū l-Kifl is "the one who got his share."

At Gen. 14:16, Melchizedeq receives one-tenth of Abraham's spoils. At Heb. 5:4 ff., Melchizedeq is considered to be ranked above the Levites, whose primary function under the Law (according to this author) was to collect tithes from the other tribes of Israel. Melchizedeq is thus a fortiori / Dhū l-Kifl /.

In the Fātiḥa (Koran I.4) God is called / *mālik yawm i d-dīn* / that is, "Possessor on the Day of Judgment." / *ṣadaqa* / is the Arabic term for "a portion given as propitiation to God." Thus *mālik ṣ—ṣadaqa* could easily serve as a synonym for / Dhū l-Kifl /. Cf. the (possibly intermediary) biblical Aramaic original of Dan. 4.24: / *malkā milkī . . . bè- ṣidqāh . . .* / = O King, my King . . . in righteousness. . . ." Note also that the El to whom Melchizedeq is chief priest has the special appellation "*Possessor* of heaven and earth" (Gen. 14:19 and 22). (. . . he [Melchizedek], together with the celestial powers, will vindicate the judgments of God so that the righteous would become his LOT [emphasis Michael Schub's] and heritage" David Flusser, *Judaism and the Origins of Christianity* [Jerusalem, 1988], p. 192.)

In sum, Muhammad saw Melchizedeq as he viewed numerous other biblical figures, through a Judeo-Christian filter of *traditio*; his *Originalität*[7] in this case consists in his conflating and condensing the various strains and in assigning Melchizedeq an appropriate Arabic name.

NOTES

1. Cf. art. EI2 for extensive bibliography.

2. Cf. L.Wittgenstein, *Tractatus Logico-Philosophicus* (London, 1961), author's preface: ". . . it is a matter of indifference to me whether the thoughts I have had have been anticipated by someone else . . ." p. 3.

3. sic. s.v. ZAL 16 (1987): 119–20.

4. Ps. 110:4: The Lord hath sworn, and will not repent. Thou art a priest for ever after the order of Melchizedeq.

5. G. W. E. Nickelsburg, *Jewish Literature between the Bible and the Midrash* (Philadelphia, 1981), p. 188, in medio. See also G. Vermes, *The Complete Dead Sea Scrolls in English* (Harmondsworth, 1998), pp. 85, 429, 500–502, 576, 618.

6. J. R. Harris, ed. *Fragments of Philo*. p. 72 on Gen. 14:18; and C. D. Yonge, *The Works of Philo Judaeus* (London, 1854), vol. 2, p. 444.

7. J. Fück, "Die Originalität des arabischen Propheten," ZDMG 90, n.f. 15 (1936): 509–25.

Part 6

EMENDATIONS, INTERPOLATIONS

6.1

Studies Contributing to Criticism and Exegesis of the Koran

J. Barth

Translated by G. A. Wells

The following studies are in the main not concerned with establishing the chronological sequence of the individual suras and the circumstances that occasioned them—matters which form the substance of the enquiries of Sprenger and Muir, and of Nöldeke's *Geschichte des Qorans*,[1] of Weil's *Historisch-kritischer Einleitung in den Koran*,[2] of Grimme's *Muhammad*,[3] and other studies.

Instead, the present author is concerned to examine the internal coherence of the suras for possible evidence of insertions, and to make other critical (also text-critical) comments. Where the coherence has been disturbed, this must have already occurred by the time of the collection and redaction of the Koran, either under Abū Bakr or under 'Uthmān; for we cannot assume that, after this, and after 'Uthmān's dispatch of the official redactions to the four provinces, there was any displacement of textual items in the Koran. On the other hand, when its individual parts were first put together—inscribed as they originally were on parchments, palm leaves, shoulder bones, broad stones, and other primitive writing material[4]—and also in the case of the further collection under 'Uthmān, it is obvious that sizable and smaller elements were inserted (as Muslims have to some extent themselves acknowledged) into passages with which they did not originally connect, so that they now disturb the pattern of the earlier sequence of ideas. Because 'Uthmān ordered that all earlier copies

---

From *Der Islam* 6 (1916): 113–48.

should be burned, so that only the versions he sponsored have reached posterity, we can adduce only internal evidence in our inquiries. Previous research into the Koran has indeed pointed to such evidence, but its main concern has nevertheless been to assign the proper chronological place to each of the suras.

So as not to have to begin with the later suras, those of Medina, the present study keeps to the sequence proposed in Nöldeke's *Geschichte des Qorans*, except that, for our present purpose, the division of the Meccan suras into three stages was not necessary.

Exegesis of the Koran is not possible without an accompanying criticism of the transmission. At times there are insertions in a single verse that interrupt its construction. Sometimes the same idea is stated twice in succession in such a way that the second mention does not presuppose the first. Again, with longer, anaphorically constructed periods, alien verses have been inserted between the indentical beginnings of the verses; and the same verses have been repeated in several suras, sometimes even in the same sura, even though they are apposite only in the one context, and in the other are left with no connection (see below on suras XXVIII and XL); and so on.

More often there are corruptions in individual words. Sometimes their nature is such that, instead of the sense to be expected, they give its very opposite. In such cases Muslims have themselves made some modest criticisms, without admitting as much (see below XIII. 30; III.147; LVII.29) One major cause of such obscurities is that the diacritical points that distinguish identical letters in the writing were lacking in the old script of the Koran, and were added only toward the end of the first century.[5] The necessary result was a series of errors in the transmission, since not many Muslims knew the text by heart (and not too much confidence can be placed in the reliability of their memories in individual instances).[6] Additionally, the written representation of the long vowels *ā*, *ī*, *ū*, was left to be effected in a number of different forms.[7]

In many instances what the context requires can be reconstituted with greater or less plausibility from what we know of Arabic linguistic usage, in particular the usage of the Koran. In many other cases the original tradition has been lost because of textual uncertainty. There is no ground for considerably greater confidence in the Muslim redaction of the text and in the earliest oral tradition, right up to the final fixation of the text, than is extended to other ancient textual witnesses of like kind, nor for accepting the text, in the Muslim manner, as canonically unimpeachable, and abandoning all criticism of it—although this is what is usually done. Admittedly, the desultory style of the Koran, the fact that there are few instances of its voicing an idea in one single passage only, and that much in it is incomplete—all this puts limits to what we are able to achieve. But although we must keep these limitations in mind, we are not entitled to ignore breaks in the nexus and insertions into close-knit sequences of ideas, or to accept obvious textual corruptions without critical comment.

For such work, help from the Arabic commentators is naturally not forthcoming. For them the canonical text of the Koran is sanctified and not to be touched. Where, in the interest of completeness, I quote the traditional Arab explanations, it was impossible to take cognizance of all, or even of the majority of, the existing commentaries for each passage. Considerations of space forbade this, as did also the regrettable imperspicuity of these editions, which often makes the hunting down of individual passages intolerably burdensome. I have therefore limited myself, for my purposes, which seldom involve reproducing the opinions of the Arabs, to three outstanding commentaries: that of Baghawī, (died 516), that of Bayḍāwī (died 685), and the Tafsīr of Al-Jalālain (whose two authors died in 864 and 911, respectively).[8] In these are compiled what the Arabs have to offer by way of explaining critical passages. Baghawī in particular conscientiously and with circumspection collects the earlier accounts given by Arabic scholars.

I. MECCAN SURAS

Sura XCVI

As is well known, this ancient sura, regarded by the Arabs as the oldest, consists of two parts that originally did not necessarily belong together,[9] namely, verses 1–8 and 9–19.

In the first part, verse 1: *ʾiqraʾ bismi rabbika*, which is given various interpretations, should in my view be rendered as: "Read in the name of thy God (the Koran, revealed to you herewith)."[10] As a parallel, Sura LXXXVII: 6 can be adduced, *sanuqriʾuka fa-lā tansā* . . . , "we give thee the Koran to read, thou wilt not forget it"; and also Sura XCVIII.2: *rasūlun yatlū ṣuḥufan muṭahharatan. . . .* , "a messenger who reads pure pages." Hence verses 3 f. have "Thy Lord is the sublime one, who has taught (the Koran) by means of the pen." That this is how *ʿallama* is to be understood is evidenced by Sura LIII. 4f.: "It is only a revelation which is revealed," *ʿallama-hu shadīdu al-quwā*, "which he who is terrible in his powers has taught," namely, by a visible revelation when he appeared to Muhammad *bi-l-ʾufuqi al-ʾaʿlā.* (the same in verse 7). Here likewise *ʿallama* means God's revealing of the Koran. Sura LXXV. 18: *fa-ʾidhā qaraʾnā-hu fa-ttabiʿ qurʾānahu* also helps to explain the first words—God or Gabriel recites the revelation to Muhammad from the divine book. He is to "follow suit," in that he likewise reads it, as indeed Bayḍāwī renders this as *fa-ttabiʿ qirāʾatahu wa takarrar fīhi ḥattā yarsukha fi dhihnika.* In the second part, Nöldeke refers verses 9–10, *alladhī yanhā ʿabdan ʾidhā ṣallā* to a slave being prevented by a powerful person from praying. But on this view, since the prophet would be in no way involved in this incident, verse 19 would not fit into the context, for here he himself is admonished, "Do not follow him (the oppressor), but bow down and draw near (to God)." Hence *ʿabdan* in verse 10 must be understood, in line with Arab commentators (Bayḍāwī, Baghawī, al Jalālain), as Muhammad himself; compare *fa-ʾawḥā ʾilā ʿabdihi mā ʾawḥā* in Sura LIII.10, and also Sura XVII.1; *lammā qāma ʿabdu llāhi yadʿū:* Sura LXXII.19.[11] An unknown powerful opponent had prevented the prophet from praying and preaching (verse 12). This opponent had a considerable following *nādiyahu* (verse 17) behind him. But Muhammad is instructed (verse 19) "Follow him not, bow down and draw near!" In verse 11 the *ʾa-raʿayta* is an erroneous addition that has found its way here from verse 9 or 13; for verse 11 is a continuation of 9 f.: "when he prays (verse 10), when he[12] is on the right path or enjoins fear of God [i.e., "preaches"]." So verse 13 speaks again of Muhammad's opponent: "Just say, when he calls (the one who proclaims) a liar [or is 'cowardly' (cf. Aghānī, V 148, 22, XV 77 ult.)], does he not know that God sees it?" Thus, the second part may well come from a quite ancient time, as there is no talk of a believing slave.

Sura LXXIV

Verses 11 ff. are spoken by a distinguished, well-situated Meccan. In the words introducing them, namely *dharnī wa-man khalaqtu waḥīdan*, *waḥīdan* is inappropriate; for neither "that God alone has created him" (Bayḍāwī), nor "that God has created him alone" ("who has no children nor wealth" Bayḍāwī), makes any sense. The latter is plainly contradicted by verse 12—what must be read is *wajīdan*, "whom I have created as a well-to do [man] [12] and to whom I have given extensive wealth [13] and children." Cf. *wujdun*: Sura LXV.6, I.Hishām 631 M., Ma'n I, 39 and *jidatun* "riches" Ḥam. 521, 4: *wājidun* "rich" Ḥam.698, 2 Kml. 199, 11 and other examples—with the old Koran script, this cannot even be called an alteration. Even the form *wajīd* need cause no surprise, in view of *faqīr wa-ghaniyy*. (cf. also *'āšyr* [rich]; *'āniy* [poor] [Hebrew]; *' -t* -r [Syriac])

Sura CXI

It seems unlikely to me that this sura, directed against Abū Lahab, the prophet's uncle, is among the oldest. Admittedly, the perfect tense *tabbat* in verse 1 may be a wish or a curse; but *mā 'aghnā 'anhu māluhu* in verse 2 points—in accordance with standard linguistic usage of the Koran—to something that has already happened (cf. Suras VII.46, XV.84, and XXVI.207, among others), whereas the imperfect *yughnī* is always used in the case of future events. For a perfect representing a curse, *lā 'aghnā* would have been used.

The sura therefore includes an expression of triumph over the death of Abū Lahab, which was already past. According to Ibn Hishām, it is supposed to have occurred about seven days after the battle of Badr.[13] Furthermore, a few Islamic authors date the sura in a fairly late period, some of them even put it in the eighth year of the Hijra (when, however, Abū Lahab was long since dead), others put it in other years.[14]

Sura XC

This has undergone manifold disruptions. To my mind, verse 2, *wa 'anta ḥillun bi-hādhā l-baladi*, refers to the capture of Mecca and excuses it,[15] and is consequently a Medinan interpolation from some time after the year 8 of the Hijra. That this is so is clear from the formal feature that in verses 1 and 2 the same *al-baladi* is used in immediate succession as a rhyming word.[16] Whether verses 5–7 originally belonged in this context is questionable; for the continuation to verse 4 ("We have created man in trouble") is given by verses 8–10 (and then by 11–16):[17] "Did we not give him two eyes and a tongue and two lips, etc.?"

In verse 17, *thumma kāna min* is a later inserion made in order to link the verse with what preceded it—to which, however, it does not belong. Moreover, the predicate of verse 17 clearly follows only in verse 18. Rather are verses 17 f. and 19 f. a small independent unit of two parts, constructed parallel and conformably to each other. The original is: verses 17, 18: *alladhīna ʾāmanū wa- tawaṣāw . . . ʾūlāʾika ʾaṣḥābu l-maymanati*; as opposite to this come verses 19, 20: *wa lladhīna kafarū bi-ʾāyātinā hum ʾaṣḥābu l-mashʾamati* ['lkh /etc.]. This little unit differs from the other contents of the sura and may have been originally independent.

Sura XCVII

Verse 1. The object of . . . *ʾinnā ʾanzalnāhu* does not refer to the Koran (as is generally supposed), so that this verb would here for the first time designate the revealing of the Koran (Nöldeke). It refers to the angel Gabriel as the carrier of the revelation; for the *nazala* is immediately repeated in *tanazzalu l-malāʾikatu wa-l-rūḥu fīhā* of verse 4 as an explanation of verse 1. What follows these words in verse 4 namely, *min kulli ʾamrin*, cannot be construed. They can neither mean *bi- kulli ʾamrin . . .* (Baghawī), nor "on account of everything" (Bayḍāwī, al Jalālain), for this would be represented by *min*. They do not belong in this context. But everything falls into place if the final words of verse 4 and verse 5 are transposed, so that they read, for verse 4, '*tanazzalu l-malāʾikatu wa-l-rūḥu fīhā ḥattā maṭlaʿi l-fajri*, and verse 5, *salāmun hiya min kulli ʾamrin*, "it [she] is not contested[18] by any [every] (evil) thing."

Sura XCI

The subject "he" of verse 15, *wa-lā yakhāfu ʿuqbāhā* . . . , has no linkage with the preceding verse 14, "God destroyed them because of their sin." Rather does it connect with verse 12: "When the unfortunate one (of the Thamūd) rose up, (15) and did not fear the consequence."

Sura LXXX

Muhammad is censured for turning grimly away from a poor blind man who had sought from him instruction about the revelation. "If (verse 5) someone is rich (6) then you turn to him." Verse 7 continues this with: *wa-mā ʿalayka ʾallā yazzakā*. It conflicts with the sequence of the ideas, to have here "it is not your concern and it does not harm you if he (the rich man) does not become pious" (. . . *laysa ʿalayka baʾsan fī ʾan lā yatazakkā.*)[19] Bayḍāwī. On the other hand, verse 7 forms a good sequel to verse 10: (8) "Whoever comes to you (9) because he fears (God), (10) with him you do not bother; (7) and you don't care whether he becomes pious."

Sura LXXIII

This sura cannot belong among the older of the Meccan ones, for the command to get up at night and recite the Koran (verse 4) already presupposes the existence in writing of a number of suras. Consonant with this is that verse 15 already designates Muhammad as "ambassador" (*rasūlan*) to his people, as was Moses to the Egyptians (All this quite apart from verse 20, which is recognized as being Medinan).

Sura LXXXII

Verse 19. The preceding verses 9–18 all rhyme on *īn*. We cannot assume that the rhyme was lacking only in the emphatic final verse. In verse 19: *li-llāhi* has dropped out after *rabbi l-ʿālamīna*[20] which is found, for example in Sura LXXXI.29; LXXXIII.6.

Sura CI

A. Fischer's[21] assumption that verses 7–8 are interpolated is not tenable; for it presupposes that the genuine threat at the end of the sura stated: verse 6 "he whose balance shall be light his mother will be childless" or "he dies." However that is an unheard of thought in the Koran, quite apart from the fact that, if it refers to the Last Judgment, it would be senseless. In the Koran, the usual punishment of the wicked is hellfire. The combination of *ṣaliya l-nāra* (*al-jaḥīma, saqara*) occurs twenty-four times. Never is anything threatened that would correspond to the *hawat ʾummuhu* as used in the general indeterminate sense by the poets. From this follows that the conclusion of the sura, *nārun ḥā miyatun*, is genuine. The preceding, *fa -ʾummuhu hāwiyatun*, is based on the traditional formula *hawat ʾummuhu*[22] and means "he is in a bad way." This general threat is then explained more precisely in verses 6, 7 as a roasting in hell. This is indicated by the *mā hiyah*, whereas, otherwise after *mā 'adrā-ka mā* . . . an explanatory individual name follows (*al-qāriʿa* in this sura, verse 2; *al-ḥuṭamatu* CIV.5; *al-ḥāqqatu*: LXIX.3) Here, however, it is not a name but the phrase *ʾummuhu hāwiyatun* that has to be explained, and moreover not in some general, unspecific sense but in the sense of burning in the fires of hell.

Sura LXXXI

Verse 6. Among the phenomenon of the Last Judgment—in which all that now exists will be changed into its opposite, so that the stars will be darkened and the mountains will move (verses 2, 3) and so on—there is here mention of *wa -ʾidhā l-biḥā ru sujjirat* (also *sujirat*), which is explained as "be set on fire"[23] (Bayḍāwī,al Jalālain). In Sura LXXXII.3, *wa-ʾidhā l-biḥā ru sujirat* appears in the same context, "when the seas are broken through and made to run into each other," which yields a more natural hyperbole. Hence in LXXXI.6 the same textual reading must be restored as the original. That is more probable than that two quite different hyperbolic statements were made for the same *wa-ʾidhā l-biḥāru* . . . , with two sounds identical in their final radicals. It is still possible to indicate what occasioned the corrupted portion of the text. In Sura LII.6, God is called *rabbu al-baḥri al-masjūri*, "the Lord of the fully swollen sea," that is, of the sea that exists now in its natural fulness. From here, the *sajirat* will have, perversely, been imported into LXXXI.6, where, however, the topic is the complete change of the nature of the sea at a future time. The words of LII.6 testify that *sujirat* at LXXXI.6, is wrong; for if this verb designates, in the former passage, the present natural condition of the sea, it cannot, at LXXXI.6, express the sea's complete transformation.

Sura LXXXIV

After verse 5 the addition to the different *ʾidhā* has probably been lost, which in the corresponding passages LXXXI.14 and LXXXII.5 on both occasions begins with *ʿalimat nafsun*. That it is given in verse 2 with *yā ʾayyuhā l-ʾinsānu* would be quite unusual. A new idea begins with this sentence. In verse 13, *masrūran* . . . is objectionable, for it cannot be alleged, as an earlier misdemeanor of the wicked man that he "was joyful among his people," when in verse 9 the pious are offered the prospect of the same thing as future happiness in verse 6. Probably *masrūran* of verse 9 is wrong and should be a participle that forbodes ill such as *shirrīran sharīran* . . . or something similar.

Sura LXXXVIII

Verse 8. Instead of *wujūhun*, which is opposed to *wujūhun* . . . in verse 2 read . . . *wa-wujūhun* as in Sura LXXV.24; LXXX.40.

Sura LXXXIII

Verses 7–9; 18–21. Here the "book" in which the deeds of the godless (7–9) are recorded, and the one that gives the deeds of the pious (18–21), are named in contrast to each other. Verses 20, 21 call the latter *kitābun marqūmun yashhaduhu l-muqarrabūna*; verse 9 calls the former only *kitābun marqūmun.* In verse 9 an addition, *yashhadu l- . . . ūna*, is obviously missing, the opposite of *yashhaduhu l-muqarrabūna,* which perhaps went "with whom the low or wicked angels are found." Otherwise precisely the characteristic and necessary counterpart to verse 21 would not be expressed. The *ʿilliyūna* of verse 18, with whom the book of the pious is to be found must be envisaged as living creatures. So much is proved by the outer plural. They are the same as the *al-muqarrabūna* of verse 21. From this it follows that the *fī sijjīnin* . . . of verse 7, which is a counterpart to *fī ʿilliyyina* . . . of verse 18,[24] was originally likewise an outer plural. As such, possibly an *taḥtiyyīna* can be inferred. Its original written form without diacritical points [نحس: rasm] could easily lead to *sijjīn* as a corruption.[25] In the Koran itself, nineteen angels are recorded in one of the oldest suras (LXXIV.30 f.) as guardians of hell and overseers of the punishment of sinners; and these are therefore likewise lower angels. Moreover, according to Sura XLIII.35, a Shaiṭān is assigned to each sinner, and is linked (*qarīn*) to him. The contrast between good and evil angels already appears in the late religious literature of the Jews and in Christian writings; for example Tobit 12, 15, "I am Raphaël, one of the seven holy angels who carry up the prayers of the holy ones." (There is no need for further examples.) On the other side there is the evil angel Asmādāj (Tobit 3, 8), the avenging angel in the Revelation of John 51, 1, and the evil spirits in the epistle of James, 2, 19, and more besides.

Sura LVI

Since verse 66 includes the words of the penitents *ʾinnā la-mughramūn ʾlkh* ((N.B. *ʾlkh* = etc.), the preceding *tafakkahūna* of verse 65, which introduces these words, probably represents an ancient error, for it means "to refresh oneself by means of something." The meanings Arab expositors read into it—"you will be surprised (*tataʿajjabūna*)," or "regret" (*tandamūna*), or "reproach each other" (*mutalāwinūna*), or "be downcast" (*taḥzanūna*), or "coverse with each other" (*tataḥaddathūna*)[26] are obviously contrived merely to meet the needs of the passage. A word like *talaffahūna* . . . , "you will feel pain at it," would fit the context. In verses 82 ff. and 85 ff., there are two periods corresponding to each other in parallel, *fa-lawlā ʾidhā* and *fa -lawlā ʾin*. The latter has, as its added element, the *tarjiʿūnahā* of verse 86. But the addition to verse 82 has been lost, and verse 84 has replaced it.

Sura XXXVII

This sura is uniformly constructed from quite short sentences with the same rhyme. Verse 30 interrupts the answer that those who are leading astray give to those being led astray—an answer given in verses 29 and 31. Verse 30 belongs after 31. The erstwhile misleading ones say (29): "You (yourselves) were not believing; you (yourselves) were wanton; (31) hence we have led you into error; for we ourselves were in error." Only after this is verse 30 appropriate: "Hence the word of our Lord afflicts us, that we shall taste (the punishment)" (refers to verse 37: "Behold, you shall taste the painful punishment").

Verse 56. The *ʾa-fa-mā naḥnu bi-mayyitīna* is a countersense. The believer (verse 54) must, on the contrary, say *mā naḥnu bi-mayyitīna ʾillā mawtatanā al-ʾūlā*, "we die but one death (i.e., only in this world) and will not be punished (as you will be)." This is in truth what is said in Sura XLIV.56 of believers: *lā yadhūqūna fīhāal-mawta ʾillā mawtata al-ʾūlā.* Hence one must read *mā* instead of *ʾa-fa-mā.* Verse 159 is disruptive between *ʾinnahum la-muḥḍarūna* . . . in verse 158 and the appropriate exception, *ʾillā ʿibāda llāhi*, in 160. It will originally have been placed before *wa—la-qad ʿ alimat* in 158 as the conclusion of the preceding section, that the possession of daughters is attributed to God (153–157).

Verse 76. In my view there is a very ancient error in the fourfold repeated *wa-taraknā ʿalayhi fī al-ʾākhirīna* (verses 76, 108, 119, 129) (in Nūh, Ibrāhīm, etc.), which, according to Baghawī, Jalālain is suposed to mean *wa -ʾabqaynā ʿalayhi thanāʾan ḥasanan,* "we left him a fine reputation from the later ones." But this sense cannot be comprised in the simple *taraka ʿalayhi*. The combination *taraka ʿalayhi* without an object in the accusative is against all Arabic usage, even against that of the Koran. Moreover *salāmun ʿalā* cannot be construed as this object (as . . . *ḥikāya*; an explanation given by Baghawī, Bayḍāwī); for it would be a decidedly feeble reward for these "prophets" that later generations say of them: *salāmun ʿalā Nūḥ*, and so on "Behold, thus do we reward those who act well" would be almost grotesque. For this language would require not (*taraknā*) *ʿalayhi* but only *lahu*. Throughout one must read, *wa-bāraknā ʿalayhi fī al-ʾākhirīna*, "we blessed him still among the later generations," as actually stands in verse 113 in *Isḥā q*, completely consonant with this is that, in all four passages there follow *ʾIbrāhīma* or, as the case may be, *salāmun ʿalā Nuḥin* etc. In Arabic, the combination . . . *bāraka ʿalayhi* is quite regular, as is well known.[27] The sense is what is to be expected here. The defective rendition of *ā* in the oldest Koran script is attested for a great number of instances, also regularly for *fāʿilūna, fāʿilīna.*[28] The diacritical points were lacking in this writing until the second half of the first century.[29] False resolution of the written signs thus goes back to an earlier period. Muhammad doubtless envisaged the promise to Abraham Gen. 22:18 (Hebrew: *w-h-t-b-r-k-w b-ẓ-r-ʿ-k k-l g-w-y-y h-ʾ-r-ʿ*: "and in thy seed shall all the nations of the earth be blessed . . ."), and the same promise to Isaac, Gen. 26:4.

Sura LXXVI

In verse 2, *nabtalīhi* between the "we created man from mixed semen" and the "and have made him able to hear and see" does not suit the context. It belongs rather in the next verse: (3) "We led him onto the (right) path, in that we tested him" ("tried" to recognize him)[30] either as some one grateful or ungrateful, that is, whether he would be grateful or ungrateful.

Sura XX

Verse 6 ("When you speak aloud"). *fa-ʾinnahu ya ʿlamu llāhu al-sirra wa-ʾakhfā*, "he (God) knows (in any case) what is secret and what is more concealed." The combination of a specific object with one that is not specific is most unnatural. It would be just as off-putting that there should be something "more concealed" (*ʾakhfā*) than the secret. Read . . . *al-sirra wa-al-khafā*, "God knows what is secret and hidden," *khafan* is, according to the lexicographers, equivalent to *khāfin, khāfiyatun*. A parallel to this is . . . *ʾinnahu yaʿlamu al-jahra wa-mā yakhfā,* Sura LXXXVII.7, which at the same time testifies to the alteration of our text.

Sura XV

Verse 12 clearly does not belong after verse 11; for both the *kadhālika* . . . and the suffix *naslukuhu* bear no relation to verse 11. On the other hand, verse 12 follows nicely after 9: (9) "Behold, we send the warning and protect it; (12) in this way we let it enter the hearts of the evildoers."

Verse 47b. *ʾIkhwānan* follows immediately from . . . *ʾāminīna* in verse 46; what stands between them, *nazaʿnā* upto *min ghillin*, is a disturbing intrusion.

Verse 56. *Qāla* is to be deleted. The verse continues the address of the angels. Abraham does not speak until verse 57.

Verse 72. The . . . *la- ʿamruka ʾinnahum*, in Lūṭ's direct speech to the Sodomites with the singular suffix *ka* and the third person plural *hum* referring to the Sodomites, does not fit this context. But it follows nicely after verse 66: (66) "We (God) imported this decision to him, that the back of these (people) would be cut off in the morning (i.e., they would be exterminated); (72) (saying) on your life, they are perplexed in their drunkenness."

Sura XIX

The son of Zakariyya is named *yaḥyā* in verses 7 and 13, with the observation (verse 8): "We have previously not given (allowed to arise) anyone of this same name." As John the Baptist is meant, I presume that *yaḥyā* is a false reading from an original, *yuḥannā*, which was then not known to the Arabs as a name.[31] Since the diacritical points were lacking in the oldest Koran script, the misreading of a strange name is understandable. The immediately following . . . *wa-ḥanānan* (verse 14) is probably an interpretation of the name Joḥanna.[32] Before verse 13 it seems that something has dropped out that concerned John's birth and early life; cf. verses 22 ff. in the case of Jesus.

Sura XXXVIII

In the narrative about Job, verses 40–44, there is some displacement. Verse 41 gives God's injunction that Job should strike the ground with his foot to assuage his pain. This belongs, without interruption, with verse 43: "and group a bundle with your hand and beat (namely your body)[33] with it" and do not sin [cf. . . . *ḥinthun* "sin," Sura LVI.45].We found him (also really) patiently persisting. Verse 42 fits (as a reward) only after this: "We gave him his family and as many gain as then (had been) with them." The Arabs misinterpreted the . . . *wa-lā taḥnath* verse 43, in accordance with normal Arab usage (but not the usage of the Koran), as "do not break your oath." Thereby there arose the absurd legend that Job had sworn to reprimand his wife because she remained absent until very late. The ridiculousness of this is already apparent from the continuation of the verse, "we found him resolute [perhaps in beating his wife?]."

Concerning the final section, verses 67 ff., Nöldeke suspected that it did not belong with the earlier ones; in addition it has a different rhyme. But this section is not itself a unity. Verses 86–88 connect with their *mā ʾasʾalukum ʿalayhi min ʾajrin,* directly with 67, 68: "It (the Koran) is a great proclamation but you turn away from it." Then, after this (86): "I require for it no reward from you." In the part preceding verse 86, the

ʿalayhi of verse 86 has, according to Nöldeke, no antecedent, and the whole verse cannot be explained. Verses 69–85 have been inserted, forming a piece complete in itself.

Sura XXXVI

Verse 4 (where *tanzīli* must be vocalized) belongs after verse 1; for verse 4 cannot refer to "you" (the prophet). Then follow 2 and 3, to which verse 5 connects ("you are sent so as to warn"). Likewise verse 46 is to be put before 45, for it terminates the three series that begin with . . . *wa-ʾāyatun lakum* (verses 33, 37, 41)with the words: "But none of these signs (*ʾāyatun* . . .) reaches them without their turning away from him." Only then do there follow two parallel units that both begin with *wa-ʾidhā qīla lahum* . . . ,verses 45 and 47. Of these, 47a has its continuation in 47 b; but the continuation of 45 has been lost.

Verses 69, 70 (that Muhammad is not a poet, and the Koran is a heavenly warning) are foreign to the context of this pericope. Verse 71 takes up the heavenly *ʾāyatun* . . . of verses 33, 37, and 41 again. On the other hand, verses 69, 70 could belong before verse 70, which otherwise stands isolated. The chain of thought would be: (69) "Muhammad is not a poet, rather is the Koran an admonition (70) and a warning for unbelievers. (76) May their chatter (that you are poet) not upset you," and so on.

Sura XLIII

Verses 15 and 18 are doublets. Hence, verse 18 cannot originally have followed so soon after 15. Its immediate continuation is, however, given by verse 20. The pair of questions *ʾashhidū khalqahum*, verse 18, and *ʾam ʾataynāhum kitāban* . . . , verse 20, belong together. Between them, verse 19 breaks the construction.

Verse 23. Instead of *qul*, read *qāla* as in 22b. For the following *qālū* . . . and *fa-nataqamnā minhum* . . . , 24a shows that here the objection of the earlier generations is mentioned, to whom a warner, verse 22, was once sent.

Verses 25–27 do not belong here. Before them, in verses 22–24, there was talk of unbelieving generations, on whom God has avenged himself.

Verse 28 accounts for why Allah has sustained the lives of the present unbelievers and their fathers, that is, those earlier ones. The two belong together. But the reminiscence of Abraham in 25–27 breaks the connection.

Verse 37 follows on with its singular *ʾidhā jāʾanā* directly after verse 35 and its singular: *wa-man . . . lahu*. Even if the idea of *man* can designate a plural, it is formally hardly tolerable that between, in *wa-ʾinnahum la-yaṣuddūnahum . . .*, both the subject and the object are plural and then the singular reappears in verse 37. Verse 36 is perhaps an early insertion to justify verse 37.

Verse 51. The *ʾam* must be changed to *ʾa-mā* (*ʾama* is said to occur in Mughni according to Lane I, 93), so that only the Fatḥ would have to be added: "Am I not better than this man ?"; it is a continuation of the *ʾa-laysa lī . . .* in verse 50.

Verses 79, 80. It is very doubtful whether both questions began with *ʾam . . .* or rather verse 79 only with *ʾa . . .*, as is the rule (e.g., Sura LXVII.16–17) Admittedly, according to Abū ʿUbayda (see Lane), *ʾam* may occur with a simple question, but only by way of exception.

Verse 88. Nöldeke notes that some words must have dropped out before 88, because *wa-qīlihi . . .* cannot be linked with verse 87 in a satisfactory way. But verse 89 connects—over the head of verse 88—well with 87. The whole of verse 88 probably belongs elsewhere.

Sura LXXII

Verse 24 forms the immediate continuation of verse 21; that is: (21) "Speak, I cannot (effect) either damage to you or proper leading for you, but only the bringing (of the revelation) of God." The *ʾillā* of verse 24 connects directly with the negative of *ʾin* of verse 21. Hence verses 22, 23 do not belong here. They have found a place here only because of the same *qul ʾinnī* in verses 21 and 22. Verse 26 also begins with *qul ʾin*, so that the verses 21, 22 will belong to our sura but to another place in it.

Sura LXVII

Verses 16, 17, 20, 21, 22 belong with their identical question figures *ʾa . . . ʾam* in uninterrupted succession. Between verses 17 and 20, verses 18, 19 are out of place. Rather is the chain of thought: "Are you secure from Him who is in heaven, that he will let the earth perish with you? (17) Or are you secure from him that he will rain stones upon you? (20) Can this thing[34] that is your army help you in the face of the All-Merciful One? (21) Or (rather) he who nourishes you (i.e., God against this army)." Likewise the further double question, verses 22 a and b with: *ʾa-fa . . . ʾam.*

That verses 18, 19 are misplaced here is clear also from the fact that here the unbelievers are addressed in the third person, whereas both before and after (verses 17, 20, 21) the second person is used for this purpose.

Sura XXIII

In verse 54 one must read *wa-ʾinna . . .* with the Kufian (see Bayḍāwī) as a continuation of *ʾinnī . . .* in verse 53 b. Verse 69 is not construable; *bihi* has nothing governing it, and the Ḥāl *sāmiran* no singular in the form of *dhū l-ḥāl.* The correct reading must be *bihā . . .* (sc. *bi-ʾāyātī. . . .* verse 68) and with the variant . . . *summuran.*

Verse 70. Instead of *ʾam jāʾahum . . .* read *ʾidh jāʾahum.* The *ʾam* has been erroneously placed earlier from verse 71. The further question sentences after *ʾa-fa-lam . . .* follow only in verse 71a, 72a; whereas here the ground is given, because of which they would have to "heed." The sense is (70): "Do they not heed the word (of God), in spite of the fact that what did not come to their earlier fathers has come to them; (71) or did they not know the (prophet) sent to them?" and so on.

In verses 89, 91 one must put the variant of many readers of the Koran, namely *Allāhu*, in place of *li-llāhi* as answer to *man*; see Bayḍāwī on this passage. The *lillāhi* is an erroneous repetition from verse 87.

Verse 101 has, with its own *ḥattā ʾidhā*, no connection with 100. There must have been mention earlier of the evil deeds or evil talk of the unbelievers.

Verse 118 and its *wa-qul . . .* must have been immediately preceded by a direct address to the prophet, to which the *wa* was linked, as in verse 95 or 99, 100.

Sura XXI

Verse 42 is isolated here. It belongs after verse 37: "When the unbelievers see you, they mock you; (42) but the ambassadors have also been mocked before you. Then punishment encompassed the mockers for their mockery." After verse 42 at this point verses 43, 44 fit well. For after, it was said in verse 37b that they "deny the mention of Raḥmān," verse 44 asks: "Say, who protects you day and night from the Raḥmān? (44) Do they have gods who can protect them from us?" On the other hand, once verses 43, 44 are moved up from their position, verse 45 fits well to 38–41. In 38- 41 they had asked why the threatened punishment does not come; and they had received the answer (41), it will suddenly and inescapably befall them. (45) "But [they ask mockingly only] because we have given them and their fathers enjoyment of life, so that their lives were long."

The direct continuation of verses 49, 50 (Reminiscence of Mūsā, etc.) is given by verse 52. Verse 51 disturbs the connection.

Sura XVII

In verse 106, the words *wa-bi-l-haqqi ʾanzalnāhu wa-bi-l-ḥaqqi nazala* . . . up to the end do not in any way belong here. The suffix in "we have sent it down" refers to the Koran, but it is not mentioned until verse 107. Those words can have stood only at some point after 107a. The rhyme here offers no lead, as it seems not to have been carried through in these verses.

Sura XXVII

Already Nöldeke[35] noted that there must be a gap before *wa-ʾūtīnā* . . . , verse 42 (since these words cannot belong to the queen of Saba). In verse 68, the first *bal* . . . has been wrongly taken in advance from *b.* The sense demands something like *hal ʾadraka ʿilmuhum mā fī al-ʾākhirati* (or *iddāraka*), "do you perhaps know what is happening in posterity?"[36]

Sura XXV

Muhammad here comes to terms firstly with objections to his status as prophet and with the way his enemies put it in question. These objections are mentioned in verses 5, 8, 9, 23a, 34a; verse 43 also, from its content, belongs here. They are introduced with the stereotype: "and the unbelievers speak" and similar phrases (5, 23, 34); "and they speak" (8). The answer to this follows for verse 5, in verse 7 with *qul*. The suffix in *ʾanzalahu* referring to the Koran, refers back to verse 5 (*iftarāhu, ʿalayhi*). Verse 6 surely did not belong between 5 and 7; for here the *ʾasāṭīru al-ʾawwalīna* are newly introduced and feminine pronouns are used for them. The verse belongs in the whole context as an argument of the unbelievers. Its continuation is probably 8b (which disrupts the connection in its present position), namely, (6) "They say, these are only old tales, which are dictated to him morning and evening [by human beings]"; (8b) "Why is no angel sent down to him, etc.?" The answer to this has apparently been lost.

Verse 8. To the objection: "Why does this ambassador [messenger] eat food and walk about in the markets? (9) Or why is no treasure alloted to him, or has he a garden, from which he can eat?" and so on. This is answered, apart from verse 11, also in verse 22: "We have sent no messenger before you who did not eat food and walk about in the markets." This characteristic repetition shows that this is to be placed with the question in verse 8.

In verse 19, *nuttakhada* is to be read, with the old Koran readers (see Bayḍāwī); but then the *min* must be deleted. It originated from a misinterpretation of this verse. The speakers are the idols (*mā yaʿbudūna*, verse 18), not their worshipers. The latter are spoken of in *b* in the third person (*hum, nasū*). In verse 20 one suspects, because of the rhyme elsewhere, that *nuṣūran*[37] (infinitive) should replace *naṣran*.

After the historical reminiscence in verses 37–41 and the polemics against the enemies in verses 43–46, there follow proofs for the true faith in God, verses 47-51, 55, 56, 63. The verses 49, 50 f., 55, 56, 63 are shown by the anaphora of *wa-huwa alladhī* to belong together.

Verses 52–54 do not fall within this context. Verse 54, with its *bihi* . . . strikes back directly to *ṣarrafnāhu* in verse 52. The suffix refers to the Koran. Verse 53 cannot originally belong between them, for otherwise the *bihi* . . . would, against all sense, refer to *nadhīran*.

Verse 61 belongs more closely to 57. Verse 60 is worded in the tone of verses that elsewhere conclude suras. Its original ending was surely *khabīran*. This rhyme suits its surround.

Verse 67b. For *wa-kāna*, which would have no subject, read *wa-kānū* . . . "and they are just between the two (the one giving too much and the one giving too little), standing quite in the middle."

Verses 64–76 give a coherent depiction of the essential nature of the believers. Something has dropped out before verse 77, for it addresses the unbelievers, and that with "Ye," while previously they and the believers were treated in the third person. The very abrupt *lawlā duʿāʾukum* between "my lord will not concern himself with you" and the "since you have designated (my messenger) a liar" is surely incorrect.[38] Perhaps we should read *wa-lā bi-duʿāʾikum,* "God will not concern himself with you, nor with your cries (in hell), since you have declared (prophet) a liar. It (the punishment) will seize you firmly."

Sura XXXII

In verse 4 something seems to be missing before *thumma yaʿruju ʾilayhi ʾlkh*, and so on. For "god" cannot very well be the subject here, too, as if he needed one thousand years to climb up to heaven. Probably there was first some mention of an angel who was sent down.[39] In verse 23, the words "be not in doubt about meeting with him" were already recognized as a foreign element by Nöldeke. But verses 23–24 are surely as a whole alien intrusions. For verse 25 presupposes, with its . . . *baynahum* in *ʾinna rabbaka huwa yafṣilu baynahum*, that the two classes of believers and unbelievers came immediately before it, and these are treated in verses 18–22. Verses 26-29 speak again of the unbelievers. Hence there is no room for the reminiscence of Moses and other imams between verses 22 and 25.

Sura XLI

Verse 7 does not belong here; for the apostrophe to the Mushrikūn (verse 5, end) in verse 6 is continued in verse 8. Between these two, the promise of reward for the believers would be an interruption. In verse 11, *wa-ḥifẓan* is fragmentary; the *min kulli shayṭānin maridin* is lacking, which follows in Sura XXXVII.7. For *wa-zayyanā* is to be read *wa-zayyana* (transferred from Sura XXXVII.7); cf. *fa-qaḍāhunna* in *a*. In verse 34, the end, from *fa-ʾidhā* to *ḥamīmun*, has come in from elsewhere. For (1) the suffix of *wa- baynahu* has no antecedent in what precedes it; (2) the suffix in *yulaqqahā* . . . verse 35a goes over the head of 34b, to the *hiya* of 34a; (3) the content is alien here. On the other hand, the first part stands quite appropriately and more completely in Sura XXIII.98, *idfaʿ bi-llatī hiya ʾaḥsanu al-sayyiʾata*, and has surely been transposed from there to our passage. In verse 41, the predicate sentence, *ʾinna*, has been lost.

Sura XVI

Verse 9. Instead of the difficult *wa-ʿalā llāhi qaṣdu al-sabīli* . . . ,[40] read *wa-ʾilā llāhi*, "the straight path leads on to God."

Verse 35, whose subject "then" refers immediately to the unfaithful, does not connect with 32–34, which treat of the faithful. Rather does it connect with verse 31.

Verses 43, 44 were already expunged as Medinan by Nöldeke. Verse 45 connects directly with 40–41 and refutes the objection to Muhammad's prophetic status therein contained: (40) "they swear to God, send no one who is mortal; oh yes ! etc. (41) So that he makes clear to them what it is they are quarrelling about. (45) We have indeed sent only men before you to those to whom we gave revelation," and so on.

Verse 42 is also alien in this context.

Verse 49b. At least the *fa-ʾinna* is an error, unless something earlier has dropped out. Because of the contrast with the first unit, one would expect *lakinna* or something similar. Verses 59 and 64, are from their sense, doublets; for in the *mā yakrahūna* of 64a, the same as . . . *al-banātu* in verse 59 is comprised (see Bayḍāwī; Jalālain). It is unlikely that in the same piece the same pronouncement with *wa-yaj ʿalūna* . . . followed twice in quick succession.

Verse 103. The insertion of *wa-llāhu yaʿlamu bi- mā yunazzalu* between the protasis and sequel of *wa-ʾidhā* is very strange. The words belong after *muftarin*: "If we insert a verse, they say, you are a liar. God knows better what he reveals. But most of them do not know it." The *Allāhu yaʿlamu* . . . and the *ʾaktharuhum lā yaʿlamūna* . . . belong together as opposites.

Verse 108. The overloading of the verse with a double subject, *man kafara bi-llāhi* . . . and *wa-lakin man sharaḥa bi-l-kufri ṣadran* . . . , shows that here a correction has been worked in. It comprises the words *ʾillā man ʾukriha* up to *ṣadran*, whereby those who have been forced into infidelity by the Meccans are exempted from the "wrath of God," which is threatened only to those who (without compulsion) "expand their chest with unbelief."

Verse 117a. Some corruption is probably included in the words *wa-li-mā taṣifu ʾalsinatukumu al-kadhiba*, which yield no understandable sense. The superfluous first *al-kadhib*, followed asyndetically[41] by a second, may be an anticipation of the same word, which follows twice more in our verse.

Sura XXX

Verse 29. The address to Muhammad with "thou" (*fa-ʾaqim*) belongs more closely together with *fa-ʾāti* (37), *fa-ʾaqim* (42), and also *fa-nẓur* . . . (49), if the latter is original. But in verses 49 and 53 the rhyme is *īr*, whereas at other points, and also elsewhere throughout, *ūn*, *īn*, so that perhaps these two verses were only secondarily positioned here. Before verse 30, where after the singular imperative the plurals *wa-ʾaqīmū, wa-ttaqūhu, munībīna*, abruptly follow, at least one verse with the imperative in the plural must have dropped out, to which these plural sentences were attached.

Verses 32 and 35 cannot originally have belonged to the same speech because the same double case is varied in both: "When what is good comes to people . . . then . . . , when what is bad comes to them, then . . ."

Verse 45. The *wa-min ʾāyātihi* belongs to the fourfold anaphora[42] of the same words in verses 21–24. The verse can be taken from its present place without introducing any disruption. Indeed, it must be put aside here, since in verse 47 the same good deed of God is repeated.

Verse 48. The *min qabli ʾan* and the immediately following *min qablihi* are not compatible in the same verse. The latter is a variant of the former sentence.

Sura XI

In this sura, the kernel of which is the narratives of the older prophets, alterations or insertions seem to have occurred at the beginning between verses 6 and 16 because of the irregular rhyme.

Verse 20 includes a corrupted element. The sequel (which Bayḍāwī and Jalālain want to add),[43] necessary to the rhetorical question *ʾa-fa-man kāna*, is missing. This addition, however, is not feasible, as it is not self-evident. One should read simply *man kāna*, which forms the contrast to *wa-man yakfur* in b: "Those who have a clear proof from their Lord, and who are followed by a witness from him (God) etc., they believe in him, but those of the multitudes who deny him, for them the fire of purgatory is their place of assembly."

Verse 37 does not belong here. For 36 and 38 are about Noah (Nūḥ), but verse 37 in between is about the Koran (*iftarā-hu*), and this has no linkage with what precedes or what follows.

Verse 90. After *ʾa-raʾaynā-hum ʾin kuntu ʿalā* there must follow, according to the usage of the Koran, a rhetorical question[44] or the imperative.[45] But here the addition is completely lacking. However, a similar case occurs in Sura XLVI.9, so a judgment on the matter is difficult. The *wa-lā ʾanhā-kum* shows, because of its *wa*, that at some time a pronouncement clause preceded that is now lacking. Moreover, the thought "I will not, in opposition to you, myself do that from which I am trying to deter you" is abstruse and alien to the Koran. The text is obviously corrupt.

Verse 113. The *lamā* (according to Tor Andrae, *lammā*, which is supposedly = *lamin mā*; according to Andrae, *lumman* = *jamī ʿan*) is not construable and is probably to be struck out.

Already Schwally rightly noted that verses 99 and 112 collide, since both treat of Moses; likewise that the review is already comprised in 102–111.

The imperative *fa-staqim* (114), *wa-lā tarkunū* (115), *wa-ʾaqim* (116), *wa-ṣbir* (117) surely belonged originally more closely to *wa-qul* (122); while the review of the narratives about the destroyed towns (verses 118, 119, 121) goes parallel to verses 103–105 and belonged closer to them.

Sura XII

Several things in this Joseph sura are so disjointed that one must suspect that something has been lost. Is, for example, Joseph's going down into Egypt to remain unmentioned before verse 100?

Verse 94. Between *wa-lammā faṣalati l-ʿīru* and the "then their father said, I sense the smell of Joseph" attached to it, there is lacking the section about their coming to their father with the coat, on which he smells something of Joseph. Only in verse 96 does "the proclaimer" bring the coat to the father. There seems to be some displacement here. Incidentally, the detail that the father smells on the coat a trace of the son is a reminiscence from the biblical story of Isaac (Gen. 27:27).

Verse 9. For the *yakhlu lakum wajhu ʾabīkum*, "the face of your father will be free for you, will alone be there,"[46] I suspect *yajlu lakum*, "then there will (again) look at you, clear and bright,[47] the face of your father." The Muslims already felt that the sense would have to be *yakhluṣu lakum wa-yaṣifu lakum (*Bayḍāwī, Baghawī) but tried to insert in *yakhlu*.

Verse 62. The double *naʿallahum* is burdensome. That they perhaps will later recognize their tools (utensils) yields no sense. Perhaps the first *laʿallahum* has come in prematurely because of the second identical word.

Verse 64. The *ʾillā* before *kamā ʾamintukum* is to be deleted. Translate as: "Am I to offer you my confidence in regard to him just as I previously trusted in regard to his brother?"

Verse 68. Before *ʾillā ḥājatan* something has probably dropped out. Perhaps *mā kāna*: "It (the advice) was nothing but a need in Jacob's soul which he satisfied."

Verse 75. There is some error in the repetition of the words *jazāʾuhu man wujida fī raḥlihi fa-huwa jazāʾuhu.* The second *jazāʾuhu* is an erroneous repetition of the first. The following clause presumably had originally something like *fa-huwa riqqun lī* or *fa-huwa -ʿabdun lī.* "let him be a slave to me" (= Gen. 44:17: *h-w-ʾ y-h-y-h l-y ʿ-b-d*: he shall be my servant. Hebrew.)

Verses 83 ff. The mechanical repetition of the same words *bal sawwalat lakum ʾanfusukum ʾamran fa-ṣabrun jamīlun* here, at the loss of Benjamin, as above, verse 18, at that of Joseph, makes one suspect that they are repeated here in place of a lost answer by Jacob. The immediately following woe cries and the "becoming white" of the eyes also do not fit the *fa-ṣabrun jamīlun.* All this is missing in verse 18 above, and also that he here weeps over Joseph (verse 84), when he should now be mourning for Benjamin. At the very least, something about Benjamin must have stood here, before he speaks in 84 of Joseph alone and in verse 87 of both sons.

Sura XL

The seemingly general statement in verse 37a interrupts Pharoah's conversation with the believer from his people, which extends from verses 29–36 before this, and from verses 38–48 after it. Moreover, the singular *kabura* in the predicate does not match the subject *alladīna* in *a*. One really expects *kaburū*. Then this offensive half-clause, *alladhīna yujādilūna fī ʾāyāti llāhi bi-ghayri sulṭāni ʾatāhum*, is strikingly repeated verbatim in verse 58a, where the predicate also fits well. It has presumably at some time been dragged from there also to verse 37. If it is deleted here, then verse 37 follows 36 perfectly: (36) *man huwa musrifun murtābun* (37) *kabura maqtan ʿinda llāhi* 'lkh /and so on, and no longer forms a disturbing enclave.

Sura XXVIII

Verse 74 repeats verse 62, and so does not originally belong here. Its continuation can also not have consisted in the words *wa-naza ʿnā min kulli ʾummatin shahīdan* (verse 75), for these have no reference to the previousn questioning about the "associates" of God, the idols. The piece about Qarun verses 76–82 need not originally have belonged to the remaining part of the sura, as Schwally already noted.

Sura XXXIX

Verses 11a and 50 agree in their thought and their expression, even in the rare *khawwalahu niʿmatan* (elsewhere only VI.94 is similar) to such an extent that they originally could not have belonged to the same piece. Both 11 and 50 can be absent without detriment to the present context.

Verses 12, with . . .*ʾamman huwa*, 20 *ʾa-fa-man ḥaqqa*; 23 *ʾa-fa-man sharaḥa*; 25, *ʾa-fa-man yattaqī*, belong by dint of their identical question form to a coherent construction that was not originally separated, as it is now, by a series of other verses. If verse 12 was clearly the first link in this series, then *ʾa-man* is probably to be read instead of *ʾamman* (for the first link in a chain of questions does not have *ʾam*.) The subject *man* is taken up again by *alladhīna yaʿlamūna*: "Is perchance he who honors God at night . . . , are they same, those who know and those who do not know?" (20), or he for whom the word of punishment stands firm; can you save him who is in hellfire ? (23) or he whose heart God has expanded to Islam . . . ? (Woe unto Them, whose heart is hard [cf.verse 20]) (25), or perhaps he who protects himself with his countenance from the grievous punishment on resurrection day (predicate is lost), while the wicked are told, taste what you have brought upon yourselves. (For . . . *wa-qīla* one must presumably read *ʾidhā qīla* or something similar. The link with *wa* to a is hardly feasible.) The predicates to verses 23a and 25a are now missing. Should they be supplied from the *hal yastawī* of verse 12? Perhaps "Are the pious and the wicked equal to each other (12) or those whose sentence of punishment stands determined (20) or those whose heart God has broadened to Islam (23), or those who fear the terrible punishment" (25) (are these perhaps the same as those worthy of punishment [verse 20] ?) But whether the verses belong together in this way is uncertain, given the nature of the tradition.

Verse 21 forms the immediate contrast to verses 17b and 18: (18) the unbelievers have tents of hellfire *lahum min fawqihim ẓulalun min al-nāri wa-min taḥtihim ẓulalun,* (21) but the believers galleries *lahum ghurafun min fawqihā ghurafun* under which rivers flow.

This contrasting reference is furthermore made visible by *lākin* (21). It is hardly a contrasting reference to verse 20. Verses 19 and 20 probably did not originally intervene.

On the position of verse 20, cf. above, verse 73. After *ḥattā ʾidhā* the sequel must begin without *wa,* as in verse 7, which corresponds to our verse; thus, *futiḥat.*

Sura XXIX

Already Noldeke had cast doubt on verses 18–22 because of their present position, for they seem to interrupt the address of Abraham to his people (16) and their reply (23). But he then took the remarkable *qul* (19) as addressed to Abraham (as in XI.37 to Noah), and withdrew his reservations about these verses. My view is that verse 17, and 18–22 with it, have been inserted here. The reference to "peoples before you who have called [their ambassadors] liars" is appropriate only on the lips of Muhammad, not on those of Abraham.

Similarly, the *al-rasūlu* . . . suits the former very well, but not the latter, who would be designated with *al-nabiyyu*. Moreover, in verse 18 the third person plural *yaraw* is out of context, when hitherto Abraham has apostrophied his enemies in the second person plural. There is also the *qul* in verse 19, which normally refers to Muhammad. And the verse in Sura XI.37 seems to me, because of its *ʾam yaqūlūna ftarāhu*, to refer to the Koran, and so to Muhammad and not to Noah, and to have been interpolated there, together with its *qul*.

In verse 22, we must surely assume an original *min raḥmatihi*, instead of *min raḥmatī,* because of the preceding *bi-ʾayāti llāhi wa-liqāʾihi.*

In verse 45 the words *ʾillā lladhīna ẓalamū minhum* must, with Schwally, be taken as a later insertion because of the double exception, and because *wa-qūlū* doesnot presuppose them. When this verse originated is uncertain.

Sura XXXI

For verse 5, the reading *li-yaḍilla* (see Bayḍāwī) is to be preferred, for it is not about one man who misleads others, but—according to verse 6—about one man who himself goes astray.

Verse 9. The transition from the threefold third person *baththa, ʾalqā, khalaqa* to the twofold first person plural *'anzalnā . . . fa-ʾanbatnā* is admittedly abrupt, the more so since, with *hādhā khalqu llāhi* in verse 10, the third person reappears. (However, the same thing occurs in, for instance, Sura XXXV.10; XLIII.10.)

Something similar is the change in the same persons in Sura XLII.11. But there, *wa-lladhī ʾawḥaynā ʾilayka* (between the revelation to Noah and to Ibrāhīm the one to Muhammad!) has been inserted later and then subsequently the following *waṣṣaynā* remodelled.

Already Nöldeke stressed that verses 13 and 14 are obviously displaced. They could perhaps, in his view, belong after verse 18.

Sura XLII

On verse 11, see above to XXXI.9.

Sura X

Verse 78. The object to *ʾa-taqūlūna li-l-ḥaqqi* is missing. Either *hādhā...* has perhaps been dropped out between the two, or possibly after *jāʾa-kum* a *siḥrun* before the similar *ʾasḥirun* has been lost.

Sura XXXV

Verse 9 is not in order; for the intermediate clause, from *fa-ʾinna llāha* to *man yashāʾu* intrudes forcibly between the first and the last part of . . .*ʾa-fa-man zuyyina*. Either the intermediate clause should be deleted, or placed after the final part, with *fa-man* instead of *ʾa-fa-man,* to be read at the beginning.

Translate as: "And if someone's evil behavior is decked out, and he thinks it fine, let not your soul expend itself in sighing about him; for God leads astray whom he will, and leads aright whom he will. Behold, God knows what they do." From the sense, *man* can refer to *ʿalayhim*; cf., for instance, Sura VII.17.

Verses 10, 12, 14 f., 16–18, which speak of God's omnipotence, belong together. But verse 13, which is inappropriate here, should, with its *wa-mā yastawī* 'ilkh/and so on; be put with verses 20 and 21, which begin in the same way. The sense is: as in nature a sweet and a bitter ocean are not the same (verse 13), so it is with the good and the bad among mankind (20, 21).

Sura VII

Verse 28, or at least the words "and direct your countenances to every mosque" upto *al-dīn* is surely a Medinan insertion, like verses 156–158, recognized as such by Nöldeke.

Verse 41. The words *tajrī min taḥtihimi l-ʾanhāru*, inappropriate here, connect with *khālidūna* of verse 40 and should follow it. Only then can *wa-naza ʿnā*, and so on, follow.

Verse 55. *Thiqālan* here belongs, as in Sura XIII.13, to *saḥāban*, which is considered to be plural. All the more striking is the masculine *bihi*,[48] which twice refers to it.

Sura XLVI

Verse 10b. The appropriate ending to the clause is missing to *wa-ʾidh*, for . . . *fa-sayaqūlūna* speaks of what the unbelievers will in the future say, whereas in the first clausal unit, with *wa-qāla lladhīna*, it is reported what they are now saying.

Verse 27. The combination of the two words *qurbānan ʾālihatan* is surely an error, and the *ʾālihah* is an explanatory gloss to *qurbānan*. On the meaning "close friends," cf. *Iqd*[2] III 53, 9 *qarābīnu llāhi banū Quṣayyin*.

In our passage, the singular (if indeed present) would be a collective.

Verse 32. The *bi* in *bi-qādirin* has nothing governing it and goes against the usage of the language.[49] There is some corruption here.

Verse 35. The word *balāghun* stands quite unconnected, and cannot belong here. (The Arab exegesists have nothing decisive to say.)

Sura VI

Verses 12 and 20. Very noticeable is, on both occasions, the unconnected *alladhīna khasirū ʾanfusahum*, which must, in the present text, be the subject of *fa-hum lā yuʾminūna*. And this linking of the predicate with *fa* is also strange. Also, one would rather expect some statement about their punishment. Perhaps there is some corruption.

In verses 17 and 18, the rhyme on *īr* between those on *ūn, īn,* is off-putting. These verses could be missing, with no disturbance to the context.

Verse 35 has been disturbed in some ways, with its double *wa-ʾin fa-ʾin* and the following *wa-law* with no clausal completions to them. The first clausal unit "and if you (yourself) should seek an exit into the earth" was surely originally followed by t he now-missing "then they would still not believe you."

In verses 66 and 69, *bihi* refers to the Koran, which, however, was not what the preceding verses were about. Verses 66 and 69 belong to some position like that after verse 92 *wa-hādhā kitābun*, or somewhere similar.

Verse 87. *Wa-min ʾābāʾihim* and so on lacks any governing verb to which *wa-jtabaynāhum* would connect. The simplest reading would perhaps be *ijtabaynā*.

Verse 109. There is surely an error in *wa-mā yushʿirukum*, which has no object. The *ʾannahā . . . lā yuʾminūna* is not suitable as an object for it.

Sura XIII

Verse 30a is defective. The essential clausal termination *lam yuʾminū* or something like it, is missing to *wa-law ʾanna qur ʾānan ʾlkh*/and so on.

In 30b, *ʾa-fa-lam yayʾasi* is a countersense. Already old authorities read here *yatabayyani*, "recognize," for those who do not believe that . . . ? (so, allegedly, ʿAlī, and Ibn ʿAbbās, see Bayḍāwī ad. loc., and this is probably correct). (Baghawī, Jalālain, explain *yayʾas* with *yaʿlamu* and say this is what it means in dialect).

In verse 33, two sentences have been run together. The continuation of the beginning of the interrogative clause . . .*ʾa-fa-man huwa qāʾimun ʿalā kulli nafsin bi-mā kasabat* is missing, but may be comprised in the words separated from it: . . . *tunabbiʾūnahu bimā lā yaʿlamu fī al-ʾarḍi.* "Will you give to him, who stands beside every soul (and sees) what it does, news of what he does not know about the occurrences on earth?"

The other part presumably went *wa-jaʿalū li-llāhi shurakāʾa qul sammūhum bi-ẓāhirin mina l-qawli*, "they put participants at God's side. Speak, name them by name in open speech !" The *ʾam . . .ʾam* presumably came in as a result of the running together of two sentences, so as to yield a superficial linkage.

MEDINAN SURAS

Sura II

Verse 19. After *qadīrun* a new verse begins. Perhaps a part containing the rhyme has dropped out.

Verse 36a is a doublet to 34, inappropriately inserted after 35.

Verse 61. The verse ends with *al-khāsirīna*; as verse 63 does likewise, with *al-jāhilīna*.

Verse 66. For *wa-lā tasqī* read *wa-tasqī*; in accordance with general usage.

Verse 79. The words *wa-ʾin yaʾtūkum ʾusārā tufdū-hum* break the connection; for the *wa-huwa muḥarramun* . . . goes over their head back to *bi-l-ʾithmi wa-l-ʿudwāni*. Those words were, then, inserted later, and only because of them was the explanation of *wa-huwa* by *ʾikhrājuhum* (which is very striking) made necessary as a further interpolation.

Verse 145a. The verbatim repetition of *wa-min ḥaythu* up to *al-ḥarām* is based on an error. The scribe wanted to continue the parallel *wa-ḥaythu mā kuntum* and stumbled anew into the sentence already written in verse 144.

Verse 261. The comparison word *ka* of *ʾaw ka-lladhī* does not link up with a similar preceding one *ka*, as one would expect it to do. Admittedly, the verse is about reanimation, like 260 and 262. But these two verses tell of Abraham, while 261 gives the legend of someone who slept for one hundred years.

Because of its reference to coming to life again after death, the verse seems to have been inserted here from another context in the course of the redaction of the Koran.

Sura XLVII

Verse 17b. Before *kaman huwa*, which has no connection with what precedes it, a sentence has dropped out, on the lines of *ʾamman huwa fī hādhā al-naʿīmi*,[50] if indeed that half sentence belongs here at all.

Sura III

Verse 66. The words *qul ʾinna al-hudā hudā llāhi* are interpolated, for they break the connection, and another *qul ʾinna ʾlkh*/and so on follows immediately in the second half verse. Once it is eliminated, the verse has "some of those who possess scriptures" (see verse 65a) saying: "Believe only such a one as follows your religion! (they say this from fear) that something like what has been given to you (the possession of the scriptures) may be given to someone, or that they could argue against you in front of your Lord."

Verse 147b. The words "and he rewarded you with trouble upon trouble" cannot be appropriately followed by "so that you may not be troubled at what you have missed (what has escaped you), nor at what has come to you."[51]

These words surely belong in the middle of the next verse, 148, after *yaghshā ṭā'ifatan minkum*: "Then he (God) sent security upon you, so that you might not be chagrined at what has escaped you," and so on.

Sura LVII

Verse 17. A relative clause with *alladhīna* and a perfect have presumably dropped out before the harsh *wa-'aqraḍū llāhu* ilkh/and so on.

Verse 20. The *wa-maghfiratun* connects not with verse 19 but with verse 17, *wa-lahum 'ajrun karīmun*; verses 18 and 19 stand loosely in their present position and did not originally belong there.

Verse 29. Instead of *li-'allā yaʿlama* there must be its opposite, "so that those possessing the scriptures know"; as the Arabs also explain this. Others actually read *li-yaʿlama* (see Bayḍāwī, Baghawī,and Jalālain). The textual error was occasioned by the immediately following *'allā yaqdirūna*, the *lā* of which came prematurely through the scribe's pen.

Sura IV

Verse 75. Between the words "if you experience something good, they say" and "if only I had been with them and had attained great gain" come the words, quite unscrutable here, "as if there had been no love between you and them." One would expect "as if there had been love between you and them." But the *lam* is attested by the Modus apocopatus *takun*. The intervening sentence belongs in verse 74:

> "When a misfortune strikes you, says he [the remnant after the battle], (75) as if between you and him there had been no love, (74b) God has done good to me, that I was not present with them there."

Verse 103. This is confused, with individual portions of the verse distorted. The original goes something like ("If you say the prayer too for them") *fa-l-taqum ṭā'ifatun minhum maʿaka fa-l-yuṣallū maʿaka wa-l-ta'ti ṭā'ifatun 'ukhrā lam yuṣallū wa-l-ya'khudhū 'asliḥatahum fa-'idhā sajadū fa-l-yadūnū min warā'ikum wa-l-ya'khudhū ḥidhrahum:* "then some of them are to stand at your side and pray with you; others, who do not pray, are to come and hold their weapons in their hand, and when they (those praying) bow down, then (the others) are to stand behind you and be on their guard." The situation is as in Neh. 4:15.

Sura XXII

There is an error in *yurid* of verse 26, because no *bi* (as in *bi-ʾilḥā din*) would govern it. The variant *yarid* (see Bayḍāwī) is better. *Bi-ẓulmin* is either a gloss to *bi-ʾilḥādin* (the more probable explanation), or *wa-bi-ẓulmin* must be read.

Verse 41b. The half sentence from *wa-lawlā dafʿu* to *kathīran* or to the end of the verse is a later addition. For it disrupts the connection of the *li-lladhīna* in verse 40, on the one hand, and of the two *alladhīna* of verse 41a and 42, on the other.

Sura XLVIII

Verse 25. The *wa-lawlā*, which has no final part to the clause and is followed in same verse once again by *law tazayyalū*, has lost its termination. What is missing is not sufficiently self-evident to constitute an aposiopese.[52] The following *li-yudkhala* may have been dependent on the missing termination.

Sura IX

Verse 113. The *al-ṣāʾiḥūna*, which stands between *al-ʾābidūna al-ḥā midūna* and *al-rākiʿūna al-sājidūna* and which must designate some behavior of service to God, is explained by Muslim tradition as "fasting ones" (*al-ṣāʾimūna*);[53] similarly with women, *sāʾiḥātin* in Sura LXVI.5, which there follows after . . . *qā ʾitātin tāʾitātin ʿābidātin*. A supposed pronouncement of Muhammad is produced: *siyāḥatu ʾummatī al-ṣawmu*. This explanation is all the more to be rejected as in verse 2 of our sura itself (the only other place where it occurs) it, with *fasīḥū fī al-ʾarḍi*, stands with the quite different meaning "wander too and fro."[54]

I suspect that, in taking in mind the neighboring verbs in both suras, one should read *al-sābiḥū na*. Or, as the case may be, *sābiḥātin* "who praise God." The word for "praise" admittedly always occurs, as in Aramaic, in the second conjugation. Also from the *subḥānun* one may—against the *Taj al -ʿArūs*—just as little infer the existence of the first conjugation as a Pe'al from *š-w-b-ḥ-ʾ* = "praise" in Syriac. But Mufaḍḍal in Karmānī (quoted in TA) gives an example of *sabaḥa* "praise" with a verse: *qabaḥa al-ʾilāhu wuj ūha Taghliba / kullamā sabaḥa al-Ḥaj ij u wa-kabbarū ʾihlālā*

[Nöldeke also found the first conjugation—as he stated in a letter — in Jarīr, II 51.4. I cannot find the passage in my edition, Cairo 1313]. This poet, constrained by the meter, could, because of the adjacent parallel participles of the first conjugation, have formed a corresponding participle of the first conjugation; and Muhammad might have done the same. This would fit very well in the context, and in the general train of thought of the Koran, with "praising ones."

For the Koran repeatedly says "what is in heaven and on earth praises (*sabbaḥa*) God (LVII.1, LXII.1, LIX.24, etc.) and what is in them (does so too) (XVII.46), mankind in the houses of God (XXIV.36), the thunder and the angels (XIII.14), the mountains (XXI.79, XXXVIII.17) and so on" It would be unnatural if the otherwise so frequently mentioned *tasbīḥ* were to be omitted in our two passages when the most diverse pious activities are mentioned.

NOTES

1. T. Nöldeke, *Geschichte des Qorans*, 2d ed., pp. 58–234.
2. Weil, *Historisch-Kritischer Einleitung in den Koran*, 2d ed., pp. 51–97.
3. Grimme, *Muhammed*, II, pp. 18–29.
4. Suyūṭī, *Itqān* in Nöldeke, *Geschichte des Qorans*, p. 191; Weil, *Historisch-Kritischer*, pp. 55 f.; Caetani, *Annali*, II, 1, p. 211.
5. Nöldeke, *Geschichte des Qorans*, as cited, p. 309
6. This indeed was what was alleged as the reason for collecting the Koran and determining its text.
7. Cf. details in Nöldeke, *Geschichte des Qorans*, pp. 248 ff.
8. The only copy of the Kashshāf of Zamakhsharī that the royal library here possesses could not be borrowed, as it stands in the reading room.
9. Tor Andrae in *Le monde oriental*, 15 assumes that the sura is all of one piece.

10. In this I agree independently with Wellhausen, *Reste*, p. 241 n. 3.

11. It would not be said of a slave that he "enjoins fear of God," verse 12.

12. Perhaps *ʾidhā* should be read instead of *ʾ in*, as in *ʾidhā ṣallā*, verse 10. The *ʾ in* can have intruded because of verse 13.

13. Cf. my article "Abū Lahab" in the *Encyclopaedia of Islam*, vol. 1, pp. 103 f.: "The sequence (i.e., verses 1–4) shows that verse 4 means that in Hell she must gather the wood for the glowing fire (comp. Bayḍāwī, ad. loc.), and not that in her lifetime she was carrying wood, that is to say, thorns, and strewing them in the way of the Prophet (as some commentators explain it; comp. for example Ṭabarī, Tafsīr, xxx.192, and Bayḍāwī, ad. loc.), nor that in her lifetime she used to spread insults on Muhammad's poverty. . . . The sura is generally considered as a Meccan one (the preterit *tabbat* used for the prediction of the future perdition; comp. Bayḍāwī to Koran, XI.17) Noldeke counts it amongst the oldest Meccan Suras. Still the wording of verse 2: *Mā aghnā ʿanhu māluhu* shows, according to the unexceptional way of expression in the Koran, something that had already happened (comp. VII.46; XV.84; XXVI.207, passim), for in case of future events the imperfect tense (*yaghnī)* is always used; neither is there any parallel to the usage of *Mā aghnā* as a preterite future. According to such a wording this sura contains consequently a triumphant outcry over the already happened death of Abū Lahab, and could be composed only some time after the battle of Badr."

14. Cf. Nöldeke, *Geschichte des Qorans*, p. 90 n. 3, and my own article already mentioned.

15. Thus also: Baghawī/Jalālain. This is already one of the alternatives suggested as explanations by Bayḍāwī. Cf. the address by Muhammad on the day after the conquest, *lam taḥlil li-ʾ aḥadin kāna qablī wa-lā taḥillu li-ʾ aḥadin yakūnu baʿdī wa-lam taḥlil lī ʾillā hādhihi l-sāʿa*. . . . I.Hishām 823.

16. Different from the magic formula CXIV.1, 2, 3, where the repetition is deliberate emphasis. However, the same rhyme follows twice in Sura XCVIII.5, 6, too.

17. If the attestation in verse 11 is correct, *fa-lā qtaḥama l-ʿaqabata* constitutes a use of *lā* in the aorist perfect (instead of *mā*), which deviates from its usage elsewhere.

18. Cf. the expression corresponds exactly with Job 21:9: *b-t-y-h-m Š-l-w-m. m-p-p-ḥ-d*: their houses are safe from fear. Also by the Arab lexicographers *salāmun* is presented as the infinitive of: *salima min al-ʾāfāti wa-l-balāʾi wa-l-ʾamri*. Lane I. 1412.

19. Likewise Baghawī: "Nothing but the bringing (of the revelation) is your concern"—Jalālain give no explanation.

20. The same in Sura LIII:62. Cf. the rhyme in verses 59–61.

21. August Fischer, "Eine Qoran-Interpolation," in *Orientalische Studien Theodor Noldeke* zum 70. Geburtstag, 1 Band, Giessen 1906, pp. 33–55; chapter 6.2 of present volume.

22. Documentary evidence for it is given by Fischer in ibid.

23. For this meaning, cf. I.Hishām 521, 7.

24. The Arab expositors are as much at a loss with this singular as we ourselves are. They interpret it as "the book which contains the deeds of the satans and unbelievers," or the "seventh and deepest earth," or "the location of the armies of Satan," or "a rock under the depths of the earth" or equivalent to *khassār wa -ḍallāl*; cf. Jalālain, Baghawī (Bayḍāwī gives only the first of these alternatives). These are obviously merely conjectures from the context.

25. The ending . . .-*iyyīn* is rendered in the oldest Koran script only with س (rasm); cf. Itqān II 167, 12 (Cairo), Nöldeke, *Geschichte Des Qorans*, p. 250. Of course, some other outer synonymous plural with corresponding letters could have stood there.

26. Baghawī instances expositors who suggest these diffferent possibilities. Cf. also Bayḍāwī

27. In the Koran, too; e.g., in verse 113 (in the same context as here): XXI.71, 81; XXXIV.17.

28. Details in Nöldeke, *Geschichte des Qorans*, pp. 248 ff. In the facsimile of a page of an old Q-manuscript in Caetani, *Annali* II, I, 712, which of course is not to be identified with the oldest script, . . . is given for *masākin, al-ʾ amthāl*, . . . : *al wāḥid*, . . . : *balāgh*, . . . : *al-aṣfād*. In the Papyri Schott-Reinh. ed. C. H.Becker (from the years after 90 A.D.) . . . = *ṣāḥib*, . . . = *ʾaṣḥāb*, . . . , . . . = *kitāb, salām*, and other examples, too.

29. Cf. Nöldeke, *Geschichte des Qorans*, pp. 306 ff.

30. Cf. TA *wa-btalaytuhu imtaḥantuhu wa-khtabartuhu* . . . ; al Rāghiba, as cited, gives as one of the meanings of the words: *taʿarrufu ḥālihi wa-al-wuqūfu ʿalā mā yujhalu min ʾamrihi*

31. Grimme, *Muhammad* II, 96 n. 4, observes about the name: "Probably arose from Jochai, the Aramaic diminutive from John." But one would first have to establish that Jochai really belonged to Jochanan as a diminutive, and also that that very unusual name was used for the Baptist in Arabia or somewhere else.

32. Cf. also Sprenger, II, p. 184 n. 3.

33. To assuage your pain; cf. Job 2:8: "He took him a potsherd with which to scrape himself."

34. Read surely *ʾaman* as the first part of the question, to which *ʾaman* ... in verse 21 forms the second part.

35. Nöldeke, *Geschichte des Qorans*, p. 106.

36. Jalālain gives *bal bi-maʿnā hal* as an explanation!

37. Cf. TA and similar words *naṣara naṣran wa-nuṣūran ka-quʿūdin*; and in the verse of the khidāsh . . . in *Lisān* VII 66, 7 *fa-tilka al-jawār ʿaqquhā wa-nuṣūruhā* . . . ; here the parallelism shows that it is infinitive.

38. How much the Arabs themselves felt this difficulty is evidenced by, for instance, the many strained interpretations in Baghawī: *(duʿāʾukum) ʿiyyāhu wa-qīla lawlā ʾaymānukum wa-qīla lawlā ʿibādatukum wa-qīla lawlā duʿāʾuhu ʾiyyākum ʾilā al-ʾislām (ʾlkh* /etc.)

39. Cf. Sura LXX.4, a passage that is close to ours: *taʿruju al-malāʾikatu wa-al-rūḥu ʾilayhi fī yawmin kāna miqdāruhu khamsīna ʾalfa sanatin*. In Sura LVII.4, the angels are designated with . . . *mā yaʿruju fīhā*

The variant *thumma yuʿraju ʾilayhi* . . . of our passage (Bayḍāwī) gives the sense correctly, but is insufficient because it lacks the active subject.

40. It would mean "the right path is the duty of God." Bayḍāwī, Baghawī, and Jalālain explain this as "explaining the right path."

41. [asyndeton (*rhet.*) *n.* a figure in which the conjunctions are omitted. - *adj.* Asyndetic.]

42. [anaphora. n. the rhetorical device of beginning successive sentences, lines, etc. , with the same word or phrase. In this instance, the phrase *wa-min ʾāyātihi*]

43. Bayḍāwī and Baghawī: "(Is he) like him who aspires to life here below"; Jalālain: "Like him who is not like this."

44. Thus verse 30: *ʾa-nulzimukumūhā*; verse 66: *fa-man yanṣurunī*; likewise *man, fa-man*. in Sura XLI.52; LXVII.28, 30.

45. *ʾArūnī* 35, 38:46, 3.

46. In this way it would mean the same as *yafrughu lakum*; as if Jacob had until then been occupied with other things and only became free again for them only afterwards.

47. Compare *jalā al-ʾamru li-l-nāsi . . . waḍaḥa* (Miṣbāḥ), *tajallati al-shamsu* (TA according to a tradition) in the Koran itself *wa- l-nahāru ʾidhā tajallā*. Sura XCII.2.

48. Bayḍāwī justifies it by saying it is constructed ad vocem (*bi-ʿtibāri al-lafẓ*)

49. According to the expositors, it is either *zāʾidah* . . . (Bayḍāwī, Baghawī), or there is a negative question: "Is he not powerful?" (Jalālain, other expositors in Bayḍāwī, Baghawī). Ja ʿqūb reads *yaqdiru*.

50. This is what Bayḍāwī and Jalālain propose as what preceded. Cf. verse 15 which is constructed in this way.

51. If the words *fa-'athābakum ghamman bi-ghammin* here are excised, there would be adequate coherence. But they must have come somewhere before verse 148, which refers back to them.

52. [aposiopesis: a sudden breaking off in the midst of a sentence.]

53. Baghawī (together with other explanations), Bayḍāwī, Jalālain. This interpretation is ascribed to Ibn Mas'ūd and Ibn 'Abbās—*'Aṭā'* in Baghawī explains *al-ghuzātu al-mujāhidūna fī sabīli llāhi.* -'Ikrima: *ṭalabatu al-'ilmi.* But how, according to these two explanations could the women in Sura LXVI.5 have been called *sā'iḥā tun* ? The explanation "fasting ones" is an ad hoc invention. To designate this, *ṣāma* is always (fourteen times) used in the Koran; and the meaning "fasting ones" for *ṣāma* is not attested elsewhere.

54. For this reason Nöldeke (in a communication by letter) suggested a reference to itinerant monks here. In this case *al-sā'iḥā tu* . . . would have to designate female itinerant monks. But, as Prof. G. Grutzmacher tells me, he knows nothing of female itinerant monks, neither in general nor for Arabia in particular. Moreover, the itinerant monks were mockingly called *Gyrovagi*, and despised for their sensual, indulgent way of living even in Christian circles, and synods promulgated prohibitions against their behavior (Grutzmacher in *Protest. Realenzykl.* 3 VII, 271 –3, I am grateful to him for what he has told me).

Even without this, one could not assume that their behaviour would have been recommended as holy to Muslims.

A passage in Clement, *de virginitate* I 10, 1 (Prof. Seeberg has kindly shown that it is there) speaks of "shameless people (monks) who under pretext of god-fearing, cohabit with virgins and thereby incur the risk of going alone with them on paths and in the wilderness (Syriac: *they go into the wilderness all alone* . . .) a course which is replete with with dangers, objectionableness, traps and pits." Here nothing more than walking together in unfrequented places is meant. In no instance is the lifestyle of these monks anywhere regarded as to be recommended or as holy. Sura LXVI.5 is also decisive in that it says "God can give you women/wives *muslimātin . . . sā'iḥātin*"; here only a Muslim, not a Christian, institution can be meant.

6.2

A Qur'ānic Interpolation

A. Fischer

Translated by Herbert Berg

To judge by the translations that are given by the Western Qur'ānic interpretations of Qur'ān CI.5-8,[1] this passage presents no particular difficulty. The four verses read: "(5) As for him whose scales are heavy, he (will have) a pleasant life (6) And as for him whose scales are light, his mother is hāwiyah (7) What will convey to you what it is? (8) A blazing fire." The best available translations for them are:

> "Moreover he whose balance shall be heavy *with good works*, shall lead a pleasing *life*: but *as to* him whose balance shall be light, his dwelling *shall be* the pit *of hell*. What shall make thee to understand how *frightful* the pit *of hell is? It is* a burning fire," with the note: "*The pit of hell*; the original word *Hawiyat* is the name of the lowest dungeon of hell, and properly signifies a *deep pit* or *gulf*." (Sale, 1764)

> Then as to him whose balances are heavy—his shall be a life that shall please him well; And as to him whose balances are light—his dwelling-place shall be the pit. And who shall teach thee what the pit (El-Hawiya) is? A raging fire! (Rodwell, 1861, agreeing almost literally; Lane Poole, 1879; and Palmer)

> Those whose works weigh heavily in the balance will have a pleasant life. Those whose works will be light will reside in the pit (*El-hawiya*),

From *Orientalische Studien*, Theodor Nöldeke zum 70, Geburtstag, 1. Band (Giessen, 1906), pp. 33–55.

Who can teach you what this pit is? It is the raging fire. (Kasimirski, 1865)

The one whose weigh-scale is heavy, will find himself in the good life, however the mother of the one whose weigh-scale is light, will be the *hāwiyah*. Also, do you know what that means? A blazing fire," with the note: "*Hāwiyah* means the fallen and also a mother robbed of her children. One says, "*hawat ummuhu*, literally, his mother is fallen or has become childless, i.e., her son fell in battle. The commentators believe that *hāwiyah* means Hell." (Sprenger, *Das Leben und die Lehre des Moḥammad*, II, 503)

Now, whose weighing will be heavy, he is in pleasure and love; And whose weighing will be light, his mother is in the depth. Do you know what this is? Heat, burning hot. (Rückert)

And whose scale sinks will be happy and healthy; but whose scale rises, falls in deep ground. What makes its nature known to you? It is a scorching fire-spitting mouth. (Klamroth)

Whose weighing is heavy (with good deeds), he will see a happy life;—but whose weighing is light, his mother is [in] the abyss(Grimme, *loc. cit.*); and so forth.[2]

These are clear and, so it seems, thoroughly plausible translations, which differ really only on one point: the majority of the translators have understood the *mother* (in verse 6) as figurative (that is, as dwelling, dwelling place, residence, and so forth), while Sprenger, Rückert, and Grimme have maintained the figure, obviously without understanding it otherwise. Sprenger's footnote reveals, at any rate, that he must have found diverse "inconsistencies" in the explanation of *his mother is hāwiyah* in the native Qur'ānic commentaries. As one can see, he quickly glided away from it, as is his nature, and contented himself with the traditional translation.

Nöldeke, *Geschichte des Qorâns* (p. 78), and Hirschfeld, *New Researches into the Composition and Exegesis of the Qoran* (p. 58), briefly classify Sura CI chronologically, without mentioning details.

From the outset, one may accept that the portrayed facts are an exact reflex of the exegesis devoted to our verses in the native Qurʾānic commentaries most used in the West. Indeed, Maḥallī (in *Tafsīr al-Jalālayn*), Bayḍāwī, Shaykh Zādah (in his *Hāshiyah* to Bayḍāwī), as well as al-Nasafī (in his commentary entitled *Madārik al-tanzīl*), Muḥammad b. Abī Rāzī (in his *Numūdhaj jalīl fī bayān asʾila wa-ajwiba min gharāʾib āy al-tanzīl*), and Abū Yaḥyā Zakarīyā al-Anṣarī (in his *Fatḥ al-Raḥmān bi-kashf mā yaltabis fi-l-Qurʾān*) give the same clear explanation as the Western translators. Compare:

Maḥāllī:

> *His mother*—his dwelling place—is *hāwiyah; And what will convey what it is?* that is, "what is *hāwiyah*?" It is *a blazing fire*, the affliction of heat.

Bayḍāwī (edited by Fleischer):

> *His mother*—his abode—is the Fire and the *hāwiyah* is one of its names. Therefore, he said, *what will convey to you what it is? A blazing fire*—possessing great heat.

Shaykh Zādah:

> Bayḍāwī's statement, "his abode is the Fire" is because the *hāwiyah* is among the names of the Fire and God's statement *his mother is hāwiyah* is a kind of simile; the Fire is likened to the mother. For their rebelliousness falls with them and attaches to them as the mother attaches to her children. They take refuge in her. God's statement *what is it* is a nominal sentence replacing the object of (the verb) *convey to you*.. . . And *it* is the pronoun for *hāwiyah*. . . . Bayḍāwī's statement "*fire*" is the predicate of an implied (dropped) subject of a nominal clause, that is, it is a fire of the affliction of heat, etc.

Nasafī:

> *His mother*—his residence and his dwelling place is the Fire. A dwelling place is called *mother* in the simile because the mother is the dwelling place of the child and his place of refuge. *And what will convey to you what it is?* is the pronoun referring back to *hāwiyah*.

Muḥammad b. Abī Bakr al-Rāzī (with whom Abū Yaḥyā Zakarīyā al-Anṣarī almost literally concurs):[3]

> God said *And as for him whose scales are light*. That is to say, his evil deeds weigh more than his good deeds. *His mother is hāwiyah* means his dwelling place is the Fire and most believers' evil deeds weigh more than their good deeds. (We say that) the God's statement *his mother is hāwiyah* does not imply their eternal residence in it. The believer dwells in it the amount of time required by his sins. Then he leaves it for the Garden. Etc.

Despite all of this, the meaning of the four verses has its problems and Muslim Qur'ānic exegesis, despite Maḥallī, Bayḍāwī, Shaykh Zādah, Nasafī, and so forth, has from the earliest times also recognized and acknowledged these problems, at least partially. One can compare al-Ṭabarī's *Tafsīr*:[4]

> His statement *And as for him whose scales are light, his mother is hāwiyah*, he is saying "as for he whose weight of good deeds is light, his dwelling place is the *hāwiyah* in which he falls on his head in Hell. The interpreters of the Qur'ān said much the same thing concerning this. Bishr related from Yazīd from Saʿīd from Qatādah:[5] *And as for him whose scales are light, his mother is hāwiyah*, it is the Fire, their abode. Ibn ʿAbd al-Aʿlā related from Ibn Thawr from Maʿmar from Qatādah, (who) said: *His mother is hāwiya*, the destiny in the Fire; it is the *hāwiyah*. Qatādah said, "It is an Arabic word. If a man fell into a harsh situation, it used to be said, 'His mother fell (*hawat*).' " Ibn ʿAbd al-Aʿlā related from Ibn Thawr from Maʿmar from al-Ashʿath ibn ʿAbd Allāh al-Aʿmā, (who) said: When a believer dies, his spirit is taken to the spirits of the believers. They [angels?] say, "Go to your brother! For he was in the affliction of the world." And they ask, "What did so-and-so do?" "He died. Perhaps he did not come to you?" They said, "Go with him to his mother the *hāwiyah*!" Ismāʿīl ibn Sayf al-ʿAjlī related that ʿAlī ibn Mushir related that Ismāʿīl from Abī Ṣāliḥ[6] said concerning *his mother is hāwiyah*: They fall (*yahwūna*) in the Fire upon their heads. Ibn Sayf related from Muḥammad ibn Sawwār from Saʿīd from Qatādah, (who) said: *His mother is hāwiyah*; He falls (*yahwā*) in the fire upon his head. Yūnus related from Ibn Wahb from Ibn Zayd, (who) said concerning *his mother is hāwiyah*: The *hāwiyah* is the Fire—it is his mother and his

abode to which he returns and in which he abides. And he recited: *And their abode is the Fire.*[7] Muḥammad ibn Saʿd related from his father from his paternal uncle from his father from his father from Ibn ʿAbbās[8] (who) said: *His mother is hāwiyah*; it is a metaphor; it represents the Fire as his mother because his abode is just as a woman giving accommodations to her son. It represents her since he does not have an abode except the residence of his mother. And the statement: *And what will convey to you what it is?* God says to his prophet Muḥammad (peace and blessings upon him): And what will impart to you, Muḥammad, what the *hāwiyah* is? Then he explains what it is. He says it is *a blazing fire*, etc.

Zamakhsharī, *Kashshāf* (ed. Lees):

[*His mother is hāwiyah*] among their teaching is, if they called destruction upon a man, then his mother falls. This is because if he falls worthless and perishes, then his mother falls into grief and is as one who has lost a child. A poem: "May his mother fall. What the morning brings (him) / And what the night conveys when he returns (home)."[9] As if it were said, "As for he whose scales are light, he is perished." And *hāwiyah* is said to be one of the names of the Fire. It is like the deep fire far into which the people of the Fire fall. As it is related, [they] fall in it for seventy autumns. In other words, his abode is the Fire. And "abode" is called "mother" allegorically because the mother is the abode of the son and his place of refuge. And from Qatādah, *His mother is hāwiyah*, his mother is his head, *hāwiyah* is in the bottom of Hell because he is cast into it upside down. *It* is the personal pronoun of the calamity which is indicated by the statement "*his mother is hāwiyah*" in the former interpretation or the personal pronoun of *hāwiyah*, etc.

al-Fakhr al-Rāzī, *al-Tafsīr al-kabīr*:

As for God's statement *His mother is hāwiyah*, it contains several meanings. (1) *Hāwiyah* is one of the names of the Fire, as though it is a deep fire far into which the dwellers of the Fire fall. It means his abode is the Fire. *Mother* refers to "abode" allegorically, since the child takes refuge only with the mother. (2) The mother of his head (his skull) is *hāwiyah* in the Fire; that is to say, al-Akhfash, al-Kalbī, and Qatādah said that they fall (*yahawūna*) into the Fire on their heads. (3) When they call

> destruction upon a person, they say "May his mother fall (*hawā*)" because when he *hawā*, that is, fell and perished, his mother fell into grieving and bereavement. Similarly, it is said regarding *and as for him whose scales are light*, he perished. Then he said *What will convey to you what it is?* The author of the *Khashshāf* said that *it* is the pronoun for the calamity indicated by the statement *His mother is hāwiyah* in the third interpretation or the pronoun of *hāwiyah*, etc.

Niẓām al-Dīn al-Ḥasan b. Muḥammad al-Naysābūrī (The edition on the margins of al-Ṭabarī's *Tafsīr*):

> As for His statement *his mother is hāwiyah*, it contains several meanings. (1) "Mother" is well-known, and *hāwiyah* is the one who perishes. This is among the usages of the Arabs. They say, "May his mother fall down (*hawā*)" that is, may she perish and fall. They mean he has a curse of affliction, ruin, shame, and disgrace on him. Al-Akhfash, al-Kalbī, and Qatādah said: The mother of his head (his skull) is *hāwiyah* in the Fire. . . . The mother is the foundation and the *hāwiyah* is among the names of the Fire because it is a deep fire and the meaning is his residence and his abode in which he abides is the Fire. This corroborates this meaning: his statement *what it is?* that is to say, "what is the *hāwiyah*?" This is the obvious meaning and the ancient [exegetes] said: the pronoun for the calamity that is indicated by the statement *His mother is hāwiyah*, etc.

Khāzin, *Lubāb al-taʾwīl*:

> *His mother is hāwiyah*, that is, his residence is the Fire. The residence is called mother because mothers are the foundation of residing. It is said that it means the mother of his head (his skull) is *hāwiyah* in the Fire and the *hāwiyah* is one of the names of the Fire. It is the abyss whose bottom is not reached. They fell in it on their heads. When a difficult situation used to befall a man, it was said, "his mother fell (*hawat*)." That is to say, she perished in grief and bereavement. *What will convey to you what it is?* It means the *hāwiyah*. Then it was explained: "*a blazing fire*," etc.

Al-Khaṭīb al-Shirbīnī, *al-Sirāj al-munīr*:

> *His mother*, that is to say, that which shelters him and embraces him just as the earth is called mother because it suggests that and one lives off of it just as one lives off of one's mother. Thus the residence is *hāwiyah*, that is to say, a very base, low fire. He does not cease falling down into it. He is in a loathsome life. The verse is an example of binding;[10] it refers to the former life indicating its being cut off in the latter, and it refers to the mother in the latter indicating her being cut off in the former. The *hāwiyah* is one of the names of Hell and it is the abyss, the bottom of which is cannot be reached. And Qatādah said it is an Arabic saying: If a difficult situation used to befall a man, it was said "His mother has fallen (*hawat*)." And it was said he intended "the mother of his head (his skull)." . . and Qatāda and Abū Ṣālih believe this interpretation. . . . *What it is?*, that is, the *hāwiyah*. . . . He said here *What will convey to you what it is?* (If it were said) that He had said [along with] first part of the sūrah, "What will convey to you what the calamity is?" and had not said, "And what will convey to you what the *hāwiyah* is?" (it would be answered) that "it is a calamity," which is a considerable matter, while "it is a *hāwiyah*," which is not like that. The distinction is obvious, etc.

Abū al-Suʿūd, *Irshād al-ʿaql al-salīm*:

> *His mother* that is to say, his abode is *hāwiyah*. It is one of the names of the Fire. Lexically it refers to the extreme limit of its depth and the farness of its abyss. . . . And it was said that it was a name for its lowest gate. . . . From Qatādah, ʿIkrimah,[11] and al-Kalbī that the meaning is: the mother of his head (his skull) is *hāwiyah* in the bottom of Hell because he is cast into it inverted. The first [suggestion] is consistent with the God's statement: *And as for him whose scales are light, his mother is hāwiyah. What will convey to you what it is? A blazing fire*. It is a clarification for it after some ambiguity. . . . It is the pronoun of the *hāwiyah*, etc.

Finally, Sulaymān al-Jamal, who in his gloss of *Tafsīr al-Jalālayn*[12] along with all sorts of excerpts out of his predecessors that contain nothing new, makes the note: "the *hāwiyah* is the last of the seven levels." Al-Shihāb al-Khafājī,[13] *Ḥāshiyah* for Bayḍāwī begins his comments to verse 6 of our sūra with the words:

(His statement, "His abode is the Fire"). The abode is called mother by mocking comparison because the mother of the child is his abode and his residence.

He concludes in connection with with Bayḍāwī's words "the *hāwiyah* is one of her names" with citations from al-Jawharī's *Ṣaḥāḥ* and Ibn Barrī's glosses.

Naturally, the Arabic lexicographers have also concerned themselves with our passage, principally regarding the term *hāwiyah*, which constitutes the real crucial point for the understanding of verses 6–8, and also regarding the nearby *His mother*. They give, all things considered, the same explanation as the Qur'ānic exegetes, but provide some features that are new and not unimportant. Compare *Ṣaḥāḥ* under the entry *hawā*:

> *Hāwiyah*[14] is one of the names of the Fire and it is definite without the definite article. God said *His mother is hāwiyah*. He is saying his dwelling place is the Fire and the *hāwiyah* is the abyss. He said:
>
> ʿAmr, had our lances found you
> You would have been like one falling to the depth (*hāwiyah*).[15]
>
> You say "May his mother fall (*hawat*)," she is *hāwiyah*, that is to say, bereaved. Kaʿb ibn Saʿd al-Ghanawī elegized his brother:
>
> May his mother fall [*hawat*]. What the morning brings (him)
> And what the night conveys when he returns (home).

Lisān al-ʿarab under the entry *hawā* (XX.25 f.):

> *Hāwiyah* and the *hāwiyah* are among the names of Hell and it is definite without the definite article. The statement of God, *His mother is hāwiyah* is to say that his abode is Hell and his dwelling place is the Fire. It is said that one who has some compensation coming, he will dwell in "a blazing fire." According to al-Farrāʾ some said concerning *His mother is hāwiyah* that this is a curse against them just as one would "May his mother fall (*hawat*)" in the speech of the Arabs. He recited the statement of Kaʿb ibn Saʿd al-Ghanawī elegizing his brother . . . [the aforementioned verse].[16] The meaning of "May his mother fall (*hawat*)" is "May

his mother perish." And one says "May his mother fall (*hawat*);" so she is *hāwiyah*, that is, she is bereaved (of a child). Some said, *His mother is hāwiyah*, (means) *hāwiyah* becomes his abode just as the woman gives shelter her son. There is no abode for him other than her, his mother. It was said the meaning of *His mother is hāwiyah* is the skull (mother of his head) falls in the Fire. Ibn Barrī said, "Had *hāwiyah* been a proper name for the Fire, then it would not be fully inflected in the verse and so the *hāwiyah* is each abyss whose bottom is not reached." ʿAmr ibn Milqaṭ al-Ṭāʾī said "ʿAmr . . . [the aforementioned verse]."

And under the entry *umam* (XIV.299):

God's statement *His mother is hāwiyah*: and it is the Fire into which he, who is made to enter it, falls, that is, perishes. And, it is said his skull (mother of his head) is *hāwiyah* in it, that is, fallen.

Tāj al-ʿarus under the entry *hawā* (X.416):

Hāwiyah without definite article is definite. Al-Jawharī restricted it to "the *hāwiyah*" also with the article. Ibn Saʿīd related it one of the names of "Hell, may God protect us from it," amen. And concerning [who is] correct, etc.

All the rest is as in *Ṣaḥāḥ* and *Lisān*; only the note to the verses is new:

"May she fall (*hawat*)," that is to say, "May his mother perish" so that she does not produce the like of him. Al-Jawharī related it from Thaʿlab: "May his mother," etc.

And under the entry *umam* (VIII.189):

(And) the mother is (the dwelling). An example is the saying of God, *His mother is hāwiyah*. That is to say, his dwelling is the Fire. And it is said that his skull (the mother of his head) is *hāwiyah* in it, that is fallen.

Thus the native exegesis gives instead of one single explanation for the passage, three different ones, of which one, as an even closer look will immediately show, is presented in four or more varieties. And their most thorough and conscientious advocates stand, as it is not possible to fail to recognize, on the point of view of *non liquet*, or, in Islamic terms, "only God knows (*Allāhu aʿlam*)." Which of these three or more explanations deserves preference? Is it really the one that the chorus of the western translators have accepted unanimously?

The explanations are:

(1) "Mother" in *his mother* stands in the meaning of "mother of the head," "skull," also "brain," and "cerebral membrane (meninx)"[17] or of only "head" and *hāwiyah* is simply the active particle of *hawā*, "to fall, to tumble" (*passim*).

(2) Mother stands metaphorically for dwelling, abode, residence, or the like (*passim*; Khafājī sees sarcasm in this metaphor), or for origin or foundation (Niẓām al-Dīn al-Naysābūrī). *Hāwiyah* denotes Hell or the Fire and to be precise either as a proper noun (*passim*) or as a common noun. As a common noun it is regarded equivalent with abyss and chasm or as a metonymy for a base, lowly fire (Khaṭīb).

(3) Mother means, as usual, mother and *hāwiyah* is the active participle for *hawat*, "his mother perished" or "lost her children" (*passim*).[18]

We will skip over without further ado the first explanation, even though it is obviously very old and is supported by names such as Qatādah, ʿIkrimah, al-Kalbī, al-Akhfash, and the like. The idea that the damned fall headfirst into Hell has obviously been influenced by Qur'ānic passages such as L.23, 25: "Cast into Hell every rebellious unbeliever . . . cast him into severe punishment"; LXVII.6: "And for those who disbelieve in their Lord there is the punishment of Hell, an evil destination. When they are cast in it they will hear the groaning even as it flares up"; CIV.4 "Nay, he will be flung into that which smashes"; XXVII.92: "And those who do evil their faces will be thrown down into the Fire"; XXV.36: "Those who will be gathered to Hell on their faces"; and the like.

The second explanation, as one has seen, is that which has achieved exclusive rule in the West. That it has also won great popularity among Muslims. In addition to the citations given above,[19] it is shown by the following not uninteresting passages as well:

Kāmil 65:

> We had said that you joined your mother falling (*hāwiyah*) into[20] the blazing Fire (the Khārijites under al-Zubayr ibn ʿAlī during their siege of Iṣfahān[21] shouted this at a brave opponent whom they believed they had killed). Muḥammad Ṭāhir al-Pattanī, *Majma ʿbiḥār al-anwār fī gharāʾib al-tanzīl wa-laṭāʾif al-akhbār*, Indian lithograph from 1314 under the entry *hawā*: Ṭ:[22] His mother is the *hāwiyah*: "Mother" is "destiny" and *hāwiyah* is the equivalent or explanation.

and Raẓālī, *al-Durra al-fākhirah*, ed. Gautier, 35:

> Perhaps a man dies a Jew or a Christian. When he arrives from the world to his people, they ask "what do you know about so-and-so?" He says to them, "He died." They say, "we are Allāh's and we return to him." He was brought low to his mother[23] the *hāwiyah*.

Its popularity is illustrated further from the fact that the Qurʾānic exegetes and theologians always list the *hāwiyah* among the names of the seven gates of hell enumerated in Qurʾān XV.44. Compare, for example, with Ṭabarī, *Tafsīr* to Qurʾān XV.44 (XIV.22)

> Al-Qāsim related from al-Ḥusayn from al-Ḥajjāj from Ibn Jurayj: It has seven gates. The first is Hell (*Jahannam*), then *Laẓā*, then the *Ḥuṭamah*, then the *Saʿīr*, then *Saqar*, then the *Jahīm*, then the *Hāwiyah*. Abū Jahl is in the *Jahīm*.

Zamakhsharī, *Kashshāf*, on the same passage:

> It is said that the gates of the Fire are its layers and levels.[24] The highest level is for the monotheists, the second for the Jews, the third for the Christians, the fourth for the Sabians, the fifth for the Magi, the sixth for the idolaters, and the seventh for the hypocrites.[25] And from Ibn ʿAbbās, Hell (*Jahannam*) is for he who feigns belief the deity, *Laẓā* is for serving the Fire, the *Ḥuṭamah*, for the serving of idols, the *Saqar* for the Jews, the *Saʿīr* for the Christians, the *Jahīm* for the Sabians, and the *Hāwiyah* for the feigners of belief in the divinity.

ʿAbd al-Raḥmān b. Aḥmad, *Daqāʾiq al-akhbār fī dhikr al-janna wa-l-nār*, ed. M. Wolff (*Eschatologie*), 89:

> [Gabriel] said: As for the first gate, in it are the hypocrites and whoever disbelieves from the companions of the table and the people pharaoh. Its name is *hāwiyah.*

and others.[26] Nevertheless, even this explanation proves itself untenable after careful consideration.

First, as Ibn Barrī correctly recognized, *hāwiyah* cannot be a proper noun, because it would then have to be diptote. (Compare with the correct form the proper nouns *ʿĀʾishah* and *Fāṭimah* and with the other names of Hell, *Laẓā* and *Saqar*). The Muslim scholars simply avoided these defects. As is apparent with the aforementioned passages, they replaced "the *hāwiyah*" or *hāwiyah* [diptote] for the traditional *hāwiyah* [triptote] without any hesitation. That is completely arbitrary!

However, if one regards *hāwiyah* as a common noun, be it in one or the other of the two accepted meanings, one also gains no usable result. Understood as abyss, chasm, gulf, and so on and with it as associated forms *hūwah* (abyss), *hūwāʾah*, *uhwīyah* (abyss), *hawāʾ*, *hawīyah* (abyss), *mahwan* (abyss), *mahwāh* (abyss), *hawt*, *hawtah*, and *hīt*[27] (compare also *hawhāʾah*, "wide fountain"), it appears very persuasive at first glance. That it can have this meaning for the old language is shown from the indigenous dictionaries citation of the verse of ʿAmr b. Milqaṭ "O ʿAmr . . . ," which I translate: "O ʿAmr, if our lances had hit you, then you would have resembled he who falls into an abyss in the deep"—for the more recent passages as *Kalīlah wa-Dimnah*, ed. Sacy, II, 1:[28]

> She said,[27] I would like you (frogs) to you go with me to a nearby deep pit. Croak in it and be noisy. When he (the elephant) hears your voices, he will not doubt that there is water (in it). He will fall (*yahwī*) in it. They agreed to that and gathered in the abyss (*hāwiyah*). The elephant heard the croaking of the frogs. Thirst overpowered him so he fell into the deep pit.

The verse from ʿAmr b. Milqaṭ is impeccable, since it is repeated not only with a second verse in *Lisān* and *Tāj al-ʿarus* (under Thaʿlab), but also appears in ʿAynī II, 458, as in Suyūṭī's *Shar shawāhid al-Murnī* (Manuscript Thorb. A 232, book XIII, folio 3a) in a larger fragment of the *qaṣīdah*, to which it belongs.[30] The Leiden manuscript of the Arabic *Kalīlah wa-Dimnah* has, just as Dozy (*loc. cit.*) cites under *hawat*, *al-hawtah* for Sacy's *al-hāwiyah*; the latter stands however, for example, also in the Mosul edition (3rd ed., 19) and has naturally its worth in any case.

Pause for thought is given by the fact that the equivalent that the Qurʾān itself employs in verse 8 for *hāwiyah*, "blazing fire," lies conceptually fairly far from *hāwiyah* (abyss). It lies far further than other instances of the Qurʾānic formula *And what will convey to you what is . . .* introducing an equivalent of the expression that it is meant to explain. Moreover, the fact that in the Qurʾān, the Prophet's authentic and characteristic interpretations that which begin with the stereotypical *And what will convey to you what is . . .*, are otherwise used just for words that he himself newly coined either in form or in content, or those that must have been entirely new for his listeners—never for common Arabic expressions such as *hāwiyah* (abyss).[31] Of even greater weight in disfavor of this interpretation is that the trope *"mother"* for "abode" (or others), understood either literally or ironically. It is less than appealing and more so to those for whom Arabic is otherwise completely foreign. As the exegetes here accept it, they do not let themselves be led by their knowledge of the language or their feeling for the language. Rather, they are led only by the acceptance that, since in verse 5 the discussion was about the future *ʿīshah rāḍiyah* (pleasant life) of the pious (that is, their life in paradise), to which stands in unmistakable antithesis verse 6, the latter must necessarily deal with the future residence of sinners in Hell. Since this residence in Hell in the Qurʾān is ordinarily expressed by means of the word "abode,"[32] "his abode" (or something else) is substituted for our *his mother*, without any hesitation.

These objections to the dominant interpretations of *his mother* naturally also brings the downfall of the identification of *hāwiyah* with a low, base fire. Apart from the fact that the latter is already in and of itself dubious.

Finally, the last of the proper modalities, the interpretation of *mother* as "origin" (*aṣl*), etc., is in itself admissible. (The meaning of *mother* as "origin," "basis," "element," and others, already exists and is fundamentally nothing more than a close metaphor).[33] So we can dismiss it because it does not bring us further in any way.

Consequently only the third explanation is left over, according to which *his mother is hāwiyah* means "his mother perishes," more correctly "becomes childless," and is regarded as a kind of euphemism[33] for "perish" (*halaka*). It seems to me that this explanation, as I will establish is the only admissible one.

That *hawā* can mean "dying, perishing," is shown, for example, by the two following verses:

> Those who rejoice at misfortune said: Ziyād is dead (*hawā*)
> Every blow of fate has a clear reason.[35]

And,

> By my life, he shouted with his loudest voice
> He announced that your chief, Ḥuyayy, died (*hawā*).[36]

However, with *mother* and others as subject, it becomes, as the majority of the old Arabic philologists recognize a synonym for *thakal*, "bereaved of a child." It means therefore "to become childless." This use cannot be surprising if, as I with Fleischer[37] want to accept that the original meaning of *hawā* is "to yawn, to gape," out of which can develop—through the intermediate meaning "to be empty"—the meanings "to die" (compare *faragha* and *khalā*) and "to become childless" in a similar manner. I can provide examples with four old verses, namely that already given above:

> May his mother become childless (*hawat*)! What the morning brings (him)
> And what[38] the night conveys when he returns (home)

and the following three others:

> May his mother become childless (*hawat*)! His grave has enclosed what is of (his) generosity and (his) good deeds when he rewards (goodness)[39]

> May his mother become childless (*hawat*)! What (ropes of glory), on the day they stretched out
> Jayshān with ropes of glory which cut through (him)

> It was said her: Exert yourself, may you become childless (*hawayti*) and hurry to obtain the pigeon lest the watersacks run out

The four verses are all well attested. The first two belong to a longer one: the Marthiyah of Kaʿb b. Saʿd al-Ranawī which is much appreciated and oft-cited by the Arabs. (According to other less reliable information it is by Sahm al-Ranawī, see *Khizānah,* loc. cit.). It is still completely or at least mostly extant, in the as yet unpublished part of the *Mufaḍḍaliyāt Aṣmaʿiyat*, no. 11.[40] *Khizana* IV, 374f, *Mukhtārāt* of Ibn al-Shajarī 27 ff., *Shuʿarāʾ al-naṣrāniya*, 746 ff., and Muḥibb al-Dīn Efendi, *Sharḥ shawāhid al-Kashshāf*, 47 f. (just the first of the two verses is also in *Ṣaḥāḥ*, *Lisān*, and *Tāj al-ʿarus* under the entry *umam*, as well as, Ibn al-Sikkīt, *Alfāẓ*, 576 and Maqqarī, *Analectes*, II, 518). The third verse comes from Abū Tammām in his *Ḥamāsah*, included with fragments of another Marthiyah, which likewise found wide circulation (compare *Ham.* 424, II ff.; Wright, *Opuscula*, 113; Yāq. II 178; and *Sharḥ shawāhid al-Kashshāf* 48; for our verse alone also Maqqarī *loc. cit.* II, 519). Finally, the fourth one is found in a particularly esteemed poem of Ḥumayd b. Thawr, that Ibn Qutaybah has preserved for us (*al-Shiʿr wa-l-shuʿarāʾ*, 231 f.). On the authenticity of these verses there can be hardly any doubt. The view of the Arabic philologists of the stereotypical *his mother fell (hawat)* in the three first verses is illustrated by the following passages. Ibn al-Sikkīt, *Alfāẓ*, 575, 5:

> It is said concerning the curse against a man . . . "May his mother become childless (*hawat*)." That is to say, "may his mother become bereaved of a child (*thakilat*). "Kaʿb ibn Saʿd al-Ghanawī said, "May his mother . . ."

with the following commentary of Tibrīzī:

> This curse employs the aspect of surprise with proficiency and skill. It excels others. It is said "may his mother become bereaved of a child" How fine is what he produces and how excellent his speech; its like is his statement "may Allāh fight him," and the statement of the Prophet (blessings upon him) "on you, of all things, is religion. Your hands are covered with dust . . ." etc.

Tibrīzī according to *Ḥamāsah*, 424:

This was said concerning being proud and being astonished. That is to say, "may their mothers be bereaved (*thakilat*) of them" And he said "may their mother fall (*hawat*)." That is to say, "may she perish." . . . Abū al-ʿAlāʾ said, "may their mother perish" is among the curses that the Arabs employed for the opposite. Namely, its obvious meaning is as disparagement and a curse on the aforementioned (person), but the intention of it is praise. It indicates their purpose with that (statement) that they do not mean anything disparaging by it.

He, his game does not make progress (that is, it dies)
What does he have? May he not be numbered among his own[41]

Khizānah IV 375:

The statement "May his mother fall (*hawat*) . . ." etc. Al-Qālī said, "That is to say, 'may his mother perish (*halakat*).' It is as though she was brought down to the *hāwiyah* and the author of the *al-Kashshāf* mentioned it. . . . The intention is not cursing someone to fall down. Rather, it is astonishment and praise like the statement "may Allah fight him" and means that he is worthy because he is envied and is cursed with destruction (*halāk*).

Sharḥ shawāhid al-Kashshāf, 48, 1:

His mother is hāwiyah is among their sayings. One curses a man "may his mother fall (*hawat*)," because then he "falls (*hawā*)." That is to say, he falls (*saqaṭa*) and perishes (*halaka*). His mother "falls (*hawat*)" bereaved and grieving. . . . And "may his mother fall" is a curse by which one does not want him to "fall down (*wuqūʿ*). Rather it is said with wonder and praise.

Lisān XIV, 296, 2 ff.

Al-Layth: When the Arabs say, "you have no mother (*lā umm la-ka*)," it is praise according to them. Against it: it is said "you have no mother," and it is a disparagement. Abū ʿUbayd: some of the scholars maintained that their statement "you have no mother" is put in the place of praise.

> Kaʿb ibn Saʿd al-Ghanawī elegized his brother "May your mother fall (*hawat*) . . ." etc. Abū al-Haytham said concerning this verse "what does this verse indicate?" Abū Ubayd: Rather the meaning of this is like their saying, "Woe to his mother," and "affliction to his mother." The affliction to her and not to the man in this (verse) indicates praise. Their saying "you have no mother" does not resemble this (verse) because their saying "you have no mother" indicates that you do not have a free mother, and this is a clear insult. This is due to the fact that the sons of a slave girl are reprehensible according to the Arabs and they do not come close to the sons of a freewoman. A man does not say to his companion "you have no mother" except in anger at him, being neglectful of him and vilifying him. He said: As for if he said "you have no father," that is not a thing of vilification. And it is said the meaning of their saying "you have no mother" is saying "you are a foundling for whom a mother is not known." Ibn Barrī said concerning the exegesis of the verse of Kaʿb ibn Saʿd "may his mother fall (*hawat*)": He employs notion of astonishment like their saying "May Allāh fight him."

(approximately the same *Tāj al-ʿarus*) and Majd al-Dīn ibn al-Athīr, *Nihāya* under the entry *umam* (ed. Cairo 1311, I, 42):

> They obeyed the two of them, that is Abū Bakr and ʿUmar (may Allāh be pleased with the two of them). They had been well guided and their mother was well guided. By "mother" he intends "community" (*ummah*). And it was said it is the opposite of their statement "may his mother fall (*hawat*)" in cursing him.

From these citations one recognizes that the conception of the Arabic philologists of "may his mother fall" is not absolutely uniform, but that the majority and most important voices identify "may she fall (*hawat*)" with "may she become childless (*thakalat*)." The reference to *hawaytī* in the verse of Ḥumayd of De Goeje in the glossary to his Ibn Qutaybah can be dealt with analogously. Whether "may his mother fall," "may you fall," and the like, over which the Arabic philologists are also of divided opinion, is merely used as antiphrasing[42] or not makes no difference for the purposes of our study; because even if, as it certainly appears that the former had been the case, the *hawā* would nevertheless have possessed exactly the same meaning outside of this optative or imprecatory formula, as (is the case with) *qātala*, *akhzā*, *tariba*, and so forth, outside the expressions *qātala-hu Allāh*, *akhzā-hu Allāh*, *taribat yadā-ka*, and so forth.

Under the circumstances no one who is very well acquainted with the peculiarities of the old Arabic lexicons would reject our explanation of *his mother is hāwiyah*, if the closing verse of the sūrah did not exist, which hangs completely in midair with this explanation. Because with Zamakhshārī and others a bridge is established on the way, it is naturally unacceptable for one to apply *hiyah* in verse 7 not to *hāwiyah* but to something inferred from verse 6 *al-dāhiyah*, "disaster," "misfortune."

Fortunately, however, there is a way out of this difficulty that must have been (and still is) closed for every Muslim, namely the possibility of striking out verses 7 and 8 as interpolations. I hold to this deletion as correct on the grounds of the following considerations. First, as we have seen, the verses 6–8 next to each other mock each literal or analogous explanation. To fall back upon Qur'ān III.5, where the Prophet appears to admit the existence of unclear or ambiguous expressions in the Qur'ān,[43] and to accept that our *his mother is hāwiyah* would be such a deliberately unclear expression, naturally would not occur to a Western interpreter because such a method would mean bankrupting all Qur'ānic exegesis. Second, whereas on each of the other thirteen passages in the Qur'ān where a new word is coined by the Prophet using "*and what will convey to you what . . . ,*" the coined word repeatedly comes after this expression. In our verse 7 instead of *hāwiyah* the pronoun *hiyah* appears (please note that the pronoun is not otherwise found in the whole Qur'ān, nor its counterpart *huwah*). This fact must be all the more disturbing, since the concerning repetition obviously constitutes a well-known rhetorical technique of the Prophet[44] and since in our passage neither the consideration of the rhyme nor any other discernible reason makes the replacement of *hāwiyah* by *hiyah* necessary. Thirdly, the content of both verses is quite meager. Verse 7 consists of an expression, that, as just mentioned, recurs not less that thirteen times in the Qur'ān. And both words, those from verse 8, *a blazing fire* (*nār ḥāmiyah*), are without doubt the most prosaic and most vapid among the numerous, partly effective rhetorical and graphic expressions with which the Qur'ān portrays Hell. They appear here all the more pathetic since they are also found in Qur'ān LXXXVIII.4, where they sound much better, so that the supposition is unavoidable that they are borrowed from there.[45] Fourth, one does not need to search far for a reason for the interpolation. The expression "his mother is *hāwiyah*" was obviously already unclear to a large, if not the largest, part of the companions of the Prophet, more precisely Meccan and Medinan companions; that is proved by a comparison of all the extant exegesis transmitted to us, particularly the first generation of the chain of transmitters (*asānid*) with which al-Ṭabarī supports his material. Obviously the blame for the uncertainly was due to the fact that the Prophet had borrowed the expression from the *ʿarabīyah*.[46] That is, at that time in the whole of Arabia the speech of the Bedouin was given classical recognition of a higher style, which differed not insignificantly from the dialects of Mecca and Medina.[47] Muḥammad, despite his animosity toward the old Arabian poets (the chief representatives of *ʿarabīyah*), repeatedly describes the language of his revelations in the Qurʾān itself as *ʿarabī*, that is, "classical Arabic."[48] In addition, it is evident from some traditions that even the oldest Qurʾānic exegetes had to let Bedouin interpret certain words and expressions in the revelations.[49] However, insofar as one was unclear over the exact meaning of the expression "his mother is *hāwiyah*," one recognized by context that it should announce the punishment of the sinner, naturally the punishment of Hell. The majority of the Qurʾānic exegetes had decided the expression to be identical with *his abode is the Fire*. This insight caused an old Qurʾān memorizer (*ḥāfiẓ*)—of course before the final redaction of the Qurʾān—to attach verses 7 and 8 to the sura, in order to make clear the intention of verse 6 as the punishment of Hell to even the dullest eyes or ears. Naturally, the aforementioned Qurʾān memorizer could thus have been led by the best of intentions.

Perhaps one could raise two kinds of objections against this solution to the problem. First, until now Qurʾānic interpolations have not been proven and so it must seem dubious, even though only the possibility of admitting such would be permissible. And second, the bare "his mother is *hāwiyah*" means "his mother becomes childless," that is, "he perishes," is not contrasted effectively enough with "He is in a pleasant life," which immediately brings to mind Paradise and to which it is supposed stand in antithesis.

To the first objection I reply that in my opinion the possibility of interpolations in the Qur'ān, even worse than that asserted by me here, absolutely must be admitted. And, if such interpolations have not been proven until now, this mainly because no one has undertaken a drastic detailed criticism of the Qur'ān. One can only imagine the absolute lack of official as well as private care for the individual "qur'āns" during the more than twenty years of Muḥammad's prophetic career. In addition, there is the uninhibitedness with which he partly retouched older revelations considerably, and partly canceled them out completely, usually replacing them with new ones according to need and mood. And there is the mendacious obsession with telling tales of many of his companions, who, as the oldest Qur'ānic exegesis and *Ḥadīth* show, even include the person and the work of the Prophet sent by God. All these things are too sufficiently well known for it to be necessary to even show them in detail here. Even a commission working with all the methods of a modern scholarly training and criticism would not have been able to produce an absolutely authentic Qur'ān from materials affected by such factors—how much less 'Uthmān's commission which was devoid of all literary practice! So few of these techniques were employed to even avoid the confusion in chronology and in content and the fragmentary composition evident in many parts of the Qur'ān. It was likewise incapable of being sure to totally eliminate small parasitic accretions that in the course of the decades—about forty years passed between the first appearance of the Prophet and the final redaction of the Qur'ān—attached themselves on individual suras. Were our Qur'ān really genuine in all its parts, the it would be truly the wonder which the orthodox Muslim belief, certainly in other respects, holds it to be.

The second objection points out that Paradise and Hell in other passages of the Qur'ān are placed in a direct, close, and (therefore at least partially perhaps) effective contrast with one another, as would be the case according to my explanation of *his mother is hāwiyah* in verse 5 and 6 of our sura. Compare LXXXII.13–14:

> As for the righteous, they will be in bliss; and as for the wicked, they will be in a fire;

LXXXI.12–13:

> And when the Fire is kindled, and when the Garden is brought near;

LXXIX.37–40:

> Then, as for him who exceeds proper bounds and preferred the life of this world, the Fire is the abode; but as for him who feared to stand before his Lord and restrained (his) soul from lust, the Garden is his abode.

XXXIX.71,73, and so forth. However, there is in no way a lack of passages where, as in our verse 6 according to my explanation, Hell and its torments are not directly addressed, rather just vaguely of a "losing the soul," a "being afraid," and others (as, on the other hand, Paradise and its blessings are not directly addressed, rather just vaguely of a "thriving," and others). Compare VII:7–8 (two verses that are also closely related to our verses 5 and 6 since they have similar wording, as already was mentioned above):

> The balance on that day will be true; those whose scale is heavy, those are the successful; those whose scale is light, those are the ones who forfeit their souls . . .

(almost exactly the same XXIII:104 f., compare also XXVIII.67); XLII.21:

> You will see the wrongdoers in fear of what they have earned and what will fall on them; those who believe and do good deeds will be in the meadows of the gardens . . .

X.46; and others. In general the threat of punishment contained in vague expressions were often as effective as the precise designation and description of the punishment.

What I have said above about *hiyah* and the general composition of the two ending verses of our sura might also suggest, among other things, that both verses are not interpolations. Rather, they are an old Qurʾānic fragment that the commission of Zayd b. Thābit and his companions or someone before them merely placed at the end of our sura, because it was less suitable elsewhere.

In conclusion I again refer to Zamakhsharī, without doubt not only the most astute and most clever of the Qurʾānic exegetes, but also the best expert on the old language, who brings the meaning of the sentence *his mother is hāwiyah* that is adopted by me to the first position.

NOTES

1. According the Flügel's numbering in his edition of the Qurʾān, which is used here by me as a basis throughout and is in the present case also consistent with Fleischer's Bayḍāwī. Others, as for example Zamakhsharī, *Khashshāf*, edited by Lees, count verse 5 and 6 as two each (see also Grimme's *Mohammed*, 12:111), but hardly correctly as the rhyme readily shows. Unfortunately, even a fairly critical edition of the Qurʾān is still lacking.

2. For he who is immersed somewhat deeper in the secrets of the *ʿarabīyah*, there can be no doubt that among all the existing translations of the Qurʾān, complete as well as partial, none satisfy very strict philological requirements. Sale's translation was a very respectable achievement for its time, and it continues to deserve to be reprinted again and again. However, it naturally now no longer stands up to the mark of Arabic studies and religious studies, especially the study of Islam. Since Sale only Sprenger, among the Qurʾān translators who have had their translations published, has seriously endeavored to penetrate deeper in the understanding of the book. Unfortunately, though he possessed a stupendous (but in no way always reliable) erudition and a wealth of spirit and imagination, he did not also possess the necessary general philological training. Nöldeke concluded the short examination of the literature of Qurʾānic translations in his *Orientalischen Skizzen*, p. 61, with the words: "Unfortunately, Fleischer's translation of the Qurʾān still awaits publication." Concerning this I would like to take this opportunity to notify, that I—in the general conviction that a translation of the Qurʾān from Fleischer's hand would necessarily greatly exceed all available translations, especially in syntactical and lexical respects—had in mind at the end of 1901 to let Brouillon print the manuscript of Fleischer. Unfortunately, I must state that it has completely disappeared. Perhaps one of the readers can give some news of its whereabouts. Thorbecke's handwritten translation of suras 50–114 (see *ZDMG* 45:480 no.131 c = Ms. Tho A. 97, e) is a cursory work without special value.

3. The same passage as a quotation out of Karkhī's commentary of *Tafsīr al-Jalālayn*, also by Sulaymān al-Jamal's *al-Futūḥāt al-ilāhīyah*, a commentary of the same works.

4. I have listed the commentators according to their seniority.

5. Qatādah b. Diʿāmah, an outstanding authority on tradition and the Qurʾān, died at the age of fifty-six around 117 A.H. I comment here only on the names of the most important and oldest informants of al-Ṭabarī.

6. Bādhām, freedman of Umm Hāniʾ, an aunt of the Prophet, source of traditions.

7. Qurʾān III.144 and XXIV.56.

8. The well-known cousin of the Prophet and the founder of the official Muslim Qurʾānic exegesis.

9. For the author of the verses [and a slightly different translation].

10. Compare to this figure of speech Mehren, *Die Rhetorik der Araber*, p. 122, n 185.

11. ʿIkrimah is the well-known transmitter, freedman of Ibn ʿAbbās, who died c. 104 A.H.

12. See above, n. 3.

13. Khafājī (d. 1069) is older than Sulaymān (d. 1204). However, because of his contact with the lexicographers, I placed him directly before them.

14. The vocalization is mine. As everybody knows, the Būlāq edition of the *Ṣaḥāḥ* that I use, unfortunately contains only consonantal Arabic.

15. For the author [and slightly different] translation see page 443.

16. In the margin, regarding:

> "May his mother fall." Al-Ṣāghānī said, replying to al-Jawharī with the report: "May his wife fall (*hawat*) and his good deeds perish when he rewards (goodness)." Al-Jawharī is correct. He is the one who emended the al-Azhar- revision of his books.

17. Mother of the head: for example, *Kāmil* 275; Yāq. I, 120. For cerebral membrane usually as "mother of the brain (*dimāgh*)," see *Kāmil* 64; 275; also mother of the head (*hām*), see ibid. Lane, *Lexicon*, see *dimāgh*, etc. Compare with all three editions of Ibn al-Athīr's *Muraṣṣaʿ*.

18. I will not allow myself to be involved with the foolish attempts at harmonization, such as that of al-Ṭabarī, who attempts to combine the first two of these three explanations with each other.

19. Tibrīzī, *loc. cit.*, can be added to them:

> In the Qurʾān, *his mother is hāwiyah*: it is said that it is a name for Hell, that is to say it is their abode just as the mother houses the child.

20. This "into (*fī*)" is missing in the five manuscripts used by Wright. In the expression is the image of the "mother" being held onto, but it means naturally a part of Hell, or rather Hell itself. Compare with the parallel report in al-Ṭabarī, *Annales*, II, 763:

They began to say: "O enemy of God, verily by God, we hope that we surround you with your mother." He said to them: "O sinners, why do you mention my mother?" They began to say: "He defends his mother to whom he will soon be brought." His companions said to him: "They mean the Fire," and he understood. He replied: "O enemies of Allah, what is most irreverent to your mother is when you are plucked from her. This is your mother and your destiny is it (the Fire)."

21. S. Brünnow, *Charidshiten*, 94 f.

22. It is explained in the forward: Al-Ṭayyibī, *Sharḥ al-mishkāh*. Compare with Brockelmann, *Gesh. d. Arab. Litt.* I, p. 364

23. Gautier has "community" (*ummah*), with the footnote, "These three words [to the community of the *hāwiyah*] is missing in BFGH; C replaces 'community' with 'people (*ahl*)'; D aj. The mother is miserable and the rank is miserable. [Gautier incorrectly has "the suspicious (*al-murība*).]" However, it is obvious that both aforementioned citations are analogous to that from al-Ṭabarī above which contains *His mother* [instead]."

24. Compare to level (*darak*) in contrast with routes (*daraj*). Ḥarīrī, *Durra*, 49.

25. Compare with Qur'ān 4:144: "The hypocrites are in the lowest level of the Fire."

26. From Western works, compare, for example, with Palmer, *Qur'ān* 1, p. LXX; Hughes, *Dictionary of Islam*, under the entry "Hell."

27. For *uhwīyah* compare, for example, with Yāq. III, 321 *Ḥamasah* 424; For *hawā'*, plural *ahwiyah*, chasm, or gulf, for example, Qazwīnī, ed. Wüstenfeld, I, 144, and al-Ṭabarī, *Annales*, Glossary; for *hīt* Yāq. IV, 997 and *ZDMG* (58): 874. I also have examples for the remaining forms, excluding *hūwā'ah* (compare however *ḥamasah*, loc. cit.), however I will refrain from citing them here, especially those that are found almost exclusively in younger sources and already by Dozy, *Supplément*.

28. I have taken this example from Dozy's *Supplément* under the entry *hāwiyah*. A second example that he gives I am not able to consider unfortunately, because the book in question (*Ajbar machmná, crónica anónima del siglo XI*, dada á luz por Don Emilio Lafuente y Alcántara) is not accessible to me.

29. That is, the lark, that wants to take its revenge on the elephant, to the frogs.

30. For ʿAmr, Aws appears in all of these passages. To *tahwī bi-hi al-hāwiyah* ʿAynī remarks: that is to say, the abyss and "you fall" with a *kasrah* under the *wāw*, that is, you fall (*tasquṭu*). Suyūṭī loc. cit. reads *tahwī ilā al-hāwiyah*, for which *tahwī* etc. would naturally be read, assuming the reliability of the manuscript with regard to *ilā*.

31. One can compare for both contentions the passages under discussion (that all stand together in Flügel's concordance under *adrā-ka*).

32. Compare with XXXII.20 "as for those who sin, their abode will be the Fire"; IV.99 "those, their abode is Hell"; V.76 "He who associates (other things) with God, God will forbid him the Garden and his abode will be the Fire," and many others. Occasionally one finds for "abode" (*ma'wā*) also related expressions such as *mathwan, maw'id, mihād, ma'āb*, etc.; compare VI.128 "the Fire is your dwelling place, abide in it for ever"; XV.43 "and verily Hell is the dwelling place for all of them"; VII.39 "for them there is Hell as a bed"; XXXVIII.55–56 "and verily, for the wrongdoers will be an evil end: Hell, they will burn in it; (it is) an evil bed"; etc.

33. Compare the lexica and for example also the *ummahāt* "mothers" or *elementa simlicia* (= *basā'iṭ*) with the *mawalladāt* "mothers," the "derived structure or compound" (= *mukarrabāt*); Qazwīnī I, 301 = Sacy, *Chrest*[2], III, 180 (see also ibid., 485 above; for *basā'iṭ* and *mukarrabāt* compare, for example, still, Ibn Ya'īsh 1122; Bayḍāwī I, 11, etc.)

34. For euphemism by curses, see Goldziher, *Abhandlgg. z̧ arab. Philologic*, I, 39 f.

35. Nābira, *Complément*, p. 54; *Lisān* and *Tāj al-'arus* under *hawā*. With the latter, *matīn*, "very solid" for *mubīn* "clear," that perhaps deserves preference.

36. *Kāmil* 727; *Ḥamasah* 382. With a few insignificant variations.

37. In Franz Delitzsch, *Kommentar zu Job*, to VI, 2.

38. Compare to *mā dhā* in the classical language the interesting chapter of Maqqarī, *Annalectes*, II, 517. The interpretation of the rest of the verses, see *Lisān* XIV 296 (= *Tāj al-'arus* VIII, 190); Ibn al-Sikkit, *Alfāẓ*, 576; *Khizānah*, IV, 375; *Sharḥ shawāhid al-Kashshāf* 48.

39. For reflection, compare Maqqarī II, 518 and 519, among others.

40. Ahlwardt—I take into account naturally only the two verses which concern us here—has the incorrect *al-ṣubha* and *al-layla* instead of *al-ṣubhu* and *al-laylu*; compare with Nöldeke, *ZDMG* (57): 209.

41. Imru al-Qays is regarded as the author; compare ed. Ahlwardt 134, no. 29; Lexika under the entry *nafar* and *namī*, Lane under *nafar*, and Maydānī, ed. Freytag II, p. 624, no. 112.

42. *'Alā 'al-aks*. This enantisemantic expression obviously belongs in the large chapter on the expression *li-l-tafā'ul* (to regard as a good omen) (see my *Marrok. Sprichwörter, Mitteilungen aus d. Sem. f. Or. Sprachen*, I, *Westas. Studien*, 203, note 1). Compare as especially relevant here "may Allāh shame him (*akhzā-hu Allāh*)" (see the Lexica), as well as "you have no father (*lā abā laka*)," Ḥarīrī, *Maqāmāt*, ed. Sacy[2] I, 165 with commentary.

43. The verse reads: "He is the one who has sent down the book to you: in it are verses of established meaning; they are the foundation (*umm*) of the book: others are ambiguous. But those in whose hearts is perversity follow the part that is ambiguous seeking discord and searching for its meaning. No one knows its meaning except Allah . . ."

44. Compare for example the beginning of our sura: "The calamity! What is the calamity? And what will convey to you what the calamity is?" the beginning of Surah LXIX: "The reality! What is the reality? And what will convey to you what the reality is?" and so forth.

45. I know very well that the Quran has no lack of reiterations (compare for example with regard to our sura itself, verse 5b with LXIX.21, verse 4 with LXX.9 and verse 5a and 6a with VII.7 f., and XXIII.104 f.). Hence, the same expressions appearing two or more times do not necessarily mean that one has been interpolated. If however one passage is already suspect, their agreement with one another naturally becomes a further suspicious fact.

46. Qatādah also acknowledged that (according to al-Ṭabarī and Khaṭīb), who calls *hāwiyah* an Arabic word (*kalimah ʿarabīyah*). Compare also according to Niẓām al-Dīn "this is from the usage of the Arabs" and so forth.

47. To a certain degree this difference is always acknowledged by the modern Arabic studies also. But that it was larger than one in general had accepted until now, I have tried to show in 1903 at the General Philologist Conference in Halle in a lecture *Zur Entstehung der Orthographie des Schriftarabischen* (see *Verhandlangen*, page 154), which I hope to be able to publish soon in expanded form.

48. See Flügel's concordance under the entry *ʿarabī*. This description that Muḥammad spoke classical Arabic is put forth more in the later official view of Muslims. Compare *Muzhir*, ed. Būlāq, 1282, I, 103:

> The most eloquent person (in Arabic) under any circumstances is our master and our lord, the Messenger of God. . . . The Messenger of God (p.b.u.h.) said: "I am the most eloquent of the Arabs." The foreign companions related it and they related it also with the wording "I am the most eloquent of those who speaks with the *ḍād*" (a letter peculiar to Arabic and hence can refer to the Arabic language).

49. See Suyūṭī's *Itqān*, Calcutta 1852–84, 267; compare also 282 ff.

6.3

Regarding Qur'ān CI.6

A. Fischer

Translated by Herbert Berg

In my article "A Qur'ānic Interpolation" I tried to show that the Qur'ānic verse: "And as for him whose scales are light, his mother is *hāwiyah*" (Qur'ān CI.6) meant for the Prophet: "And whose scale is light, his mother will become childless (that is, he perishes)." And I tried to show that the meaning of *hāwiyah* as hell, as it is presented in the two final verses of the sura: "What will convey to you what it is? A blazing fire," was only brought in artificially. I wish here to further support my argument through reference to the Muslim Qur'ānic exegetes. To be precise, even the oldest of them usually forcibly interpreted the term "hell" into the Qur'ān. Obviously this is because their religious imagination, unfruitful in coming up with other ideas, always preferred the image of the unbelievers in damnation (as contrasted with the believers in paradise). One can compare in this connection, how the Qur'ānic commentary expresses itself to *wayl* (woe) in Qur'ān II.73

> Woe to those who write the Book with their hands and then say: "This is from Allāh" in order to buy with it (something) of little value! Woe to them for what their hands write and woe to them for what they earn.

For example, al-Ṭabarī (I, 286):

From *ZDMG* 60 (1906): 371–74.

Fa-wayl: the interpreters differed with respect to the statement *fa-wayl*.

Some of them advocated what Abū Kurayb related from ʿUthmān ibn Saʿīd from Bishr ibn ʿUmārah from Abū Rawf from al-Ḍaḥḥāk from Ibn ʿAbbās, (who) said: *fa-wayl la-hum*, "Punishment is upon them."

Others advocated what Bashshār related from Ibn Mahdī from Sufyān from Ziyād ibn Fayyāḍ, (who) said, "I heard Abū ʿIyāḍ say, 'The *wayl* is the pus[1] that flows in the base of Hell (*jahannam*).' " Bishr ibn Abān al-Khaṭṭāb related from Wakīʿ from Sufyān from Ziyād ibn Fayyāḍ from Abū ʿIyāḍ, (who) said concerning the statement *fa-wayl*, "A cistern in the base of Hell in which flows their pus." ʿAlī ibn Sahl al-Ramlī related from Zayd ibn Abī al-Zarqāʾ from Sufyan from Ziyād ibn Fayyāḍ from Abū ʿIyāḍ, (who) said, "The *wayl* is a river of pus in Hell." Ibn Ḥumayd related from Miḥrān from Shaqīq, (who) said, "*Wayl* is water which flows with pus in the base of Hell."

Yet others advocated what al-Muthannā related from Ibrāhīm ibn ʿAbd al-Salām ibn Ṣāliḥ al-Tumtari from ʿAlī ibn Jarīr from Ḥammād ibn Salamah from ʿAbd al-Ḥamīd ibn Jaʿfar from Kinānah al-ʿAdawī from ʿUthmān ibn ʿAffān from the Messenger of Allāh (p.b.u.h.) (who) said, "The *wayl* is a mountain in the Fire." Yūnus related from Ibn Wahb from ʿAmr ibn al-Ḥārith related from Darrāj from Abū al-Haytham from Abū Saʿīd from the Prophet (p.b.u.h.), (who) said, "*Wayl* is a river in Hell into which the unbeliever falls for forty autumns before he reaches its bottom."

Abū Jaʿfar [al-Ṭabarī] said, "The meaning of the verse based on what was related above concerning the interpretation of *wayl* is that the punishment of drinking pus by the people Hell in the lowest part of the *Jahīm* is for the Jews who write falsehood with their hands and then say, 'This is from Allāh.' "

Bayḍāwī:

Fa-wayl, that is, the sighing and destruction. Whoever said that it was a river or a mountain in Hell, he means that in it (Hell) is a place which is occupied it by the one for whom the *wayl* is made. Perhaps it is called that metaphorically.

There are also other examples. Naturally, this exegesis has its echo in the lexicography; compare al-Jawharī under *wayl*:

ʿAṭaʾ ibn Yasār said, "The *wayl* is a river in Hell. If the mountains were sent into it, they would melt from its heat."

Lisān al-ʿarab under *wayl* (XIV, 266):

Wayl is a river in Hell and *wayl* is one of its gates. In the *Ḥadīth* from Abū Saʿīd al-Khudrī, he said, "The Messenger of Allāh (p.b.u.h.) said, 'The *wayl* is a river in Hell into which the unbeliever falls for forty autumns. If the mountains were sent into it, they would melt from its heat before they reached its bottom. Al-Ṣaʿūd[2] is a mountain of fire in which he (the unbeliever) ascends seventy autumns. Then he falls likewise. . . .' " Ibn al-ʿAnbārī said, "The *wayl* of Satan and his lamenting. Concerning the *wayl* are three teachings: Ibn Masʿūd said, 'The *wayl* is a river in Hell,' " etc.

Qāmūs under *wayl*:

Wayl is the word "punishment" and a river in Hell, or a spring, or a gate to it."

(See also *Tāj al-ʿarus* under *wayl*). Here therefore, a whole crowd of old—indeed the oldest traditionalists and Qurʾānic—exegetes, among them a man such as al-Ṭabarī himself (whom one would not easily assess as a dimwit), have construed a word as well known as *wayl*, which outside the Qurʾān and the pious tradition no one would have given a meaning for other than "woe," without much circumlocution to be a place in Hell: a river or a cistern of pus[3] that flows from the damned, a fountain, a river valley, a mountain, a section of hell, and so on. Indeed, they have not shrunk from putting these interpretations partly in the mouth of the Prophet himself. How, then, is one supposed to make much with the rare *hāwiyah* in Qurʾān CI, with which one does not know how to start?

Actually we are justified in believing the oldest Muslims, by their own lack of training in literary things in matters of Qurʾānic interpretation, capable of every stupidity. It is obvious the Prophet himself was not conceptually completely clear over all kinds passages in his revelations!

Vollers (who agrees in the remainder of my explanation of Qurʾān CI.6–8) referred me to Wellhausen's German Wāqidī ("Muhammed in Medina") at the bottom of page 35. There Wellhausen translates the expression "he comes to his mother" *al-hāwiyah*: "(ʿUmar . . . requested him to be allowed to chop off a head,) whereupon he returned nothingness home to his mother." At this point Wellhausen gave the notice: "Compare to Job 1:21, Psalm 9:18 and perhaps תהו to *al-hāwiyah* (Qur'ān 101:6)." However, *al-hāwiyah* is nowhere called "the nothing" and תהו has nothing to do etymologically with *al-hāwiyah* (Qur'ān CI.6 calls it only *hāwiyah*!); also the notion, that the man had emerged from nothingness and with his death returns to nothingness, would not be Muslim, but pagan. I explain the expression as the closely related:

> They went to his mother. He was brought low by it to his mother *al-hāwiyah*. You united with your mother *al-hāwiyah al-hāwiyah*.

For other examples that I have dealt with elsewhere, see pages 397–422.

NOTES

1. Compare Qur'ān XIV.19, "In front of him is Hell and he is made to drink from festering (*ṣadīd*) water."
2. Compare with Qur'ān LXXIV.17.
3. *Ṣadīd*. See the Qur'ānic commentaries and the lexicons.

6.4

THREE DIFFICULT PASSAGES IN THE KORAN

C. C. Torrey

I. "RAQĪM" AND DECIUS

XVIII. 8–25

In the first part of the eighteenth sura Muhammad alludes, in a characteristically cryptic way, to the Seven Sleepers of Ephesus, Christians who took refuge in a cave, at a time of severe persecution, and after being walled in by their pursuers slept there for about two hundred years, at the end of which time they were awakened and came forth.

It is plain that Muhammad has heard the story recently and been interested by it; that he has tried to tell it for the edification of his followers, but has been embarrassed by the questions of certain unbelievers, who very possibly knew the story better than he did. He accordingly produces a "revelation," in which he tiptoes around the story, incidentally giving his divine authority for refusing to answer foolish queries.

In verse 8 he introduces the subject with the question, "What think you of those associated with the cave *and with al-Raqīm*? Was not their experience a wonderful sign?" What the word *raqīm* means here has been an unsolved mystery. Some commentators explain it as the name of the mountain in which the cave was, others regard it as the name of the valley below. Others, starting from etymology, suppose it to designate a tablet or

---

From *A Volume of Oriental Studies Presented to E. G. Browne* (Cambridge, 1922), pp. 464–71.

scroll, something *inscribed* (verb *raqama*), which may have been put up over the mouth of the cave in which they lay. But the popular explanation, approved by the majority of native commentators (always with express caution, however), is this, that, *al-raqīm* is the name of *the dog* that accompanied the sleepers, mentioned in verses 17 and 21. This explanation is intrinsically most unlikely. "Raqīm" is all but impossible as a name; moreover, Muhammad could hardly have chosen the form of words which he uses, if this had been his meaning. The dog himself was *ṣāḥıb al-kahf*, or one of "those of the cave," and he plays no important part in the story in any of its forms. It is true that Muhammad shows some interest in this dog, and it is therefore no wonder that his oriental followers, with their love of the whimsical and their own interest in domestic animals, should have given the preference to this explanation of the strange word. But very few scholars, either oriental or occidental, have expressed themselves as really persuaded.

The second of the passages in which the dog is mentioned is interesting as exhibiting Muhammad's somewhat anxious eagerness to show himself well acquainted with the legend. Verse 21: "They will say, Three, and the fourth was their dog; others will say, Five, and the sixth was their dog (guessing wildly [or, as the Arabic might be rendered, 'throwing stones in the dark']); still others will say, Seven; the eighth was their dog. Do *thou* say, My Lord knows best how many there were, and very few others know." It is plain that the Prophet felt "shaky" as to some details of the story; yet it is quite evident on the other hand that he had heard it in a complete version, and knew it well. There was indeed variation in the versions current at that time as to the number of the sleepers; for example, a Syriac manuscript of the 6th century gives the number as eight (Wright's *Catalogue of the Syriac MSS in the British Museum*, 1090).

There is, however, one important and constant feature of the legend, apparently omitted in the Koranic version, which is perhaps really present here in a curious disguise. In all the extant ancient versions of the tale, the tyrant who was the author of the persecution, before whom the seven youths appeared and from whom they fled to their cavern, is the emperor Decius. He is made very prominent in the story, and his name occurs many times. See, for instance, the texts published in Guidi's important monograph, *I Sette Dormienti di Efeso*, where the name Decius is found (repeatedly in each case) in two Coptic (Sahidic) versions, pp. 5 ff., 13 f.;

three Syriac versions, 18 ff., 24 ff., 36 ff.; two Ethiopic versions, 66 f., 87; and two Armenian versions, 91, 96 ff. In two Syriac manuscripts the name is miswritten as Dūgs, or Dūkus, and in still other ways, and in the Christian Arabic version printed by Guidi (51 ff.) the form is Decianus (daqyānūs); but such occasional corruptions count for nothing.

The ordinary way of writing the name Decius in Aramaic would be דקיס, ܕܩܝܘܣ , and this is the orthography which occurs uniformly in the oldest and best Syriac texts, as in the version of this legend in Land's *Anecdota Syriaca*, III, 87, 6, 10; 90, 12 ; 91, 3; 93, 7, etc., and in the version published by Guidi, 36, 2 a f. It is therefore a tempting hypothesis, and to me at least it seems very probable, that when Muhammad's informant, who read or narrated to him this legend of the Seven Sleepers saw in the text before him the name רקיס he read it רקיס instead of דקיס. Not only the Hebrew characters, but also the Aramaic characters of that time and region, could very easily be a ambiguous, as any extensive table of ancient Semitic alphabets will show,[1] and the coincidence appears too striking to be accidental, in view of the supporting circumstances.

2. THE EXCEPTION IN FAVOR OF "THE BLIND, THE CRIPPLE, AND THE SICK"

XXIV.60

A considerable part of Sura XXIV is taken up with prescriptions concerning decent behavior. Muhammad and his immediate circle of followers have been greatly disturbed by the Ayesha scandal, and in dealing now with this most important matter the Prophet takes occasion also to lay down rules in regard to general considerations of chastity, modesty, and allied subjects. According to his mental habit, illustrated in a multitude of Koranic passages, he passes abruptly from one subject to another, and occasionally returns again suddenly to a theme he had previously discussed and seemingly finished.

In verse 27 Muhammad introduces the subject of intruding on the privacy of men or women—but especially women—in their own houses or apartments. He then goes on to speak, in verse 31, of the duty of believing women to avoid uncovering themselves before those who are not members of their families. These are matters lingered in his mind, for he returns to them in this sura and also treats them, in this same order, in Sura XXXIII. The translation (24, 27 ff.): "O ye who believe! enter not into other houses than your own, until ye have asked leave and have saluted its people. That is better for you; perhaps ye will be mindful. 28 And if ye find no one therein, enter not until permission is given you; if it is said to you, 'Go back,' then go back. That is more decent behavior on your part; and God knows what ye do. 29 It is no trespass for you to enter uninhabited houses, if ye have need to do so; God knows what ye reveal and what ye conceal. 30 Say to the believers that they should restrain their eyes and guard their chastity. That is more decent behavior for them; verily God knows what they do. 31 And say to the believing women that they should restrain their eyes and guard their chastity; they should not display their ornaments, except those which are outside; they should pull their veils over their bosoms and not show their ornaments, except to their husbands or fathers, or their husbands' fathers, or their sons, or their husbands' sons, or their brothers, or their brothers' sons, or their sisters' sons, or their women, or their slaves, or the male attendants who are incapable, or to children who do not notice women's nakedness."

In Sura XXXIII.53 ff. he brings forward the same two closely related subjects, in a looser and less concise mode of presentation: "O ye who believe! enter not into the houses of the prophet, unless permission is given you, to partake of food, without awaiting his convenient time. When ye are bidden, then enter; and when ye have partaken, then disperse; without being familiar in conversation, for this would annoy the prophet and he would be ashamed for you; but God is not ashamed of the truth. And when ye ask them (the prophet's wives) for anything, ask it from behind a curtain; that is purer for your hearts and for theirs. . . . 54 Whether ye reveal a thing or conceal it, verily God knows all things. 55 It is no trespass for them (the wives of the prophet) to show themselves unveiled to their fathers, or their sons, or their brothers, or their brothers' sons, or their sisters' sons, or their women, or their slaves; but let them fear God, verily God is witness over all. . . . 59 O thou prophet! say to thy wives and thy daughters, and to the wives of the believers, that they should let down their veils over them. That is more likely to make them understood aright and to protect them from annoyance; God is forgiving and merciful."

The way in which the one of these two passages parallels the other is very noticeable; presumably the passage in Sura XXXIII is the older of the two. As has already been remarked, Muhammad returns again to these subjects farther on in Sura XXIV, namely at verse 57: "O ye who believe! let your slaves and those of you who have not reached puberty ask permission of you (before coming into your presence) at three times in the day: before the prayer of dawn, and when ye put off your garments at midday, and after the evening prayer; three times of privacy for you. It is no trespass for you or for them, after these times, when you are going about from one to another. Thus God makes clear to you the signs, and he is knowing and wise. 58 But when your children arrive at puberty, then let them ask leave of you, as did those before them. Thus God makes clear to you his signs, and he is knowing and wise. 59 As for those women who are past childbearing and have no hope of marriage, it is no trespass for them if they put off their garments, but in such a way as not to display their ornaments; yet if they abstain from this, it is better for them; and God both hears and knows."

The next verse is commonly rendered, and the text seems to require that it be rendered, as follows: 60 "It is no sin for the blind, nor the cripple, nor the sick, nor for you yourselves, to eat in your own houses, or in those of your fathers, or your mothers, or your brothers, or your sisters, or your uncles on the father's side, or your aunts on the father's side, or your uncles on the mother's side, or your aunts on the mother's side, or in those houses of which ye possess the keys, or in the house of your friend; there is no trespass for you in eating either together or separately."

In spite of all attempted explanations of the first part of this verse, the fact remains that "the blind, the cripple, and the sick" have nothing whatever to do with this prescription in regard to eating. Goldziher, in his *Vorlesungen über den Islam*, 33 f., in expressing his conviction that some passages in the Koran have been misplaced with very disturbing result, points to this clause at the beginning of XXIV.60 as the outstanding example. He proceeds: "*Jedoch bei näherer Betrachtung gewahren wir, dass der in diesem Zusammenhange fremdartige Passus aus einer anderen Gruppe von Verordnungen hierher verschlagen wurde. Er bezieht sich ursprünglich nicht auf Teilnahme an Mahlzeiten ausser dem eigenen Hause, sondern auf die an den kriegerischen Unternehmungen des jungen Islams*"(p. 34). He then points out that these same words, " There is no compulsion for the blind, nor for the cripple, nor for the sick," are found also in XLVIII.17, where the Prophet, after threatening those who hold back from the warlike expeditions of the Muslims, makes this exception in favor of those who are effectually hindered by physical disability, and he draws the conclusion that the phrase has somehow been taken from XLVIII.17 and forced into this context in XXIV.60 where it is now so disturbing: "*Dieser Spruch ist nun als fremdes Element in jenen anderen Zusammenhang versprengt worden und hat augenscheinlich die Redaktion des Verses beeinflusst, dessen ursprünglicher Anfang nicht in sicherer Weise rekonstruiert werden kann.*"

Goldziher is certainly right in holding that the clause, as it has traditionally been understood both by Arab commentators and by occidental scholars, is out of place and inexplicable, but it cannot be said that he has accounted for its presence in Sura XXIV. It is hardly conceivable that either Muhammad or any one of his followers should have introduced here purposely the exception as to participants in the holy war, for it is not merely isolated from every context dealing with that subject, but as it stands it quite plainly means something else. On the other hand, no theory of the accidental transfer of the clause to this place could be made to seem plausible. But we are not reduced to any such desperate straits as Goldziher's suggestion would imply. Is not the solution of the difficulty rather this, that the troublesome clause is to be connected with the preceding context, and that the dispensation in favor of "the blind, the lame, and the sick" refers to the regulations regarding modesty with which the Prophet has been so variously busied? We have seen how, in each place where he treats of these matters, he makes some provision for the natural exceptions, those members of the family to whom the freedom of the house must of necessity be given, or who cannot be held under the same restriction as others in regard to privacy and the exposure of their persons in clothing and unclothing themselves; not making the same exceptions in each case, but giving utterance to them as they happen to occur to him. In XXXIII.55 he excepts (of course) the nearest members of the family, and adds that the women of whom he is speaking have no need to be careful about unveiling or unclothing themselves before other women or before their own slaves. In XXIV.31 he makes similar exceptions (but in considerably different terms, showing that he had not formulated the matter carefully for himself), and adds to the list eunuchs and children. And finally, in the passage under discussion, XXIV.57 ff., he mentions as exceptions the slaves and children, and then adds that the restrictions do not apply in their stringency to women who have passed the age of marriage. To this he further adds as an afterthought (if I am right), that a similar liberty is to be allowed to the members of a household who are under serious physical disability. The justice of this, even its necessity, is quite obvious.

The one objection that could be urged is the abruptness of the transition from the first clause of verse 60 to the passage that immediately follows, treating of a different subject but in its grammatical construction a continuation of the closest description. But this sudden and unexpected leap is, I would contend, thoroughly characteristic of Muhammad's mental habit. The verse granting dispensation to old women is brought to an end with the usual rhyming appendix; a new verse is then begun as follows:

laysa ʿalā-l-ʾaʿmā ḥarajun walā ʿalā-l-marīḍi
ḥarajun walāʿ alāʾanfusikum ʾan taʾkulū min buyūtikum . . .

"Upon the blind, the cripple, and the sick there is no strict prohibition. Nor is there (such prohibition) upon you yourselves, against your eating in your own houses, or the houses of your fathers," and so on. This is the mental habit—essentially dramatic—of him who composed the oft-quoted verse XII.29, in which the transition is equally unexpected and even more abrupt, taking place, as in the present instance, in the middle of a sentence. Other illustrations of the same general character will occur to all those who are familiar With the Koran. As for the verbal agreement of the clause with XLVIII.17, this is by no means the only instance in which Muhammad repeats an extended phrase in widely different contexts.

3. "HIS MOTHER IS HĀWIYA"

CI.6–8

In an essay entitled "Eine Qoran-Interpolation" contributed to the Nöldeke *Festschrift*, I, 33–55, August Fischer attempts to demonstrate that the last two verses, 7 and 8, of Sura CI are a later interpolation. He returns to the subject in the *ZDMG* (62 [1910]: 371–74), bringing some additional evidence in support of his contention, which he regards as sufficiently established. Goldziher, in his *Vorlesungen über den Islam* (1910), p. 33, refers to this demonstration of Fischer's in a way that seems to show that he regards it as conclusive. Any modern critical edition of the text of the Koran, he says, "wird . . . auf Interpolationen (vgl. August Fischer, in der Nöldeke *Festschrift*, 33 ff.) ihr Augenmerk richten müssen."

The matter is one of considerable importance for the early history of the Koran, inasmuch as interpolations in the sacred book (excepting those made by Muhammad himself) have not hitherto been demonstrated in a convincing way. Fischer's examination of the evidence is in some particulars very thorough, and makes a first impression of being exhaustive. He has failed, however, to take into account one or two factors of capital importance, as I shall endeavor to show.

Sura CI is one of the most vigorous and picturesque of Muhammad's early utterances, a veritable gem. It is a terse characterization of the coming Dies Irae, when the last hour strikes, in the universal crash of dissolving heavens and earth, and the just and unjust of mankind are sent to the abodes they have deserved. It also has the external appearance of being a very characteristic specimen of the Prophet's peculiar rhetoric. It begins and ends with brief, exclamatory phrases, while the middle portion is made up of slightly longer sentences. There are two rhymes, of which the principal is the "asonante" termination with the vowels *ā-i-ah*, the woeful *ah!* in particular, with its voiced *h*, being just suited to the theme. This rhyme, after appearing in verses 1 and 2, is replaced by another in the purely descriptive verses 3 and 4, and is then resumed in 5–8. The text of these last four verses reads as follows:

(5) *fa ʾammā man thaqulat mawāzīnuhu fahuwa fī ʿīshatin rāḍiyatin*
(6) *waʾ ammā man khaffat mawāzīnuhu fa ʾummuhu hāwiyah*
(7) *wa mā ʾadrāka mā hiyah*
(8) *narun ḥāmiyah*

This is ordinarily translated somewhat as follows: " 5 Then as for the one whose balances are heavy, he (enters) into a joyful life; 6 but as for him whose balances are light, his abode is the pit. 7 And how dost thou know what this is? 8 A raging fire!"

The starting point of Fischer's argument is the difficult phrase at the end of verse 6, *fa ʾummuhu hāwiyah*. He urges, very justly, that the current renderings (similar to the one just given) are more than questionable.

Hāwiyah (without the article!) ought not to be rendered "*the* pit." There is indeed a well-known Arabic noun appearing in a variety of forms, of which this is one, meaning "pit, abyss, precipice," and the like; but there are good reasons why we cannot believe that Muhammad is using it here. He could not have omitted the article, in such a context, unless he intended Hāwiya as a proper name, and it seems quite unlikely that he would have made this transformation of a noun of the native speech. More important still is the fact, emphasized by Fischer (*Festschrift*, 45), that the immediately following phrase, *mā adrāka* . . . , is always used in a very significant way by Muhammad, in connection with new and strange vocables of his own introducing: "*sonst stets nur an Wörter angeknüpft, die er entweder selbst der Form oder dem Inhalt nach neu geprägt hatte, oder die doch für seine Zuhörer völlig neu sein mussten.*" Fischer argues further, that *ʾummuhu* (literally "*his mother*") with the meaning " his *abode*" or "his *lot*," is not a natural use of the word, but sounds artificial. Finally he shows, with a thoroughness of demonstration that leaves nothing to be desired, that the phrase *hawat ʾummuhu*, as used by the Arabs in and before Muhammad's time, meant "his mother is bereft (of him)." That is—and to this every Arabic scholar must give assent—the only natural translation of verse 6 *taken by itself* is: "And as for the one whose balances are light, his mother is (now to be) childless." But verses 7 and 8 are absolutely incompatible with this rendering, for they presuppose a reference in the phrase to the place of abode of the wicked. Hence Fischer sees himself forced to the conclusion that the sura originally ended with verse 6, and that verses 7 and 8 are a later, mistaken addition.

The argument seems a strong one at first sight, but the more one thinks it over the less convincing it appears. The very considerations that make the present reading difficult stand opposed to the hypothesis of an interpolation; just in proportion as it is strange that *ʾummuhu* should mean "his abode," and evident that *hāwiyah in its present context* is an anomaly, does it become improbable that any later hand should have created this manifest incongruity deliberately, making a stupid and quite useless addition to what was clear, and changing the meaning of the sacred words. Sura CI, be it remembered, is one of the oldest of Muhammad's Meccan utterances, and from its contents, as well as from its striking form, we should suppose it to have been one of the most widely familiar. Very many of his Companions and followers must have known it by heart, from the first. Fischer attempts to break the force of this obvious objection to his theory by arguing (p. 51 f.) that Muhammad's Companions and their contemporaries in Mecca and Medina were unfamiliar with the phrase *ummuhū hāwiya*, and did not know that it meant "his mother is bereaved." The Prophet, he thinks, got this idiom from the classical speech (*'arabīya*), which was too high-style for his Companions generally. I do not believe that many Arabic scholars will find help in this extraordinary suggestion of Professor Fischer. It is easy to show, as he does by the citations in Tabari, that some of the Companions were more or less perplexed by the phrase *as it stands in this sura*, but this gives no evidence whatever that they were ignorant of its "classical" use. Moreover, Mecca and Medina were not beyond the reach of the *'arabiya*; if Abu Bekr and Omar did not know the classical idioms of their day, as Muhammad used them in the Koran, they had only to ask their meaning; there were plenty at hand who knew. It should be added, with emphasis, that if the sura had originally ended with verse 6, as Fischer contends, its concluding words would never have made any difficulty. Everyone who knew the typical meanings of the verb *hawā* (and did not the Companions of the Prophet know as much as this?) could have guessed without fail the signification of the idiom. Fischer explains (p. 52), that when they were perplexed by it, they "saw from the context" that the words must contain an allusion to the place of punishment. Thereupon some Koran expert, "*von den besten Absichten geleitet*," added verses 7 and 8—in order to make everything plain! But the context, up to the end of verse 6, gives no such indication nor is there anything in either form or content of any of Muhammad's other utterances in the Koran that could naturally lead the reader to infer from CI.1–6a that verse 6b contained a designation of hell.

The supposed motive of the interpolation, then, is certainly not cogent; when closely examined it is not even plausible. We are left simply with the fact of a difficult reading and the question whether the supposition of two writers, one of whom misunderstood the other—always a desperate expedient—is the probable solution.

Examination of the two verses, 7 and 8, supposed by Fischer to have been added by a later hand, shows that, apart from the postulated incongruity with verse 6, they give no support whatever to his theory, but rather testify strongly against it. Fischer remarks (p. 51) on the strangeness of *hiyah*, at the end of verse 6: "*sonst nicht im ganzen Qorān!*"

But the very strangeness is testimony that Muhammad, and not another, wrote it. This is one of the rhymes in which he especially revels, in some of the earliest and most fiery passages of his book. A good example is LXIX.4–29, where for the sake of this very same "asonante" rhyme *ā-i-ah* he builds out the suffix of the first person singular, changing *kitābī sulṭanī* and so on into *kitābiyah sulṭāniyah*, and so on, in six different instances. The *mā hiyah* of CI.7 is merely another case of exactly the same sort. We can recognize in it at once the voice of Muhammad, knowing his rhetorical habits as we do; but it would not readily have suggested itself as an imitation of the Prophet, and no mere interpolator would ever have produced it. The imitator, had there been such, would infallibly have written : (or *al-hāwiyah*) *wa mā ʾadrāka mā hāwiyah*, since this is the way in which Muhammad proceeds in every other instance of the kind. It is from the originator of these forms, not from lesser scribblers, that we expect such sporadic yet characteristic variation.

Fischer's assertion (ibid.) in regard to verse 8 is so astonishing that one is tempted to see in it a virtual admission of the weakness of his argument as it touches the verses supposed to be interpolated.[2] In the process of attempting to show that this "appendix" to the sūra is made of inferior stuff, he says that the phrase *narum ḥamiyah* is the weakest and least poetical of all the expressions for "hell" in the Koran ("*der prosaischste und platteste Ausdruck*") and designates it again as "*armselig*." If this is a deliberate judgment and not a mere hasty utterance, we can only be thankful that the impassioned Meccan suras were composed by Muhammad and not by his critic. It would be possible, of course, to employ six words, or a dozen, or more, instead of the two used here; or to search out strange locutions, or circumlocutions, instead of taking the most familiar noun in the Arabic language and the adjective made obvious by sense and meter; but the man who thinks "*raging fire*" not forcible enough as a description of the future abode of the wicked is the one who is laboring with an argument, not the one who (like many of Muhammad's contemporaries) thinks himself in danger of going there. The fact is, it is impossible to conceive a more powerful ending of the little chapter than that which it has. From the standpoint of rhetoric, the termination with verse 6 would have been very tame in comparison.

The whole sura was composed by Muhammad himself, whatever may be the solution of the difficulty at the end of verse 6. This is the conclusion very strongly indicated by all the evidence at hand. We can then hardly escape the further conclusion, that *hāwiyah* was intended by him as a proper name, as it certainly was intended as a designation of hell. But if the word was familiar to him and his fellows as a common noun, why did he not treat it as such, using the article; and—an equally puzzling question—why did he choose the strange *ʾummuhu* instead of *maʾwāh* or a similar word?

It seems to me that Professor Fischer has left out of account, in his argument, one of the most important characteristics of the Prophet's literary art, namely his singular fondness for mystifying words and phrases. This tendency is especially conspicuous, and often especially crude in its manifestation, in the oldest portions of the Koran. He coins words of his own, and far more often borrows them from foreign languages, with what seems to us an almost childlike delight in the awesome riddles that he thus furnished to his hearers. We certainly have an example of the kind, and apparently a twofold example, in the passage before us.

Muhammad chose the phrase *ʾummuhu hāwiyah* not because the people of Mecca did not know the meaning of the idiom *hawat ʾummuhu*, but precisely because he knew it was so familiar to them all. Whoever heard Sura CI for the first time would suppose verse 6 to contain the threat: "He whose balances are light shall perish (his mother shall be bereaved)." But as the Prophet went on, the hearer would see that the threat was far more terrible. *Hāwiyah*, instead of being the participial adjective, was a mysterious *name* of a blazing fire, while *ʾummuhu* contained the grimly ironical assurance that his acquaintance with Hāwiya would not be merely temporary; she would be his permanent keeper and guardian. This is wordplay of a kind in which the Arabs have always taken special delight; but it is more than this, it is Muhammad through and through, in its combination of mystery and threat. The quality of strangeness, in fact, is present in every part of this little Sura, not by accident.

Finally, in regard to the word *hāwiyah*, I believe that the supposition of a borrowed word, always the most probable hypothesis when a strange theological term is encountered in the Koran, has not in this instance been given the attention it deserves. I should not deny the possibility that Muhammad may have created the proper name from a native Arabic noun, but the supposition is an unlikely one, as Fischer and others have argued with good reason. The only excuse for such a proceeding here would be the wish to make the wordplay just described, but even this could hardly have seemed a sufficient reason. Moreover, it is not likely that Muhammad would have used his *mā ʾadrāka* with reference to a *noun* whose meaning was already known; the case of *adjectives* such as *al-gāriʿa al-ḥāqqa*, and the like is obviously quite different. He employs the very significant phrase only after using words whose meaning must really have remained obscure without the interpretation which he—by the help of Gabriel—proceeded to give them.

Among the old Hebrew words for the final catastrophe that is to overtake the wicked, there is one that corresponds *exactly*, in both form and meaning, to Muhammad's *Hāwiya*. The passage in which it occurs most significantly is Isa. 47:2, in a chapter that describes in very striking and picturesque language the doom of Babylon. Hebrew: *tippol ʿālayikᵉ howāh lōʾ tūkᵉlīy kapporah*, "There will fall upon thee *Disaster* which thou wilt not be able to propitiate." In form, this word *howāh* [Hebrew] is the active participle feminine of the *qal* stem of *hwh* [Hebrew] "to fall." Just what sort of "disaster" the Prophet had in mind is made plain in the following verses, in which Babylon's helpers and advisers are promised a share in her doom; verse 14: "They shall be as stubble, the fire shall burn them; they shall not deliver themselves from the grasp of the flame. It will not be coals to warm at, nor a fire to sit before!" We have, then, in one of the most striking passages in the Hebrew Bible, the same word, with the same meaning, that we find in our Koran passage. It occurs in the Old Testament also in Ezek. 7:26, *howāh ʿal howāh* [Hebrew], "Disaster upon disaster," and is therefore not a word upon which any doubt can be thrown.

It would be interesting to discuss the corresponding or most nearly related words in Hebrew and the Aramaic dialects, the complicated questions of borrowing from one language by another, and so on; but all this would be a mere waste of time as concerns the present question. We have before us a perfect explanation of the troublesome passage in Sura CI, and have no need to look further. In every detail of the composition we can see Muhammad's own well-known habits and mental processes: his high-sounding rhetoric, his fondness for strange vocables, the gleaning of new terms from Jewish sources—of whatever sort. There is not the slightest difficulty in explaining how Muhammad got hold of this particular word; every educated Jew had it at his tongue's end. The whole splendid passage in Isaiah may well have been recited to Muhammad many times, with appropriate paraphrase or comment in his own tongue, for his edification. The few " hellfire passages" in the Hebrew Scriptures must have been of special interest to him, and it would be strange if some teacher had not been found to gratify him in this respect.

Observe further—and the fact is most important—that the pet phrase *mā ʿadrāka*, is used here in the very same significant way as elsewhere, that is, after a truly *cryptic* utterance; see especially Fischer's own words, quoted above. Note in particular that in *seven* of the ten other occurrences of the phrase in the Koran, the strange term to which it calls attention is either a designation of the Last Judgment or else (twice; 83, 8, 19) of certain definite features of the judgment scene; three of the terms, *saqar*, *sijjīn*, and *ʿilliyyūn*, are *proper names*, apparently created by Muhammad himself; three of them, *sijjīn*, *ʿilliyyūn*, and *yawm ad-dīn*, are borrowed from Jewish sources.

As for the word *ʾummuhu*, scholar Khafājī was quite right in regarding it as an example of Muhammad's "sarcasm" (Fischer, p. 41), and the wordplay I have described above, with its sudden and ironical transformation of the familiar into the strange and terrible, is as characteristic as anything in the Koran. The word *Hāwiya* should, of course, be written *hāwiyatu*, as a diptote. As originally used in this Koran passage, by Muhammad and his followers, it had the ending of neither diptote nor triptote, but merely the rhyming termination *ah*. That the native commentators, even the oldest, should have stumbled over the phrase was not only natural but also quite inevitable. The word was Muhammad's own, and they had no means of knowing where he got it.

The translation of verses 6 ff.:

As for him whose balances are light his mother is Hāwiya! And how knowest thou what that is? A raging fire!

NOTES

1. For the Hebrew characters, see Euting's *Tabula Scripturae Hebraicae* (accompanying Chwolson's *Corpus Inscriptionum Hebraicarum*), cols. 67–83, fifth and sixth centuries A.D.; and for the Aramaic, *Euting's Tabula Scripturae Aramaicae* (1890), cols. 41–53, and also 33–40. The ambiguity might have

occurred in any one of several varieties of the West Semitic script of about Muhammad's time; but it is perhaps most probable that the document in question was written in Hebrew characters.

2. A similar tacit admission is to be seen in the suggestion on p. 52, that verses 7 and 8 may, after all, have been "an old Koran fragment"!

6.5

A Strange Reading in the Qur'ān

C. C. Torrey

The wonderful book is, of course, full of strange readings. The Prophet himself warned his hearers that there were *āyāt* that no mere human being could fully understand (III.5), and aside from these deeper mysteries there are difficulties that every student of the Qur'ān encounters. The new dress of new ideas, and the background of shifting conditions, provide obscurities enough; just what was it, we ask in this or that case, that the Prophet had in mind?

The example here to be considered is of quite another character. We seem to be sufficiently informed about the circumstances, and the matter treated is one of a familiar nature. It concerns the duty and the behavior of Muslims in times when the cause of Islam calls for the active service of all its able-bodied men. Muhammad's practical wisdom is unfailing, and the advice, or command, to be issued in this case seems, by whatever knowledge we possess, to be definitely suggested; that which is actually said, however, leaves us in some bewilderment.

The passage in question is LXIV.14,[1] near the end of a short sura that is built around the command to believe and obey God and his messenger (verses 8 and 12). In the concluding portion of this sura, verses 14–18, the Prophet introduces again a subject upon which he touches in numerous other places, namely, the danger that the cares and joys of family life will turn aside the Muslim from his duty to the Muhammadan cause.

C. C. Torrey, "A Strange Reading in the Qur'ān," in *Ignace Goldhizer Memorial Volume*, ed. S. Lowinger and J. de Somogyi (Budapest: Globus, 1948).

It is a typical situation, illustrated in many places. An especially familiar example is afforded by the advice given by the apostle Paul to his converts in Corinth. Persuaded that the time was short, while much remained to be done, he would prefer that the men in his churches should not marry. "The unmarried man," he says, "is anxious about the affairs of the Lord, how to please the Lord; but the married man is anxious about worldly affairs, how to please his wife, and his interests are divided" (1 Cor. 7:32–34).

Muhammad's treatment of the matter, in the present context, is typically just and considerate. Worldly goods and children are a temptation (verse 15); but if a man is saved from his own self-seeking, he is one of the really prosperous. The true believer must give both himself and his substance to the holy cause, serving God "*as much as he can*" (verse 16). That which is lacking of his achievement will be mercifully overlooked, for "If you lend to God a goodly loan, he will double it for you, and will forgive you: for God is gratefid and element" (verse 17).

But in verse 14 we find the following singular utterance: *yā ayyuhā ʾlladhīna āmanū inna min azwājikum wa aulādikum ʿaduwwan lakum fa ʾḥdharūhum wa-in taʿfū wa taṣfaḥū wa taghfirū fa-inna ʾllāha ghafūrun raḥīmun*. "O you who believe! Verily among your wives and children are foes of yours, so beware of them! *But if you forgive, and overlook, and pardon, verily God is forgiving and merciful.*" I am not aware that any commentator, ancient or modern, has found difficulty in this last sentence, though some undertake to explain it. Every utterance of sacred scripture that is clearly expressed in unequivocal and familiar language, with the text of the passage under no suspicion of corruption, is readily accepted and easily "explained," as we all know. But the sentence before us, if it were in a less sacred book than the Qurʾān, would be pronounced mere nonsense.

The wives and children of many a Muslim were dangerous "enemies" to him, it is true, but simply because they were so strong a temptation, as verse 15 reiterates. Temptation can be resisted. The man with a wife and family, with a duty to his home, must inevitably fall short of his full effort for the common cause, at the time when active service for Islam is demanded of all those who can render it; but *if he turns away from the temptation*, doing for God and his Prophet "as much as he can," (verse 16, he can be pardoned.

The woman commits no crime by marrying a true believer, nor by continuing to perform the duties and enjoy the privileges of a wife; nor are the children to blame for being born into the Muslim world and continuing for years to be a burden of care and expense. They do not require to be "forgiven" for the strong attraction they exert. They are enemies to loyal Muslims in the same way that strong drink is an enemy to the man addicted to it. He could not acquire merit by "forgiving" his bottle. Nor would it follow, by any means, that the delinquent and self-indulgent Muslim who should "pardon" his wife and children for keeping him from his duty, would be let off, inasmuch as "God is forgiving and merciful"; neither Muhammad nor any other leader in his place ever uttered such folly. The apostle Paul did not say that if the Christian would forgive his wife, all would be well.

In view of this plain condition of things, it is all the more noticeable that three successive words meaning "forgive" are employed here (where there is nothing to forgive!), as though for special emphasis. Muhammad very frequently uses two synonyms in emphatic statement: indeed, two of the three verbs now before us, *ʿafā* and *ṣafaḥa*, are thus joined in three other passages in the Qur'ān, always with the same meaning, "forgive" (or, "forgive and pass over"). In II.103 (B 108) the form is the plural of the imperative, *waʿfū wa'ṣfaḥū*; in V.16 (B 12) it is the imperative singular, *waʿfu wa'ṣfaḥ*; and in XXIV.22 (B 21), the jussive plural, *wa'l-yaʿfū wa'l-yaṣfaḥū*. The phrase was evidently fixed in the mind of the Prophet. In each of the three cases the reason for emphasis is obvious, but in no one of the three could a student of the Qur'ān imagine the Prophet employing *three* verbs.

There are still other points of difficulty in the passage. The *fa-inna* clause enters rather abruptly, and its meaning is not made quite clear. It appears to say that if the Muslim will forgive his wife and children for their evil influence, Allah also will forgive them; but we know that this cannot be the meaning, for the person to be forgiven (if he deserves it) is the householder himself, no one else.

In short, as was said above, the verse as it stands is bewildering. It does not sound like an utterance of the Prophet, either in its rhetoric or in its practical content.

In Sura VIII, with its atmosphere of the battle of Badr, Muhammad gives to his followers the same warning that is given in Sura LXIV. Islam needs all its men and all their resources, and there must be no paltering;

it is no time for a Muslim to be taking his ease at home. Verse 27 (B 26), "O you who believe! Do not play false (*lā takhūnū*) with God and his messenger, nor betray your trust! Know that your possessions and your children are a temptation (*wa'lamū innamā amwālukum wa auladukum fitnatun*)," the same words which occur in LXIV:15. And he concludes by saying in effect: "If you will serve God, he will repay, and forgive."

The situation is serious enough. The Prophet's words to his adherents are not a mere recommendation, they are a stern warning. The Muslim who is the head of a family is at best handicapped in the effort to do his duty, and is in real danger of betraying his trust and playing false with Allah and his Prophet. "Beware of the foes in your own household!" Thereupon would be expected: "*But if you restrain yourselves, and turn away* (from the temptation), you will be forgiven" (*wa-in ta'iffū wa taṣfaḥū yughfar lakum*).

The two verbs in the protasis of this conditional sentence are precisely the ones to expect, neither one could be improved upon. The verb *'affa* is typical in classical Arabic for the expression of *abstinence*, and *ṣafaḥa*, "turn away, retrain, refuse," and the like, is definitely the verb to be associatcd with it in the present context. The resemblance of this phrase to the words of LXIV.14, *wa in ta'fū wa taṣfaḥū wa taghfirū*, is startling, and the temptation to examine the matter further is too strong to be resisted.

As far as the Qur'ānic usage is concerned there is very little that needs to be said. Muhammad does not happen to use the first stem of the verb *'affā*, elsewhere in the Qur'ān, but employs other stems (the fifth and tenth) several times, of course with the usual meaning. Aside from the examples already mentioned, the verb *ṣafaḥa* occurs in the Qur'ān in two passages, XV.85 and XLIII.4. In both of these, the verb appears to have its original signification, "turn away," rather than the derived meaning, "forgive."

Sura XLIII is a fairly early utterance, belonging to the Meccan period. A *Qur'ān* in the Arabic language is announced in the first verses, and the Prophet is istructed to say: "Shall we, then, turn away from you utterly (*ṣafḥan*) the admonition?" The meaning of the complementary object (*al-maf'ūl al-muṭlaq*) is assured.

Sura XV, also of the Meccan period and of about the same time as the preceeding, is concerned with those peoples who in the past had rejected the message of Islam; and the Prophet is instructed how to deal with the obdurate and scoffing Meccans. The unbelievers of old met their fate, in spite of all that they had relied upon (verse 84, B 83). Those who now do not receive the truth, and accept Islam, are in the same grievous error. The Meccans mock, as did their predecessors, at the messenger of God who preaches to them (verses 6–15); but his possessions are greater than theirs. He who created the heavens and the earth had determined all things, and the day of reckoning is surely coming (verse 85). The injunction is laid upon Muhammad: *fa'ṣfaḥi 'ṣ-ṣafḥa 'l-jamila.*

Regarding the meaning of *ṣafaḥa* in this phrase, there has been difference of opinion. Al-Baiḍāwī, whose word is law, chose "forgive"; and accordingly all the modern translations of the Qur'ān render: "So forgive with a gracious forgiveness."

It must be said, however, that this rendering seems out of keeping with the character of the Sura. Muhammad is being heckled by some of the leading men of the city, who do their best *to prevent the truth from gaining converts*; who make sport of the Prophet's teaching and pronounce him a lunatic (verse 6). The whole chapter is a rebuke and a threat directed against such men. Verse 94 gives to the Prophet the final instruction: "So do what you have been bidden to do, and *turn away* from the mushriks." This command seems much better suited to the circumstances.

One might conjecture that al-Baiḍāwī's choice was more than a little influenced by the pleasing word *jamīl* and by the ancient and well-founded tradition that XV.85 was abrogated by "the verse of the sword" (IX.5). Neither of these considerations can he given weight, however, as will appear. There are other commentators whose judgment should be taken into account.

We read in *Jalālain*, as the paraphrase of XV.85: *aʿriḍ ʿanhum iʿrāḍan lā jazaʿa fīhi*, that is, "Turn away from them, *but without inipatience*." In the face of persecution and ridicule the Prophet is to maintain his equanimity; here the word *jamīl* has its rightful meaning. The *Kaššāf* says the same thing, more explicitly: *faʿriḍ ʿanhum fa'ḥtamil mā talqā minhum iʿrāḍan jamīlan bi-ḥilmin wa iʿḍā'in.* It is what the circumstances required; the Prophet was not to pay attention to these men, nor to envy them (verse 88), nor to show irritation. Much earlier, in aṭ-Ṭabarī's great *Tafsīr*, the interpretation "turn away" is given the foremost place, and more than one of the commentators he quotes make the connection of verse 85 with verse 94.

Instead of the translation "So forgive (your people) with a gracious forgiveness," the authorities above quoted would suggest "So turn away (from the unbelievers) in calm avoidance." Permitting the Prophet to interpret himself, this rendering of *ṣafḥan jamīlan* is given very strong support by the two passages LXX.5 and LXXIII.10, in which the same adjective is used in the same way, under the same circumstances. The modern renderings of XV.85 need to be revised.

In any case, and by any interpretation, the verse XV.85 is certainly abrogated by the *āyatu 'S-sayfi*, in which there could be no place for the idea expressed by the adjective *jamīl*.

Before returning to the passage LXIV.14, there may be mentioned a derivative of the root *ṣafaḥa* that has its bearing on the present inquiry. The verbal adjective *ṣafūḥ* describes the woman who turns away from the man, forsaking his society (*Qāmūs: al-mar'atu 'l-muʿriḍatu 'ṣ-ṣāddatu 'l-hājiratu*). The stereotyped use shows how the verb would naturally be suggested in speaking of the man who (as far as is reasonable) turns away from the society of his wife and children and gives himself to the service of Islam.

Let us suppose that the original reading of LXIV.14 was the following: *yā ayyuhā 'lladhīna āmanū inna min azwājikum wa aulādikum ʿaduwwan lakum fa'ḥdharūhum wa-in taʿiffū wa taṣfaḥū yughfar lakum fa-inna 'llāha qhafūrun raḥīmun.* "O you who believe! Verily among your wives and children are foes of yours, so beware of them! But if you restrain yourselves and turn away from them, you will have pardon, for God is forgiving and merciful." Here is an *āyat* that at least reflects the Prophet's practical wisdom and his justice.

The question now is, whether the present reading of the Qur'ānic text is readily explained as derived, in the ordinary process of manuscript copying, from this original. The answer is that the explanation is easy and natural if it is assumed that the alteration took place in the earliest period, while there were still Muslim scribes who could make a mistake in copying and allow the slip to pass. The script at that time was continuous, there was no interval between words. The copyist wrote *wa taṣfaḥū wa*, under the influence of the *wāw* just preceding. Once written, the *w* made it necessary to continue with *taghfirū* and to omit *lakum*: unless the copyist was willing to discard the quire and take a new one. A *wāw* introduced by mistake has proved a fatal error in very many Semitic transcriptions.

We have need to bear in mind what Nöldeke wrote in his *Geschichte des Qorans* (1860), page 203: "*Die Muslimen legen der ersten Sammlung des Qorāns eine zu grosse Bedeutung bei. Denn vor Allem Müssen wir anerkennen, dass jene* durchaus keine öffentliche Auktorität *hatte, sondern eine blosse* Privatsache *Omar's and Abu Bekr's war. Nur dadurch ward ihr Ansehen so gross, dass sie unter ʿOthmān der, kanonischen Gestaltung des heiligen Buchs zur Grundlage diente*." A false reading, such as the one here supposed, could easily have gained its place in the sacred book in the time of Abu Bekr, or even of Omar. This is all that can be said.

Our revered teacher and mentor, Professor Goldziher, in his *Muhammedanische Studien*, II, 242 f., made passing mention of those Muslim scholars—not a few—who would remove the difficulty of this or that verse in the Qur'ān by rewriting it: and he cited the remark of Ibn Jinnī, that such "improved" readings are, after all, only designed to interpret, not to emend (*dass sie "nur commentirende, nicht corrigirende Bedeutung haben wollen*"). It is needless to say that the present criticism of Sura LXIV, verse 14 (13), is offered merely as comment.

NOTE

1. I use the verse numbers of Flügel's edition, generally appending to them the numbers given in the official Būlāq edition of 1342 A.H., designated by the letter B. In the present case, the verse number in the latter edition is 13.

6.6

Some Proposed Emendations to the Text of the Koran

James A. Bellamy

In this article, eleven difficult passages in the Koran, which have defied the efforts of both Muslim commentators and orientalists to explain them, are interpreted as corruptions resulting from faulty copying by scribes. Emendations of the text are proposed to bring it as close as possible to the form it had when first spoken by the prophet Muḥammad. At the end, a few changes are made in the author's old hypothesis that the Mysterious Letters at the head of some of the suras are old abbreviations of the *basmalah.*

A curious feature of studies on the Koran in the West over the last 150 years is the scant attention paid by scholars to the Koranic text as such. Orientalism has many excellent works on the Koran to its credit, but one seeks in vain for a systematic application of the techniques of textual criticism to the textual problems of the Koran, although classicists and biblical scholars have for centuries made continuous efforts to improve the quality of the texts that are the bases of their disciplines. It is difficult to see why this should be so. Early Koran scholars such as Fleischer, Nöldeke, and Goldziher were good textual critics; they were all well educated in classical and biblical studies, and they made good editions of later Arabic texts that are still in use today.

Whatever the reasons, Western scholarship, with very few exceptions,[1] has chosen to follow the Muslim commentators in not emending the text. When faced with a problem, the Westerners have resorted to ety-

James A. Bellamy, "Some Proposed Emendations to the Text of the Koran," *JAOS* 13 (1993): 562–73. Reprinted with permission.

mologizing and hunting for foreign words and foreign influences. They have produced a great deal of valuable scholarship important for our study of the Koran and the origins of Islam, but where they exercised their skill on corrupt texts, they, of course, produced only fantasies.

The Arabs, on the other hand, tend to paraphrase, stating in different terms what they think the passage must mean. However, their Arabic was very good, so we find sometimes that they sensed the correct meaning of a problematical passage, and then defined, or, better said, "redefined," the crucial word accordingly even when lexically it was impossible. This is of great help to the modern textual critic, who has only to carry the process one step further and make the necessary emendation. We shall see below several instances of this sort of redefinition.

The earliest generation of Muslim commentators, although they did not emend the text, had no doubt that it did contain mistakes. Our sources list several acknowledged errors, and—if we are to believe the Arab tradition—the first textual critics of the Koran were ʿUthmān, ʿAlī, and ʿĀʾishah. The caliph ʿUthmān, when the recension of the Koran that he had sponsored was presented to him, looked it over and noticed some mistakes (*laḥn*), and said, "Don't correct them for the Bedouin Arabs will correct them with their tongues." ʿĀʾishah, responding to a question about them, said that they were the work of the copyists, who had made mistakes in writing.[2] ʿAlī is credited with an astute emendation. In LVI.29 the blessed in paradise are portrayed as strolling among heaped-up bananas (*ṭalḥ manḍūd*). ʿAlī said that this made no sense and one should rather read *ṭalʿ* "blossoms," and, like a good critic, he pointed to a parallel text in XXVI.148, which reads *ṭalʿ*. When asked if he would change the reading, he replied that today the Koran cannot be disturbed or changed.[3]

Ibn ʿAbbās, cousin of the Prophet and a famous early commentator, is credited with detecting and correcting several errors in the text. In XIII.31 we find *a-fa-lam yayʾasi lladhīna āmanū*, "Have not those who believed despaired?" Ibn ʿAbbās, following Ibn Masʿūd, read *yatabayyan*, "Have they not seen clearly?" and said that the copyist must have been sleepy when he wrote *yay'as*. In XVII.23, *wa-qaḍā rabbuka allā taʿbuda illā iyyāhu*, "Your lord has decreed that you should not worship any except him," he read *wa-waṣṣā*, "Your lord advised," explaining that the copyist had taken up too much ink in his calamus, and that the *wāw* had flowed into the *ṣād*, turning it into a *qāf*.[4]

Probably none of the anecdotes cited above is really true, but they are important in that they show that about a generation after the promulgation of the Uthmanic recension, some readers noted that there were mistakes in the Koran, and suggested corrections, though they prudently did not try to alter the official text. They also show us that the Arab commentators were well acquainted with drippy pens and copyists' errors brought on by fatigue.

In addition to the errors noted above, there are in the Koranic text many variant readings (*qirā'āt*), which do not involve errors, but each of which is evidence that a mistake was made in the tradition at some time or other. Otherwise we must admit that the Prophet may have recited a passage in a certain way when it was first revealed, but then changed it in a subsequent recitation—not impossible, but this could not account for all the variants. Most of the *qirā'āt* derive ultimately from the fact that the Uthmanic recension was published without diacritics—though they did exist at that time—and without vowel signs, which were not invented until some years later. They are important to us here because they prove that there was no oral tradition stemming directly from the Prophet strong enough to overcome all the uncertainties inherent in the writing system.

Given the fact that the Koran contains acknowledged errors and, in the *qirā'āt*, evidence of many more, it is impossible to deny that still more mistakes, as yet undetected, may lie hidden in the text. In this article I shall attempt to isolate several errors and then to emend the text in order to restore it as nearly as possible to its original form. In the Koran "original form" means, of course, the form the word or phrase had when it was first uttered by the prophet Muḥammad.

The first step in this process is the isolation of possible errors. The most important clue that an error may have been made is the lack of good sense in the word or passage and the resulting variety of opinion among scholars as to what it means. Another clue is when the word is transmitted in more than one form. In general, different views about the meaning and/or form of a particular word make it likely that the word is wrong. Still another clue is when the word in question is said by the lexicographers to be dialectal or foreign. Some such claims may be the result of academic pretentiousness, but others indicate that the word was not known to the Meccans and the Medinese and hence is probably a mistake.

In proposing emendations, I shall follow rules laid down by classicists. In order to be acceptable, an emendation must make good sense, better than the received text; it must be in harmony with the style of the Koran; it must also be palaeographically justifiable; and finally, it must show how the corruption occurred in the first place.

The cases examined below share a common feature; each occurs in a context of simple, everyday words, which makes it most unlikely that the difficult word represents something mysterious, arcane, or foreign. Indeed. in some cases, as noted above, the meaning required is obvious, or nearly so, so all we have to do is search for a simple, everyday word that will fill the slot and, at the same time, meet the requirements for emendation listed above. The results are likely to be dull and commonplace, since they will lack the ambiguity of the mistakes that allows the imagination of scholars to soar.

1. ḤAṢAB: FUEL

We shall begin with a case in which, by a lucky accident, both the original and the error have been preserved. In XXI.98 we read: *innakum wa-mā taʿbudūna min dūni llāhi ḥaṣabu jahannama*, "You and what you worship other than God shall be the fuel of hell." However, Ubayy read *ḥaṭab* instead of *ḥaṣab*, as did ʿAlī and ʿĀʾishah.[5] Bell translates, "coals," but in a note says it literally means "pebbles";[6] Paret has "Brennstoff" with a query.[7]

Ḥaṣab, in the meaning of fuel, is found only here. The basic meaning of the verb *ḥaṣaba* is "to pelt with pebbles" or "to scatter pebbles." From this sense the lexicographers redefine it to mean "to throw pebbles (i.e., fuel) on a fire"; others limit it to fuel that is thrown into an oven, or used as kindling, but they offer no *shawāhid* in support of any of these meanings. In order to explain its strangeness, they hold that *ḥaṣab* is Ethiopic, or in the dialect of Nejd or the Yemen;[8] the word is also said to mean "the fuel of hell" in Zanjīyah.[9] All this only goes to show that it was not known to the Meccans and Medinese. Rabin[10] apparently takes the Yemeni ascription seriously, but does not mention Nejd or Ethiopia. He relates it to the Hebrew *ḥaṣabh*, the agent noun of which, *ḥōṣēbh*, occurs in Isa. 10:15, as the hewer or chopper with an ax. However this is the only occasion on which the word "apparently" refers to cutting wood, the other instances refer to hewing stone.[11] We note, too, that the regular Old Testament verb for cutting or gathering firewood is *ḥaṭabh* = Arabic *ḥaṭaba*.

Obviously correct is *ḥaṭab*; it is the regular word in Arabic for firewood and occurs elsewhere in the Koran (CXI.4 and LXXII.15) in that meaning. Closely parallel to XXI.98 is LXXII.15: *wa-ammā l-qāsiṭūna fa-kānū li-jahannama ḥaṭaban*, "As for the unrighteous, they shall be fuel for hell." It is easy to see how the mistake occurred; in copying *ḥaṭab*, the scribe forgot to write the vertical stroke of the *ṭ*, turning it into a *ṣ*. This is much like our forgetting to cross a *t* or dot an *i*, something that everyone does from time to time.

2. UMMAH: TIME, WHILE

The word *ummah* appears twice in the Koran in the apparent meaning of "while, time": XI.8 reads *wa-la-in akhkharnā 'anhumu l-'adhāba ilā ummatin ma'dūdatin la-yaqūlunna mā yaḥbisuhu*, "And if we postpone for them the punishment for a reckoned (amount of) time, they will surely say, 'What is holding it back?'" And in XII.45: *qāla lladhī najā minhumā wa-ddakara ba'da ummatin*, "And the one of them who was saved remembered after a time and said."

These two occurrences have not attracted much attention from Western scholars. Paret, in a note on XI.8 says only that here and in XII.45, *ummah* means "Frist, Weile," thus accepting the meaning given by the majority of the commentators.[12] Blachère translates XI.8 by "jusqu'à un moment compté,"[13] and XII.45 by "s'amendant après réflexion," and notes that he translates by intuition, and that the commentators take it to mean "après un temps," which has little relation to the sense of the root.[14]

Ummah, of course, cannot mean "time, while," but this is one of the cases in which the commentators instinctively grasped the meaning necessary and went on to redefine the word accordingly. In XI.18 they all assert that the word means "time, while" (*ḥīna, ẓamān*), but there is some variety of opinion on XII.45. In addition to "time," some suggest *immah* "favor"[15] (poorly attested), and *amah* or *amh* "forgetting."[16] *Ummah* makes its way into the list of dialect words in the meaning *sinīn* "years" (Azd Shanū'ah) and as "forgetting" (Tamīm).[17]

The meaning plainly must be "time, while," as the majority of the commentators held, and this we can restore simply by emending *h* to *d*, and reading *amad*, which means "time, term, period of time." The addition of the feminine ending to *maʿdūd* would occur naturally to anyone reading *ummah* for *amad*; the copyist may have thought he was correcting the text, but he may have done it instinctively without being aware of it. *Amad* occurs four times elsewhere in the Koran, III.30, XVIII.12, LVII.16, and LXXII.25.

3. *ABB*: FODDER, PASTURAGE

In a brief passage in Surah LXXX:26-32 God enumerates some of the blessings—specifically foodstuffs—that he has bestowed on mankind. *Thumma shaqaqnā l-arḍa shaqqan* 26, *fa-anbatnā fīhā ḥabban* 27, *waʿinaban wa-qaḍban* 28, *wa-zaytūnan wa-nakhlan* 29, *wa-ḥadāʾiqa ghulban* 30, *wa-fākihatan wa-abban* 31, *matāʿan lakum wa-li-anʿāmikum* 32; "Then we split the earth and caused to grow in it grain, grapes, and clover, olives and date-palms, and luxurious orchards, and fruit and *abb*, as a benefit for you and your livestock."

The crux in this passage is the word *abb* in verse 31, though there is some uncertainty about *qaḍb* in verse 28 as well. Blachère translates the latter as "cannes" (canes; possibly he means sugar-cane), apparently tacitly emending *qaḍb* to *qaṣab*.[18] Paret translates: "Futterpflanzen" and marks the Arabic word with a query.[19] Neither annotates the word. I believe that *qaḍb* is correct here; the word is well attested in the dictionaries where it is defined as "clover" (*raṭbah, fiṣfiṣah*), "lucern" (*qatt*), or anything that is cut and eaten while it is green. There are several *shawāhid* and several other words with related meanings derived from the same root.[20] It may be that Blachère preferred *qaṣab* to *qaḍb* because he felt that the needs of the livestock were taken care of by *abb*, but this is not so. They were taken care of by *qaḍb*.

The word abb is glossed by the commentators as "fodder, pasturage" (*marʿan, kalaʾ*), as "grass" (*ʿushb*), "straw" (*tibn*), and "dried fruit."[21] They were doubtless influenced by verse 32, and since they could not know what *abb* really meant, "fodder, pasturage" was the best choice under the circumstances. There are hints, however, in our sources that some were not sure of the meaning and admitted their ignorance. Abū Bakr, when questioned about *abb*, exclaimed, "What heaven will cover me, or what earth will carry me, if I say about the book of God something I do not know?"[22] ʿUmar after reciting the verses remarked, "I know what *fākihah* is, but what is *abb*?" Then at once he checked himself and exclaimed that this was presumptuousness (*takalluf*). In another version of the same story he states, "Sufficient for us is what we already know."[23] *Abb* was assigned by some to the dialect of the People of the West (*ahl al-gharb*), presumably the Berbers![24]

Among commonplace words such as grain, olives, and date-palms, *abb* was very cryptic, so scholars felt obliged to work hard to give it similar currency. In addition to redefining the word, they invented *shawāhid*, both prose and verse, trying to show that *abb* meant pasturage. An anonymous poet is quoted as saying: "Our tribe is Qays and our home is Najd; we have there pasture (*abb*) and a watering place."[25] In the list of poetic *shawāhid* falsely ascribed to Ibn ʿAbbās we find another anonymous verse: "You see in it pasturage (*abb*) and gourds mingled together, on a way to water beneath which willows run."[26] Zamakhsharī cites the following expression: *Fulānun rāʿa lahu l-ḥabbu wa-ṭaʿa lahu l-abbu*,[27] which Lane translates: "Such a one's seed-produce [or grain] increased and his pasture became ample."[28] Another statement is ascribed to the legendary Quss b. Sāʿidah: *Fa-jaʿala yartaʿu abban wa-aṣīdu ḍabban*, "And he proceeded to graze on *abb* while I hunted for lizards."[29] The prose expressions may not have been invented to deceive, but may have been coined after *abb* as "pasture" had been absorbed into the vocabulary of educated people. One should not underestimate the power of the Koran to generate new expressions such as these.

A. Jeffery, following earlier scholars, relates *abb* ultimately to Hebrew *ʾbb* "to be green," but assumes that it came into Arabic directly from Syriac *ʾbʾ*,[30] which means "fruit" = *fākihah*.

Despite these attempts at redefinition and etymologizing, the fact remains that *abb* was not understood by the first commentators on the Koran. The word is not found in Arabic literature before or after its occurrence here (except the spurious verses and the proverbial expressions cited above) and it stands in the midst of common words that everyone could understand. Stylistically it is disturbing. What could be the purpose of reminding people of God's blessings using a word that not even the experts could understand? Everything points toward its being a word as commonplace as grain, olives, fruit, and so forth. In short, *abb* has to be a mistake.

We can restore the text with a very simple emendation, by reading *lubban* instead of *abban*. The copyist's pen, as it turned to the left after the *lām*, for a split second ceased to flow, thus breaking the connection with the following *bā'* and converting the *lām* into *alif. Lubb* is a common word meaning "kernel" or, according to the dictionaries, anything of which the outside is thrown away and the inside eaten; specifically mentioned are pistachio nuts and almonds. Today, if one buys *libb* from a street vendor in the Near East, he gets sunflower seeds or pumpkin seeds. Stylistically, fruit and nuts go together much better than fruit and pasturage.

4. *SIJILL*: WRITER OF A DOCUMENT

In XXI.104 God describes how he is going to proceed on the last day: *yawma naṭwī l-samā'a ka-ṭayyi l-sijilli lil-kutubi*, "The day on which we shall fold up the heavens as the *sijill* folds up the writings."

The meaning of *sijill*, a well-known word in Arabic, is "document," consequently the "document" could not do any folding or rolling up of other documents. This problem has been approached from two directions. Some of the commentators realized that *sijill* had to be the subject of the *maṣdar ṭayy*, so they interpreted it as the name of an angel, a man's name, or the name of the prophet's scribe. Others, however, held that *sijill* was a sheet of vellum or papyrus (*ṣaḥīfah*) and redefine the phrase to mean: *ka-ṭayyi l-sijilli 'alā mā fīhī mina l-kitāb*, "as the *sijill* is folded over the writing that is on it." Ṭabari prefers the latter explanation since he says *sijill* is well known, and that there is no angel or scribe known by this name.[31] The redefinition of the function of the preposition *li-*, however, is too drastic to be credible.

The Westerners generally follow Theodor Nöldeke's opinion that Muḥammad mistakenly took the name of the document for the writer of it.[32] This idea, however, is untenable. Although he may have been illiterate, the Prophet was nevertheless surrounded by writing. He was a merchant and so was his wife. He dictated portions of the revelations to scribes, and he doubtless dictated his correspondence as well, and must have received letters that were opened and read before him. He had a share in the drafting of two important legal documents, the Constitution of Medina, and the Treaty of Ḥudaybiyah. In short, writing was so widely employed at that time that Muḥammad could not have confused the document with its writer.

Those commentators who saw in *al-sijill* the writer and the subject of *ṭayy* were correct, although they could not take the last step necessary for reaching the correct reading. This problem can be solved with a simple emendation, by changing *al-sijill* to *al-musjil* or *al-musajjil*. The loss of the *mīn* is easy to explain. In older hands the *mīm* after the definite article does not turn back under the *lām* as it does in later hands, but is often no more than a thickening of the connecting line between the *lām* and the letter following. Here, too, a leaky pen may have run the *mīm* into the first tooth of the *sīn*, causing the *mīm* to lose its identity; and possibly one of the teeth was indistinct, thus facilitating the misreading.

5. *ḤIṬṬAH*: FORGIVENESS

This and the following emendation are of mistakes that arose from the inability of the writing system to indicate all the *hamzahs* that had been lost in the Ḥijāzī dialect[33] but were added at a later time when it was decided that the Bedouin pronunciation should prevail. Usually the absence of *hamzah* is indicated by one of the consonants *alif*, *wāw*, or *yā'*, but not always. In these two cases the absence of a possible carrier for the *hamzah* had already resulted in the erroneous readings that we find, so the revisers did not suspect that *hamzahs* were etymologically justified.

In Sura II.58 God recalls that he told the children of Israel to enter the village and eat from it wherever they wished in ease, and then says: *udkhulū l-bāba sujjadan wa-qūlū ḥiṭṭatun naghfir lakum khaṭāyākum*, "Enter the gate prostrating yourselves and say *ḥiṭṭatun'* and we shall forgive your sins." In VII.161 we find essentially the same phrase repeated.

Bell and Paret leave the word untranslated,[34] but Bell says it may come from Hebrew *ḥēṭ'* "sin," and Blachère translates "dites, Pardon!"[35] On page 645 he refers it to the Hebrew *ḥaṭṭā*, "sinners." Of the translators Blachère comes closest to the Muslim exegetes, who take the word to mean "forgiveness," that is, a "pulling down" of the burden of sin. Some commentators say that *ḥiṭṭah* means "speak the truth" (imptv., masc. pl.) in Zanjīyah.[36]

The word, however, must surely be the Arabic *khiṭah*, the Ḥijāzī form of the Classical *khiṭʾah*, which is a maṣdar of *khaṭiʾa*, "to commit a sin." The spelling is like that of *shṭh* = *shaṭʾahu*, "its sprout, shoot" (XLVII.29); cf. *GdQ*, 3:43. The people, of course, are appealing for forgiveness but to obtain this they must first confess their sins. *Khiṭatan* < *khiṭʾatan* with the implied omission of the verb *khaṭīnā* < *khaṭiʾnā* is the equivalent of "We have sinned!" The word may have been pronounced *khiṭṭatan*, since some readers read *al-marri* for *al-marʾi* (VIII.24) and *juzzun* for *juzʾun* (XV.44).[37] Usually, however, this doubling is limited to *wāw* and *yāʾ*.[38]

We note finally that *ḥiṭṭah* is the only word in the Koran derived from the root *ḥṭṭ*, which means basically "put down," that is, from a higher to a lower level. There are twenty-two words, however, derived from *khṭʾ*, all of which have some meaning related to sin.

6. *ṢURHUNNA ILAYKA*: INCLINE THEM (THE BIRDS) TOWARD YOU

In II.260 Ibrahim asks God to show him how he raises the dead. At first God doubts that Ibrahim really believes, but he insists that he wants to see the process only to ease his heart, so God gives him the following instructions: *fa-khudh arbaʿatan mina l-ṭayri faṣurhunna ilayka thumma jʿal ʿalā kulli jabalin minhunna juzʾan thumma dʿuhunna yaʾtinaka saʿyan*, "Take four birds and incline them toward yourself, then put a part of them on each mountain, then call them, and they will come to you flying."

The crux lies in the words *fa-ṣurhunna ilayka*, which is the reading of the seven canonical readers without exception, but one finds also *ṣir*; rare and late seem to be *ṣurrahunna*, "tie them," and *ṣirrahunna*, "shout at them."[39]

Blachère translates: "et serre-les contre toi (pour les broyer),"[40] and says that he translates by intuition. Bell has "incline them to thyself," noting that the sense is uncertain.[41] Paret: "richte sie (mit dem Kopf?) auf dich zu (und schlachte sie?)."[42] In *Kommentar*, he notes that the commentators either read "incline them," which is not understandable, or "cut them up," with which the following "to yourself" does not fit.[43] In short, neither of the accepted readings makes good sense. The meaning "cut up" is said to be Nabataean; others take it to be Greek.[44]

Ṭabarī devotes several pages to these words.[45] He cites the two major views on the meaning of *ṣur*, "incline" and "cut up," and decides emphatically for the latter, because the overwhelming majority of the exegetes hold this opinion, and he takes issue with a few Kufan lexicographers who insist that *ṣāra*, *yaṣūru* never means "cut up" in the language of the Arabs.

Both these groups are right, each in its own way. The lexicographers are right in denying that *ṣāra* means "cut up"; the *shawāhid* are late or suspicious, so it looks as if the exegetes had redefined the word in the way we have noted before. However, the context clearly demands that the phrase read "cut to pieces," so the exegetes are "right" as well. One of them even goes so far as to insist that the pieces of the birds are all mixed up: "The wing of this one is with the head of that one, and the head of that one is with the wing of this one."[46] Others say that the flesh and feathers are mingled.[47]

Since the meaning must be "cut them to pieces and mix them up," we can restore the text as follows: *fa-jazzihinna (wa-)lbuk*, which, not surprisingly, means "make them into pieces and mix (them) up." The emendation of *ṣad* to *jīm* is no problem since the two letters resemble each other closely enough for such a misreading to occur. *Jazzi*, of course, is the classical *jazzi'*; the change of final-hamzated verbs to final-*ya'* verbs is well known, and was doubtless universal in the Ḥijāzī dialect, where, as noted above, all the *hamzahs* had been lost. The meaningless *ilayka* is removed by reading *ulbuk* without any change in the *rasm* at all; the *wa-* was dropped when the word was misread as *ilayka*. Another possibility is that this phrase originally read *wa-labbik*, which has the same meaning, on the assumption that the *wāw* was mistaken for an *alif*. This is not impossible if the handwriting was small.

7. *SAB'AN MINA L-MATHĀNĪ*: SEVEN MATHĀNĪ (?)

This and the following two emendations are of special interest since, in addition to correcting the text, they depend on assuming the same mistake. One could argue from this that all three were copied by a single scribe with a certain peculiarity in his handwriting.

The mysterious word *mathānī* occurs twice in the Koran, first in XV:87: *wa-la-qad ātaynāka sabʿan mina l-mathānī wal-qurʾāna l-ʿaẓīm*, "We have given you seven *mathānī* and the mighty Koran." It is found in a group of verses (86–97) in which God comforts the prophet in his disappointment at the doings of those who pay no attention to his message. The verse seems to be a reminder that God has favored him above all others with these special gifts.

Mathānī is also found in XXXIX.23: *Allāhu nazzala aḥsana l-ḥadīthi kitāban mutashābihan mathāniya taqshaʿirru minhu julūdu lladhīna yakhshawna rabbahum thumma talīnu julūduhum wa-qulūbuhum ilā dhikri llāh*, "God has sent down the best account, a book alike (in its parts), *mathānī*, at which the skins of those who fear their Lord creep, then their skins and hearts become soft to the remembrance of God."

The problem of the *mathānī* has generated much scholarly writing, most of which shall be ignored here.[48]

Muslim authorities derive the word from the root *thny*, and most of them assign it the meaning of something repeated, as can be seen in two of the translations above. However, the verb *thanā* means "to double, to fold, to make something twofold by adding a second element to the first," but the idea of repetition easily follows. One of the meanings ascribed to Form II of the verb is "repeat, iterate."[49] Others suggest that it comes from the Form IV verb *athnā* "to praise."

An early suggestion by A. Geiger that the word is derived from the Hebrew Mishnah, or, as preferred by Nöldeke, the Aramaic *mathnīthā*, has been accepted by many Western scholars, but the word as used in the Koran does not reflect the character of the Mishnah.

The number seven has caused as much trouble as the word *mathānī* itself. The exegetes say that the seven *mathānī* are the seven longest suras of the Koran, or the seven verses of the Fātiḥah, which is the most popular view, or they are the suras that have less than a hundred verses but more than the shortest, which are called *al-mufaṣṣalāt*; all of these definitions reflect the idea of repetition in some way. We note further that *sabʿan* is a masculine numeral, so it demands a feminine singular. The only word that approaches the idea of repetition would be the past participle of Form II, *muthannāh*, but this would take a plural *muthannayāt*, not *mathānī*.

Western scholarship has mostly accepted the theory that they are seven punishment stories that are scattered throughout the Koran because of the effect they have on the hearers. This is only speculation, but it is not refuted by our emendations.

I believe that the word in XV.87 should be emended to read *al-matālīyi*, and in XXXIX.23 to *matālīya*, meaning "recitations," literally, something that has been, or is to be, recited. This is the broken plural of *matlūwun*, as in *maktūbun*, *makātību* "writings" and *mazmūrun*, *mazāmiru* "psalms," and others. The copyist mistook the *lām* for a *nūn* because it was too short; having accepted *nūn* the only other word that could be formed from the *rasm* was *mabānī*, which could not be right, so he had to decide for *mathānī*, and so initiated the idea of redoubling or repeating.

One reason that the scribe failed to read *matālī* is that the word does not appear in the Koran nor does the singular *matlūw*. The verb *talā*, "recite," however, is very common, occurring more than sixty times in a variety of forms both active and passive, so the past participle is surely possible. It is likely that the verb *talā* was not much used in the common speech of Mecca, but came suddenly into extensive use only in the Koran, so the copyist was not alert to the possibility here. In the dictionaries, the space allotted to *talā* in this meaning is quite small and there are no *shawāhid*. Additional evidence that the word was little used is provided by a *mukhaḍram* poet, Khufāf b. ʿUmayr al-Sulamī, who in describing his beloved's campsite misuses the agent noun under the impression that it means "scribe": *ka'annahā ṣuḥufun yakhuṭṭuhā tālī*, "as if they were pages written by a *tālī*."[50]

Talā is usually used with *āyāt* "signs" as its object or passive subject, but we find it with other words as well, including *kitāb* (seven times, see concordance), so there is no discrepancy in XXXIX.23 in equating the *kitāb* and the *matālī*. The distinction, however, between *kitāb* and *qur'ān* (XV.87) is found elsewhere in the same sura (v. 1): *tilka āyātu l-kitābi wa-qur'ānin mubīn*, "Those are the signs of the book and (of) a clear Koran."

It is also necessary to emend *sabʿan*, which I believe should be read *shay'an*. The mistake occurred when the scribe carelessly wrote a small loop resembling an *ʿayn* instead of the minim of the *yā'*. This is comparable to our writing a small *e* when we intend to make the shaft of an *i*. The next copyist, seeing *sʿ'*, could hardly do anything other than add the *bāʾ*. Seven was also doubtless congenial to him; it is virtually a sacred number in the Near East, and many things come in sevens. Since he did not know what *mathānī* meant, he must have felt that the number seven was appropriate for such a mystery.

So XV.97 should read: *wa-laqad ātaynāka shayʾan mina l-matālīyi wal-qurʾāna l-ʿaẓīm*, "We have given you some recitations and the mighty Koran."

8. *TAMANNĀ; FĪ UMNIYATIHI*: TO DESIRE; IN HIS DESIRE

In XXII.52 God points out that Satan distorts the message brought by messengers and prophets: *wa-mā arsalnā min qablika min rasūlin wa-lā nabīyin illā idhā tamannā alqā l-shayṭānu fi umniyatihi fa-yansakhu llāhu mā yulqī l-shayṭānu thumma yuḥkimu llāhu āyātihi*, "We have not sent down before you any messenger or prophet but that when he desired, Satan injected (something) into his desire, but God cancels what Satan injects, then God makes his signs strong."

Tamannā and *umniyatihi* in the meaning "desire" (verb and noun) have caused problems for the translators. Bell has "but when he formed his desire Satan threw (something) into his formulation," with a note saying that the meaning is doubtful.[51] Paret has "ohne dass ihm, wenn er etwas wünschte, der Satan (von sich aus etwas) in seinen Wunsch unterschoben hätte."[52] Blachère has "sans que le Démon jetât [l'impurité (?)] dans leur souhait, quand ils (le) formulaient."[53] All three rely on the dictionary definition of *tamannā*, but none of them annotates the passage.

Ṭābarī devotes most of his commentary on this verse to the reason for its revelation;[54] it was sent down as a comfort to the prophet for having inadvertently, because of Satanic interference, spoken favorably of the pagan goddesses Allāt, ʿUzzā, and Manāt. But on pages 113 f. he quotes from exegetes who hold that *tamannā* here means *qaraʾa, talā*, and *ḥaddatha*. Ibn Hishām reports on the authority of Abū ʿUbaydah that the Arabs used *tamannā* in the meaning of *qaraʾa*, and cites two *shawāhid*, obviously spurious since both refer to the recitation of the book of God.[55]

This is another example of the redefinition by the exegetes and/or lexicographers of the crucial word in a problematic passage in which the redefinition is correct. One should emend *tamannā* to read *yumlī*, "dictates" and *fī umniyatihi* to *fī imlāʾihi*, "in his dictation"; the latter was originally written *ʾmlyh*, with no *alif* for the long *ā*, a common feature of Koranic spelling. The *nūn* was written for *lām* because the latter was too short, as in *mathānī*, and one of the minims was lost. The word was probably pronounced *imlāyihu* or *imlāyhu*.[56] After reading *tamannā*, *umniyatihi* was, of course, inevitable. The copyist may have felt more comfortable with the perfect *tamannā*, since *idhā yumlī* does not appear in the Koran; *idhā tutlā*, however, is found a number of times, and the two words mean much the same thing.

9. *ILLĀ AMĀNĪYA*: EXCEPT DESIRES

Sura II.74–79 is a polemic against the Jews but directed to Muslim listeners. The Jews are denounced for perverting the true scriptures and for pretending to believe when they really do not. In verse 78 we read: *wa-minhum ummiyūna lā yaʿlamūna l-kitāba illā amānīya wa-in hum illā yaẓunnūna*, "And among them are *ummiyūna* who do not know the book except desires and they can only guess." The passage then ends with an imprecation against those who write a book with their own hands and say that it is from God just to make a small profit.

The meaning of *ummiyūna* has been much discussed by scholars and need not delay us here, since in this context it must mean ignorant people who do not know the scriptures. The problem for us is the meaning of *illā amānīya*. Bell, p. 11, translates, "except as things taken on trust, and who only cherish opinions," and notes that the meaning of the word is uncertain.[57] Blachère has "qui ne connaissent point l'Écriture [*mais*] seulement des chimères, et [*qui*] ne font que conjecturer."[58] Paret translates "Unter ihnen [i.e., the Jews] gibt es Heiden (*ummīyūn*), die die Schrift nicht kennen, (ihren Ansichten und Behauptungen) vielmehr (eigene) Wünsche (zugrunde legen) und nur Mutmassungen anstellen."[59] It is very unlikely that this one word can carry all the nuances that are heaped on it in the last translation.

Some exegetes define *amānīya* as lies (*kadhib*), talk (*aḥādīth*). Others cite the phrase *yatamannā ʿalā llāhi al-bāṭila wa-mā laysa lahum*, which seems to mean "and they want to get vain things from God and what is not due them." Ṭabarī himself prefers the meaning "lies, falsehood" and in arguing for it has to maintain that *tamannā* here cannot mean *talā* (= *amlā*), which as we have seen, was derived from XXII.52, nor have its usual meaning "desire," but must mean *takhallaqa*, *ta kharraṣa*, and *ifta'ala*, all of which mean "falsify, fabricate." He accuses the *ummiyūna* of committing such sins because of their ignorance of the book, that is, the Torah.[60] It seems, however, that the meanings other than "to desire" and "to ask, i.e., someone to satisfy one's desire" all derive from this passage in the Koran. Here we get more help from the lexicographers than the exegetes, since the former redefine the word as "recitation." Abū Isḥāq al-Zajjāj (d. 311/923), in discussing this verse, says plainly: *ma'nāhu l-kitāba illā tilāwatan*, "its meaning is: (they do not know) the book except by recitation."[61]

I believe that *amānīya*, like *mathānī* and *tamannā*, is a result of the copyist's mistaking *lām* for *nūn*, and should be emended to read *amālīya* "dictations." So the passage should run: "And among them are *ummiyūna* who do not know the book except dictations (from it) and so they can only guess." These poor ignorant people know of the scriptures only what the evil perverters of the word and the forgers mentioned in the following verse will let them know. They are victims to be pitied and not reproached. Since they had no scriptures at all, they could not be the perverters of it, nor could such ignorant people be so effective as forgers as to write out the book with their own hands, as mentioned in verse 79. The perverters and the forgers must be the same group and the people they deceive are the *ummiyūna*, certainly not the Muslims, who now have the true scriptures.

10. *ṢIBGHAT ALLĀH*: GOD'S RELIGION

Sura II.134–41 is a segment in which God answers the Christians and Jews who urge people to be Christian or Jewish in order to be rightly guided: *qul bal millata Ibrāhīma ḥanifan wa-mā kāna mina l-mushrikīna* 135, *qūlū āmannā billāhi wa-mā unzila ilaynā* . . . 136, *fa-in āmanū bi-mithli mā āmantum bihi fa-qadi htadaw wa-in tawallaw fa-innamā hum fi shiqāqin fa-sa-yakfikahumu llāhu wa-huwa l-samī'u l'alīm* 137, *ṣibghata llāhi wa-*

man aḥasanu mina llāhi ṣibghatan wa-naḥnu lahu ʿābidūn 138. "Say (sg., addressed to Muḥammad), no, rather the community of Ibrāhīm, a *ḥanīf*, for he was not one of the polytheists. Say (pl. addressed to the Muslims), we believe in God and what has been sent down to us . . . (here follow the names of all the prophets whose messages the Muslims believed in). . . . And if they believe in the same things you believe in, they are rightly guided, but if they turn away, they are in schism, but God will take care of them for you (sg.), for He hears and knows; the *ṣibghah* of God! and who is better at *ṣibghah* than God? so we worship Him."

Bell translates: "The savour of Allah, and in savour who is better than Allah? Him are we going to serve," and notes that the exact meaning is uncertain. ("Savour" is singularly ill chosen.)[62] Blachère has "Onction (?) d'Allah! qul donc est meilleur qu'Allah en [*Son*] onction? [*Dites*] Nous sommes Ses adorateurs." In a note he rejects the explanations offered by the exegetes (see below), but admits that "onction" is not satisfactory, and suggests it might mean: "L'allure procurée par Dieu à l'homme converti au Monothéisme d'Abraham."[63] Paret translates: "Das baptisma (? ṣibga)"; in *Kommentar* he cites the commonly held views, and adds the opinion of E. Beck (from *Le Muséon* 65 [1952]: 92) that the word, which means baptism (Taufe) is used here in a more general sense for religion, which agrees with the exegetes' views.[64] Jeffery derives it from the Syriac but does not discuss its meaning in the Koran.[65]

The word gave considerable trouble to the exegetes. They knew it meant the Christian baptism, but because in the passage the Jews are referred to as well, some of them expanded its meaning to include circumcision.[66] However, it is the Muslims who receive the *ṣibghah* of God and so neither baptism or circumcision can apply—the Jews and the pagan Arabs already practiced circumcision. The exegetes therefore redefine the word as *fiṭrah*, *dīn* "religion," *īmān* "faith," or they equate it with the *millata Ibrāhīm* in verse 135, which they take to mean Islam. Thus Ṭabarī paraphrases: *bali ttabiʿu millata Ibrāhīma ṣibghata llāh*; and Qatādah says: *wa-inna ṣibghata llāhi l-Islām*.[67] With this interpretation, however, the comparison at the end makes little sense; can one really ask, "Who is better at Islām or *īmān* than God?" Other redefinitions of *ṣibghah* are *sharīʿah* "law," and *khilqah* "constitution, make-up."[68] Grammatically, most of the commentators take *ṣibghah* to be in apposition with *millah*, even though the two are rather far apart. Those who take *ṣibghah* to mean *īmān* take it as the acc. internal object of *āmannā* in verse 136.

In this case I believe that the exegetes were far off track. It is to me inconceivable that one should find in the Koran the name of a Christian sacrament used—even metaphorically—for Islām or *īmān*. The whole idea runs counter to the general attitude toward Christianity and Judaism in the Koran, and is so disturbing that the word practically announces itself as a mistake.

Neither the exegetes nor the orientalists have considered that *ṣibghata llāh* might refer simply to the words immediately preceding: *fa-sa-yakfikahumu llāh*. Taken thus, *ṣibghah* is an exclamatory acc., used in praise of God's action in sparing the prophet the trouble of dealing with his own enemies. There are two emendations that would give this sense. The first is to read *ṣanīʿah*, "favor." This emendation can be effected without altering the *rasm* at all if we assume that the original *ṣād* did not have the little nub on the left—this is often omitted in manuscripts—but that the next copyist took the *nūn* to be the nub. Otherwise we can add a minim to the *rasm*, a minor change which is easily acceptable.

The second possibility is to read *kifāyah*, the *maṣdar* of *kafā*, which would have been spelled *kfyh*, the long *ā* without *alif*. In older MSS and inscriptions the initial *kāf* is often written without the diagonal stroke that we add separately. The line of the letter runs parallel to the line of writing so that it sometimes closely resembles *ṣād* and *dāl*. The copyist first misread *kāf* as *ṣād*, and then carelessly took the loop of the *fāʾ* as a minim. *Kifāyah* is what we should most likely expect grammatically, given *fa-sa-yakfikuhum* above, but on the whole I prefer *ṣaniʿah* since fewer changes are required to bring it into line. Both "favor" and "sufficiency" are stylistically better in this position than any of the other meanings proposed, and the comparison at the end of verse 138 makes good sense with either of them.

11. *AṢḤĀB AL-AʿRĀF*: THE PEOPLE OF THE HEIGHTS

Sura VII.46 and 48 speak of a group of men who are situated in some coign of vantage from which they can observe both the blessed in heaven and the damned in hell: *wa-baynahumā ḥijābun wa-ʿalā l-aʿrāfi rijālun yaʿrifūna kullan bi-sīmāhum wa-nadaw aṣḥāba l-jannati an salāmun ʿalaykum lam yadkhulūhā wa-hum yaṭmaʿūna* 46, "Between them is a curtain and on the *aʿrāf* are men who know each by their mark and they call to the people of heaven, Peace be with you; they have not entered it but they hope to." However, these same men, when they look at the people of hell, pray to God not to put them with the sinners, and we then read: *wa-nadā aṣḥābu l-aʿrāfi rijālan yaʿrifūnahum bi-sīmāhum qālū mā aghnā ʿankum jamʿukum wa-mā kuntum tastakhbirūna* 48, "and the people of the *aʿrāf* call to men whom they know by their mark; they say, Your collecting (of money) has not helped you nor has your arrogance."

The word *aʿrāf* is the plural of *ʿurf*, which means "mane" or "comb of a cock," so if correct here it must be used metaphorically. Bell, however, translates "men of recognition," reading *iʿrāf* instead of *aʿrāf*.[69] However *iʿrāf* does not mean "recognition" but only "inform someone of his misdeeds and forgive him," and "to have a sweet odor" (from *ʿarf*), and "to have a long mane" (from *ʿurf*).[70] Bell's *iʿrāf* is rejected by Blachère, who leaves the word untranslated, but has a long note in which he reviews the opinions of some of the exegetes, he makes no suggestion as to the lexical meaning of the word.[71] Paret translates simply, "auf den Höhen" and "die Leute der Höhen."[72]

The problem in this passage is both textual and eschatological. The eschatological problem concerns who the *aṣḥāb al-aʿrāf* really are. Some orientalists, notably Bell and Tor Andrae, think that they are the inhabitants of the highest realm of heaven, but in order to get this out of the text they have to take the people of heaven as the subject of *lam yadkhulūhā wa-hum yaṭmaʿūna* 46. This results in very clumsy Arabic and the exegetes are doubtless correct in keeping the *aṣḥāb al-aʿrāf* as subject here and in the following verse (47). The *aṣḥāb al-aʿrāf* are men who are not yet sure whether they are going to heaven or to hell.

I would first point out that *aʿrāf* may not be incorrect. The word might be used here metaphorically of some high place on which these observers are located. What makes it a bit suspicious is that the metaphor does not appear to have been used in Arabic either before or after the revelation of this passage. Furthermore, if the word refers to the top of the *ḥijāb*, as some think, one would expect *ʿalā aʿrāfihi*. We can propose two emendations here, neither of which has to be metaphorical, though the second one may be.

The first is *ajrāf*, plural of *juruf* or *jurf*, which means "bank," specifically of a wadi that has been undercut by the current, or simply, "a bank or ridge that rises abruptly from the bed of a torrent or stream."[73] Such a position would allow the observers an unimpeded view of what was going on below. Palaeographically there is no difficulty. Sometimes in early manuscripts and papyri initial *ḥā'* begins with a lead-in line like a small arc with the concavity facing right, which then continues downward to the right completing the main body of the letter. If this arc is exaggerated, the whole letter can easily be taken for an *'ayn*.

The other suggestion is *aḥruf*, plural of *ḥarf*, which means, among many other things, "point, ridge, brow, ledge, of a mountain."[74] The same emendation, *'ayn* to *ḥā'*, is needed here as in *ajrāf*, and the *alif* presents no problem. It might have been introduced at the time of the Uthmanic recension, or it could have been added by 'Ubaydallāh b. Ziyād, who, during his governorship of Kufah (53–59/673–679), instituted a reform in Koranic orthography that consisted of the introduction of about two thousand *alifs* into the text.[75] Taken this way, *aḥruf* is not metaphorical, but we find the singular, *ḥarf*, used metaphorically in Sura XXII.11: *wa-mina l-nāsi man ya'budu llāha 'alā ḥarfin fa-in aṣābahu khayruni ṭma'anna bihi wa-in aṣābahu fitnatuni nqalaba 'alā wajhihi khasira l-dunyā wal-ākhirata*, "And among the people there are those who serve God on a *ḥarf*, and if good comes to them they are at ease with it, but if trouble comes to them, they turn back to their (old) ways. They lose both this world and the next." These people who serve God "on a ridge" are fence-sitters and summer soldiers who are not sure which way they will jump, since circumstances can vary. The same is true of the *aṣḥāb al-a'rāf*, who are not sure whether they will end up in heaven or hell, since it depends on God's will, which they do not yet know. The two usages are not exactly parallel since *al-a'rāf* is plural and def. and *ḥarf* is singular and indefinite; nevertheless, the similarity is striking. In general, I prefer the reading *aḥruf*, but would suspend judgment on whether it should be taken metaphorically or not.

12. AGAIN THE MYSTERIOUS LETTERS

Some years ago I wrote an article[76] in which I argued that the Mysterious Letters (the *fawātiḥ al-suwar* or *al-ḥurūf al-muqaṭṭaʿah*) of the Koran were old abbreviations of the *basmalah.* The argument was based on the assumption that these abbreviations, like the words studied above, had been corrupted through copyists' errors, so it is not inappropriate here to add a few additional observations on the *fawātiḥ*, and, in particular, to record a change of opinion with regard to some of them.

At that time I was anxious to avoid any suggestion that the emendations proposed might be arbitrary, so I left out of account those groups of letters that might, as they stood, be considered abbreviations of the *basmalah.* In so doing I relegated ḤM to a footnote (p. 280, no. 72), although I was convinced that it derived from an original BM or BSM. I think now that I was somewhat overcautious, since ḤM—to be read BSM and not BM—is the best evidence in favor of the hypothesis.

The derivation is well supported palaeographically. The *bāʾ* of the *basmalah* often begins with a flourish, which in some cases, especially in carelessly written manuscripts and papyri, starts above the line to the left, proceeds to the right and then turns under to form the rest of the letter, giving it a form that can easily be mistaken for *ḥāʾ*. Today in printed texts the *bāʾ* is written taller than usual and bends slightly to the left. This practice probably descends from the ancient practice, which in handwriting could be exaggerated.

The *sīn* of the *basmalah* is often flattened out to such an extent that it appears to be omitted altogether. Tradition tells us that Zayd b. Thābit disapproved of writing the *bsm* of the *basmalah* without the *sīn*, and Ibn Sīrīn did not like people to stretch the *baʾ* to the *mim* until the *sīn* had been written. The caliph ʿUmar is said to have beaten a scribe for omitting the *sīn* from the basmalah.[77]

These anecdotes date from a time when interest was growing in how the Koran should be written, and in which the Kufic hand was in the course of development. In fact, Ibn Sīrīn (ha. 110/728) might well have taken an interest in such matters.

Tables 3 and 4 (p. 282) can now be largely ignored since they make the process of corruption much more complicated than it really was. In

ḤM ʿSQ, I would now keep the two "words" separate as they regularly appear in the Koran. Both segments I believe represent an original BSM. The first to be written was the second segment, which was eventually corrupted to read ʿSQ; this was not understood by a subsequent copyist or editor who added at the beginning another BSM, which was later misread as ḤM. The copyist may have been the same one who wrote BSM (> ḤM) in all the suras where the latter appears.

The original BS was misread as ʿS by the Uthmanic editors and as simple S by Ibn Masʿud because of uncertainty as to the number of minims. The first two were probably badly written as well since they resembled an initial *ʿayn*. Ibn Masʿūd's SQ is closer to the original than the Uthmanic ʿSQ.

KHYʿṢ turns out to be less of a problem than I had originally thought. The real crux is in the *hāʾ*, but this can be solved by dividing the letters into two segments, KH and YʿṢ, following the example of ḤM ʿSQ.

In discussing the word *kifāyah*, we pointed out how *kāf* closely resembles *dāl* and *ṣād* in some early hands; it may also resemble the carelessly written *bāʾ* that we have seen in ḤM. I believe that this *kāf* was originally a *bāʾ*, and with this reading all the other difficulties vanish. The resulting BH—which could have been an original BSM—is a good abbreviation of the basmalah, and in YʿṢ we can see how the *yāʾ* and the open-topped *ʿayn* were miscopied from an original *sīn* in which the teeth were not clearly written. There may even have been a fourth minim representing *bāʾ*, which could have been swallowed up when the two segments were combined later on. The original form was like Ibn Masʿūd's variant SQ (= SM < BSM).

Similarly, I conclude that YʾṢ was written first, then not understood by a later copyist, who added BH or BSM (> KH) to represent the *basmalah.*

The final point concerns those abbreviations in which the letter *ṭāʾ* is found. In the article referred to (p. 280), I assumed that these *ṭā*'s all went back to an original BA. This, however, is not satisfactory, for since the *basmalah* in XXVII.30 at the head of Solomon's letter to the Queen of Sheba is spelled without *alif*, it is not likely that any abbreviation of the phrase would contain that letter. I now believe that the vertical strokes of the *ṭā*'s were originally cancellation marks, added by some copyist when he went through his old surahs to write out the *basmalah* in full. The vertical cancellation mark is well known from later manuscripts and there is no reason why it should not have been employed here. One should keep in mind that the Arabs at the time of Muḥammad were not an ignorant people struggling toward literacy; writing was widely used, though not for literature apparently, especially in urban centers such as al-Ḥīrah, where a chancery style must have been employed. The heads of the *ṭā*'s, now unencumbered by *alifs*, become simple *bā*'s, written in the same careless way as the others that are concealed under ḤM, and the resulting BS, BSM, and BH are all good abbreviations of the *basmalah.* Although it is not necessary for the argument, I believe further that BS and BH also go back to an original BSM. The final flourish of the *sīn* and the final *hā*ʾ could both easily have been miscopied from a *mim.*

I am now more than ever convinced that the *fawātiḥ* are indeed old abbreviations of the *basmalah* that suffered corruption at the hands of later copyists. And, after all, what can more properly stand before a surah than the *basmalah*?

* * *

It should not be assumed that in making these emendations I am in any way trying to diminish the remarkable achievement of Zayd b. Thābit and his colleagues in producing the Uthmanic recension of the Koran. When one considers that the Arabs at that time had no literary culture based on written texts, their accomplishment becomes truly monumental, and one can readily believe that Zayd really said when ordered to do the editing, "By God, if they had charged me with carrying a mountain, it could not have been heavier for me than this." Without any experience of editing or, indeed, of reading a book of similar size and content, they were able to publish a work that has taken its place as one of the three or four greatest books that mankind has produced. It remains for modern scholarship to correct the few mistakes that they overlooked, and to restore the text to the form it had when first spoken by the prophet Muḥammad.

NOTES

1. In the *cruces* discussed below I have found only one proposed emendation, that of R. Bell, who wanted to read *iʿrāf* for *aʿrāf*; see section 11; this does not effect the *rasm*.

2. See T. Nöldeke et al., *Geschichte des Qorans* [hereafter *GdQ*] (Hildesheim: Georg Olms Verlagsbuchhandlung, 1961), 3:2f.

3. I. Goldziher, *Die Richrungen der islamischen Koranauslegung* (Leiden: E. J. Brill, 1952), p. 36.

4. Abd al-Raḥmān al-Suyūṭī, *Al-Itqān fi ʿulūm al-Qurʾān*, ed. Muḥammad Abū l-Faḍl Ibrāhīm (Cairo: Maktabat al-Mashhad al-Ḥusaynī, 1387/1967), 2:275, where other mistakes are noted. The scribe who wrote *yayʾas* was probably not sleepy but confused by similar consonantal outlines. The words *yayʾas* and *yatabayyan* are so different that such a mistake could not have occurred in the oral tradition, so we have to look to the written tradition for an explanation. However, the Uthmanic *rasm* of *yayʾas* is *yʾys*, so it is equally difficult to see how it could be a mistake for *yatabayyan*, or vice versa. My guess is that *yayʾas* was originally written *yʾys*, and so the two words are virtually identical. Each has four minims: *yys* (probably pronounced *yayyas*) with the two *yā*'s and the first two teeth of the sīn, and *yatabayyan* with its *ytby*. The final flourish of the *sīn* was mistaken for a *nūn*, or vice versa. For the loss of *hamẓah* in the Ḥijāzī dialect and compensatory lengthening of a preceding *wāw* or *yāʾ* with *sukūn*, see section 5.

A minim—the term is borrowed from medieval Latin palaeography—is the shortest vertical stroke in any given hand. The word is not wholly suited to Arabic, since in good Arabic manuscripts adjacent minims are often written with slightly differing heights to show that they belong to different letters. It is convenient, however, since it can be used of the teeth of the *sīn*, the nub of the *bāʾ*, *tāʾ*, etc., and also of those nubs that are mistakes, even those that are omitted: Next to the omission or misplacement of dots, minim errors, that is, copying more or fewer minims than are in the original, are the most common mistakes in Arabic MSS.

5. R. Bell, *The Qurʾān: Translated with a Critical Re-arrangement of the Surahs* (Edinburgh: T. & T. Clark, 1937), p. 313.

6. R. Paret, *Der Koran: Übersetzung* (Stuttgart: Kohlhammer, 1962), p. 269.

7. A. Jeffery, *Materials for the History of the Text of the Qurʾān* (Leiden: E. J. Brill, 1937), p. 147.

8. Muḥammad Murtaḍā al-Ḥusaynī al-Zabīdī, *Tāj al-ʿarūs min jawāhir al-Qamūs*, ed. ʿAbd al-Sattār Aḥmad Farrāj. Kuwayt: Matbaʿat Ḥukūmat Kuwayt,

1385/1965), 2:283; E. W. Lane, *Arabic-English Lexicon* (London: Williams and Norgate, 1863–1893), p. 581

9. Suyūṭī, *Itqān*, 2:111.

10. C. Rabin, *Ancient West Arabian* (London: Taylor's Foreign Press, 1951), p. 26.

11. F. Brown et al., *Hebrew and English Lexicon of the Old Testament* (Oxford: Clarendon Press, n.d.), p. 345.

12. Paret, *Übersetzung*, p. 23.

13. R. Blachère, *Le Coran: Traduction nouvelle* (Paris: G. P. Maisonneuve, 1949), p. 433.

14. Ibid., p. 471.

15. ʿAbdallāh b. ʿUmar al-Bayḍāwī, *Anwār al-tanzil wa-asrār al-taʾwīl*, ed. H. Fleischer (Osnabrück: Biblio Verlag, 1968), 1:462.

16. Muḥammad b. Jarīr al-Ṭabarī, *Jāmi ʿal-bayān fi tafsīr al-Qurʾān* (Būlāq, 1323; Beirut: Dār al-Maʿrifah, 1409/1989), 11:135.

17. Suyūṭī, *Itqān*, 2:97, 101.

18. Blachère, *Le Coran*, p. 36.

19. Paret, *Übersetzung*, p. 500.

20. Zabīdī, *Tāj,* 4:49–52; Lane, *Arabic-English Lexicon*, p. 2538.

21. Zabīdī, *Tāj,* 2:5 f.; Lane, *Arabic-English Lexicon*, pp. 3 f.

22. Suyūṭī, *Itqān*, 2:4.

23. Ṭabarī, *Jāmi ʿal-bayān fi tafsīr al-Qurʾān*, 30:38.

24. Suyūṭī, *Itqān*, 2:108.

25. Zabīdī, *Tāj,* 2:5.

26. Suyūṭī, *Itqān*, 2:84.

27. Maḥmūd b. ʿUmar al-Zamakhsharī, *Asās al-balāghah* (Beirut: Dār Ṣādir, 1399/1979), p. 9.

28. Lane, *Arabic-English Lexicon*, pp. 3 f.

29. Zabīdī, *Tāj,* 2:6.

30. A. Jeffery, *The Foreign Vocabulary of the Qurʾān* (Baroda: Oriental Institute, 1938), p. 43.

31. Ṭabarī, *Jāmi ʿal-bayān fi tafsīr al-Qurʾān*, 17:78 f.

32. Theodor Nöldeke, *Neue Beiträge zur semitischen Sprachwissenschaft* (Amsterdam: APA Philo Press, 1982), p. 27; Jeffery, *Foreign Vocabulary*, p. 164.

33. This feature of Ḥijāzī Arabic is discussed at length by Rabin, *Ancient West Arabian*, pp. 130 ff.

34. Bell, *The Qurʾān*, pp. 9, 143; Paret, *Übersetzung*, pp. 12, 137.

35. Blachère, *Le Coran*, pp. 645, 742.

36. Suyūṭī, *Itqān*, 2:111.

37. Rabin, *Ancient West Arabian*, p. 134.
38. See no. 2, above.
39. Zabīdī, *Tāj,* 12:361 f.
40. Blachère, *Le Coran*, p. 309.
41. Bell, *The Qur'ān*, p. 39.
42. Paret, *Übersetzung*, p. 39.
43. R. Paret, *Der Koran: Kommentar und Konkordanz* (Stuttgart: Kohlhammer, 1971), p. 56.
44. Suyūṭī, *Itqān*, 2:114.
45. Ṭabarī, *Jāmi ʿal-bayān fi tafsīr al-Qur'ān*, 3:36 f.
46. Ṭabarī, *Jāmi ʿal-bayān fi tafsīr al-Qur'ān*, 3:37 ult.
47. Ibid., 3:38.
48. For a summary and extensive bibliography, See Paret, *Kommentar*, pp. 279 f.; also Jeffery, *Foreign Vocabulary*, p. 26. Paret (*Übersetzung*) translates XV.867: "Sieben Erzählungen"; Blachère (*Le Coran*, p. 223), "Sept des répétitions"; Bell (*The Qur'ān*, p. 243), "Seven of the repetitions."
49. Lane, *Arabic-English Lexicon*, p. 360.
50. Abū Ghālib b. Maymūn, *Muntahā l-ṭalab*, MS Laleli 1941, facsim. ed. by F. Sezgin. (Frankfurt am Main, 1986), p. 23.
51. Bell, *The Qur'ān*, p. 322.
52. Paret, *Übersetzung*, p. 276.
53. Blachère, *Le Coran*, p. 1043.
54. Ṭabarī, *Jāmi ʿal-bayān fi tafsīr al-Qur'ān*, 17:131–34.
55. ʿAbd al-Malik Ibn Hishām,. *K. Sīrat rasūl Allāh*, ed. F. Wüstenfeld (Frankfurt am Main: Minerva, 1961), pp. 370 f.
56. For the Ḥijāzī suffix *-hu*, where Classical Arabic has *-hi*, see Rabin, *Ancient West Arabian*, pp. 99, 151; for the loss of *hamzah* in Ḥijāzī, see above, pp. 783–84.
57. Bell, *The Qur'ān*, p. 11.
58. Blachère, *Le Coran*, p. 748.
59. Paret, *Übersetzung*, p. 14.
60. Ṭabarī, *Jāmi ʿal-bayān fi tafsīr al-Qur'ān*, 1:297 f.
61. Ibn Manẓūr al-Ifrīqī, *Lisān al-ʿArab* (Beirut: Dār Ṣādir. 1374–1376/ 1955–1956), 15:294.
62. Bell, *The Qur'ān*, p. 18.
63. Blachère, *Le Coran*, p. 767.
64. Paret, *Übersetzung*, p. 21; *Kommentar*, p. 34.
65. Jeffery, *Foreign Vocabulary*, p. 192.
66. Ifrīqī, *Lisān*, 8:438.

67. Ṭabarī, *Jāmi ʿal-bayān fi tafsīr al-Qurʾān*, 1:444.

68. Ifrīqī, *Lisān*, 8:438.

69. Bell, *The Qurʾān*, pp. 141 f.

70. Lane, *Arabic-English Lexicon*, p. 2014.

71. Blachère, *Le Coran*, pp. 618 f.

72. Paret, *Übersetzung*, p. 126 f. For further bibliography on this much-discussed point, see Paret, *Kommentar*, p. 160, and Jeffery, *Foreign Vocabulary*, p. 65.

73. Lane, *Arabic-English Lexicon*, p. 411.

74. Ibid., p. 550.

75. Nöldeke, *GdQ*, 3:255 f.

76. A. Fischer, "The Mysterious Letters of the Koran: Old Abbreviations of the *Basmalah*," *JAOS* 93 (1973): 267–85.

77. Suyūṭī, *Itqān*, 4:159.

Part 7

Richard Bell: Introduction and Commentary

7.1

INTRODUCTION TO RICHARD BELL

Ibn Warraq

The Rev. Dr. Richard Bell was born in Scotland in 1876, and educated at Edinburgh University, where he studied Semitic languages and divinity. He became a minister of the Church of Scotland in 1904, and ordained to the parish of Wamphrey in 1907. After fourteen years in the parish ministry, Bell returned to Edinburgh as lecturer in Arabic, attaining the position of reader in Arabic in 1938, a position he held until his retirement in 1947. He died in 1952.[1]

Bell seems to have a led an uneventful life, having dedicated his entire life to the church and his scholarly pursuits. After an initial interest in Arabic mathematical manuscripts,[2] Bell switched to and concentrated on the Christian influences on the development of Islam, and the structure, chronology and composition of the Qur'ān. He gave the Gunning Lectures at the University of Edinburgh in 1925, and these were published the following year as his first book, under the title *The Origin of Islam in its Christian Environment*.'[3] In the latter book Bell argued that "the key to a great deal both in the Qur'ān and in the career of Muhammad lies . . . just in his gradual acquisition of knowledge of what the Bible contained and of what Jews and Christians believed."[4]

Henceforth, Bell concentrated on the Qur'ān, producing seven articles on various aspects of Qur'ānic studies, before bringing out his English translation of the Qur'ān, *The Qur'ān Translated, with a Critical Rearrangement of the Surahs*.[5]

Further articles followed,[6] and finally what had been his class lectures on the Qur'ān appeared posthumously in 1953 as *Introduction to the Qur'ān.*[7]

But as Bosworth and Richardson point out it is the "*The Qur'ān Translated* which may be regarded as Bell's magnum opus. . . . By closely examining the Qur'ānic text verse by verse, observing the lengths of verses, their external and internal rhymes and assonances, etc., he came to believe that the structure of the Qur'ān was far more complex than had hitherto been believed. He concluded that the revelations underwent considerable revision, including expansion, replacement of certain portions by others, re-arrangements, etc;, and that the use of written documents was involved, under the Prophet's guidance, so that the Qur'ān as we know it took shape in the last eight years or so of Muhammad's mission at Medina, i.e. from A.H. 2–10 / C.E. 624–32. This corresponded to what Bell called "the Book period," when a written scripture was produced out of the revelations previously used largely for liturgical purposes. His *The Qur'ān Translated* endeavored therefore to show schematically on the printed page, by the use of significant indentation, dotted lines separating passages, parallel columns, and so on, in order to show which pieces of revelation had been substituted for others or written on the back of one fragment of writing material, whilst at the same time retaining the traditional order of what Bell nevertheless now regarded as highly composite suras."[8]

Bell explains his objectives in the preface to his translation of the Qur'ān:

> "The main object has been to understand the deliverances of Muhammad afresh, as far as possible in their historical setting, and therefore to get behind the traditional interpretation. But the Moslem commentators have not been ignored. Bayḍāwī has constantly, and other standard commentaries have occasionally,been consulted. But dogmatic prepossessions sometimes vitiate their exegesis, and in many passages the grammatical construction is evidently difficult even to them."[9]
>
> "The translation goes frankly on the assumption that the Qur'ān was in written form when the redactors started their work, whether actually written by Muhammad himself, as I personally believe, or by others at his dictation. . . . .

All the possibilities of confusion in written documents have had to be considered—corrections, interlinear additions, additions on the margin, deletions and substitutions, pieces cut off from a passage and wrongly placed, passages written on the back of others and then read continuously, front and back following each other."[10]

For Bell, the Qur'ān was revealed in short passages. Rippin sums up Bell's views thus:

"Abrupt changes in rhyme patterns, repetition of rhyme words, rupture in grammatical structure, sudden variation in verse length, and unwarranted shift in personal pronouns all point to revisions undertaken by Muhammad due to a change in purpose sometime during his career. Bell suggests that three periods may be separated in Muhammad's career: the early period in which "signs" and praise of God play the predominant role; next, the Qur'ān period which covers the later Meccan and Medinan era up to the year 2 A.H.; and finally the Book period which is from the year 2 A.H. on."[11]

Watt also sums up Bell's hypothesis and then examines Sura LXXXVIII.17–20 to bring out Bell's meaning:

[Bell's] theory was not simply that parts of the Qur'ān had been written down at a fairly early stage in Muhammad's career, but more particularly that the occurrence in the middle of a sura of a passage wholly unrelated to the context was to be explained by the supposition that this passage had been written on the back of the 'scrap of paper ' used for one of the neighbouring passages which properly belonged to the sura. . . .

Bell's arguments can be presented most clearly in the case of sura LXXXVIII.17–20:

"The sura begins with a description of the Judgement and the fate of the wicked, and then continues with a picture of the righteous

(10) in a garden lofty (*ʿāliya*)
(11) wherein they hear no babbling; (*lāghiya*)
(12) therein is spring running; (*jāriya*)
(13) therein are couches upraised (*marfūʿa*)

(14) and goblets set out (*mawdūʿa*)
(15) and cushions in rows (*maṣfūfa*)
(16)and carpets spread. (*mabthūtha*)
(17) Will they not look at the camels, how they have been created (*khuliqat*)
(18) at the heaven, how it has been uplifted; (*rufiʿat*)
(19) at the mountains, how they have been set up; (*nuṣibat*)
(20) at the earth, how it has been laid flat? (*suṭiḥat*)
(21) So warn. You are only a warner. . . . (*mudhakkir*)

The argument here is as follows. The passage 17–20 has no connection of thought either with what goes before or with what comes after; and it is marked off by its rhyme. It is thus difficult to know why it has been placed here. If one assumes that its position has been given to it by a collector, one may still ask whether a responsible collector could not have found a more suitable place for it. Bell's hypothesis is that verses 17–20 have been placed here because they were found written on the back of verses 13–16. He further holds in this particular case that 13–16, which are marked off by rhyme from the preceding verses, were a later addition to these, and happened to have been written on the back of a "scrap" which already contained 17–20."[12]

In his preface to the translation of the Qurʾān, Bell regretted that "owing to the cost of printing, the mass of notes which have accumulated in the course of the work have had to be suppressed. . . ." These notes were eventually reworked into a commentary, but were never published during Bell's lifetime. Sometime in the early 1970s, a microfilm of the typescript of this commentary was entrusted to Professor C. E. Bosworth by the then secretary of the Edinburgh University Press. The microfilm was taken home, and then lay forgotten in a cupboard for nearly twenty years, until a chance remark brought the existence of the microfilm back to mind.[13] As a result, we have the two volumes of Bell's Commentary, edited by Bosworth and Richardson.

Welch, in his article on the Qurʾān in the *Encyclopaedia of Islam*, 2nd edition,[14] considers Bell a pioneer, and Bosworth and Richardson think that it "would be hard to imagine the radical, contemporary approaches to Qurʾānic scholarship represented, in differing ways, by e.g. John Wansbrough and Angelika Neuwirth, without the pioneering work of Bell."[15]

Muslim scholars consider him a "Scottish crackpot";[16] and Rippin, while admitting that Bell's *Commentary* is valuable for his efforts at determining meaning in the Qur'ānic text "in terms of providing a reading strategy for the Qur'ān, however, the work reveals its age." Rippin ends his article on a positive note, however: "What merit there is in [Bell's *Commentary*] lies in its emphasis on discerning the meaning of the text; we will be able to consider the appearance of the book worthwhile if, as a result of its circulation, it helps move scholarship away from a preoccupation with theories about the Qur'ānic text and turn attention to the actual text itself."[17]

WORKS BY RICHARD BELL:[18]

Full-Length Works

The Origin of Islam in its Christian Environment. London: Macmillan, 1926; reprint, London: Frank Cass, 1968.

The Qur'ān Translated, with a Critical Re-arrangement of the Surahs. 2 vols. Edinburgh T. & T.Clark, 1937–39.

Introduction to the Qur'ān, Language and Literature No. 6, Edinburgh: Edinburgh University Press, 1953. Reprinted as Bell and Watt, *Introduction to the Qur'ān,* revised and enlarged by W. M.Watt (Edinburgh: Edinburgh University Press, 1970).

A Commentary on the Qur'ān. Manchester, 1991.

Articles

"A Duplicate in the Koran; The Composition of Surah xxiii." *MW* 18 (1928): 227–33.

"Who were the Ḥanīfs? *MW* 20 (1930): 120–24.

"The Men of A'rāf (Surah vii: 44)." *MW* 22 (1932): 43–48.

"The Origin of the 'Id al-Adhā'. *MW* 23 (1933): 117–20.

"Muhammad's Call." *MW* 24 (1934): 13–19.

"Muhammad's Visions." *MW* 24 (1934): 145–54.

"Muhammd and previous Messengers." *MW* 24 (1934): 330–40.

"Muhammad and Divorce in the Qur'ān." *MW* 29 (1939): 55–62.

"Sūral al-Ḥashr: A Study of Its Composition." *MW* 38 (1948): 29–42.

"Muhammad's Pilgrimage Proclamation." *JRAS* (1937): 233–44.
"The Development of Muhammad's Teaching and Prophetic Consciousness." *School of Oriental Studies Bulletin* (June 1935): 1–9.
"The Beginnings of Muhammad's Religious Activity." *TGUOS* 7 (1934–5): 16–24.
"The Sacrifice of Ishmael." *TGUOS* 10: 29–31.
"The Style of the Qur'ān." *TGUOS* 11 (1942–44) 9–15.
"Muhammad's Knowledge of the Old Testament." *Studia Semitica et Orientalia* 2 (1945): 1–20.
"Critical Observations on the mistakes of Philologers. . . ." *JRAS* (1904): 95–118.
"List of the Arabic Manuscripts in the baillie Collection in the Library of Edinburgh University." *JRAS* (1905): 513–20
"John of Damascus and the controversy with Islam." *TGUOS* 4 (1913–22): 37–38
"Notes on Moslem Traditions." *TGUOS* 4 (1913–22): 78–79.
"Some early literary contacts between Moslem Spain and the East. *TGUOS* 13 (1947–49): 48–51.
"A Moslem Thinker on the Teaching of Religion: al-Ghazzali A.D.1058–1111." *Hibbert Journal* 42 (1943): 31–36.

ARTICLES ON OR DISCUSSIONS OF BELL

Merrill, J. E. "Dr. Bell's Critical Analysis of the Qur'ān." *MW* 37 (1947):134–48.
Nagel, Tilman. "Vom Qur'ān zur Schrift: Bells Hypothese aus religionsgeschichtlicher Sicht." *Der Islam* 60 (1983): 143–65.
Parvez Manzoor, S. "Method against Truth: Orientalism and *Qur'ānic* Studies." *Muslim World Book Review* 7, no. 4 (1987): 35.
Rippin, A. "Reading the Qur'ān with Richard Bell." *JAOS* 112, no. 4 (1992): 639–47.
Tritton, A. S. "Obituary." *JRAS* (1952–53): 180.
Watt, W. M. "The Dating of the Qur'ān: A Review of Richard Bell's Theories." *JRAS* (1957): 46–56.
Welch, A. T. s.v. *EI2* 5: 418a, s.v. "dur'ān."

REVIEWS OF BELL'S *INTRODUCTION TO THE QUR'ĀN*

Vahiduddin, S. "Richard Bell's Study of the Qur'ān." *IC* 30 (1956): 263–72.
Jeffery, Arthur. *MW* 44 (1954): 254–58

Paret, Rudi. *ZDMG* 105 (1954): 497–501.
Schacht, Joseph. *Oriens* 7 (1954): 359–62
Arberry, A.J. *BSOAS* 17 (1955): 380–81.

NOTES

1. C. E. Bosworth and M. E. J. Richardson, "Introduction," Bell's *A Commentary on the Qur'ān* (Manchester, 1991), pp. xiii–xiv. Almost all the details of Bell's biography come from this introduction.

2. According to A. S. Tritton, "Obituary," *JRAS* (1952–53): 180, quoted by A. Rippin, "Reading the Qur'ān with Richard Bell," *JAOS* 112, no. 4 (1992): 639.

3. R. Bell, *The Origin of Islam in its Christian Environment* (London: Macmillan, 1926; reprint, London: Frank Cass, 1968).

4. Ibid., pp. 68–69, quoted by Rippin, "Reading the Qur'ān with Richard Bell," p. 640.

5. R. Bell, *The Qur'ān Translated, with a Critical Re-arrangement of the Surahs*, (Edinburgh: T & T. Clark, 1937–39).

6. For a complete list of his articles see the bibliography.

7. R. Bell, *Introduction to the Qur'ān,* Language and Literature No. 6 (Edinburgh University Press, Edinburgh 1953.

8. Bosworth and Richardson, "Introduction" pp. xiv–xv.

9. Bell, *The Qur'ān Translated*, vol.1, p. v.

10. Ibid., p. vi.

11. Rippin, "Reading the Qur'ān with Richard Bell," p. 641.

12. Bell and Watt, *Introduction to the Qur'ān* (Edinburgh: Edinburgh University Press, 1970), pp. 101–102.

13. Bosworth and Richardson, "Introduction," p. xiii.

14. A. T. Welch, EI2 5: 418a, s.v. "dur'ān"

15. C. E. Bosworth and M. E. J. Richardson, Introduction to Bell's *A Commentary on the Qur'ān,* Manchester, 1991, pxvi

16. At least one does: S. Parvez Manzoor, "Method against Truth: Orientalism and *Qur'ānic* Studies," *Muslim World Book Review* 7, no. 4 (1987): 35; quoted in Rippin, "Reading the Qur'ān with Richard Bell," p. 640

17. Rippin, "Reading the Qur'ān with Richard Bell," pp. 645, 647.

18. All the bibliographic details come from ibid. and Bell and Watt, *Introduction to the Qur'ān.*

7.2

FROM *INTRODUCTION TO THE QUR'ĀN*

Richard Bell

THE STRUCTURE AND STYLE OF THE QUR'ĀN

R*hymes.*— The Qur'ān, then, presents itself in the form of suras divided into verses. The questions arise whether the suras are unities, and, if so, whether they show any organic structure; or, if they are not unities, whether we can discern how they have been built up. In approaching these questions, if we follow the method of starting from externals, it will be well to be clear as to the nature of the rhyme that marks the close of verses.

There is no attempt in the Qur'ān to produce the strict rhyme of poetry. In an Arabic poem each verse had to end in the same rhyme-consonant surrounded by the same vowels—an interchange of *i* and *u* was allowed, though considered a weakness. Short, inflectional vowels following the rhyme-consonant were usually retained, and, if retained, were pronounced long at the end of the line. Only in very exceptional cases is it possible to find this type of rhyme in the Qur'ān. What we find is, rather, assonance, in which short, inflectional vowels at the end of a verse are disregarded, and for the rest, the vowels, particularly their length, and the fall of the accent, that is, the form of the end word of the verse, are of more importance than the consonants. Of course the consonant may remain the same, but that is not essential. Thus in CXII the four verses

From Richard Bell, *Introduction to the Qur'ān* (Edinburgh: Edinburgh University Press, 1958). Reprinted with permission.

rhyme in *-ad*, if we disregard the inflections; in CV we have the rhyme in *-īl*, if we disregard end vowels and allow *ū* in place of *ī* in the last verse. In CIII *r* is rhyme-consonant, but the inflections vary and have to he disregarded, though, for pronunciation, we require a short vowel sound of some kind after the *r*, or, alternatively, a short vowel before it which is not in the form. In LIV, where *r* as the rhyme-consonant is carried through fifty-five verses, we have not only to disregard the end vowels but to accept variations of the preceding vowel, *i* and *u* and even *a* occurring in that position; the assonance is *-faʿil*, that is, an open syllable with a short vowel that takes the accent, followed by a syllable with a short vowel closed by *r* that thus becomes a rhyme-consonant. On the other hand, the accusative termination *-an* is often retained, being probably pronounced as *-ā*; for example in XVIII, LXXII, and C, where the accusative termination seems to be essential to the rhyme. Further, the feminine termination *-atun* dropped not only its inflections but also its *t* sound; cf. CIV, where, if we drop end vowels and pronounce the feminine termination as *ā* or *ah*, we get a consistent assonance formed by an accented syllable followed by a short unaccented syllable and the ending, that is *fāʾalah*, in which both vowels and consonants are variable, but the place of the accent and the ending *-ah* remain the same. The actual rhyme-words are: *lúmazah, ʿáddadah, ákhladah, al-ḥúṭamah, al-ḥúṭamah, al-mūqadah, al-ʾáfʾidah, múʾṣadah, mumáddadah*; this illustrates the retention of the same sound formation with variation of consonant, and even of vowel. In XCIX we have a similar assonance, formed by a long accented *ā*, followed by a short syllable, and the feminine suffix *-hā*, that is, *-ā́lahā*, the *-hā* being in one verse replaced by the plural suffix *-hum*. The assonance of XLVII is the same, but with greater variation of suffix.

The structure of the Arabic language, in which words fall into definite types of forms, was favorable to the production of such assonances. But even in the short suras we find a tendency to rely for the assonance on grammatical terminations, for example, the suffix *-hā* as in XCIX above, and in XCI assonance *-ī́hā*. In the longer suras this tendency increases. Thus in LV the assonance depends very largely upon the dual-ending *-an̄*. Fairly often in the longer suras, though hardly ever carried through unbroken, we find the assonance *-ā(l)*, that is, a long *ā* vowel followed by a (variable) consonant; so in parts of II, III, XIV, XXXVIII (almost complete), XXXIX, XL, and sporadically elsewhere. But in the great majority of the suras of any length, and even in some of the short ones, the prevailing assonance is *-ī(l)*, that is, a long *ī* or *ū* sound (these interchange freely) followed by a consonant. This depends very largely on the plural endings of nouns and verbs, *-ūn* and *-īn*, varied by words of the form *faʿīl*, one of the commonest forms in Arabic. By far the greater part of the Qurʾān shows this assonance.

With an assonance depending thus upon grammatical endings there may occasionally be doubt as to whether it was really intended. The varying systems of verse numbering depend to some extent, though not entirely, upon varying judgment as to where the rhyme was intended to fall in particular cases. But that assonance at the end of verses was intended and deliberately sought for can hardly be questioned. In passages with short verses and frequently recurring assonances the intention is unmistakable. But even in suras in which the verses are long, we find special turns of phrase employed in order to produce the assonance. Thus the preposition *min* with a plural participle is often used where a participle in the singular would have sufficiently given the sense; so that we get phrases like "one of the unbelievers" instead of simply "an unbeliever" because the former gives the rhyming plural ending, while the latter does not: for example, III.53, 75;VII.103. *Kānū* with an imperfect or participle in the plural often takes the place of a simple perfect plural; for example in II.54, VII.35. Or an imperfect plural may be used where a perfect might have been expected, as in V.74. Occasionally a phrase is added at the end of a verse that is really otiose as regards sense but supplies the assonance, as in XII.10;XXI.68, 79, 104. Sometimes the sense is strained in order to produce the rhyme, for instance in IV, where statements regarding Allah are inappropriately thrown into the past by the use of *kāna* in front of them, the accusative ending on which the rhyme depends being thereby obtained. The form of a proper name is occasionally modified for the sake of rhyme, as *Sīnīn*, XCV, *Ilyāsīn*, XXXVII.130.

Rhyme-phrases.—Statements regarding Allah occur frequently at the end of verses, especially in the long suras, where the verses also are of some length. Where the verses are short, the word or phrase that carries the rhyme forms as a rule an integral part of the grammatical structure and is necessary to the sense. But in some passages we find that the phrases that carry the rhyme can be detached without dislocating the structure of what remains, as in XLI.8 ff. Sometimes, in fact, the rhyme phrase interrupts the sense, as in VI.142 ff.; but this is exceptional. Usually the phrase is appropriate enough but stands apart from the rest of the verse. These detachable rhyme phrases—most of which carry the assonance in *-ī(i)*—tend to be repeated, and to assume a set form that recurs either verbally or with slight changes in wording. Thus, *inna fī dhālika la-'āyatan li-l-mu'minīn* often closes the account of a "sign." *'Alā llāhi fa-l-yatawakkal il-mu'minūn* (*il-mutawakkilūn*) occurs nine times. *Wa-llāhu 'alīm ḥakīm* occurs twelve times, or, if we include slight modifications, eighteen times. There are other combinations of adjectives referring to Allah that are frequently used in the same way. Perhaps the most frequent of all such phrases is *inna llāha 'alā kulli shai'in qadīr*, "verily Allah over everything hath power," which is used six times in II, four times in III, four times in V, and some eighteen times in other suras. To have a stock of such phrases was no doubt a convenience for a busy man who had adopted a rhyming style of utterance. But there is also a certain effectiveness in their use. These sententious phrases regarding Allah are most often used to close a deliverance, and serve at once to press home a truth by repetition and to clinch the authority of what is laid down. They act as a kind of refrain.

Refrains.—The use of actual refrain, in the sense of the same words occurring at more or less regular intervals, is sparse in the Qur'ān. It is anything but effectively used in LV, where the same words "Which then of the benefits of your Lord will ye twain count false?" occur in verses 12, 15, 18, 21, 23, 25, 28, and from there on in practically each alternate verse, without regard to the sense, which they frequently interrupt. The same tendency to increasing frequency and disregard of sense appears in the use of the words, "Woe that day to those who count false!" as a kind of refrain before sections of Sura LXXVII. Didactically effective, on the other hand, is the use of refrain in the groups of stories of former prophets that occur in various suras. The stories in these groups not only show similarities of wording throughout, but are often closed by the same formula; cf. those in XI, XXVI, XXXVII, and LIV.

Internal Rhymes.—In addition to the rhymes that occur at the end of the verses, we can occasionally detect rhymes, different from the end rhymes, occurring in the middle or elsewhere in the verse. These give the impression of a varied arrangement of rhymes. R. Geyer pointed out some of these in an article in the *Göttinger Gelehrte Anzeigen* (1901), and argued that stanzas with such varied rhymes were some times deliberately intended in the Qur'ān. If that were so, we should expect the same form to recur. But in going through Geyer's examples we do not get the impression that any preexisting forms of stanza were being reproduced, or that any fixed forms of stanza at all were being used. There are no fixed patterns. All that can he said is that in some passages we do find such mixtures of rhymes, just as, quite often, we find, within a sura, breaks in the regular recurring rhyme at the end of the verses. But, as we shall see, these facts are to be otherwise explained.

Strophes.—A similar argument applies to the contention of D. H. Mueller in his book, *Die Propheten in ihrer ursprünglichen Form* (Vienna, 1895). He sought to show that composition in strophes was characteristic of prophetic literature, in the Old Testament as well as in the Qur'ān. From the Qur'ān he adduced many passages that appear to support such a view, for example, LVI. But if we are to speak of strophic form, we expect some regularity in the length and arrangement of the strophes. Mueller, however, failed to show that there was any such regularity. What his evidence does show is that many suras of the Qur'ān fall into short sections or paragraphs. But these are not of fixed length, nor do they seem to follow any pattern of length. Their length is determined not by any consideration of form, but by the subject or incident treated in each.

Short Pieces.—Interpreted in this way, Mueller's contention brings out a real characteristic of Qur'ān style. It is disjointed. Only very seldom do we find in it evidence of sustained unified composition at any great length. The longest such pieces are the addresses found in some of the later suras. The address before Uḥud has become broken up and is now difficult to unravel from the middle of III. But the address after the Day of the Trench and the overthrow of the Quraiẓah, XXXIII.9–27, and the assurance to the disappointed Muslims after the truce of Ḥudaibiyah, XLVIII.18–29, may be taken as examples of fairly lengthy pieces evidently composed for one special purpose. Some of the narratives, too, in the Qur'ān, especially accounts of Moses and of Abraham, run to considerable length. But they tend to fall into separate incidents, instead of being recounted straightforwardly. This is particularly true of the longest of all, the story of Joseph in XII. In other suras, even where we can trace some connection in thought, this paragraph arrangement is very evident. In LXXX, for instance, we can persuade ourselves that a line of thought governs the collection of the separate pieces, running from the Prophet's dissatisfaction with his cajoling of the wealthy, through the sublimity of the message that ought to commend itself, but is thwarted by man's ingratitude for religious and temporal benefits, up to the description of the final Judgment day. But one has a stronger impression of the distinctness of the separate pieces than of their unity; and one of them, verses 24–32, bears evident traces of having been fitted into a context to which it did not originally belong. In the longer suras devoted largely to political and legal matters we find, as is natural enough, that subjects vary, and, while we do find here and there considerable blocks of legislation devoted to one subject, for example, the rules regarding divorce in II.228 ff., we do not get the impression that an effort has been made to produce a sura dealing systematically with any subject. One sura may contain passages dealing with many different subjects, and the same subject may be treated in several different suras.

The Qur'ān itself tells us that it was delivered in separate pieces, XVII.107, XXV.34. Neither of these passages tells us anything as to the length of the pieces. But Muslim Tradition, which assigns different 'occasions ' to passages consisting of a verse or two, favors the assumption that the pieces were short. We were led to this by consideration of Muhammad's method of composition. It corresponds to what we actually find in the Qur'ān. Not only are there a considerable number of short pieces standing alone as separate suras, but the longer suras contain many short pieces that are complete in themselves, and could be removed without serious derangement of the context. Consideration of the passages introduced by formulae of direct address will show that. II.173–175, for instance, deals with retaliation; it comes indeed among other passages addressed to the believers and dealing with other subjects, but it has no necessary connection with them. V.14 stands quite by itself, clear enough, if only we knew the event to which it refers, but if it had been absent we should never have suspected that something had fallen out. XLIX.13 may be quoted as illustrating the form of these passages: "O ye people, We have created you of male and female and made you races and tribes, that ye may show mutual recognition; verily, the most noble of you in Allah's eyes is the most pious; verily Allah is knowing, well-informed." Here, following the address, we have an indication of the subject that has called for treatment, then comes a declaration regarding it, and finally the passage is closed by a sententious maxim. This form is found not only in passages with direct address, but in a multitude of others. They begin by stating their occasion; a question has been asked, the unbelievers have said or done something, something has happened, or some situation has arisen. The matter is dealt with shortly, in usually not more than three or four verses; at the end comes a general statement, often about Allah, which rounds off the passage. Once we have caught this lilt of Qur'ān style it becomes fairly easy to separate the suras into the separate pieces of which they have been built up, and this is a great step toward the interpretation of the Qur'ān. It is not, of course, to be too readily assumed that there is no connection between these separate pieces. There may, or there may not, be a connection in subject and thought, and where that is absent there may still be a connection in time. On the other hand, there may be no connection in thought between contiguous pieces, or the sura may have been built up of pieces of different dates that have been fitted into a sort of scheme.

Style of the Qur'ān.—It is only when we have unravelled these short units of composition that enter into the structure of the suras that we can speak of the style of the Qur'ān. The insistence so frequently met with on its disjointedness, its formlessness, its excited, unpremeditated, rhapsodical character, rests too much on a failure to discern the natural divisions into which the suras fall, and also to take account of the displacements and undesigned breaks in connection, which, as we shall see, are numerous. We have to remember, too, that Muhammad disclaimed being a poet, and evidently had no ear for poetry.[1] He claimed that he had messages to convey. We have to seek, therefore, for didactic, rather than for poetic or artistic, forms.

Slogans.—One of these forms, the prevailing one in later suras, has been spoken of above. But the simplest form of the kind is the short statement introduced by the word "say." There are about 250 of these scattered throughout the Qur'ān. Sometimes they stand singly; here and there we find groups of them standing together, though really quite distinct from each other, for instance in VI.56 ff.; sometimes they are worked into the context of a passage. These statements are of various kinds, answers to questions, retorts to arguments or jeers of his opponents, statements of Muhammad's own position; there are one or two prayers, for example III.25; there are two credal statements for his followers to repeat, the word "say" being in the plural, II.130, XXIX.45, to which may be added CXII, though the verb is singular; finally, there are a number of phrases suitable for repetition in various circumstances, such as, " Allah's guidance is the guidance," II.114; "Allah is my portion; on Him let the trusting set their trust," XXXIX.39.

It is evident that these phrases were designed for repetition; they were not composed originally as parts of suras, they were of the nature of slogans devised for public use, and found their way into suras later. Where a context is given, usually in the later parts of the Qur'ān, we get a hint of how they were produced. A question has been asked, II.185, 211;V.6;VIII.1; and so on, or some argument or jeer has come to the Prophet's knowledge, and he has thought over it until the '"suggestion" of the answer has come. He has "sought guidance" and has been told what to say. The statement thus becomes a part of one of the paragraphs already described as characteristic of Qur'ān style.

These slogans are difficult to date, and it is doubtful if any of those that appear in the Qur'ān are very early, though some of them may quite well be so. But they are so common that the presumption is that they were a constant element in Muhammad's methods of propaganda, and that from the first he made use of carefully prepared formulas for repetition.

The use of assonance in such formulas would be natural. But those that actually occur hardly support the idea that it was by this route that assonance became a feature of Muhammad's deliverances. Most of them fall naturally enough into the rhyme of the sura in which they occur, but few of them rhyme within themselves. XXXIV.45 and XLI.44 possibly do, and CII.1, 2 looks like an early rhymed slogan, though not preceded by "say." It is more likely that the suggestion of rhyme came from the *saj*ʿ of the soothsayers.

Kāhin–Form.—Muhammad protested against being classed as a soothsayer, LII.29, LXX.42, and, as the form and content of his deliverances developed, the disclaimer was justified; but to begin with, his position was similar enough to that of a *kāhin* to suggest that he may have taken a hint from the soothsayers as to the form of his utterances. Actually, there are five passages in the Qur'ān that are quite in *kāhin* manner, XXXVII.1–4, (5); LI.1–6; LXXVII.1–7; LXXIX.1–14; C.1–6. In these we have a number of oaths by females of some kind, forming a jingle, leading up to a statement which does not rhyme with the oaths. The statement is mostly quite short; but in LXXIX it is of some length and may have been extended. The feminine participles are usually thought to apply to angels; the Qur'ān itself gives some support to this, XXXVII.165. But this is probably an afterthought, and it may be doubted if originally any definite meaning was attached to these asseverations. The soothsayers, no doubt, often used a string of cryptic oaths without much sense, simply to prepare the way for the statement and make it impressive.

Asserverative Passages.—Muhammad apparently found these random oaths unsatisfactory. LXXXIX.1–4, which is so cryptic as to be unintelligible, may indicate this. LII.1–8 still shows the same device of making the statement stand out by having a different assonance from the oaths, but the oaths, though still difficult to interpret, had evidently a clear enough sense in the prophet's own mind. In other asseverative passages, of which there are not a few,[2] the oaths are chosen as having some bearing on the statement to which they lead up, and this statement in the same assonance makes an effective close to the passage. The best example is perhaps XCI.1–10, where four pairs of oaths by contrasted things, sun and moon, day and night, heaven and earth, and what formed the soul and implanted in it its wickedness and piety, lead up to the statement of the contrast between him who purifies his soul and him who corrupts it. This asseverative style seems to have gradually been discarded. There are a number of passages where a single oath appears at the beginning, but in pasages certainly Medinan oaths hardly appear at all.

"When" Passages.—A modification of the asseverative passage is seen in the use of a number of temporal clauses, introduced by *idhā* or *yawma*, leading up to a statement pressing home the fact of the Judgment upon the conscience. In one passage, LXXV.26–30, it is a death scene that is described in the temporal clauses, but usually it is the Last Day that is conjured up by a selection from its awe-inspiring phenomena. In LXXXIV.1–6 the statement of the main clause is left unrhymed, but in all the others it has the same rhyme as the clauses that lead up to it. The longest of these passages is LXXXI.1–14, where twelve *idhā* clauses lead up to the statement: " A soul will know what it has presented," that is, the deeds laid to its account. The effectiveness of such a form is even more evident in some of the shorter pieces, and there can be no doubt that they were carefully designed for repetition to impress the conscience of hearers.[3]

Dramatic Scenes.—This homiletic purpose is evident throughout the

Qur'ān. The piling up of temporal clauses did not continue, but at all stages of the Qur'ān the scenes of the Judgment and the future life are evoked, not for any speculative purpose, but in order to impress the conscience and clinch in argument. With all the details which the Qur'ān gives of the future abodes of the blessed and the damned, we nowhere get a complete description. Where such a picture seems to have been attempted, as in LV, LXXVI, and LXXXIII, the attempt appears to break down in confusion. On the other hand, we get short well-polished pieces describing luscious attractions or lurid terrors. The same applies to the descriptions of the Judgment; Muhammad evidently is interested in these scenes not for their own sake but for their homiletic value. Only once or twice does he make any attempt to describe the theophany, and it is not sustained, XXXIX.67 ff., LXXXIX.23 f. Attention should, however, be called to the dramatic quality of many of these scenes, which is often unrecognized, but which is really very effective. Some of them are difficult to understand, because, being designed for oral recitation, they do not indicate by whom the various speeches are made; that was left to be made clear by gesture or change of voice as the passage was delivered. As examples may be cited, L.19–25 and XXXVII.48–59; in both of these passages we have to use our imagination to supply the accompanying action of the speeches, but are rewarded by little dramatic scenes which must have been very telling if delivered with dramatic action. This dramatic quality is, in fact, a pervading characteristic of Qur'ān style. Direct speech is apt to be "interjected" at any point, and we have to imagine the personages spoken of in the narrative as expressing themselves in words. If, for instance, we look at the story of Moses in XX, we find that more space is occupied by the spoken words of the actors than by actual narrative. Even where narrative does predominate, the story is hardly ever told straightforwardly, but tends to fall into a series of short word-pictures, the story advancing incident by incident, and the intervening links being left to the imagination of the hearers.

Narratives and Parables.—In narratives, too, the homiletic element is apt to intrude. Thus in the story of Joseph in XII, we find every now and then an aside introduced to make clear the intention of Allah in what happened. This homiletic element is also apt to intrude unduly into Qur'ān *mathals* or parables. The best of these is the parable of the Blighted Garden in LXVIII; that of the Two Owners of Gardens is less clear and more didactic, XVIII.31–42. Others are little more than expanded similes, XIV.29 ff., XVI.77 f., XVIII.43 f., XXX.27, XXXIX.30. That of the Unbelieving Town, XXXVI.12 ff., is difficult to classify; it is perhaps a simile expanded into a story.

Similes.—The Qur'ān contains a good number of similes. These occur in all contexts. In descriptions of the Last Day, when the heavens are rolled up like a scroll, XXI.104, when the people are like moths blown about, and the mountains are like carded wool, CI.3, 4, the similes are sometimes borrowed with the rest of the material, but the Prophet had at all of his career a gift of coining vivid and sometime grimly humorous comparisons. Jews who have the Torah but do not profit by it are compared to an ass loaded with books, LXII.5. Some who in the early days in Medina made advances to Muhammad and then drew back are likened to those who have lit a fire that has then gone out and left them more bewildered in the darkness than ever, II.16; cf. 18 f. Polytheists who imagine other gods besides Allah are like the spider weaving its own frail house, XXIX.40. The works of unbelievers, from which they hope to benefit at the Judgment, are like ashes blown away by the wind, XIV.21, or like a mirage that appears to be water, but, when one comes to it, turns out to be nothing, XXIV.39. People who pray to gods other than Allah are like those who stretch out their hands to water, which, however, never reaches their month, XIII.15; the prayer of unbelieving Quraish at the Kaʿbah is only whistling and clapping of hands, VIII.35. Lukewarm supporters, asked for their opinion and getting up to speak, no doubt hesitatingly, are compared to logs of wood propped up, LXIII.4. For other comparisons, see II.166, 263, 266, 267; III.113; VII.175; X.25; XVIII.43; LVII.19; LXXIV.51. Where the simile is complicated by an attempt at allegory, the result is not so happy, XXX.27, XXXIX.30.

Metaphors.—Metaphors are still more common. T. Sabbagh[4] has collected well over four hundred metaphorical uses of words. Many of these, however, were, no doubt, already so much a matter of course as to be no longer felt as metaphorical. It is not easy to say how far the Qur'ān added new metaphors to the language. The number of commercial terms transferred to the religious sphere is noteworthy.[5] It is, of course, only what might be expected from Muhammad's upbringing, and his taking up his mission in a commercial town, but it did help to stamp its legalistic character upon Islam. The deeds of men are recorded in a book; the Judgment is the reckoning; each person receives his account; the balance is set up, and men's deeds are weighed; each soul is held in pledge for the deeds committed; if a man's actions are approved, he receives his reward, or his hire; to support the Prophet's cause is to lend to Allah. From Bedouin life come the designation of the delights of Paradise as *nuzul*, "reception-feast," and the application of the verb *ḍalla*, "to go astray," to those who follow false gods. The application of bodily functions to spiritual matters is almost unavoidable; thus unbelievers are deaf, unable to hear, blind, unable to see; they cannot discern the truth; they have veils over their hearts, heaviness in their ears; they are in darknesses. The revelation is guidance and light, and the function of a messenger is to lead people out of the darknesses into the light. Doubtful supporters are said to have disease in their hearts; after their conduct at Uḥud they are dubbed *munāfiqīn*, "jinkers," "those who dodge back into their holes like mice."

Borrowed Metaphors and Words.—Many of these metaphors can be paralleled in Jewish and Christian literature. It must not, however, be too readily assumed that that is proof of their having been borrowed. Some of them are so obvious that they may quite well have been employed independently. Borrowed words, on the other hand, generally show their foreign origin by some peculiarity. That the Qur'ān contains a number of words that are not native Arabic was, a little reluctantly, recognized by Muslim scholars, though, in their lack of knowledge of other languages, they often failed to elucidate their origin. Modern scholarship has devoted a good deal of attention to these words, and with wider knowledge of the languages and dialects prevailing in the Near East in pre-Islamic times has for the most part succeeded in tracing their source. Here again, however, we must be on our guard against assuming that every word of foreign origin used in the Qur'ān was by that use introduced into Arabic. Apart from proper names, Dr. Jeffery[6] has collected some 275 words that have been regarded as of foreign origin. The majority of these, however, can be shown to have been in use in Arabic in pre-Islamic times, and many of them had become regular Arabic words. Of only about seventy can we say that the use was new, or that they were used in new senses. Of these seventy, half come from Christian languages, many from Syriac and a few from Ethiopic; some twenty-five come from Hebrew or Jewish-Aramaic; the rest, of little religious importance for the most part, come from Persian, Greek, or unknown sources. It must, however, be remembered that between Syriac and Jewish-Aramaic the decision is often difficult, and the exact provenance of some of these words is still in dispute.

Language.—That there occur unfamiliar words and words used in an unfamiliar sense is shown by the fact that explanations are sometimes added. But it is only natural to assume that the Qur'ān was delivered in the language of the people so far as possible, and that even these borrowed words were already known to Muhammad's followers from their intercourse with Jews and Christians. As a matter of fact, the language of the Qur'ān, so far as we can judge, is on the whole the classical Arabic language. We have seen that in assonance at the end of verses inflectional vowels were dropped and the feminine ending modified, as in colloquial speech. How far this was done in the middle of the verses, we have no means of knowing. For, as the Qur'ān is now pointed and recited, these vowels and terminations are strictly exhibited and pronounced. This may be due to later revision and assimilation to the classical poetry, as Vollers[7] argues, and many dialectical forms may have. been removed in the process. A few irregular forms, which we may perhaps assume to be colloquial or dialectical, still remain, for example, *'yazzakkā* for *yatazakkā* (LXXX.3, 7), *yadhdhakkaru* for *yatadhakkaru* (II.272, III.5, LXXX.4), *iddāraka* for *tadāraka* (VII.36, XXVII.68).

The style of the Qur'ān is held to be unique and inimitable. It certainly is characteristic and unmistakable, in spite of its variations from sura to sura and from section to section.[8] Its artistic, dramatic, pictorial, imaginative qualities have often been lost sight of in theological treatment of the 'the inimitability' of the Qur'ān, but they have always exercised a spell upon the Muslim worshiper.

THE COMPILATION OF THE SURAS

Revisions and Alterations

We have seen that the unit of composition in the Qur'ān is not the sura, but the short piece. The suras, except the very short ones, have been constructed rather than composed. The question then arises whether they were put together by Muhammad, or by those who collected the Qur'ān after his death. The tradition as to the collection of the Qur'ān seems to leave the latter possibility open, and there are even special traditions that ascribe the placing of certain passages to Zaid b. Thābit. On the whole, however, tradition seems to take it for granted that the suras were found much in their present form. The question is one that has really never been thoroughly discussed, and which we shall probably never be able to answer with complete certainty. There is, however, a great deal of evidence that the Prophet himself had more to do with the compiling of the suras than has been usually assumed. Some general considerations already mentioned argue against the collectors having had a free hand in the matter. The great variation in the lengths of the suras is hardly to be accounted for by difference of subject or rhyme or form, though that may explain why some of the short pieces were kept as separate suras. The occurrence of the *bismillah*, which we found reason to think belonged to the composition, would mark at least the beginning of a sura. The occurrence of the mysterious letters also seemed to imply that not only suras, but also groups of suras, were already in existence when the Qur'ān came to be arranged in its present order. The existence of suras is borne out, too, by the challenge the Prophet gave to his opponents that, if they believed that he had invented the Qur'ān, they should produce ten suras like it, XI.16. He must, at that time, have had at least ten pieces of the nature of suras that he could produce if the challenge were taken up. The date is indeterminate, but is probably not later than early Medinan times, and many other suras may have taken shape within the Prophet's subsequent lifetime. But the most conclusive proof of the Prophet's part in the compiling of the suras comes from a detailed study of their structure, which discloses evidences of revisions and alterations such as could hardly have been made without his authority, and for which we can, in many cases, assign a reason in his own changing circumstances and aims.

That passages were not only placed in certain suras, but were sometimes adapted to their position in them, is shown by the occurrence of hidden rhymes. The real explanation of what led Geyer to the assumption of a kind of sonnet formation is that passages that had originally rhymed in one assonance have been adapted to stand in a sura, the assonance of which is different. For example, XXIII.12–16 rhyme in *-ī(l)*, the assonance of the sura as a whole; V.14, however, is long, and breaks up into five short verses rhyming in *-ah*, with a rhyme phrase added carrying the *-ī(l)* assonance, but not entering into the structure of the verse. The rhyme

-ah can be found also in verses 12 and 13 by dropping the end words of each, and this can he done with advantage to the sense. Thus we get in verses 12–14 a complete little piece rhyming in *-ah* describing the generation of man as a sign of Allah's creative power. This has been fitted into the surah by adding rhyme phrases and verses 15, 16, which speak of the resurrection. The passage that follows, XXIII.17–22, has been similarly dealt with. The rhyme phrases are detachable, and, when they have been removed, traces of an assonance in *fāʿil* can be found underneath. Quite a number of other passages have been treated in this way.[9]

Attention may be called to a few cases in which the rhyme of the sura changes. The beginning of III rhymes in *-ā*(*l*), as does also the end; the middle, however, has the rhyme in *-ī*(*l*). Near the point at which the change occurs stands a passage, verses 30 ff., dealing with the story of Mary and Jesus, which has originally rhymed in *-ā*(*l*) but into which phrases have been inserted to carry the rhyme *-ī*(*l*). It is as if a portion with the latter rhyme had been inserted into a sura that had originally rhymed in *-ā*(*l*) and an attempt had been made to dovetail the two pieces together at the start. The impression is strengthened it we notice that the rhyme *-ī*(*l*) occurs at the end of verse 16, carried by a phrase the construction of which causes some difficulty and which leads over to verse 20 f. rather than to verses 17 f. In XIV also the rhyme changes in the middle of the sura and at the junction there is a passage, verses 29 ff., in which the original rhyme has been altered. In XIII something similar appears to have happened at the beginning, verses 2–4, and In XIX near the middle, verses 52–58, 59, but these cases are not quite so clear.

There are many passages in which the rhyme phrases can be detached without revealing an older rhyme underneath. In these cases it is not quite so certain that revision has taken place, for, as we have seen, the detachable rhyme phrase often appears as the mark of the close of a passage. When, however, it appears at the end of a number of consecutive verses, as in VI.95 ff., it is reasonable to assume that it has been inserted into an originally unrhymed passage in order to give it the rhyme of the sura. In two cases this seems to have been done with a list of names, VI.84 ff. and XXXVIII.45 ff.; cf. also XIX.52–58.

Nor is this the only way in which passages have been adapted. VI.142–145 cannot be grammatically construed as they stand, but by taking the first part of each verse we get a list of Allah's bounties in produce of the soil and animals; into this, sentences have been introduced combating heathen food taboos. In VII.55 f. the sign of Allah's revival of dead land and the varying response of different soils—perhaps a simile of the varying response of men to the divine message—has been transformed by inserted sentences, marked by a sudden change of pronoun, into a corroboration of the resurrection.

If passages could be adapted to their place in a sura, they could also be adapted to the needs of a different situation. The Qur'ān itself practically tells us that such revisions were made, for we are told that Satan may influence a prophet's formulation of his message, but Allah adjusts his signs and abrogates what Satan has thrown in, XXII.51 ff. And the Prophet is assured that if he is made to forget a verse, he will be given a similar or a better one, II.100. Muslim theology, too, founding on these and other passages, has always recognized that a deliverance may be modified or completely annulled by a subsequent one.[10] This is usually regarded as applying to separate deliverances, but XXII.51 ff. seems to imply that alterations were made upon actual passages, and examination of the Qur'ān shows that both methods of revision were freely used.

Now, it is no doubt possible to revise a passage so carefully that no sign of patching remains, but as a rule a critical reader will detect the modification from some unevenness in the style. As a matter of fact, there are many such roughnesses in the Qur'ān. There are not only hidden rhymes and rhyme phrases not woven into the texture of the passage, but there are abrupt changes of rhyme, and repetition of the rhyme word or phrase in adjoining verses. Abrupt changes of subject are natural to the paragraph style of the Qur'ān, but often we find a quite extraneous subject intruding into a passage apparently meant to be homogeneous. Or the same subject will be treated in somewhat different ways in neighboring verses, often with repetition of words and phrases. There are breaks in grammatical construction that trouble the commentators. There are abrupt changes in the length of verses, and sudden changes of dramatic situation involving changes of pronoun from singular to plural, or from second to third person and vice versa. Sometimes apparently contradictory statements appear side by side. Passages of different dates stand together, and late phrases enter into earlier verses. So common are these things in the Qur'ān that they have often been regarded as characteristic of its style not calling for further study, but they certainly demand an explanation. The explanation may, of course, vary in each case, but in the great majority of cases it will be found in some revision or alteration of an earlier text.

Glosses, that is to say, short explanations occasioned by some obscurity, which may be supposed to have been written on a manuscript by some later reader, are not numerous in the Qurʾān. Examples may be found in VI.12, 20; VII.90; XXX.48, 104; XXVII.7; XLI.16; LXXVI.16. How these have originated it is impossible to say, but in II.79 we find one that is evidently considerably later than the writing of the original passage. Here, the word *ikhrājuhum* is inserted to explain the pronoun *huwa*, but immediately in front of that is a phrase that evidently belongs to the preceding verse; when that is removed to its proper position, there is no difficulty about the reference of the pronoun; the insertion of *ikhrājuhum* must, therefore, be subsequent to the misplacement of the preceding phrase.

Explanations are sometimes added[11] in the form of an extension of the passage. In twelve places[12] we find after a rather unusual word or phrase the question: "What has let thee know what . . . is?" and this is followed by a short description. That in some the description has been added later is clear from the fact that it does not correspond to the sense in which the word or phrase was originally used. The most striking case is CI.7 ff., but XC.12 ff. and CIV.5 ff. are similar, and the addition is never an exact definition.

There are additions and insertions of other kinds, of which the following are examples taken from the shorter suras. In XCI it is evident that the passage, when composed, ended at verse 10 (see above, p. 836), but this is followed by a summary of the story of Thamūd, which may have been added to illustrate the moral, or placed here just because of the similar rhyme. LXXXVIII.6, 7 are marked as an insertion by the different rhyme, LXXVIII.33, 34, by breaking the connection between 32 and 35. In LXXXVII a sudden change in the dramatic situation in verse 16 marks an addition that might possibly be contemporary—as if the Prophet, having recited his revelation, had turned to impress its point upon his audience—but is probably much later. In LXXIV, verses 31–34 are clearly marked as an insertion by the different style and length of verse. Some of these examples already suggest that Muhammad himself was responsible for the addition, though it is possible to hold that they were due to some later collector or reader.

There are, however, other additions that can hardly have been made without authority. The misplaced phrase of II.79, for instance, though it looks like a gloss written on the margin and taken in by a copyist at the wrong place, makes a real addition to the regulation laid down. There are not many such misplacements, but short additions that make substantial alterations to the sense are frequent enough. In LXXIV.55 we have a limitation of the freedom of man's choice that virtually takes back what had been stated in 54; cf. LXXVI.30 f., LXXXI.29. This corresponds to the hardening of the doctrine of predestination that took place in Medinan days. Reservations introduced by *illā*, "except," are especially frequent. We must not, of course, assume that every such reservation is a later addition, but in quite a number of cases[13] there are independent reasons for such an assumption, as in LXXXVII.7, and XCV.6, where *illā* introduces a longer verse with characteristic Medinan phraseology into an early passage with short rhythmic verses. Such additions, making as they do a distinct modification of the statement, must have been deliberately introduced. In at least some of them we can discern the motive for making the exception.

Longer additions can sometimes be easily distinguished. Thus in LXXIII a long verse occurs at the end that, by containing a reference to Muslims being engaged in fighting, is clearly marked as Medinan, and is recognized by everyone as being so. But the rest of the sura, and especially the beginning, is in the short crisp verses characteristic of early passages. The reason for the addition is that the passage at the beginning, which really refers to the composition of the Qur'ān,[14] had been adapted so as to recommend night-prayer; but as this was being overdone, it became necessary in Medina to counsel moderation.

Additions in the middle of suras are very common. A few examples will suffice. The, first part of XIX has the assonance in *-īyā*, but this is interrupted by verses 35–41, which have the common *-ī(l)* assonance. These verses follow an account of Mary and Jesus, and, by rejecting the idea of Allah having offspring, were evidently meant to combat the Christian doctrine of the Son of God. III.125–128 warn against the taking of excessive interest, and promise heavenly reward to those who act generously. The passage evidently closed with the rhyme phrase of verse 128, but two verses follow giving a further description of those who do well by repenting and asking forgiveness, and a promise of heavenly reward that is practically a repetition of that already made. Those who have transgressed but are prepared to reform are thus included. XXII.5–8 argue for the resurrection as in line with Allah's power otherwise manifest, and close with a scoff at those who "without knowledge, guidance, or light-giving book" argue to the contrary. Verses 9, 10 join to this rather awkwardly and threaten not only future punishment, but "humiliation in this life," a Medinan threat, to those who so act. The change of tone and attitude shows clearly enough that these verses did not belong to the original passage. In XXXVII we have accounts of various biblical persons, closing in the first four cases with the refrain: "Thus do We reward those who do well. Verily he is one of Our servants believing." But in the case of Abraham this refrain is followed by a statement about the posterity of Abraham and Isaac. This must have, been added after the passage was composed.

Then we often find that a passage has alternative continuations, which follow each other in the present text. This will be marked by a break in sense, and by a break in grammatical construction, the connection being not with what immediately precedes, but with what stands some distance back; there may also be the repetition of a word or phrase. Thus in XXIII we find following upon verse 65, which speaks of men continuing a defective course of conduct, three passages introduced by *ḥattā idhā*, 'until when.' verse 66, verse 79, and verse 101. It is possible, with some straining, to join verse 79 to verse 78, but verse 101 will not join to verse 100. But *ḥattā idhā* requires before it a reference to something continuing. Verses 101 f. are in fact the proper continuation of verse 65, as is evident if we read them together; the other verses introduced by *ḥattā idhā* are substituted for them. In V, verse 46 begins with a phrase *sammāʿūna li-l-kadhib*, which is entirely out of connection. The same phrase occurs in verse 45, and we can quite well replace it and what follows of verse 45 by verse 46. At the end of XXXIX there is a verse that appears isolated. It follows a Judgment scene and evidently belongs to it; but the scene is already finished; judgment has been given, the unbelievers have been sent to Gehennah, the pious have entered the Garden; then we find ourselves back at the scene of Judgment where judgment will be given with truth. This phrase, which has already occurred in verse 69, indicates what was the original position of verse 75; it followed the first phrase of verse 69 and completed the scene; at some later stage it was displaced by the much longer description in verses 69–74.[15] Occasionally a change of rhyme may accompany such a substitution as in LXXX, where verses 34–37 have their assonance in *-īh*, while verses 38–42, which join equally well to verse 33, have the *-ah* assonance that runs through the whole of the rest of the sura. More frequently the occurrence of the same rhyme word or phrase is a sign that such a substitution has been made, the new version being made to end with the same rhyme as that which it replaced. Thus in II, verses 96 and 97 both end in *law kānū ya'lamūna*, which gives a presumption that verse 97 was intended to replace verse 96; in III, the similar ending indicates that verse 138 is a substitute for verse 139. See also IX.118 and 119, XXXIV.51 and 52, XLV.27 and 28, and LXXII.25 and 26–28. It may be noted that in such cases the alternative continuations often stand in reverse order of date, though one cannot take this as all invariable rule. It is as if the paper[16] had been cut and the alternative inserted. Occasionally we may find a substitution made at the beginning or in the middle of a passage, as if an alternative had been written above or between the lines, or two versions may be interwoven, as in III.122–124, as if the substitution had been somehow written through a text already written down; cf. XXXVI.1–4.

The conviction that we have here written documents grows upon us as we deal with these evidences of revision, and an assumption that such is the case seems necessary to explain another phenomenon of frequent occurrence in the Qur'ān. There remains a multitude of disconnected pieces, sudden changes of subject, even grammatical breaks, which no discursiveness of style or additions or alternative continuations will explain. Take, for instance, LXXXIV.16–19; here we have a little piece in *kāhin* style, a number of cryptic oaths, followed by in emphatic statement. It is evidently complete in itself, has its own rhyme, and has no apparent connection in thought with the rest of the sura. How did it come to stand where it does? A collector may have thrown it in at random, but a responsible collector would, one might think, have sought a more suitable place. The same thing appears ln LXXXV.16–19 and LXXXVIII.17–20. In these two cases it is fairly evident that immediately before the unconnected piece an addition has been made to the preceding passage, for the added verses have a different rhyme. In LXXXIV there is no abrupt change of rhyme, but if we consider carefully we shall see that verses 13–15 destroy the balance of the preceding piece, verses 7–12, which is complete as it stands, two verses being given to describe the fate of each class. In each case, then, all addition has been made, and the addition occupies approximately the same space as the extraneous passage that follows. The presence of this latter would be explained if we were to suppose that it had stood on the back of a scrap of paper on which the addition was written, and that both sides of the paper had been read and copied consecutively when the Qur'ān came to be made up in the form of a codex. Similar examples may be found throughout the Qur'ān. To take an example from near the beginning: II.16 compares those who have accepted the Prophet's guidance and then gone back upon it to people who have lit a fire, and then it has gone out, leaving them blinded in the darkness. Verse 17, "Deaf, dumb and blind, they do not return," evidently closes the passage, but verses 18, 19 contain another simile: they are like people in a thunderstorm, the rain pours down, the thunder deafens them, the lightning blinds them. Evidently this is a parallel to verse 16 and should have preceded verse 17. It has been added later. There follows a passage, verses 19b, 20, quite unconnected with the context, appealing for the worship of Allah and adducing signs of his power and bounty. This appears to be continued, after a break, in verses 26, 27. Now verse 25, while not evidently in addition, is probably so, for verse 24 finishes with a reference to the "reprobates," which is conclusive enough. But verse 25 proceeds to describe a special class of "reprobates," who violate a covenant after having made it. Further, we find in verses 158–160a a passage that, by the use of the rather unusual word *andād*, "peers," is marked as almost certainly a continuation of verses 19b, 20, 26, 27. Here we have, not preceding but following, a passage, verses 160b–162, which returns to the theme of verses 156, 157, and must have been intended as an addition to that passage. This whole section is an interesting example of how a passage has been expanded by additions. The point, however, here is that we find a passage originally dealing with the worship of Allah apparently cut up, and the back of the pieces used for making insertions into other passages.

An interesting example of the same kind is found in Sura IX. The last two verses of this sura are said by tradition to have come to the knowledge of Zaid b. Thābit when he had almost completed his task of collecting the Qur'ān, and were placed here as the most convenient position at the time. This is evidently an attempt to account for the fact that there is a break in connection between verse 128 and verse 129, and between verse 129 and verse 130. These two verses seem to stand isolated, but verse 130 will connect well enough with verse 128, though the latter verse ends as if nothing more were to be said. It is a case of something having been later added to a passage, and we may suppose that the back of verse 129 was used to write it on. By some accident (verse 128 had itself been used for the writing of another passage) the back was read by the compilers before the addition. But this is not all; verse 40 of the same sura stands isolated, though it evidently requires something in front of it. The pronoun "him" must evidently refer to the Prophet, of whom there has been no mention in the context, but verse 129 speaks of the Prophet, and if we read verse 129 and verse 40 together we get a moving appeal for loyalty to the Prophet addressed to his followers. This has evidently been cut in two, one part being added to verse 128 and the other placed after verse 39.

The reverse seems also to have taken place; scraps of paper were somehow pasted together to form a sheet. XIV.8–17—an evident addition to the account of Moses—in which he addresses his people in regular Qur'ān style, is followed by a series of disjointed pieces, verses 18–20, 21, 22, 24–27, 28, which together occupy practically the same space. In fact, it is almost a rule in the later parts of the Qur'ān that an addition or connected deliverance of any length is preceded or followed by a number of disconnected pieces that together make up approximately the same length. An interesting instance of this occurs at the end of II. There we find a long deliverance dealing with the recording of debts, verses 282, 283. This occupies approximately the same space as verses 278–281, a deliverance forbidding usury, verse 284 a separate verse, and verses 285, 286 a profession of faith of the believers. Into this piece two little sentences intrude at the junction of the verses; they have no connection with each other or with the context and break the connection of verse 285 and verse 286, which must have originally formed one verse. If now we suppose the deliverance regarding debts, verse 282 f., to have been written on the back of a sheet (or part of a sheet) which contained the deliverance on usury, verses 278–281, and on that of a second sheet containing verses 284, 285 f., we find that the intrusion into the latter piece comes practically opposite a proviso introduced into the debts deliverance excepting from its scope transactions in the market where goods pass from hand to hand. This we may suppose was written on the back of two scraps and inserted into the deliverance. To do so, the sheet was cut and the proviso pasted in. Hence the appearance of two extraneous scraps on the other side of the sheet.

The same thing occurs in IV, where, if we suppose verses 90–93 to have been written on the back of verses 81–89, a proviso introduced by *illā*, verse 92a, will come opposite verse 84 which breaks the connection between verse 83 and verse 85. This passage is further interesting in that the passage verses 81–83, 85, 86 is almost certainly private and was not meant to be publicly recited. There are quite a number of passages of this kind included in the Qur'ān. The most striking of them is III.153, which can hardly have been intended for publication either at the time or later; cf. also verses 148c and 155.

As further proof that these alterations and revisions belong to Muhammad's lifetime, we may consider some of the passages dealing with subjects and situations we know to have presented critical problems to him. It is just at these points that the Qur'ān becomes most confused.

A simple case is that of the ordinance concerning fasting. When he removed to Medina, Muhammad hoped for support from the Jews and showed himself willing to learn from them. Tradition says that he introduced the Jewish fast of the *'Āshūrā*, which was the Day of Atonement, preceded by some days of special devotion. Later, the month of Ramaḍān was prescribed. Now, in II.179–181 these two things lie side by side: verse 180 prescribes a fast of a certain number of days, verse 181 the month of Ramaḍān. The two verses are, of course, generally read consecutively, the certain number of days of verse 180 being regarded as made more precise by the mention of the month of Ramaḍān in verse 181. But a certain number of days is not naturally equivalent to a month, and the repetition of phrases in the two verses shows that the one was intended to replace the other. We have, in fact, a case of alternative continuations of verse 179. Further, we find that verse 182 is entirely unconnected; not only has it no reference to fasting, but whereas in the preceding verses the believers are being addressed and Allah spoken of in the third person, in it Allah is speaking, the Prophet is being addressed, and men spoken of in the third person. Verse 183 returns to the subject of fasting and the dramatic setting of verses 179–182. If we consider the length of verse 181, we shall find that when written out it occupies approximately the same space as verse 180 and verse 182 together. The presence of this latter verse seems to have arisen from the necessity of adding to the space afforded by the back of verse 180 by using the back of a verse from some other context.

The marriage laws in Sura IV are a clear case of alternative continuations. Verse 27 lays down the forbidden degrees of relationship, and reproduces the Mosaic list with some adaptation to Arab custom. That this was deliberate is shown by verse 31, which states that "Allah desireth . . . to guide you in the customs of those who were before you." At a later time, however, some relaxation appeared necessary, and verses 29, 30, and perhaps 32a were substituted for verse 31, allowing marriage with slaves. Finally verse 28, which gives ample liberty, was substituted for verses 29, 30, and verse 32b was added to give a verse ending. The similar endings of verses 31, 32a, and 32b show that substitutions have been made.

The change of *qiblah* affords another example. The passage dealing with it, II.136–147, is very confused; verses 139–147 especially are unintelligible as they stand. When analyzed, however, they turn out to contain (a) a private revelation to the Prophet of the solution to his problem, verses 139a, 144 ; (b) a public announcement, using part of (*a*) accompanied by an appeal for obedience based on gratitude, verses 139a, 145–147; and (*c*) the final form of the ordinance, 139a, 139b.

The process of the introduction of the religion of Abraham is outlined for us in II.124–135. It takes the form of answers to the assertion of Jews and Christians: verse 129a, "They say: 'Be ye Jews or Christians and ye will be guided.'" This is followed by three retorts introduced by "say." Verses 133–135 claim that the Prophet and his followers have a perfect right to serve Allah in their own way, as did Abraham and the patriarchs who were an independent religious community long since passed away. This passage was cut off and replaced by verses 130, 132, in which it is claimed that Muhammad and his followers stand in the line of Abraham and the patriarchs, Moses, Jesus, and all the prophets. It was again modified by the insertion of verse 131 in place of verse 132. Finally, the short retort of verse 129b was written in, professing the creed of Abraham, who was a *ḥanīf* and no polytheist. The back of the discarded passages was then utilized to add an account of the transmission of the religion of Abraham to his sons. This now stands as verses 124–128, having been put before verse 129, and not after it as was evidently intended.

The question of the pilgrimage, which was part of the religion of Abraham, also caused difficulty. The ceremony was recognized and Muhammad's followers were counselled to take part in it, but as *ḥanīfs*, followers of the religion of Abraham, not as polytheists, XXII.32. Sacrificial animals were to be sent to Meccah, verses 35a, 34. But the bloodshed to which Muslim attacks on Meccan caravans, and especially the clash at Badr, led made it dangerous for any Muslim to visit Mecca. It was therefore laid down that the animals dedicated for sacrifice might be slaughtered at home and their flesh given to the poor. This we can deduce from XXII.30–38.[17]

Fighting in the sacred months also caused difficulty. Muhammad's attitude is made clear by the analysis of Sura IX. They were at first recognized as a period of truce, by a deliverance which consisted of IX.36a, 2, 5, but as the intercalary month, which kept the Arab lunar year in conformity with the seasons, was decreed from Mecca, misunderstandings as to what months were sacred would soon arise. Hence the deliverance that now stands as IX.36, 37, abolishing the intercalary month and decreeing that war with the polytheists was to be carried on continuously.

The discarded verses dealing with the sacred months now appear as verses 2 and 5, because the back of them was used, with other material, for the writing of a renunciation of agreements with polytheists, in fact the denunciation of the treaty of Ḥudaibiyah, which stands at the beginning of IX. As the heading informs us, however, this is also a proclamation to be made at the pilgrimage. It has been altered and added to for this purpose after the fall of Mecca.[18]

The defeat of the Muslims at Uḥud was naturally a severe blow to the prestige of the Prophet. The passage dealing with the battle, III.97 ff., is in great confusion. Analysis shows that there was an address intended for delivery before the battle, which consisted of verses 97, 98, 99, 106a, 111–113, 119, 133–137, 139–144, 152, 154. Part of this, perhaps from verse 133 onward, was redelivered, with a few alterations, some time after the battle. Reactions to the defeat appear in a reproof to the Prophet himself for having, without authority, promised the assistance of angels, verses 117, 120, 121 and parts of verses 122–124. That was later revised as an explanation and rebuke to his followers. That he had been inclined to speak angrily to them is indicated in the private verse, 153. Part of this "rough" speech may be embedded in verses 145–148, a passage that has been revised and added to in a milder sense later. In fact, we can see the attitude to the defeat growing gradually calmer and more kindly toward the faithful. Finally, when the setback had been overcome, part of the original address was used again, with a new continuation added after verse 106a, in preparation probably for the attack on the Jewish tribe of Naḍīr, verses 106b–110; and the back of a discarded piece was used for the writing of an ordinance prohibiting usury, which has thus come to be mixed up with the Uḥud material.[19]

Treated in this way the Qur'ān certainly becomes much more intelligible. Much remains obscure, not only because the analysis is uncertain, but because we do not know enough of the circumstances. But we can at least discern something of the way in which Muhammad inspired and guided the nascent community of Islam. Occasionally we even get a glimpse into the inner mind of the Prophet, and learn something of his plans, his occasional misgivings and self-reproaches, and his ever-renewed assurance.

It seems clear, then, that the present form of the Qur'ān, which is practically the form given to it at the revision in the reign of ʿOthman, rests upon written documents that go back to Muhammad's lifetime. Whether these were written by his own hand is really immaterial. We know that in his later years he employed secretaries, and there are even traditions that tell of them being employed in writing the revelation. It is, in fact, difficult to believe that no record was made of the legal deliverances, often of some length, that were given in Medina. But if we read between the lines of LXXXVII.1–9, we may gather that he distrusted his memory, and suspect that he very early took to writing out his Qur'āns and memorizing them beforehand. That he kept the fact secret is possible, though XXV.6 implies that it was at least suspected in Mecca. Secrecy may help to explain the scarcity of writing material that led to backs of sheets and scraps being used, though perhaps the fact that Medina was not a trading community like Mecca may be sufficient to explain it. That the ʿOthmanic recension was based upon *ṣuḥuf*, or "sheets," which were found in the possession of Ḥafṣah, we know. Tradition asserts these to have been the collection of the Qur'ān made by Zaid b. Thābit after Muhammad's death. We have seen above that this tradition is open to various criticisms, and in particular it is difficult to see how such an official collection, if it was made, came to be in the possession of Ḥafṣah, even though she was the daughter of the caliph ʿOmar. She was, however, also one of the widows of the Prophet, and as likely as any of his wives to have been entrusted with the care of precious documents. The *ṣuḥuf* may have been in her possession not as ʿOmar's daughter, but as Muhammad's widow.

NOTE ON THE MOSLEM DOCTRINE *OF NĀSIKH AND MANSŪKH*

This doctrine is based on verses of the Qur'ān: :

II.100: "For whatever verse We cancel or cause (the messenger) to forget, We bring a better or the like."

XIII.39: "Allah deleteth or confirmeth what He willeth; with Him is the mother of the Book."

XVI.103: "When We substitute one verse for another—Allah knoweth best what He sendeth down—they say: 'Thou art simply an Inventor'; nay, most of them have not knowledge."

XXII.51 : "We have not sent a messenger or prophet before thee, but when he formulated his desire Satan threw (something) into his formulation; so Allah abrogateth what Satan throweth in, then Allah adjusteth His signs."

What is referred to in the last verse is supposed to have been completely removed, so as not to occur in the Qur'ān.

The doctrine has been voluminously discussed in Islam, not from the point of view of literary criticism, but from that of Law, it being important for Islam to decide what ordinances of the Qur'ān were abrogated and what remained valid. In some respects the doctrine was extended, on the one hand to include the abrogation of laws of the Pagan Arabs, or of Jews or Christians, through the revelation of the Qur'ān, and on the other to admit the possibility of an ordinance of the Qur'ān being abrogated by the Sunnah. Ash-Shāfiʿi, however, laid it down that when this happened there must be something in the Qur'ān to confirm the Sunnah. Others held that, the proper sense of *naskh* was that one verse of the Qur'ān abrogated another, and that in regard to this we must not follow the opinions of exegetes or the founders of legal schools, but have the authority of a direct statement of the Prophet or of one of the Companions, though it might be possible to infer *naskh* from plain contradiction of two verses, combined with a knowledge of their dates. Other restrictions of the doctrine were introduced; it applies only to commands, not to narratives or promises or threats; alterations of practice, such as the recommendation of patience in Mecca and fighting in Medina, are not properly included under abrogation, but are rather instances of postponement of promulgation of the full law of Islam because of unsuitable circumstances. There are other cases in which, though a different law is laid down, it remains allowable to act according to the earlier one. As-Suyūṭī in his *Itqān*, adopting these restrictions, reduces the number of cases of abrogation proper to twenty, of which he gives a list.

One should not perhaps expect the result of such legal discussion to confirm results of literary analysis, though in a few instances it does. What interests us is that Islam does recognize that deliverances were sometimes replaced by others. Further, the fact that these abrogated deliverances have been retained in the Qur'ān as it has come down to us affords a strong presumption that no attempt was made to adapt it to any preconceived ideas. The retention of the recitation, with abrogation of the ordinance, is a difficulty for Islam. As-Suyūtī gives two grounds, (a) the abrogated verses were the Word of Allah, which it was meritorious to recite; (b) abrogation was generally directed to making things easier, and the earlier ordinance was retained as a reminder of God's mercy.

NOTES

1. See the story in Ibn Hishām, p. 882.

2. A list of the chief asseverative passages may here be given: XXXVI.1 ff.; XXXVII.1–4; XXXVIII.1; XLIII.1; XLIV.1 ff.; L.1 ff.; LI.1–6; LII.1–8; LIII.1 ff.; LVI.74 ff.; LXVIII.1 ff.; LXIX.38–43; LXXIV.35–40; LXXV.1–6; LXXVII.1–7; LXXIX.1–14; LXXXI.15–19, 22, 24, 25, 27; LXXXIV.16–19; LXXXV.1–7; LXXXVI.1, 4, 11–14; LXXXIX.1–4; XC.1–4 ff.; XCI.1–10; XCII.1–4 ff.; XCIII.1–3 ff.; XCV.1–5; C.1–6; CIII.1 f.

3. "When" passages, introduced by *idhā*: LVI.1–9 (LXIX.13–17); LXXIV.8–10; LXXV.7–12, 26–30; LXXVII.8–13; LXXIX.34–41; LXXXI.1–14; LXXXII.1–5; LXXXIV.1–6; XCIX.1–6 (CX.1–3); introduced by *yawma*: LXX.8–14; LXXVIII.18–26; LXXX.34–37 (CI.3–6).

4. T. Sabbagh, *La Métaphore dans le Coran.*

5. C. C. Torrey, *The Commercial-Theological Terms in the Koran.*

6. Arthur Jeffery, *The Foreign Vocabulary of the Qur'ān.*

7. K. Vollers, *Volkssprache und Schriftsprache im alten Arabien.*

8. For the use of these as evidence of date, see Introduction to the Qur'ān, chap. 6.

9. See III.30 ff, 40 ff.; VII.160 ff.; XIII.2 ff.,; XIV.29 ff.; XVI.10 ff., 50 f., 53.; XXV.47 ff., 55 ff., 62 f.; XXVII.60 ff.; XXXII.15–20; XL.59 ff., 71 ff.; XLI.8 ff.; XLIII.8 ff.

10. See note on the Muslim doctrine of Abrogation (pp. 865–867).

11. See p. (843–849).

12. LXIX.3; LXXIV.27; LXXVII.14; LXXXII.17; LXXXIII.8, 9; LXXXVI.2; XC.12; XCVII.2; CI. 2, 7; CIV.5.

13. II.155, 229, 282; III.83; IV.145; XI.14; XIX.61, 90; XXIII.6 f.; XXV.70; XXVI.227; LIII.27; LXXVIII.25; LXXXIV.25; LXXXVII.7; LXXXVIII.23 f.; XCV.6; CIII 3.

14. See Bell, *Origin of Islam in its Christian Environment*, pp. 97 f.

15. To give a full list of such substitutes is tedious and unnecessary. some of the more striking cases may be here listed: II.95 ff., 129 ff., 139 ff., 179 ff., 192 ff.; III.43 f., 61 ff., 97 ff., 106 ff., 137 ff., 145 f., 164 f., 177 ff.; IV.27 ff., 130 f.; V.45 f., 52 ff., 76 ff., 92 f.; VI.87 ff.; VII.38 f., 163 ff; VIII.73 f.; IX.87 ff. (82 ff.), 112 f., 118 f., X.104 ff.; XI.42 ff.; XIII.19 ff.; XV.87 ff.; XVI.16 ff.; XVII.47; XXVII.38 ff.; XXXIV.50 ff; XXXV.26 ff.; XXXVI.79 ff.; XXXIX.48 f., 69 ff.; XL.31 ff.; XLV.26 ff.; L.21 ff.; LIV.43 ff.; LVII.13 f.; LIX.5 ff.; LXIII.7 f.; LXXII.26 ff.; LXXIV.31 ff.; LXXX.33 ff.

16. "Paper" is used in the general sense of writing material of whatever nature that may have been. Papyrus sheets seem probable.

17. See my article "The Origin of the*, ʿīd al-aḍḥ a*," *Moslem World* 23 (1933): 117 ff.

18. See my article "Muhammad's Pilgrimage Proclamation," *JRAS* (1937): 233 ff.

19. For my analysis of other complicated passages, see "The Men on the Aʿrāf" (VII.44), *The Moslem World*, 22 (1932); "'Sūrat al Ḥashr" (LIX), 38 (1948).

7.3

From *A Commentary on the Qur'ān*

Richard Bell

PREFACE

Some explanation of the form of these notes on the Qur'ān is required, and may best be given in a short account of their origin.

When I began to prepare my lectures on the origin of Islam, my investigations were directed to the background and surroundings of early Islam rather than to the Qur'ān itself. The results of European scholarship at that time seemed to point to Muhammad's dependence on some form of Christianity for the initiation and early content of his prophecy. I hoped to sum up the results, and perhaps by reading in Christian literature to extend them. Quite suddenly, when one day I was verifying a reference to the Qur'ān, it dawned upon me that I was on the wrong track; that Muhammad could never have been in close contact with any form of Christianity. The echoes of Christian language, which one hears occasionally in the Qur'ān, must have come to him in the course of his mission. Time pressed, but a fresh study of the Qur'ān had to be undertaken.

In this study, the aim—impossible, of course, to realize—was to get away from previous interpretations, both Muslim and non-Muslim, and to read the book as openmindedly as possible, with the help of dictionary, grammar, and above all the Concordance. Nöldeke's order of the suras was retained. The first form of the notes consisted of short jottings of my impressions of the man behind the book, his teachings and his aims;

From Richard Bell, *A Commentary on the Qur'ān* (Manchester: Manchester University Press, 1991), vol. 1, pp. 5–61. Reprinted with the permission of C. E. Bosworth and M. E. J. Richardson, editors, *Journal of Semitic Studies Monographs*.

answers to the questions “What was aimed at by this deliverance?” and “How would it be understood by those who heard it delivered?”

Interest in the Qurʾān having been thus aroused, I set myself as soon as my lectures were off my hands to work through the book, making a translation and keeping notes of difficulties, and any tentative solutions at which I arrived. I now made use of commentaries, especially that of Baydāwī, and of European studies, so far as they were available to me, but I aimed always at an independent interpretation. I aimed further at dividing the suras into their component parts; for I was convinced that they consisted of short pieces, and that verses were not to be assumed to be connected simply because they happened to be placed together. Here perhaps I should acknowledge a special debt to Barth's article in *Der Islam* 7 (1916), which first called my attention to the grammatical unevennesses and interruptions of sense that occur in the Qurʾān. That interpretations were sometimes adopted for their novelty and that breaks were discerned where there was no necessity to assume them, were natural. But this working over did bring out the main divisions and the breaks in connection. So far there was little attempt to explain how the dislocations had occurred. My aim was analysis, not reconstruction. The notes consisted largely of philological and exegetical matter, along with discussions of date. There was no attempt at a systematic commentary,

The idea had, however, been growing in my mind, and now I began to type out the translation and notes simultaneously, making drastic revisions, omissions, and additions. By this time I was fairly sure that I was dealing with written documents, and was on the outlook for explanations of confusions and displacement of verses. The suras were still being dealt with in Nöldeke's order, and it must have been in working through his Medinan suras that the idea that sheets and parts of sheets might have been covered with writing on both sides and later read consecutively, began to take shape in my mind. Used as a tentative solution, it worked in many passages. When by its help I was able to solve to my own satisfaction the confusion at the beginning of Sura IX, the truth of the hypothesis seemed to be assured. From then on I used it freely, and found that it often gave a simple explanation of passages that had formerly seemed difficult and complicated.

Before publication could be thought of, however, it was necessary to work through the whole again. For it was only toward the end of revision that this idea had become clear to me, and it had now to be applied throughout the Qur'ān. Besides, the notes, filled out with discussions and gropings after solutions of difficulties, had expanded to a rather formidable length. I therefore began to revise both translation and notes, compressing the latter as much as possible. I worked now in the traditional order of the suras, but before I had proceeded very far, I lost hope of finding a publisher for the notes. They were laid aside, except for my own use, and were no longer revised to correspond with changes made, not so much in the actual translation as in the arrangement of the contents of the surahs.

After the publication of my translation, regrets at the suppression of the notes were expressed by most of the reviewers, and inquiries about them were made from various sides. But no way to their publication appeared, and I felt I had spent enough time and labor on the Qur'ān and had no mind to take up these notes and revise them again. So matters rested until the autumn of 1947. The Justice Faiz B. Tyabji, who had written me from Bombay about my *Translation*, paid a visit to this country and came to see me in Edinburgh. By his friendly interest and encouragement, he persuaded me to resume the work I had put aside, in the hope that the notes might have an interest not only for *Christians** but for Muslims as well. Should this hope—which, presumptuous as it is, I could not in the light of my friend's example entirely reject—ever be fulfilled, and a Muslim consult the opinion of one of another faith on the meaning of the Qur'ān, I must apologize for any offense to Muslim sentiment in the form and manner of expression. These notes were not written with any polemical object. They are simply the deposit of an honest effort to understand Muhammad and the Qur'ān.

The work of revision has gone slowly; it has not been so thorough as it might have been. Evidence of the haphazard way in which *the work*† took shape, no doubt, remains. There are perhaps repetitions; there may even be inconsistencies. Of the latter I hope there are not many. But varied ideas found expression in the notes at different times. Some variation may remain. I have thought, however, to bring the whole into conformity with my final results expressed in the arrangement of my *Translation*. The notes are meant to be used along with the *Translation*, paragraph by paragraph, and to explain shortly and clearly why the arrangements of the materials of the suras were adopted.

---

*The typescript is not at all clear; there is room for another word.

†There is not quite enough room for both these words in the unclear typescript.

SURA II

Verses 1–6

The introduction consists of three parts.

Verses1–4 describe the true believers for whom the book is being delivered. The description is duplicated in verses 2 and 3. With verse 3 compare verse 130, which dates probably a little before the adoption of the religion of Abraham. Verse 2 is later, but the date cannot be determined.

Verse 1

ʾalif lām mīm. This combination of letters occurs at the beginning of Suras II, III, XXIX, XXX, XXXI, XXXII, accompanied by other letters in VII and XIII. Other combinations occur at the beginning of many other suras. No satisfactory explanation of these mysterious letters has yet been given, though many attempts to explain them have been made. The fact that they come after the bismillāh indicates that they belong to the sura and not to the editorial heading. In nearly every case they are followed as here by some reference to the book.

dhālika. The reference is uncertain; it would naturally refer back to the mysterious letters, but it may refer forward to what is to follow. It is also uncertain whether it should be taken as demonstrative pronoun, or as adjective, "that Book."

lā raiba fīhi. Usually in connection with "day" or "hour" of the Book, in X.38, XXXII.1.

Verse 2

al-ghaib, "that which is absent, hidden, or unseen" is frequent in the Qurʾān, generally in an eschatological sense.

Verses 5–6

alladhīna kafarū, "those who have been ungrateful" or "have definitely disbelieved," is often applied to the Meccans, sometimes to the Jews of Medina. The reference here is not certain.

For phraseology of verse 6, cf. VI.46, XLI.22, and the like.

Verses 7–19a

These verses describe unsatisfactory believers among the people of Medina.

Verse 9, however, does not continue verse 8, but the conduct of those who try to deceive Allah and the believers is described in verse 13. This evidently refers to Jews who hover between joining Muhammad and keeping on good terms with the Jewish leaders; cf. III.65. A more pronounced attitude on their part is indicated in the gibe recorded in verse 12, which probably displaced verses 13–14 as the continuation of verse 8. verses 10–11 begin and end similarly to verse 12, having been modelled upon it. verses 9–11 therefore displaced verses 8–12 as the continuation of verse 7.

Verses 15–17 may be the continuation of verses 13–14, though in some ways the simile is more appropriate to those who had definitely gone back upon Muhammad, as is implied in verse 12.

The simile of verses 18–19 fits those who are hesitating in their attitude and support him so far, but are doubtful as to where he is leading them. It is therefore an addition referring to "those in whose hearts is disease."

Verse 9

This phrase designates those who were later dubbed Munāfiqīn.

Verse 10

'alsada, "to cause corruption" and **'alsaḥa**, "to set things right," refer to secular actions that affect the morale of the community.

Verse 13

For "satans'" as applying to Jewish rabbis, cf. verse 96; VI.112, 121.

Verse 15

cf. verse 170; III.170, 184, and the like.

Verses 19–20

These are quite out of connection; their presence here is explained by the addition of verses 18–19, having been written on the back of them. They are regarded by *NS*, i, p. 173) as of Meccan date, but the address "O ye people" is prevailingly Medinan.

Probably the same "sign" arguments were used in Medina as had been used in Mecca, and we have here the beginning of one of these early Medinan addresses.

"Dome" is Bḍ.'s explanation of **binā'**, "building."

Verses 21–22

These do not connect with the general context, nor with verses 19b–20. The back of them has been used for the addition of verse 23.

"Scripture," for the derivation of **sūrah**, the word here used, cf. Bell, *Origin of Islam*, p. 52. For similar challenges cf. X.39; XI.16; XXVIII.19.

"Witnesses," that is divine testimony to the truth of the revelation, as Muhammad claimed Allah as his witness.

For people as "fuel of the Fire" cf. III.8; LXVI.6.

Bḍ. interprets "the stones" as "idols," but quotes the explanation, attributed to Ibn ʿAbbās, "sulphur" or "brimstone."

The date of this passage is uncertain. Its presence is due to the introduction of verse 23.

Verse 23

This is an addition, probably later than verses 18 f., designed to balance the condemnation of opponents and uncertain followers by an assurance to believers. It has been written on the back of verses 21–22.

For "pure spouses" cf. III.13; IV.60.

Verse 24

This belongs perhaps to about the same time as verse 16; it may have been occasioned by some discussion of the simile of that verse.

Verses 25

This is an addition making the epithet **fāsiqīn** of the previous verse apply to a particular section of the people, that is, probably to the Jews.

For their "violating the covenant of Allah," cf. verses 77 ff.

What is meant by "separating what Allah hath commanded to be conjoined" is not clear, but it may refer to their rejection of part of the book, (verse 79) or to their rejection of Muhammad while claiming to believe in Allah.

Verses 26–27

These are directly addressed to the people. They are the continuation of verses 19a–20 and have been used for the addition of verse 25, which therefore probably belongs to about the same time as verses 18 f.

Verse 26

The Resurrection here takes its place not as a doctrine to be argued for, but, alongside the production of living men in the first half of the verse, as a sign or proof of the supreme power of Allah.

With verse 27 cf. XLI.10.

Verses 28–37

The story of Adam has come from different sources, as is still shown by the change from "thy Lord" (verse 28) to "We" (verse 32), and the change from **'Iblīs** (verse 32) to "Satan" (verse 34). It has, however, probably been placed here as a whole, having already taken its shape at an earlier period; cf. VII.10–18; XV.28–44; XVII.63–68; XX.115ff; XXVIII.71–86. Verse 37 has perhaps been added at this time.

Verse 28

khalīfah, "vice-gerent," cf. XXXVIII.71, where it is applied to David; the variant **khalīqah**, "creature," is of no authority.

Verse 31

For Adam giving names, cf. Gen. 2:20, and the passage quoted by Geiger, p. 98, from Midrash Rabbah on Numbers, par. 19; cf. XX.115a, XXXVIII.74.

'Iblīs is probably a corruption of Greek διάβολος (cf. Jeffery, *Foreign Vocabulary*, s.v.).

Verse 33

Cf. VII. 18.

Verse 34

Cf. VII.23, from which it is clear that the mutual enemies are mankind, not man and Satan.

Verses 35 f.

Cf. XX.120 f. The change of pronoun and apparent repetition (Barth) come from there.

In the Syriac *Cave of Treasures*, God makes a promise to Adam when he leaves the Garden (Budge's translation, p. 67); but it may be doubted if it is necessary to go beyond the biblical account for an explanation.

'immā, the enclitic **mā** makes the conditional particle more indefinite, "if ever."

Verses 38–69

These are in the form of an appeal to the Children of Israel, the Jews of Medina being probably specially in mind. In the main this will be earlier than the introduction. But the passage is not homogeneous, as is evident from the two beginnings, verses 38 and verse 44, and the appearance of revisions and additions within the sections.

Verses 38–43 appear on the whole to be later than verses 44 ff., and may at one time have displaced that passage. It is, however, composite.

Verse 38

This is long and there is a verse ending at **fa-rhabūni** very similar to that at the actual end of the verse. This indicates that a substitution has been made.

Verse 39

It is not clear whether the covenant referred to is the Covenant of Sinai or the covenant made with the people of Medina after the Hijrah; cf. verses 77 f; cf. also III.70; VI.153; XVI.93.

Verse 40

The **zakāt** is the legal contribution for the support of the community. The date of its enactment is uncertain, but was probably toward the end of the year 2 or beginning of the year 3.

Verses 42–43

These seem to be addressed to the believers rather than to the Jews, and verses 39–48 are probably later than the rest. The arrangement is not certain, but probably verse 38b, **wa-'awfū . . . fa-rhabūni** has been substituted for the rest of verse 38 and verse 39; verses 40–41 have then been added later on the back of verses 42–43.

Verse 42

Cf. verse 148. The pronoun has nothing to refer to, the verse being out of its context.

Verses 44–45

These recognize the privileged position of the **Banī Isrā'īl**, and are probably earlier than the preceding; but cf. verses 116 f., also VII.136 and XLV.15. It is not certain that the Christian doctrine of atonement or of intercession is aimed at in verse 45, but it seems probable.

'adl is interpreted by Bḍ. as "ransom," some take it as "substitute"; cf. VI.69.

Verses 46–50

The deliverance of the Children of Israel from Egypt and giving of the Law at Sinai are recalled as the basis of the appeal for gratitude and belief.

Verse 50

furqān, from Syr. **purqānā**, "salvation," cf. Bell, *Origin of Islam*, pp. 118 ff.; Jeffery, *Foreign Vocabulary*, s.v.; as it is here associated with the book, it is evidently thought of as of the nature of law or what distinguishes between right and wrong or between believers and unbelievers. Possibly the Heb. **pərāqîm** may have influenced its use, as well as the meaning of the Arabic root; cf. XXI.49.

Verse 51

This repeats the incident of the Golden Calf, already referred to in verse 48, and is possibly a substitute, somewhat less friendly, for verses 48–50.

fa-qtulū 'anfusakum, "slay yourselves"; it is interpreted by Bḍ. in a spiritual sense of humiliation and mortifying of the body, but cf. Exod. 32:26 f., on which this is probably founded.

Verses 52–58

These are the continuation of verse 51, rather than of verses 48–50, as they recount the perversities of the Children of Israel, rather than Allah's benefits to them.

Verse 52

Cf. Exod. 19:17 ff., 33:18 f.; Moses' request to see God's glory has perhaps been transferred to the people; cf. IV.152.

Verse 53

Rodwell refers to Sanhedrin v, for the statement that the Israelites who had died were restored to life.

Verse 54

Cf. Numbers 11; as the guiding pillar of cloud is referred to in Num. 10:34, that, rather than the clouds and thick darkness at Sinai, may be what is meant here.

The change of pronoun at the end of the verse may be due to following VII.166.

Verses 55–56

Cf. VII.161 f.; there is no certain explanation of this, but probably there is a reminiscence of the failed attempt to enter the Promised Land at Kadesh-Barnea mingled with something else, whether the High Priest's entrance into the Holy of Holies on the day of Atonement, as Hirschfeld suggests, or the parable of the Pharisee and the Publican, is doubtful.

ḥiṭṭah, probably an attempt to reproduce the Heb. **ḥēṭ'** "sin"; (see Jeffery, *Foreign Vocabulary*, s.v.); cf. the reference in Ibn Hishām, p. 741.

Verse 57

Cf. Numbers 20

Verse 58

This is founded on Num. 11:4 ff.; the second half of the verse is, however, later in tone and phraseology and there is an abrupt change of pronoun at **wa-ḍuribat ʿalaihim**. It is a later insertion. Possibly the original end of the verse is found at verse 285b.

For the charge of killing the prophets cf. III.20, 108, 177; IV.154; Matt. XXIII.31.

Verse 59

This has no connection with the context; the back of it has been used to make the insertion of verse 58b.

alladhīna hādū, a pun on the name **Yahūd**, "Jews." **Naṣārā**, "Christians."

ṣābiʾīn has baffled all investigators. The verse aims at a recognition of all monotheists.

Verses 60–61a

These return to Sinai, and would be in place after verse 50. But as the account in VII is to some extent being followed in this, we may note that VII.170, which corresponds to this, is also out of its proper place as referring to the Covenant of Sinai. It may be that the continuation of verses 51–58a begins here.

Verses 61b–62

These seem to be based on VII.163 ff.; see notes on that passage. It may be noted that the particular story there referred to has disappeared, probably because it had caused difficulty as not being scriptural, and the charge becomes the general one of "transgressing in the matter of the Sabbath."

Verses 63–68

Hirschfeld's suggestion that this rests on a confusion of Num. 19:1–10 and Deut. 21:1–9, is probably correct. No source has been discovered for the questioning of Moses by the people. It probably reflects Muhammad's own experience with the Jews.

Verse 69

This is the close of the appeal, and indicates that Muhammad has now given up hope of gaining the Jews. The reproach is perhaps of Christian suggestion, cf. Ahrens, *ZDMG*, 84 (1930): 16 f., though there are sufficient references to the Jews' hardness of heart in the Old Testament.

The reference in "stones which have fallen in reverence for Allah" is enigmatical; the idols of the Philistines (?), Dagon, I Sam. v (?).

Verses 70–76

These are addressed to believers, but are directed against the Jews.

Verses 70–72 accuse them of double-dealing, cf. verses 7–8, 13 f.

Verse 70

kalām Allāh is interpreted by Bḍ. as meaning the Torah, which gives the ordinary charge of perverting the Scriptures; more probably it is Muhammad's deliverance, which they listen to, and then pervert to ridicule behind his back.

Verse 71

This seems to imply that Muhammad's followers have been getting information from Jews.

The sense of "dispute with you in the presence of your Lord" is not clear. It probably implies that the Jews wish to withhold information out of jealousy, lest Muhammad's followers should be rivals in the favor of God.

Verse 73

This might be interpreted to mean that some Jews had attempted to palm off writings on Muhammad that were not Scripture; but more probably it refers to Jewish writings, such as the Mishnah, which the "common people" are allowed to regard as Scripture.

'ummiyyūn, belonging to the **'ummah** or community, possibly therefore, Arabs, but perhaps the Jewish phrase **'am ha-'āreṣ** has influenced the meaning here. The meaning of **'amāniyya** is not certain. Bḍ. takes it as plural of **'umniyyah** (XXII.51), but in spite of the fact that the word is there connected with the verb **tamannā**, "to wish," it is doubtful if we should take the word here as derived from the root **mny**. It would more naturally come from **'mn**, and would then mean something like "tradition, dogma, a thing taken on trust." This would suit the context here, and also in verse 105; IV.122.

Verses 74–76

These are the conditions of salvation. There is no need to assume that this refers especially to the Christian doctrine of purgatory. For the Jewish belief that no Israelite would be consigned permanently to Gehenna, cf. Weber, *Lehren des Talmuds* i, pp. 326 ff.

Verses 77–81

These are addressed to the Jews and interrupt the argument of verses 70–76, which is continued in verses 82 ff. Their position suggests that they were written on the back of that passage. They are hostile in spirit, and probably belong to the same time as Job. The Jews are charged with breaking the covenant.

Verses 77

This refers to the Covenant of Sinai. The contents of this covenant, as given here, reproduce some of the Ten Commandments, but correspond still more closely to the essentials of Muhammad's teaching; the Jews had, of course, perverted their religion after having received it.

The mention of the **zakāt** as a recognized institution is evidence of fairly late date.

Verses 78

This refers to the compact made with the inhabitants of Medina, including the Jews, shortly after Muhammad's settlement there (see Ibn Hishām p. 341 ff.); some of its provisions are reproduced, and the phrase **'ithm wa-'udwān** actually occurs in it.

The prohibition of shedding their own blood refers to the prosecuting of blood feuds within the community.

Verse 79

wa-'in ya'tūkum 'usārā tufādukum. This clause evidently belongs to verse 78, as one of the provisions of the compact. It seems to have been written on the margin, and taken in by a copyist at the wrong place.

'ikhrājukum is a gloss rendered necessary by the misplacing of the clause.

The beginning of the verse charges the Jews with breaking the compact. Unfortunately it is impossible to say on what specific actions this charge is founded, but it must refer to conduct after Muhammad's settlement in Medina, and the making of the compact. From the time of the battle of Badr and the attack on the Banī Qainuqā' that followed, the attitude of the Jews must have been suspect, and the intrigues of some of them with the Quraish may have given occasion for this charge.

For the second half of the verse cf. verse 108; verse 37, 45; XXII.9; XXXIX.27; XLI.15.

Verse 80

lā yukhaffafu ʿanhum ul-ʿadhābu, cf. verse 157; III.82; XVI.87; XXXV.33.

Verse 81

This recounts the privileges given to the Jews, and their perversity. The giving of the book to Moses is frequently cited. The following up by messengers is mentioned in LVII.27 (a reference to the prophets, cf. Jer. 25:4). Jesus is also sent to the Banī 'Isrā'īl (III.15) but rejected by the Jews.

al-bayyināt may refer to the miraculous "evidences" there associated with Jesus, **rūḥ al-qudus**, the "spirit of holiness," cf. verse 254, verse 109, both of which passages refer to Jesus. In XVI.104, the only other occurrence of the phrase, it is associated with the revelation of the Qurʾān and is interpreted as referring to Gabriel. But as associated with Jesus, it no doubt refers to the Holy Spirit of Christian belief.

For the charge of killing the prophets, cf. verse 61.

It may be recalled that the occasion for the attack on the Banī Naḍīr was an alleged plot to kill Muhammad. Ahrens (*Muhammad*, pp. 191 f.), however, thinks, probably rightly, that in these and similar passages we have an echo of Christian polemic against the Jews.

Verses 82–87

These continue the attack upon the Jews interrupted by the preceding passage.

Verse 82

This puts in the mouth of the Jews a New Testament charge against them (cf. Acts VII.51); it is also found in the Old Testament (cf. Jer. 9.26). If actually used by the Jews, it must have been in mockery.

Verse 83

contains a repetition **lammā jā'ahum**, which is broken in construction, at **wa-kānū**, or, if we take this as a circumstantial clause, there is a break at **fa-lammā**. The first clause was inserted, after Muhammad had begun to deliver the book, as a substitute for the second, **wa-kānū . . . 'arafū**.

The sense of **yastaftahūna** is not clear, but it looks as if Jews had appreciated Muhammad's deliverances against idolators and had asked for more of them.

"What they recognized," that is, as being the same as what was in their own Scriptures.

Verse 84

Their refusal to accept Muhammad's deliverances as revelation is attributed to jealousy.

Verses 85–87

These meet the Jewish refusal to accept any new revelation, while accepting their own Scriptures, by pointing out that they have always been unbelieving, even in Moses' time.

Verse 87

This refers to the covenant of Sinai, cf. verse 60.

samiʿnā wa-ʿaṣainā is a punning reproduction of the Hebrew **shāmaʿnû wəʿāśînū** (Deut. 5:27).

Verses 88–90

These deal with the claim of the Jews to be the exclusive people of God in a grimly humorous fashion., cf. LXII.6.

In verse 90 the mention of the idolators is probably later, as the phrase comes in awkwardly and is difficult to construe.

Verse 92

This was perhaps the continuation of this passage, though the rhyme phrase of verse 90 is one that often closes a passage. If so, angels were probably at this stage thought of as the channel of revelation, by the rejection of which the Jews show their enmity. This is confirmed by verse 91, which begins in the same way as, and is evidently intended as a substitute for, verse 92. It is an assurance to the Prophet of the reality of the revelation through Gabriel, who now, but not untill now, appears as the medium of the revelation. As what is given to Muhammad still confirms previous Scriptures, the change must have been made not all too long afterward; perhaps before the time Muhammad assumed complete independence.

Verse 93

This continues verse 91. As the back of verse 92 did not give sufficient space, another scrap, verse 94, was used. This is out of place where it stands, but inasmuch as it charges the Jews with breaking covenant, it belongs to this context; where is uncertain.

Verses 95–97

These ascribe the rejection of the Messenger to the rejection of Scripture and the adoption of "what the satans recited in the reign of Solomon, and what had been sent down to the two angels in **Bābil**, **Hārūt** and **Mārūt**." This has given rise to much speculation and investigation. On **Hārūt** and **Mārūt** cf. Wensinck in *EI*, s.v. It must be confessed that no satisfactory explanation has been found.

"Those to whom the Book has been given" is a frequent designation, which includes both Jews and Christians. The context suggests that the "part" of them here referred to is the Jews. This leads us to think of the Rabbinic Law as what is referred to at the beginning of verse 96, cf. the use of "satans" of the Jewish rabbis in verse 13.

The mention of **Bābil** may further suggest the Babylonian Talmud. But the whole verse is obscure. It has been extended to undue length by the insertion of clauses designed to obviate misconceptions:

wa-mā kafara are . . . as-siḥr;
wa-mā yuʿallimāni . . . takfur;
wa-mā hum . . . Allāh.

Finally the verse, having perhaps given rise to misconceptions, was discarded, and the short verse 97 substituted for it; this is, shown by the repetition of the rhyme phrase.

Verses 98–104

These are addressed to the believers, presumably in Allah's name, and are probably designed to prepare the way for a definite break with the Jews.

Verse 98

The objection to **rāʿinā** is said to have been that the Jews laughed at it as meaning "our bad one"; but cf. IV.48, which implies that it was a Hebrew word, possibly mispronounced. Hirschfeld suggests **re'ēh-nā**, "see now"; in any case, the sense must have been similar to that of the Arabic word to be substituted for it.

Verse 99

"Idolators" may again be a later insertion, the grammar is uneven; cf. verse 90; for the sense cf. verse 84.

Verse 100

The alteration of verses may have been noticed, or the way is being prepared for the changes that are to come.

Verse 102

Cf. verses 63 ff. for the questioning of Moses.

'ahl al-kitāb, "the People of the Book," may include both Jews and Christians, but probably refers here mainly to Jews.

Verse 103

Their criticism is discounted as arising from envy, and is to be suffered in the meantime.

'amr, in the sense of "affair," that is, special intervention.

The rhyme phrase would be the natural end of a passage, verse 104, with its mention of the **zakāt**, is therefore a somewhat later addition.

Verses 105–111

These resume the theological attack, interrupted by the preceding passage. It now definitely includes Christians as well as Jews.

Verse 105

This deals with the exclusive attitude of both religions; note the form **hūd**, apparently a plural, only here and in verses 129, 134.

Verse 106

This introduces the idea of Islam, conjoined with good conduct, as the criterion of acceptance with God.

The sense of **'aslama** is no doubt the Arabic one of "surrender," that is, humble obedience. While this might theoretically be found in all three religions, it was inevitable that, as Muhammad claimed to be delivering the message of Allah, it should soon come to imply the acceptance of his directions.

Verses 107–109

These deal with the mutual enmity of Jews and Christians, who reject each other's claims.

"Those who have no knowledge" must refer to the Arabs, who agree in rejecting the claims of both.

Verse 108

This is difficult to understand.

Bḍ. suggests that it refers to

(a) the Romans who raided the Temple at Jerusalem, or
(b) the Meccans who prevented the Muslims from visiting the Ka'bah at the time of Ḥudaibiyah.

This latter event is too late, but the charge of barring the way to the Ka'bah was brought against the Meccans much earlier, cf. VIII.34, though probably not before the change of **qiblah**, for which the following verse 109 is a preparation. Bḍ.'s first suggestion is ruled out by the fact that the context is directed against Jews and Christians.

The use of the plural **masājid**, "places of worship," causes difficulty. The Ka'bah is usually distinguished as **al-masjid al-ḥarām**, and it is doubtful if there was more than one definitely Muslim "mosque" in existence at this time. **Masjid**, however, is not limited to this, cf. XXII.41 and particularly XVIII.25. The reference might therefore quite well be to Christian churches in Jerusalem. Jerusalem was still the **qiblah**, but was in Persian hands, the Jews having aided them in its capture.

Even this, however, seems far-fetched; we should expect the verse to report some contemporary conditions affecting the Muslim community; VII.28, 29 seem to imply that believers may worship at any shrine provided they consciously direct their worship to Allah. It may be that the Jews objected to such use of their synagogues.

Verses 110 f.

This distinctly rejects the Christian doctrine of the divine sonship.

Verse 112

This belongs in form to what precedes, but deals not with Jews and Christians, but with some among the Arabs (cf. verse 107) who are asking why no revelation or "sign" has come to them. They do not, of course, recognize Muhammad as a prophet, and probably he, at this stage, claimed simply to confirm previous revelations and to make clear the signs, that is, the evidence of God's being and acts.

"Those who were before them," that is former unbelieving peoples.

Verses 113–115

These follow this up by an assurance to him that he has really been sent by Allah. This is addressed to him personally and was probably not intended for public recitation. He was no doubt disturbed by his disagreement with the followers of both religions, who, as monotheists, he had expected to agree with him, but he cannot doubt the truth of his own mission.

Verse 114

Cf. verses 195, 129, and for the latter part of XIII.37.

millah from Syr. **melthā'**, "word," that is, creed or form of religion.

"The guidance of Allah," that is, the divine promptings that come to the Prophet; he must follow these.

Verse 115

It would be possible to translate, "Those to whom We have given the Book recite it as it should be recited; they believe in it," but in that case the verb **yatlūna** would more naturally have come first; as it stands it is to be taken as circumstantial.

The pronoun "it" in **yu'minūna bihi** refers to Muhammad's own message. He has not yet given up the idea that he is in fundamental agreement with previous revelation, properly interpreted, and some of the People of the Book still support him.

Verses 116–123

The first two verses repeat verses 44 f. almost verbatim and lead up to a reference to Abraham as an example to follow. The idea may have been to make a final appeal to Jews and Christians to agree with him on the basis of Abraham, whom both claim, but who was "neither a Jew nor a Christian."

Verse 118

kalimāt, "(certain) words," is probably a reference to the command to offer his son.

'imām, here in the sense of model or example.

Verse 119

This attributes the establishment of the Kaʿbah as a place of worship to Abraham. The attempt to find a basis for this in the traditions of local Jews or Christians fails for want of evidence; cf. Snouck Hurgronje, *Het mekkansche Fest*, p. 33 ff. But the introduction of Abraham and the Kaʿbah in place of Moses and the blessing bestowed through him, is here abrupt and unprepared for (see below). It is, however, evidently connected with the change of **qiblah**.

"The House" is the Kaʿbah. It may be doubted whether the "station of Abraham" meant any other place. The name is now applied to a small building to the east of the Kaʿbah. The circling of the Kaʿbah was an ancient Arab rite.

"Cleave" seems to be the sense of the verb **ʿakafa**; in XXII.5 it seems to refer to those who live near the Kaʿbah, but one would expect some religious action to be referred to here.

In XXII.27 the word **al-ʿākifīn** is replaced by **al-qāʾimīn**, "those who stand" in prayer. Whether bowing and prostrating themselves was an ancient Arab custom is doubtful, but these actions must have been part of Muslim worship before this time.

Verse 120

The security of the **ḥaram** of Mecca is represented as having been established in response to Abraham's prayer.

Verse 123

The sending of Muhammad is similarly represented. One is tempted to translate **zakkā** here as "impose the **zakāt** on"; but unless this passage be considerably later, it is doubtful if it had yet become a legal prescription.

Verses 124–135

This is a confused but important passage that shows, when unraveled, some of the steps by which Islam was freed from dependence upon Judaism and Christianity.

We have seen the widening rift between Muhammad and the People of the Book, known from tradition, reflected in the preceding passages from verse 44 on. But we have had nothing to prepare us for the virtual substitution of Abraham and the Kaʿbah for Moses and the deliverance from Egypt, which appears in verses 116–25. For some of the intervening steps we have to turn to III, especially verses 57 ff., but others will be found here. Even with verses 116–23 preceding, the mention of "the religion of Abraham" in verse 124 comes in abruptly.

This question would certainly be more in place if it followed the statement at the end of verse 129, where the "religion of Abraham" appears again. But if we place it there, we are struck by the fact that the beginning of verse 129 carries us back to the context of verses 1054 ff, where statements of Jews and Christians are being controverted. Here in answer to a claim of Jews and Christians, we have again the religion of Abraham abruptly introduced.

Now the "Say" of verse 129b is twice repeated in what follows.

Verse 130 does not join in verse 129 as it at present stands, but is in place if we take "Say ye," like the "Say" of verse 129b, as introducing the reply to the "They say" of verse 29a. So also "Say" in verse 133 which is unmotived as it stands. The rhymes also confirm that some substitution has taken place, for verses 128, 134, and 135 have all the same rhyme word; in fact, verses 128 and 135 are practically the same.

Taken as answers to the claims of Jews and of Christians in verse 129, these passages arrange themselves best by taking verses 133 ff. as the earliest. Here the assertion is that Muhammad's followers serve the same God as the Jews and Christians and have an equal right to claim his guidance. Their works may differ, but are equally based on service to the One

God. This is the claim of verse 114, and reminds us of Saint Paul in Rom. 14:26.

Curiously enough, Abraham, who serves Saint Paul in his argument against the bondage of the law (Rom. 4:1 ff.), comes in here also as a stepping stone to the freedom of Islam. But the approach is so different that we cannot attribute this to borrowing. The point of verse 134 is that Abraham and his family were not Jews or Christians, seeing they lived prior to both the law and the Evangel, and if they were accepted of God, as was admitted, his grace could not be confined to Jews or to Christians, cf. III.58 ff.

Verses 138 f. goes a step further. The claim that Muhammad's followers are to make (note the plural qūlū) is that they believe in God, and accept whatever he has revealed, be it through Muhammad, Abraham and the Patriarchs, Moses, Jesus, or any other prophet, without distinction—provided, of course, they could be sure that it really came from God. This attempt at accommodation, cf. III.57, having failed, we find the religion of Abraham put forward by itself in verses 129b, 124–126; cf. 116–123.

The present arrangement of the passages may be explained as follows: verse 129a belonged somewhere in the context of verse 105, and was followed by verse 133, probably not by the whole of verses 133–135 (see below). This was detached and verses 130 and 132 were substituted for it. A later alteration was made on this that introduced verse 131 (see below). This again was discarded, verse 129a being still retained, and now verse 129b was added to it and the continuation, verses 124–128, written on the back of the discarded passages.

The disparity in length may be accounted for by the additions made to these passages, having been crowded onto the same sheets. As it so happened, this was left in such a way that verses 124–128 appeared to come before verse 129 and that verse appeared to be followed by 130 ff.

Verse 124

safiha nafsahu, the accusative causes difficulty, some take it as direct object, "has rendered himself stupid," others as accusative of respect, "has become stupid in soul."

millat 'Ibrāhīm is pretty much equivalent to Islam. The idea of Islam has already appeared in verse 106.

Verse 126

"Jacob" is read as nominative and also as accusative; the former perhaps to be preferred. The implication seems to be that the religion of Abraham was handed on and ought therefore to have been accepted by his descendants.

Verse 128

This rather conflicts with the above (see below); it is really repeated from verse 135 and ends the substitution.

Verse 129

hūd as a name for the Jews appears in verse 105; in verse 107 the usual form **yahūd** appears, another indication that this verse originally belonged to the neighborhood of verse 105.

hanīf is the singular of **ḥunafā'**, the Syriac **ḥanəphē**, "heathen," the term applied by Syriac-speaking Christians to the Arabs. As the founder of the Arab religion, Abraham was a **ḥanīf**; but that religion, according to Muhammad's ideas, had been, to begin with, pure monotheism. It had degenerated into idolatry, as the other two religions had degenerated from the purity of their beginnings. It is futile to look for the ḥanīfs as a pre-Islamic sect in Arabia. The use of this phrase shows that the idea of an original Arab monotheism, and the break with the People of the Book, were already complete.

Verse 130

This is a profession of faith for Muhammad's followers, when confronted with Christian and Jewish assertions, cf. verse 285; III.78.

"Abraham . . . and the Patriarchs" are grouped together, apparently on an equal footing; indeed, the gist of the declaration is that all revelation from Allah is accepted equally. Patriarchs, asbāṭ, properly "tribes," sing. sibṭ, Heb. šebeṭ.

Verse 131

This cannot be part of the declaration, but is addressed to the believers, of course through the Prophet, as the singular pronoun at the end shows. The attitude also differs, for implicitly the belief of the Muslim community is now made the standard, from which to differ is to be in "schism."

shiqāq, "separation," "cleavage"; cf. IV.39, but usually in the Qur'ān of reprehensible separation from the community, cf. XXII.52; XLI.52.

Verse 132

This is apparently unconnected.

Zam. connects **ṣibghata llāhi** with **'āmannā bi-llāhi**, verse 130, as absolute object. This would be possible if verse 131 were absent, which, as we have seen, is different in attitude from verse 130.

Now the present rhyme-phrase of verse 130 is very similar to that of this verse differing by the use of **muslimīn** instead of **'ābidīn**. This, then, which fits in quite well as part of the declaration, was the original end of verse 130, which has been displaced by the present end phrase and verse 131.

ṣibghah has been frequently derived from Syriac **ṣba'** "baptize." But that is not the usual verb for "baptize" in Syriac, and there is no need to go beyond the Arabic, in which **ṣabagha** means to "dye," "color," or "flavor" a thing; note especially the use, cited by Lane, as applied to a girl brought into the household of someone. To believe in a revelation from Allah is to take the flavor or color of Allah and to become, as it were, one of his household servants.

Verse 133

This an answer for the Prophet to use against the assertions of Jews and Christians. It is based on common service to Allah; cf. XLII.14.

For the point of verse 134a, cf. above.

Note the form **hūd**, a confirmation that verses 105, 129a, and this originally belonged closely together.

Verse 134b

Introduced by another "Say," this does not continue verse 134a, but gives a retort to a claim, more likely to be made by Jews than by Christians, that Abraham belonged to them. To say so is to claim to know better than Allah. For Allah has made clear in the revelation given to Moses, that is, in the Torah, that Abraham, Ishmael, Isaac, Jacob, and the Patriarchs lived before the time of Moses and the establishment of the Jewish religion. This revealed fact, **shahādah**, the Jews are accused of having concealed, a tacit admission that it had not been known to Muhammad until recently.

Verse 135

This is the original continuation of verse 134a; note the similarity of the rhyme words of verses 134 and 135 as an indication that a substitution has taken place. Abraham and his descendants were neither Jews nor Christians, but were a community that had passed away, for whose works, or code of conduct, no one was now responsible. This seems to exclude any claim even by Muhammad and his followers to have historical continuity with Abraham and his followers. Islam is an independent revival of the religion of Abraham; cf. III.60 f.

Verses 136–147

These deal with the change of **qiblah** or direction of prayer. The date of this is given sometimes as Rajab, sometimes as Shaʿban of the year 2. Possibly the change was not carried through all at once, but there was an interval during which no specified **qiblah** was followed.

Verse 139a seems to imply that, cf. verses 109, 172. Perhaps verses 136–138 belonged to this interval, but the position of verse 137 is doubtful. The repetitions in verses 139, 144, and 145 indicate that revisions have taken place.

The suggested reconstruction is that verse 144 was the original continuation of verse 139a., and that this was private. When the new **qiblah** was promulgated, it was done in verse 139a (which was retained) and verses 145–147. These latter were written on the back of verses 141 and 142, (a scrap that probably has no reference to the **qiblah**), verses 143 and 144, (now detached from verse 139a). This deliverance counts on a certain amount of reluctance on the part of his followers, and argues and appeals for the adoption of the change.

Finally, when the need for argument was past, the shorter prescription, verse 139b, was substituted as the continuation of verse 139a. This was written on the back of verse 140, which was also probably private, and belonged to about the same time as verse 144, that is, the time when the adoption of the new **qiblah** was privately decided upon. It is recognized that this meant a final break with the Jews and the Christians.

Verse 136

As the future is explicitly indicated, the change has not yet taken place, or at least is so recent as not to have attracted outside attention.

as-sufahā' min an-nās will most naturally be Arabs, not Jews, cf. verse 12.

Verse 137

On the other hand, this implies that the change is past; unless, as may quite well be, it belongs to what the Prophet is to say in answer to the "stupids."

By the change of **qiblah**, the Muslims have become a "community." This sense of **'ummah** seems to belong to North Semitic, cf. Heb. **'ummah**, but is pre-Islamic.

wasaṭ, only here, is usually taken as an adjective, unchangeable for gender and number, and is given the sense of "good," "best," that is, following the mean and avoiding extremes, or sometimes, especially by European translators, "middle," "intermediate." We thus get the sense "a good community" or "an intermediate nation" (Sale), between the Arabs and other nations, or between the Jews and the Christians. This latter seems to suit the historical situation.

But **wasaṭ** is really a noun, and is here in apposition to **'ummah**; so that what we have here is a statement that the Muslims have now become an independent community, and that they as a community are "an intermediate (body)" between Jews and Christians, or better as giving due weight to what follows, between the Prophet and the rest of the people (of Medina); he is to watch over them, and they are to watch over the rest of the people.

The Muslims appear as an **'ummah** in the Constitution of Medinah, but that document belongs probably to about this time (see Buhl-Schaeder, *Das Leben Muhammads*, pp. 211 f).

Verse 138

"The **qiblah** which thou hast been observing" can only refer to the Jerusalem **qiblah**; the Prophet is being addressed as the representative of the community. As its appointment is represented as a test of the loyalty of his followers, it cannot have been popular, and must have been introduced after the Hijrah in the endeavor to conciliate the Jews.

Verse 139

The change of pronoun may be explained by the Prophet being the representative of the community, but the beginning of the verse seems more personal, while the second part ordains the people to turn in the direction of "the Sacred Mosque," that is the Kaʿbah at Mecca. If the above reconstruction be adopted, "turn thy face" is repeated from verse 144 or verse 145. Note also the repetition of the rhyme phrase from verse 144.

Verse 140

This refers to the **qiblah**, and seems also personal to the Prophet. It stresses the separation from the People of the Book, which the introduction of the new **qiblah** will cause.

Verses 141 f.

These do not connect closely with any verse in the context; so it is not clear that what the people of the Book recognize, as they recognize their own sons, is the new **qiblah**. That would be a bold statement, and in VI.20 where similar words occur, the reference is to the Qur'ān, or the revelation given to Muhammad. Probably it is the same in this detached verse. The similar statement in verse 139 repeats this and is to be similarly interpreted as referring to the revelation, which now includes the new **qiblah**.

Verse 143

"Each" would most naturally refer to individuals, and the verse would imply that when it was revealed there was no fixed **qiblah**. If "each" refers to communities, the Muslims must have had their own fixed **qiblah**.

Verse 144

This is similar to verse 139b, but seems more personal to the Prophet. It is probably the original continuation of verse 139, which was displaced by verses 145–147.

"As thou hast gone forth" or "from where thou hast gone forth," that is, from Meccah.

Verse 145

This begins with the same phrases as verse 144, but evidently the community is now in mind.

For the use of ḥujjah, cf. IV.163; the Arabs had evidently been critical of the Jerusalem **qiblah**; the ground of their criticism will now be removed.

"Those of them who have done wrong" possibly refers to the Jews.

Verses 146 f.

These make an appeal to the loyalty and gratitude of the believers, the effect of which is heightened by the change from "We" to "I" at the end.

zakkā, "purify" by almsgiving; the **zakāt** has probably not yet become a definite impost.

Verses 148–162

The basis of this passage is a short deliverance dealing with those slain at Badr (Ramaḍān II), consisting of verses 148, 149, 156, and 157. The part dealing with the Muslim dead was expanded, probably after Uhud, by the addition of verses 150–152, which were written on the back of the scraps verses 153 and 154 f. That dealing with the Meccan dead was expanded by the addition of verses 160–162, written on the back of verses 158–160a.

The date of these verses is uncertain. As the rhyme is different, they were not added at the same time as verses 150–152. The scrap on which they were written seems to be connected with the discourse verses 19b, 20, 26, 27; note the recurrence of "peers" in verses 20 and 160a. If so, it was probably made shortly after verses 18 f were added.

If it were certain that "those who have done wrong" referred to the Jews, (see verse 145), one might surmise that it referred to some of them killed at the siege of the Banī Qainuqā', though we are not told of any casualties at that time.

Verse 148

Cf. verse 42.

Verses 150–152

As *NS* point out, the Muslims are in adversity.

Verse 153

This is an addition to the regulations for the pilgrimage, apparently in answer to a question. The date is uncertain.

Permission is given to perform the run between Ṣafā and Marwah, two heights in the neighborhood of the Ka'bah. This was, therefore, an Arab custom.

sha'ā'ir, "manifestations," things that make Allah known.

The **'umrah** was the lesser pilgrimage or visit to the Ka'bah.

Verses 154 f.

These refer to the Jews' concealment of things in Scripture; the date is again uncertain. It is also uncertain whether "the Book" refers to the book in the hands of the Jews, or to that which Muhammad was now delivering; probably the former, the concealed fact perhaps being that of Abraham's priority to Moses.

Verse 160

This is evidently broken in the middle.

Verse 161

"Those who have been followed" would most naturally refer to religious leaders, but might possibly refer to false gods; cf. XXVII.63.

Verses 160b, 161, and 162

These have the assonance in -ā(l) while the context has it in -ī(l).

The rest of the sura is mainly taken up with legislation. First we have in verses 163–219 revisions of previous regulations, rendered necessary by the changed attitude toward the People of the Book, and the independence of Islam. These revisions will date from the period between Badr and Uhud, though still later revisions have sometimes been made.

Verses 163–171

These verses deal with food.

The earlier regulation, stating Muhammad's original attitude of unrestricted freedom, is contained in verses 163–164; the revised law in verses 167–168 and probably verse 169, though the connection of this latter verse is not certain. This was written on the back of the discarded verses 163 f., and, as that did not give sufficient space, verses 165–166 were also used. These seem to belong to the early Medinan discourse of which we have found other portions in the sura and probably were the continuation of verse 160a.

Verse 171 is a later addition of uncertain date, suggested by verse 169. It has been written on the back of verse 170, of which the connection is uncertain.

Verse 163 f.

khuṭuwāt ash-Shaiṭān, "footsteps of Satan"; the sense is not clear, cf. verse 204; VI.143; XXIV.21, but probably the reference is to heathen customs. It can be hardly be to Jewish customs, as this, though Medinan, presumably dates from before the break with them.

Verses 165 f.

These refer to heathen, and "what Allah has sent down" is revelation in general; for the Jewish attitude cf. verse 85.

nazaqa, only here, "to croak," with **bi** "to call to" (animals).

Verse 167

This repeats the sense of verse 163, which it replaces.

The restrictions in verse 168 are Christian rather than Jewish, cf. Acts 25:20, 29.

'uhilla probably refers to invocations of the name of the god when an animal was slain, cf. Robertson Smith, *Religion of the Semites*, pp. 340, 431. This restriction will correspond to "meats offered to idols."

Verse 169

This, no doubt, refers to the Jews and their concealment of Scripture, but the phrase "eat nothing but fire in their bellies" probably shows that it is connected with this passage, and it may imply rejection of Jewish food laws.

Verse 170

This is out of rhyme. The exact reference is lost.

Verse 171

This appears to be later, cf. verse 131. Allah has now revealed the book to Muhammad, so that the real content of revelation is known.

Verse 172

This must originally have belonged to the period when the **qiblah** was indefinite, but the reference to the bestowal of wealth led to its being revised to include others than those originally specified.

What exactly has been added to the verse is difficult to say. It may have ended originally with **al-masākīn**, "the poor," and the rest has been added now, though the mention of captives and the **zakāt** suggests even later addition, for zakāt must here be a fixed impost, as almsgiving has been already mentioned. Or the concluding clauses may also have belonged to the original.

'alā ḥubbihi. The suffix would naturally refer to wealth, but it might refer to Allah.

ibn as-sabīl, "son of the way," probably refers to those whose presence in the community is due to their adherence to the "way" or cause of Allah, that is, those who have migrated to Medina to join the Muslims, and who have thereby been impoverished.

Verses 173–175

The original prescription consisted of verses 173a, and 175. The latter was rejected, and verses 173b-174 (no verse ending at 'iḥsān) substituted. The revision is an alleviation of the original Jewish and Arab *lex talionis*, recommending forgiveness of injuries within the Moslem community rather than revenge.

kutiba 'alaikum probably implies scriptural authority.

Verses 176–178

These prescribe the making of a will before death, for which also scriptural authority is assumed. There is no mention of writing. The revision consists of verse 178, which allows interference, probably at the time the will is being made, on the part of a hearer for the purpose of preventing injustice.

jinf, only here, "inclining" away from the right, "unjust partiality."

Verses 179–186

These deal with fasting. The original consisted of verse 179, which may have stood alone, but was probably followed by verse 180, which in any case belongs to the time between the Hijrah and the first occurrence of the Jewish fast of ʿĀshūrah, which is here adopted.

For this latter verse, verse 181, prescribing the fast of Ramaḍān, was now substituted, being written on the back of it. As more space was required, the back of another scrap, verse 182, was utilized. Verse 183 was added later as a relaxation, written on the back of verses 184, 185, and 186(?). The date of this is uncertain; the mention of "judges" in verse 184 probably implies a fairly late date and if verse 186 was used for the insertion, it must date from the year 7 at the earliest.

Verse 179

Fasting is Medinan, not Meccan.

"Those before you" are the People of the Book, as is implied in **kutiba**; here particularly the Jews, as being most closely in contact.

Verse 180

The junction with verse 179 is not quite smooth, but, if we regard the rhyme phrase of verse 179 as parenthetical, or possibly later added, the two verses join quite well.

'ayyāman maʿdūdātin is accusative of time to **ṣiyām**, a fixed, and probably small number of days.

If we take this verse by itself, and as belonging to the early months in Medina, when approaches were being made to the Jews, there is no reasonable doubt that what is here in view is something corresponding to the Jewish fast of ʿĀshūrah, or the Day of Atonement on the tenth day of the Jewish year, in preparation for which the preceding nine days were kept sacred. Provision is made for those who are sick or on a journey. Those who can afford it may redeem the fast by feeding a poor man, but this is a pious duty that should be done voluntarily, and not as substitute for a fast. Fasting is, in any case, better.

Verse 181

This institutes the fast of Ramaḍān. The general similarity of form, and the actual repetition of the provision regarding sickness or absence, show that this was intended as a substitute for verse 180. This agrees with the historical tradition, which asserts that the fast of Ramaḍān took the place of the ʿĀshūrah. It is noteworthy that the provision as to buying off the fast is not repeated.

shahr is read as nominative; Bḍ. suggests several constructions, none of them satisfactory; he records, however, a reading as accusative, which would correspond to **'ayyāman** in verse 180.

There has been considerable discussion as to why Ramaḍān was thus distinguished, but no satisfactory reason has been suggested; (see *EI*, sverses *Ramaḍān, Ṣawm*). The battle of Badr was fought in Ramaḍān II, and in spite of the difficulty as to the traditional date of the institution of the fast, we may surmise that it was that important victory that led to it.

The reason given is that the Qur'ān was sent down in that month. This is often interpreted as the sending down of the Qur'ān to the lower heaven on **lailat al-qadar**, which is placed in Ramaḍān. But cf. VIII.42, from which we learn that something had been sent down on the day of Badr. Probably that is here referred to; for the Qur'ān is several times spoken of as something special, cf. XV.87, and the later suras speak of the revelation of the book, not of the Qur'ān.

furqān, cf. verse 50.

Verse 182

has no reference to fasting, but rather to prayer, which Allah is ready to hear and to answer.

Verse 183

This returns to the subject of the fast, which is now, however, an established institution. The Muslims have assumed that marital intercourse was forbidden during the [nights of the] fast; it is now explicitly permitted. This must be considerably later. The method of keeping the fast is also laid down. The rule of abstinence by day and breaking the fast at night is said by NS, i, p. 179 (note 1) to have prevailed only among the Manichaeans and to have presumably been adopted from them. But it seems to have been fairly common among Oriental Christians to end fasts at nightfall or even earlier in the day (see *ERE*, s.v. "Fasting").

rafath, only here and in verse 193, "sexual converse."

"What Allah hath prescribed for you" may refer simply to the relaxation here laid down, but is usually interpreted as meaning "offspring."

'akafa, cf. verse 119 and Goitein, in *Der Islam* 18 (1929): 192. The sense seems to be that this relaxation is not to interfere with times of devotion in the mosque.

Note **'āyāt** in this and similar phrases, not in the sense of "wonderful sign" nor exactly in that of "verses," but rather "deliverances" or "pieces of revelation."

Verse 184

This is quite detached. It refers to gambling and bribery. For the mention of judges, which implies a fairly advanced date, cf. IV.39, 61 f.

Verse 185

This is also quite detached. It answers a question as to new moons, and condemns some pagan custom connected with them.

Verse 186

This deals with fighting. It has no connection with what precedes, but the following verse continues the subject. Considerations of space however, require the use of this verse also for the insertion of verse 183, so that it was probably a separate piece. It shows a peaceable disposition and would suit well the attitude adopted on the expedition that ended at Ḥudaibiyah.

iʿtadā, "to transgress" or "to show oneself hostile"; cf. verse 89.

Verses 187–191

Verses 187 ff. display a much more bellicose attitude than verse 186, and cannot belong to the same time. They belong to the time of the final expedition against Mecca, and stand here because verse 186 had introduced the subject of fighting.

Verse 189, however, does not connect with verse 188, but with verse 187. Verse 188 is a substitute for it, inserted when negotiations had opened the prospect of a peaceable entry into Mecca. This deliverance was written on the back of verses 190 and 191.

That verse 190 belongs, as Snouck-Hurgronje argues (*Verspreide Geschriften*, i, p. 38), to the time of Ḥudaibiyah, is possible but not certain. The sacred months had been broken much earlier, for example, by the Quraish raid after Badr.

The verse is later than IX.5, but earlier than IX.37b.

Verse 191 is surely not so late as the year 6, but is more likely to belong to the period between Badr and Uhud, when the danger of Quraish attack was pressing, and contributions had not yet been regularized.

Verse 187

"From whence they have expelled you," that is, from Mecca, or more particularly, the Kaʿbah.

Verse 189

fitnah has several meanings; here probably it has the sense of "persecution." The object is to put an end to Quraish persecution of Muslims, and establish the religion of Allah in Mecca.

Verse 191

For the meaning of the second clause of the verse, cf. A. Fischer and P. Schwarz, in *ZDMG*, 65 (1911): 794–96, and 66 (1912): 136–38, 294–99, "hand not yourselves over to destruction," "put your hands in the power of destruction."

Verses 192–203

Passages dealing with the pilgrimage have become mixed with verses dealing with another subject. Rhymes also are mixed. The confusion is perhaps inextricable; the following suggestion is at best tentative.

The pilgrimage was probably dealt with at the time of the adoption of the religion of Abraham; verses 119 ff. prepare for it. But after Badr, it must have been extremely dangerous for Muslims from Medina to visit Mecca, and the pilgrimage could no longer be insisted on as a duty. The original deliverance is perhaps to be found in verses 192a and 199, which recommend the performance of the pilgrimage "to Allah" and the spending of at least two days in this act of remembrance.

A question having arisen as to taking part in the trade which was usually combined with the pilgrimage, verse 199 was detached from verse 192a, and verses 194–195 substituted. This permits trading and substitutes for the two days' remembrance of Allah, a special act of remembrance at the Sacred Monument, and the doing otherwise as the rest of the people do. Or verses 194 and 195 may simply have been added to verses 192a and 199.

Badr having intervened, a new deliverance altogether was given, consisting of verses 193, 196, 197, and 198. This has the rhyme in -āl and perhaps did not belong to this sura; but this rhyme occurs in other parts of the sura in additions made about this time, cf. verses 160 ff. This deliverance is permissive only, and, by its insistence on strictness of conduct, discouraging rather than encouraging. It was, of course, essential in the circumstances that Muslims should give no offense. The connection in the middle of verse 196 is doubtful, but verses 196b–198 are perhaps in place here as enforcing the pious attitude Muslims should observe, and discouraging too great eagerness to take part in trade at the pilgrimage.

This gave the model for verses 200–203, which were probably written on the back of verses 196–198 (now detached from verse 193), and of the detached verse 199 (see above). This passage was evidently occasioned by some event, and, from the reference to destruction of tillage and stock, it may be surmised that it was the assistance rendered by some of the Banī n-Naḍīr to the raid of the Quraish after the battle of Badr.

The final regulation, verse 192, retained verse 192a and continued on the back of verses 193, 194, and 195. It is much later, but its exact date is difficult to determine. The sense is in some parts uncertain.

The injunction not to shave their heads until the gift, that is, the animals for sacrifice, has reached its place, would naturally refer to those who have been prevented but have sent a gift, but it might refer to those who actually perform the pilgrimage; and the exact sense of "making use of the time between the ʿumrah and the ḥajj," is not clear. As it refers to those whose families are not present, it would seem to be a permission to absent themselves from Mecca, or engage in trade if they so desire and feel that they can safely do so. The regulation is late, for the way to Mecca is evidently open; all that can be said is that it must be later than the conquest of Mecca.

Verse 193

"Specified months" may refer to the one particular month of each year, or to the three sacred months in each year in the middle of which the pilgrimage fell; more naturally the latter.

Verse 194

"Seek bounty from your Lord," that is, engage in trade. The "Sacred Monument" is a height on the eastern side of Muzdalifah on which a minaret has been built. It is probably a pre-Islamic place of worship; see Rutter, *Holy Cities*, i, p. 166.

Verse 195

The Muslims are evidently at this time inconspicuous members of the crowd.

Verse 196

khalāq, "portion" probably Heb. ḥēleq (Hirschfeld); the phrase is Medinan.

Verse 197

Cf. VII.155 and, for the rhyme phrase, III.14, 188.

Verse 199

The actual pilgrimage usually occupied three days; Muslims are permitted to omit one day.

Verse 200

This would appropriately refer to Jews, who claim to worship Allah, but dispute Muhammad's claims.

Verse 201

Abū Sufyān, the leader of the Quraish raid, having obtained information from one of the leaders of the Banī n-Naḍīr, destroyed some palm plantations and then withdrew (Ibn Hishām, p. 545). Possibly, however, this is too early a date for the passage. Muslim commentators make it apply to an individual, al-Akhnas b. Sharīq, but the indefinite pronoun, **man**, though construed as a singular, may refer to a group, and the reference is perhaps to Muhammad's opponents in Medina, especially some of the Jews who, between Badr and Uhud, and even later, were intriguing with Quraish and others, stirring up enmity against the Muslims.

Verse 203

This also describes a group, the true believers.

Verses 204–210, 212, 213 and 215(?)

For the address in verses 204, cf. 98, 148, 173, 179.

The two latter passages suggest that verses 212 f. originally followed the address here, as verse 212 is in the same form as these verses. Fighting is prescribed as a duty for believers.

Whether verse 215 followed verse 213 is not certain, but is possible. It promises the "mercy of Allah" to those who have left their homes and fought in Allah's cause. These verses were cut out later and replaced by an appeal for unity, the present verses 204–205.

silm occurs only here; **salm**, in VIII.63; XLVIII.37. According to Bḍ. the meaning is "resignation" or "obedience"; but cf. the verse of al-Aʿshā quoted by Lane, s.v., which gives the sense as "peace," "living in accord with each other," as opposed to war.

Verse 210, which prepares believers for suffering and disappointment, probably formed part of this declaration, or may have been added after Uhud. This verse was later discarded, and the philosophical explanation of the disunity among the followers of revealed religion, verse 209, was attached to the appeal for unity in verses 204–205. It ascribes the division not to any difference in the revelation, but to jealousy arising among them after the revelation had come. This cannot be dated with any certainty, but is probably still fairly early Medinan. The verse was written on the back of scraps that now stand as verses 206–208.

These verses are entirely out of connection here, are out of rhyme and are not even connected with each other. They cannot be placed.

For the form of verse 206, cf. VI.159, VIII.51, X.102, XVI.35, XXXV.41, XXXVI.49, XLIII.66, XLVII.20, especially VI.159 and XVI.35; it is just possible that "the angels" may be an afterthought here.

For the theophany, cf. XXXIX.69 and LXXIX.25. As the verse is detached, it is impossible to say to whom it refers.

Verse 207

This must date from before the complete break with the Jews, though there is already a hint of the charge that they change the good gift of Allah, that is, the revelation; cf. XIV.33.

Verse 208

This might be Meccan, but is more likely to be early Medinan, while the believers were suffering poverty and distress.

Verses 211, 214, and 216–222

These are a series of answers formulated to questions that believers ask, or are likely to ask. The earliest of them, at least, were not intended to form part of the book, and were not in rhyme. These are verses 216 and 217, wrongly divided in Flügel, in an attempt to get rhyme. The rhyme phrase in verse 217 has been inserted later. So probably also the rhyme phrases of verse 219 (verses 218–219 should be only one verse), verse 221 (verses 200–221, only one verse), and possibly verse 222.

Verse 211

This was written on the back of verses 212–213 (see above); it took the place of verses 216b–217; note the similar beginning and that here we have an answer not to the question "what," but "for what." The rhyme phrase may have been added later here also.

ibn as-sabīl, see verse 172.

Verse 214

This deals with the question of fighting in the sacred month. This would arise in consequence of ʿAbdallāh b. Jaḥsh having attacked a Meccan caravan on the first of Rajab of the year 2; so Bḍ. and *NS* i, p. 182. It apologizes for this on the ground of the continued persecution of Muslims who had remained in Mecca, and the prevention of others from declaring themselves.

The phrase in the middle of the verse **wa-l-masjid** . . . **minhu**, is an insertion from a later date, when the duty of pilgrimage had been recognized, and the Meccan opposition was preventing the duty being fulfilled; note that **wa-l-masjidi** depends upon **ṣaddun ʿan**, not upon **kufrun**; the latter phrase was probably intended to be omitted when the change was made.

This verse was written on the back of verses 215, 216, 217 (the latter probably not at the time having the rhyme phrase). The concluding phrase was written on the other side below verse 217, and now stands at the beginning of verse 218. Later, when a rhyme phrase was added to verse 214, the former concluding phrase was rewritten along with it at the foot.

Verse 216

This must have been discarded when verse 214 was written. Wine and **maisir** were afterward forbidden altogether, verse 92. The answer to the question about contributions was also discarded. It must belong to the early days of the demand for contributions, verse 211 being considerably later.

maisir, an old Arab gambling game.

Verse 217

For **al-ʿafw**, "the redundant," cf. VII.198, and Lane, s.v. The rest of the verse is a formal rhyme phrase, which was probably added at a much later revision.

Verse 218

For the first phrase, see above. It is difficult to say whether these two verses belong to the time of verses 216 f. or to that of verse 214; most probably to the former. They seem earlier than IV.2, but Bḍ. makes them subsequent to IV.11. The rhyme phrase has again been added later.

Verse 220 f.

This is not, like the surrounding verses, an answer to a question, but it may belong to the same period. If, however, "idolaters" includes Jews and Christians (so Bḍ.) the verse must be large, but this is hardly correct. The rhyme clause is again formal and has no doubt been added later.

Verse 222

This perhaps implies that some regulation concerning marital relations had preceded, but not necessarily. For a similar attitude to menstruation, cf. Lev. 18:19; 20:18.

Verse 223

This may, then, be earlier than verse 222. It declares marital intercourse to be unrestricted. From this verse 222 excepts the period of menstruation.

'annā is indefinite in meaning, "how" and "when." The use of the simile of cultivated land shows that it is natural intercourse that is thought of.

qaddimū is usually interpreted as recommending the doing of some meritorious act or uttering a pious phrase before coition. The concluding phrase is again loosely attached, and out of construction; cf. IX.113, and verses 23, 150.

Verses 224–225

These are placed by Bḍ. at the time of the trouble with ʿĀʾishah and made to refer to the oath of Abū Bakr not to have anything more to do with Mirtaḥ, who had harbored suspicions against ʿĀʾishah. That would suit well as an occasion, but the words are quite general. The similar rhyme phrases argue that the verses were modeled on verses 226 f., but the phrase "setting things right amongst the people" is against taking them as a later treatment of the same purely private matter; especially as that follows in verses 228 ff.

The sense seems to be that people are not to plead oaths, which may have been hastily uttered, as an excuse for not doing what is right and for the public good, cf. verse 91.

Verses 226–227

The verses deal with divorce, and recommend a waiting period of four months from the cessation of intercourse before divorce is finally determined on. The continuation is probably to be found in verse 242. The verses were discarded in favor of the fuller treatment that follows.

Verses 228–243

These also deal with divorce, the treatment of divorced women, and that of widows. This is later than verses 226 f., whether it belongs to the same time as verses 224 f. is doubtful, but it can hardly be earlier than that time. Muslim law as it finally took shape hardly does justice to the spirit of these regulations; see my article in *The Moslem World*, 29 (1939): 55–62.

Verse 228

This verse is really a substitute for verses 226 f. and the intention evidently is that there should be an interval of between three and four months (**qurū'**, "menstrual courses of women") before divorce becomes final, and that, during that interval, both spouses should keep the way open for the resumption of marital relations.

Verse 229

Divorce of this kind, which has not been made final, may occur twice, with the option each time of reconstituting the marriage during the period, or of finally dismissing the wife at the end of it. Presumably if it occurs a third time, the parties are to separate finally. If the divorce be made final, the woman's dowry must be paid up in full.

The clause **'illā** . . . **bihi** is a later insertion; it shows a mixture of pronouns.

The pronoun in **khiftum** is usually taken as referring to the judges who deal with the case; it probably, like preceding second persons, refers to the Muslim community, as representing who the Prophet is here being addressed.

The idea of the insertion probably is that if the payment of the dowry is an obstacle to the dissolution of marriage otherwise desired, the woman may sacrifice part of her dowry to purchase her freedom, cf. verse 231.

Verse 230

This would naturally refer to the case in which divorce has been actually carried through, on any of the occasions on which it may have been contemplated. Muslim law, however, regards it as the consequence of a third complete divorce. Muhammad's intention apparently was to make divorce a serious step, by allowing a period for reflection and ordaining that, if a man at the end of that period still insisted on divorce, he had to reckon with the probability that it would never be allowable for him to take the woman as his wife again.

Verse 231

This condemns unfair advantage being taken of the option stated in verse 229; the woman is not to be retained against her will. It is earlier than the insertion in that verse that recognizes a method adopted by women to avoid what is here condemned.

'ajalahunna, that is, the term stated in verse 228.

al-kitāb wa-l-ḥikmah, cf. verses 123, 146; III.158, and so on.

Verse 232

This is usually taken as addressed to the woman's relatives, forbidding them to interfere and prevent her returning to the husband who has divorced her. More naturally it would be the complement of verse 231; a woman provisionally divorced is not to be retained by force, nor is she to be vexed if she chooses to marry another husband at the conclusion of her **'iddah**.

Verse 233

This deals with the case in which there is a child of the marriage. The husband can demand that the divorced wife suckle the child until it is two years old, but he must during that time provide for her according to his means. They may, however, agree to make other arrangements.

Verse 234

This verse extends the principle of the **'iddah** to widows.

Verse 235

Marriage with them may meantime be contemplated, but must not be actually carried through, nor must there be any binding promises, until the expiry of the **'iddah**.

"Until the book has reached its term" must mean "until the term prescribed in the book has been reached." The book is here that given to Muhammad of which the preceding regulations are part.

Verses 237 f.

These deal with divorce taking place before the marriage has been consummated, and are perhaps a somewhat later addition. The marriage portion would normally be settled at the time of the marriage, so that in all probability the marriage of minors is here contemplated. This is confirmed by the phrase "he in whose hand the bond of marriage is" (verse 238). It is usually taken as referring to the husband and as meaning that he may give more than half the dowry. But the use of **'fw** in this sense is unusual. More probably it refers to the girl's guardian, who may remit part of the demand on her behalf. These two verses were probably written on the back of discarded scraps.

Verses 239 f

These have no connection with the context. They seem designed for those on some military expedition. They are earlier than IV.102 f. (*NS*). The middle prayer is said to be the afternoon prayer, but though the verse might possibly include the five canonical prayers, it would be more natural to take it as referring to three, morning and evening, and a prayer during the day, perhaps recently introduced and therefore more liable to be omitted. In danger, the prayers may be performed without the customary formality, and supplemented by special remembrance of Allah later; cf. verses 192, 194.

Verse 241

This verse deals with the same subject as verse 234, and was discarded in favor of that verse. It must be earlier also than the detailed regulations for inheritance in IV.12 ff.

Verse 242

This may have been the continuation of verses 226 f. and was discarded in favor of the fuller treatment of divorce in verses 228 ff.

Verse 243

This is formal, and it is impossible to say whether it was originally connected with verse 242 or not; cf. verses 112, 183, 217, and 221.

Verses 244–259

The kernel of this lengthy passage is a parable drawn from the history of the Children of Israel designed to illustrate and enforce the duty of fighting, verses 247–252.

Verse 247 is perhaps earlier than the rest. It was written on the back of scraps, verse 244 (which suggested the beginning), verse 245, and verse 246.

Verses 248–252, which illustrate the victory of a small band and conclude by inculcating the duty of defense may have been revealed before Uhud. It was written on the back of a number of older passages, verses 253, 254, 255, 256, and 257–59.

Verse 244

This is enigmatic; it is unconnected with the context (but cf. verse 260), and the reference is unknown.

Bḍ. gives two stories:

> (a) that of the people of Dawardān, said to be a village near Wāsiṭ associated in legend with Ezekiel, who were stricken by a pestilence and fled; Allah caused them to die, but afterward brought them to life;
>
> (b) that of some of the Israelites who refused to fight when summoned to do so by their king; they were caused to die but restored to life after eight days.

The latter is evidently founded on a wrong interpretation of the verse, which has no connection with fighting, but is designed to enforce the doctrine of the resurrection. The former is perhaps founded upon Ezekiel's vision in Ezekiel 47. Something of the kind may lie behind the verse. Muhammad Ali takes the reference to be the exodus of the Children of Israel from Egypt, but that can hardly be, unless the verse be pretty early in date.

ʾulūf, probably plural of **ʾalf**, "thousand," but possibly an unusual plural of **ʾilf**, "intimate friend."

Verse 245

This is an unconnected scrap, and as recommending fighting, is Medinan in date.

Verse 246

This is also unconnected, and also Medinan; cf. verse 263; LVII.ll. It is an appeal for funds for war and other purpose.

Verse 247

This evidently refers to the demand of the Israelites to Samuel to appoint a king over them, 1 Sam. 8:5; the second half of the verse is suggested by the position of the **Muhājirīn**, rather than by any biblical incident. The initial reluctance of Muhammad's followers to fight is reflected in it.

Verse 248

The form **Ṭālūt** for Saul is influenced by **Jālūt** for Goliath in verse 250. Objections to Muhammad's authority in Medina are perhaps reflected in the objections to Saul as king.

Verse 249

The return of the Ark, 1 Samuel 6, is associated with Saul.

tābūt for the Ark of the Covenant is late Hebrew; cf Geiger, pp. 45 f. and Jeffery, *Foreign Vocabulary*, s.v.

It ought to be feminine, and Bḍ. therefore takes **fīhī** as referring to the coming of the Ark, and **sakīnah** "assurance" as in other passages, cf. IX.26, 40; XLVIII.4, 16, 26. But as **sakīnah** is coordinate with **baqiyyan**, it is more natural to take **fīhi** as referring to the Ark itself, and **sakīnah** as something which was supposed to be contained in it. The word is the Heb. **shəkīnah** and this is no doubt the earliest use of it in the Qur'ān; in the other passages the sense has been influenced by that of the Arabic root.

For the relics of the family of Moses and Aaron contained in the Ark, cf. Exod. 25:6 ff.; I Kings 8:9; and especially Heb. 9:4. That the angels carry the Ark is probably a reminiscence of the cherubim.

Verse 250

This mixes the story of Gideon, Judges 7:5 f., with that of Saul. Goliath is regarded as leader of the opposing forces. The end of the verse combats the feeling of weakness in face of a stronger force, possibly before Uhud.

Verse 251

cf. VII.123; VIII.ll.

Verse 252

Cf. XXII.41; there was still some aversion to war among the people of Medina.

Verse 253

This is quite detached, though it may have originally preceded verse 254.

Verse 254

This is out of connection; it must have followed some list of previous messengers; cf. XVII.57. It belongs to the period of controversy with Jews and Christians, cf. verse 81. It deals with the problem of the differences between the monotheistic religion.

man kallama llāh, "to whom Allah spoke" as to Moses, but **Allāh** is sometimes read as object, "who spoke to Allah"; cf. verse 208.

Verse 255

This is also unchanged, but may be complete in itself. For the address cf. verse 204, and for parallels, XIV.36; LXIII.10. The rhyme phrase is loosely attached.

Verse 256

The famous verse of the throne, also stands by itself.

al-ḥayy al-qayyūm, cf. III.1; XX.110.

qayyūm is by Muslim interpreters derived from Arabic **qāma bi**, and taken in the sense of "all-sustaining," but it is probably the Aramaic **qayyām**, "eternal."

NS suggests that the verse may be the translation of a Jewish or Christian hymn, see *NS*, i, p. 184, n., for references to Jewish literature, from which phrases may have been borrowed. More probably, it has been composed on the basis of knowledge acquired in early Medinan days, particularly of the Psalms, cf. Ps. 121:3, 24:1, 50:10 f., 139, 11:4; also Isa. 40:13, 28; 66:1. The verse may have formed part of the early Medinan address in praise of Allah, portions of which have already appeared in the sura, cf. verses 19b, 20, 26, 27, and 158–160a.

The intercessors referred to seem to be angels, cf. XIX.65.

Verses 257–259

These might possibly connect with verse 256, but are probably separate. This seems to be the only passage in which compulsion in religion is deprecated; it is probably early Medinan.

For the opposition of **ar-rushd** and **al-ghayy**, cf. VII.143, also LXXXII.2.

ṭāghūt from late Heb. **ṭaʿūth** (Geiger), Aram. **ṭaʿyūthā** (Grimme); Jeffery decides in favor of Ethiopic as the source from which the required sense of "idols" may be derived. The occurrence of the word in early Medinan passages would, however, favor Jewish influence. From verse 259 it appears that the word was regarded as plural.

al-ʿurwah al-wuthqā, cf. XXXI.21.

"bring out of the darkness into the light," cf. V.18; XIV.1, 5; XXXIII.42; LVII.11.

Verses 258–259 should form only one verse.

Verses 260–268

These verses consist of a series of deliverances dealing with contributions, verses 263–268, which have been written on the back of verses 260–262, which belong to the same context as verse 244. The disparity in space is perhaps to be explained by verse 265, and the close of verse 266 being later insertions. The fact that verse 244 was evidently detached when verses 247 ff. was written may perhaps argue that these deliverances were earlier than the preceding passage.

Verse 260

This begins in the same way as verse 244, and like it, deals with the revival of the dead. Bḍ. says the reference is to Nimrod, but no satisfactory source has been discovered.

Verse 261

This verse connects with verse 260, and also deals with the resurrection.

The reference is quite uncertain. Ezekiel's vision may have suggested the first part of the verse (Muhammad Ali); others find in it a reference to Nehemiah's restoration of Jerusalem. A. Müller, in *ZDMG* 42 (1888), recalls the story in the Ethiopic Book of Baruch, according to which the friend of Jeremiah falls asleep for years, and when he is restored, finds his provisions still fresh. The verse may be based on a confusion of the two stories.

For the phrase **khāwiyah ʿalā ʿurūshinā**, cf. XVIII.40; XXII.44;

kam labithta, cf. XVIII.18; XXIII.114 f.

Verse 262

This is perhaps founded on a verse recollection of Gen. 15:9 ff. It belongs to the same context as verses 260–261.

ṣur, in **ṣurhunna**, is variously pointed; it is usually taken as imper. of **ṣwr**, used here in the sense of "cause to come." This is an unusual meaning of the verb, but no better suggestion has been made.

Verse 263

This is an appeal rather than a command for contributions, and is complete in itself. The simile perhaps shows a recollection of the parable of the sower. For the close of the verse, cf. verse 246.

Verse 264

This is a similar appeal.

mann, properly "favor" or "bounty," must be here in the sense of presuming upon favors bestowed to affect superiority, playing the bountiful. The concluding phrase shows that the verse was originally complete in itself.

Verse 265

This is probably a later addition.

Verses 266–267

These probably originally formed only one verse. The concluding clause of verse 266 interrupts the parable, and breaks the construction; it was probably introduced later to give a rhyme and break an overlong verse. The parable contained in the verses seems to show reminiscences of the parable of the sower and Matt. 7:24 ff.; perhaps also Isa. 6:1 f.

"For the sake of appearances," cf. Matt. 6:1.

Verse 268

This seems to be another parable emphasizing the point of the preceding one. Those who contribute for show may seem to have a nice garden of good works, but when they need it most, it is suddenly swept away.

Verses 271–274a

These verses are complicated, and the arrangement adopted in my *Translation* is not satisfactory. Verse 272 is out of rhyme. Verse 273 has a verse ending in the middle, which would give the same rhyme as as that of verse 272. A similar rhyme is found in verse 271a and verse 272a; verse 274a has no connection with the context, while verse 271 and verse 272 have very little connection with the subject of contributions. The rhyme phrase of verse 271 is loosely attached and rather disrupts the connection. It was probably inserted later to divide the verse and introduce the assonance of this surah. If it be removed, verses 271–272 may be read as one verse, with assonance in -ā followed by a consonant, or as consisting of at least three verses. verse 271a (**bi-l-faḥshā'**); verse 271b (**faḍlā[n]** [?]); verse 272a (**yashā'**); verse 272b (**al-albāb**).

The presence of this passage, which deals with Allah's free bestowal of wisdom, is no doubt due to verses 269–270 having been written on the back of it.

Though verse 273a does not connect with verses 271–272, it has the assonance and probably belongs to the earlier strand. The back of it was used for the writing of verse 273b, which forms a (perhaps later) annex to verses 269–270; as that did not suffice, the concluding phrase was written on the back of another short phrase, which stands isolated at the beginning of verse 274.

Verse 271

Cf. verse 164; XXIV.21.

al-faḥshā' can hardly mean "nigardliness," which is the usual interpretation here, but is an attempt to adapt the passage to the present context.

Verse 272

Cf. verse 252, XXXI.11.

Verse 273a

For rhyme phrase, cf. III.189.

Verse 273b

Cf. Matt. 6:4; verse 275.

Verse 273c

kaffara is the Hebrew **kippēr**, and is a Medinan word; the subject to the verb here is usually taken to be Allah, but may be the action described.

For the phrase, cf. IV.35; III.194; verse 15, 70; VIII.29; XXIX.6; XLVIII.5; LXVI.8.

Verses 274b–275

Verse 274

This verse is long, even after detaching the initial phrase, which does not belong to it, and has a break, with a rhyme, in the middle, at **tuẓlamūna**.

li-l-fuqarā' has nothing to depend on in its present position. It is parallel to **li-'anfusikum**, and the second part of the verse is a substitute for the first, beginning at the latter word. For additional space, the back of verse 275, itself a separate deliverance on alms-giving, cf. XIV.36, was utilized.

"Restricted in the way of Allah," Bḍ. takes to mean "occupied with the **jihād**," but more probably it refers to **Muhājirīn**, who have been reduced to poverty and for some reason or other cannot engage freely in trade. Whether the fact that they can be recognised by their mark implies that they devoted themselves to pious exercises is doubtful; cf. VII.44, 46; XLVII.32, (XLVIII.29); LV.41.

Verses 276–277

These verses deal mainly with usury, but are not uniform.

Verse 277 consists really of two verses, with an ending at **'athīm**. The second half has no connection with usury.

Verse 276

This is long, but has a break at **al-mass**.

Up to here the verse is a dissuasion from taking usury because of its moral consequences at the Judgment. The rest of the verse implies that usury has already been forbidden, and repeats the prohibition more emphatically. This previous prohibition may be that of Jewish Law, or that contained in verse 277, which possibly may have been the original continuation of verse 276a. The sense seems to be that usury is done away with; it is alms freely given that bear interest, that is, in spiritual reward.

Verse 276b

This has been written on the back of the two separate verses contained in verse 277.

Verse 276

"Arise," that is, at the resurrection.

takhabbaṭa, only here in the Qurʾān, "to strike obliquely," as a camel with the forefoot, "to overthrow."

The "touch" of Satan probably refers to demoniacal possession or insanity.

"Retains what is past," that is, the prohibition is not to apply to what has already been received, of which no account is to be taken.

Verses 278–286

The main part of this is a long and probably late enactment dealing with borrowing and the recording of debts, verses 282–283, which may have been designed to replace previous deliverances dealing with usury. In any case it was written on the back of

> verses 278–81 (a prohibition of usury),
>
> verse 284 (a verse from some other context setting forth Allah's knowledge),
>
> verses 285a–286b (a profession of faith and prayer).

A modification excepting ordinary business transactions from the necessity of being recorded was inserted into verse 282, **'idhā . . . tabāya'tum**. This was written on the back of the scraps verses 285b–286a, and when it was inserted in its proper place in the new enactment, these scraps interrupted the connection of verse 285a and verse 286b on the other side.

Verses 278–281

These verses are very peremptory in tone and, being addressed to believers, are difficult to date. They are probably later than verse 276b. They forbid, under threat of war, the collecting of interest that has already been agreed upon, but has not been paid. One would be inclined to regard this a directed against the Jews, but they could hardly be addressed as believers. Tradition says it was the Thaqīf who demanded usury from some of the Quraish; this would imply a later date.

The pronoun in verse 280 refers to the debtor; the indulgence to be granted refers to the repayment of capital, not interest.

Verses 282–283

These imply that writing was a fairly common accomplishment in Medina, but not in the country districts. For similar regulations regarding the recording of bequests, cf. V.105 f., which is perhaps earlier than this.

alladhī ʿalaihi l-ḥaqqu, that is, the debtor; by dictating the agreement he acknowledges the debt.

waliyyuhu is not the other party to the contract, but the representative of the debtor.

tijārah ḥāḍirah is read by **ʿĀṣim** as accusative, by all the other readers as nominative, without much difference in sense.

tijārah must be in the concrete sense of "merchandise." The exception introduced refers to goods passing from hand to hand in the ordinary course of business.

yuḍārra may be either active or passive, that is, either those who write the agreement or witness it are not to do an injury by writing or testifying what is false, or they are not to suffer an injury by being involved in the transaction. The latter seems preferable on account of the following clause. But perhaps "ye" is to be taken as including the writer and witness; that is, if writers and witnesses from among you do an injury.

Verse 283

On a journey amongst the Bedouin, it might be difficult to find a "writer"; there are variants, **kitāb**, **kutub**, **kuttāb**; but the context supports **kātib**. In that case a pledge may be taken, as equivalent, or as evidence of the debt. Or the lender may dispense with formalities and simply trust the debtor, in which case the debtor must, as a pious duty, fulfill his obligation.

Verse 284

This verse is almost certainly Medinan, because of its insistence on Allah's knowledge of concealed opinions, but its context is uncertain.

Verse 285 f.

This dates from about the time of the break with the Jews, cf. verse 92 and verse 130, also IV.135. The end of verse 285 is, however, out of connection; note the grammatical break at **wa-qālū.**

There is also a grammatical break at **ktasabat** in verse 286, and the beginning of this verse is also quite out of connection,

The introduction of these two scraps is explained by the insertion of the exceptive clause in verse 282. With their removal, verse 285 and verse 286 join together as a declaration of belief on the part of the messenger and the believers, followed by a prayer.

With the declaration of belief cf. verse 130; the date must be somewhere about the time of the change of **qiblah**.

For verse 285b

Cf. verse 87. It may have been the original ending of verse 58, but that is uncertain.

The original context of verse 286a is still more uncertain. A similar idea occurs in the second part of the verse; cf. also VI.153; VII.40; XXIII.64.

BIBLIOGRAPHY AND ABBREVIATIONS

Ahrens, K. "Christliches im Qoran. Eine Nachlese." *ZDMG*, 84 (1930): 15–68, 148–90.

———. *Muhammad als Religionsstifter*. Leipzig, 1935.

Andrae, Tor. *Die Ursprung des Islams und das Christentum*. Uppsala–Stockholm, 1926.

Archer, J.C. "Mystical Elements in Islam." in *Essays in Philosophy Presented in His Honour*, edited by A. R. Wadia. Bangalore 1954.

al-Balādhuri, *Futūḥ al-buldān.* edited by M. J. de Goeje, *Liber expugnationis regionum.* Leiden, 1866.

Barth, J. "Studien zur Kritik und Exegese des Qorāns." *Der Islam* 6 (1916): 113–48.

Baumstark, A. "Jüdischer und christlicher Gebetstypus im Koran." *Der Islam* 16 (1927): 229–48.

Bd. = al-Bayḍāwī, *Commentary.*

Bell, *Translation* = R. Bell. *The Qur'ān Translated.* 2 vols. Edinburgh, 1937–39.

Bell, R., *The Origin of Islam in its Christian Environment* (The Gunning Lectures, 1925). London, 1926.

———. "A Duplicate in the Koran; the Composition of Surah XXIII." *MW* 18 (1928): 227–33.

———. "The Men of the A'rāf (Surah vii: 44)." *MW* 22 (1932): 43–48.

———. "Muhammad's Pilgrimage Proclamation." *JRAS* (1937): 233–44.

———. "Muhammad and Divorce in the Qur'ān," *MW* 29 (1939): 55–62.

———. "Muhammad's Knowledge of the Old Testament." in *Studia Semitica et Orientalia* 2 (= *A Presentation Volume to William Barron Stevenson*, ed. C. J. Mullo Weir). Glasgow, 1945.

Bevan, A. R. "Mohammed's Ascension to Heaven." *ZATW* 27 (1914) (= *Studien J. Wellhausen gewidmet*): 49–61.

Blachère, R., *Introduction au Coran. Traduction nouvelle.* 3 vols. Paris, 1947–51.

Bräunlich, E. "The Well in Ancient Arabia," *Islamica* 1 (1925): 41–76, 288–343, 454–528.

Buhl, F. *Das Leben Muhammads.* Translated by H. H. Schaeder. Leipzig. 1930.

al-Bukhārī, Ṣaḥīḥ = *Le recueil de traditions musulmanes.* Edited by L. Krehl and F. W. Juynboll. 4 vols. Leiden, 1862–1908.

Burkitt, F. C. *Jewish and Christian Apocalypses* (The Schweich Lectures, 1913). London, 1914.

Casanova, P. *Mohammed et la fin du monde, étude critique sur l'Islam primitif.* Paris, 1911.

Charles, R. H. *A Critical and Exegetical Commentary on the Revelation of St. John* (The International Critical Commentary). 2 vols. Edinburgh, 1920.

Clermont-Ganneau, Charles. "La lampe et l'olivier dans le Coran." *RHR* 81 (1920): 213–59.

Doutté, E. *Magie et religion dans l'Afrique du Nord.* Algiers, 1908.

EI = *Encyclopaedia of Islām.* First edition. Edited by M. Th. Houtsma et al. 4 vols. and supplement. Leiden, 1908–36.

ERE = *Encyclopaedia of Religion and Ethics*. Edited by J. Hastings. 13 vols. Edinburgh, 1908–20.

Fischer, A. "Eine Qorān-Interpolation." In *Orientalische Studien Theodor Nöldeke zum siebigsten Geburtstag gewidmet*. Edited by C. Bezold. 2 vols. Giessen, 1906.

———. "Sure 2,191." *ZDMG* 65 (1911): 794–96.

———. "Noch einmal Sure 2,191." *ZDMG* 66 (1912): 294–99, 410.

———. "Der Werth der vorhandenen Koran-Übersetzungen und Sure 111." In *Berichte über die Verhandlungen der Sächsischen Akademie der Wissenschaften zu Leipzig*, Phil.-hist. Kl., lxxxix, 2. Heft, 1937.

Fluegel, G. *Corani textus arabicus*. Leipzig, 1831.

Fraenkel, S. *De vocabulis in antiquis Arabum carminibus et in Corano peregrinis*. Leiden, 1880.

———. *Die Aramäischen Fremdwörter im Arabischen*. Leiden, 1886.

Geiger, A. *Was hat Mohammed aus dem Judenthume aufgenommen?* Bonn, 1833.

Goitein, [S.D.] F. "Zur Entstehung des Ramaḍāns." *Isl*am 18 (1929): 189–95.

Goldziher, I. *Muhammedanische Studien*. 2 vols. Halle a. S., 1889–90.

———. *Vorlesungen über den Islam*. Heidelberg, 1910.

———. *Die Richtungen der islamischen Koranauslegung*. Leiden, 1920.

Goosens, E. "Ursprung und Bedeutung der Koranischen Siglen." *Islam* 13 (1923): 191–226.

Grimme, H. *Mohammed. I. Das Leben. II. Einleitung in den Koran. System der koranischen Theologie*. 2 vols. Münster i. W, 1892–95.

———. "Über einige Klassen südarabischer Lehnwörter im Koran." *ZA*, 26 (1912): 156–68.

———. *Der Koran, ausgewählt, angeordnet, und im Metrum des Originals übertragen*. Paderborn, 1923.

Hennecke, E. *Neutestamentliche Apokryphen, in Verbindung mit Fachgelehrten und mit Einleitung*. 2d ed. Tübingen, 1923.

Hirschfeld, H. *New Researches into the Composition and Exegesis of the Qoran*. London, 1902.

Horovitz, J. "Das koranische Paradies." In *Scripta Universitatis atque Bibliothecae Hierosolymitanum. Orientalia et Judaica*, i. Jerusalem, 1923.

———. "Die paradiesischer Jungfrauen im Koran." *Islamica*1 (1925): 543.

———. *Koranische Untersuchungen*. Berlin, 1926.

———. "Bemerkungen zur Geschichte und Terminologie des islamischen Kultus." *Isl.* 16 (1927): 249–63.

Hurgronje, C. Snouck. *Het Mekkaansche Fest*. 2 vols. Leiden, 1880.

Ibn Hishām. *Sīrat Al-Nabī*." In *Das Leben Muhammed's nach Ibn Ishâk bearbeitet von Abd elMalik Ibn Hischâm.* Edited by F. Wüstenfeld. 3 vols. Göttingen, 1858–60.

Ibn Khaldūn, Muqaddima. "Les Prolegomènes d' Ebn Khaldoun. In *Notices et extraits des manuscrits de la Bibliothèque Impériale*, edited by E. Quatremère. 3 vols. Paris, 1858.

Isl. = *Der Islam*. Strassburg, Berlin and Leipzig, Berlin.

Jeffery, A. *The Foreign Vocabulary of the Qur'ān*. Baroda, 1938.

JRAS = *Journal of the Royal Asiatic Society*. London.

Künstlinger, D. "Sū Sura 95." *OLZ* 29 (1936): cols. 1–3.

Larmmens, H. *La Mecque à la veille de l'Hégire*. Beirut, 1924.

Lane, E.W. *Selections from the Ḳur-án . . . with an Interlinear Commentary, . . .* London, 1843.

———. *An Arabic-English Lexicon*. 8 vols. London, 1863–93.

Le Strange, G. *Palestine under the Moslems, a Description of Syria and the Holy Land from* A.D. *650 to 1500*. London, 1890.

Lidzbarski, M., and A. Fischer. "Zu arabisch faḫḫār." *ZDMG* 72 (1918): 189–92, 328–39.

Margoliouth, D.S. *Mohammed and the rise of Islam*. Heroes of the Nations. New York, 1905.

———. *The Early Development of Mohammedanism*. London, 1914.

Montet, E. *Le Coran, traduction nouvelle et intégrale*. Paris, 1929.

Müller, A. "Zu Koran, 2, 261." *ZDMG* 42 (1888): 80.

Muhammad Ali, Maulvi *The Holy Qur-án, Containing the Arabic Text with English Translation and Commentary*. Woking, 1917.

Muir, Sir William. *The Life of Mahomet*. 3 vols. London, 1858–61.

———. *The Life of Muḥammad*. New and revised edition by T. H. Weir. Edinburgh, 1912.

MW = *Moslem World* (*Muslim World*).

Nöldeke, Theodore. *Delectus veterum carminum arabicorum*. Berlin, 1890.

———. "Beiträge zur Geschichte des Alexanderromans." In *Denkschriften der Kaiserlichen Akademie der Wissenschaften zu Wien*. Phil-hist. Cl., xxxvii, Nr. 5 (1890), 1–56.

———. "Fünf Moʿallaqât, übersetzt und erklärt." in *Sitzungsberichte der Kaiserlichen Akademie der Wissenschaften zu Wien*. Phil.-hist. Cl.. cxl Nr. 7 (1899), 1–84, cxlii Nr. 5 (1900), 1–94, cxliv Nr. 1 (1902), 1–43.

———. "Arabs (Ancient)," in *ERE*, vol. 1 659–73.

———. *Geschichte des Qorāns*. 2 vols. 2nd ed. F. Schwally. Leipzig, 1909.

———. *Neue Beiträge zur semitischen Sprachwissenschaft*. Strassburg, 1910.

NS = Nöldeke-Schwally, *Geschichte des Qorāns.*

O'Leary, De Lacey. *Arabia Before Muhammad.* London, 1927.

OLZ = *Orientalistische Literaturzeitung.* Berlin, Leipzig, Berlin.

Palmer, E. H. *The Qur'ān.* Sacred Books of the East, VI, IX. Oxford, 1880.

Paret, R. "Der Plan einer neuen, leicht kommentierten wissenschaftlichen Koran übersetzung." In *Orientalische Studien Enno Littmann zu seinem 60. Geburtstag . . . überreicht. . . .* Leiden, 1935.

Pautz, O. *Muhammeds Lehre von der Offenbarung.* Leipzig, 1898.

Praetorius, F. "Zur 12. Sure." *ZDMG* 76 (1917): 447.

Reckendorf, H. *Arabische Syntax.* Heidelberg, 1921.

RHR = *Revue de l'histoire des religions.*

Rodwell, J. M. *The Koran, Translated from the Arabic.* London and Edinburgh, 1861.

Rückert, F. *Der Koran, im Auszuge übersetzt.* Edited by A. Müller. Frankfurt a. M., 1889.

Rudolph, W. *Die Abhängigkeit des Qorans von Judentum und Christentum.* Stuttgart, 1922.

Rutter, E. *The Holy Cities of Arabia.* London, 1928.

Sale, G. *The Koran: Commonly Called the Alcoran of Mohammed, Translated into English . . . to which is Prefixed Preliminary Discourse.* London, 1734.

Schrieke, B. "Die Himmelreise Muhammeds." *Isl.* 6 (1915–16): 1–30.

Schwarz, P. "Zu Sūre 2, Vers 191." *ZDMG* 66 (1912): 136–38.

———. "Zur Erklärung von Sure 2, Vers 191." *ZDMG* 66 (1912): 411–13.

Sidersky, D. *Les origines des légendes musulmanes dans le Coran et dans les vies des prophètes.* Paris, 1933.

Smith, W. Robertson. *Lectures on the Religion of the Semites: The Fundamental Institutions.* 3rd ed. Edited by S. A. Cook. London, 1927.

TGUOS = *Transactions of the Glasgow University Oriental Society.*

Torrey, C. C. "Three Difficult Passages in the Koran." In *ʿAjabnámah. A Volume of Oriental Studies Presented to Edward G. Browne on His 60th Birthday.* . . . Edited by T. W. Arnold and R. A. Nicholson. Cambridge, 1922.

———. *The Jewish Foundation of Islam.* The Hilda Stich Stroock Lectures at the Jewish Institute of Religion. New York, 1933.

Vollers, K. *Volkssprache und Umgangssprache im alten Arabien.* Strassburg, 1906.

Weber, F. *Die Lehren des Talmuds quellenmässig, systematisch und gemein verständlich dargestellet.* Edited by F. Delitzsch and G. Schneidermann. Leipzig, 1886.

Weil, G. *Mohammed der Prophet, sein Leben und seine Lehre.* Stuttgart, 1843.

Wellhausen, J. *Reste arabischen Heidentums*. 2nd ed. Berlin, 1897.
———. "Zum Ḳoran." *ZDMG* 47 (1913): 630–34.
Wright, W. *A Grammar of the Arabic Language*. 3rd ed. 2 vols. Cambridge, 1896–98.
ZA = *Zeitschrift für Assyriologie*.
Zam. = al-Zamakhsharī, *Commentary*.
al-Zamakhsharī. *al-Mufaṣṣal*. Edited by J. B. Broch. Christiana, 1879.
ZATW = *Zeitschrift für alttestamentlichen Wissenschaft*.
ZDMG = *Zeitschrift der Deutschen Morgenländischen Gesellschaft*.

Part 8

Poetry and the Koran

8.1

The Strophic Structure of the Koran

Rudolf Geyer

Translated by G. A. Wells

The purpose of this article is to draw attention to a few perhaps not unimportant observations pertaining to the strophic structure of the Koran—observations I myself cannot pursue further as I am fully occupied with other tasks. D. H. Müller based his division of various Koran suras into stanzas on purely stylistic and rhetorical considerations, whereas I came to my all too brief study of the Koran rhymes a propos of reading Vollers's *Volkssprache und Schriftsprache.*[1] The results of my investigations were nevertheless surprising, and will soon be published in my review of Vollers's book in *Göttinger Gelchite Anzeige.* In many respects what I say there overlaps with what I am putting forward here. But here I am making some additional observations, which are not included there because they go beyond what is relevant in that context. Also, quite a few points touched on there are taken up again here and stated with greater clarity and precision.

The Koran text appended by W. N. Lees to his edition of Zamakhshārī's *Kashshāf* gives a division into verses that differs from the text of Flugel's edition. Zamakhshārī's text (designated Zam. henceforth) does not merely record the division into suras, and into Juzʾ[2] and verses, as Flügel does, but also makes the rulings concerning pauses and prostrations (Arabic, Rukūʿ) when the text is read out ritually. The Juzʾ divisions are marked with all manner of signs, corresponding to the extended system

From *WZKM* 22 (1908): 265–87.

of Ibn Ṭayfūr as-Sajāwandī and enumerated by Nöldeke in *Geschichte des Qoran*,[3] while the rukūʿ are given the siglum, *ʿayn* ع (the Arabic letter). It is a priori obvious that these prostrations must mark the more forceful sections of the recitation and hence also of the textual content.

And this is indeed almost invariably the case, at least in Lees's case. When in some few instances there is deviation from this rule, we are justified in assuming that either the rukūʿ has been put in the wrong place, or that there has been some disruption of another kind. That this assumption is correct is confirmed in that we find, on the one hand, that no break between two suras is without rukūʿ, and on the other, that every rukūʿ coincides with the ending of a verse (according to the division in Zam.) [4] It is then striking that the end of a verse that comes at a rukūʿ often departs from the rhyming context, as with XIII.26; XIV.6, 32; XVI.72; XIX.41 (from verse 35 on in *-ūn*); XXII.34; XXIV.56; XXVIII.28; LXXXIX.30; XC.20; XCIII.11; XCVI.19; XCVIII.8; CXI.5 (further examples in my review in the *Gott. Gel. Anz.*). Finally, the change in rhyme not infrequently coincides with a rukūʿ (I give numerous examples in my review in that journal).Whether the distribution of the rukūʿ is identical or variable in all recensions of the Koran, or in all Islamic rites, would still have to be investigated. However, that there are fluctuations and differences between the individual recensions is suggested by the fact that Zam. shows in Sura II.19 after *qadīran*, a verse division not present in Flügel—one which at the same time is provided with a rukūʿ. If we now consider those suras that, in the view of D. H. Müller, show strophic divisions, and take into consideration the rukūʿ noted in Zam., then such prostrations are prescribed in Sura VII before verses 57, 63, 71, 83, 92, 98, 106, 124, 127, 138, 146, and 151; in Sura XI before verses 27, 38, 52, 64, 72, 75, 85, and 99; in Sura XV before verses 16, 26, 45, 61, and 80; in Sura XIX before verses 16, 42, 52, 67, and 86; in Sura XXVI before verses 9, 33, 52, 69, 105, 123, 141, 160, 176, and 192; in Sura XXXVI before verse 33; in Sura XLIV before verses 29 and 43; in Sura LI before verses 24 and 31; in Sura LIV before verses 23 and 41; in Sura LVI before verses 38 and 74; in Sura LXIX before verse 38; in Sura LXXV before verse 31; and in Sura LXXVIII before verse 31. In the remaining four suras considered by D. H. Müller, only the beginning and the end are given rukūʿ. Thus, of the fifty-two rukūʿ enumerated here, only seven—namely those before Sura

VII.98, 124, 127, 151; XIX.86; XLIV.29; and LVI.38—are internal to Müller's stanzas, whereas forty-five coincide with the strophic divisions posited by Muller. The textual division conjectured by Müller from the stylistic and rhetorical premises agrees, then, within the thirteen suras being considered, at forty-five out of fifty-two points with the sections marked with prostration in the recension in Zam. What is true of rukūʿ that do not fall on strophic divisions remains to be discussed in the relevant individual instances. But before I move onto this, I must indicate two features of importance for the strophic structure also of the Koran which I have treated at length in my article in the *Gott. Gel. Anz.*, and to which, in consequence, I need only briefly refer here. In the article I have shown, by comparing Flügel's text with Zam., that the division of the Koran into verses varies considerably in the different recensions; and I believe that from this, we may confidently infer that this division was introduced at a relatively late stage. On the other hand, I have shown there that the division into verses in at any rate these two recensions—probably also in all others—does not keep strictly to the rhyming units of the text, but ignores all manner of internal rhymes and often—intentionally or otherwise—obscures beyond recognition quite complicated rhyme-strophe complexes. I have made it clear with various examples that the rukūʿ divisions frequently coincide with these complexes. And so all these various features must be kept in mind when studying the poetic forms of the Koran; and in this sense I will now discuss the suras treated by Müller.

SURA I

Sura I shows, in its short construction, an ending in verse 6 that deviates from the rhyme. If we take the rhyme as our criterion, we obtain six lines, with verses 6 and 7 comprised in the final one. The sura divides into two equal parts of three lines each, and in each part the rhyme sequence is as follows: *īn, īm, īn*. The first half praises God; the second gives the prayer for proper guidance. Possibly the division of the sixth line into two verses was effected in order to bring about the holy number seven in the Fātiḥah.

SURA VII

A regular division into stanzas is not visible in this sura, as Müller already showed. But if we consider the distribution of the ruku‘, we can discern a more or less definite subdivision in the contents, which develops in the following way:

(a) verses 1–9. Threat of being called to account at the Last Judgment
(b) verses 10–24. Rebellion of ʾIblīs, and the Fall
(c) verses 25–29. The ordering of apparel
(d) verses 30–37. Punishment of unbelievers in hell
(e) verses 38–45. Distinguishing the just and the unjust
(f) verses 46–51. Tardy repentance of unbelievers
(g) Verses 52–56. Evidence of God in nature
(h) verses 57–62. Noah
(i) verses 63–70. Hūd
(k)[5] verses 71–82. Ṣāliḥ (71–77) and Lot (78–82)
(l) verses 83–91. Shuʿayb
(m) verses 92–97. The scheme according to which the prophets were [are] sent
(n) verses 98–123. Practical (moral) applications following therefrom (98–100); dispatch of Moses and conversion of the magicians (101–123).
(o) verses 124–126. Pharaoh's resistance and Moses' encouragement of his people
(p) verses 127–137. Unbelief of the Egyptians and Exodus of the Israelites
(q) verses 138–145. Moses on Sinai
(r) verses 146–150. The Golden Calf and Moses' anger
(s) verses 151–156. Moses' giving of the Law
(t) verses 157–162. Israel in the wilderness
(u) verses 163–170. Legend of Elath
(v) verses 171–180. God's signs in history [or in the story]
(w) verses 181–188. God's punitive court and judgment
(x) verses 189–205. God the refuge of believers.

The rukūʿ seems not always to occur in the correct place; for instance, it should surely be moved from verse 150 to the division between 152 and 153. The prostration after verse 97 is also noteworthy, and would really be expected after verse 100, which is where Müller places the divide. It comes as no surprise that in this sura, sloppily put together as it is, Müller's divisions are not always confirmed by the positioning of the rukūʿ. It is all the more to be noted that, where the division according to content, marked by responsion,[6] is more evident, Müller's sections coincide exactly with the rukūʿ. Thus it is precisely the irregularities of this sura that give visible indication that his theory is correct. Closer study of the way the rhymes are arranged would perhaps eliminate many of those irregularities. But such a study would lead us too far afield, and is also made very difficult by the sura's rhyming in the characteristic un-sound. (The [austretenden] rhymes that drop out of 139, 143, 146, 157, 186, are dropped in the distribution given in Zam.)

SURA XI

Müller's strophes verses 27–98 coincide exactly with the rukūʿ sections, with only the rukūʿ after verse 46 missing. In this way the Noah legend would divide into only two sections of 11 ($2 \times 6 - 1$) and 14 (2×7) lines, and so is strongly analogous to the following legends of Hūd, Abraham and Shu'ayb.[7] If one takes note of the rhyme formation, the legend of Salih divides likewise into two parts; the first comprising four lines rhyming in *īb (ūb)*, as verse 66 forms a single line with verse 67 because the rhyme has dropped out. The second part consists of two lines (verses 69 and 70 + 71), rhyming in *īz (ūd)*[8] and introduced by the responsion formula *fa-lammā jāʾa* . . . (when our decree issued . . .]. The whole is thus made up of six lines which fits the remaining stanzas (as half?). Incidentally, the structure of the Abraham strophe changes considerably if the rhyme is taken into consideration. It then divides—by splitting verse 84 after *manḍūdin*—into two equally long sections of seven lines each, which incidentally are linked by terminal responsion *fa-lammā dhahaba . . . ar -rawʿu wa jāʾ-athul bushrā* [verse 77] and *fa-lammā jāʾa amrunā* (verse 84). The rhyme is formed by the elements *īd* and *īb* in all manner of combinations, while in the Shu'ayb strophe, constructed in the same way, two elements terminating in *īn* are entwined additionally in each half. The rest of this sura (not discussed by Müller), which contains practical applications from the Moses legend, also falls—by the rukūʿ mark after verse 111—into two equally long strophes, linked by their initial *wa la-qad ʾarsalnā Mūsā bi-ʾ āyātinā . . .* [verse 99] = *wa la-qad ʾātaynā Mūsā l –kitāba* [verse 112], and their final responsion *wa innā la-muwaffūhum naṣībahum ghayra manqūṣin* [verse 111] = *wa mā rabbukā bi-ghāfilin ʿammā taʿmalūna* [verse 123], each comprising fourteen lines (if one adds the new verse endings indicated in Zam.: *mubīnin* in verse 99, *mukhtalifīn* in verse 120, and *ʿāmilūna* in verse 122). The first of the two strophes begins with non-rhyming line (*mubīnin*) and then has two sequences of five lines each, the first four of which in each case terminate in *ūd*, while the fifth (verses 103 and 108) departs from the rhyme but both assonate among themselves (īb = īq). An abgesang (concluding section) of three lines forms the end of the strophe, the first two lines rhyming again in *ūd*, while the third and final line departs completely from the rhyme (*manqūṣin*). The second strophe is much more simply constructed. It begins likewise with a nonrhyming line *murībin*, followed by a distich in *īr (u)* but the remaining eleven lines terminate in the all-purpose rhyme *ūn*.

SURA XV

The rukūʿ here also come at Müller's strophic divisions, but in such a way that a different division into groups is formed from that advocated by Müller. The first rukūʿ division accords with Müller's group 1, whereas group 2 would extend only to verse 25, and group 3 begins already at verse 26. In this distribution, groups 2 and 3 would correspond through their initial words—on the one hand *wa la-qad ja ʿalnā fī s-samāʾi burūjan* (verse 16) and on the other *Wa la-qad khalaqnā l-ʾinsāna* (verse 26). This grouping is also justified because of the content, for in group 1 the disposition of the whole sura is given, while group 2 tells of God's care in his creation, and group 3 of the angelic fall of the Iblis. Müller's linking strophe (verses 45–50) is not divided off by the rukūʿ division in Zam., but belongs there to a group that extends to verse 60 and which, beginning with mention of the joys of paradise, narrates Abraham's visitation by the angels. The next rukūʿ strophe (verses 61–79) repeats the punishment of the Sodomites, while the final one (verses 80–99), after a brief reminiscence of the affair with Ḥijr, draws the moral and gives an exhortation to fear of God and to faith. The number of lines in the individual rukūʿ strophes form the following series: 15 + 10 + 19 + 16 + 19 + 20. Nothing much can be inferred from brief consideration of the rhymes terminating in the *an* sound. From the distribution of the rukūʿ, it would seem that that the construction of the strophes is somewhat irregular. But I would stress the possibility that larger or smaller units have been lost, bearing in mind that the reports of punitive judgments, known from other suras, have been substantially abbreviated and sharpened into pure exemplifications. In verses 78 and 79, which Müller[9] wishes to eliminate, there may be a residual fragment of a longer account. Müller's divisions into groups are not further impaired by the results of the comparison. In particular, to include the linking strophe verses 45–50 (which quite looks as though it did not originally belong in the context of the sura) in the following rukūʿ section is quite intelligible from its origin as an interpolation. As the sense of the section between verses 44 and 51 was already firmly fixed, the intrusion could be reckoned as well with the preceeding as with the following section; the latter was preferred, as the substance of the interpolated piece could just about be suitable as an introduction to the mention of the "friend of Allah," whereas it had no point of contact with the naming of hell, which concludes the earlier section.

SURA XIX

Here, too, the division proposed by Müller is on the whole confirmed. But study of the disposition of the rhymes makes the strophes much more regular than Müller himself assumed them to be, retaining as he did the division into verses of Flügel's edition of the text; for if we eliminate verse 3,[10] which deviates from the rhyme, by joining it to verse 4 (so as to make a line comparable in length to verse 5); and if we take note of the internal rhyme *taqiyyan* verse 14, which in Zam. appears as a special break, so that the correspondence with verse 33 is even more forcefully stressed; then the principal group concerning the Baptist episode (verses 1–15) becomes divided into three equally long strophes of five lines each, assuming that the end of verse 7 (drawn in Zam. together with verse 8) in *Yaḥyā* (in the not impossible pronunciation *Yaḥiyyā*) rhymes with *samiyyan.* Even if this assumption is not tenable, the sequence of lines 5 + 4 + 5 remains symmetrical. In the Mary episode, making verses 26 and 27 into one (effected also in Zam.) is justified by the absence of rhyme, and then the lines are distributed in the individual strophes in the ratio of 6 + 5 + 7. Closer comparison of the third strophe of each of the two principal groups shows that the address of Yaḥyās in verse 13 has no proper link with what precedes it, and the analogy of verse 30 would lead one to expect here a question of the people to Zakariyyā. If one may assume for this reason that a line has dropped out before verse 13, then we obtain the following distribution of units to the two principal groups: Yaḥyā 5 + 4 + 6; ʿĪsā 6+5+7, and the stanzaic structure is firmly secured by manifold interlocking of responsion elements. The additional strophe verses 35–41 is appended by the rukūʿ positioning of the Mary episode, as with D. H. Müller. The process is here the same as with the interpolation in verses 45–50 in sura XI. Müller's Abraham strophe (verses 42–51) is bounded by two rukūʿ marks, whereas there is no such mark after verse 58, and, on the other hand, the two strophe verses 52–58 and verses 59–66, which Müller regards as belonging together, are kept apart from each other by a rukūʿ. The uncertainty here is due not to Müller—even though he stresses (*Proph.* I.29) the difficulties obtaining here—but to those considerations which were dominant in distributing the rukūʿ. So much is clear from the notable absence of a rukūʿ after verse 75, where both the division according to content and the change of rhyme suggest that there would be one here. Study of the disposition of the rhymes shows that Müller's division remains in essence secure also for the final section of the sura, prominent by virtue of its novel rhyme—in spite of the badly misplaced rukūʿ after verse 85. For if we allow for the internal rhymes *waladan* in verses 91 and 93 and *ʿabdan*[11] in verse 94, all moved to the end of new verses by the division of the verses in Zam., then we obtain three strophes, of which the first (verses 76–83) has eight, the second (verses 84–90) seven, and the third (verses 91–95) eight lines, while verses 96–98 form a special coda to the great symphony and solemnly summarize the promise of eternal bliss for the godfearers, and eternal punishment for unbelievers. The rukūʿ inserted here between verses 85 and 86 can, as already said, make no difference to this, because it blatantly disturbs the content, and also because verses 84–87 are shown to be closely linked by the intertwinement of the rhymes *ʿizzā–ḍiddā-ʾazzā—ʾaddā*. Additionally there is the fact that—characteristic of the sense of form documented in the structure of the whole sura—the rhyme termination *-zzā*, which otherwise occurs only in this passage (verses 84 and 86), turns up once again in the final verse of the coda. Whether the distribution of the rukūʿ in this sura reappears in other recensions of the Koran would have to be determined by comparison, which I am at present unable to make. But even if all rites agreed, this would not make the striking displacement of the two final prostration marks any more acceptable. Both have obviously been moved too far back, and probably belong after verse 58 or, as the case may be, after verse 75. Comparison of the division into stanzas of this sura proposed by Müller (*Proph.* I.33) with the one that emerges from the above discussion yields the following configurtion:

First section (verses 1–15). Birth of John 5 + 4 + 5(6) (M. 6 + 5 + 4)

Second section (verses 16–34). Birth of Jesus 6 + 5 + 7 (M. 6 + 6 + 7); addendum (verses 35–41) Polemics against Christianity 7 (M. 7)

Third section (a) (verses 42–58) Various prophets 10 + 7 (= 17); and (b) (verses 59–75). Period without prophets, resurrection 8 + 9 (=17) (M. 10 + 7 + 8 + 9)

Fourth section (verses 76–95). Polemics against those of other faiths, 8 + 7 + 8 and coda (verses 96–98). The reward of faith, punishment of infidelity 3 (M. 8 + 7 + 8).

The comparison shows clearly how surprisingly the results of the two so different methods of observing the data agree.

SURA XXVI

In this sura the rukūʿ marks fall invariably on Müller's intervals between the strophes, and also, with one single exception (after verse 32) on those that Müller emphasizes with division marks. A section marked off in this manner with the rukūʿ distribution placed also between verses 32 and 33, which are not separated in this way by Müller, seems justified to me because of the introduction of the Egyptian medicine men in the next section. The part played by the number eight in the line numbering of the Moses legend is striking and was already stressed by Müller. If one eliminates the nonrhyming verse 59[12] by combining it with verse 60, one then obtains a regular eight-line stanza instead of the nine-line one. There then remains only the irregularity of the seven-line strophe, verses 33–39, explicable as the result of a line dropping out, as one misses any mention between verses 38 and 39 of the persons speaking in the latter verse. Müller's division gives irregular strophes in the Abraham legend. In spite of what he says (*Proph.* I.41), I would place the division of the second from the third strophe after verse 86, where a new theme begins; and I would put verse 96 with the fourth strophe, to which its subject matter is better suited. In this way we obtain four equally long strophes of nine lines each—a number that reappears in the strophes of the following legends of Noah and Hūd. The story of Ṣāliḥ covers—if one allows for the internal rhyme *yufsidūna* in verse 152—two equally long strophes of ten lines each, while the legends of Lot and Shuʿayb return to the regularity of eight lines in each of two strophes—a regularity dominant in the final part of the sura. I would advocate taking the units of five and three lines together—Müller makes them alternate—because of verse 197, which because it does not rhyme must be fused with verse 198, whereas verse 194 divides into two lines after the internal rhyme *litakūna*. To be sure, a fresh five-line unit could end with verse 195 and the three-line unit begin at verse 196. The subject matter would allow this. Müller makes the final section into a unit of five lines; but with the fusion of verses 227 and 228, justified by the subject matter, since the mention of the Shayāṭīn in verse 221 leads on immediately to verses 224 ff. to the polemics against the poets inspired by him. In fact, no prostration is prescribed at this point. Our analysis, while strikingly confirming Müller's divisions, demonstrates that this sura possesses a far more regular form, one that is completely rounded off, apart from the insignificant aberration the fourth strophe, as the following tabulation makes clear:

I.	Introduction		1. Strophe (v.1–8)	8 lines
		Rukūʿ!		
II.	Moses and Pharaoh		{ 2. Strophe (v.9–16)	8 lines
			{ 3. Strophe (v.17–32)	8 + 8 lines
		Rukūʿ!		
III.	Moses and the Magicians		4. Strophe (v.33–39)	7 (8 – 1) lines
			5. Strophe (v.40–47)	8 lines
			1. Halfstrophe (v.48–51)	4 lines
		Rukūʿ!		
IV.	Exodus		6. Strophe (v.52–60)	8 lines
			7. Strophe (v.61–68)	8 lines
		Rukūʿ!		
V.	Abraham		8. Strophe (v. 69–77)	9 lines
			9. Strophe (v. 78–86)	9 lines
			10. Strophe (v.87–95)	9 lines
			11. Strophe (v. 96–104)	9 lines
		Rukūʿ!		
VI.	Noah		12. Strophe (v. 105–109, 111–113, 110)	9 lines
			13. Strophe (v. 114–122)	9 lines
		Rukūʿ!		
VII.	Hūd		14. Strophe (v. 123–131)	9 lines
			15. Strophe (v. 132–140)	9 lines
		Rukūʿ!		
VIII.	Ṣāliḥ		16. Strophe (v.141–150)	10 lines
			17. Strophe (v. 151–159)	10 lines
		Rukūʿ!		
IX.	Lot		18. Strophe (v. 160–167)	8 lines
			19. Strophe (v. 168–175)	8 lines
		Rukūʿ!		
X.	Shuʻayb		20. Strophe (v. 176–183)	8 lines
			21. Strophe (v. 184–191)	8 lines
		Rukūʿ!		
XI.	Practical application (or drawing the moral)		22. Strophe (v. 192–199)	8 lines
			23. Strophe (v. 200–207)	8 lines
			24. Strophe (v. 208–215)	8 lines
			25. Strophe (v. 216–223)	8 lines
			2. Halfstrophe (v.224–228)	4 lines
		Rukūʿ!		

That a literary configuration that is so well-proportioned in its form could not have risen by chance is quite obvious.

SURA XXVIII

Müller gives only a brief analysis of this sura, without quoting the text. The rukūʿ in Zam. are distributed in the intervals after verses 12, 20, 28, 42, 50, 60, 75, and 82. I am not attempting any more accurate account, but should like to refer briefly to the third section (Moses' adventure in Midian), the eight lines of which have their rhymes embraced as follows: first and last verse *īl*; second to fifth verse *ūn, īr, īr, īn*; sixth and seventh verse *īn*. Müller's divisions accord approximately with the rukūʿ marks.

SURA XXXVI

Müller's division, established by the responsion, overlaps with the arrangement of the rukūʿ only insofar as the second rukūʿ of the sura does in fact fall on the inteval between strophes 1 and 2; here, too, I have no desire to anticipate a closer study of the structure.

SURA XLIV

Here the first of the rukūʿ noted in Zam. falls in the middle of Müller's strophe 4, while the second, following the sense, comes to stand between strophes 5 and 6. But the position of the first rukūʿ is hardly tenable, because the legend of Pharaoh's punishment is thereby cut into two in a quite unintelligible way. In this instance, light will come only from comparison of the various recensions.

SURA LI

If we ignore the nine (really eight) verses of the initial invocation that deviate from their rhyme—I discuss them in *Gott. Gel. Anz.*—then the sura divides first into a fourteen-line proclamation of punishment and reward (verses 10–23), then into a legend section of twenty-three verses in all (verses 24–46), followed by fourteen lines of pointing the moral (verse 47–60). In the legend section fourteen lines are devoted to the birth of Isaac and the judgment on Sodom. There are those Müller discusses in his "Prophets." The remaining nine lines comprise fragments of the other well-known judgment legends, and here the question arises as to what extent the abbreviating is original or attributable to later mutilation. No one can fail to recognize the rhythmic role of the number seven in the other parts. The three rukūʿ that have been entered come after verses 23, 30, and 46 and confirm Müller's division.

SURA LIV

Here, too, the principle on which Müller bases his sectionalization is confirmed by the positioning of the rukūʿ. For the rest, the sura seems to be in a pretty mutilated condition. (See *Proph.* I.54)

SURA LVI

The rukūʿ after verse 37 is seemingly without proper sense, and placed where it really disturbs the recitation. But it may indicate that at this point something is not right with the text. It is in fact the case that in the preceding section, verses 13 and 14, which clearly form a responsion, stand in a quite different context. From the tafsir literature the sense of these verses is that many of those who were pious before Muhammad was active will belong to the foremost in paradise, and only a few of those who came later, namely, the oldest and most faithful members of his community. These verses thus answer the question: Who really are the *sābiqūna* (foremost)? Verses 38 and 39 must have a similar sense and reference. It is very natural to suspect that originally they also had an analogous position. Accordingly, they would belong between verses 26 and 27 as an answer to the question: *mā aṣḥābu l-yamīni*? What will be the companions of the Right Hand? That a remark of this kind is not to be expected from "the people of the left hand," the sinners, lies in the nature of things. Of such people there were countless numbers before and after Muhammad's call. But the answer to the relevant question lies in the words of verse 49: *ʾinnā l-ʾawwalīna wa-l-ʾākharīna*; Yea, those of old and those of later times. Here, too, we find responsion to the passages just discussed, which gives fresh support to Müller's theory, even if in certain details I sectionalize in a different way. Above all it is significant that in Zam., verse 22 divides after *ʿīnun,* and verse 40 after the first *ash-shimāli,* whereas Müller makes verses 46 and 47 into a single verse. It is important to stress the division of verse 40, because by analogy it leads to dividing verses 8, 9, 10, and 26 in the same way—something justified also by the rhyme dispositions of these units. If we further take cognizance that this latter is valid also for verses 3 and 32, we then obtain for verses 1–56 of the text a series of 63 lines to encompass these into strophic configurations, one must note that: verses 1–7 form an eight-line introductory strophe, in which the first four units have a uniform rhyme and the two middle lines only an assonating one, while the second half comprises three assonating lines and finally a nonrhyming one. Then there follows a transition strophe (verses 8–10) of six lines consisting of identical rhyme pairs. Here the three categories of wretched souls on the day of the Last Judgment are enumerated.

(In verse 10 the interrogative *mā* has presumably dropped out and must be supplied.) Each one of these three groups is then discussed with reference to the fate awaiting it. Each strophe begins by repeating the question that is put in the transitional strophe. Only the first strophe (verses 11–25) which treats of the group of the "foremost ones" named there in third place, is linked with it, appropriately to the sense, merely with a connecting demonstrative clause. The second strophe (verses 26, 38, 39, 27–37) discusses "the people of the right hand," the third (lines 40–55), "the people of the left." Each of these three principal strophes comprises, if one takes into consideration the features indicated above, sixteen lines. Verse 56 stands quite isolated at the end, giving a résumé of the portrayal of Judgment Day, and in my view it refers not merely to the third group but to the whole. The isolated framework verses, which Müller posits for the second and the third main division of the sura, thus finds here, too, in the first part, something corresponding to them. By dividing the strophe in this way the rukūʿ that Müller places in the middle of the second strophe (after verse 37) comes at its end, and so confirms, if a minor uneveness is eliminated, the correctness of his proposals as a whole. What Müller (*Proph.* I.24 ff.) says to justify his proposal that verses 24 and 25 should come after verse 39 is obviated by isolating verse 56 (or is obviated because it implies isolating verse 56). Rather does verse 37 come to a satisfactory and natural conclusion with the words

Li-ʾaṣḥābi l-yamīni. Its relation to the recapitulation in the final strophe, verses 89 and 90, is thereby disturbed only in respect of a minor detail, and otherwise retains its full force. Müller's sectionalizing of the second main group is so firmly vindicated by the responding components that there can be no doubt about it.

Concerning the third main division, it is above all noteworthy that the isolation of verse 73 is assured by the positioning of the rukūʿ after it. Zam.'s drawing of verses 91 and 92 together into one, on the basis of their sense (double rhyme at the end of verse occurs again and again in the Koran), would seemingly upset the progression of the number of lines posited by Müller for the strophes of this section. But if one takes verse 95 with the final strophe, which the sense makes perfectly feasible (in that such a conclusion, which strongly reaffirms the recapitulation, also rounds off the strophe's content), then not only is the progression restored, but also the identity of the framing verses 73 and 96 is more forcefully emphasized by the isolation of the latter. And so here, too, we have on a purely formal basis—in spite of some seeming displacement of Müller's presuppositions in individual instances—striking confirmation of his fundamental arguments.

SURA LXIX

The principle operative in Sura LVI, of framing strophes by means of isolated verses, is seen again here in a different form, in that the principal section (verses 4–29) distinguished by its rhyme from the final section of the sura, is framed by two framework elements of three lines each. These vary in their rhyme both from the main section and from the final one, and also from each other, and the length of their lines becomes progressively longer. The principal section, marked out in this way, divides, for its part, into two subsections, the structure and rhyme dispositions of which are clarified by Müller (*Proph.* II.49 ff.). Müller puts a line of demarcation between verses 12 and 13, but I think this gives too sharp a division. I also think that the line drawn after verse 32 is misplaced, because it cuts into two the speech of the judgment angel, which all belongs together. It is better transferred to after verse 37, where it coincides with the rukūʿ marked in Zam. The strophe verses 33–37 thereby still forms part of the principal section, and forms a sort of coda to it, the rhyme of which is continued in the tripartite *abgesang*[13] (the final unit) that follows: If verse 44 is put with verse 45, because there is no rhyme, then the *abgesang* yields the symmetrical strophic sequence of 5 + 4 + 5 lines that Müller has found in so many instances.

SURA LXXV

Müller's division, so clearly confirmed by the change in rhyme, is further supported by the rukūʿ after verse 30. The sura thereby divides into a principal section and a two-strophe *abgesang*. When the internal rhymes are taken into account, the distribution of the lines turns out to be even more regular than it is with Müller. Verse 16 seemingly deviates with its ending from the rhyme pattern, but in fact consists of two halves, rhyming with each other and dividing after the first *bihi*. In this way the third strophe comes to consist of seven lines, like the second. The fifth strophe has—taking the internal rhyme in verse 29 *as-sāq/as-sāqu* into account—six lines. The number of lines in the different strophes is thus, in sequence, 6 + 7 + 7 + 6 + 6 in the *aufgesang* [the initial sections], and 5 + 5 in the *abgesang*. Each strophe has its own particular rhyme. Only the third has a more complicated rhyme configuration (a + a, b+b, c+c+c), and the two strophes of the *abgesang* rhyme identically.

SURA LXXVIII

This strophe, too, is divided into an *aufgesang* and an *abgesang* by a rukūʿ after verse 30. While the former discusses God's signs in nature and threatens with the punitive Last Judgment, the latter begins by depicting the joys of paradise and repeats the admonition about the judgment of the world. Each of the two parts divides again into two (unequal) halves: the first after verse 16; the second after verse 36. The line count gives 5 + 6 + 5; 4 + 6 + 4 for the *aufgesang*; and 6 + 4 (verse 40 does not not rhyme and forms a single line with verse 41, as in Zam.) for the *abgesang*. The arrangement of the rhymes is noteworthy. The first strophe (verses 1–5) rhymes in *ūn,* the remainder of the first half of the principal section in *ādā,* with various assonating deviations, which are nevertheless so ordered that again and again a rhythm is discernible. Thus, in the second strophe (verses 6–11); in each case the first two and last two verses have pure rhymes with each other, while the third assonates more closely with the final ones (*ājā: āshā*), and the fourth more closely with the initial ones (*ātā: ādā*). In the third strophe (verses 12–16), *ādā* assonates with *ātā* in the first and fourth verse, the second and third verses rhyme with *ājā*, and the fifth ends with an assonace equally remote from both groups. In the whole of the rest of the sura the rhyme *ābā* is dominant, likewise punctuated with rhythmically ordered assonances, which on the one hand serve as intimations of *ādā*, and on the other as suggesting *ājā.* It is worth stressing that the deviations from the principal rhyme *ābā* are consistently put at the beginning or at the end of the strophes (half-strophe in the *abgesang*). The fourth strophe (verses 17–20) begins in its first verse with *ātā* followed by the second with *ājā* (assonance with *āqā*).[14] The third and fourth verses have *ābā.*The fifth strophe (verses 21–26) has *ādā, ābā, ābā, ābā, āqā, āqā*; the sixth (verses 27–30), *ābā* throughout; the seventh (verses 31–36, beginning of the *abgesang*) has *āzā* (assonance with *āqā*), *ābā, ābā, āqā, ābā, ābā*; the eighth (verses 37–41), has *ābā* throughout. If we note that *āfā* in verse 16 sounds closer to *ābā*; there results the following rhymes and strophe scheme for the sura, in which the exponent *x* designates the assonance with the basis in general, and the exponent *e* the approach of the basis to the basis *e*:[15]

Aufgesang	1. Strophe	v. 1	a	
		v. 2	a	
		v. 3	a	
		v. 4	a	
		v. 5	a	
	2. Strophe	v. 6	b	
		v. 7	b	
		v. 8	ex	
		v. 9	bx	
		v. 10	ce	
		v. 11	ce	
	3. Strophe	v. 12	b	
		v. 13	ex	
		v. 14	ex	
		v. 15	bx	
		v. 16	dx	
	4. Strophe	v. 17	b	
		v. 18	ex	
		v. 19	d	
		v. 20	d	
	5. Strophe	v. 21	b	
		v. 22	d	
		v. 23	d	
		v. 24	d	
		v. 25	e	
		v. 26	e	
	6. Strophe	v. 27	d	
		v. 28	d	
		v. 29	d	
		v. 30	d	
		Rukūʿ!		
Abgesang	7. Strophe	v. 31	ex	half strophe
		v. 32	d	
		v. 33	d	
		v. 34	e	half strophe
		v. 35	d	
		v. 36	d	
	8. Strophe	v. 37	d	
		v. 38	d	
		v. 39	d	
		v. 40 + 41	d	

SURA LXXX

Here, too, it is quite apparent that Müller's ordering of the strophes is confirmed by the rhyme. One needs to add that verse 15 is to be divided off after the internal rhyme *safaratin/safarah*, as is the case in Zam. In this way the strophic schema for the first part is improved to 4 + 6 + 6. It is not feasible to terminate verse 18 with the nonrhyming *nuṭfatin*. It presumably extends to *khalaqahu* in verse 19, whereby a rhyme identical with verse 17 is achieved. In the fifth (nine-line) strophe (verses 24–32) it is notable that every third verse departs from the strict rhyme scheme. The framing of this strophe with the verse endings *taʿāmihi* and *li ʾanʿāmikum* is also of interest. They can be taken as rhyming with each other by analogy with Sura XLVII. The rule according to which the different pronoun suffixes do duty for each other here has yet to be investigated. Whether, on the other hand, verse 33 may be taken as a particular line seems doubtful to me, because it lacks any rhyme. If we put it with verse 34, the strophic scheme of the second part becomes 8 + 9 + 9 (i.e., compared with that of the first part; $2 \times 8 + \frac{1}{2} \times 6 + \frac{1}{2} \times 6$).

SURA LXXXII

Müller's divisions, justified by the content and the rhymes, would become even more rounded by dividing verse 12 after the internal rhyme *yaʿmalūna*. The sura would then fall into two parts, the first comprising a strophe of five lines, the second consisting of two equally long strophes of seven lines each. It is of no significance that the final verse deviates from the rhyme structure.

The divisions of Suras XC and CXII are quite clear and need no further confirmation.

* * *

I deliberately omit any summary of the observations made in this paper, since many details need further study, with recourse to recensions of the Koran that have not been considered here, and to possible ritual deviations. Moreover, as already stated, my illumination of the relevant rhyme patterns are not put forward as definitive. One thing, however, must be stressed; namely, from this study, only two of the seven rukūʿ enumerated above that clash with Müller's proposals concerning divisions—namely, those postioned in the difficult Sura VII after verses 12 and 126—have stood firm (have survived criticism), and therefore serve to refute those proposals decisively. In all other instances—that is, in fifty out of fifty-two—Müller is proved right.

From the evidence I have given it does seem to emerge that closer study of the Koran's poetic forms will be able to disclose all manner of not unimportant facts. Above all, I think I have shown how correct the presuppositions are from which Müller proceeded. I myself was for long, if not skeptical, then at any rate indifferent toward his observations. All the more forcefully has the agreement of facts chanced upon, and unknown to Müller himself, with his examples of strophic divisions in the text of the Koran, convinced me that his views are correct. I regard it as fairly certain that in the future, following what has already been established, a whole series of strophe like configurations will be demonstrated going far beyond Müller's own expectations. To be sure, it is equally certain that not all such forms will evince the characteristics of concatenation and responsion that formed Müller's point of departure. But he himself stressed as much in the case of some of the individual texts that he discussed. On the other hand, one thing seems to to me to result irrefutably from my account; namely that the whole science of Koran study is forced to operate on very insecure ground so long as a principal requirement to its apparatus is lacking, that is, a European edition of the Koran that is really scholarly, meeting all the demands of criticism, and containing all relevant historical, philological, religious and liturgical material, set out discursively and with the appropriate comparisons. Without this, all individual research into the Koran must remain disjointed patchwork. This is how I regard my own contributions here, and I publish them only to stimulate further study after the manner of Müller's work, and to demonstrate how unsatisfactory the existing text editions are.

NOTES

1. Karl Vollers, *Volkssprache und Schriftsprache im alten Arabien* (Strassburg, 1906).

2. [Juz' = One of the thirty portions into which the Koran is divided.]

3. [Theodor Nöldeke, *Geschichte des Qorans* (1860), p. 352. [Geyer obviously could only have been referring to the first edition.]

4. In contrast, there are Juz' sections without rukūʿ, as, for instance, before Juz' 3, 5, 6, 7, 9, 10, 11, 12, 14, 16, 20, 23. Juz' 21 coincides (according to the division in Zam.) with a rukūʿ (after Sura XXIX.43), whereas, from Flugel, it would be after verse 44 without R.

Further deviant 'Ajzā' in Zam.: Juz' 20 after Sura XXVII.56 and Juz' 23 after Sura XXXVI.20.

5. [Geyer does not have (j). I have kept his notation.]

6. ["An answer or reply; a response. Now rare." O.E.D. Cf. "Responsory: A liturgical chant traditionally consisting of a series of versicles and responses, the text usually taken from Scripture. The arrangement was designed for alternate singing of sentences or lines by different people." CODCH.]

7. David H. Müller, *Die Propheten in ihrer ursprünglichen Form. Die Grundgesetze der ursemitischen Poesie, erschlossen und nachgewiesen in Bibel, Keilinschriften und Koran und in ihren Wirkungen erkannt in den Chören der griechischen Tragödie,* 2 vols. (Vienna, 1896), vol. 1, p. 43 n.

[Other works of Müller on strophic composition include: *Strophenbau und Responsion*. Neue Beiträge. (5. Jahresbericht der israelisch-theologischen Lehranstalt in Wien 1897/1898) Wien, 1898; "Die Formen der jüdischen Responsenliteratur und der muhammedanischen Fetwas in den sabäischen Inschriften," *WZKM* 14 (1900): 171; "Komposition und Strophenbau." *Alte und neue Beiträge* (Wien 1907).]

8. The different dental sounds rhyme (assonate) with each other in the Koran. Examples in my review of Vollers, R. Geyer, review of Karl Vollers, Volkssprache und Schriftsprache im alten Arabien, *Göttinger Gelehrter Anzeiger* 171 (1909): 10–56.

9. Müller, *Die Proheten in ihrer ursprunglichen Form*, vol. 1, p. 48.

10. In my frequently mentioned article I assumed that *shayban* could be included in the rhyme by softening of the *b*. But closer scrutiny has convinced me that such a development is improbable.

11. On the capacity of *faʿla, fiʿla, fuʿla* to rhyme with *faʿal, fa ʿil, faʿul, fiʿal, fiʿil, fiʿul, fuʿ il, fuʿal, fuʿ ul*, see Vollers, *Volkssprache*. pp. 97ff.

12. There is nothing notable in the fact that the same verse ending in verse 16 must be counted in, as there is often a nonrhyme at the end of a strophe.

13. [German *Aufgesang* = the first two sections of ternary strophe; German *Abgesang* = its concluding part.]

14. In the coinciding of these I discern a sort of anticipatory approach in the pronunciation of the *q* (Arabic letter, *qaf*) to the palatization to *z* effected in the later language. Compare with this what Vollers has to say about the pronunciation of the *q* (*qaf*) in the Koran.

15. Concordance of the rhyme types and rhyme syllables:

a = ūn, īm
b = *ādā*
bx = *ātā*
ce = āsā, āshā
d = ābā
dx = āfā
e = āqā
ex = ājā, azā

8.2

On the Koran

Julius Wellhausen

Translated by G. A. Wells

The divine name *ar-raḥmān* is generally translated as "the merciful one" and regarded as a Jewish-Aramaic foreign word. But how it was formed does not seem at all clear. If the word means "merciful" it cannot derive from the Pe῾al,[1] the meaning of which is "to love." Also, the ending *an* for the nomen agentis does not occur in the Pe῾al. Rather is it the case that: raḥmān = meraḥmān (Hebrew).

In Syriac the prefix *me* of the nomen agentis is absent only from roots with four sounds, except for [*raḥmān*] itself. But in Palestinian-Jewish-Aramaic, it is surely also missing from those with three sounds, which are really equivalent in the Pe῾al to those with four. For instance, *naḥmān* (Hebrew), "comforter" [*Menahem*; Christian-Palestinian: *mnḥmnʾ* (Syriac), παράχλητος (Greek)], [*paršān* (Hebrew), "expositor"; *Šaddeḵān* (Hebrew), "marriage broker," which German Jews distort to "schadchen" used as a neuter. There is also *qanneʾan* (Hebrew) = zealot, ζηλωτής (Greek). In the New Testament, *qnʾnʾ* (Hebrew) has become κανααναίος (Greek) Canaanean; likewise *perīšāʾ* (Hebrew), Φαρισαιος (Pharisee). These are the only examples I have at hand, but probably more can be found.

* * *

From *ZDMG* 67 (1913): 630–34.

In the *al-Aṣmaʿiyyāt*, ed. Ahlwardt[2] No. 20, there is a poem ascribed to the Jew Samaual, and its relation to the Koran deserves attention. I translate it here, adding a few comments in brackets:

(i) I originated in my time as a drop of semen. It was given a destiny, and I grew in it.
(ii) God preserved it in a secret place (the mother's body); and its place is hidden, if I were hidden (?).[3]
(iii) I am dead in that (drop?), then alive, then after life (again) dead, in order to be awakened.
(iv) If my understanding leaves me, then consider, O woman, that I am old and defective.
(v) Make, O God, for my upkeep, what of acquisitions is permissible, and make purity my innermost substance, for all my life.
(vi) Make my conscience tight against deception. May penury never impel me to grasp at goods entrusted to me, so long as I am preserved.
(vii) I have heard much abuse in silence, have not demurred at much that is improper, and have rested content in the face of it.
(viii) If only I knew—when in due course it will be said, "Read the inscription," and I read it—
(ix) whether the surplus is in my favor or goes against me (i.e., whether I have a plus or minus) when I am called to account. My lord is empowered to call me to account.
(x) I was dead for an eternity, then I entered into life, but my life stands surety for the fact that I will die.
(xi) And tidings have reached me that, after death, when my bones have rotted, I am to be awakened.
(xii) Shall I say . . . when my mind . . . and collapses upon me, that I am surprised,
(xiii) either with grace and kindness from the heavenly king, or with a burden of guilt, which I have sent before me and for which I now pay the price?
(xv[4]) And tidings have reached me of the Kingdom of David, and this pleases and delights me.
(xiv) Permitted, limited sustenance is profitable, but not so the sustenance that is abundant and shameful.

(xvi) The rich man does not obtain too much, nor the poor and lonely one too little.
(xvii) Rather everyone allotted what is his due, even if the greedy man toils excessively.

I cannot understand the second half of verse 2, nor really the end of verse 17 (cf. Noldeke, *Bietrage,* p. 72). I cannot translate the words omitted in verse 12 even literally, Sura XXVII.68 notwithstanding. For ʾ-nn-y (9), I read, following a suggestion in the Lisān,[5] r-bb-y, Verses 4 and 15 stand isolated. The latter breaks the the connection between 14 and 16, 17, and comes as a parallel to 11, with the same introduction. The theme of 1–3 recurs in 10–13, and that of 5–7 reappears in 14, 16, 17.

The reason why the poem is ascribed to Samaual lies in verse 6, where it is said "May I never grasp at goods entrusted to me." That seemed to point to the famous Samaual of Taima, memory of whom was linked with his faithful preservation of the weapons given by him by the prince of poets, Imruʾ al-Kays.[6] But the statement in verse 6 is worded quite generally and timelessly, and our poem certainly does not come from the Samaual whose poem stands as no. 49 in the Hamasa.[7] From this latter it differs both in form and content: in form because of *q-r-y-t* (8) instead of *q-r-ʾ- t*; and because of *m-b-ʿ-w-t, kh-b-y-t* (11, 14), instead of *m-b-ʿ-w-th, kh-b-y-th* (see Abu Zaid, *Nawadir* 104). These Aramaisms are admittedly preserved only in the rhymes, whereas the interior of the verse now has the correct Arabic pronunciation *ʾ-q-r-ʾ* (8) and *b-ʿ-th, th-mm,* (4). As to its material, our poem differs from that other one because of its striking contacts with the Koran: Thus *b-ʿ-th* (awaken from death, 4, 11), *muqīt*: (empowered 9; Sura IV.87), *t-d-ʾ-r-k ḥil-m-y* (12; Sura XXVII.68); further, the equating of the first procreation leading to earthly life with the second leading to the future life (1–3, 10), the sending on into eternity of good and evil actions (13), and, in particular, the note that is handed to the resurrected person and which allocates him his place in heaven or hell (8; Sura LXIX.19; cf. Revelation 2:17). However, this latter idea differs, in its externals, quite markedly from the corresponding one, in the Koran, and so is not taken from it. Altogether, the poem ascribed to Samaual in the Aṣmaʿiyyāt is too original to be regarded as a Muslim forgery based on the Koran. Rather, does it stem from the same tradition from which Muhammad also drew. The Kingdom of David (15) also seems to be

Jewish. It cannot be understood as the historical Kingdom of David, but only as the future one; that is, the messianic kingdom. Admittedly, such a late Jewish writer might not be expected, as is the case in some passages, to regard the resurrection not as an established doctrine, but only as a secret hope, of which he has tidings (11, 15).

* * *

A propos of Sura LV.46–78, Noldeke[8] observes: "The normal form of the words, and even their sense is at times changed for the sake of the rhyme. For instance, in Sura LV. there is mention of two heavenly gardens, each with two springs and two types of fruit, and additionally of two other similar gardens; and it is clear that here these duals have been used for the sake of the rhyme."

Surely strangest of all are two other similar gardens (LV.62–77) that follow the first two (LV.46–61) and have the same dual in the rhyme both in their described features and in the refrain repeated as a stereotype after each individual feature. Also in the contents, the individual features described in 46–61 are repeated in almost the same sequence in the description of 62–77, as indicated below:

46.62 two gardens,
48.64 two overhanging branches, with deep green foliage;
50.66 with two murmuring springs,
52.68 with different types of fruit,
54.76 with cushions on which one lies,
56–58.70–74 with beautiful girls.

This doubling of the double paradise can hardly be the original conception. Rather, it is the clearest example of two variants of the same revelation, which came to be regarded as different and were then placed the one after the other. To make this sequence possible, an editor has inserted *wa min dūnihimā* into verse 62 and thereby effected what is at least an external, spatial differentiation of the two really identical descriptions of paradise.

* * *

The word *buhtān*, which occurs in the Koran in what is called the homage formula of the woman (LX.12), is strange. It is supposed to mean "slander" and occurs in this sense also in Aghānī XV, 118, 1,[9] again in *qawmun buhtun* Ibn Hishām, 353, 13[10] and also in Kāmil 685, 2.[11] Then it has nothing to do with the genuine Arabic *b-h-t*, for that means "suddenly attack" or "make frightened," like Hebrew *b-ʿ-t* and Arabic *b-gh-t* (e.g., Aghānī, II. 28, 20.[12] Ṭabarī, I. 877, 12. 3182, 11. III, 821, 5.). On the other hand, it can readily be linked with Aramaic *b-h-t* = Hebrew *b-w-š* (as *r-h-ṭ* = *r-w-ṣ*), for which there is no Arabic equivalent. The idea of slander would then be traceable to that of what is disgraceful.

That *buhtān* in Arabic is a loan word is shown also by its form. Admittedly, *fuʿlān* as an infinitive is surely genuinely Arabic, as is also *ruḍwān*. But the correct nouns of this form are not. There are not very many of them. The origin of *ʿunwān* is obscure. *Burhān* derives from the Abyssinian; *sulṭān*, *ṭūfān*, *furqān*, *qurbān*, from Aramaic. The vocable *buhtān* cannot, it is true, be found in extant Aramaic literature; but it will nevertheless surely be Aramaic, if the verb form which it derives is also Aramaic. One then has to assume that it was used by Arabic Jews or Christians whose ancient mother tongue was Aramaic; or perhaps that it was newly constructed from the type which very frequently occurs in Aramaic.

The noun *qurʾān* will likewise go back to Arabic Jews or Christians. It seems to come from giving a slight Arabic twist to *qeryānā*; cf. Schwally in his edition of Nöldeke's *Geschichte des Koran*, I 33.34. Also the verb qaraʾa in the sense of "read aloud, recite" (e.g., the greetings formula) is not genuinely Arabic. The Arabs have other expressions for "to call," from which "to read" derives. Perhaps *ʿunwān* is also connected with ʿinyānā.

NOTES

1. [Peʿal = "Most verbs in Syriac have three consonants. These root consonants appear in a number of patterns or stems. The basic pattern is called the simple stem of the verb. This simple stem of the verb is described as peʿal on the basis of the set of root letters *pʿl*: Syriac [*pʿl* being the 3rd masc.singular of the root in this stem)." J. Healey, *First Studies in Syriac* (Birmingham, 1994), p. 27. Cf. Arabic stem *faʿala*.]

2. Al-Aṣmaʿī, "al-Aṣmaʿiyyāt," in *Sammlungen alter arabischer Dichter*,

ed. Ahlwardt (Berlin, 1902). This anthology by the Basran philologist Al-Aṣma'ī (died 213/828) contained seventy-two fragments attributed to pre-Islamic poets, or those who lived in the first half of seventh century. Poem number 23 (according to the *EI2* article "al-Samaw'al," though Wellhausen says it is number 20) is attributed to al-Samaw'al b. ʿĀdiyā, a Jew, who lived in the middle of the sixth century. This poem "contains reflections on birth, death and the Day of Judgment which may be . . . references to Aggadic literature . . . thus pointing to the Jewish religion of its poet. The authenticity of the poem was defended by J. W. Hirschberg (*Der Diwan as as-Samau'al ibn ʿAdija*, Cracow, 1931) against Noldeke's negative verdict (T. Nöldeke, *Beitraege zur Kenntnis de Poesie der Alten Araber*, Hanover 1864, pp. 52–86). Levi Della Vida ("A proposito di as-Samaw'al," in *RSO* 13 (1931): 53–72) drew up the very probable hypothesis that the poem was in fact created by one of al-Samaw'al's descendants, who had already converted to Islam but still was acquainted with Jewish tradition." T. Bauer, "al-Samaw'al b. ʿĀdiyā," *EI2*.

3. [It is indeed Wellhausen's question mark in brackets.]

4. [Wellhausen does give 15 before 14 in the original.]

5. *Lisān al-ʿArab*, Arabic Lexicon of Ibn Manẓur, 20 vols. (Cairo, 1308).

6. [Here is the story of Imruʾ al-Qays: The poet and Kinda Prince Imruʾ al-Qays entrusted his arms to al-Samaw'al. When the Ghassanid phylarch al -Ḥārīth b. Jabala heard about this, he set out against al-Samaw'al, who dug in inside his castle. al -Ḥārīth managed to kidnap al-Samaw'al's son, threatening to kill him unless the father handed over the consigned weapons. Al-Samaw'al remained faithful to his promise, preferring to see his son killed than to betray his friend.]

7. [*Dīwān al-ḥamāsa* (Book of Valor) was an anthology of texts compiled by Abū Tammām (died 231/846). It includes mainly pre-Islamic and early Islamic poets, though also some from the ʿAbbāsid period.]

8. T. Nöldeke, *Geschichte des Korans*, 1st ed., p. 30 = 2d ed., p. 40.

9. Abūʾl-Faraj ʿAlī ibn al-Ḥusayn al-Iṣbahānī, *Kitāb al-aghānī*, 20 vols. (Cairo, 1285).

10. Abū Muḥammad ʿAbd al-Malik Ibn Hishām, *Sīrāt Rasūl Allāh*, ed. F. Wustenfeld, 2 vols. (Gottingen, 1858–1860).

11. *The Kāmil of al-Mubarrad*, ed. W. Wright (Leipzig, 1864–1892).

12. Abū Jaʿfar Muḥammad al-Ṭabarī, *Ta'rīkh al-rusul wa'l-mulūk*, ed. M. J. de Goeje et al., 15 vols. (Leiden, 1879–1901).

8.3

On Pre-Islamic Christian Strophic Poetical Tests in the Koran
A Critical Look at the Work of Günter Lüling

Ibn Rawandi

INTRODUCTION

Gunter Lüling was born in Varna, Bulgaria, in 1928. The first period of his academic life was spent at the University of Erlangen, Germany, between 1956 and 1961. His original intention was to work as a theologian on the theological themes of the Koran, but owing to the opposition of his professor to this idea, he agreed to work on the theme of the adoption of Greek science by Arab scholarship. Due to continuing bad relations between himself and his supervising professors, he was forced to leave the university in 1961, "without any achievement to show for those years."[1]

This bad experience, however, was in reality a blessing in disguise, in that it led to him obtaining the post of director of the Goethe Institute at Aleppo, Syria, in the years 1962 to 1965. It was here that he learned what he could not have learned if he had remained in academic life at a German university: a deep acquaintance with the Arabic vernacular. It later turned out that knowing the Arabic vernacular was one of the essential requirements for critically analyzing the text of the Koran. In 1966 Lüling seized the opportunity to return to academic life in Germany: first, as assistant professor at the Faculty of Medicine at Erlangen, supervising studies in the history of antique and early medieval Arab medicine, and then transferring at the end of 1967 to the post of assistant professor at the Erlangen Institute of Arabic and Islamic Studies. He was now in a position to freely pursue the dogma-critical approach to the Koran that he had always intended.[2]

The chief result of Lüling's research was that underlying about one-third of the Koran text there are pre-Islamic, antitrinitarian Christian, strophical hymns, dating from the beginning of the sixth century C.E., approximately one hundred years before the time of Muhammad; the postulated background to this discovery being a predominantly Christian central Arabia, including a Christian Mecca, Kaaba, and Quraish. In 1970 Lüling submitted a 180-page dissertation on his research as a thesis for a Ph.D. degree. The official reports on the thesis were enthusiastic, stating that: "the proof for strophical ur-texts, which can be reconstructed, can be regarded as established. . . . The work places the history of the origin of Islam and the history of the dogmatics of early Oriental Christianity into new dimensions," and was consequently awarded the highest possible note of *eximum opus*. Within a fortnight, however, the tone of the university authorities changed and he was told that he could no longer look forward to the habilitation that an *eximum opus* entitled him. According to Lüling, his ideas had incurred the wrath of the Arabist Anton Spitaler of Munich, the leader of the pure philology school of German Arabic studies. Spitaler refused to give up the conventional method of judging the Koran by the laws of Classical Arabic, and feared that Lüling's results would, "certainly turn upside down the hitherto existing notions about the history of the origin, the text and the contents of the Koran." Such was Spitaler's influence that by the end of 1972 Lüling was officially dismissed from the University of Erlangen.[3]

The implementation of this decision, however, could be delayed by legal proceedings against it, and this was the course that Lüling took. He was encouraged in this move by the support of the French Koran expert Regis Blachère. After studying Lüling's dissertation, Blachère wrote to him: "Highly eminent colleague. In this way (i.e., with Lüling's methods) the tradition continues of that German school of scholarship to which we owe so much grateful appreciation. I hope that owing to your generation there will be kept alive a curious speciality of worldwide importance with regard to Islamic studies which alone offers the chance for a global understanding of the problems." Unfortunately, Blachère died a few months after he wrote this letter, but Lüling persisted in arguing his case. In 1973 he presented the whole of his collection of restored Christian strophic texts, under the title *On the Pre-Islamic Christian Strophe Poetical Texts in the Koran*, to the Faculty of Philology at Erlangen as his Habilitationsschrift, essential for the continuation of his academic career. In February 1974 this, too, was voted against by a majority of faculty members, according to Lüling, after much politicing on the part of the "pure philology" faction. The decision was disputed in court, but without success, and Lüling was finally dismissed from the university in July 1978.[4]

In 1974, however, he had published his Habilitationsschrift under the title *Uber den Ur-Quran*, which was well received by many outside the academic establishment in Germany. It is this work, revised and expanded for the English edition under the title *On the Pre-Islamic Christian Poetic Texts in the Koran*, that forms the basis for the present exposition and critique of Lüling's ideas. In addition, Lüling has also published a work on the Prophet Muhammad: *Die Wiederentdeckung des Propheten Muhammad, The Rediscovery of the Prophet Muhammad*, which will be referred to occasionally.

THESES AND METHODOLOGIES

Lüling's approach to the text of the Koran is based on four fundamental theses.

Thesis 1

About one-third of the present day Koran text, as transmitted by Muslim orthodoxy, contains as a hidden groundlayer an originally pre-Islamic Christian text.

(a) Difficulties in interpreting the old Arabian script.

Every Arabic text today, as for the past fourteen or fifteen centuries, consists of three different layers. First, the basic letter shape, or drawing (*rasm*). Second, the diacritical points (*nuqaṭ*), the function of which is to differentiate the otherwise similar letters of the *rasm*. And third, the strokes for the vowels, (*ḥarakāt*), which are not shown in the basic consonontal text of the *rasm*. The crucial point here is that in pre-Islamic and early Islamic times the diacritical points were not set at all in everyday writing, because they were not yet known or not commonly accepted. In the Koran text, at least during the first century of its existence, diacritical points were even forbidden, ostensibly out of pious reverence for the holy text. All the older Koran codices that have come down to us display the text without diacritical points and signs, not to speak of the strokes for the vowels, which were introduced even later. This means that finding the originally intended sequence of consonants, and hence the originally intended meaning of the text, becomes something of a lottery, often determined by the preconceptions of the redactor as to what the text ought to mean.[5]

(b) The difference between strophic poetical structures and prose texts in the Koran as a very important key to the reconstruction of the pre-Islamic Koran hidden in the present-day Koran.

It has always been recognized that in the traditional Koran some suras very clearly contain strophic refrains, although the repetition of these refrains mostly does not follow a perceptible, strict metric measure. This fact has for a long time been taken by some Islamicists as an indication that the Koran originally contained strophic structures, the strict order of which has been destroyed by later redaction of the text. This converted the old strophic or hymnodic speech into prose and changed the wording and meaning of the older material. This apparently occurred when texts were collected and redacted to serve as the holy book of the nascent Islamic community.

According to Lüling, uncovering these old strophic texts requires a threefold methodology: (1) philological (grammatical and phraseological), (2) strophe-metrical, and (3) dogma critical; the last two methods having been neglected since the 1930s, this approach represents a fresh start. The special genre of religious hymnody detectable in the groundlayer of the Koran belongs, form historically, to a chain of strophe-poetical traditions reaching from Old Egyptian, Old Testamentarian, pre-Islamic old Arabian, and Old Jewish models, across the equivalent Byzantine, Coptic, Syriac, Arabic, and Ethiopian hymnody of pre-Islamic and early Islamic times, up to late medieval and modern strophic poetry.

Lüling regards it as beyond question that the rich Christian Ethiopian hymnody of the early sixth century goes back in the main to a Christian

Coptic original, sometimes word-for-word across hundreds of strophes, the sequence of which is neatly maintained. Frequent misunderstandings of the Coptic original in the Ethiopic translations result from typical misunderstandings of an ambiguous Arabic text minus its diacritical points and vowel strokes. To Lüling, this indicates that these voluminous Ethiopic strophic texts of c. 500 C.E., which stem from Coptic sources, must have passed through a central Arabian stage of a likewise voluminous, but now lost, pre-Islamic Christian strophic hymnody. This thesis involves regarding as authentic the strophic poetry of the purportedly pre-Islamic Imru ʿul-Qays, and an almost complete recasting of the original Christian hymnody by the earliest Koran text collectors and redactors, who changed poetry into prose and altered its original meaning.

(c) Different languages in the Koran.

The language of the Christian strophic texts that Lüling finds underlying the Koran is without diacritical points or vowel strokes, and resembles what he calls "Old Arabian," indicating a tradition of literate education and erudition. This non-Classical, vernacular, though nevertheless literary Christian Arabic had many grammatical equivalents to the language of early Christian literature; a middle-standard, educational, and literate Arabic which served as an intertribal lingua franca, or koine, over the whole Arabian peninsula. Lüling regards the grammatical license and rules for medieval strophic poetry, conveyed to us by medieval Arabic philologists, as applying also to the pre-Islamic Christian hymnody in the Koran.

(d) The techniques of the Muslim reinterpretation of the erstwhile Christian ur-Koran hidden in the ground layer of the transmitted orthodox Koran.

(1) The deviating reading of vowels, which would later mean the deviating setting of vowel strokes, but nevertheless maintaining correctly the original groundlayer layer of the Arabic script.

(2) The deviating reading of consonants, which would later mean the deviating setting of diacritical points for ambiguous consonant signs, but nevertheless, out of piety, correctly retaining the *rasm* groundlayer.

(3) The slight alteration or deformation of the consonontal signs of the groundlayer (*rasm*), while simultaneously reading alternative consonants and vowels, and eventually changing the diacritical points and vowel strokes.
(4) The omission, addition, or replacement of single characters of the consonontal text of the groundlayer (*rasm*), of single words, sentences and sections.
(5) Taking advantage of varying or different (vernacular or high-standard) orthography.
(6) Taking advantage of the concurrence of different meanings of one and the same word or word root within Hebrew, Aramaic (Syriac), and vernacular and high-standard Arabic.
(7) Giving a deviating meaning to single words on the basis of vague associations, so that a series of Koranic lexical meanings must be classed as invented.
(8) The disregarding of grammatical and particularly syntactical rules during the initial deviating reading of the erstwhile Christian hymnody.

This last technique, in order to defend the peculiarities of language it produced, led some Arabic grammarians to assert that the content of the Koran is not defined by Arabic grammar, but that Arabic grammar is defined by the Koran. Thus the Koran, in part, not only contradicts the rules of common secular Arabic, but itself, when it says: "We (God) never sent any messenger but with the speech of his people, that he might make (things) clear to them" (XIV.4); and: "This is clear Arabic language" (XVI.103) In view of these texts, the further explanation of the grammarians that the grammatical peculiarities of the Koran are due to the ecstatic utterances of the Prophet is hardly convincing.

Thesis 2

According to the statements of thesis 1 the transmitted text of the Koran contains four different kinds, or layers, of text.

These four kinds of text are:

First, because historically the oldest, the texts of the pre-Islamic Christian strophic hymnody. These are called "erstwhile Christian texts."

Second, and historically later, the texts of the new Islamic interpretation pressed on the groundlayer of erstwhile Christian texts. These are called "second-sense Koranic texts."

Third, and historically parallel to the second layer, the originally pure Islamic texts; that is to say, texts that are to be attributed to the Prophet Muhammad. These are called "single sense Koranic texts." They make up about two-thirds of the whole Koran, the remaining third being the erstwhile Christian texts transformed into second-sense Koranic texts.

Fourth, and historically post-Muhammad, are the single-sense Koranic texts that have been reinterpreted by Koran editors in such a way that the original ideas of the Prophet have been distorted. These texts are called "texts of the post-Muhammadan Koran editors."

Further analysis of these four different textual layers.

(a) The Islamic scholarly terminology for different layers of Koran text.

(1) *al-mutashābihat*: "texts that are similar to something else," or "texts that contain different aspects of interpretation." These are the original meanings of the term, but later it was interpreted as referring to "the anthropomorphic expressions of the Koran," probably to divert attention from awkward texts, such as those containing an original Christian hymnody.

(2) *al-muḥkamat*: "texts that are decided, firm, unambiguous." This came to mean the whole of the Koran, but originally referred to the third kind of text listed above, those attributable to the Prophet and without any underlying erstwhile Christian text.

(3) *al-mufassal*: "texts that are commentary." This term must be a subcategory of *al-muḥkam* since not all *muḥkam* texts are *mufassal*, but a *mufassal* text is always *muḥkam* If *muḥkam* denotes the third layer identified above, *mufassal* must denote the glosses and commentaries inserted into the texts of the first and third layers in order to pin down the eventually preferred meanings of those layers to prevent the original sense from showing through. Such insertions would have been indispensable at the time when diacritical points and vowel strokes were not yet permitted in Koran texts. A clear example of such an inserted commentary is IX.16.

(b) On the characteristically distinct contents of the different kinds of Koran text.

It is in the distinct contents of the different kinds of Koran text that the dogma-critical aspect of Lüling's threefold methodology comes into play. He argues that the Islamic intellectual content that was pressed on the erstwhile Christian *rasm* groundlayer was determined by pagan Arabian conceptions, in fact, by the old Arabian tribal religion of pre-Islamic times, and that it is from this position that these texts are turned against Christian and Jewish dogmatics. Lüling regards this classification of these earliest Islamic texts as pagan not as a slight upon them but as a positive evaluation.

Lüling sees original Christianity, not that of the later, trinitarian-imperialist Hellenistic church, as the resurfacing of popular pagan/tribal religion from the underground of peasant religion. It was, in fact, the revival of the old Semitic and old Israelite tribal religion at the High Places or Holy Groves, where the cult at the shrines of the primeval Messianic Heroes of the tribes had blossomed. This old religion was persecuted and stamped out by the imperialist Jewish religion of Yahweh, and after a brief revival by Jesus, stamped out again by imperialist Christianity. Lüling sees the old religion as having spread very early into tribal society all over Arabia, and even surviving there until the twentieth century.

Contrary to the portrayal of the central motive of the ur-Islamic movement by later Islamic orthodoxy, depicting it as the defeat of central Arabian paganism, Lüling sees the ur-Islamic movement led by Muhammad as a movement away from central Arabian Christian, especially trinitarian conceptions, toward the old Semitic pagan/tribal religion, under the slogan: "Return to the religion of Ismail and the tribes." This shift toward tribal religion is detected in an ur-Islamic reinterpretation of the Hellenistic Christian groundlayer of the Koran text, especially in those sections that fight against the "Garden," the pagan-Arabic Grove of Fertility, condemned by Judaism as the cult at the High Places. These Hellenistic Christian antipagan passages, originally contained in the *rasm* text of the Koran, have each, with the exception of XVIII.40, been reinterpreted by early orthodox Islamic redactional devices, so that the pagan "Garden" thereafter appears as the revered Islamic "Paradise," with its pagan religious erotic pleasures, differing so markedly from the Christian heaven.

Another example of this ur-Islamic shift away from Christian conceptions is that texts of the Christian groundlayer referring to salvation in Christ were reworked to apply to the Koran, or supplied with editorially added negative signs, interpreted as applying to foes of the Prophet.

The Islamic single-sense Koran texts are also considerably influenced by these pagan Arab tribal ideas, and can be identified above all in the ur-Islamic prose texts pressed on the *rasm* groundlayer of the erstwhile Christian hymnody. Such single-sense texts were often inserted as glosses and commentaries into the reinterpretation of the Christian texts, and often appear as new, textually neat versions or doublettes of lexically and grammatically clumsy texts, resulting from the original reinterpretation of the strophic texts. Such new versions or doublettes are usually placed at some distance from the clumsy originals, which they repeat in a linguistically neat form. This gives rise to the suspicion that these new neat text versions are not only located far from their clumsy originals in terms of textual space, but also in terms of time of composition. That is to say, they have been composed much later than the original clumsy interference with the *rasm*, which necessitated their eventual composition for sake of clarification.

(c) On the literary form of the different kinds of Koran text.

The Islamic second- and single-sense Koran texts were originally designed and then handed down as prose texts. In the second-sense texts, as a consequence of the disregard or dropping of the internal rhymes of what was once a Christian strophe, a type of verse or sentence has been developed for which the term "Koranic rhymed prose" came into use in Western scholarship; the later, originally single-sense Koran texts, emulate this type of early Koranic rhymed prose. From the time of the Islamic reinterpretation and elimination of the strophic hymnody onward, each Koranic prose verse, or sentence, now rhymes with its last word, though now far remote from the preceding and next-to-last words of its surrounding long prose verses or sentences; these are now long and monotonous because of the annulment of the internal rhymes. In the latest of the single-sense texts, emulating the oldest so-called Islamic rhymed prose, the sentences became so long that, although each of them finishes with a remote rhyme word, one can hardly speak any longer of a rhyming effect. This underlines the fact that the so-called rhymed prose of the Koran is not a genuine form of poetic art, but a peculiar technique developed from the leveling out of the sophisticated Christian strophic poetry, and the necessity of disguising the strophical structure of the Christian hymnody.

As a result of his research, Lüling holds that the equation of the terms "rhymed prose" and *sajᶜ,* which has been made here and there in Western scholarship, must be abandoned. The *sajᶜ* is a longer, emphatically pronounced sentence, usually uttered by a pagan soothsayer, consisting of very short syntactic parts, the endings of which are not arranged to rhyme according to a strophe-metrical order, although the *sajᶜ* shows alliterations and unsystematically scattered rhymes.

In the Koran the *sajᶜ* comes across only as an Islamic single-sense text, often placed before or after an erstwhile Christian strophic groundlayer, on which a new Islamic interpretation has been pressed. Since Lüling attributes the single-sense texts to Muhammad, and they are usually in the form used by soothsayers, he sees this as a confirmation of his thesis that the ur-Islamic movement led by the Prophet had actually been a movement away from Western, Hellenistic, trinitarian, imperialist Christianity, toward the ur-Semitic tribal religion, symbolized by its progenitors Abraham and Ismail. This use of *sajᶜ* by the Prophet would explain why his Meccan opponents, who Lüling considers to have been trinitarian Christians, considered him to be a *kāhin* or soothsayer. Those sections of the Koran that are hostile to poets, such as XXVI.224–226, are to be attributed to pre-Islamic Christian invective against the people of the pagan Holy Groves or High Places, which, of course, included the pagan soothsayers.

(d) On the linguistic aspects of the different texts of the Koran.

Lüling's linguistic analysis of the different Koran texts yields the result that despite the fact that the canonic Koran is written in what is usually called high-standard or classical Arabic, it in fact contains four different types or standards of Arabic that, insofar as they can be distinguished, follow each other in time, and can be labeled as language strata, or language layers.

(1) The oldest Arabic language layer is that of the erstwhile Christian strophic hymnody. This Arabic, in itself a highly literate vernacular, differs considerably and in several respects from high-stan-

dard classical Arabic. First of all, the grammatical case endings of nouns and the grammatical modal endings of verbs are either missing, or appear arbitrarily to fill in gaps in the rhythm of the strophe lines, and to supply secondary rhyme endings; all this without regard to the grammatical correctness of such endings. Indeed, it seems very often that the rhyme composer misuses classic grammatical endings intentionally and humorously, as a skillful poetic device. This is a feature of popular and vernacular poetry in many languages, and underlines the literary form of the pre-Islamic strophic poetry. But this vernacular yet literate language not only differs from high-standard classical Arabic in its grammar, but also lexically in its vocabulary. Besides the expected difference in word choice and meaning between vernacular and classical, there are also a lot of Semitic words that have intruded into this, as Lüling calls it, pre-Islamic central Arabian Christian Arabic, from neighboring Semitic Christian literatures, especially from contemporary biblical Aramaic, Syriac, and, less frequently, Hebrew. These are words that, although stemming from the same Semitic word root, had in the long-term development of these different Semitic languages assumed slightly different meanings, but sometimes even essentially different ones.

To sum up: the language of the Christian hymnody in the groundlayer of the Koran is grammatically a vernacular Arabic, and moreover, a vernacular language the lexicography of which is thoroughly impregnated by neighboring Semitic Christian literatures. It is therefore absolutely indispensable for research into this ur-Koranic Christian hymnody to use both a grammar of early Christian Arabic,[6] and to consult all the available lexica of all the neighboring Semitic Christian literatures.

(2) Second comes the language of the second-sense Koran texts. This language is actually not a language in the true sense of the word, but a selective and unique conception of speech for the occasion, a consequence of the attempt to force a new interpretation on an ambiguous but decisive script. The erratic nature of this speech has been, and is still, being excused unconvincingly, by orthodox Islamic Koran scholarship and by many Western Islamicists, as resulting from the ecstatic state of the Prophet during his experiences

of revelation. The explanation, however, of how ecstatic speech was transformed, on the spot, into the text of scripture, is still missing.

(3) The third language is that of the early editorial glosses and commentaries, inserted into or added on to the second-sense texts, in order to pin the new interpretation to the underlying groundlayer of the *rasm*. This language, with its conspicuous preference for nominal instead of verbal constructions, forms a striking contrast to the literate language of both the underlying Christian hymnody, and old and present-day classical Arabic. This mostly nominal language discloses by its lack of elegance its identity as a nonliterate language; at least as a language without a discernible distinct literary tradition.

(4) The fourth language is that of the late and latest single-sense texts. That is, those originally Islamic texts that are neither immediately nor directly related to the erstwhile Christian *rasm* groundlayer, but which present larger cohesive complexes of prose texts in classical Arabic. This language, in its phraseology and grammatical sophistication, and in its skilful and therefore elegant appearance, is to be thoroughly distinguished from the language defined in the preceding paragraph.

Based upon information transmitted in Islamic tradition, Lüling concludes that this language must be attributed to the Prophet himself or, rather, to the literate secretaries who were charged with recording his pronouncements.

While for languages 1, 2, and 3, it is beyond question that they do not present high-standard classical Arabic and should not originally have been read as such, it still remains an open question whether the fourth and last type of language was originally intended to be so read, including case endings (*Iʿrāb*). Lüling presumes not, but as even this last language has been distorted and reinterpreted by post-Muhammadan Koran editors it is, again, a language especially created for the occasion. This fourth and last language layer is not Lüling's major concern, since he is most intent on uncovering the vernacular Christian hymnody of the ground-layer.

Thesis 3

The transmitted Islamic Koran text is the final of several successive editorial revisions.

Three essential motives for the different successive Koran-text editorial processes can be discerned. These processes obviously went on over several decades, and in all probability three successive periods of editorial work on the Koran.

(1) The first and main motive for the editorial reworking of the Koran is dogmatic.

It is the motive for both the Islamic reinterpretation of the erstwhile Christian hymnodies and for the collection and recording of the original Islamic revelation texts. In Lüling's view it has its cause in a national-Arabian/pagan-Arabian antagonism toward a central Arabian, and especially Meccan Hellenistic trinitarian Christianity of the Prophet's time. This Christianity had kept good relations with the trinitarian Christianity of all the neighboring nations and, like them, was split into different parties and confessions. Lüling considers that this national-Arabian/tribal-Arabian countermovement against the foreign-dominated Christianity of central Arabia, as not necessarily originating with Muhammad, but that it could have begun even with his grandfather ʿAbd al-Muṭṭalib. Likewise, the editorial reworking of the Christian hymnody may have begun before the Prophet's time, being in no way initiated by him, and then added to the text of the Koran after his passing.

This pagan or tribal-Arabian ur-Islamic movement, would have been incited by discord between the different factions and confessions of Christians in Mecca, which had been established there for some two centuries before Muhammad, during which time the Kaaba had been a Christian church. Lüling pictures Mecca as containing quarrelsome parties from all the different Christian church denominations of the surrounding countries—Mesopotamia, Syria, Palestine, Egypt, and Ethiopia. The Christian groundlayer of the Koran, in the view of Lüling, contains an archaic ur-Christian angel-christology, involving the idea that

Christ is an angel and therefore a created being. This Judaic or Ebionite Christianity had been condemned as heretical by all the Christian confessions extant at Mecca, who were still controlled by their Hellenistic mother churches. Only the central Arabian heretics (*ḥanīf*), the few descendants of the earliest ur-Christian and therefore angel-christological communities in central-Arabia, continued to stick to their creed. This nontrinitarian, ur-Christian angel-christology, found by Lüling in the strophic hymnody of the ur-Koran, was also eventually abandoned by ur-Islam in its turn to its own tribal-religious traditions under the slogan: "The religion of Abraham, Ismail and the tribes." This would explain the curiosity that Muhammad was considered both champion and betrayer of hanifdom.

(2) Historically, the second motive for a renewed editorial overworking and enlargement of the Koran comes from the victory of Islam over the Meccan "associators" (*mushrikūn*), whom Lüling sees as the Christians of Western trinitarian theology, who deified Jesus as God's son. The effect of this reworking was to tone down the original defection from central Arabian Christianity in order to appease former enemies, and to propagate the idea that there had never been any institutionally established Christian community in central Arabia, least of all in Mecca, the inhabitants of which were thereafter portrayed as pagan idolators.

(3) The third fundamental motive for the editorial reworking of the Koran derives secondarily from the national Arabian/tribal motivation and becomes gradually autonomous. That is, the motive of overworking the Koran text in order to make it read from beginning to end as a high-standard classical Arab prose text. This relatively late linguistic redaction consists, therefore, on the one hand, in the removal of the strophic structure of the original Christian text of the *rasm* groundlayer, and on the other, in the linguistic reworking of the entire Koran text, including all the second- and single-sense texts, in order to replace the hitherto vernacular reading without case endings, by a high-standard classical Arabic reading with case endings. The time when this redaction took place would be the time when the diacritical consonant points and diacritical vowel strokes had become accepted as permissible in Koran codices.

The motivation for changing the Koran into a classical Arabic prose text, as opposed to a strophic text, was probably to erase the memory of its original Christian contents, in the form of hymnody and responsories; to do this, rhythm and rhyme, the twin pillars of memory, had to be erased. Whether the Prophet himself ever knew and performed the Christian hymnody in its original form is impossible to say for sure, but Lüling is inclined to the opinion that he did.

The predilection of rising Islam for the national-Arabian cause brought about a preference for high-standard classical Arabic over the international Arabic vernacular, spoken beyond central Arabia in the surrounding nontribal countries with an urban culture; this "national" high-standard Arabic was pressed on the *rasm* groundlayer in a gradual process of grammatical and orthographical reworking. While in the earliest phase of developing Islam the lexical and grammatical differences between the Christian Arabic koine and the Old Arabian high-standard language had been used for the reinterpretation of the Koran, it seems that the high-standard Arabic reworking was relatively late, probably long after the death of the Prophet. This exclusively linguistic, as opposed to dogmatic, reworking was not only chronologically the last, but also, in its effect on the meaning of the Koran text, the least significant.

Thesis 4

The presence of the successive layers in the Koran text can be confirmed by material in Muslim tradition that has hitherto gone unnoticed or been misinterpreted.

On the basis of Lüling's findings of an ur-Christian and ur-Islamic groundlayer beneath the text of the present-day Koran, the existence of Koranic ideas, thoughts, and expressions in the pre-Islamic Old Arabian poets would cease to be anomalous. It would then appear that the pre-Islamic poets were indeed influenced by the Koran, but it was the much older Christian ur-Koran contained in the *rasm* groundlayer of the Islamic Koran. The thesis of Louis Cheikho that the pre-Islamic old Arabian poetry had been largely Christian would then be confirmed, since innumerable pre-Islamic Christian poems would have been reinterpreted using the same editorial techniques as those used on the erstwhile Christian texts of the ur-Koran. Furthermore, on the basis of Lüling's uncovering of the history of the formation of the Koran text, Islamic traditions can be read in a new light and exposed to a historicocritical analysis from a new perspective.

EXEMPLIFICATION: UNCOVERING THE HYMNODY

The evidence for the theses outlined above is laid out by Lüling in five chapters of over five hundred pages of small print. These contain examples from some seventeen different suras and long footnotes on related topics, together with numerous "excursuses" on related topics. The scholarship is overwhelming, and unless one can retain a sure grasp of the theses being argued for, the average reader is likely to get lost in an endless forest of detail. Because of limitations of space we must confine ourselves to two brief summaries of this material from the first and final chapters.

In the Koran as transmitted by Muslim orthodoxy, the text is divided into numerous sections. These sections are interpreted by Muslim tradition according to an extra-Koranic frame narrative, which assigns them to some purportedly historical incident to give the text a particular meaning. These interpretations are such that they cannot be legitimately derived from the text section alone and in itself on the basis of grammar and lexicography. Indeed, they are often so fantastic that they furnish no parallel, either from non-Koranic or from pre-Koranic Arabic texts.

On the other hand, a word-for-word interpretation of such texts, relying on nothing other than the transmitted *rasm* text, neglecting even the transmitted pointation, which is in effect the first commentary, yields a cohesive and self-contained text which needs no supplementary elucidation, and certainly no reference to allegedly historical incidents. As a rule, the acribic analysis of the broader *rasm* text, that is to say, the text sections before and after a dubious section, uncovers one long line of thought, whereas the traditional Islamic interpretation yields several short sections with, as to their content, independent and extremely short lines of thought, usually with totally disconnected ideas.

Lüling begins the demonstration of this thesis in chapter 1 with an examination of Suras XCVI and XXX. Sura XCVI is a particularly suitable place to begin, since it is a Sura where the original pre-Islamic Christian sense of the *rasm* groundlayer can be uncovered without the necessity of changing a single letter of the *rasm* script. Sura XCVI can also be said to be the pivot upon which the whole edifice of Islam rests, since this text has been taken by Muslim tradition as the first instance of Koranic revelation, the purported historical context of which forms the guarantee of the Koran's transcendental origin. If Sura XCVI turns out to be other than what Muslim tradition has portrayed it as being, that tradition will be shown to be false, indeed, to be a knowing and deliberate falsification, and the Koran to be not a revelation but a man-made text like any other.

According to the traditional Islamic interpretation, Sura XCVI falls into three thematic parts: verses 1–5, 6–8, and 9–19. In the cases of the first and last sections, a frame narrative has been attached to the text that has no basis in the actual words of the texts themselves. In the first and crucial section the frame narrative has the angel Gabriel appearing to Muhammad and appointing him Prophet, first of the Arab nation and then of all mankind, and presenting him with a script and commanding him to read. By this non-Koranic, pseudohistorical narrative, the interpretation of the introductory imperatives: *ʾiqraʾ* "read" (XCVI.1, 3), are pinned down in a definitive fashion. The text immediately following these two imperatives is then taken for the text Gabriel presented to the eyes of the Prophet-to-be to recite.[8] Yet the idea that the two commands to read are the only words of Gabriel, and that the rest is the script to be read by Muhammad is not indicated in the text in any way at all; moreover, the actual names "Gabriel" and "Muhammad" are wholly gratuitous and likewise do not appear in the text. The late and spurious nature of the references to Gabriel in Islamic tradition is confirmed by the fact that in the only other places in the Koran where Gabriel is mentioned (VI.97 f.; LVI.4) are so marginal in content as to be classified as glosses added later; also, in Islamic tradition concerning the life of the Prophet, texts that deal with Gabriel display an unproblematic Arabic grammar and lexicography, whereas surrounding passages apparently dealing with facts of history show many such problems.

In a similar fashion, the frame narrative attached to the third and final section of Sura XCVI (verses 9–19), has obviously been concocted to supply an acceptable meaning to an otherwise incomprehensible text. This time it concerns a member of the developing Muslim community, either a slave or even Muhammad himself, who is hindered in the performance of the ritual prayer. Between these two larger sections, 1–5 and 9–19, the short section, 6–8, is of such general significance that it could be attached to either the preceding or following sections, or even to any religious statement whatever. The curious thing is that although this middle section can, because of its general relevance, be understood as a proem to the third section, it is instead joined by Muslim tradition to the preceding section, to which it is much less suited because of its postponed position. It is a strange rule of the Arabic grammarians, in fact derived from this crude Koranic interpretation, that the expression *kallā*, meaning "not at all," which introduces this middle section, is only ever used as a negation of a preceding sentence, which merely compounds the hardly understandable connection between the middle and final sections of Sura XCVI.

At this point it will help to have before us both a conventional translation of Sura XCVI and Lüling's reconstruction. The following is a simplified English version of Rudi Paret's translation:

(1) Recite in the Name of your Lord who has created
(2) has created man out of an embryo!
(3) Recite! Your Lord is magnanimous as nobody else in the world
(4) [He] who has taught the use of the writing cane
(5) has taught unto man what he didn't know.
(6) Not at all! Man is really rebellious
(7) since he considers himself independent,
(8) however, to your Lord everything returns.
(9) What do you think about him who restrains
(10) a slave when he performs the ritual prayer.
(11) Do you believe that he is following the guidance
(12) or gives the order to be god-fearing.
(13) Do you believe that he pronounces lies and turns away.
(14) Does he not know that God sees.
(15) Not at all! If he doesn't cease we shall definitely grab him by the forelock
(16) a forelock full of lies and sinful.
(17) May he then call for his clique.
(18) We will call up the bailiffs.
(19) Not al all! Do not obey him! Prostrate and approach.

It should be obvious to everyone that this text is, for the most part, incoherent nonsense, and makes a mockery of the Koran's description of itself as "of clear Arabic language." Indeed, what little coherence this text has in translation is only achieved by supplying numerous words that are not in the original Arabic text at all, but drawn from the wholly spurious frame narrative supplied by Islamic tradition. Other illustrious translators, such as Arberry or Bell, only achieve whatever fluency their translations have by the same dubious method. It is impossible to produce a coherent translation because there is no coherence in the original Arabic, and it is precisely this fact that necessitated the invention of the traditional Islamic frame narrative. Muslims themselves had no idea what this text meant until an orthodox interpretation was concocted and spread abroad in Koran commentaries.

According to Lüling this incoherence results from the fact that the basic *rasm* text has been manipulated in order to disguise its original form as a pre-Islamic Christian strophic hymn. Lüling's translation and reconstruction follows, arranged in its original strophic form:

Verse	Strophe	Line
1	1	Invoke the Name of your Lord
	2	who created,
2	3	created man from clay.
3	1	Invoke! For thy Lord is the most generous
4	2	who taught by the writing cane,
5	3	taught man what he didn't know.
6	1	Not at all that man should be presumptuous
7	2	When ever he sees Him overbearingly independent!
8	3	Behold, to God is the recourse
9	1	Have you ever seen
	2	that He denies
10	3	a servant when he prays?
11	1	Have you ever seen
	2	—when he clung firmly to the creed?
12	3	—or spoke as a God-knower?

13	1	Have you ever seen
	2	that He betrayed and turned away?
14	3	Have you not learned that God sees?
15	1	Not at all! If He is not given peace
	2	truly He will be seized
	3	by His forelock
16		("a lying sinful forelock." Late gloss to be canceled.)
17	1	So call for His High Council!
18	2	You will then call up the High Angelship!
19	3	Not at all! Be you not presumptuous against Him!
		Prostrate and approach!

The strophic or poetic nature of this text is apparent from the frequent repetition of words, phrases, ideas, and synonyms. Moreover, it now appears as a single text with a theme common to all its parts, rather than three separate texts arbitrarily stitched together. However, there is still much that would strike the ordinary reader as obscure and puzzling. Lüling justifies his translation and rearrangement of Sura XCVI in sixty pages of small print in which every word and line is discussed at length. For reasons of space we can only report briefly some of the more important parts of this analysis.

The first thing to be considered is the opening word of Sura XCVI, *ʾiqraʾ*, which is usually translated "read," or "recite." It is upon this interpretation that the whole idea of the Koran as a revealed text rests, as well as the idea of Muhammad as its passive recipient. Lüling takes his cue for reading *ʾiqraʾ* as "Invoke," rather than "read," or "recite," from the relatively early Arab philologist Abū ʿUbayda (d. 203/818). ʿUbayda remarked that the verb *qaraʾa* in XCVI.1 has the same meaning as the verb *dhakara*: "invoke, laud, praise." While in the West, long before Lüling, the scholars Gustav Weil (1808–1899) and his contemporary Hartwig Hirschfield had stressed the point that the Hebrew expression *qārāʾ be shem Yahwe*, "to invoke (with) the name Yahwe," widespread in the Old Testament, must be taken into account in the interpretation of Sura XCVI.

Understanding *ʾiqraʾ* as "invoke," rather than "read" or "recite," becomes plausible when it is realized that in the ancient world reading was invariably reading aloud, so that the distinction between reading and invoking would not have been what it is today. If it was unfamiliar or even totally unknown to an Arab of the sixth and seventh centuries to read silently, the Arabic expression *qaraʾa* must have meant "to articulate loudly." One can therefore easily understand the significance of "Articulate loudly the Name of God!" (XCVI.1) as being the equivalent of "Invoke the Name of God!" and, as far as the "name of God" is here a hypostasis, as equivalent to "Invoke God!" At the time of the rise of Islam there must still have existed a self-evident sense of magic in the solemn utterance of words with a religious connotation, which virtually excludes the interpretation of *qaraʾa* as a merely aesthetic reciting of something to be stated.

A significant consequence of abandoning the traditional Islamic frame narrative for XCVI.1–5, and taking up Abū ʿUbayda's interpretation of *ʾiqraʾ* as "invoke (your Lord)," is that there is no longer any need to treat the first five verses as a separate section. One then realizes the striking fact that scattered throughout the whole sura there are a total of seven references that equally, but in different words, express the meaning of "prayer": in XCVI.1 and XCVI.3, *qaraʾa* "invoke"; in XCVI.10, *ṣallā* "perform the ritual prayer," in XCVI.17 and XCVI.18; *daʿā* "call for or intercede in prayer"; in XCVI.19 *sajada* "prostrate for prayer"; and in the same verse, *iqtarib* "apprach (God)." These seven verbs with the meaning "to pray," could be the thread that runs through the whole sura as its unifying theme.

A word that cries out for explanation is *kallā*, "not at all, by no means," which occurs no less than three times in Sura XCVI. Its first appearance at XCVI.6 is senseless, since it cannot be a negation of the preceding section no matter how those verses are interpreted. Against the stipulation of Arabic grammarians and Koran commentators that *kallā* can only apply to a preceding sentence, Lüling, following H. L. Fleischer (1801–1888), treats *kallā* as a negating particle equally applicable tp preceding as well as following sentences, preferably to the latter. For XCVI.6 this means that a vocal sign from the third layer of the Arabic script must be changed to establish the relation of the negation to the following sentence, so that XCVI.6 will read: "Not at all that man shall be presumptuous," rather than the awkward: "Not at all! Behold: man is presumptuous." This use of *kallā* is important since it not only makes sense out of the otherwise incoherent Sura XCVI but, as we shall see, performs the same function in Sura LXXIV, the other sura that is sometimes claimed by Islamic tradition as the first to be revealed. The stipulation of the grammarians that *kallā* can only apply to a preceding sentence thus appears to be deliberately devised to block a return to the erstwhile Christian reading of texts.

The other phrase that draws attention to itself by a triple repetition is *a-ra'aita*, "have you (ever) seen?" or "do you believe?" which introduces verses 9, 11, and 13. The strophic structure underlying the prose text shines through particularly clearly here, since the three *a-ra'aita* would make up the anaphoric initial word of three successive strophes. This being the case it would reveal the application of an artistic device that is common in strophic poetry everywhere.

In explanation of the curious reference to a "forelock" in verses 15 and 16, Lüling uses the dogma-critical aspect of his threefold methodology. He observes that in the simile "to seize God by the forelock," there appears not only an anthropomorphism offensive to the Islamic understanding of God, but an attitude toward God that is foreign to the whole world of orthodox Islamic religious ideas. It is, however, familiar in Jewish and Christian conceptions of God, and was carried over from the Old Testament to the New and on into evangelical Protestantism. For Lüling, pre-Islamic Arabian Christianity, as far as dogma was concerned, had an archaic Jewish-Christian or quasi-Arian character, so that in it we are entitled to take an understanding of prayer as an appropriate pestering of God for granted. The topos of struggling with God in prayer belongs to the oldest Jewish and Christian eschatological attitudes, and thus, on Lüling's hypothesis, to the earliest form of the Koran text. The forelock in old Arabian normally had a positive meaning as the seat of honor, so the Koran redactors had to stress that the forelock of the reinterpretation of XCVI.15 had an unfamiliar negative significance instead, just for this special and extraordinary case. The redactors could not make such a curious switch without inserting a gloss or commentary to the word "forelock"; hence, the addition of the spurious "a lying sinful forelock," as verse 16.

The reference to "His high Council" in XCVI.17, also betrays the Christian origin of the text, in that *nādī*, "council," has the Koranic synonym *mala*, which is applied in at least two cases (XXVII.8 and

XXVII.69) to the High Council of the archangels. This council is in the Greek Septuagint version of Isa. 9:6, called the *megata boula*, "the Great Council," where God consults with the highest angels, the highest of which is the Messiah, the angel kataxochen: *megalos boulos angelos*, "the Angel of the High Council of God." It is in this biblical sense that the word *nādiyah*, of XCVI.96:17, is to be understood. As a hypostasis, this High Council of Angels appears almost to be a synonym for God, so that to call for the "Council of God," means practically the same as to call for God. In the following line the mysterious word *z-zabāniyata*, a Koranic hapax legomenon, translated by Paret as "bailiffs of hell," and by Richard Bell as "imps of hell," is reconstructed by Lüling to read *ar-rabbāniya*, "ruling, governing, or powerful angels." This reading is achieved by only the slightest change to the pointation of the *rasm*, removing one point and setting one additional doubling sign. To reinforce these interpretations, Lüling then goes into a lengthy excursus on the significance of the *rabbānīyūn*, the Angels of the High Council of God, in early Near Eastern theology, the Koran, and early Islamic literature.

Lastly, there is a remnant of two words that in the orthodox Koran text are counted as verse 19. Both these words have endings that offer no possibility for a rhyme on long *a* to fit the previously uncovered strophic order of Sura XCVI. However, these words: *wa-sjud wa-qtarib*, "and prostrate, and approach," can easily be understood as the title or "headline" of the sura. Historically, the convention was to have a "footline," instead of a "headline," that is, the title was normally given at the end of a poetic or literary piece, and this seems to be the case here. They therefore do not belong to the body of the strophic hymn and should be eliminated along with verse 16. The effort to bring the number of verses up to nineteen in the sura designated as the first to be revealed may be not unconnected to the matter of nineteen in Sura LXXIV. This is not noted by Lüling.

This brief but, we hope, representative selection from Lüling's case for a Christian strophic hymn underlying Sura XCVI must suffice for the moment; all readers should consult Lüling's own text for the argument in full. At this point we must turn from the first to the final chapter of Lüling's book for a resume of his analysis of Sura LXXIV.1–30. Suras XCVI and LXXIV.1–30 are related in that they have both been considered by orthodox Muslim tradition as candidates for the first to be revealed; they may also be related for a more controversial reason, as we shall see.

Sura LXXIV.1–30 is of primary importance in Lüling's analysis, since it not only exemplifies all the techniques of his methodology but brings to the fore his contentions about the nature of the Christianity he finds underlying the Koran. According to Lüling, the pre-Islamic Christian hymnody contained in the Koran is theologically and dogmatically highly heretical, and unacceptable to the official trinitarian Christianity contemporary with the rise of Islam. With regard to the central issue of understanding the person of Christ in his relation to God, the pre-Islamic Christian hymnody confesses the blunt heresy that Christ is created. For Lüling, this so-called heresy is in fact the original truth of Christianity, and the victorious trinitarian creed, its falsification. Lüling maintains that Sura LXXIV.1–30 contains an extraordinary pre-Islamic hymn in which, in the form of a formulaic confession of faith, there occurs the explicit statement that God created Jesus Christ. This pre-Islamic hymnody is therefore of inestimable value as a residue of ur-Christianity, and the archaic biblical dogmatics of central Arabia in pre-Islamic times, which, again according to Lüling, formed the starting point for the new world religion of Islam.

As a whole, Sura LXXIV contains fifty-six verses in its orthodox recension. The restriction to verses 1–30 is justified by the fact that verse 31 is acknowledged, even by Islamic scholarship, to be a late insertion. Even the layman can recognize this from the length of verse 31 in comparison with the preceding and following verses. While verses 1–30 have an average of about four to six words each, verse 31 has no less than sixty-six words, and the following verses again small quantities. So verse 31 is quite obviously a commentary on the enigmatic number nineteen, mentioned in the previous verse: "Over it are Nineteen." Nevertheless, this over-length commentary in verse 31 is not an insertion into a large pre-Islamic text unit, because the second half of Sura LXXIV, although of a seemingly similar structure to 1–30, is in fact different in kind. Sura LXXIV.32–56 is what Lüling calls a single-sense Islamic text, made up of phrases that occur elsewhere in the Koran in slightly different form, sometimes as reinterpreted sentences of pre-Islamic Christian hymn texts. The possibility cannot be ruled out that LXXIV.32–56 contains some scattered fragments of the hymn in LXXIV.1–30, since that is only the introductory part of a larger text, but the last part of Sura LXXIV is too damaged for a fruitful reconstruction.

At this point it will help to have the text of Sura LXXIV.1–31 before us in its canonical form. The following translation is Lüling's depending on Bell and Arberry:

(1) O thou who shrouds himself in the mantle,
(2) arise, and warn!
(3) And thy Lord magnify.
(4) And they garments purify.
(5) And defilement flee!
(6) And bestow not favour to gain many.
(7) And for thy Lord wait patiently.
(8) For when the trumpet shall be sounded
(9) that day will be a harsh day.
(10) For the unbelievers far from easy.
(11) Leave me with him who I have created alone.
(12) And for whom I have appointed wealth extensive,
(13) and sons as witnesses.
(14) For whom I have made everything smooth.
(15) Who then desires that I shall do more.
(16) Nay, to Our signs he has become obstinate.
(17) I shall constrain him to a hard ascent.
(18) Lo, he reflected and determined!
(19) Blast him! How he determined.
(20) Again, blast him! how he determined!
(21) Then he looked,
(22) Then he frowned and scowled
(23) Then he turned his back and looked great
(24) And said: "This is nothing but magic made impressive,
(25) This is nothing but human speech,"
(26) I shall roast him in hellfire (*saqar*).
(27) And what will teach thee what is hellfire?
(28) It leaves not over and it leaves not off.
(29) Scorching the flesh,
(30) Over it are Nineteen.
(31) We have appointed only angels to be masters of the fire, and their number we have appointed only as a trial for the unbelievers, that those who were given the Book may have certainty,

> and that those who believe may increase in belief, and that those who were given the Book and those who believe may not be in doubt, and that those in whose hearts there is sickness, and the unbelievers, may say: "What did God intend by this as a similitude?" So God leads astray whomsoever He will, and he guides whomsoever He will; and none knows the hosts of thy Lord but He. And it is naught but a Reminder to mortals.

As with Sura XCVI, it is the introductory words of Sura LXXIV that led it to be considered a candidate for a first revelation; in both cases this interpretation rests on a reinterpretation, or even a misrepresentation, of the underlying *rasm* text. A further parallel is that the traditional interpretation of these two suras derives from extra-Koranic frame narratives that have only a minimal basis in the text itself. Sura LXXIV is divided into different sections, seemingly without any coherence as to their content, each of them receiving its general idea from its respective frame narrative adduced in the commentaries of later orthodox Islamic Koran scholarship. The two basic sections of Sura LXXIV.1–30 are 1–10 and 11–30, each with its own frame narrative; the most curious of these is that attached to the crucial second section. This frame narrative has it that God himself utters threats to a Meccan foe of the Prophet named al Walīd ibn al Mughīrah, a distinguished, extraordinarily rich Qurayshite, friendly to Christians. Not much is known of this person other than that he is very rich and, in addition to some daughters, has no less than seven sons; all this conjured from the contents of verses 12 and 13, in the orthodox form of the text.

Lüling's point of departure for a christological reading of Sura LXXIV.1–30 lies in verses 11–17. As in Sura XCVI.6, the key to uncovering the original meaning of the *rasm* text is to ignore the arbitrary rule of classical Arabic grammar that *kalla*, "not at all," can only relate to a preceding sentence, even if there is no preceding sentence, and never to a following sentence. As was seen in the analysis of Sura XCVI, this rule seems to have been deliberately devised to prevent a return to the original reading of the text. The annulment of this theoretical rule, which has practically no support in vernacular Arabic, results in the change of *kallā inahu*, "Not at all behold him . . . ," to *kallā annahu*, "Not at all that he . . . ," which requires no change in the *rasm* and results in a reverse of meaning; this provides the clue for a reconstruction of the whole context about Jesus Christ, closely corresponding to the usual Christian phraseology. This means that Sura LXXIV.16, instead of reading: "Nay! He has rebelled against Our signs" (Paret), will read, "Not at all that He was rebellious against Our signs." Paret's translation, "he has rebelled," is simply wrong, and the correct translation provides a christological topos: the suffering servant of Isa. 52:13, 53:7, and 53:12; Phil. 2:6–11; and Heb. 5:1–10.

This reading is confirmed by the following verse, LXXIV.17, which in its orthodox form is an exemplary case of a fantastic interpretation with no lead in the text. This verse consists of only two words: *sa-ʾurhiquhū ṣaʿūdan*, and the key word is *ṣaʿūdan*, "a height, hill, ascending path." According to orthodox Koran scholarship this refers to the central mountain of hell, up which sinners will be rushed until, after seventy years, they fall off in order to begin the process again, but none of this can be derived from the accompanying verbal stem *r-h-q*.

The solution to the problem lies again in interpreting both these words as literally as possible, but with the freedom of changing the punctuation, which is a late phenomenon and as such highly dubious. The *rasm* of *ṣaʿūdan* [ṣʿwd] is comparatively unproblematic, because there are no reasonable variants on the basis of another punctuation, so its general significance of "height, hill, ascending path," remains valid; there only needs to be found a plausible christological topos involving the key word "height." This emerges when the first word is read as *sa-ʾazhaqahu*, rather than *sa-ʾurhiquhū*, which can be done with no change of the *rasm*. This means, quoting Lane's lexicon word for word: "He [God] caused his soul to go forth, pass forth, or depart." If this meaning is added to the second word, we get the sentence for LXXIV.17: "finally He [God] made him pass through death to height," which is the christological topos of Christ ascending, or being elevated after his death. Moreover, the word *ṣaʿūd* in LXXIV.17, is a technical term in the Arabic-speaking church: the Ascension of Christ in the Christian Arabic Church was from of old called *ṣaʿūd ar-rabb*, "the ascending of the Lord," and the feast of the Ascension was known as *ʿīd as ṣaʿūd*

The traditional interpretation of LXXIV.11–15 has a series of statements by God expressed in the first person singular, supposedly referring to some anonymous evildoer, the details of which are supplied by the highly imaginative extra-Koranic frame narrative; this in itself is highly suspicious. It seems likely that this person was only invented to give the transmitted *rasm* text, within the very limited range of deviating punctuation possible, a fundamentally different meaning because the original christological content had to be eliminated.

The second half of the transmitted text of LXXIV.11 reads: *wa man khalaqtu waḥidan*, and is interpreted as: "(the evil doer) whom I (God) created as a single being." This is nonsense, and does not even correspond grammatically to the text as it stands. The first person singular here is almost certainly due to the Koran editors, and to get back to the original christological hymnody needs to be changed to the third person: *wa man khalaqahu waḥidan*, "and whom He (God) created (him) as a unique being." This makes it easier to understand the first half of LXXIV.11, which traditionally reads: *dharnī*, "let me go, dismiss me," but which Lüling reads as: *dhara'anī*, "He has created Me," making *dhara'a* a synonym for *khalaqa*, "to create"; this has precedence elsewhere in the Koran at Suras VI.136; VII.179; XVI.13; XXIII.79; XLII.11; and LXVII.24. Sura LXXIV.11 now reads: "He has created me and whom he has created as a unique being," a clear christological statement.

This grammatical reconstruction of LXXIV.11 is justified on dogma-critical grounds by the fact that in most of the Christian creeds there is the custom of first mentioning God's creation of the cosmos in general and man in particular, and only afterward to mention Jesus Christ. In the case of Sura 74:11 ff. we have, according to Lüling, an ur-Christian, angel-christological creed. Whereas in the trinitarian creeds, the statement about Christ's creation cannot occur at all, because Christ is identified with the creator; the ur-Christian angelogical creed, preserved uniquely in LXXIV.11 ff., has the two statements following each other. God created Jesus Christ as the lastly added remedy for the entire creation, so that Christ might become, as God's suffering servant, the salvation of the world. This explains why, even in the old creeds of trinitarian Christianity, Jesus Christ is only mentioned after the creation of the cosmos and mankind. The ur-Christian creed of Sura LXXIV.11 ff. would be the original form of all Christian creeds before the triumph of trinitarianism. Lüling regards the designation of the Quraish of Mecca as *mushrikūn*, "associators," as evidence that they had converted to a Hellenistic-Christian trinitarian creed, and had rejected the pre-Islamic angel-christological hymnody. The early Islamic movement abandoned faith in Jesus Christ as a central issue and reinterpreted the hymnody to fit a wholly Islamic Koran. The only people who remained faithful to the pre-Islamic hymnody were the *ḥanīfs*, or heretics, who were eliminated by victorious Islam.

In a similar manner to those analysed above, verses 12–15 of Sura LXXIV can be reconstructed to read as parts of a pre-Islamic, angel-christological hymn, and the reader is referred to Lüling's text for the lengthy and detailed arguments. After verses 11–17, Lüling turns his attention to section LXXIV.18–30, and in particular to the crucial section LXXIV.26–30, which concerns Christ's descent into hell.

Attention is first drawn to a conspicuous inconsistency in the text of LXXIV.18–30, in that in the closely following verses 25 and 29, the word *bashar*, "flesh," is in the first instance given its normal significance of transitory human being, while in the second it is given the context: "and is scorching the flesh (in hell)." The latter is especially suspicious in that the *rasm, lawwāḥatun*, interpreted as yielding the verbal predicate "is scorching," cannot mean this since the verb *l-w-ḥ* always means elsewhere in Arabic, apart from this single Koranic instance, "to shine, to beam," and has nothing to do with fire and burning heat. The only plausible alternative reading of the *rasm* is as *la-wāḥatun*, "verily, an oasis," so that the whole of LXXIV.29 would read: *la-wāḥatan li-l-bashar*, "verily, an oasis for the transitory flesh." This is a very suitable expression for the underworld, the place of the dead until the day of Last Judgment. It also unites the two instances of the word *bashar*, in verses 25 and 29, with a single meaning.

If there is no reference to hellfire in LXXIV.29, we are led to suspect that the word *saqar* in LXXIV.26 does not refer to hellfire either, since the spurious nature of LXXIV.29 is only constructed to provide an answer to the question: "What has let thee know what *saqar* is?" in LXXIV.27.; if *saqar* does not mean: "the heat of hellfire," as the traditional interpretation of the *rasm* would have it, then the accompanying verb *s-l-w* will not mean: "to roast, to stew." The word *saqar* holds a key position in the interpretation of the section LXXIV.26–30, and thus of the whole section LXXIV.1–30; Lüling devotes some fifteen pages of fine print to its analysis, of which we can only give an indication here.

Saqar, with the meaning: "hellfire, heat of hell," as assigned to it by Islamic tradition, has no certain origin in Arabic or any other Semitic language. If Lüling is right in his theory that the original *rasm* of Sura LXXIV.1–30 contained a pre-Islamic christological hymn, and that that hymn concerned Christ's descent into hell, then it is reasonable to assume that the word *saqar* had some connection with the idea of an underworld or realm of the dead, rather than simply of hell or hellfire. This underworld would be hell in the older sense of a receptacle for the dead, good as well as bad; a realm ruled by Death, into which Christ would bring salvation and the sacraments of the New Covenant for the benefit of the deceased of earlier, pre-Christian times. If this line is taken one stumbles upon remarkable connections and coincidences in the Arabic language, which are at the same time probably etymological relations.

Lüling suggests that the Koranic word *saqar*, which he interprets as meaning "underworld" or "place of the dead," is an irregular derivation from the tenth verbal stem of the verb *q-r-r*, "to be stationary," "to be cool/cold," an appropriate description of both the dead and the place where they reside. The direct phonetic parallel to *saqar* in Hebrew is *shaqar*, which probably originally meant the womb as the underworld, the receptacle of the dead as well as the place of rebirth and resurrection. As such this is an archaic messianic concept, originally centred in the cult of the heroic ancestors at the High Places, which as burial sites represented a womb. This was a wholly positive idea of the underworld, the notion of eternal punishment in hellfire being an innovation of the newly invented monotheisms, which sought to destroy the old religion of the High Places and turn the *saqar* idea into its opposite: deceit, delusion, illusion, hallucination, lie. The positive idea of the underworld as womb and place of resurrection can also be traced in Akkadian, Assyrian, and Babylonian, where it has no connotation of heat or hellfire, but, on the contrary, that of coolness.

So the reconstructed meaning LXXIV.27 now reads: "And what has taught you what the underworld is?" which makes more sense of the following enigmatic verse LXXIV.28 when translated: "it (the underworld) doesn't let remain and doesn't let go"; it doesn't leave anyone remaining on earth and doesn't let anyone go until the final judgment. In conformity with these reconstructions, LXXIV.26: *sa-aṣlāhu saqara*, can now be translated: "So He (God) has finally exposed him (Christ) to the underworld," the verbal root *s-l-y* being given its core meaning of: "to turn oneself or something toward something," as in the verb *salla*, to pray.

We are now in a position to consider some of the ramifications of the controversial verse LXXIV.30: *ʿalayhā tisʿata ʿashara*: "Over it are Nineteen." As noted above, Sura LXXIV.1–30 is composed in a very homogeneous form, in that every verse has the same rhythmic style and approximately the same length of, on average, three to four words, which in itself is a good indication that it was originally a strophic text. This makes the contrast between LXXIV.1–30 and the following verse LXXIV.31, which is a prose text taking up half a page, so conspicuous that it could not fail to draw the attention of commentators. Even traditional Islamic Koran scholarship has classified LXXIV.31 as a late insertion into an earlier text; late and early in that context referring of course to Medinan and Meccan. Lüling proposes that this traditional classification should be abandoned in favor of the contrast: "pre-Islamic Christian strophic texts," and "Islamic texts." However, the essential point to grasp about the juxtaposition of verses LXXIV.30 and 31 is that, although they are quite clearly different types of text, it is also quite clear that the latter is a commentary on the former. This raises all sorts of questions about how this could have come about.

The traditional interpretation of Sura LXXIV.31 is that it is a commentary on the immediately preceding words of LXXIV.30, yet in order to make sense of that text it utilizes the frame narrative of verses 11–30, which, if Lüling is correct, is a late interpretational device of those wishing to disguise the meaning of the original *rasm*. Since verse 31 twice mentions "those who were given the Book," presumably meaning the Koran, when, according to the traditional picture of events, the Koran was not assembled into a book until long after the Prophet's death, we have in this verse a major anomaly. Why would the Prophet, at Medina or anywhere else, receive a revelation about a book that did not yet exist, even a particular verse of that book?

The whole idea of a book, and that book being the Koran, arises out of the text of verses 25 and 26: "This is nothing but magic made impressive. This is nothing but human speech," which is taken by the commentary of verse 31 as an insult by the protagonist of the frame narrative to the revelatory utterances of the Prophet, for which he is condemned to roast in hellfire (*saqar*). But if Lüling's interpretation of *saqar* is correct there is no hellfire and no roasting, only an underworld. Moreover, there is still no explanation for the appearance of the number nineteen. Even if nineteen refers to angels who watch over the underworld or over hellfire, why would "their number" be a "trial for unbelievers," and why would it give certainty to those that have the book, and cause the unbelievers to say: "What did God intend by this similitude?"

According to Lüling the number nineteen arises from a misreading of the *rasm* of LXXIV.30, the true meaning of which must be sought in conformity with the whole preceding section, 1–29, and in particular to the section 26–29, which concerns Christ's descent into the underworld. Most probably LXXIV.30 should be seen as still part of the answer to the question set in LXXIV.27: "and what has let thee know what *saqar* is?" Verses 28 and 29 are the first two answers to that question, and verse 30 would be a third.

Everyone whose job it is to read old Arabic manuscripts, which are very poorly supplied with diacritical dots, will have been in the situation of being unable to decide whether to read *tisʿa*, "nine," or *sabʿa*, "seven," because these two numbers, when written in words, are indistinguishable in a *rasm* without dots. This means that the original *rasm* of LXXIV.30 could have read "On it are seventeen," rather than the traditional "On it are Nineteen," and apparently there is at least one record of a variant reading of this kind.[9] It is therefore quite possible that there could have existed in verse LXXIV.30 solely the number seven, so that the following word, which is written separately, need not have been ten, extending the preceding seven to become seventeen, but a noun designating something that is counted by the preceding number seven. So the text of LXXIV.30 may have originally read: "on it there are seven *x*," where *x* stands for something expressed by a noun hidden behind the *rasm* of *ʿashara*. It so happens that there is a very plausible candidate for this hidden noun, bearing in mind Lüling's translation of *saqar* as "underworld."

It was a common idea in the old Orient as well as in Islam that the underworld had seven sections or levels, corresponding to the seven heavens above, and that these seven levels had seven gates. Referring to "Gehenna," which originally meant the underworld, Sura XV.44 reads: "it has seven gates to every one of which belongs a section partitioned off." This brings to mind the fact that the Semitic and Arabic word *ʿashar*, "ten," very much resembles in both its script and its sound the Hebrew word *sha'ar*, "gate." It would not be exceptional if the Hebrew word *sha'ar* had an offshoot in pre-Islamic old Arabic, where the Arabic word would have had the form *sa'ar*, or *sa'r*. The difference between the alternative words "ten" and "gate," consists in Arabic script of the metathesis of only one consonant: *s-ʿ-r ʿ-s-r*. It therefore appears quite possible that the early Koran editors, in the course of their reinterpretation of the whole section LXXIV.1–30, "corrected" the original rasm of the Hebrew loanword "gate" to get "ten." So the original text of LXXIV.30 may well have read "On it are seven gates," rather than "On it are Nineteen."

On this reading of LXXIV.30 the number nineteen arises solely from a deliberate misreading of the original *rasm*, which could have been read as either seventeen or nineteen. Apparently it was sometimes read as seventeen, but this was dropped in favor of nineteen, presumably, if Lüling's diagnosis is correct, to further remove it from the original seven of the *rasm*. The commentary in the following verse 31 is read by Lüling as a threat against those who still remembered the Christian hymn and the number seven hidden in the original *rasm*, but this hardly seems an adequate explanation for all the nuances of the text of verse 31.

Even if Lüling is correct about the substitution of nineteen for seven or seventeen, why would the redactors deliberately draw attention to it by incorporating such an obvious and anomalous commentary into the text? Presumably the "correction" of the *rasm* of verse 30 was one of the first editorial acts perpetrated on the material that eventually formed the Koran, perhaps even before the life of Muhammad, whatever dates are give to that life. The commentary, however, is quite obviously late, and must have been concocted by those engaged in one of the final stages in the production of the canonical Koran, *a time when the Koran was already some form of book*. Verse 31 appears to be there to draw attention to some feature of that book that would cause problems for unbelievers and convince believers of its supernatural nature. This feature is of such a kind that it can be called a "similitude." Of what could the number nineteen possibly be a similitude? There appears to be only one plausible answer: nineteen is a similitude of the book's supposed author, the One God, Allah.

By the *abjad* system of substituting numbers for letters, nineteen is the number of the Arabic word *wāḥid*, meaning one. If the Koran was formed in a sectarian milieu of competing forms of Christianity in which the trinity was a bone of contention, the oneness of the One God of emergent Islam would have been its distinguishing feature. What better similitude of this One God could there be than that his revealed book be permeated throughout by recurring patterns of the number nineteen. This would be especially telling in a milieu where it was well-known that Jewish and Christian books were based on numbers revelatory of their nature; for instance, Ecclesiastes was based on the number fifty-six, the number of the word *hebel*, "vanity." This feature of the holy book of the Muslims may have been most prominent and pervasive in its early recensions, only the ruins of such a scheme being apparent in the Koran as we have it today. The idea of nineteen in the Koran has lingered in the corners of the Muslim mind for centuries, and has become a matter for dispute in recent times, but is too detailed to be pursued here.[10]

Having shown in some detail Lüling's method of reconstruction of LXXIV.11–17 and 26–30 in order to show the underlying pre-Islamic Christian creed in the form of a strophic hymn, the remaining text LXXIV.1–10 and 18–25 needs less attention. This is because the main points that identify this underlying text as a Christian angelological creed have already been made, and the remaining sections, although not without puzzling elements in need of explanation, simply confirm the preceding analysis; the reader is referred to Lüling's own text for his punctilious line-by-line and word-by-word argumentation.

We are now in a position to present Lüling's reconstruction of the whole pre-Islamic hymn present in LXXIV.1–30:

Verse	Strophe	Line	
1		1	O thou hesitating one!
2		2	Arise and solemnly promise!
3		3	And say that thy Lord is great!
4	1	4	And thy garments purify!
5		5	And defilement flee!
6		6	And bestow not favor to regain many!
7		7	And for thy Lord wait patiently!
8		1	And when the trumpet will be sounded.
9	2	2	That day will be a harsh day
10		3	For the unbelievers not easy.

11		1	He (God) has created me and whom he created as a unique being.
12		2	And He (God) made him (Chr.) a property obedient to his will.
13		3	And He testified him by witnesses.
14	3	4	And he pave him the way.
15		5	Then he (Chr.) desired that he (Chr.) might be increased.
16		6	Not at all that he was rebellious against his signs (commandments).
17		7	Finally He (God) made him pass through death to height.
18		1	Behold him! He (Chr.) was tortured and despised.
19	4	2	So he (Chr.) was killed as it was decided.
20		3	He (Chr.) accomplished. He (Chr.) was killed as He (God) had decided.
21		1	He stopped looking around reflectively.
22	5	2	He stopped scowling and making a stern face.
23		3	He stopped disputing and said "God is great."
24		1	And he said: "What else is this but the seducer who desires.
25	6	2	What else is this but the voice of the transitory flesh!"
26		3	So He (God) has finally transferred him to the underworld.
27		1	And what has let thee know what *saqar* is?
28	7	2	It doesn't let remain and doesn't let go.
29		3	Indeed an oasis for transitory flesh.
30		1	On it are seven gates.

The reader should be aware that there is a caesura before the last line of each strophe, since this was sung by the lay audience as a response to the preceding lines which were usually sung by a soloist priest or deacon.

It should also be noted how the content of the hymn is arranged by strophe. Strophe 1 being a prelude admonishing the congregation to be vigilant; strophe 2, a reminder of doomsday; strophe 3, a creedlike assessment of God's preparing Christ for the salvation of mankind; strophe 4, a description of Christ's Passion and death as decided by God; strophes 5 and 6, a description of Christ in Gethsemane giving up his will to the will of God; and strophe 7, a description of the nature of the underworld..

THE HISTORICAL CONTEXT

The question of whether Lüling's uncovering of a pre-Islamic Christian hymnody underlying about one-third of the Koran is in the end convincing, must be left to specialists in the field of Arabic language and philology. However, these linguistic and textual problems are only half of Lüling's thesis about the origin of Islam. Just as important is the historical and geographical context in which he envisages this adaptation of Christian texts to have taken place.

His position might be characterized as at once traditional and revisionist. He is traditional in that he accepts without question the Muslim account of the origin of Islam in central Arabia and the Ḥijāz towns of Mecca and Medina. He also accepts that a major role in the birth of Islam and the Koran was played by a prophet called Muhammad, who had roughly the dates and a good part of the biography assigned to him by Muslim tradition. The most radical difference Lüling has with this traditional picture is that he sees practically the whole of the Arabian peninsula as thoroughly Christianized, even to the extent of Muhammad's own tribe of the Quraysh being Christian. This view of the religious allegiance of the people of central Arabia is, in a sense, forced upon him by trying to reconcile the fact of the Koran having Christian hymns hidden in its *rasm*, with the fact of its having originated in central Arabia or the Ḥijāz. Where could these Christian hymns have come from if there was not a widespread Christian population at hand already making use of them?

To bolster this assumption of a thoroughly Christianized central Arabia, even to the extent Mecca being a center of Christianity for some two centuries before the birth of Muhammad, Lüling has to make the most of every piece of Muslim tradition that can be interpreted in a way that would support his thesis. Chief among these are the stories that the Kaaba at Mecca contained biblical pictures, including Jesus and Mary, as well as architectural features that Lüling interprets as indicating a Christian church oriented toward Jerusalem. He also reads the Koranic term *mushrikūn*, meaning "those who adjoin a companion to God," as referring not to the idol-worshiping polytheists of the *jāhiliyya*, as Muslim tradition would have it, but to trinitarian Christians. Now, all these items of information may be significant for assessing the origin of Islam, but none of them necessitate the interpretation given them by Lüling as backing his thesis of a Christianized cental Arabia; indeed, the very opposite may well be the case.

The inherent implausibility of Lüling's assumption of a widespread Christianity in central Arabia in pre-Islamic times is shown by the paucity of contemporary scholarship that he can adduce in support of the idea. Apart from some German Protestant theologians, he only mentions J. S. Trimingham as insisting on the existence of organized Christian communities in that area in pre-Islamic times, but if Trimingham's book on the subject is actually consulted nothing substantial is found that supports Lüling's thesis.

In discussing the presence of monotheism in West Arabia, Trimingham remarks that: "Christianity was non-existent among the Arabs of western Arabia south of the Judham tribes." In a chapter headed "Christians in the Ḥijāz," after describing the history of Mecca according to the Muslim sources, plus its geographical location, he concludes that "these factors are sufficient to explain why Christianity in any of its available forms could have no influence upon its inhabitants."[11] The following section is promisingly entitled "Christians in Central Arabia," but is concerned mostly with the nomad alliance state of Kinda. The main body of Kinda lived in the Ḥaḍramawt, but early in the fourth century some sections separated and moved into the Najd area of central Arabia among clans of Ma'add, with whom they formed alliances; because of a subsequent alliance with the Byzantines it is assumed that the Kinda confederation must have adopted some form of Christianity. This would at least appear to be true of the ruling clan, judging by an inscription found in a convent church at Ḥīra on the Euphrates.[12] Ḥīra is over six hundred miles from Mecca and can hardly be called central Arabia.

The other scholar to whom Lüling refers is Irfan Shahid. In his

Byzantium and the Arabs in the Fifth Century, Shahid makes the remark, "Places with distinctly Christian association, such as Maqbarat al Nasara, the cemetery of the Christians, are attested in Mecca in later Islamic sources and these could not possibly have been fabricated."[13] To which one is inclined to reply: Why not? When so much other material in Muslim tradition has been either invented or transposed, why not a Christian cemetery at Mecca? The source of the information is Azraqī's "Meccan Reports," *Akhbār Makka*, assembled some two hundred years after the supposed lifetime of the Prophet and published a hundred years after that, so there is no reason to think it any more trustworthy than any other literature produced at the same time. Moreover, if it is true, as many scholars believe, that much of the material referring to Mecca in the southern Ḥijāz has been transferred there from somewhere much farther north, then the whole picture changes. The elements of Muslim tradition that Lüling attributes to a Christian milieu in the midst of which Islam emerged, need not indicate the Ḥijāz and central Arabia at all, but a place where we know for a fact, rather than unsubstantiated hypothesis, that such a society existed.

These considerations bring us to the crucial point that is likely to make Lüling's thesis unacceptable to the majority of scholars. It is not that the posibility of a Christian hymnody hidden in the *rasm* of parts of the Koran is inherently unlikely or unacceptable, but that the historical context of this possibility, as postulated by Lüling, is simply too far-fetched and involves too many unverifiable presuppositions. There is also the problem that all those who adopt a skeptical attitude to a body of tradition cannot at the same time use that tradition to reconstruct "what really happened," since the criteria for selection from that tradition will then be entirely arbitrary; whatever supports the favored hypothesis is treated as true and genuine tradition, while the rest is ignored or dismissed as irrelevant fabrication. Also, a conscious burying or falsification of history that is generally known to be true, as Lüling's hypothesis requires, seems inherently less likely than a gradual, unconscious, construction of a tradition that no one knows to be false.

It is now well-known that the consensus of scholarly opinion on the origins of Islam underwent something of a seismic shift in the last quarter of the twentieth century.[14] This change of view was initiated by John Wansbrough in his *Quranic Studies*, published in 1977; behind the scenes

Wansbrough had also been a crucial influence on Patricia Crone and Michael Cook, who published their *Hagarism: The Making of the Islamic World* in the same year. These two books made a radical break with the traditional picture of the origins of Islam. The shift is one of both place and time, in that the location for that origin is no longer the Ḥijāz in the lifetime traditionally attributed to Muhammad, but the Fertile Crescent some time after his death and subsequent to the Arab conquests.

The key to the thinking behind this new view of things is to be found in the following passage from *Quranic Studies*:

> The frequently adduced view that the text of revelation was easily understood by those who had witnessed its first utterance, as well as by their immediate successors, but by later generations would not be, is in my opinion not merely ingenuous, but belied by the many stories of early efforts towards the interpretation of scripture associated with the figures of ʿUmar b. Khaṭṭāb and ʿAbdallāh b. ʿAbbās. Whatever the reasons for production of those stories, it seems hardly possible that at the beginning of the third/ninth century the Muslim community had to be reminded of what it had once known. *Tafsīr* traditions, like traditions in every other field, reflect a single impulse: *to demonstrate the Ḥijāzi origins of Islam* [our italics].[15]

In other words, the whole Muslim tradition of the origin of the Koran, including both the "occasions of revelation," (*asbāb an nuzūl*), and their meaning, is a fabrication of the ninth century. The purpose behind this literary effort was to convince both Muslims and non-Muslims that Islam had its origin not in the civilized region of the Fertile Crescent conquered by the Arab tribes, as contemporaries might presumably have supposed, but in the Arab homeland desert region of the Ḥijāz. This set Islam apart, both geographically and theologically, from the Judaism and Christianity with which it obviously had so much in common.

The final divine revelation had descended not upon the corrupted Hellenes of the north, but upon the unspoiled Arabs of the pristine desert of the south, the final chosen people whose divinely guided destiny it was to rule the civilized world in the name of the one true God, Allah.

Because so much of the Koran and Hadith is obviously dependent upon a historical context in which the presence of Jews and Christians is taken for granted, it was necessary for Islamic apologists to populate the Ḥijāz with Jewish and Christian communities for which there is little or no evidence outside Muslim literature; Lüling's attempt to fill central Arabia and the Ḥijāz with Christians is just a continuation of this project into modern times. Remarking on this phenomenon with regard to the necessity for postulating Jewish influence on the collection of and commentary upon the Koran, Wansbrough says:

> Some scholars . . . have been excessively generous in their assessment of the documentary value of Islamic source materials for the existence and cultural significance(!) of Jewish communities in the Ḥijāz about which Jewish sources are themselves silent. References in Rabbinic literature to Arabia are of remarkably little worth for purposes of historical reconstruction, and especially for the Ḥijāz in the sixth and seventh centuries. The incompatibility of Islamic and Jewish sources was only partially neutralised, but the tyranny of the "Ḥijāzi origins of Islam" fully demonstrated, by insistence upon a major Jewish immigration into Central Arabia.[16]

Lüling's insistence on a major Christian immigration into central Arabia is just as undocumented and unlikely, and just as much a product of a dogmatic insistence upon the "Ḥijāzi origins of Islam." In this matter Lüling takes Muslim tradition wholly at face value, regardless of how much he wishes to undermine and call it into question in other respects.

If a plausible Mecca is necessary to account for all the material in the Muslim sources, a suitable candidate would be Moka, a town in Arabia Petraea mentioned by Ptolemy; not far distant was a "Kaaba" toward which Muslims prayed in early times, as witnessed by Jacob of Edessa.[17] Such locations in northwest Arabia, far north of Mecca in the Ḥijāz, provide a suitable environment for the origin of Islam, which obviates the necessity to postulate large-scale migrations of Jews and Christians into Arabia. Indeed, anywhere in the arc of the Fertile Crescent would provide a suitable location for the notorious foreign vocabulary of the Koran, which indicates familiarity with a cosmopolitan environment far removed from the southern Ḥijāz.[18]

However this may be, there is a sense in which the geographical location of the original Mecca or Medina is irrelevant, in that the only fact about which there can be no doubt is that in the second quarter of the seventh century there was a large-scale occupation of the Hellenic Middle East by Arabs. The crucial point at issue is the exact nature of this event: was it simply an act of political opportunism, taking advantage of an exhausted opponent, or was it driven by some kind of religious zeal? The first alternative is favored by Wansbrough, who sees the development of Islam as wholly subsequent to the establishment of a religiously unspecific polity: "Both the quantity and quality of source materials would seem to support the proposition that the elaboration of Islam was not contemporary with but posterior to the Arab occupation of the Fertile Crescent and beyond."[19] Both the Muslim and Christian accounts of "what happened" are read by Wansbrough as indicating "the persistence of Judaeo-Christian sectarianism in the Fertile Crescent under Arab political hegemony, the establishment of a *modus vivendi* between the new authority and the indigenous communities, and the distillation of a doctrinal precipitate (a common denominator) acceptable initially to an academic elite, eventually an emblem of submission (*islam*) to political authority."[20] Thus, one of the few "facts" that we have about early Islamic history is that "the religious movement later identified with the state begins as the sectarian expression of a scholarly elite."[21]

If the "doctrinal precipitate" that we know as Islam first appears to us in documents produced by a literary elite c. 800 C.E., it seems reasonable to suppose that there were earlier documents that have not survived. "What really happened" may not be what the literary elite would have liked us to think happened, but whatever the exact process, the emergence of Islam involved a gestation of at least 170 years, which left traces other than documents. It is perhaps significant that such documentary evidence as survives from the Sufyanid period (661–684) makes no mention of Muhammad as the messenger of God, and the coinage invokes Allah without mentioning his prophet, but by the Marwanid period (684–744) coinage was being struck which identified Muhammad as *rasūl Allāh*, and thereafter reference to Muhammad as messenger of God becomes standard on Arab coins. It was the caliph ʿAbd al Malik (685–705) who devised the classical solution for Arabic/Islamic coinage, when he produced a coin with no images, only Arabic script containing a distinctly Islamic message: "There is no God but God and Muhammad is his messenger who He sent with guidance and the religion of Truth to make it supreme over all others whether the polytheists like it or not."[23] Since the caliph was in effect the state, the crystallization of the idea of Muhammad as messenger of God and Islam as a distinct religion had been adopted by that institution within seventy years of its foundation. At the same time, there was at least an incipient version of a collection of texts that was eventually canonized as the Koran, as witnessed by the inscriptions on the Dome of the Rock, also completed in the reign of ʿAbd al Malik.

None of this is, of course, sufficient to validate the picture of the origin of Islam that was propagated by the literary elite of the ninth century, but does indicate that more history is available to us than can be derived from documents. This issue constitutes the main difference between the approaches of Wansbrough, on the one hand, and Crone and Cook, on the other, to the origins of Islam. While Wansbrough eschews any attempt at a reconstruction of "what really happened," beyond such gnomic utterances as those quoted above, Crone and Cook put forward a positive thesis that contradicts the traditional account and lays itself open to refutation and critical attack; but even Wansbrough's sparse assertions are vulnerable to the hard facts of architecture and numismatics.

Once the traditional picture of the origin of Islam is laid aside the problem resolves itself into two questions: (1) Did Islam as a religious phenomenon begin before or after the Arab conquests? (2) Was it a development from or against Judaism or Christianity or both? Crone and Cook would answer the first question "before," and the second "from Judaism"; Wansbrough would answer the first question "after," and the second question, probably, "from and against both"; Lüling would answer the first question "before," and the second question "from and against Christianity." When scholars who have spent their lifetimes examining the same source material in the original languages can come up with such contradictory conclusions, the problem is obviously not easily solved, and is perhaps susceptible to whatever bias is brought to the subject. The old Pascalian adage may apply here as elsewhere: There is always enough evidence for those who want to believe (whatever), and never enough for those who do not.

If the Koranic texts on the Dome of the Rock and the inscriptions on the coinage are taken as our hardest evidence for what counted as "Islam" at the end of the seventh century, there is a case for taking the Koran and the Prophet as fundamental elements of the faith from the beginning, remembering that "Koran" simply means "reading" or "recitation," and that *rasūl Muhammad* could be an office that never had an incumbent. The danger is that given the existence of these ideological shibboleths we read into them, at the seventh-century stage, all that the scholarly elite of the ninth century would like us to believe about them. It has been argued, for instance, that because the inscriptions on the Dome of the Rock resemble phrases and short passages from the canonical Koran, that text must have existed in the reign of ʿAbd al Malik as a perfect exemplar from which it was permitted to deviate in order to form an argument against Christians.[25] The logic of this assertion is hard to follow. Why could not a fixed text have been assembled later from already existing fluid and fragmentary texts? All the inscriptions on the Dome of the Rock and the coinage demonstrate is that Koranic sentiments and phraseology were in circulation at the end of the seventh century. This is hardly surprising and does not contradict Wansbrough, since he never denied the existence of Koranic logia from an early period. Apart from these considerations it is obviously impermissible to argue from the existence of fragments of a text to the existence of the whole, especially when those fragments are either polemical or of a type used in prayer and thus most likely of all to have existed from the beginning.

If the sentiments of the Dome of the Rock and coinage inscriptions are anti-Christian, in their assertion of one God as a refutation of "polytheists" in the sense of trinitarians, this could be in favor of monotheist Judaism, as Crone and Cook might argue, or of a nontrinitarian aboriginal Christianity, as argued by Lüling. Whichever the case, it could have begun either before or after the conquests, either in northern Arabia or the Fertile Crescent. What the role of Muhammad might have been in such a development is, again, a matter of choice. In Wansbrough's account of postconquest developments, the Prophet appears as little more than a cipher, a more or less inevitable feature of any religious evolution from Middle Eastern monotheism, necessary as a channel for revelation and as a moral example for the nascent community. Basing themselves on Syriac and Greek sources contemporary with the conquests, Crone and Cook have no doubts about Muhammad's historicity.[26] Indeed, Crone seems most enamored of the traditional, not to say Romantic, image of the Prophet: "There is no doubt that Muhammad lived in the 620s and

630s A.D., that he fought in wars, and that he had followers some of whose names are likely to have been preserved,"[27] and even goes as far as to declare that "it is a fact that whichever way the origins of Islam are explained, Islamic civilization is the only one to begin in the mind of a single man."[28] In this respect, if in no other, Crone is in agreement with Lüling, the difference resides in their wholly opposed conceptions of the nature of ur-Islam.

As already noted, the companion volume to Lüling's *On the Ur-Koran* is his *Rediscovery of the Prophet Muhammad: A Criticism of the "Christian" Orient*. We have already had occasion to mention most of the features of Lüling's "rediscovered" Muhammad when illustrating his reconstruction of the Christian hymnody in the text of the Koran. The chief feature of Lüling's newly discovered Prophet is that he is the messenger for an Ebionite Judaeo-Christianity, which is taken as the ur-Christianity of Christ himself. This ur-Christianity is also an ur-Judaism in the form of a cult of the Hero Messiah at the groves on the High Places of the northern kingdom of Israel, a cult known to Lüling's Muhammad as the religion of Abraham, Ishmael, and the tribes; this ur-Christianity is opposed to the Hellenistic trinitarian Christianity of the imperial Roman Church. Both these Christianities are imagined by Lüling as existing in central Arabia and the Ḥijāz during Muhammad's lifetime.

Now, in comparison with the views of Wansbrough, Crone, and Cook, this is obviously a very different kind of thesis; one not so much drawn from the sources usually utilised for establishing the origins of Islam, as one born elsewhere and brought to those sources seeking confirmation wherever it can be found. It is in fact a thesis that brings with it a lot of baggage carried over from a German Protestant, liberal theological study of the Old and New Testaments, and a psychologically driven reading of anthropology, linguistics, and world religions; a thesis born of an obssessional program extraneous to Islam as such. Lüling's Muhammad is, in effect, the embodiment and protagonist of his own preoccupations; not so much a "rediscovery" as a reinvention in his own image.

Extraordinary as it might seem, the mission for world peace and understanding of Muhammad in seventh-century Arabia turns out to be the same as that of Günter Lüling at the beginning of the third millenium: the abandonment of the imperialistic orthodoxies of Judaism, Christianity, and Islam, and a return to a prehistoric henotheism. Even more extraordinary, Lüling appears to expect modern Muslims to welcome his rediscovery of this previously unknown Muhammad, along with his uncovering of Christian hymnody at the base of their holy book, and embrace his vision of a new/old religion as spiritual inspiration in the new millenium, even though it is not a new millenium for them. For a man who has spent a large part of his life in the Middle East, this shows a surprising naïveté about the mentality of Muslims.

Lüling's view of Muhammad and the origin of Islam is not only opposed to the traditional account, but also to the "revisionist" hypotheses of Wansbrough, Crone, Cook, and Hawting. In a lengthy preface written for the English edition of his book on the ur-Koran, Lüling makes an attempt to refute the revisionist approach to the origins of Islam. In general terms, the revisionists are castigated for dismissing the huge body of Islamic literature, dating from 800 C.E. and later, as historically worthless, rather than painstakingly sifting through it, using the source-separating and text-separating methods of linguistic, literary, historical, and theologico-dogmatic text criticism. These are the methods, presumably, that enabled Lüling to come to his equally revisionist conclusions about Muhammad and the origins of Islam; the difference being that whereas Lüling questions everything in the Muslim sources apart from their overall geographical and chronological framework, the anglophone revisionists question this, too. The problem with the methods advocated by Lüling is that the researcher tends to end up with evidence for whatever prejudice he starts out with. If he takes it for granted that the traditional Islamic account of events must be basically true, he will find evidence for that; if, like Lüling, he assumes there has been a massive coverup of what really happened, he finds evidence for that, and so on. Lüling manages to find evidence for both the traditional account with regard to the framework, and his own idiosyncratic version of revisionism, as it suits him.

A contemporary scholar whose methods Lüling would probably approve is Michael Lecker,[29] who has sifted throgh mountains of detailed source material about early Medina in search of "hidden pearls" of historical truth, the assumption being that it all has to be either true or fabricated, since "it would be absurd to argue that the fine, detailed information we have on certain aspects of early Islamic Medina is unusable or entirely the outcome of later inventions."[30] Unfortunately, as Patricia Crone has pointed out,[31] Lecker's "hidden pearls" of historical truth turn out to be nothing of the kind, but simply endless contradictory anecdotes that make no difference to the overall picture of events. Anecdote piled upon anecdote is in fact what makes up the bulk of historical material on early Islam, all carried by the basic framework of a Ḥijāzi origin at Mecca and Medina, if that goes the rest goes with it, at least in that context.

Lüling also objects to the revisionist thesis on the grounds that it shows a superficial understanding of such concepts as monotheism, polytheism, Judaism, and Christianity, as well as plain ignorance of the religio-historical situation in central Arabia, so that it has to be conjectured that a religion such as Islam could not possibly have originated there. A further complaint is that the "mainstream of oriental monotheism" (Wansbrough), out of which Islam is supposed to have emerged, is chiefly identified by the revisionists with Judaism rather than Christianity; the classic texts of C. C. Torrey and A. Katsch on Judaism on Islam,[32] are said to have been long since disproved, but we are not told how, where, when, or by whom. Gerald Hawting is especially singled out for attention, seemingly because in his book on idolatry and early Islam,[33] he is seen as having trespassed on Lüling's patch without giving him due recognition, especially with regard to his insistence upon a Christian presence at Mecca and elswhere in central Arabia. Hawting lists Lüling's book on Muhammad in his bibliography, but does not refer to him in the text, probably because he had already published his views on Lüling's theories almost twenty years previously, when they first appeared in their German editions.

In his review of *The Rediscovery of the Prophet Muhammad*, Hawting acknowledges that Lüling has made several important points with which he can agree:

> for example, the drawing of attention (pp. 153 ff.) to the tension which is observable in Muslim sanctuary traditions and practises between, on the one hand, the concept of the sanctuary as something which is entered and within which rituals are performed and, on the other, the idea that the sanctuary is closed and venerated externally, seems perceptive and important. I also share Lüling's views on the importance of the traditions about the area of the sanctuary called *al ḥijr* (pp. 133 ff.) and the curiously unconvincing nature of the reports about the idols said to have been destroyed by the Prophet at the time of the *fatḥ* (pp. 168 ff.). Again, I find attractive the argument (pp. 183 ff.) that words

> like *shirk* and *mushrikūn* may, in the Qur'an and elsewhere, be understood as polemic and not as references to polytheists or idolators in the literal sense. More generally, his view that the Qur'an can be seen as containing material which cannot all be attributed to one individual is, when expressed in this way, in keeping with recent Qur'anic studies, and the similarity between Muslim prophetology and what we know of the prophetology of Judaeo- Christianity, which Lüling adopts from H. J. Schoeps, is striking and, as Schoeps presents it, persuasive.[34]

However, the way in which these points are elaborated and developed into a wider thesis show "significant weaknesses in argumentation and in method."[35]

Now, Lüling's thesis about the origin of Islam, no less than that of the revisionists, involves the rewriting history; what, up to now, is generally thought to have happened, is not what either party thinks really happened. The main difference between them being that Lüling is convinced he has found the truth; there is only one right way of reading the evidence, his way. In Lüling's writing arguments are always "proven," or "clearly demonstrated," and counterarguments are long since "disproved," and unworthy of attention; nothing is put forward as a hypothesis for consideration, but as established fact resulting from an infallible method, while those who disagree are either ignorant or ill-motivated. Lüling accuses the revisionists, Hawting in particular, of dismissing Muslim tradition as unreliable while at the same time relying on it when it suits them. *But this is precisely what he does himself.* According to Lüling there has been a massive rewriting of history by the Muslim traditionists themselves, but he still relies on that tradition to confirm his favored theses about Christians in Mecca, the appearance and use of the Kaaba, Muhammad's biography, and so on. Moreover, if both parties are guilty of at once dismissing and using the tradition as it suits them, Lüling is the more guilty in that he assumes that the truth of "what really happened" was generally known, but that a massive amnesia was somehow imposed by "orthodox" Islam, whereas the thesis of the revisionists is that "what really happened" was *not* known, which is precisely the circumstance that favored the invention of so many conflicting stories. The traditional Islamic picture of the origin of Islam was not a massive rewriting of events that were common knowledge, but the pious filling of an embarrassing void.

The problem with Lüling's general method of arguing was well diagnosed by Hawting as a failure to distinguiush between evidence which unambiguously says what he wants it to say, of which there is hardly any, and evidence that can somehow be made to support his hypotheses:

> Having argued, for instance, that the *mushrikūn* were not really polytheists (and there is no way of proving this), Lüling then goes on to show that they were Hellenistic, trinitarian and iconodule Christians. His proofs for this, though, seem to be entirely external, in the sense that they depend on other arguments, which themselves start from questionable presuppositions; the identity of the *mushrikūn* is not clearly or persuasively shown from the information pertaining to them in the Muslim traditions. . . . Again, the traditions about al-Hijr do not themselves lead to Lüling's conclusion that it was once the apse of a church.
>
> This conclusion . . . is rather imposed on the material and rests on ideas which depend on other evidence and the inferences drawn from it. In short, it seems to me, that there is a failure to maintain a proper relationship between the author's ideas and the evidence, and one is involved in a sort of circular argument where conclusions about one body of evidence constantly depend upon conclusions about another.[36]

If these strictures apply to Lüling's arguments for the historical background of early Islam, they must apply also to his reasoning on the nature of the material he thinks he finds in the *rasm* of the ur-Koran. As Hawting goes on to say, describing Lüling's methods of restoring this supposed ur-Koran:

> In general the method of restoration consists of the reinterpretation of certain key words, slight changes in the vocalisation or consonant structure of the text which has come down to us, and sometimes in the relationship which has traditionally been accepted between certain sentences or clauses. Again, it seems to me that the argument is essentially circular and that since there is no way of controlling or checking the recomposed *Ur-Qurʾan*, there is a danger that it will be recomposed to suit one's own preconceptions about what one will find in it.[37]

In short, Lüling's case for finding Christian hymnody in the ur-Koran is unverified and unverifiable. Perhaps this is overstating the case against.

The material in the Koran has to have come from somewhere and, as we have seen, Hawting himself admits that it cannot all be attributed to one individual. If Lüling is right about central Arabia being full of Christians, or, more likely, if the revisionists are right about the milieu of early Islam being the predominantly Christian Hellenistic north, the likelihood surely is that at least some of the underlying material in the text of the Koran would be of Christian origin. There is evidence that this could have been the case that does not involve any of Lüling's dubious speculations and circular arguments, as we hope to indicate in the conclusion.

Without his grand plans for the spiritual future of mankind, and without his assumption of a large Christian presence in central Arabia, Lüling's main thesis on the ur-Koran is not implausible. The main problem is his insistence upon Mecca and the *Ḥijāz* as the location where it all happened. Once again the crucial objections to his postion have been well stated by Hawting when he points out that Lüling

> accepts that all of the material which Muslim tradition preserves and applies to the Ka'ba at Mecca did in fact originate with regard to the Meccan Ka'ba.
>
> In other words, he accepts the view that in the time of the Prophet Islam took over the Meccan sanctuary, and that all the many reports, often difficult to understand and sometimes contradictory, about the develoment of the sanctuary in the early Muslim period, in fact refer to the sanctuary at Mecca. If one is starting from a sceptical position, then there is no reason why one should accept this, and it seems to me to make more sense to envisage that some of the sanctuary material did not originally relate to the Meccan sanctuary but that it has been adapted by Muslim tradition and made to apply to Mecca at a secondary stage.
>
> Again, the general point is that if one believes, as Lüling does, that Muslim tradition has deliberately falsified the historical record, why should we accept the main framework which that tradition provides?[38]

This is not only the main argument against Lüling, it is the main revisionist argument against the traditional Muslim picture of the origin of Islam, and all the Western scholarship that has taken it at face value.

A final point worth noting is one upon which Lüling is more radical than the revisionists. In his newly composed preface to the English edition of his book on the ur-Koran, he criticizes Wansbrough for taking the

Islamic tradition seriously with regard to there having been an oral tradition in the transmission of Koran texts. Basing himself on the work of Fritz Kernow and others, Lüling declares that there was in principle no oral tradition at all, neither for old Arabic poetry nor for the Koran, and that Wansbrough, in using this traditional idea in his revisionist theory, goes against his own principles. If Lüling is right about this it would explain the role of the *quṣṣāṣ*, the storytellers of early Islam, who appear to have had a free hand in inventing the provenance and meaning of Koran texts; they could say whatever they liked because there was no one who knew any better in order to contradict them. Once a text was known to be "Koran" it would be remembered for use in prayers, sermons, and polemic, but it was not remembered as issuing from the mouth of "the Prophet."

CONCLUSION

That there was a pre-Islamic Koran is something about which Lüling and the revisionists can agree. Speculating on the reasons for there being so much that is obscure in the text of the Koran, not only to us but also to the earliest Muslim commentators, Michael Cook proposes two possible explanations:

> One is to suppose that the materials which make up the Koran did not become generally available as a scripture until several decades after the Prophet's death, with the result that by the time this happened, memory of the original meaning of the material had been lost. The other is to speculate that *much of what found its way into the Koran was already old by the time of Muhammad* [our italics]. The two approaches do not exclude each other. Each has its attractions, and each has its problems—notably the need to reject much of what our narrative sources tell us.[39]

As far as the revisionists are concerned, what most needs to be rejected from the narrative sources is the origin of Islam at Mecca and Medina in the Ḥijāz.

Remaining true to the fundamental thesis of *Hagarism*, Cook draws attention to several factors that indicate a non-Ḥijāzi region as the background for Islam. The Koran often speaks of seafaring, when there is no record in the *sira* of Muhammad ever having been to sea. In this connection it is curious to note that the most plausible etymology of "Quraysh," the Prophet's tribe, is that it means "shark," or at least some kind of fish.[40] Why would a central Arabian tribe be named after a fish? There is also the curious fact that XXXVII.133–38 refers to the site of the destruction of Sodom and Gomorrah (Genesis 19), which is traditionally located on the borders of Palestine, as a place that "you," presumably meaning Muhammad, pass by "in the morning and the night." Why would he do this if he was centered in the Ḥijāz? It is from this same region that we have the important testimony of the fifth-century Christian historian Sozomenus, who tells of a group of Arabs who had come into contact with Jews and learned from them their biblical descent from Abraham's son Ishmael, and who thereafter adopted Jewish laws and customs.[41] As Cook acknowledges, this would not amount to Islam as we know it, but it provides a plausible location for the acquisition of a fusion of monotheism and Arab identity, long before the Koran and the Prophet.

In conformity with the drift of these facts is the archaeological evidence from the Negev desert, marshaled by Y. D. Nevo and J. Koren. They note that, despite extensive excavations in the Syro-Jordanian desert, the Arabian peninsula, and especially the Ḥijāz, no remains of pagan sanctuaries from the sixth and seventh centuries have been found, and that in fact there are very few indications that the Ḥijāz was much inhabited in the fifth to seventh centuries C.E., and certainly not by any people using any form of classical Arabic. On the other hand, there is evidence for an active pagan cult in the central Negev that existed from Nabatean times down to the start of the ʿAbbasid period in the second half of the second/eighth century. Moreover, many features of the material remains of this cult resemble the Muslim descriptions of the shrine at Mecca, while there is also literary and epigraphical evidence of a monotheistic cult of Abraham in the Negev. The largest pagan sanctuary at Sde Boqer shared its site with a sect of monotheistic Arabs whose many rock inscriptions in classical Arabic in the Kufic script reveal a Judaeo-Christian flavor. These features conform to elements in the traditional account of early Islam, for which they could well have served as models, and then transferred to Mecca and the Ḥijāz in the literary sources, as suggested by Hawting and others.[42]

We have already seen how Lüling cites J. S. Trimingham's *Christianity Among the Arabs in Pre-Islamic Times* as confirming his thesis of widespread Christianity in the Ḥijāz and central Arabia, and how, in fact, it does nothing of the kind; not only that, but this work in reality provides much evidence for the revisionist thesis of a northern origin for Islam.

To take a few points more or less at random, we may note the following: "The particular form *Allāh* need not be thought of aṣ an Arab contraction of *al-ʿilāh*, but as a proper name for God, coming through Aramaic, as the absolute state of *Alāhā*, the most used form in Syriac (see Payne Smith, *Thesaurus Syriacus*, I. col. 195–96). This was the name of God among Nabateans and other north-Arabian inscription writers. Its usage in compound names like *whbʾlh* necessitates vocalising as *Wahb Allāh*, "Gift of God," not "gift of the god," showing the divine name to be *Allah* and not a contraction of *al-ʾilāh*."[43]

While discussing the spread of Christianity in the Syro-Arab region, Trimingham refers to two tribes that are mentioned in a number of inscriptions: the Khasētēroi and Audēnoi of the villages of Merdoch and Rimea in the Hawrān east of Palestine. Of the Khasētēroi he says: "It has been suggested that they were a clan of the Azd who migrated to southern Syria around A.D. 200 under chiefs Jafna, Mujālid, ʿAws and Khazraj (clan names). The last two groups of ʿAws and Khazraj returned later to settle in the Ḥijāz, but other clans stayed in Syria to make their reappearance as the Banū Ghassān."[44] How do we know any of this? If it is only from Muslim sources, it must be regarded as suspect. The ʿAws and Khazraj were parties to the notorious "al Aqaba" and "Constitution of Medina" agreements. Why could they simply have never moved from the Hawrān region on the borders of Palestine, and this be the real location where the "Constitution of Medina" was contracted, "Medina" being any town in the region?

When discussing the heads of the Tanūkh tribe, Trimingham mentions Jadhīma (or Judhaima) al Waḍḍāh al Abrash, who, Ṭabarī (I.750) reports Ibn Kalbī as saying, ruled the territory that "lay between Ḥīra, Anbār, Baqqa, Hīt, and district."[45] Ḥīra, Anbār, and Hīt all lay along the Euphrates, but the location of Baqqa appears to be unknown. Could this be the location of the Baqqa mentioned in the Koran (III.90), which most exegetes are eager to identify with Mecca in the Ḥijāz, but which really lay somewhere between Anbār and Hīt, on the Euphrates? It may also be significant that the Arabic script known as Kufic was in common usage among the Ibād, the Arab Christians of al Iraq al Arabi. Ṭabarī (*Ta'rīkh*, I. 206) reports that when the Arabs of that region were asked, "From whom did you learn letters?" they replied, "We learned the script from the Iyād." Trimingham goes on to say: "It is claimed that the script through which the Qur'an was preserved was taken from the Christian Arabs of Ḥīra and Anbār, carried to Dūma and from there to Mecca."[46] Perhaps, in reality, the last part of that journey was unnecessary.

The Syriac influence on the Koran has long been noted. A crude word count of the foreign vocabulary shows a predominance of Syriac words, closely followed by Aramaic;[47] the latter was the Middle Eastern lingua franca, and Syriac the language of the semi-independent Syriac church, split into the factions of Monophysites and Nestorians. Of particular significance is the influence of Syriac on the Koran's religious terminology, almost all of which is derived from that language, including the words for God, soul, last judgment, salvation, sacrifice, resurrection, heaven, angel, priest, Christ, and prayer; this influence also appears in such theological expressions as "light upon light," and upon semibiblical quotations and biblical events and facts. In comparison, the Jewish influence upon the religious vocabulary of the Koran is negligible. Alphonse Mingana, who is the source of these observations, also remarks on the fact that, given the proximity and alleged intimacy between the Ḥijāz and Abyssinia, "the only Ethiopic religious influence on the style of the Kur'an is in the word *ḥawāriyūn*, 'Apostles.' "[48]

The Syriac church regarded itself as descended from Saint Thomas rather than Saint Peter, and had many distinctive features that may account for the odd character attributed to Christianity in the Koran. From the beginning the church emphasized that there is one God, the God of the Old Testament, who sent the Messiah. Doctrinally it was divided between the factions of the Nestorians and Monophysites, regarded as heresies by the parent Greek church. Monophysitism, the idea that Christ had one nature, not two as defined by the Council of Chalcedon (451), produced, in the territory of the Arab tribe of the Banū Ghassān, a reaction in the form of a farther heresy, tritheism, the idea that since the divine nature belongs to each of the hypostases (Father, Son, and Holy Ghost) there are in reality three gods. This could have contributed to the Koranic notion that Christians worship three gods (e.g., V.116).[49] This point gains credibility when the widespread presence of the *Diatessaron* in the Syriac church is taken into account.

The *Diatessaron* (Gr. "through [the] four [gospels]") is a gospel harmony created about the year 172 by the Mesopotamian scholar Tatian.[50] Its importance lies in the fact that it is the earliest extant collection of second-century gospel texts, and is probably the form in which the gospels first appeared in Syriac, Latin, Armenian, and Georgian. The importance of this work for the study of the Koran rests on the fact that, in addition to the four canonical gospels, it incorporated Judeo-Christian elements, most probably from the *Gospel of the Hebrews*.[51] It is from this source incorporated in the *Diatessaron* that the Koranic notion of tritheism in the form of God, Jesus, and Mary most probably derives, since it is in this gospel that an assimilation of Mary to the Holy Spirit took place. Origen, in a commentary on the *Gospel of the Hebrews*, tells us that it depicts Jesus as saying: "Even now did my mother the Holy Spirit take me by one of mine hairs, and carried me away unto the great mountain Thabar." Such an expression probably derived from the fact that in Hebrew the word for "spirit" is feminine.[52]

The *Diatessaron* sets sections of Matthew, Mark, and Luke into John's framework. It begins with the Johannine prologue about the Word, continues with Luke's account of the angelic annunciations to Zechariah and Mary, and follows with Matthew's report of how Mary was found to be pregnant by the Holy Spirit. This is similar to the Koran's view of Jesus as God's Word, which he casts into Mary, and with the apparent identification of the angel Gabriel with the Holy Spirit. It is also worthy of note that the *Diatessaron* says of Mary that no man had known her, rather than that she did not know a man (Luke 1:34), making the male the active partner, reflected in III.47 and XIX.20.[53]

Familiarity with the *Diatessaron* in the hands of Nestorian and Monophysite Christians may well have given the impression to non-Christian Arabs that the gospel (*injīl*) was one book. In addition, it would explain several features of the Koranic view of the Old and New Testaments, particularly the fact that the Old Testament personages are, with few exceptions, of the patriarchal period. Adam, Abel, Noah, Abraham, Lot, Isaac, Jacob, Moses, David, Elijah, Elisha, and Jonah, are all mentioned in the Koran and the *Diatessaron* with either complete identity of spelling or a close relationship.[54]

Knowledge of the *Diatessaron*, or even the canonical gospels in their Syriac interpretation, is not of course sufficient to account for all the features of Jesus and Christianity to be found in the Koran; much is obviously drawn from the apocryphal infancy gospels such as the Protevangelium of James, the Infancy Story of Thomas, and the Gospel of Pseudo-Matthew. Nor is it possible to say that the influence is more Monophysite than Nestorian. As Neal Robinson has said of the Koran: "In agreement with the Nestorians it stresses the full humanity of Jesus and Mary. In agreement with the Monophysites it emphasises that God is One. In opposition to both it rejects all Trinitarian language and all talk of divine Sonship no matter how it is understood."[55] What is clear, however, is that the milieu in which much of the Koran took shape was strongly Christian, albeit of a somewhat less than orthodox nature.

Such a conclusion is hardly new or radical.[56] In the days of the old scholarship, before the appearance of the revisionists, when the Ḥijāzi origin of Islam and the traditional biography of the Prophet was more or less taken for granted, all such conjecture as those above would have been accompanied by speculations as to where, when, and how Muhammad could have acquired all the diverse and obscure information in the Koran, usually on his trading trips to the north. Günter Lüling, in a move that is at once revisionist and traditional, solves the problem by shifting all those influences into the Ḥijāz, making Mecca a cosmopolitan center for practically every religious faction existing in the seventh-century Middle East. Since the evidence for this is either nonexistent or susceptible to alternative explanations, the solution of the revisionists appears to hold the field.

Without the Ḥijāz, and without the Prophet as sole source for the Koran text, many new hypotheses become possible, including that of pre-Islamic hymnody in the *rasm* of the ur-Koran. If the milieu of Koran formation was antiorthodox Christian, as we have seen that it probably was, Lüling could even be right that the Christian element underlying the Koran was not straight forward Hellenic orthodoxy, but was antitrinitarian and considered Jesus as both created and angelic. The provenance of such views, however, is already known in the arc of the Fertile Crescent. To postulate an unverified and unverifiable location in the Ḥijāz appears an unnecessary extravagance that jeopardises the acceptance of valuable insights. Lüling needs the revisionists, and the revisionist should regard Lüling as one of their own.

NOTES

1. See G. Lüling, "Preconditions for the Scholarly Criticism of the Koran and Islam, with some Autobiographical Remarks," *Journal of Higher Criticism* 3, no.1 (spring 1996): 81.

2. Ibid., pp. 89–90.

3. Ibid., p. 95.

4. Ibid., pp. 96–99.

5. See also M. Cook, *The Koran: A Very Short Introduction* (Oxford, Oxford University Press, 2000), chap. 7, and Y. H. Safadi, *Islamic Calligraphy* (London: Thames & Hudson, 1978).

6. First and foremost that of Joshua Blau, *A Grammar of Christian Arabic* (Louvain, 1966), based mainly on South Palestinian texts of the first millenium.

7. Also Noldeke, *Geschichte des Qorans*, I, pp. 78 ff.

8. See Guillaume, trans. *The Life of Muhammad* (Oxford: Oxford University Press, 1978), pp. 104–107.

9. See Ibn Hishām, *Sīra*, ed. Wustenfeld, vol. 2, p. 67, lines 4–16. Ibn Hishām quotes this "seventeen" as a tradition of *ahl at tafsīr*, "people of Koran exegesis." The late Koran commentary *Tafsīr al Jālālain* also refers to this variant reading "seventeen" in Sura LXXIV.30.

10. For a preliminary examination of some of the problems involved in the idea of nineteen in the Koran see Ibn al Rawandi, *Islamic Mysticism: A Secular Perspective* (Amherst, N.Y.: Prometheus Books, 2000), pp. 201–24.

11. J. S. Trimingham, *Christianity Among the Arabs in Pre-Islamic Times* (London: Longman, 1979), pp. 249–58.

12. Ibid., pp. 276–77.

13. Irfan Shahid, *Byzantium and the Arabs in the Fifth Century* (Washington, D.C.: Dumbarton Oaks, 1989), p. 387.

14. For a brief overview of these developments see Ibn al Rawandi, "Origins of Islam: A Critical look at the Sources," in *The Quest for the Historical Muhammad*, ed. Ibn Warraq (Amherst, N.Y.: Prometheus Books, 2000, pp. 89–124.

15. J. Wansbrough, *Quranic Studies: Sources and Methods of Scriptural Interpretation* (Oxford: Oxford University Press, 1977), p. 179.

16. Ibid., p. 51.

17. See P. Crone, *Meccan Trade and the Rise of Islam* (Oxford, Blackwells, 1987), pp. 134–37, and P. Crone and M. Cook, *Hagarism: The Making of the Islamic World* (Cambridge: Cambridge University Press, 1977), pp. 24, 173 n. 30.

18. See A. Jeffrey, *The Foreign Vocabulary of the Qur'an* (Baroda: Oriental Institute, 1938).

19. J. Wansbrough, *The Sectarian Milieu: Context and Composition of Islamic Salvation History* (Oxford Oxford University Press, 1978), p. 99.

20. Ibid., p. 127.

21. Ibid., p. 124.

22. See P. Crone and M. Hinds, *God's Caliph: Religious Authority in the First Century of Islam* (Cambridge: Cambridge University Press, 1978), p. 99.

23. See F. Robinson, ed., *The Cambridge Illustrated History of the Islamic World* (Cambridge: Cambridge University Press), 1996, p. 13.

24. For Wansbrough's view of Crone and Cook see the remarks on *Hagarism* in *The Sectarian Milieu*, pp. 116–19, and the review of same in *The Bulletin of the School of Oriental and African Studies* 41 (1978): 155–56; also the review of *Meccan Trade*, in *BSOAS* 52 (1989): 339–40. For a reply, see Michael Cook's review of *The Sectarian Milieu*, in *Journal of the Royal Asiatic Society* (1980): 180–82.

25. See Whelan, E., "Forgotten Witness: evidence for the early codification of the Qur'an," *Journal of the American Oriental Society* (January–March 1998): 5.

26. See M. Cook, *Muhammad* (Oxford: Oxford University Press, 1983), p. 74, and Crone and Cook, *Hagarism*, chap. 1.

27. P. Crone, *Slaves on Horses: The Evolution of the Islamic Polity* (Cambridge: Cambridge University Press, 1980), p. 15.

28. Ibid., p. 23.

29. M. Lecker, *Muslims, Jews and Pagans: Studies on Early Islamic Medina* (Leiden: E. J. Brill, 1995).

30. Ibid., p. 49.

31. See P. Crone, review of *Muslims, Jews and Pagans*, *JSS* 42 (1997): 182–85

32. See C. C. Torrey, *Jewish Foundations of Islam* (New York: Ktav Publishing House, 1967), and A. Katsch, *Judaism in Islam* (New York: New York University Press, 1954).

33. G. R. Hawting, *The Idea of Idolatry and the Emergence of Islam: From Polemic to History* (Cambridge, Cambridge University Press, 1999).

34. G. R. Hawting, review of *Die Widerentdeckung des Propheten Muhammad*, *JSS* 27 (1982): 109.

35. Ibid., p. 110.

36. Ibid., pp. 110–11.

37. Ibid., p. 111.

38. Ibid., p. 112.

39. Cook, *The Koran: A Very Short Introduction*, pp. 137–38.

40. See Jeffrey, *The Foreign Vocabulary of the Qur'an*, pp. 236–37.

41. See Shahid, *Byzantium and the Arabs in the Fifth Century*, pp. 167–80, 332–49.

42. See Y. D. Nevo and J. Koren, "The Origins of the Muslim Descriptions of the Jahili Meccan Sanctuary," *Journal of Near Eastern Studies* 49 (1990): 23–44.

43. Trimingham, *Christianity Among the Arabs*, p. 251 n. 14.

44. Ibid., p. 78.

45. Ibid., p. 154.

46. Ibid., p. 227.

47. See Jeffrey, *The Foreign Vocabulary of the Qur'an*, pp. 298–311. Alphonse Mingana estimated that "taking the number 100 as a unit of the foreign influences on the style and terminology of the Kur'an Ethiopic would represent about 5 per cent. of the total, Hebrew about 10 per cent., the Graeco-Roman languages about 10 per cent., Persian about 5 per cent., and Syriac (including Aramaic and Palestinian Syriac) about 70 per cent." "Syriac Influences on the Style of the Kur'an," *Bulletin of the John Rylands Library* 11 (1927): 80 (chapter 3.1 of this volume.)

48. Ibid., p. 87.

49. Trimingham, *Christianity Among the Arabs*, pp. 183–84.

50. See the essay "Tatian's Diatessaron," by W. L. Pearson, in *Ancient Christian Gospels: Their History and Development*, ed. H. Koester (London: SCM Press, 1990), pp. 403–30.

51. Ibid., p. 412 n. 2.

52. M. R. James, *The Apocryphal New Testament* (Oxford: Clarendon Press, 1969), p. 2. See also G. Parrinder, *Jesus in the Qur'an* (London: Sheldon Press, 1965), pp. 134–37.

53. See N. Robinson, *Christ in Islam and Christianity* (New York: SUNY, 1991), pp. 18 ff.

54. See J. Bowman, "The Debt of Islam to Monophysite Christianity," *Nederlands Theologisch Tijdschrift* 19 (1964–65): 177–201.

55. N. Robinson, *Christ in Islam and Christianity*, p.20.

56. See R. Bell, *The Origins of Islam in Its Christian Environment* (New York: Macmillan & Co., 1926).

Part 9
MANUSCRIPTS

9.1

The Problem of Dating the Early Qur'āns

Adolf Grohmann

In 1947 Prof. Dr. Giorgio Levi della Vida[1] published a valuable and interesting contribution to Arabic palaeography by editing fragments of parchment Qur'āns, acquired by the Vatican Library in 1946; they formerly belonged to the collection of Tammaro de Marinis, and were probably acquired in Egypt. This publication was made with the usual thoroughness and accuracy characteristic of all the works of Levi della Vida. In his customary cautious manner, he avoids taking a definite position on the difficult problem of dating, especially since it is just this dating of the oldest Qur'ān-manuscripts that is still controversial and undecided. However, I think I am right in assuming that he is more inclined to prefer an earlier dating, proposed by Bernhard Moritz and Nabia Abbott, for he considers the early dating, namely, the second half of the first century of the Islamic era, as at least not impossible, since inscriptions and papyri of this period show a type of writing completely analogous to that of the earliest Qur'ān copies.

So Levi della Vida has, in passing, indicated the only passable way in which the problem of dating the oldest extant copies of the Qur'ān can be solved in a satisfactory manner; and when I here—in a limited way—enter into a discussion of the problem, I would, first, like to express my thanks to the learned scholar on the occasion of his jubilee[2] for his above-mentioned contribution, and then, to explain what more new material, recently brought to light, has contributed toward the solution of this problem of dating.

Adolf Grohmann, "The Problem of Dating the Early Qur'āns," *Der Islam* 33 (1958): 213–31.

While—with one exception[3]—we hitherto possessed Qur'ānic texts on papyrus written only for subsidiary purposes, i.e. in pericopes and included in magic texts,[4] real leaves from a Qur'ān codex have made their appearance in the Collection of George Michaélidès in Cairo, which put scientific research on quite a different basis. As a welcome completion thereto I discovered in the National Egyptian Library in Cairo quite a good number of valuable fragments of early parchment Qur'āns, which had apparently been collected and mounted between two glass plates by the former director of the Egyptian Library, my ever memorable friend B. Moritz, but which obviously had not been utilized by him for his studies. Finally, the last finds of Arabic papyri in Khirbet Mird (Palestine-Jordan) which were liberally made accessible to me by G. Lankester Harding, have enriched our knowledge of the early Arabic script used outside Egypt, and furnished new, hitherto unknown material for palaeographic investigation. I now give a short survey of the state of the problem of dating the oldest Qur'ān manuscripts up to the present.

Since Jacob Christian Lindberg[5] made the first attempt at dating the parchment Qur'ān manuscripts in the Royal Collection in Copenhagen in 1830, and Johann Heinrich Möller,[6] in the appendix to his collection of thirty-one facsimiles of Qur'ān fragments from various centuries in the Ducal Library in Gotha, laid down the first principles and distinctive marks for dating these manuscripts in 1842, showing a fine comprehension of this hazy problem, definite dating of old parchment Qur'āns was practiced by Josef Balthasar Silvestre.[7] He dated specimens from Kufic Qur'āns, formerly belonging to the collection of Michelangelo Lanci (Rome), in the seventh (Pl. iv), ninth (Pl. v, vi), and tenth centuries (Pl. vii, , viii), while William Wright[8] dated the parchment Qur'ān Or. 2165 in the British Museum in the eighth century C.E. But the most important and extensive contribution to Qur'ān palaeography is due to B. Moritz,[9] in whose monumental work Qur'ān manuscripts formed the overwhelming majority. He dated, for example, the big parchment Qur'ān in the Egyptian National Library (formerly in the ʿAmr-Mosque in Old-Cairo) and the copy of the mosque of Sayyidna Husein in Cairo into the first to second century of the Higra, and a Qur'ān from the mosque in Fuwwah (Delta) in the second/third century.

His datations met with a severe criticizm from the part of J. v.

Karabacek, who dated the parchment Qur'āns in Pl. i–xii in the third century A.H. (instead of the first suggested by B. Moritz), xvii–xxx into the third century A.H. (instead of the second, as Moritz did), and Pl. xxxix, xl, xliv in the second century A.H. (eighth century C.E.) instead of Moritz's third century.[10] The monumental publication on the masterpieces of Muhammadan Art, exposed in Munich in 1910, contained Qur'ān manuscripts also, among them Codex Gothanus no. 565, ascribed to the eighth century A.D.,[11] which dating was contested by J. v. Karabacek,[12] who suggested the ninth century C.E. In 1914 Eugen Tisserant[13] published four plates containing Qur'āns of the eighth to the sixteenth century C.E., and in the following year Eugenio Griffini,[14] one page of a Kufic parchment Qur'ān without dating it. An important contribution to Arabic palaeography and especially also the palaeography of Koranic writing was then published in 1919 by Prof. Gotthelf Bergsträsser,[15] who, nevertheless, gives relative datings only ("*älteste, altertümliche Korane*"), qualifying Arabic palaeography Pl. 44, Brit. Mus. Or. 2165 and Paris. Arabe no. 328 (1) and 328 (4) as the oldest or most archaic Qur'ān-copies. Some years later[16] he published a short survey of the script of the Qur'ān manuscripts of the first four centuries of the Higra, and stated that dated copies occur more frequently after the third century A.H.[17] He discerns three styles of writing: (1) Lapidary *Kūfī* (e.g., Arabic Palaeography Pl. 1); (2) a script between this lapidary style and the cursive writing known from the papyri (*ḥijāzī*), e.g., the Qur'ān in the British Museum Or. 2165; and (3) Maghrabi writing. Eight plates with ten photographs complete his short essential survey.

Therewith the main bulk of material, available for the study of the question of dating this kind of Arabic bookscript, was concluded.

The main difficulty for dating this material is obviously formed by the fact that clearly dated copies of the Qur'ān, which could serve as landmarks for dating, are still exceedingly rare: one dated copy exists from the first century and two exist from the second,[18] seven only from the third century of the Hijra.[19] Among the Qur'āns of the first century A.H. there should be—according to I. Y. Kratchkovsky[20]—also included the Qu'rān from Samarqand.[21] At any rate, the opinion about the age of early Qur'āns differs considerably; I shall quote only some of the most important examples: on one hand, Nabia Abbott,[21] for example, considers the

Qur'āns reproduced in B. Moritz's Arabic Palaeography, Pls. i–i2, 31–34 as "the very earliest extant Korans," while Arthur Jeffery is inclined to doubt "whether any fragments we have are from so early a period as the first Islamic century, and one would hesitate to date more than a very few in the second century."[23] I shall come back to these statements later.

But the most spectacular announcement was made by M. Minovi in his "Outline History of Arabic Writing,"[24] where he said that the extant early Qur'ānic specimens are *all* either *forgeries* or *suspect*, and that there was a widespread use of the various *cursive* scripts in early Qur'ānic writing. This spectacular and autoritative statement deserves closer investigation. *Minovi* starts from the illustration of the Meccan-Medinan script in the Chester-Beatty codex no. 3315 of *Ibn an-Nadīm's Kitāb al-Fihrist* in the National Library of Ireland (Dublin), fol. 3 verso last line (see Fig. 1), which he classifies as *cursive*, and concludes thereform that early Qur'āns, said to be written in the Meccan-Medinan scripts, were written in *cursive* scripts.[25] He then refers to the *Galīl*, *Ṭūmār*, *Thuluthain*, and *Thuluth*, all of which he considers as predominantly and equally cursive scripts, restricted to Qur'ānic writing since the coming of the ʿAbbāsids, that is, since the second half of the eighth century C.E. He further says that even the new Qur'ānic scripts, developing at this time, *were also cursive*, for example, the *muḥaqqaq*, and that cursive scripts were widely used for early Qur'ānic writing. Then he says that not many early Qur'āns have survived from the early centuries, and that these Qur'āns were *wholesale forgeries* in Kufic script, which was considered by the forgers as the script current in the first centuries of Islam. He corroborates this theory by pointing to instances of forged documents and some Qur'āns attributed to the Caliph ʿAlī ibn Abī Ṭā lib.

Naturally enough, these suppositions of Minovi met with a severe and just criticizm by N. Abbott, who, in her article already quoted,[26] gave her opinion extensively on Minovi's statements.

a. b.

Fig. 1. The Basmala in Meccan-Medinan script.

a. facsimile drawn by Minovi (*Survey* II, p. 1710. fig. 580)

b. the drawing in the original

(1) She surmises that the illustrative Basmala in the Chester Beatty codex of the *Kitāb al-Fihrist* is in a different script from that of the whole text (p. 70a).

(2) If this specimen represents *the true cursive variety of the Meccan-Medīnan script*, other specimens in this script *should be easily found* in documents dating from these centuries or even from the third. As a matter of fact, N. Abbott could not find any documents from these early centuries written in the script of the sample of the Meccan-Medīnan script in the Chester-Beatty codex. The peculiar Alif of this sample, with its sharp-hooked bend to the left of the top is to be met with in the fourth- and fifth-century script (p. 70 b).

(3) Although Minovi is convinced that this sample really corresponds to the description of the Meccan-Medīnan script given by *Ibn an-Nadīm*, N. Abbott is convinced that it does *not*. Minovi has obviously misunderstood and misinterpreted this description when he says, "the Mecca and Medina scripts were charcterized by an *alif* with a slightly oblique *lower terminus*, slanting to the right, and a *final hooked in the opposite direction*, together with a slightly swaying rhythm."[27] The *correct* interpretation is that there is in its alifs a turning to the right and a raising high of the fingers (i.e., the upright strokes) and there is in its form a slight slant (p. 71).[28]

(4) In contradistinction of Minovi's supposed mass destruction of old Qur'ānic copies, Miss Abbott (p. 72) surmizes that a good number of early Qur'ānic manuscripts have survived, although the extant number of manuscripts is not *suspiciously* large.

(5) While Minovi states his conviction that the great majority of extant Qur'ānic specimens are forgeries of later centuries, he gives no *real* proofs for this supposition, but promises to do so in a forthcoming monograph. Miss Abbott correctly states that even *forged* specimens are expected to give a fair reprensentation of Qur'ānic scripts and practices of the earlier centuries (p. 72b). Although cases of forged deeds and letters are recorded in Arabic literature,[29] she has not come across any references to Qur'ānic forgeries *in general*, and even if a few such references would appear, they would not prove that our extant Qur'ānic specimens are *all*, or almost all, forgeries, and although one should be reasonably suspicious of extant Qur'ān copies attributed to ʿAlī, ʿUthmān, or Ibn Moqla and Ibn al-Bawwāb, it would be oversuspicious to extend these suspicions to all extant Qur'āns of the angular types, as does Minovi.[30]

So far Miss Abbott's objections.

It was clear from the beginning that the capital point in the discussion is the sample of the Basmala occurring in the Chester-Beatty codex of *Ibn an-Nadīm's Kitāb al-Fihrist*, published in facsimile by Minovi[31] (see Fig. 1). Miss Abbott has not had the opportunity to see the original drawing, which obviously forms the cornerstone of Minovi's statements. Since every and even minute detail could be of great importance for the questions under discussion, I asked for photographs of the pages referring to Arabic script in the Chester-Beatty codex no. 3315, and especially also of the Basmala in Meccan-Medīnan writing, and I am greatly obliged to Mr. J. V. S. Wilkinson, librarian of the Chester-Beatty Library in Dublin, for sending me the respective films. A close inspection of the photographs had the following results:

(1) The text of the locus classicus concerning the oldest Arabic scripts given by *Ibn an-Nadīm* (fol. 3 verso) is obviously identical with that offered in the Edition of G. Flügel, p. 63 ff. and the edition of Cairo, Raḥmāniyya Press, 1929/30, p. 8 ff.; it runs:

> *Qāla Muḥammadu'bnu Isḥāqa: fa-'awwalu'l-ḫuṭūṭi'l-ʿarabīyati'l-ḫaṭṭu 'l-Makkīyu wa-baʿdahu ʿl-Madanīyu ṯumma 'l-Baṣrīyu ṯumma 'l-Kūfīyu. Fa-'amma ʿl-Makkīyu wa-'l-Madanīyu fa-fī alifātihi taʿwīgun 'ila yamani 'l-yadi wa-'iʿlā'u 'l-'aṣābiʿi wa-fī šaklihi inḍiǧāʿun yasīrun wa-hāḏā miṯluhu: Bismi 'llāhi'r-Raḥmāni'r-Raḥīmi.*
>
> "Muhammad ibn Isḥāq says: The first Arabic scripts are: the Makkī-script, and after it the Medīnan, then the Baṣran, then the Kūfan. As far as the Meccan and Medīnan are concerned, there is in its Alifs a bend to the right side of the hand, and a raising high of the vertical stokes (*hastae*, fingers) and in its shape a moderate inclination to the side."

So it is quite evident that Minovi's translation is incorrect and misleading (cf. above p. 218); for nothing is said of an oblique lower terminus and a final hooked in the opposite direction, and the translation of *wa-'iʿlā' ul'aṣābiʿi* (a raising high of the *hastae*) is missing.[32]

(2) It is surprising that the Basmala sample in this codex is not, as should have been expected, in a quite *different* script from that of the whole text, but in a hand not essentially differing from the text in which it

is included. This becomes clear from a comparison of the Basmala on fol. 1 verso line 1 and the Meccan Basmala on fol. 3 verso last line; the former differs only in the shape of the slightly curved Alif, and vertical Lām, both of which lack the hooked tops; but those barbed Alifs and Lāms recur several times within the text, just as in fol. 3 verso. Besides, Minovi's copy of the Meccan-Medīnan Basmala sample is not quite exact; it shows throughout barbed tops of the Alifs and Lāms, which really occur in Lām of *ir-Raḥmāni r-Raḥīmi* and in the Alif of *ar-Raḥmāni* only, while the Alif in *allāhi* shows a thickened head as in the Muṣḥaf, no. 77 in the Egyptian National Library. The initial Ḥā has, in Minovi's facsimile, a small loop coming down below the basic line of the letters, quite different from the form in the original, which shows a pointed triangle *on* the basic line. The tail of the Mīm in *Bismi* shows a slight swing in the facsimile, while in the original it is straight, and finally, the flat, slightly curved tail of final-Mīm in *ar-Raḥīmi* is too short in Minovi's facsimile. All these are inaccuracies that should be avoided in such an important sample of writing.

But is there really any chance that the sample of the Basmala in Meccan-Medīnan writing in fact represents this script?

If we compare it with the description if the Meccan-Medīnan script given by Ibn an-Nadīm, we must state that two main characteristics are completely missing in the Alifs of the facsimile, that is, the bend to the right and the pronounced height. Furthermore, the thickened head of the Alif, which may ressemble either a fishing hook or a knob, does not occur before the third century of the Higra, for example, in PER Inv. Ar. Pap. 1920, APEL II no. 50 1 Pl. vi (third century A.H., ninth century C.E.), and is more frequently found only in the second half of the fourth century A.H., for example, in APEL I no. 37 (Pl. III); that is just about the time when Ibn an-Nadīm composed his *Kitāb al-Fihrist* and the first copies thereof came into existence. So it seems doubtful whether the facsimile in the Chester-Beatty codex could be considered as a real representative of the old and original Meccan-Medīnan style of writing. Already Prof. Dr. A. Jeffery[33] has referred to the fact that Ibn an-Nadīm's illustration of the Ḥimyaritic *musnad*-script does not encourage confidence that his information regarding early Arabic script was much more accurate. Although the illustration of this *musnad*-script is much better in the Chester-Beatty codex (fol. 3 verso) than in the Cairo edition (p. 9), even here some characters are obviously misunderstood and others completely ficticious.

The illustration of the Meccan-Medīnan script offers therefore no criterium for the dating of early Qur'ān copies, and gives no clue respecting the genuinity of these copies.

But have we really to give up any hope of dating these Qur'ān copies or to content ourselves with general and somewhat vague characterisations as, for example, "oldest, most archaic," and so on?

In the first place we have to state that it is in fact very difficult to date the first group of Qur'āns, written in a "lapidary style."[34] The hieratic character of this script, the intention to create something special and extraordinary, has led the creative and ingenious calligraphists to develop a copious set of different styles, of which Ibn an-Nadīm[35] gives a long list. I refer only to plates I, iii–vi, viii in G. Bergsträssers treaty in the *Geschichte des Qor'āns* to give a general idea of some of the rich possibilities prevailing for the purpose of rendering the Book of God conspicuous and to distinguish it from other, secular books by a special type of large writing, which is significant of the large-sized Qur'āns of the mosques.

But the second style, called *ḥijāzī* by Bersträsser and others, allows dating, owing to its affinity with the script of papyri. Dated papyri can thereby serve as landmarks,[36] and it is quite important to state that this style of writing is—in contradistinction to the hieratic lapidary script—a *secular* script, used even for economic purposes, as, for example, PER Inv. Ar. Pap. 11077 and 11154, two lists of payments, 11161 a list of persons, 11163 a receipt, and so on, all representing Egyptian writing and coming from the ruins of al-Fusṭāṭ. If we compare the Qur'āns Brit. Mus. Or. 2165, Mss. Paris. Arabe 328 (1), 328 (4)[37] Codex Vat. Ar. 1605,[38] Arabic Palaeography Pl. 44, Istanbul, Saray, Medina 1a,[39] the parchment no. 1700 in the Papyrus-collection of the National Egyptian Library in Cairo (Plate III a) and Inv. Perg. Ar. 2 in the Archduke Rainer Collection in the National Austrian Library in Vienna (Plate Va) with these papyri, it is fairly possible to ascribe them to the first century of the Islamic era (seventh or beginning of eighth century C.E.). Also the papyrus fragment Arabic Palaeography Pl. 43, ascibed by B. Moritz to the third century of the Higra, belongs still to the first century of the Islamic era. Anyhow, this fragment is severely mutilated. But the Qur'ān fragment no. 32 in the Collection George Michaélidès in Cairo is large and much better preserved,

Plate I

Recto

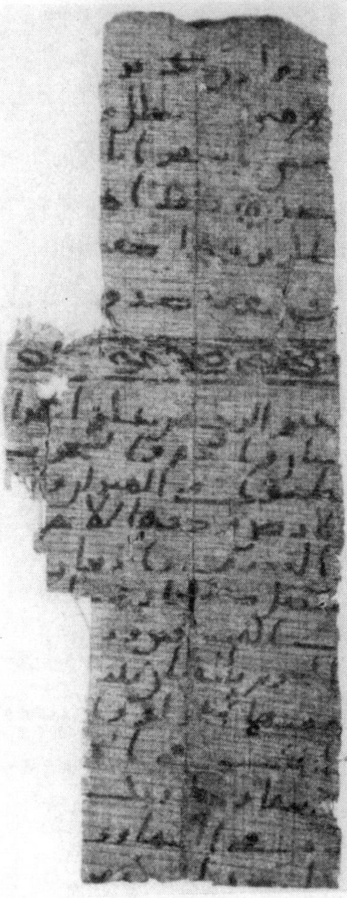

Verso

P. Michaélidès no. 32.

and may therefore serve as a good example of the early Koranic book-hand on papyrus.

Qur'ān LIV.11–38, 45–55, LV.1–32

Brown, fine papyrus. 14.8 x 5.9 cm. On the recto twenty lines, containing Sura LIV.11–38, are written in black ink parallel to the horizontal fibres, the verso bears eighteen lines, running at right angles to the vertical fibres, containing verses 45–55 of Sura LIV, and verses 1–32 of Sura

On the recto:

[(١١) ففتحنا ابواب السمآء بمآء] منهمر(١٢) وفجرنا [الارض عيونا فالتقى المآء]
[على امر قد قدر](١٣) وحملناه [على ذات الوا]ح ودسر(١٤) تجرى باعيننا]
[جزآء لمن كان كفر](١٥) ولقد تر[كنها آياة فهل [من مدكر](١٦) فكيف كان]
[عذابى ونذر](١٧) ولقد يسرنا [القران للذكر فهل [من مدكر](١٨) كذبت عا[د]
[فكيف كان عذابى ونذر](١٩) انا ارسلنا علي[هم ريحا صرصرا فـ[ى]
[يوم نحس مستمر](٢٠) تنزع النا[س كأنهم اعجا[ز نخل منقعر](٢١) فكيف]
[كان عذابى ونذر](٢٢) ولقد يسرنا القران] للذكر فهل من مدكر]
[٢٣ كذبت ثمود بالنذر](٢٤) فقالوا ا[بشرا منا و[احدا نتبعه انا اذا]
[لفى ضلال وسعر](٢٥) ءألقى] الذكر عليه من بيننا [بل هو كذاب اشر]
[(٢٦) سيعلمون غدا من] الكذاب الاشر(٢٧) انا [مرسلوا الناقة فتنة
[لهم فارتقبهم وا]صطبر(٢٨) ونبئهم ان [الماء قسمة بينهم كل]
[شرب محتضر](٢٩) فنا]دوا صحبهم فتعا]طى فعقر(٣٠) فكيف كان]
[عذابى ونذر](٣١) إنا ار]سلنا عليهم صي[حة واحدة فكانوا]
[كهشيم المحتظر](٣٢) ولقد يسرنا القران للذ]كر فهل من مدكر(٣٣)
[كذبت قوم لوط بالنذر](٣٤) انا ارسلنا علي[هم حاصبا الا آل لوط]
[نجيناهم بسحر](٣٥) نعمة [من عندنا كذلك [نجزى من شكر](٣٦) ولقد
[انذرهم بطشتنا فتماروا با]لنذر(٣٧) ولقد راودوه] عن ضيفه فطمسنا
[أعينهم فذوقوا عذابى ونذر](٣٨) ولقد صبحهم بكرة عذاب مستقر(٣٩)

---

8. Ms. منا (dotted). — **9.** Ms. بيننا (fully dotted). — **11.** Ms. وا]صطبر.—

17. Ms. با]لنذر (with a dash instead of a dot above the D̲āl).

On the verso:

1 [منتصر (٤٥) سيهزم الجمع] ويولون الدبر (٤٦) [بل الساعة موعدهم والساعة]

2 [ادهى وامر (٤٧) ان المجرمين في ضلل [وسعر (٤٨) يوم يسحبون في]

3 [النار على وجوههم ذوقوا] مس سقر (٤٩) انا [كل شى خلقناه بقدر (٥٠) وما]

4 [امرنا الا واحدة كلمح بالبصر (٥١) ولقد اهلكنا اشياعكم فهل من مدكر]

5 [(٥٢) وكل شى فعلوه في] الزبر (٥٣) وكل صغير وكبير مستطر (٥٤) ان المتقين]

6 [في جنات ونهر (٥٥)] في مقعد صدق [عند مليك مقتدر]

7 [بسم الله الرحمن الرحيم (١) الرحمن علم القران (٢) خلق الانسان (٣) علمه]

8 [البيان (٤) الشمس والقمر بحسبان (٥) والنجم والشجر يسجدان (٦) والسماء رفعها]

9 [ووضع الميزان (٧) الا تطغوا في الميزان (٨) واقيموا الوزن بالقسط]

10 [ولا تخسروا الميزان (٩) والارض وضعها للانم (١٠) فيها فاكهة والنخل ذات]

11 [الاكمام (١١) والحب ذو العصف والريحان (١٢) فباى آلاء ربكما تكذبان]

12 [(١٣) خلق الانسان من صلصل كالفخار وخلق الجان من مارج من نار (١٥) فباى]

13 [آلاء ربكما تكذبان (١٦) رب المشرقين (١٧) ورب المغربين (١٨) فباى آلاء]

14 [ربكما تكذبان (١٩) مرج البحرين يلتقيان (٢٠) بينهما برزخ لا يبغيان (٢١) فباى آلاء]

15 [ربكما تكذبان (٢٢) يخرج منهما اللولو والمرجان (٢٣) فباى آلاء ربكما]

16 [تكذبان (٢٤) وله الجوار المنشات في البحر كالاعلام (٢٥) فباى آلاء ربكما]

17 [تكذبان (٢٦) كل من عليها فان (٢٧) ويبقا وجه ربك ذو الجلال والاكرام (٢٨) فباى آلاء]

18 [ربكما تكذبان (٢٩) يسأله من في السموت والارض كل يوم هو في شان]

19 [(٣٠) فباى آلاء ربكما تكذبان (٣١) سنفرغ لكم اية الثقلان (٣٢) فباى]

---

14. يلتقيان is fully dotted in the Ms. — 15. Ms. منهما. — 16. Only ت (which is dotted) is certain of the first word. — 17. ربك is dotted in the original.

Plate II

c)

b)

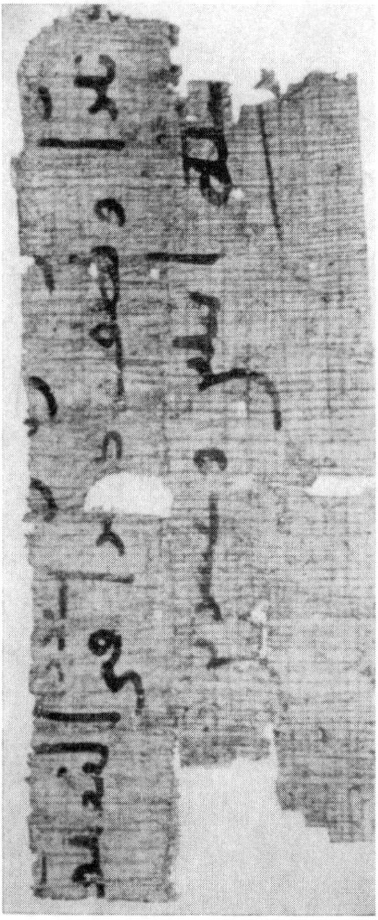

a)

a) P. Mich. 6704 (22–75 A.H., 643–694 A.D.) b) P. Berod. 15002 (22 A.H., 643 A.D.) c) PERF N. 573 (57 A.H., 677 A.D.)

LV. In line 4, at the end of verse 50, a verse-division mark is visible. Sura 54 is divided from LV by two parallel horizontal lines running over the full width of the page, and filled in with an ondulating line with pearls in the compartments.

Place of discovery unknown.

The script has become obliterated in some places and the papyrus is torn upon all sides. The fragment shown here (Plate 1) comes from the middle of the page, which as the line originally contained about three-times as much as at present, would have been about 17.7 cm. wide. This Qur'ān was certainly destined for private use only, and belongs to the small, oblong sizes, particularly used for private owners already in very early times.

Before entering into the question of dating[40] it will be recommendable to give a palaeographical analysis of the script of P. Michaélidès no. 32. The *Alif* (line 8), the most significant letter of the Arabic alphabet, as J. v. Karabacek has said,[41] shows a definite bend to the right side, as it is already the case in PER Inv. Ar. Pap. 94 (ca. 30 A.H., 650 C.E.).[42] It differs, therefore, from the straight, vertical Alif in PERF no. 558,[43] in the bilingual protocol BM 1473,[44] in Arabic Palaeography P1. 43 and in the Qur'ān Paris. Arabe 328[45] as well as from the Alif, curved to the right at the basis, shown by the Qur'ān Medīna 1a in the Saray in Istanbul.[46]

The *Dāl* corresponds to the form offered by PERF no. 558, P. Berol. 15002 (Plate IIb), P. Mich. 6714 (Plate IIa), P. Berol. 9177 (124 A.H., 742 C.E.) and the parchment Qur'ān Paris. Arabe 328 (1).

The *Rā* (*Zāy*) is similar to the same letter in PERF no. 558, P. Berol. 15002, PERF no. 573 (Plate IIc, 57 A.H., 677 C.E.).

In *Sīn*, the tail of the final letter (recto line 6) goes down in an almost straight line, as in the Nūn occurring in PERF no. 558, 573, PER Inv. Ar. Pap. 94. It therefore differs from the final Sīn with a curved tail occurring, for example, in PERF no. 558.

The *Ṭā* has a rectangular body and a vertical stroke bending to the right side, as, for example, in Paris. Arabe 328 (4).[47] The latter characteristic feature already occurs in PERF no. 558 and P. Loth II, further in the legend of copper coins from the second decade of the first century of the Higra[48] and in the Qurra-papyri,[49] where it interchanges with the straight form. This characteristic feature is preserved in the third century of the Higra (ninth century C.E.) in the papyrus script,[50] and in early Christian

Plate III

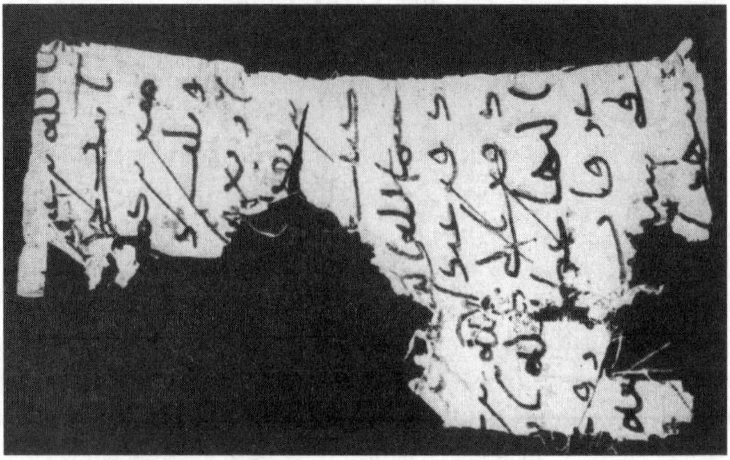

b) PER Inv. Ar. Pap. 11154

a) P. Cair. B. É. Inv. N0. 1700

Arabic manuscripts forming the transition to *Maghrabī*-writing,[51] in which it is preserved until recent times. Possibly this form of the Ṭā was also significant for the Makkī-script, while the old scripts of al-Kūfa, al-Baṣra and Damascus preferred the *vertical* stroke.

The *Nūn* has about the same form as in PER Inv. Ar. Pap. 94.

An additional characteristic feature is the reverted Yā (e.g., in على recto line 2 and in ـخ verso lines 9, 16).

All these characteristics show, together with the general impression of the writing, that the script of P. Michaélidès no. 32 cannot be dated later than the first century af the Higra (end of the seventh or beginning of the eighth century C.E.).

Some orthographical peculiarities should be added here.

The Alif madda is frequently omitted:

On the recto line	3	تركنها	for	تركناها
	12	صحبهم	for	صاحبهم
	12	فعطى	for	فتعاطى
	17	رودو[ه	for	راودو[ه
On the verso line	2	ضلل	for	ضلال

A remarkable thing here is السماوت in line 18 for السماوات and السموت in P. Michaélidès no. 235 line 2 (first century A.H., seventh century C.E.). *Diacritical dots* are used sparingly and are formed in the same way as in PERF no. 558 already described in CPR III, 1/i, pp. 70–71. Once a short dash is used in *Dāl* (on the recto line 17 in بالنذر instead of a dot. Such diacritical dashes are used very early. We find them—apart from the parchment Qur'ān Paris. Arabe 328 (1)[52]—in PER Inv. Ar. Pap. 8181 (first cent. of the Higra, seventh century C.E.), 10136 (second century of the Higra, eighth century C.E.), Inv. Perg. Ar. 186, in P. Mich. 6714 (22–75 A.H., 643–694 C.E.), where the short dashes are similar to oval dots. There can be no doubt whatever that in all these examples the dots or dashes respectively are set *by the original hand.*

The occurence of dots in such an early Qur'ān as P. Michaélidès no. 32 is of some importance, since Prof. A. Jeffery,[55] the greatest living Western authority in Qur'ānic science, emphasizes the fact that the oldest Qur'ānic codices were *generally* without diacritical points, and the lines

Plate IV

P. Michaélidés No. 190 recto (Qur'an, Sūra 60s–63s)

replacing dots (occuring only in some old codices and fragments) may well be nothing more than scribal fantasy.

It is quite possible that the dashes, used as diacritical marks in some old Qur'ān manuscripts, for example, Arabic Palaeography Pl. 1 ff., were added later. But the occurence of such dashes—and dots—would no longer militate *in se ipso* against a dating in the first century of the Higra, since dashes are not unusual in papyri of the first century of the Higra and the use of dots is proved by papyri as early as even the *first half* of the first century of the Higra.[54]

Another important statement, made by Prof. A. Jeffery[55] is that the oldest Qur'āns had no rubrics or marks for divisions, which were reproved by traditions traced back to early authorities, and that the occurrence of marks indicating divisions of ten verses would argue against so early a dating as the first to second century of the Higra, attributed by Miss N. Abbott to some specimens in the collection of the Oriental Institute in Chicago University.

As a matter of fact, there is one mark indicating the ending of a group of ten verses after verse 50 of Sura LIV on the verso of P. Michaélidès no. 32 line 4. It consists of a ه surrounded by dots.[56] It is said[57] that the marking of the endings of groups of five or ten verses was introduced by al-Ḥaggāg ibn Yūsuf, the governor of the ʿIraq (75–95 A.H., 674–714 C.E.) or by Naṣr ibn ʿĀṣim al-Laithī (died 89/90 A.H., 708/709 C.E.).[58] The occurence of a ten-verses division mark in P. Michaélidès no. 32 argues in favor of these authorities, and shows that Qur'ān copies containing these marks could well be placed in the time suggested by Miss N. Abbott. Another question is the origin of these marks.

I have suggested already in 1929 that these division marks were an imitation of the use of plain circles as punctuation marks in Pahlawi literary papyri, for example, PERF no. 446 and P. Berol. 4442.[59] Such plain circles recur still in Arabic papyri of the second and third centuries of the Higra (eighth/ninth century C.E.),[60] and when it is just an ʿIrāqī governor who is credited with its introduction, Persian influence is thereby very probable.

Still more important is the occurrence of an ornamental sura division after Sura LIV on the verso of P. Michaélidès no. 32 between lines 6 and 7. It is formed by two parallel horizontal lines, framing an undulating line, the curves of which are filled in with pearls.

Plate V

a) PER Inv. Perg. Ar. No. 2 (Qur'an, Sūra 28 61–73)

b) PERF No. 582 (65–86 A.H., 685–705 A.D.)

The oldest extant parchment Qur'āns are apparently destitute of any rubric or indication of the ending of a sura or the beginning of a new one, and there are even several traditions disapproving such a practice, which, nevertheless, made its way into copies of the Qur'ān of the first century of the Islamic era, and even those destined for private use, as the example of P. Michaélidès no. 32 shows. A comparison with another fragment of a papyrus Qur'ān in the Collection Michaélidès (no. 190, Pl. IV), forming the leaf of a quire, comprising two columns on each side, folded in the middle, which contains Sura LIX.11 to LXV.4, furnishes interesting details for the early adornment of Qur'ān manuscripts (see Plate IV). This fragment is apparently considerably later than P. Michaélidès no. 32, and may, according to the script, appartain to the end of the second or beginning of the third century of the Higra (first half of the ninth century C.E.).

Here we see a simple intertwined band ornament at the end of Sura LXI (on the recto, left column, line 8) and perhaps also at the end of Sura LXIV (on the verso, right column, line 16). The end of Sura LX (on the recto, right column, line 14) is marked with a hexagram and an intertwined band ornament. The simple design in this papyrus codex was obviously more elaborate in large copies of the Qur'ān, destined for the use in the mosque; a good example of an ornamented band concluding the sura is offered by the codex Saray no. 50395 in Instanbul.[61]

The development of the practice of emphasizing the division of the chapters in Qur'ān manuscripts may have happened in the following way:

The first step was to an *empty space* between the end of a preceding sura and the beginning of the following sura;[62] such empty spaces divide also the various parts of documents and occasionally of letters.[63]

Then a simple ornament, for example, a composition of intertwined or intersecting lines, as we see it in P. Michaélidès no. 32, 190, marked the end of a sura. Possibly such bands were taken over from Greek or Syriac manuscripts, in which they marked the beginning of a new chapter or paragraph.

In a more elaborate execution, an intertwined band, beautifully ornamented, extended over the whole lenghth of a page in big liturgical copies of the Qur'ān, as we see it in the Qur'ān from the ʿAmr-Mosque[64] or that from Sarmaqand.[65] These ornamental flourishes are often a clear imitation of the *clavi* in late Roman textiles.

In the meantime, it had probably become customary to mark the beginning of as sura by a special formula mentioning its origin (whether Meccan or Medīnan), the name of the sura and the number of its verses.

In P. Michaélidès no. 190 فاتحة سورة الممتحنة ثلث عشرة آية,[62] accompanied by a simple intertwined band, opens sura LX (on the verso, left column, line 13), while the same plaited band is repeated after the Basmala (line 14).

The opening of sura LXI is unfortunately partially destroyed. It begins with the Basmala, followed by an intertwined band, then a lacuna and مدنية وهى اربع تعشرآية (on the recto, right column, LINES 14–15).

Still more damaged is the beginning of sura LXIV (on the verso, right column, line 3), where [مكية وهى ثمان عشرة آية, followed by an intertwined band and the Baslama, opens the chapter. It is not to be made out, whether also here فاتحة سورة الصف and فاتحة سورة التغابن, respectively, are to be supplemented in the lacuna.

Since this fragment comes apparently from a Qur'ān destined for private use, the scribe was not restricted to the observation of a severe tradition of adornment, but was able to apply a liberal selection of various ways of indicating the beginning of a sura.

Finally, the title of the sura, including the mentioning of its place of origin and the number of its verses, thus forming a real rubric, was set within the intertwined band, which now formed its ornamental frame. This last step of a long development was then standardized, and survived in the old lapidary style of writing within the embellished copies of Qur'ān, now written in beautiful, big *Thuluth* or other, younger scripts.

We may summarize our article under the following headings:

(1) The supposition of Minovi, that the extant early Qur'āns are wholesale forgeries, is not only unjustified, but in itself highly improbable.

(2) The sample of Meccan-Medīnan writing in the Chester-Beatty codex of the *Kitāb al-Fihrist* by Ibn an-Nadīm does not really represent the original Meccan-Medīnan script, but we can form an opinion of this script by a close study of the writing in the papyri of the first century.

(3) These papyri can indeed form the basis for the dating of early Qur'āns, and it is fairly possible to date some of them in the first century of the Islamic era.

(4) The existence of diacritical dots or dashes, or even of punctuation and verse-decade marks and rubrics in those early Qur'ān manuscripts

would not prejudice a dating in this period, and Arabic sources, mentioning these peculiarities as existing in Qur'ān codices of the first century of the Higra, are reliable.

So a small fragment of a simply adorned Qur'ān leaf has contributed essentially to our knowledge of the early history of the Holy Book of Islam, and it is to be hoped that future finds may widen this knowledge and help to solve the problems whose solutions are still pending.

LIST OF ABBREVIATIONS

APEL	Arabic Papyri in the Egyptian Library ed. A. Grohmann I–V (Cairo 1934–1956)
CPR III	*Corpus Papyrorum Raineri Archiducis Austriae* III, Series Arabica ed. A. Grohmann (Wien 1923–1924)
JNES	*Journal of Near Eastern Studies*
Inv. Ar. Pap.	Inventory numbers of Arabic papyri
Inv. Perg. Ar.	Inventory numbers of Arabic parchments
P. Berol.	Papyri in the collection of the State Museum, Berlin
P. Cair. B. É.	Papyri in the collection of the Egyptian National Library, Cairo
P. Mich.	Papyri in the collection of the University of Michigan, Ann Arbor
P. Michaélidès	Papyri in the collection of George Michaélidès, Cairo
PER	Collection of the Papyrus Erzherzog Rainer, Austrian National Library, Vienna
PERF	Papyrus Erzherzog Rainer. Führer durch die Ausstellung. Wien, 1894
PSI	Papiri della Società Italiana per la richerca dei Papiri, Florence
Sb. Ak. Wien	Sitzungsberichte der Akademie der Wissenschaften in Wien, philosophisch-historische Klasse
WZKM	Wiener Zeitschrift für die Kunde des Morgenlandes
ZDMG	Zeitschrift der Deutschen Morgenländischen Gesellschaft

NOTES

1. Frammenti Coranici in carattere Cufico nella Bibliotheca, Vaticana, (Codici Vaticani Arabi 1605, 1606), Studi e testi no. 132, Città del Vaticano, 1947.

2. The present article was originally destined as a contribution to the Scritti offerti a G. Levi della Vida, but could not be completed in time for reasons of health.

3. *Arabic Palaeography* by B. Moritz, Pl. 43, containing Sura XXVIII. 48–57. J. V. Karabacek, WZKM 20 (1906): 137 expressed his doubts concerning the existence of papyrus Qurʾāns, since this plate did not convince him owing to the bad state of the verso of the papyrus.

4. Loth II, cf. ZDMG 34 (1880): 688.

5. Lettre à M. le Chevalier P. O. Brönsted sur quelques Médailles cufiques dans le Cabinet du Roi de Danemark . . . et sur quelques manuscrits cufiques, Copenhagen, 1830, paragraph 8, pp. 33 ff.

6. Paläographische Beiträge aus den herzoglichen Sammlungen in Gotha, fasc. 1, Erfurt, 1842.

7. *Paléographie universelle*, Paris, 1839, English edition by Frederic Madden (London, 1850), Pl. xxxii–xxxvi.

8. Facsimiles of Manuscripts and Inscriptions, Palaeographical Society, Oriental Series, London 1875–1883, Pl. xlix; the date is accepted by J. v. Karabacek, WZKM 5 (1891): 324, 20 (1906): 137 who places the piece in *early* eighth century C.E. or end of the first century and beginning of the second century A.H., respectively.

9. *Arabic Palaeography, A Collection of Arabic Texts from the First Century of the Hidjra till the Year 1000* (Cairo, 1905), Publications of the Khedivial Library no. 16; cf. B. Moritz's remarks on Kufic Writing in Qurʾāns in *Encyclopaedia of Islam* 1, p. 388. In his article "Ausflüge in der Arabia Petraea," *Mélanges de la Faculté Orientale* (Université Saint Joseph, Beyrouth) III (1908), p. 430, B. Moritz, dated the Qurʾān from the ʿAmr Mosque ca. 100 A.H.

10. WZKM 20 (1906): 133 ff., Sb. Ak. Wien 184/3 (1917): 12f., 33 n. 2. In Th. W. Arnold and A. Grohmann, *The Islamic Book* (Florence 1929), p. 22, I have tentatively dated the Qurʾān manuscript reproduced in Pls. I–XII at about 107 A.H. (725 C.E.) and that reproduced in Pls. XXXI–XXXIV at 102 A.H. (720 C.E.).

11. *Die Ausstellung von Meisterwerken muhammedanischer Kunst* 1 (München 1910), Pl. 1.

12. Sb. Ak. Wien 172 (1913): 35 n. 1. Karabacek (in a note in his posthumously examined manuscripts) bases his contestation on the form of the Alifs,

the foot of which shows a curved turn to the right, which form can not be eighth century according to him. But the evidence of the papyri disproves this argument.

13. *Specimina codicum Orientalium* (Bonn 1914), Pl. 41, 42.

14. ZDMG 64 (1915): 80 and Pl. xvi.

15. "Zur ältesten Geschichte der kufischen Schrift," *Zeitschrift des Deutschen Vereins für Buchwesen und Schrifttum* 5/6 (1919): 54–66, especially pp. 55a n. 3, 66.

16. Nöldeke-Bergsträsser-Pretzl, *Geschichte des Qorāns* III (Leipzig 1936), S. 251–257.

17. Ibid., p. 253.

18. E. Herzfeld has mentioned a Qur'ān copy, dated 94 A.H. (712/13 C.E.), among the collections of valuable books in Persia (cf. Ephemerides Orientales O. Harrassovitz 28. 1. 1926). For two copies, dating 102 A.H. (720 C.E. B. Moritz, *Arabic Palaeography*, Pl. 31–34) and 107 A.H. (725 C.E., ibid., Pl. 1–12), respectively, according to information obtained in the Egyptian National Library cf. Arnold and Grohmann, *The Islamic Book*, p. 22. Cf. also I. Y. Kratchkovsky, *Among Arabic Manuscripts* (Leiden, 1953), p. 150: "Kufic Qorans of the first-second century A.H. are extremely rare. . . ." The Qur'ān Maṣāḥif no. 387 in the National Egyptian Library (*Arabic Palaeography*, P1. 18) dated by B. Moritz, basing his conclusion on the *waqfiyya*, in the second century A.H., is, according to J. v. Karabacek, WZKM 20 (1906): 135, 136, from the third century A.H. Moritz read the date 168 instead of 268 (882 C.E.).

19. Codex Paris. Arabe no. 336 229 A.H. (843/44 C.E.); Cairo National Egyptian Library General number 40160 256–264 A.H. (870–877 C.E.), 33910 270 A.H. (883/84 C.E.), 33910 277 A.H. (890/91 C.E.); two fragments of parchment Qur'āns in the National Museum in Damascus 265–271 A.H. (878–885 C.E.) and 298 A.H. (910/11 C.E.); one Qur'ān manuscript in Persia, dated 260 A.H. (873/74 C.E.), is recorded by E. Herzfeld, op. cit.; cf. B. Moritz, *Encyclopaedia of Islam* 1, p. 388, G. Bergsträsser, *Geschichte des Qorāns*, III, p. 270.

20. Kratchkovsky, *Among Arabic Manuscripts*, p. 150.

21. S. Pissaref, Reproduction exacte du célèbre Coran Coufique écrit, d'apres la tradition, de la propre main du troisième Calife Osman (644–656) et se trouvant maintenant dans la Bibliothèque Impériale publique de Saint-Pétersbourg (St. Pétersbourg, 1905).

22. "Arabic Palaeography," *Ars Islamica*. 7 (1941): 73, 74 n. 14.

23. *Moslem World* 30 (1940), p. 192.

24. A. V. Pope, *A Survey of Persian Art* II (1939), p. 1718 and note 4. Cf. N. Abbott, op. cit., p. 68.

25. Pope, *A Survey of Persian Art*, p. 1710.

26. *Ars Islamica* 8 (1941): 70 ff.

27. Pope, *A Survey of Persian Art*, p. 1710.

28. Apparently Minovi found his "final hooked (terminus) in the opposite direction" substantiated in the fishing-hooks or barbs of the Alifs in the Basmala of the Chester-Beatty codex of the *Kitāb al-Fihrist*. We have to return to this point again later.

29. E.g., in *aṣ-Ṣū lī, Adab al-Kuttāb* (Baghdad 1922), pp. 43f. cf. also F. Krenkow, "The Grant of Land by Muḥammed to Tamim ad-Dāri," *Islamica* 1 (1924): 529–532.

30. Pope, *A Survey of Persian Art*, p. 1718.

31. Ibid., p. 1710, fig. 580.

32. The same has happened to Karabacek in WZKM 5 (1891): 323.

33. *Moslem World* 30 (1940): 193.

34. This expression is not very luckily chosen, but if we compare, e.g., the inscription B of al-Medina (Gebel Salaʿ) published by M. Hamidullah in *Islamic Culture* 13 (1939): plate opposite p. 435, the resemblance with the Kūfī Qurʾāns is very striking. The rich collection of photographs of old Qurʾāns in the Bavarian Academy of Sciences in Munich would have been very useful for a more detailed classification of this style of writing.

35. *Kitāb al-Fihrist*, pp. 9 ff., 10 ff.

36. Apart from the well-known Qurra-papyri (90–96 A.H., 709–714 C.E.) the following date from the first century of the Higra:

PERF no. 558	22 A.H.. (643 C.E.)
P. Berol. 15002	22 A.H. (643 C.E.) Plate II b.
PER Inv. Ar. Pap. 94	first half of the first century A.H. (second half of the viith cent. C.E.)
P. 'Augā' el-Ḥafir	54–57 A.H. (674-677 C.E.)
PERF no. 573	57 A.H. (677 C.E.) Plate II c
P. Mich. 6714	22–75 A.H. (643–694 C.E.) Plate II a
PERF no. 585	75 A.H. (695 C.E.)
PERF no. 582/83	65–86 A.H. (685–705 C.E.) Plate V b
PER Inv. Ar. Pap. 3678	65–86 A.H. (685–705 C.E.)
PERF no. 591	87 (89) A.H. (706/708 C.E.)
PSI xii/2 (1951) no. 1273, pp. 105–106 (P1. iv verso)	first century A.H. (seventh century C.E.)

The parchment letter from Sogdiana about 100 A.H. (719 C.E.) V. A. Kratchkovskaia and I. Y. Krachkovski, *Recueil Sogdien* (Leningrad, 1934), pp. 52–90.

37. Cf. above, n. 8, E. Tisserant, op. cit. P1. 41 a, b.

38. Scritti offertia G. Levi della Vida, P1. 1, pp. 1 f.

39. Bergsträsser, *Geschichte des Qorans*, P1. viii.

40. The dating second/third century of the Hijra, given in *From the World of Arabic Papyri*, p. 229 n. 268, refers to the papyrus Qur'ān leaf P. Michaélidès no. 190 (not to no. 32).

41. WZKM 5 (1891): 323.

42. Cf. my "Aperçu de papyrologic Arabe," *Études de papyrologie* 1 (1930): Pl. ix.

43. Cf. the Table of Writing in CPR III, 1/2, p. xxii.

44. Cf. ZA 22 (1908): Pl. 1 line 6.

45. Cf. Bergstrāsser, *Geschichte des Qorans*, Pl. vii.

46. Ibid., P1. viii.

47. E. Tisserant, op. cit., Pl. 41b.

48. Cf. J. v. Karabacek, *Beiträge zur Geschichte der Mazjaditen* (Leipzig 1874), p. 35; WZKM 5 (1891): 324.

49. APEL III no. 147, 3, 5 P1. II (91 A.H., 710 C.E.).

50. APEL III no. 167, 94, 06 Pl. xi (140 A.H., 757 C.E.); 180, 5, 7 Pl. xv (113 A.H., 731/32 C.E.); 201, 26 Pl. xxi (ca. 116 A.H., 734 C.E.); APEL 11 no. 79, 8, 9 Pl. iv (third century A.H., ninth century C.E.), 82, 4 Pl. vi (253 A.H., 867 C.E.); 91, 3 Pl. vii (second/third century A.H., ninth century C.E.); 120, 4 Pl. xix (third century A.H., ninth century C.E.), APEL IV no. $233^{r}_{5,7}$ Pl. vii (third century A.H., ninth century C.E.); J. D. Weill, *Le Djâmi'd'Ibn Wahb* 1 (Cairo 1939), Pl. 5, 7 (second half of the third century A.H., ninth century C.E.).

51. E.g., in the translation of the New Testament, which H. L. Fleischer, "Beschreibung der von Prof. Dr. Tischendorf zurückgebrachten christlich-arabischen Handschriften," ZDMG 8 (1854): 585, dates in the eighth, at the latest the ninth century C.E.

52. E. Tisserant, op. cit., P1. 41a.

53. *Moslem World* 30 (1940): 195, 198.

54. PERF no. 558, P. Berol. 15002 (both 22 A.H., 643 C.E.); PERF no. 573 is dated 57 A.H. (677 C.E.), one year before the inscription of the dam near aṭ-Ṭā'if, in which diacritical dots occur frequently (cf. G. C. Miles, "Early Islamic Inscriptions near Ṭā'if in the Ḥijāz," *JNES* 7 (1948): 237 and Pl. xviiiA). Diacritical dashes also occur in Christian Arabic manuscripts, e.g., in the fragment of an Arabic translation of Job from the ninth century C.E.; cf. H. L. Fleischer, "Zur Geschichte der arabischen Schrift," ZDMG 18 (1864): 288–291 and plate in front of pag. 288.

55. Op. cit., p. 196.

56. Cf. CPR III, I/I, p. 73. In the codex Vaticanus Arabicus 1605 the verse-decade mark consists of a red circle surrounded by black dots with a numeral filling in the circle (cf. Scritti Offerti a G. Levi della Vida, p. 2).

57. Cf. A. Jeffery, *Two Muqaddimas of the Qur'ānic Sciences* (Cairo 1954), p. 276 ff. Some historians traced the use of such verse-decade marks back to the Caliph al-Ma'mūn (198–218 A.H., 813-833 C.E.), but this is obviously too late.

58. Cf. Bergstrāsser, *Geschichte des Qorans*, III, p. 258.

59. Arnold and Grohmann, *The Islamic Book*, p. 23.

60. E.g., PERF no. 712, 734, PER Inv. Ar. Pap. 814; J. D. Weill, *Le Djâmiʿd'Ibn Wahb*, Pl. xxx pag. 61 line 15. Such a very regular circle also occurs in the parchment Qur'ān Paris. Arabe 334, cf. Bergstrāsser, *Geschichte des Qorans*, III, Pl. 1, fig. 2.

61. Bergstrāsser, *Geschichte des Qorans*, III, Pl. V, fig 6a.

62. Ibid., p. 259.

63. Cf. my *From the World of Arabic Papyri*, p. 89.

64. Cf. Moritz, *Arabic Palaeography*, Pl. 1ff.

65. See n. 20

66. For this formula cf. Or. 2166 in W. Wright, Palaeographical Society, Oriental Series, Pl. xLix line 17

فاتحة سورة طس النمل وهى اربع وتسعين آية فيها سجدة

N. Abbott, *The Rise of the North Arabic Script*, Pl. xvii no. 11 verso and Berstrāsser, *Geschichte des Qorans*, III, p. 259. He also mentions a Qur'ān codex in the possession of the grandfather of Malik ibn Anas (died 179 A.H.), written in the time of the Caliph ʿUthmān, containing sura subscriptions, written in black ink on an ornamental band, which ran over the whole line

(فرأينا خواتمه من حبر
على عمل السلسلة فى طول السطر ورأيته معجوم الاى)

9.2

Observations on Early Qur'ān Manuscripts in Ṣan'ā'

Gerd-R. Puin

The plan of Bergsträsser, Jeffery, and later Pretzl to prepare a critical edition of the Qur'ān was not realized, and the collection of variants derived from real old codices failed to survive the bombs of World War II.[1] Many more old manuscripts are accessible now, which would justify a new approach, but no such undertaking is in sight. It is true, unfortunately, that the (scriptural) variants are hardly helpful for a better understanding of much of the text which is still far from being as *mubīn* ("clear") as the Qur'ān claims to be! Thus, even if a complete collection of variants could be achieved, it will probably not lead to a breakthrough in Qur'ānic studies. Certainly, though, it will help to reveal the stages of Qur'ānic (and Arabic) orthography.

An exciting "excavation" of old Qur'ānic fragments took place in the Yemeni capital of Ṣan'ā' from 1980 onward.[2] The fragments were discovered in 1972 in the loft of the Great Mosque. Subsequently the (then) *General Authortiy for Antiquities and Libraries* took care of them in the *Dār al-Makhṭūṭāt*. Meanwhile, the many thousand pieces of parchment have been cleaned and identified according to *Muṣḥaf*, *Sūrah*, and *Āyah*; at this stage a complete microfilm documentation is needed in order to make the fragments available for study and for the preparation of a catalog. Unfortunately, the priorities of neither the German sponsor of the restoration project (Ministry of Foreign Affairs) nor of the Yemeni antiq-

Gerd-R. Puin, "Observations on Early Qur'ān Manuscripts in Ṣan'ā'," in *The Qur'ān as Text*, ed. Stefan Wild (Leiden: E. J. Brill, 1996), pp. 107–11. Reprinted with permission.

uities administration seem to favor the idea. Hopefully better times will come. Since no complete microfilm documentation is available,[3] the details presented below are left without exact reference to the manuscripts from which they are taken.

Among the fragments of roughly nine hundred different parchment *Muṣḥafs*, about 10 percent are written in a peculiar "pre-Kufic" variety of script, *Ḥijāzī* or *Māʾil*. It is this group of manuscripts that was examined in a preliminary way in order to prepare a questionnaire for a more comprehensive investigation. Examples of these observations are recorded here according to the type of deviation from the *Rasm* of the Egyptian standard edition of the Qurʾān. My observations do not claim to be either new or unexpected,[4] except for the last paragraph, which discusses the different arrangements of the *Sūrahs*.

(1) *Defective writing of the Alif* constitutes the most common "deviation" from the *Rasm* of the printed standard edition. The scriptural appearance of the following examples presupposes an established oral tradition of correct reading, much more than the familiar *Rasm*—which has the *plene Alif*—does:

فلوا	فل	فلت	كنوا	سحر	نصحبكم
qālū	*qāla*	*qālat*	*kānū*	*sāḥir*	*bi-ṣāḥibikum*

The standard *Rasm* اماوكم is easily recognized as *ʾābāʾukum*, whereas ابوكم in the *Ḥijāzī* manuscripts, again, requires the oral tradition for the same pronunciation! In cases like بلحق *bi-l-ḥaqqi* or كلجواب *ka-l-jawābi* the *Alif* of the article is written defectively, but there can be no doubt about the correct reading. Evidently, no orthographic convention was connected with the *Alif al-wiqāyah*, either (راو instead of راوا *raʾaw*). On the other hand, does كلدى *ka-lladhī* imply that the second letter *Yāʾ* should not be pronounced at all?

(2) If it is true that the defective writing of the *Alif* is more archaic than the *plene* version, then the same is true for those cases where the *Alif* is written *in lieu of* (Semitic) *Hamzah*: ساى for *shayʾin* (as if *shaʾyin* was intended), سات for *sīʾat*, and even السا for *as-sayyiʾa*.

(3) Most of the *canonical "readings"* (*Qirāʾāt*) of the Qurʾānic text do not presuppose a different *Rasm*; but although the proportion of the cases that deviate from the standard *Rasm* is relatively low, it is amazing how many of these cases of deviations—in absolute figures—are reported! We can now easily check any variation of the *Rasm* with the accumulated tradition of Muslim scholarship on the *Qirāʾāt*, thanks to the eight-volume dictionary *Muʿjam al-qirāʾāt al-qurʾāniyyah*.[5] By doing this we discovered that 'our' manuscripts contain many more *Qirāʾāt* than are recorded by the old authorities. These examples may suffice: In XIX.62 the original لا تسمع *lā tasmaʿ* was later corrected to *lā tasmaʿūna* (instead of the usual *lā yasmaʿūna*). Instead of *qul jāʾa l-ḥaqqu* in XXXIV.49 we find قيل جا الحق *qīla jāʾa l-ḥaqqu*. The systems of the seven, ten, or fourteen *Qirāʾāt* are, consequently, younger than the variants observed in *Ṣanʿāʾ*.

4. The same is true for the variants in *counting the verses*. Even in the most archaic manuscripts, the end of a meaningful portion of the text is marked by dots, strokes, *Alifs*, or similar signs. Many of the separators in the Yemeni manuscripts are placed in positions, however, that are not counted as the "end of a verse" according to the "Kūfan" counting. The Islamic tradition is aware of different regional counting systems, of which Spitaler has compiled a condensed, easy-to-handle survey;[6] all together, twenty-one systems are distinguishable according to his sources. The Ṣanʿānī early manuscripts in question seem to favour the "Kūfan" counting, but in a substantial number of manuscripts we find no thorough correspondence with any of the other traditional systems. If we compare, for example, the verse separators/verse counting realized in one archaic manuscript (no. 00–25.1) with the traditional systems of verse counting, the ratio of identical (+) or diverging (-) countings can be summed up as follows:

Baṣra 10 + /5 - , Kūfa 4 + /11 - , Makka 11 + /4 - , Madīna 11 + /4 - .

It is noteworthy that in some of the Ḥijāzī manuscripts the *Basmalas* at the outset of the Sūrahs are always marked by a verse separator. Would these manuscripts reflect the opinion that the *Basmalas* are primordial parts of the Qurʾānic text?

In general the number of separators seems to exceed the number of verses counted, which is clear from contradictory use of separators and markers for groups of five or ten verses. Separators are observed even at places where the Egyptian standard edition has the recitation mark (صلى) (*al-waṣlu awlā*, "enjambement is preferable")!

(5) Two early Qur'ān authorities are reported to have kept their "private" Qur'ān manuscripts, which they refused to destroy or harmonize with the official version promoted by the caliph ʿUthmān: Ibn Masʿūd and Ubayy b. Kaʿb. Lists of the *different arrangements of the Sūrahs* in their respective *Muṣḥafs* have been preserved,[7] but until now no such differing arrangement has been traced in a manuscript. The implications of the "validity of these reports" are far-reaching and apt to shed some light on the question of what the Qur'ān looked like at the time of, say, the "Righteous Caliphs." "But if most of the *sūras* were written down and put into approximately their final form during Muḥammad's lifetime, then there would be no strong reason for rejecting the validity of these reports [i.e., on different arrangements) outright," A. T. Welch[8] connects the two issues of the arrangement and the time of the Qur'ān's composition. Now, since we do have examples of different arrangements in *Ṣanʿaʾ*—are we allowed to invert Welch's argument, concluding from their existence that *most of the* Sūrahs *were not written down and put into approximately mately their final form during Muḥammad's lifetime?*—The Ṣanʿāni specimens are, however, not only proofs for their existence, but allow for the hypothesis that even more arrangements were in use which differed from the official sequence as well as from those reported to go back to the two authorities Ibn Masʿūd and Ubayy:

In one case, the end of Sūrah XXVI is followed by the beginning of Sūrah XXXVII (on the same page, of course!), which corresponds exactly with the leap reported about Ibn Masʿūd's arrangement—while Ubayy's *Muṣḥaf* is said to have lept from Sūrah XXVII to XXXVII. Two other leaps observed, namely, from Sūrah XIX to XXII and XXXVI to XXXVIII are close to the Ubayy list (who has the sequences 11–19–26–22 and 27–37–38–36), while the leap LXVII to LXXI is somewhat closer to Ibn Masʿūd's codex (49–67–64–63–62–61–72–71–58), again. Finally, there are the leaps LXXII to LI and LXVII to LXXXIII. which are not even remotely reflected in one of the lists. The last three "leaps" are, of course, not of the same importance as the preceding ones, as they are situated in the higher numbers of *Sūrahs* where the placement is rather arbitrary and not as easily determined as with the, say, first fifty *Sūrahs*.

NOTES

1. Information about the ambitious project can be gathered from scattered sources, like Arthur Jeffery, *Materials for the History of the Text of the Qur'ān* (Leiden: Brill, 1937), pp. vii, 3–4 (esp. n. 6); Otto Pretzl in *Geschichte des Qorāns. Dritter Teil: Die Geschichte des Korantexts*, ed. Theodor Nöldeke, G. Bergsträsser, and O. Pretzl (Leipzig, 1938; reprint, Hildesheim: Olms, 1981), pp. 249–251, 274; Anton Spitaler, "Otto Pretzl, 20. April 1893–28. Oktober 1941. Ein Nachruf," *ZDMG* 96 (1942): 161–170; A. Fischer, "Grammatisch schwierige Schwur- und Beschwörungsformeln des klassischen Arabisch," *Der Islam* 28 (1948): 5–6 n 4; Arthur Jeffery, *The Qur'ān as Scripture* (New York, 1952), p. 103.

More recently, Angelika Neuwirth in her *GAP* article "Koran" (p. 112, see fn. 3) has given the impression that it was the photographs taken in order to build up the "Koran-Archiv" in Munich which were destroyed at the end of World War II. This impression is false, and thus it is an amazing fact that evidently no attempt has been made since to study the photographs!

2. Under the supervision of Albrecht Noth, Hamburg; the present writer was in charge of the scholarly as well as practical organization of the project from 1981 until 1985, when he was succeeded by his collegue H.-C. v. Bothmer for another two years.

3. Meanwhile, microfilms have been made for the *Dār al-Makhṭūṭāt* in Ṣan'ā', and one copy is with my colleague, Dr. H.-C. Graf v. Bothmer, Saarbrücken.

4. Cf. especially Nöldeke, Bergsträsser, and Pretzl, *Geschichte des Qorāns,* Werner Diem, "Untersuchungen zur frühen Geschichte der arabischen Orthographie," *Orientalia. Roma.* 48 (1979): 207–257; 49 (1980): 67–106; 50 (1981): 332–383; 52 (1983): 357–404.

For a detailed bibliography see Angelika Neuwirth, "Koran," in *Grundriß der Arabischen Philologie. Band II: Literaturwissenschaft*, hrsg. von Helmut Gätje (Wiesbaden: Reichert, 1987), pp. 98–135, *passim.*

5. 'Abd al-'Āl Sālim *Makram* (wa-) Aḥmad Mukhtār *'Umar* (I'dād), *Mu'jam al-qirā'āt al-Qur'āniyyah, ma'a maqaddimah fī l-qirā'āt wa-ashhar al-qurrā'*, 8 vols. (al-Kuwayt: Dhāt as-Salāsil 1402–1405/1982–1985).

6. Anton Spitaler, *Die Verszählung des Koran.* München 1935 (Sitzungs-

berichte der Bayer. Akad. d. Wissenschaften. Philos.-histor. Abt., Jg. 1935, Heft 11).

7. Jeffery, *Materials*, pp. 20–24; Hans Bauer, "Über die Anordnung der Suren und über die geheimnisvollen Buchstaben im Qoran," *ZDMG* 75 (1921): 1–20; Muḥammad b. Isḥāq an-Nadīm, *The Fihrist of al-Nadīm. A Tenth-Century Survey of Muslim Culture*, trans. Bayard Dodge (New York, London: Columbia University Press, 1970), vol. 1, pp. 53–57, 58–61.

8. "al-Ḳurʾān," in EI2 V 407 b.

Appendices

A Abbreviations

AO	*Ars Orientalis.* Washington, D.C., Ann Arbor, 1954–.
AcO	*Acta Orientalia.* Copenhagen.
BSOAS	*Bulletin of the School of Oriental and African Studies.* London, 1917–.
CODCH	*The Concise Oxford Dictionary of the Christian Church.* Ed. E. A. Livingstone. Oxford, 1980.
CSCO	*Corpus scriptorum christianorum orientalium.* Ed. J. B. Chabot, I. Guidi, et al. In six sections: Scriptores Aethiopici; Scriptores Arabici; Scriptores Armeniaci; Scriptores Coptici; Scriptores Iberici; Scriptores Syri (various publishers). Paris, Leuven, 1903–.
EI	*Encyclopaedia of Islam.* Ed M. T. Houtsma et al. 4 vols. Leiden and London, 1913–1934.
EI2	*Encyclopaedia of Islam*, 2d ed. Ed. H. A. R.Gibb et al. Leiden and London, 1960–.
ER	*Encyclopedia of Religion.* Ed. M. Eliade. New York: Macmillan, 1993.
GAL	C. Brockelmann. *Geschichte des Arabischen Literatur*, 2d ed. 2 vols. Leiden, 1943–49; Supplementbände. 3 vols. Leiden, 1937–42.
GAS	Fuat Sezgin. *Geschichte des arabischen Schriftums.* Leiden, 1967–.
GdQ/GdK	Theodor Nöldeke. *Geschichte des Qorans.* Göttingen, 1860. 2d ed. Ed. Friedrich Schwally, G. Bergstrasser, and O. Pretzl. 3 vols. Leipzig, 1909–1938.

IC	*Islamic Culture*. Hyderabad, 1927–.
IJMES	*International Journal of Middle East Studies*. Middle East Studies Association of North America, New York. Vol. 1, 1970–.
JA	*Journal asiatique*. Paris, 1822–.
JAATA	*Journal of the American Association of Teachers of Arabic*
JAL/ZAL	*Journal for Arabic Linguistics*. Wiesbaden.
JAOS	*Journal of the American Oriental Society*. New Haven, Ann Arbor, 1842–.
JESHO	*Journal of the Economic and Social History of the Orient*. Paris, 1957–.
JNES	*Journal of Near Eastern Studies*. Oriental Institute, University of Chicago. Vol. 1, 1942–. Supersedes *American Journal of Semitic Languages and Literatures.*
JPHS	*Journal of the Pakistan Historical Society*
JRAS	*Journal of the Royal Asiatic Society*. London, 1834–.
JSAI	*Jerusalem Studies in Arabic and Islam*. Jerusalem, 1979–.
JSS	*Journal of Semitic Studies*. Oxford, 1956–.
MW	*Muslim World*. Hartford Seminary Foundation, Hartford, Conn. Vol. 1, 1911–. Published as *Moslem World*, 1911–1947.

REI	*Revue des Etudes Islamiques*. Paris
REJ	*Revue des Etudes Juives*
RHPR	*Revue d'Histoire et de Philosophie Religieuses.* Strasbourg.
RHR	*Revue de l'histoire des religions. Annales du Muséé Guimet.* Paris. Vol. 1, 1880–.
RSO	*Rivista degli studi orientali.* Rome. Vol. 1, 1907–.
RSPT	*Revue des Sciences Philosophiques et Théologiques.* Paris
RSR	*Revue des sciences religieuses.* Strasbourg, 1921–.
SEI	*Shorter Encyclopaedia of Islam.* Ed. H. A. R. Gibb and J. H. Kramers. Leiden, 1953.
SI	*Studia Islamica.* Paris, 1953–.
TGUOS	*Transactions of the Glasgow University Oriental Society*. Glasgow.
TLS	*Times Literary Supplement*. London.
THES	*Times Higher Education Supplement*. London.
Wellhausen *Reste*	J. Wellhausen. *Reste arabischen Heidentums*, 2d ed. Berlin, 1897.
WI	*Die Welt des Islams.* Berlin, 1913–.
WZKM	*Wiener Zeitschrift für die Kunde des Morgenlandes.* Vienna.

ZAL / JAL	*Zeitschrift für Arabische Linguistik.* Wiesbaden.
ZATW	*Zeitschrift für alttestamentliche Wissenschaft*
ZDMG	*Zeitschrift der deutschen Morgenlandischen Gesellschaft.* Leipzig, Wiesbaden, 1847–.

B CONVERTING FLÜGEL KORANIC VERSE NUMBERS INTO STANDARD EGYPTIAN

The left–hand column gives Flügel's numbers; the corresponding numbers in the Egyptian text are obtained by adding or subtracting as shown. At the points of transition this applies only to part of a verse in one of the editions.

I	1–6	+1
II	1–19	+1
	19–38	+2
	38–61	+3
	61–63	+4
	63–73	+5
	73–137	+6
	138–172	+5
	173–212	+4
	213–216	+3
	217–218	+2
	219–220	+1
	236–258	−1
	259–269	−2
	270–273	−3
	273–274	−2
	274–277	−1
III	1–4	+1
	4–18	+2
	19–27	+1
	27–29	+2
	29–30	+3
	30–31	+4
	31–43	+5
	43–44	+6
	44–68	+7
	69–91	+6
	92–98	+5
	99–122	+4
	122–126	+5
	126–141	+6
	141–145	+7
	146–173	+6
	174–175	+5
	176–179	+4

III *cont.*	180–190	+3
	191–193	+2
	194	+1
	196–198	+1
IV.	3–5	+1
	7–13	−1
	14	−2
–	15	−3
	16–29	−4
	30–32	−5
	32–45	−4
	45–47	−3
	47–48	−2
	49–70	−3
	70–100	−2
	100–106	−1
	118–156	+1
	156–170	+2
	171–172	+1
	174–175	+1
V	3–4	−1
	5–8	−2
	9–18	−3
	18–19	−2
	20–35	−3
	35–52	−4
	53–70	−5
	70–82	−4
	82–88	−3
	88–93	−2
	93–98	−1
	101–109	+1
VI	66–72	+1
	136–163	−1
VII	1–28	+1

VII *cont.*	28–103	+2
	103–131	+3
	131–139	+4
	140–143	+3
	144–146	+2
	147–1 57	+1
	166–186	+1
	191–205	+1
VII1	37–43	−1
	44–64	−2
	64–76	−1
IX	62–130	−1
X	11–80	−1
XI	6	−1
	7–9	−2
	10–22	−3
	22–54	−2
	55–77	−3
	77–84	−2
	84–87	−1
	88–95	−2
	96–99	−3
	99–120	−2
	120–122	−1
XII	97–103	−1
XIII	6–18	−1
	28–30	+1
XIV	10–11	−1
	12–13	−2
	14–24	−3
	25–26	−4
	27–37	−5
	37	−4
	37–41	−3
	41–42	−2

XIV *cont.*	42–45	–1
	46–47	–2
	47–51	–1
XVI	22–24	–1
	25–110	–2
	110–128	–1
XVII	10–26	–1
	27–48	–2
	49–53	–3
	53–106	–2
	106–108	–1
XVIII	2–21	+1
	23–31	+1
	31–55	+2
	56–83	+1
	83–84	+2
	85–97	+1
XIX	1–3	+1
	8–14	–1
	27–76	–1
	77–78	–2
	79–91	–3
	91–93	–2
	93–94	–1
XX	1–9	+1
	16–34	–1
	40–41	–1
	42–63	–2
	64–75	–3
	75–79	–2
	80–81	–3
	81–88	–2
	89–90	–3
	90–94	–2
	94–96	–1
	106–115	+1
	115–121	+2
	122–123	+1
XXI	29–67	–1
XXII	19–21	–1
XXII *cont.*	26–43	–1
	43–77	+1
XXIII	28–34	–1
	35–117	–2
	117	–1
XXIV	14–18	+1
	44–60	+1
XXV	4–20	–1
	21–60	–2
	60–66	–1
XXVI	1–48	+1
	228	–1
XXVII	45–66	–1
	67–95	– 2
XXVIII	1–22	+1
XXIX	1–51	+1
XXX	1–54	+1
XXXI	1–32	+1
XXXII	1–9	+1
XXXIII	41–49	+1
XXXIV	10–53	+1
XXXV	8–20	–1
	20–21	+1
	21–25	+2
	25–34	+3
	35–41	+2
	42–44	+1
XXXVI	1–30	+1
XXXVII	29–47	+1
	47–100	+2
	101	+1
XXXVIII	1–43	+1
	76–85	–1
XXXIX	4	–1
	5–9	–2
	10–14	–3
	14–19	–2
	19–63	–1
XL	1–2	+1
	19–32	–1
XL *cont.*	33–39	–2
	40–56	–3
	56–73	–2
	73–74	–1
XLI	1–26	+1
XLII	1–11	+2
	12–31	+1
	31–42	+2
	43–50	+1
XLIII	1–51	+1
XLIV	1–36	+1
XLV	1–36	+1
XLVI	1–34	+1
XLVII	5–16	–1
	17–40	–2
L	13–44	+1
LIII	27–58	–1
LV	1–16	+1
LVI	22–46	+1
	66–91	+1
LVII	13–19	+1
LVIII	3–21	–1
LXXI	5–22	+1
	26–29	–1
LXXII	23–26	–1
LXXXIV	32	–1
	33	–2
	34–41	–3
	41–42	–2
	42–51	–1
	54–55	+1
LXXVIII	41	–1
LXXX	15–18	+1
LXXXIX	1–14	+1
	17–25	–1
XCVIII	2–7	+1
CI	1–5	+1
	5–6	+2
	6–8	+3
CVI	3	+1

C Glossary

Abū l -Qāsim. Father of Qasim, i.e., Muhammad, the Prophet; a *kunya* for Muhammad, the Prophet.

adab. *Belles-lettres*; refinement, culture.

ʿadālah. Probity; synonym of **taʿdīl.**

adīb. Writer of **adab;** man of letters.

ʿahd. Covenant, treaty, engagement.

Ahl al-Bayt. The people of the house, Muhammad's household (the family of the Prophet).

ahl al-Ḥadīth. Those collecting and learned in the **Ḥadīth**.

Ahl al-Kitāb. "People of the Book," especially Christians and Jews.

ahl al-ra'y. People of reasoned opinion; those using their own opinion to establish a legal point.

ahl as -ṣuffa. The people of the bench, of the temple at Mecca; they were poor strangers without friends or place of abode who claimed the promises of the Apostle of God and implored his protection.

akhbār. Reports, anecdotes, history.

ʿalām. Signs, marks, badges.

amān. Safe conduct.

amārāt al-nubūwwa. Marks of prophethood.

ʿāmm. Collective or common words.

anṣār. The helpers; early converts of Medina, and then later all citizens of Medina converted to Islam; in contrast to the Muhajirun, or exiles, those Muslims who accompanied the Prophet from Mecca to Medina.

ʿaqīqah. The custom, observed on the birth of a child, of leaving the hair on the infant's head until the seventh day, when it is shaved and animals are sacrificed.

ʿarabiyyah. The standard of correct Arabic usage of the sixth and seventh centuries C.E., as envisaged by the eighth-century grammarians.

'aṣabiyyah. Tribal solidarity.

asbāb al-nuzūl. The occasions and circumstances of the Koranic revelations.

aṣḥāb al-nabī. Companions of the Prophet. (A single companion is a **sahabi.**)

assonance. A repeated vowel sound, a part rhyme, which has great expressive effect when used internally (within lines), e.g., "An old, mad, blind, despised and dying king," Shelley, "Sonnet: England in 1819." It consists in a similarity in the accented vowels and those which follow, but not in the consonants, e.g., creep/feet skin/swim. Examples in the Koran at VI.164; XVII.15, etc., e.g., *wa-lā taziru wāzir -atun wizra ukhrā.*

Awā'il. The ancients; the first people to do something.

āyah (pl. **āyāt**). Sign, miracle; verse of the Koran.

ayyām al- 'Arab. "Days" of the Arabs; pre-Islamic tribal battles.

bāb. Subchapter, especially in **Ḥadīth** literature.

basmalah. The formula "In the name of God, the Merciful, the Compassionate" (*bi-'smi 'illahi 'l-Rahmani ' l-Rahim*).

bint. Girl; daughter of.

ḍa'īf (pl. **ḍu'afā'**). Weak, as classification of a **Ḥadīth**; traditionist of dubious reliability.

dalā'il. Proofs, signs, marks.

dār. Abode.

Dār al -Ḥarb. The Land of Warfare, a country belonging to infidels not subdued by Islam.

Dār al –Islām. The Land of Islam, the Islamic world.

dhimmah. Security, pact.

dhimmī. Non-Muslim living as a second-class citizen in an Islamic state; Christian or Jew.

diglossia. A situation where two varieties of the same language live side by side. The two variations are high and low: High Arabic and Low Arabic.

dīn. Religion.

dīwān. Register; collection of poetry by a single author or from a single tribe.

du'ā'. Prayer; generally used for supplication as distinguished from **ṣalāt** or liturgical form of prayer.

faḍā'il. Merits.

fakhr. Boasting, self-glorification or tribal vaunting.

faqīh (pl. **fuqahā'**)**.** One learned in **fiqh**.

fātiḥah. The first **sura** of the Koran.

fiqh. Islamic jurisprudence.

al-fiṭaḥl. The time before the Flood.

fitnah. Dissension, civil war; particularly the civil war ensuing on the murder of the Caliph 'Uthmān.

fuṣḥā. The pure Arabic language.

futūḥ. Conquests; the early Islamic conquests.

ghārāt. Raids.

gharīb. Rare, uncommon word or expression; a rare tradition, or such traditions as are isolated, do not date from one of the companions of the Prophet, but only from a later generation.

ghazwah (pl. **ghazawāt**)**.** Early Muslim military expeditions or raiding parties in which the Prophet took part; synonym of **maghāzī**.

ḥabl. Covenant, treaty, engagement.

Ḥadīth. The corpus of traditions of the sayings and doings of the Prophet.

ḥadīth (with a small initial)**.** Such a tradition

ḥajj. The annual pilgrimage to Mecca in the month of Dhu 'l-Hijjah.

ḥalāl. Licit, permitted; opposite of **ḥarām**.

ḥanīf. A Koranic term applying to those of true religion; seeker of religious truth.

ḥaram. Sacred enclave; esp. those of Mecca and Medina.

ḥarām. Forbidden, illicit; opposite of **ḥalāl**.

ḥarakāt. Vowels.

ḥasan. Category of **ḥadīth** between sound (**ṣaḥīḥ**) and weak (**ḍaʿīf**).

hijrah (**hijra**)**.** Muhammad's migration from Mecca to Medina in 622 C.E.

ḥukm. Judgment.

ibn. Son of.

i ʿjāz. Inimitability of the Koran.

ijāzah. License given by a scholar to his pupil, authorizing the latter to transmit and teach a text.

ijmāʿ. Consensus; the consensus of the Islamic community.

illah (pl. **ilal**)**.** Cause; defect; esp. gap in chain of authentic transmission of a **ḥadīth**.

imām. Leader, esp. religious leader; leader in communal prayer.

Injīl. The Gospel.

Iʿrāb. Usually translated as "inflection," indicating case and mood, but the Arab grammarians define it as the difference that occurs, in fact or virtually, at the end of a word, because of the various antecedents that govern it.

isnād. Chain of authorities; in particular in **Ḥadīth** and historical writings.

isrāʿ. Journey by night; the famous night journey of Muhammd to Jerusalem

Jāhiliyyah. Period before Muhammad's mission; era of ignorance; pre-Islamic period.

jihād. Holy War.

jizyah. Poll tax; capitation tax.

kāfir. Unbeliever.

kāhin. Pre-Islamic soothsayer.

kalāla. (a) one who dies leaving neither parent nor child, or, all the heirs with the exception of parents and children; (b) a bride, daughter-in-law, or sister-in-law.

kalām. Scholastic theology.

karshūnī. Syriac alphabet adapted to suit the Arabic language.

khabar (pl. **akhbār**)**.** Discrete anecdotes, reports.

khafī. Sentences whose meanings are hidden

khajī. Sentences in which other persons or things are hidden beneath the plain meaning of a word or expression contained therein.

Khāṣṣ. Words used in a special sense.

khāṣṣīya, **khaṣā'iṣ.** Privilege, prerogative, feature, trait.

khaṭīb. Orator; person pronouncing the Friday **khuṭbah.**

khulq. Disposition, temper, nature.

khuṭbah. Oration; address in the mosque at Friday prayers.

kiblah. *See* **qiblah**.

kissa. *See* **qiṣṣah**.

kitāb (pl. **kutub**). Writing; Scripture, book; in **Ḥadīth**, a division approximating a chapter.

kufic. Style of Arabic script, used in early Koran codices.

kunya (**konia, kunyah**). A patronymic or name of honor of the form Abu N or Umm N (father or mother of N).

kussas. *See* **quṣṣāṣ**.

mab 'ath. Sending; the Call, when Muhammad was summoned to act as God's Prophet.

maghāzī. Early Muslim military expeditions or raiding parties in which the Prophet took part.

majlis (pl. **majālis**). Meeting, session, scholarly discussion.

manāqib. Virtues, good qualities.

mansūkh. Abrogated.

mashhūr. Well known, widely known; a statement handed down by at least three different reliable authorities.

mathālib. Defects.

matn. Main text; narrative content.

mawlā (pl. **mawālī**). Client, non-Arab Muslim.

Midrash. (Hebrew for "exposition or investigation.") A Hebrew term for the method of biblical investigation or exegesis by which oral tradition interprets and elaborates on the scriptural text. This investigation became necessary because the Written Law in the Pentateuch (the first five books of the Old Testament) needed to be reinterpreted in the light of later situations and disagreements. The Midrashim are usually divided into two broad groups:

1. **Halakha Midrash**, which is the scholastic deduction of the Oral Law (Halakha) from the Written Law; the totality of laws that have evolved since biblical times regulating religious observances and conduct of the Jewish people; tend to be rather dry and legalistic.

2. **Haggada Midrash**, which consists of homiletic works whose purpose is edification rather than legislation; while less authoritative than halakhic ones, they are often highly imaginative stories, with a great deal of charm.

mi ʿrāj. Ascent; the Prophet's vision of heaven.

Muʿallaqah (pl. **Muʿallaqāt**). A collection of supposedly pre-Islamic poems.

Mu'awwal. Words that have several significations, all of which are possible.

mubtada'. Beginnings.

Mufakharah. Contests of vaunting, a war of words constituting a literary genre.

Mufassar. Explained. A sentence that needs some word in it to explain it and makeit clear.

Mufaṣṣal. Set forth or described minutely or in great detail.

muḥaddith Ḥadīth. Scholar, collecting and studying the **Ḥadīth**.

muhājirūn. Those who went with the Prophet from Mecca to Medina at the time of the *hijrah*.

Muḥkam. Perspicuous; a sentence the meaning of which there is no doubt.

Mujmal. Sentences that may have a variety of interpretations.

muruwwah. Manliness, chivalry, prowess; the qualities of the ideal pre-Islamic Arab.

musannaf. Classified, systemized compilation. **Ḥadīth** compilations arranged according to subject matter.

muṣḥaf. Koran codex.

mushkil. Sentences that are ambiguous.

mushtarak. Complex words that have several significations;

musnad. Work of **ḥadīth** in which individual **ḥadīth** can be attributed to the Prophet himself.

mut'ah. Temporary marriage.

mutakallim. Scholastic theologian.

mutashābih. Intricate sentences or expressions, the exact meaning of which it is impossible for man to ascertain.

Mu'tazilah. Theological school that created speculative dogmatics of Islam.

mutawātir. A report handed down successively by numerous Companions, which was generally known from early times, and to which objections have never been raised.

nabī. Prophet.

nahḍah. Renaissance.

nasab (pl. **ansāb**). Genealogy.

nāsikh. Passage in the Koran or Sunnah that abrogates another passage.

Nuqaṭ. The diacritical points, the function of which is to differentiate letters of the basic ***rasm***; there are seven letters that are the unmarked members of pairs where the other member has over-dotting.

Peshitta (Pšiṭṭā). The official text of the Bible in Syriac.

Poetical koinē. The written but not spoken language common to pre-Islamic poetry. (Not a happy term, as Rabin says (chap. 3.4) since the Greek *koinē* was a spoken language; thus Classical Arabic resembles more closely the status of Homeric Greek.)

Qaddarites. A group of teachers during ther Abbasid period who championed free will against the theory of predestination.

Qāḍī. Judge of a sharī'ah court.

qara'a 'alā. Literally, read aloud to; study under.

qāri' (pl.**qurrā'**). Reader, reciter of the Koran.

qiblah. Direction of prayer.

qirā'ah. Recitation of the Koran; variant reading of the Koran.

qiṣṣah (pl. **qiṣaṣ**). Story, fable, narrative tale; the narrative tales of the Koran.

qiyās. Analogy; the process of arriving at a legal decision by analogy

quṣṣāṣ. Storytellers, relaters of **qiṣaṣ**.

Rāshidūn. The first four caliphs (the orthodox or rightly guided caliphs), that is, Abū Bakr, ʿUmar, ʿUthmān and ʿAlī.

Rasm. The basic (unpointed) form, shape, or drawing of the individual word.

Rasūl. Messenger; apostle.

Rāwī (pl. **ruwāh**). Reciter, transmitter.

ra'y. Opinion.

rijāl (sing. **rajul**). Men; trustworthy authorities in **Ḥadīth** literature.

risālah (pl. **rasā'il**). Epistle.

riwāyah. Transmission (of a nonreligious text); recension; variant reading in poetry.

Ṣadaqa. Alms, charitable gift; almsgiving, charity; legally prescribed alms tax.

Ṣaḥābah. The group of the Companions of the Prophet.

ṣaḥīfah (pl.**ṣuḥuf**). Page leaf; in the plural: manuscripts, documents containing **Ḥadīth** material.

ṣaḥīḥ. Sound (category of **Ḥadīth**); name of the **Ḥadīth** collections of al Bukhārī and Muslim.

sajʿ. Balanced and rhyming prose.

sarāyā. Early Muslim military expeditions at which the Prophet was not present.

shādhdh. Peculiar; esp. unacceptable variants of the Koranic text.

shamā'il. Good qualities; character, nature.

sharīʿah. The corpus of Islamic law.

shawāhid. Piece of evidence or quotation serving as textual evidence.

Shīʿah. Sect that holds that the leadership of the Islamic community belongs only to the descendants of ʿAlīand Fāṭima.

Shuʿūbiyyah. Anti-Arab political and literary movement, especially strong in Iranian circles.

Sīra/sīrah (pl. **siyar**). Biography, esp. of the Prophet.

Sitz im leben. (German: situation or place in life.) A term used initially in biblical criticism to signify the circumstances (often in the life of a community) in which a particular story, saying, etc., was created or preserved and transmitted.

stanza/strophe. Some poems are divided into groups of lines that stricly speaking are called "stanzas"; though in popular language they are often called "verses." The stanza will have a predominating meter and pattern of rhyme. For example, the Omar Khayyam stanza has four iambic pentameters, rhyming AABA; it receives its name from its use by E. Fitzgerald in his translation of the *Rubaiyat*.

sunnah. Way, path; customary practice, usage sanctioned by tradition, the sayings and doings of the Prophet that have been established as legally binding.

sura/sūrah. A chapter of the Koran.

ṭabaqāt. Historical works organized biographically.

tābiʿūn (sing. **Tābiʿ**). Followers, the generation after the Prophet's Companions (**ṣaḥā bah**).

ta ʿdīl. Confirming the credibility of a **muḥaddith**.

tafsīr. Koranic exegesis.

tafsīr biʾl-maʾthūr. Interpretation or exegesis of the Koran following tradition.

tafsīr biʾl-raʾy. Interpretation or exegesis of the Koran by personal opinion.

tajwīd. The art of reciting the Koran, giving each consonant its full value, as much as it requires to be well pronounced without difficulty or exaggeration.

tanzīl. The divine revelation incorporated in the Koran; occasionally, the inspiration of soothsayers.

taʾrīkh. History.

tawḥīd. The doctrine of the unity of God.

ta'wīl. Interpretation; sometimes used as a synonym for **tafsīr**; later acquired specialized sense of exposition of the subject matter of the Koran, in contrast to the more external philological exegesis of the Koran, which was now distinguished as **tafsīr**.

ummah. Folk; the Islamic community.

Ur-. (German origin; prefix.) Primitive, original.

uṣūl. The fundamentals of jurisprudence.

warrāq. Paper seller, stationer, bookseller, copyist.

waḍū'. Ablution.

zakāh. Alms tax of prescribed amount.

zuhd. Asceticism.

D THE GENETIC RELATIONSHIP AMONG SEMITIC LANGUAGES

Merritt Ruhlen

Languages are given in capital and lower-case letters; language groups, in all capitals. Languages and language groups preceded by a dagger are extinct. The number of extant languages in each genetic group is given in brackets following the name of the group. Languages preceded by an asterisk are discussed by Merritt Ruhlen in volume 2, *Language Data,* of his work *A Guide to the World's Languages* (Stanford, forthcoming.)

VI. SEMITIC [19]:
[0]: †Eblaic
A. †EAST [0]: *†Akkadian
B. WEST [191:
1. CENTRAL [6]:
a. ARAMAIC [2]: *†Old Aramaic, †Syriac, *Assyrian, Aramaic
b. ARABO-CANAANITE [4]:
i. CANAANITE [1]: *†Classical Hebrew, *Hebrew, †Phoenician, *†Ugaritic, †Moabite
ii. ARABIC [3]: *†Classical Arabic, *Eastern Arabic, *Western Arabic, *Maltese
2. SOUTH [13]:
[1]: †Epigraphic South Arabian, *South Arabian
a. ETHIOPIC [12]:
i. NORTH [2]:
[0]: *†Geez
α. NORTH PROPER [2]: *Tigre, *Tigrinya
ii. SOUTH [101:
α. TRANSVERSAL [4]:
I. AMHARIC-ARGOBBA [2]: *Amharic, Argobba
II. EAST GURAGE-HARARI [2]: *Harari, East Gurage
ß. OUTER [6]:
I. N-GROUP [2]:
[0]: *†Gafat
A. N-NORTH GURAGE [2]: Soddo, Goggot
II. TT-GROUP [4]:
A. TT-NORTH GURAGE [1]: *Muher
B. WEST GURAGE [3]:
[1]: Masqan
1. CENTRAL & PERIPHERAL [2]: *Central West Gurage, Peripheral West Gurage

E Semitic Languages Family Tree

AFRO-ASIATIC PHYLUM

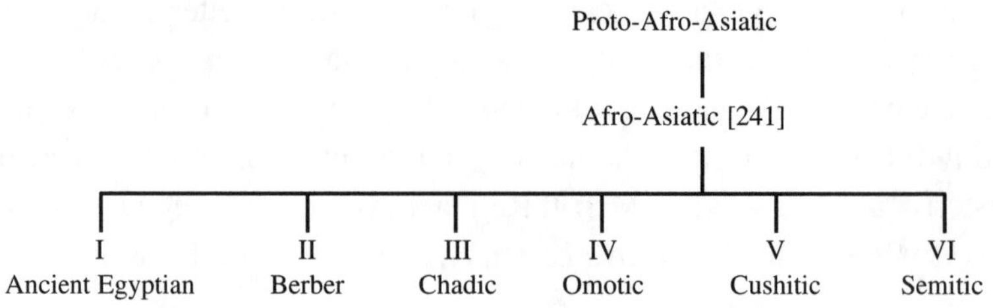

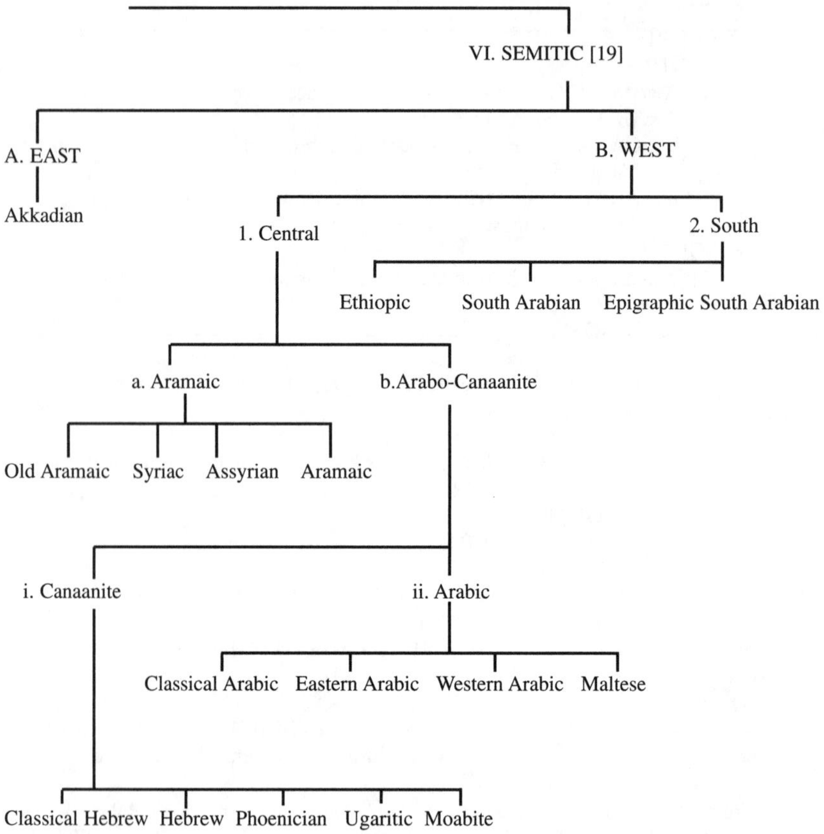

F ORIGIN OF THE ALPHABET

I. J. Gelb

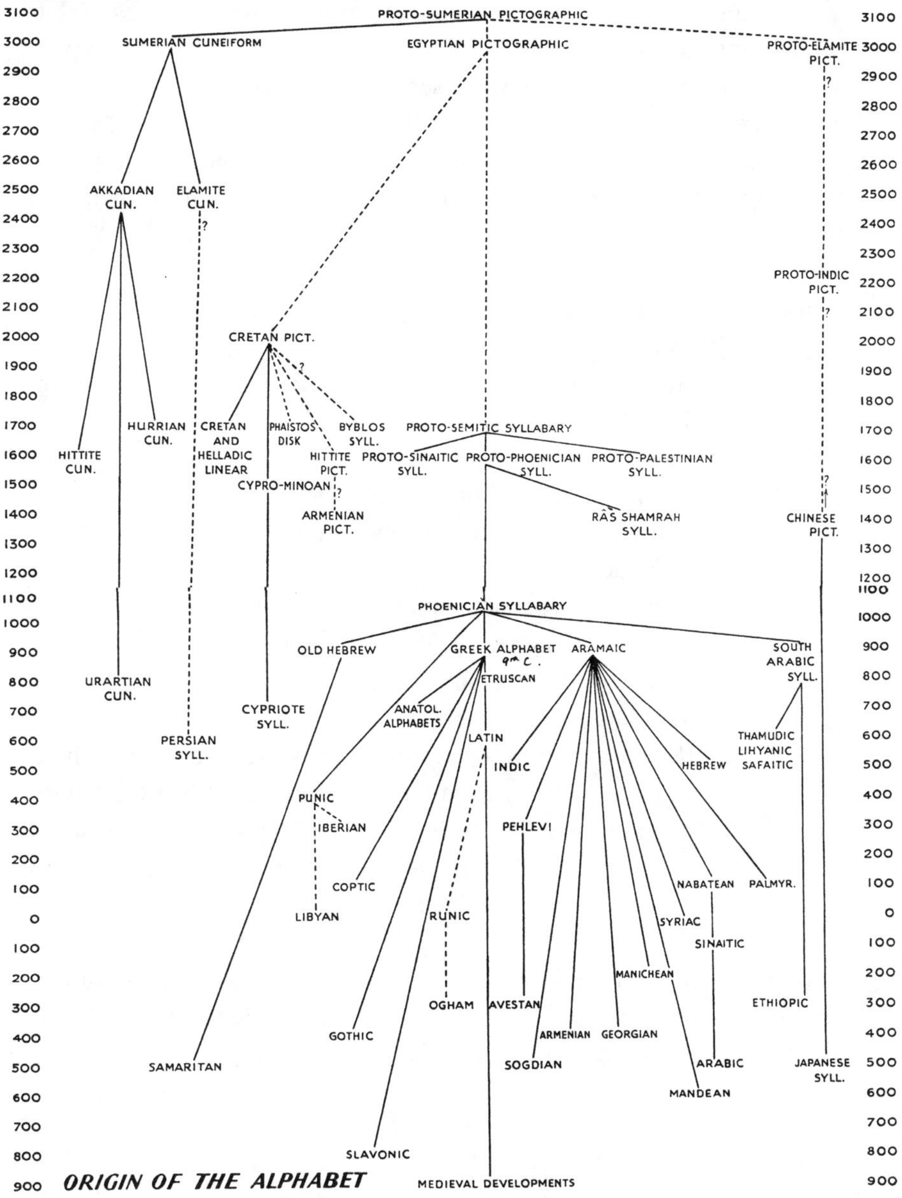

From I. J. Gelb, *A Study of Writing* (Chicago: University of Chicago Press, 169), pp. x–xi.

G DEVELOPMENT OF ARAMAIC SCRIPTS

Aramaic was used as an official language by the Assyrians, Babylonians, and Persians. After the collapse of the Persian Empire, the Imperial Aramaic language and script, which had been more or less unified across the empire, began to break up, and local dialects and scripts developed, such as (Square) Hebrew; Nabataean, from which Arabic eventually emerged; Palmyrene; Hatran, Syriac (several forms); and Mandaic.[1]

Column 1:Transcription
- 2: [Modern Square] Hebrew
- 3: Aramaic inscription on stele of King Zakkur of Hamath, 780–775 B.C.E.
- 4: Aramaic, sixth century B.C.E.
- 5: Aramaic, cursive form, fifth century B.C.E.
- 6: Palmyrene, first/second century C.E.
- 7: Nabataean, first century C.E.
- 8: Nabataean, second century C.E.
- 9: Syriac-Estranghelo, fifth century C.E.
- 10: Syriac-Jacobite, eighth century C.E.
- 11: Mandaic
- 12: [Samaritan, developed from Old Hebrew script, which, in turn was derived from Early Phoenician. While the Jewish community as a whole abandoned the Old Hebrew script in favor of the Aramaic script, certain Jewish sects, such as the Samaritans, retained it.]

Reproduced with the kind permission of Père Jean-Hugo Tisin o.p. Père Tisin also helped, with much generosity and patience, with all matters Aramaic and Syriac, for which I thank him warmly.

NOTE

1. John F. Healey, *The Early Alphabet* (London /Berkeley, 1990), p. 42

The Development of Aramaic

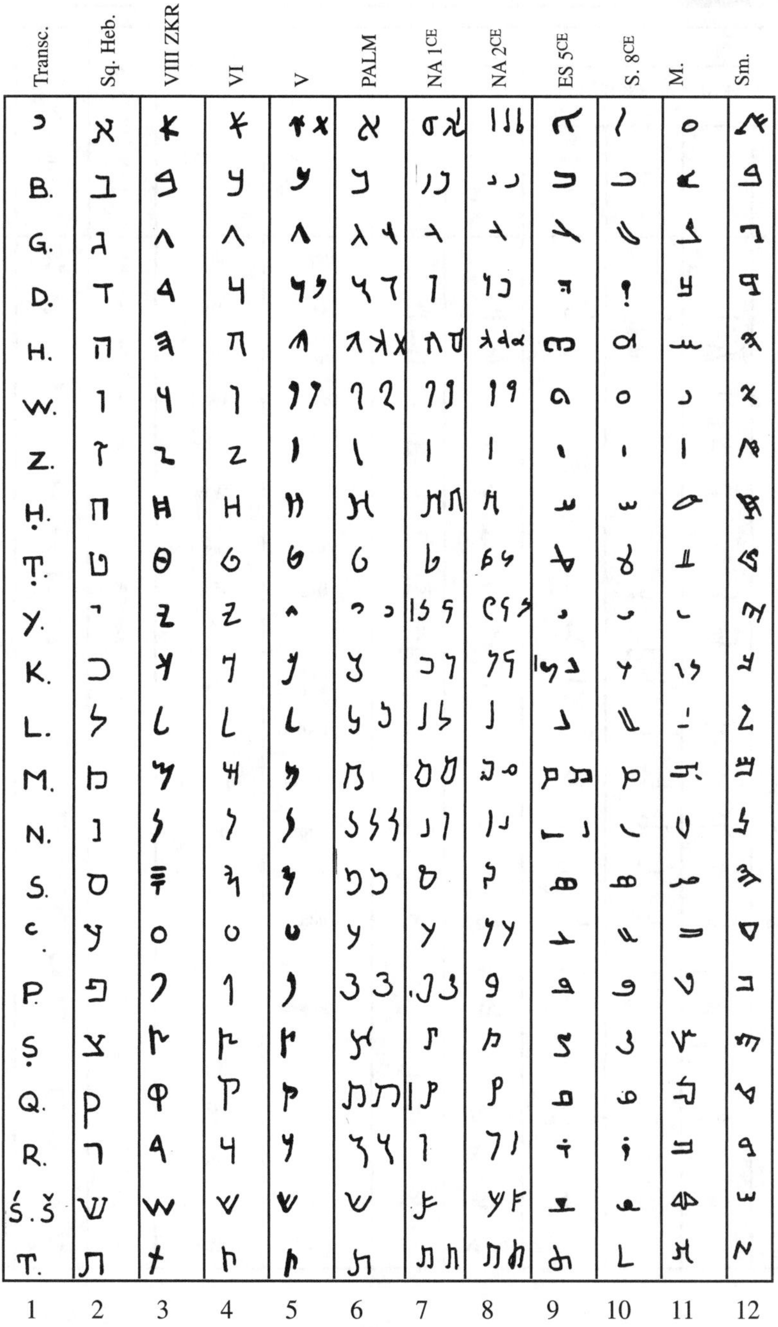
Transc.
Sq. Heb.
VIII ZKR
VI
V
PALM
NA 1CE
NA 2CE
ES 5CE
S. 8CE
M.
Sm.
ʾ
B.
G.
D.
H.
W.
Z.
Ḥ.
Ṭ.
Y.
K.
L.
M.
N.
S.
ʿ
P.
Ṣ.
Q.
R.
Ś.Š
T.
1
2
3
4
5
6
7
8
9
10
11
12

H A Comparative Table of Syriac, Hebrew, and Arabic Scripts

SYRIAC						NAME		TRANSCRIPTION	HEBREW	ARABIC
SERTO OR JACOBITE				NESTORIAN OR CHALDAEAN	ESTRANGHELO	SYRIAC	HEBREW			
ALONE	FINAL	INITIAL	MEDIAL							
ܐ	ܐ			ܐ	ܐ	ʾālap̱	ʾālep̱	ʾ	א	أ
ܒ	ܒ	ܒ	ܒ	ܒ	ܒ	Bēṯ	Bēṯ	b	בּ	ب
ܓ	ܓ	ܓ	ܓ	ܓ	ܓ	Gāmal	Gīmel	g	ג	ج غ
ܕ	ܕ			ܕ	ܕ	Dālaṯ	Dāleṯ	d	ד	د ذ
ܗ	ܗ			ܗ	ܗ	Hē	Hē	h	ה	ه
ܘ	ܘ			ܘ	ܘ	Waw	Wāw	w	ו	و
ܙ	ܙ			ܙ	ܙ	Zayn	Zayin	z	ז	ز
ܚ	ܚ	ܚ	ܚ	ܚ	ܚ	Ḥēṯ	Ḥēṯ	ḥ	ח	ح
ܛ	ܛ	ܛ	ܛ	ܛ	ܛ	Ṭēṯ	Ṭēṯ	ṭ	ט	ط
ܝ	ܝ	ܝ	ܝ	ܝ	ܝ	Yōḏ	Yōḏ	y	י	ى
ܟ	ܟ	ܟ	ܟ	ܟ	ܟ	Kāp̱	Kāp̱	k	כּ	ك خ
ܠ	ܠ	ܠ	ܠ	ܠ	ܠ	Lāmaḏ	Lāmeḏ	l	ל	ل
ܡ	ܡ	ܡ	ܡ	ܡ	ܡ	Mīm	Mēm	m	מ	م
ܢ	ܢ	ܢ	ܢ	ܢ	ܢ	Nūn	Nūn	n	נ	ن
ܣ	ܣ	ܣ	ܣ	ܣ	ܣ	Semkaṯ	Sāmeḵ	s	ס	س
ܥ	ܥ	ܥ	ܥ	ܥ	ܥ	ʿē	ʿayin	ʿ	ע	ع
ܦ	ܦ	ܦ	ܦ	ܦ	ܦ	Pē	Pē	p	פּ	ف
ܨ	ܨ			ܨ	ܨ	Ṣāḏē	Ṣāḏē	ṣ	צ	ص
ܩ	ܩ	ܩ	ܩ	ܩ	ܩ	Qōp̱	Qōp̱	q	ק	ق
ܪ	ܪ			ܪ	ܪ	Rēš	Rēš	r	ר	ر
ܫ	ܫ	ܫ	ܫ	ܫ	ܫ	Šīn	Šīn / Śīn	š	שׁ	ش
ܬ	ܬ			ܬ	ܬ	Taw	Tāw	t	ת	ت ث

I A Comparative Table of Nabataean and Arabic

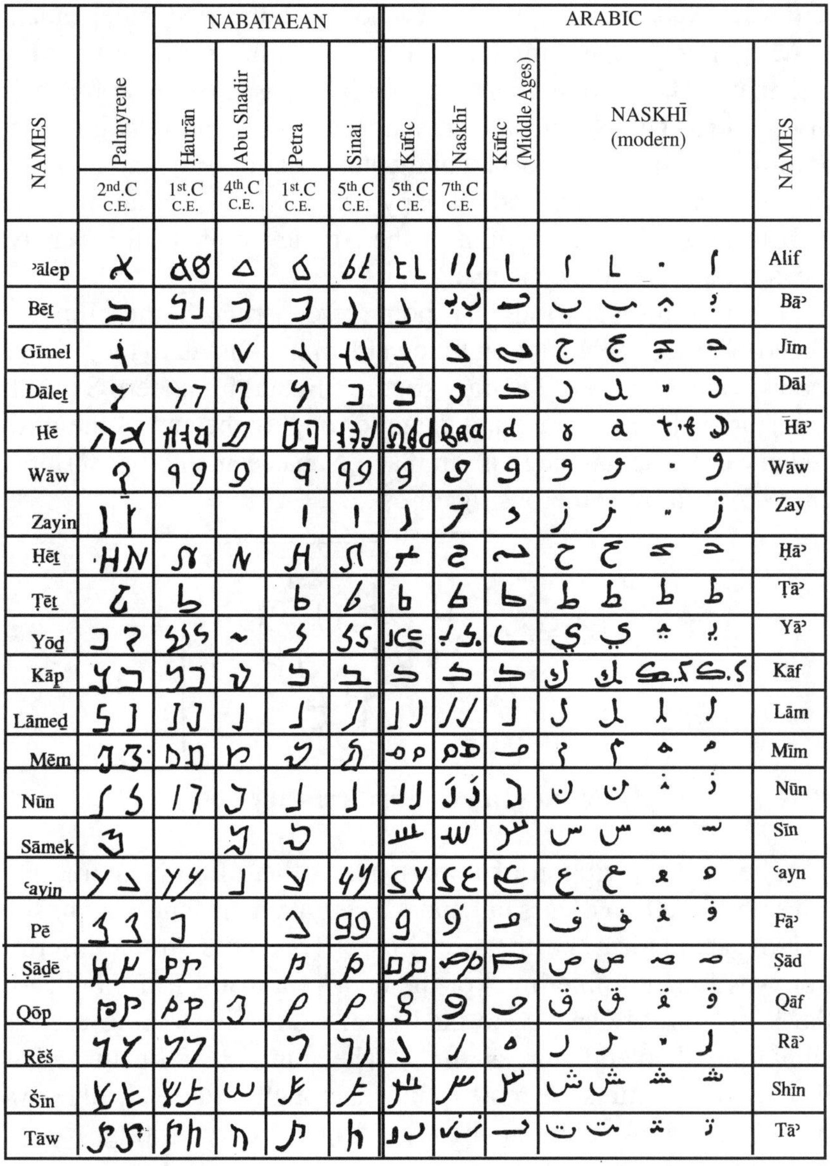
NAMES
NABATAEAN
ARABIC
Palmyrene
2nd.C C.E.
Ḥaurān
1st.C C.E.
Abu Shadir
4th.C C.E.
Petra
1st.C C.E.
Sinai
5th.C C.E.
Kūfic
5th.C C.E.
Naskhī
7th.C C.E.
Kūfic (Middle Ages)
NASKHĪ (modern)
NAMES
ʾālep
Bēt̲
Gīmel
Dālet̲
Hē
Wāw
Zayin
Ḥēt̲
Ṭēt̲
Yōd̲
Kāp̱
Lāmed̲
Mēm
Nūn
Sāmek
ʿayin
Pē
Ṣād̲ē
Qōp
Rēš
Šīn
Tāw
Alif
Bāʾ
Jīm
Dāl
Hāʾ
Wāw
Zay
Ḥāʾ
Ṭāʾ
Yāʾ
Kāf
Lām
Mīm
Nūn
Sīn
ʿayn
Fāʾ
Ṣād
Qāf
Rāʾ
Shīn
Tāʾ

Adapted from *Dictionanaire de la Bible*, vol. I, Paris, 1895.

J NABATEAN AND ARABIC INSCRIPTIONS

The Nabataeans were the founders of the first independent northern Arab kingdom centred on Petra in modern Jordan (see map). They spoke a form of Arabic but used Aramaic for their inscriptions. The Nabataean Aramaic script is found in two forms: a formal script used for monumental inscriptions, and a more flowing cursive script used on papyrus. It is fairly certain that the Nabataean script is the origin of the Arabic script. Unfortunately, the epigraphic evidence is meager.

In modern discussions, the point of departure is the bilingual Greco-Nabataean inscription found at Umm al-Jimāl, to the west of the volcanic plateau of Hauran (south of Bosra) in modern Syria. It was studied by Littmann, and dated to roughly the end of the third century C.E. The language is Aramaeo-Nabataean, and the script is characterized by numerous ligatures.

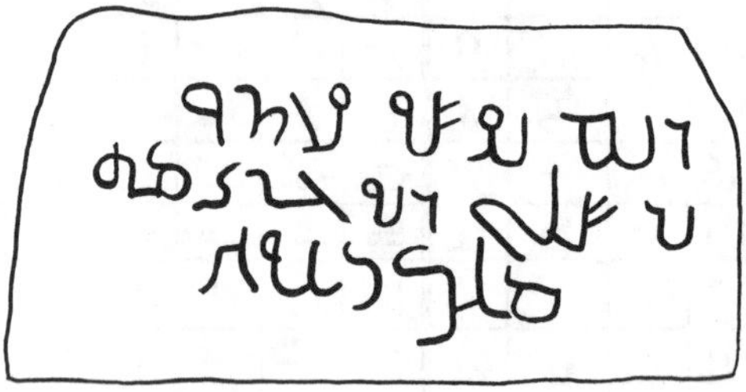

Umm al -Jimal, third century C.E.

The next inscription of importance is that of an-Namāra, discovered in 1901 by Dussaud and Macler at an ancient Roman site east of Jabal Druze (northeast of Bosra) This proto-Arabic inscription was found on the lintel of the door of a mausoleum, built for the King Imruʾ-l-Qays, who died in 328 C.E. The writing used is similar to that at Umm al-Jimāl. The number of ligatures has increased, the letters are more rounded, though certain, like the ʿ*ayn* or the final *īn* of the plural already prefigure Kufic writing.

From J. Catineau, *Le Nabatéen* (Paris, 1930); Regis Blachère, Histoire de la Littérature Arabe, vol. 1 (Paris, 1952); John F. Healey, The Early Alphabet (Berkeley, 1990).

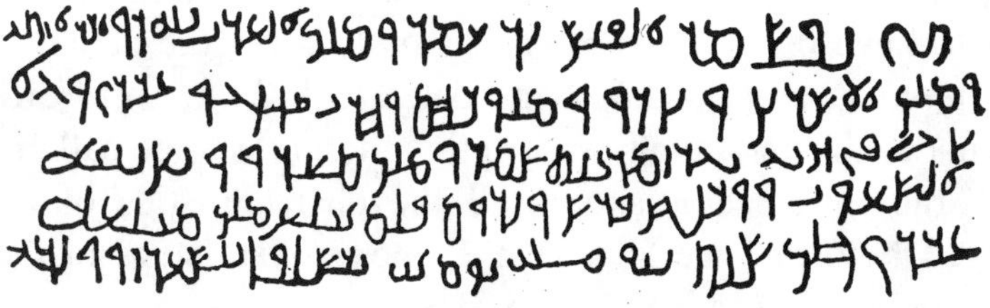

Namāra Inscription, 328–329 C.E.

1 تِي نفسُ امر. القيس بر عمرو مَلِك العرب كُلّه ذو أَسَرَ التاج

2 وَمَلَكَ الاسدين وَنَزارو وُملو كهم وَهَرَّبَ محجو عكدِي وجاءَ

3 يَزَجاى فى حبَج نجران مدينت شُمَّر وَمَلَكَ معدّو وَبَين بَنيه

4 الشعوب وَوَكَّلَهُنَّ فارسو لرُوم فَلَم يبلغ مَلِكُ مبلَغَهُ

5 عكدى هَلَكَ سنت 223 يَوم 7 بِكسلول بالسعد ذو وَلَدَهُ

Transcription

Translation:

This is the tomb of Imru-I-Qays, the son of Amr, king of all Arabs, who assumed the crown (2)which subdued (the two tribes) of Asad, and Nizār and their kings, who scattered MHDJ until now, who carried the day (3) at the siege of Najrān, the town of Chammār, who subdued the tribe of Ma'add, who divided among his sons (4) the tribes and organized that the latter like a cavalry corps for the Romans. No other king attained his glory, (5) to this day. He died in the year 223 [328. C.E.], the seventh day of Kesloul. May happiness reign over his descendants.

The third epigraphic piece of evidence was discovered in 1879 by Sachau on the lintel of a door of a sanctuary dedicated to Saint Sergius, in the small village of Zabad. The Arabic text, engraved next to two inscriptions, one in Greek and the other in Syriac, seems to have been added later. It simply gives the names of the founders, all Aramaic. The script, dated to 512 C.E., very different from that of the an-Namāra inscription, deserves to be called properly "Arabic," since it shows all the characteristics of cursive writing. Obviously, we lack all the intermediate steps in the evidence that leads from Namāra to Zabad.

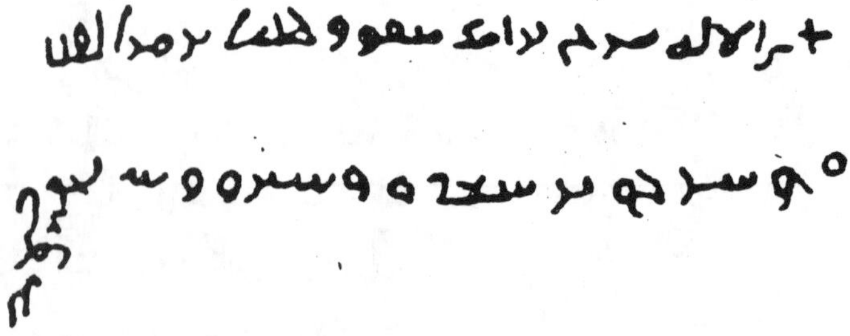

Zabad, 512 C.E.

The fourth piece of evidence is a bilingual inscription discovered by Wetzstein in 1864, at Ḥarrān, northwest of Jabal Druze on the borders of the plateau Leja. It represents the dedication of a martyrium, which the Greek text tells us was consecrated to Saint John the Baptist, and the door bears the date 463, the era of Bosra (568 C.E.). The style can be called "kufic." With this document clearly dated, we have a specimen of a system of writing definitively established. (Notice the Christian context.)

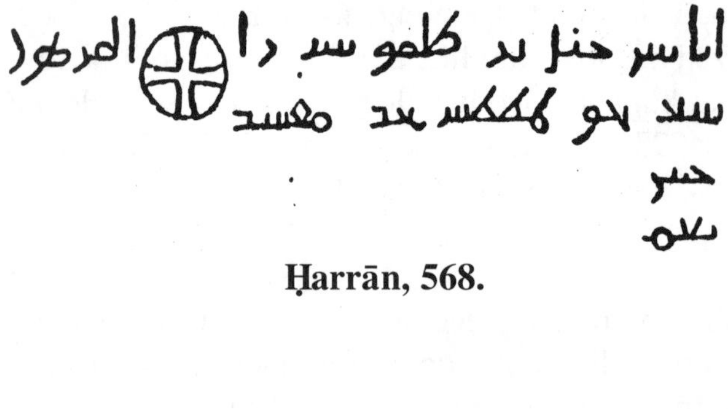

Ḥarrān, 568.

Transcription

1 انا شراحيل بر طلمو بنيت ذا المرطول

2 سنت 463 بعد مفسد

3 حينئذ

4 نعم

Translation:

I, the Sharaḥīl, the son of Ṭalemū, built this, (2) in the Year 463; after the corruption (3,4), prosperity.

K The Arabic Alphabet

The form of the Arabic letters varies according to whether the letter is in initial, final, or medial position in a word.

Alif	ا	ا ا ا
Bā	ب	ببب
Tā’	ت	تتت
Thā’	ث	ثثث
Jīm	ج	ججج
Ḥā’	ح	ححح
Khā’	خ	خخخ
Dāl	د	د د د
Dhāl	ذ	ذ ذ ذ
Rā’	ر	ر ر ر
Zay	ز	ز ز ز
Sīn	س	سسس
Shīn	ش	ششش
Ṣād	ص	صصص
Ḍād	ض	ضضض
Ṭā’	ط	ططط
Ẓā’	ظ	ظظظ
‘ayn	ع	ععع
Ghayn	غ	غغغ
Fā’	ف	ففف
Qāf’	ق	ققق
Kāf	ك	ككك
Lām	ل	للل
Mīm’	م	ممم
Nūn	ن	ننن
Hā’	ه	ههه
Wāw	و	و و و
Yā’	ي	ييي

Final Medial Initial

Final Medial Initial

L A Dot or Two Can Make All the Difference

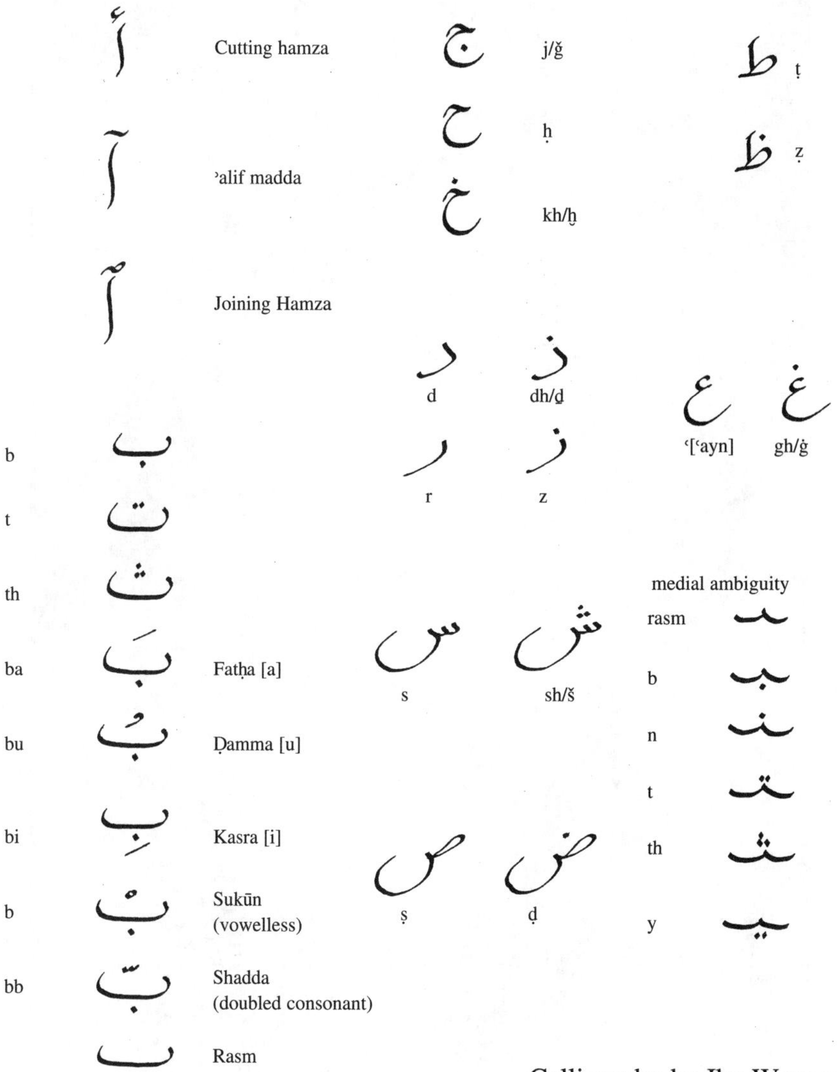

Calligraphy by Ibn Warraq

M ARABIA AND THE NEAR EAST

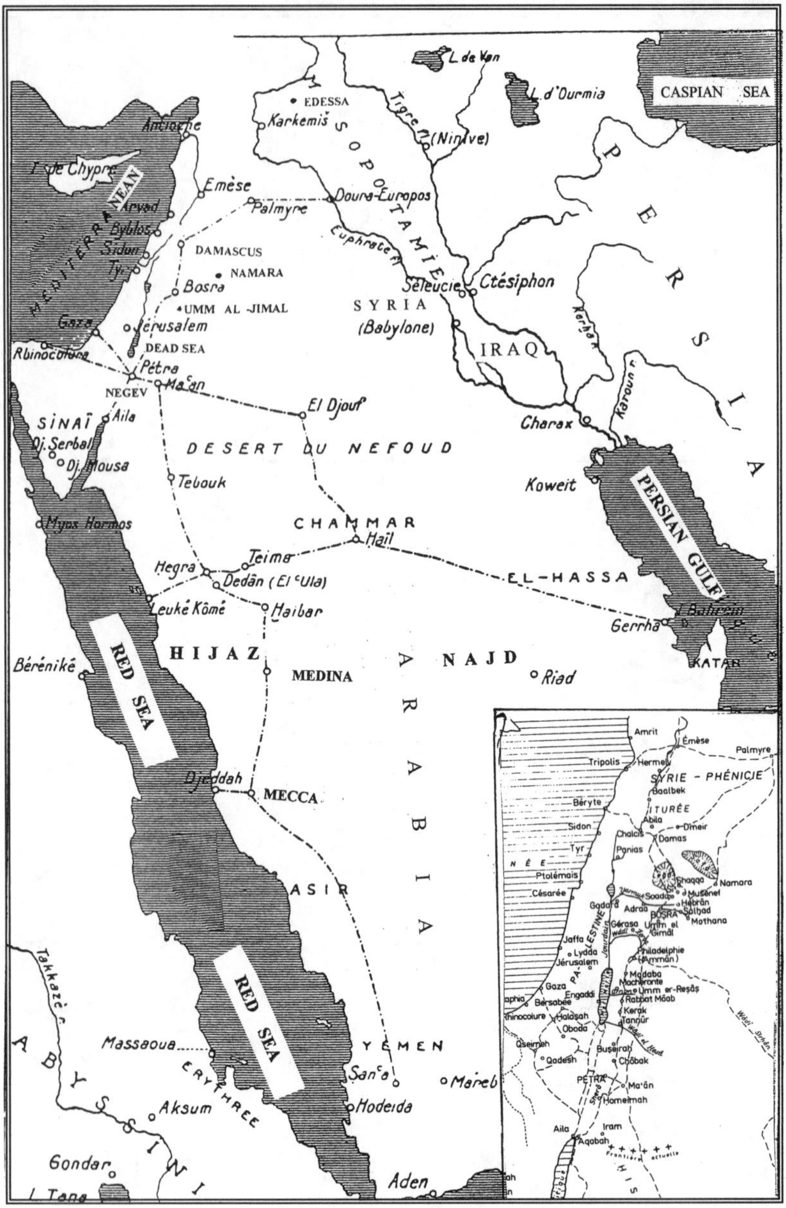

Map adapted from J. Catineau, *Le Nabatéen*, Paris, 1930. Inset adapted from *Dictionnaire de la Bible*, Supplement. Ed. Pirot, Robert et al. Tome 7. Paris, 1966.

List of Contributors

Jacob Barth (1851–1914), from a Jewish family, was a teacher from 1874 onward at the newly founded Seminary for the Orthodox Jewish Education of Rabbis in Berlin. Later, Barth taught Semitic philology at Berlin University, and became well known for his works on Semitic grammar (*Die Nominalbildung in Semitischen*) and for his edition of the Arabic commentary of Maimonides on the Mishnah tract Makkoth. The latter was one of the first Middle Arabic texts to be published.

Rev. Dr. Richard Bell (1876–1952) was educated at Edinburgh University, where he studied Semitic languages and divinity. He became a minister of the Church of Scotland in 1904, and ordained to the parish of Wamphrey in 1907. After fourteen years in the parish ministry, Bell returned to Edinburgh as lecturer in Arabic, attaining the position of reader in Arabic in 1938, a position he held until his retirement in 1947.

J. Bellamy is professor emeritus in the Department of Near Eastern Studies, University of Michigan.

A. Ben-Shemesh taught at the University of Tel Aviv, and edited and translated a well-known Arabic work on taxation: Yahya b.Adam, *Kitâb al-kharâj* (Leiden, 1967).

Dr. Bishai graduated from the Johns Hopkins University in 1959, with a dissertation entitled "The Coptic Influence on Egyptian Arabic." Dr. Bishai taught at the Johns Hopkins University and then at Harvard University, where he retired as senior lecturer of Arabic in 1973.

The Reverend E. F. F. Bishop was formerly principal of the Newman School of Missions in Jerusalem and senior lecturer in Arabic at the University of Glasgow.

Joshua Blau is professor emeritus of Arabic at the Hebrew University of Jerusalem, and author of *The Emergence and Linguistic Background of Judaeo-Arabic* vol. 5 of *Scripta Judaica* (Oxford, 1965), and *A Grammar of Christian Arabic*, CSCO Subsidia 27–9 (Louvain, 1966–67).

M. Bravmann taught at the Hebrew University in Jerusalem, and is author of *The Spiritual Background of early Islam* (Leiden, 1972) and *Studies in Semitic Philology* (Leiden, 1977).

Claude Cahen (1909–1991). Following research in Turkey in 1936, Cahen taught, after the war, at the University of Strasbourg, where he founded the first journal devoted to the social and economic history of the East. In 1959 he went to the Sorbonne, where he taught for twenty years. Hourani described Cahen's work as "perhaps the most systematic attempt to apply mature sociological concepts to the realities of Islamic society."[1]

August Fischer (1865–1949), a disciple of H. L. Fleischer, was a professor in Leipzig. His particular talent for linguistic analysis led him to write some Koran-critical essays (e.g., "Der Wert der vorhandenen Koranübersetzungen und sure 111," *Berichte über die Verhandlungen der Sächsischen Akademie der Wissenschaften [BVSAW] zu Leipzig* 89, Heft 2 [1937]). Also worth mentioning is his monograph "Der Koran des Abu l-'Alâ al-Ma'arrî," *BVSAW* 94, Heft 2 (1942), and the establishment of the Shawahid Indices, which were completed in 1945 by his disciple and successor, Erich Bräunlich.

Rudolf Geyer (1861–1929) was a disciple of D. H. Müller. On Müller's retirement, Geyer became professor of Semitic languages at the University of Vienna. Geyer also continued Müller's work on strophic poetry in the Koran, though his main interest remained Arabic poetry.

Adolf Grohmann (1887–1977) was professor of Semitics and cultural history of the Near East in Prague and Vienna. His main field of interest was Ethiopic and South Arabic of pre-Islamic times. One of his discoveries was that the Old Ethiopic Hymnody was derived from an Old Arabic, pre-Islamic translation, carried out before 500 C.E., and which, in turn, was derived from a Coptic original (*Âthiopische Marienhymnen*, Abhandlungen der Sächsischen Akademie der Wissenschaften, Phil.-hist. Klasse, Bd.33 No.4, Leipzig 1919.) He was also the author of two further important works: *Arabien. Handbuch der Alterumswissenschaft* (Munich 1963), which is a reference book on Arabian cultural history throughout the ages; and "Arabische Palägraphie," in *Sitzungsberichte der Österre-*

ichischen Akademie der Wissenschaften Wien, Phil.-hist. Klasse, Denkschriften, 94. Bd., 1. Abhandlung (Wien 1967–1971).

C. Heger, after studies at the universities of Cologne and Bonn, and research at the Ruhr-University in Bochum, worked with the Council of Environmental Experts. He is currently engaged in research on early Islam, and the textual criticism of the Koran.

Paul Kahle (1875–1964) began his academic career as a Protestant theologian working on the textual tradition of the Hebrew Old Testament. Kahle spent five years in Cairo as pastor of the Protestant parish in Egypt; this stay brought him closer to the field of Arabic and Islamic studies. He eventually became professor of Semitic languages at the University of Bonn. He was advised to leave Germany in 1938 since he and his family had helped persecuted Jews. Kahle's knowledge of Christian theology gave him a different perspective on the Koran than was usual in Germany. Under the influence of Carlo de Landberg and Karl Vollers, Kahle regarded the language of the Koran as not Classical Arabic.

M. J. Kister is professor emeritus at the Hebrew University of Jerusalem. He is the author of *Studies in Jahiliyya and Early Islam* (London, 1980).

Rev. Professor Raimund Kobert was researcher and teacher at the Pontifical Biblical Institute, Rome. He was the author of numerous articles in learned journals such as *Der Islam* ("Zur Lehre des Tafsīr über denbösen Blick (Mk.7.22par)," *Der Islam* 28, 111–121), *Biblica*, and *Orientalia*.

Toby Lester is a writer and editor whose articles have appeared frequently in the *Atlantic Monthly*. From 1988 to 1990 he was a Peace Corps volunteer in North Yemen, and from 1992 to 1994 he worked for the United Nations in Jerusalem and the West Bank.

David S. Margoliouth (1858–1940) was professor of Arabic at the University of Oxford, and a member of the Council of the Royal Asiatic Society. He was the author of numerous articles and books on Islam, including *Muhammad & the Rise of Islam* (London, 1905), and *The Early Development of Mohammedanism* (London, 1914). His research into the history of Early Islam led him to compare the life of Joseph Smith, the founder of Mormonism, to that of the Prophet of Islam, and forced him to conclude that human beings with unusual powers fall easily into dishonesty.

Alphonse Mingana (1881–1937) was a great scholar of Semitic languages, especially Syriac and Arabic. He was a member of the Chaldaean Church in Iraq, where he was also professor of Semitic languages and literature in the Syro-Chaldaean Seminary at Mosul. He collected invaluable Arabic and Syriac manuscripts that became the foundation for the famous Mingana Collection, now housed in Birmingham, U.K. The last twenty years of his life were spent in England, where he taught Semitic languages. His essays were collected in *Woodbrooke Studies: Christian Documents in Syriac, Arabic, Karshuni* (1927).

Yehuda D. Nevo was a freelance archaeologist, whose discovery in the Negev Desert (Israel) of Kufic inscriptions, four hundred of which were published in *Ancient Arabic Inscriptions from the Negev*, led him and Judy Koren to reexamine the origins of Islam and early Islamic history. At his death, Nevo left the manuscript of *Crossroads to Islam*, which Judy Koren is revising with a view to its publication soon. Koren and Nevo have also published together "The Origins of the Muslim Descriptions of the Jahili Meccan Sanctuary, *Journal of Near Eastern Studies* (1990).

M. Philonenko is professor at the University of Strasbourg, and one of the directors of the journal, *Revue d'Histoire et de Philosophie Religieuses*. He is the author of many articles on the Dead Sea Scrolls, and edited *La Bible; Ecrits Intertestamentaires* (Paris: Gallimard, 1987), for which he also translated from the Hebrew into French, *The Testament of Job; the Apocalypse of Abraham; and The Book of Secrets of Enoch,* among others.

Gerd-R. Puin is a member of the Institute of Oriental Studies at the Universität des Saarlandes, Saarbrücken, Germany. During the 1980s he was in charge of a German cultural aid project in the Yemen concerned with the restoration of Koranic fragments written on parchment.

Chaim Rabin, Ph.D. (1939, London), D.Phil. (1943, Oxford), was lecturer in post-biblical Hebrew at the University of Oxford and Professor of Hebrew Language at the Hebrew University of Jerusalem. He is the author of *Ancient West-Arabian* (London, 1951), and *Qumran Studies* (Oxford, 1957).

Ibn al-Rawandi is a freelance writer on philosophical and religious subjects. He has a special interest in the mystical and esoteric aspects of the world's religious traditions, and has personal experience of Sufism, Christian Theosophy, and Jewish Qabalah. He is the author of *Islamic Mysticism: A Secular Perspective* (Prometheus Books, 2000) and numerous articles and book reviews.

F. Rosenthal completed a Ph.D. on the language of the Palmyrenian Aramaic inscriptions under H. H. Schaeder in 1935. He left Germany at the end of 1938 for Sweden, England, and the United States, where he arrived in February 1940. Rosenthal taught at the Hebrew Union College in Cincinnati, Ohio, served in the US Army, and was appointed professor at the University of Pennsylvania in 1948 and at Yale University in 1956. Professor Rosenthal retired in 1985. He has translated Ibn Khaldūn's *The Muqaddimah* and the first part of Ṭabarī's *History*, and is the author of *A History of Muslim Historiography* (Leiden, 1952).

Uri Rubin is a professor of Arabic and Islam at Tel Aviv University. He is the author of over twenty articles published in learned journals such as BSOAS, JRAS, and JSS, and of the full-length study *The Eye of the Beholder: The Life of Muhammad as Viewed by the Early Muslims* (*A Textual Analysis*) (Princeton, 1995), and is working on *Between Bible and Quran: The Children of Israel and the Islamic Historical Self-Image.*

Michael Schub, Ph.D. was lecturer in Arabic language and literature at Yale University for three years. He now teaches at Trinity College in Hartford, Connecticut.

C. C. Torrey (1863–1956) was professor of Semitic languages at Yale University. He worked with the American Schools of Oriental Researchin the Near East, helping to excavate a Phoenician Necropolis at Sidon. He was an expert on Palestine antiquities in general, and a formidable biblical scholar with more than fifteen works to his credit, including *The Four Gospels* (1947); *The Apocryphal Literature* (1945); and *The Second Isaiah* (1928).

Julius Wellhausen (1844–1918), German biblical scholar and orientalist. In his pioneering work on the Old Testament, which he began publishing in 1876, Wellhausen showed that the Pentateuch was a composite work in which one could discern the hand of four different writers. His research completely transformed Old Testament studies. Wellhausen then turned his critical mind to the sources of early Islam. His works include *Prolegomena zur ältesten Geschichte des Islams* (Berlin, 1899), and *Das Arabische Reich und sein Sturz* (Berlin, 1902).

NOTE

1. A. Hourani, "Islam and the Philosophers of History," in *Europe and the Middle East* (Berkeley, 1980), p. 73, quoted in *The Jewish Discovery of Islam*, ed. M. Kramer (Tel Aviv, 1999), p. 35.

DATE			